Mercedes-Benz Diesel Automotive Repair Manual

by Larry Warren and John H Haynes
Member of the Guild of Motoring Writers

Models covered:

200D, 220D, 240D, 240TD, 300D, 300CD, 300TD models with 1988cc, 2197cc, 2404cc and 2399cc 4-cylinder engines and 2998cc 5-cylinder engine. Coupe, Sedan and Station Wagon (Estate) body styles designated W123 Series.

Covers diesel models including turbodiesel versions

 (4C7 - 63012)
(697)

ABCDE
FG

2

Haynes Publishing Group
Sparkford Nr Yeovil
Somerset BA22 7JJ England

Haynes North America, Inc
861 Lawrence Drive
Newbury Park
California 91320 USA

Acknowledgements

We are grateful for the help and cooperation of Mercedes-Benz for their assistance with technical information and certain illustrations.

A book in the **Haynes Automotive Repair Manual Series**

Printed in the USA

ISBN 0 85696 697 5

Library of Congress Catalog Card Number 86-080525

Contents

Introductory pages
About this manual   5
Introduction to the Mercedes-Benz 123 Series Diesel   5
Use of English   8
General dimensions   9
Vehicle identification numbers   9
Buying parts   10
Maintenance techniques, tools and working facilities   10
Booster battery (jump) starting   17
Jacking and towing   17
Safety first!   18
Automotive chemicals and lubricants   19
Conversion factors   20
Troubleshooting (fault diagnosis)   21

Chapter 1
Routine maintenance   28   1

Chapter 2 Part A
Engine   58   2A

Chapter 2 Part B
General engine overhaul procedures   81   2B

Chapter 3
Cooling, heating and air conditioning systems   107   3

Chapter 4 Part A
Fuel and exhaust systems   114   4A

Chapter 4 Part B
Turbocharger   124   4B

Chapter 5
Engine electrical systems   128   5

Chapter 6
Emissions control systems   134   6

Chapter 7 Part A
Manual transmission   136   7A

Chapter 7 Part B
Automatic transmission   147   7B

Chapter 8
Clutch and driveline   152   8

Chapter 9
Brakes   162   9

Chapter 10
Suspension and steering systems   174   10

Chapter 11
Body   185   11

Chapter 12
Chassis electrical system   202   12

Wiring diagrams   213

Index   300

Mercedes Benz 300TD station wagon

About this manual

Its purpose

The purpose of this manual is to help you get the best value from your vehicle. It can do so in several ways. It can help you decide what work must be done, even if you choose to have it done by a dealer service department or a repair shop; it provides information and procedures for routine maintenance and servicing; and it offers diagnostic and repair procedures to follow when trouble occurs.

It is hoped that you will use the manual to tackle the work yourself. For many simpler jobs, doing it yourself may be quicker than arranging an appointment to get the vehicle into a shop and making the trips to leave it and pick it up. More importantly, a lot of money can be saved by avoiding the expense the shop must pass on to you to cover its labor and overhead costs. An added benefit is the sense of satisfaction and accomplishment that you feel after having done the job yourself.

Using the manual

The manual is divided into Chapters. Each Chapter is divided into numbered Sections, which are headed in bold type between horizontal lines. Each Section consists of consecutively numbered paragraphs.

The two types of illustrations used (figures and photographs), are referenced by a number preceding their caption. Figure reference numbers denote Chapter and numerical sequence within the Chapter; (i.e. Fig. 3.4 means Chapter 3, figure number 4). Figure captions are followed by a Section number which ties the figure to a specific portion of the text. All photographs apply to the Chapter in which they appear and the reference number pinpoints the pertinent Section and paragraph; i.e., 3.2 means Section 3, paragraph 2.

Procedures, once described in the text, are not normally repeated. When it is necessary to refer to another Chapter, the reference will be given as Chapter and Section number i.e. Chapter 1/16). Cross references given without use of the word ''Chapter'' apply to Sections and/or paragraphs in the same Chapter. For example, ''see Section 8'' means in the same Chapter.

Reference to the left or right side of the vehicle is based on the assumption that one is sitting in the driver's seat, facing forward.

Even though extreme care has been taken during the preparation of this manual, neither the publisher nor the author can accept responsibility for any errors in, or omissions from, the information given.

NOTE

A **Note** provides information necessary to properly complete a procedure or information which will make the steps to be followed easier to understand.

CAUTION

A **Caution** indicates a special procedure or special steps which must be taken in the course of completing the procedure in which the **Caution** is found which are necessary to avoid damage to the assembly being worked on.

WARNING

A **Warning** indicates a special procedure or special steps which must be taken in the course of completing the procedure in which the **Warning** is found which are necessary to avoid injury to the person performing the procedure.

Introduction to the Mercedes-Benz 123 Series Diesel

These models are available in 2-door coupe, 4-door sedan and 4-door station wagon (touring wagon) body styles and feature four wheel independent suspension.

The 4-or 5-cylinder diesel engines used on these models drive the rear wheels through a choice of 4-or 5-speed manual or 4-speed automatic transmission. Some models are available with turbocharging. Certain models also feature automatic self-leveling of the rear suspension. Steering is of the recirculating ball-type with power assist

as standard. Servo assisted disc brakes are used on all four wheels and some models are equipped with an Anti-locking Brake System (ABS).

There are some detail differences between UK and US models due to local laws and regulations. Some models were available in certain areas, i.e. the 123 series 200D, 220D and 240TD were distributed only in the UK market.

Vehicle identification number locations on earlier US 240D and 300 models

1 Certification tag
2 VIN number
3 Chassis number
4 Body number, paint code number
5 Engine number
6 Emission tag
7 Emission control catalyst information

Vehicle identification number locations on US station wagon models

1 Certification tag
2 VIN number
3 Chassis number
4 Engine number
5 Body number, paint code number
6 California version emission vacuum line routing
7 Emission control tag
8 Emission control catalyst information

Vehicle identification number locations on UK models

1 Identification plate	3 Body number, paint code number
2 Chassis number	4 Engine number

Vehicle identification number locations on US models

1 Certification tag	5 Body and paintwork number
2 VIN number	6 Emissions tag (California 300TD turbo diesel only)
3 Chassis number	7 Emission control tag
4 Engine number	8 Emission control catalyst information

Use of English

As this book has been written in England, it uses the appropriate English component names, phrases, and spelling. Some of these differ from those used in America. Normally, these cause no difficulty, but to make sure, a glossary is printed below. In ordering spare parts remember the parts list may use some of these words:

English	American	English	American
Accelerator	Gas pedal	Locks	Latches
Aerial	Antenna	Methylated spirit	Denatured alcohol
Anti-roll bar	Stabiliser or sway bar	Motorway	Freeway, turnpike etc
Big-end bearing	Rod bearing	Number plate	License plate
Bonnet (engine cover)	Hood	Paraffin	Kerosene
Boot (luggage compartment)	Trunk	Petrol	Gasoline (gas)
Bulkhead	Firewall	Petrol tank	Gas tank
Bush	Bushing	'Pinking'	'Pinging'
Cam follower or tappet	Valve lifter or tappet	Prise (force apart)	Pry
Carburettor	Carburetor	Propeller shaft	Driveshaft
Catch	Latch	Quarterlight	Quarter window
Choke/venturi	Barrel	Retread	Recap
Circlip	Snap-ring	Reverse	Back-up
Clearance	Lash	Rocker cover	Valve cover
Crownwheel	Ring gear (of differential)	Saloon	Sedan
Damper	Shock absorber, shock	Seized	Frozen
Disc (brake)	Rotor/disk	Sidelight	Parking light
Distance piece	Spacer	Silencer	Muffler
Drop arm	Pitman arm	Sill panel (beneath doors)	Rocker panel
Drop head coupe	Convertible	Small end, little end	Piston pin or wrist pin
Dynamo	Generator (DC)	Spanner	Wrench
Earth (electrical)	Ground	Split cotter (for valve spring cap)	Lock (for valve spring retainer)
Engineer's blue	Prussian blue	Split pin	Cotter pin
Estate car	Station wagon	Steering arm	Spindle arm
Exhaust manifold	Header	Sump	Oil pan
Fault finding/diagnosis	Troubleshooting	Swarf	Metal chips or debris
Float chamber	Float bowl	Tab washer	Tang or lock
Free-play	Lash	Tappet	Valve lifter
Freewheel	Coast	Thrust bearing	Throw-out bearing
Gearbox	Transmission	Top gear	High
Gearchange	Shift	Torch	Flashlight
Grub screw	Setscrew, Allen screw	Trackrod (of steering)	Tie-rod (or connecting rod)
Gudgeon pin	Piston pin or wrist pin	Trailing shoe (of brake)	Secondary shoe
Halfshaft	Axleshaft	Transmission	Whole drive line
Handbrake	Parking brake	Tyre	Tire
Hood	Soft top	Van	Panel wagon/van
Hot spot	Heat riser	Vice	Vise
Indicator	Turn signal	Wheel nut	Lug nut
Interior light	Dome lamp	Windscreen	Windshield
Layshaft (of gearbox)	Countershaft	Wing/mudguard	Fender
Leading shoe (of brake)	Primary shoe		

General dimensions

Overall length

Coupe and 4-door sedan . . . . 186 in
Station wagon . . . . 190.9 in

Overall width

All models . . . . 70.3 in

Overall height

Coupe. . . . . 54.9 in
4-door sedan . . . . 56.6 in
Station wagon . . . . 57.9 in

Wheelbase

Coupe. . . . . 106.7 in
Sedan and station wagon . . . . 110 in

Vehicle identification numbers

Modifications are a continuing and unpublicized process in vehicle manufacturing. Since spare parts manuals and lists are compiled on a numerical basis, the vehicle numbers are essential to correctly identify the component required. On these models in particular, the chassis and engine numbers are critical when ordering parts. Consequently it is a good idea to record these numbers and keep this information in a convenient location. The accompanying illustrations show the locations of the various identification numbers.

The body and paintwork number information is located on a tag riveted to the radiator brace

The VIN number (US models only) is located on the drivers side windshield post

Buying parts

Replacement parts are available from many sources, which generally fall into one of two categories – authorized dealer parts departments and independent retail auto parts stores. Our advice concerning these parts is as follows:

Retail auto parts stores: Good auto parts stores will stock frequently needed components which wear out relatively fast, such as clutch components, exhaust systems, brake parts, tune-up parts, etc. These stores often supply new or reconditioned parts on an exchange basis, which can save a considerable amount of money. Discount auto parts stores are often very good places to buy materials and parts needed for general vehicle maintenance such as oil, grease, filters, spark plugs, belts, touch-up paint, bulbs, etc. They also usually sell tools and general accessories, have convenient hours, charge lower prices and can often be found not far from home.

Authorized dealer parts department: This is the best source for parts which are unique to the vehicle and not generally available elsewhere (such as major engine parts, transmission parts, trim pieces, etc.).

Warranty information: If the vehicle is still covered under warranty, be sure that any replacement parts purchased – regardless of the source – do not invalidate the warranty!

To be sure of obtaining the correct parts, have engine and chassis numbers available and, if possible, take the old parts along for positive identification.

Maintenance techniques, tools and working facilities

Maintenance techniques

There are a number of techniques involved in maintenance and repair that will be referred to throughout this manual. Application of these techniques will enable the home mechanic to be more efficient, better organized and capable of performing the various tasks properly, which will ensure that the repair job is thorough and complete.

Fasteners

Fasteners are nuts, bolts, studs and screws used to hold two or more parts together. There are a few things to keep in mind when working with fasteners. Almost all of them use a locking device of some type, either a lockwasher, locknut, locking tab or thread adhesive. All threaded fasteners should be clean and straight, with undamaged threads and undamaged corners on the hex head where the wrench fits. Develop the habit of replacing all damaged nuts and bolts with new ones. Special locknuts with nylon or fiber inserts can only be used once. If they are removed, they lose their locking ability and must be replaced with new ones.

Rusted nuts and bolts should be treated with a penetrating fluid to ease removal and prevent breakage. Some mechanics use turpentine in a spout-type oil can, which works quite well. After applying the rust penetrant, let it work for a few minutes before trying to loosen the nut or bolt. Badly rusted fasteners may have to be chiseled or sawed off or removed with a special nut breaker, available at tool stores.

If a bolt or stud breaks off in an assembly, it can be drilled and removed with a special tool commonly available for this purpose. Most automotive machine shops can perform this task, as well as other repair procedures, such as the repair of threaded holes that have been stripped out.

Flat washers and lockwashers, when removed from an assembly, should always be replaced exactly as removed. Replace any damaged washers with new ones. Never use a lockwasher on any soft metal surface (such as aluminum), thin sheet metal or plastic.

Fastener sizes

For a number of reasons, automobile manufacturers are making wider and wider use of metric fasteners. Therefore, it is important to be able to tell the difference between standard (sometimes called U.S. or SAE) and metric hardware, since they cannot be interchanged.

All bolts, whether standard or metric, are sized according to diameter, thread pitch and length. For example, a standard 1/2 — 13 x 1 bolt is 1/2 inch in diameter, has 13 threads per inch and is 1 inch long. An M12 — 1.75 x 25 metric bolt is 12 mm in diameter, has a thread pitch of 1.75 mm (the distance between threads) and is 25 mm long. The two bolts are nearly identical, and easily confused, but they are not interchangeable.

In addition to the differences in diameter, thread pitch and length, metric and standard bolts can also be distinguished by examining the bolt heads. To begin with, the distance across the flats on a standard bolt head is measured in inches, while the same dimension on a metric bolt is sized in millimeters (the same is true for nuts). As a result, a standard wrench should not be used on a metric bolt and a metric wrench should not be used on a standard bolt. Also, most standard bolts have slashes radiating out from the center of the head to denote the grade or strength of the bolt, which is an indication of the amount of torque that can be applied to it. The greater the number of slashes, the greater the strength of the bolt. Grades 0 through 5 are commonly used on automobiles. Metric bolts have a property class (grade) number, rather than a slash, molded into their heads to indicate bolt strength. In this case, the higher the number, the stronger the bolt. Property class numbers 8.8, 9.8 and 10.9 are commonly used on automobiles.

Strength markings can also be used to distinguish standard hex nuts from metric hex nuts. Many standard nuts have dots stamped into one side, while metric nuts are marked with a number. The greater the number of dots, or the higher the number, the greater the strength of the nut.

Metric studs are also marked on their ends according to property class (grade). Larger studs are numbered (the same as metric bolts),

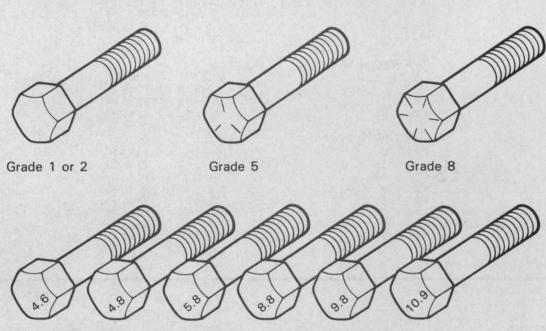

Grade 1 or 2   Grade 5   Grade 8

4.6   4.8   5.8   8.8   9.8   10.9

Bolt strength markings (top — standard/SAE/U.S.; bottom — metric)

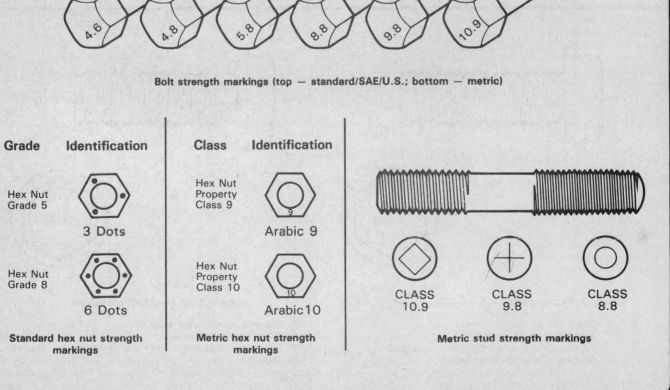

Grade	Identification
Hex Nut Grade 5	3 Dots
Hex Nut Grade 8	6 Dots

Standard hex nut strength markings

Class	Identification
Hex Nut Property Class 9	Arabic 9
Hex Nut Property Class 10	Arabic 10

Metric hex nut strength markings

CLASS 10.9   CLASS 9.8   CLASS 8.8

Metric stud strength markings

while smaller studs carry a geometric code to denote grade.

It should be noted that many fasteners, especially Grades 0 through 2, have no distinguishing marks on them. When such is the case, the only way to determine whether it is standard or metric is to measure the thread pitch or compare it to a known fastener of the same size.

Standard fasteners are often referred to as SAE, as opposed to metric. However, it should be noted that SAE technically refers to a non-metric *fine thread* fastener only. Coarse thread non-metric fasteners are referred to as U.S.S. sizes.

Since fasteners of the same size (both standard and metric) may have different strength ratings, be sure to reinstall any bolts, studs or nuts removed from your vehicle in their original locations. Also, when replacing a fastener with a new one, make sure that the new one has a strength rating equal to or greater than the original.

Tightening sequences and procedures

Most threaded fasteners should be tightened to a specific torque value (torque is the twisting force applied to a threaded component such as a nut or bolt). Overtightening the fastener can weaken it and cause it to break, while undertightening can cause it to eventually come loose. Bolts, screws and studs, depending on the material they are made of and their thread diameters, have specific torque values, many of which are noted in the Specifications at the beginning of each Chapter. Be sure to follow the torque recommendations closely. For fasteners not assigned a specific torque, a general torque value chart is presented here as a guide. As was previously mentioned, the size and grade of a fastener determine the amount of torque that can safely be applied to it. The figures listed here are approximate for Grade 2 and Grade 3 fasteners. Higher grades can tolerate higher torque values.

Metric thread sizes	Ft-lb	Nm/m
M-6	6 to 9	9 to 12
M-8	14 to 21	19 to 28
M-10	28 to 40	38 to 54
M-12	50 to 71	68 to 96
M-14	80 to 140	109 to 154

Pipe thread sizes		
1/8	5 to 8	7 to 10
1/4	12 to 18	17 to 24
3/8	22 to 33	30 to 44
1/2	25 to 35	34 to 47

U.S. thread sizes		
1/4 — 20	6 to 9	9 to 12
5/16 — 18	12 to 18	17 to 24
5/16 — 24	14 to 20	19 to 27
3/8 — 16	22 to 32	30 to 43
3/8 — 24	27 to 38	37 to 51
7/16 — 14	40 to 55	55 to 74
7/16 — 20	40 to 60	55 to 81
1/2 — 13	55 to 80	75 to 108

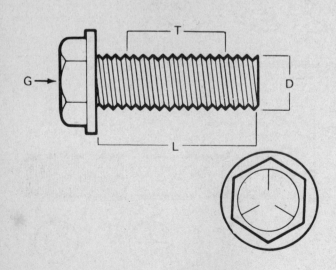

Standard (SAE and USS) bolt dimensions/grade marks

G Grade marks (bolt strength)
L Length (in inches)
T Thread pitch (number of threads per inch)
D Nominal diameter (in inches)

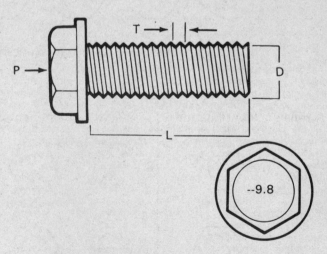

Metric bolt dimensions/grade marks

P Property class (bolt strength)
L Length (in millimeters)
T Thread pitch (distance between threads in millimeters)
D Diameter

Fasteners laid out in a pattern, such as cylinder head bolts, oil pan bolts, differential cover bolts, etc., must be loosened or tightened in sequence to avoid warping the component. This sequence will normally be shown in the appropriate Chapter. If a specific pattern is not given, the following procedures can be used to prevent warping.

Initially, the bolts or nuts should be assembled finger-tight only. Next, they should be tightened one full turn each, in a criss-cross or diagonal pattern. After each one has been tightened one full turn, return to the first one and tighten them all one-half turn, following the same pattern. Finally, tighten each of them one-quarter turn at a time until each fastener has been tightened to the proper torque. To loosen and remove the fasteners, the procedure would be reversed.

Component disassembly

Component disassembly should be done with care and purpose to help ensure that the parts go back together properly. Always keep track of the sequence in which parts are removed. Make note of special characteristics or marks on parts that can be installed more than one way, such as a grooved thrust washer on a shaft. It is a good idea to lay the disassembled parts out on a clean surface in the order that they were removed. It may also be helpful to make sketches or take instant photos of components before removal.

When removing fasteners from a component, keep track of their locations. Sometimes threading a bolt back in a part, or putting the washers and nut back on a stud, can prevent mix-ups later. If nuts and bolts cannot be returned to their original locations, they should be kept in a compartmented box or a series of small boxes. A cupcake or muffin tin is ideal for this purpose, since each cavity can hold the bolts and nuts from a particular area (i.e. oil pan bolts, valve cover bolts, engine mount bolts, etc.). A pan of this type is especially helpful when working on assemblies with very small parts, such as the alternator, valve train or interior dash and trim pieces. The cavities can be marked with paint or tape to identify the contents.

Whenever wiring looms, harnesses or connectors are separated, it is a good idea to identify the two halves with numbered pieces of masking tape so they can be easily reconnected.

Gasket sealing surfaces

Throughout any vehicle, gaskets are used to seal the mating surfaces between two parts and keep lubricants, fluids, vacuum or pressure contained in an assembly.

Many times these gaskets are coated with a liquid or paste-type gasket sealing compound before assembly. Age, heat and pressure can sometimes cause the two parts to stick together so tightly that they are very difficult to separate. Often, the assembly can be loosened by striking it with a soft-face hammer near the mating surfaces. A regular hammer can be used if a block of wood is placed between the hammer and the part. Do not hammer on cast parts or parts that could be easily damaged. With any particularly stubborn part, always recheck to make sure that every fastener has been removed.

Avoid using a screwdriver or bar to pry apart an assembly, as they can easily mar the gasket sealing surfaces of the parts, which must remain smooth. If prying is absolutely necessary, use an old broom handle, but keep in mind that extra clean up will be necessary if the wood splinters.

After the parts are separated, the old gasket must be carefully scraped off and the gasket surfaces cleaned. Stubborn gasket material can be soaked with rust penetrant or treated with a special chemical to soften it so it can be easily scraped off. A scraper can be fashioned from a piece of copper tubing by flattening and sharpening one end. Copper is recommended because it is usually softer than the surfaces to be scraped, which reduces the chance of gouging the part. Some gaskets can be removed with a wire brush, but regardless of the method used, the mating surfaces must be left clean and smooth. If for some reason the gasket surface is gouged, then a gasket sealer thick enough to fill scratches will have to be used during reassembly of the components. For most applications, a non-drying (or semi-drying) gasket sealer should be used.

Hose removal tips

Caution: *If the vehicle is equipped with air conditioning, do not disconnect any of the A/C hoses without first having the system depressurized by a dealer service department or an air conditioning specialist.*

Hose removal precautions closely parallel gasket removal precautions. Avoid scratching or gouging the surface that the hose mates against or the connection may leak. This is especially true for radiator hoses.

Because of various chemical reactions, the rubber in hoses can bond itself to the metal spigot that the hose fits over. To remove a hose, first loosen the hose clamps that secure it to the spigot. Then, with slip-joint pliers, grab the hose at the clamp and rotate it around the spigot. Work it back and forth until it is completely free, then pull it off. Silicone or other lubricants will ease removal if they can be applied between the hose and the outside of the spigot. Apply the same lubricant to the inside of the hose and the outside of the spigot to simplify installation.

As a last resort (and if the hose is to be replaced with a new one anyway), the rubber can be slit with a knife and the hose peeled from the spigot. If this must be done, be careful that the metal connection is not damaged.

If a hose clamp is broken or damaged, do not reuse it. Wire-type clamps usually weaken with age, so it is a good idea to replace them with screw-type clamps whenever a hose is removed.

Tools

A selection of good tools is a basic requirement for anyone who plans to maintain and repair his or her own vehicle. For the owner who has few tools, the initial investment might seem high, but when compared to the spiraling costs of professional auto maintenance and repair, it is a wise one.

To help the owner decide which tools are needed to perform the tasks detailed in this manual, the following tool lists are offered: *Maintenance and minor repair*, *Repair/overhaul* and *Special*.

The newcomer to practical mechanics should start off with the maintenance and minor repair tool kit, which is adequate for the simpler jobs performed on a vehicle. Then, as confidence and experience grow, the owner can tackle more difficult tasks, buying additional tools as they are needed. Eventually the basic kit will be expanded into the repair and overhaul tool set. Over a period of time, the experienced do-it-yourselfer will assemble a tool set complete enough for most repair and overhaul procedures and will add tools from the special category when it is felt that the expense is justified by the frequency of use.

Maintenance and minor repair tool kit

The tools in this list should be considered the minimum required for performance of routine maintenance, servicing and minor repair work. We recommend the purchase of combination wrenches (box-end and open-end combined in one wrench). While more expensive than open end wrenches, they offer the advantages of both types of wrench.

Combination wrench set (1/4-inch to 1 inch or 6 mm to 19 mm)
Adjustable wrench, 8 inch
Feeler gauge set
Brake bleeder wrench
Standard screwdriver (5/16-inch x 6 inch)
Phillips screwdriver (No. 2 x 6 inch)
Combination pliers — 6 inch
Hacksaw and assortment of blades
Tire pressure gauge
Grease gun
Oil can
Fine emery cloth
Wire brush
Battery post and cable cleaning tool
Oil filter wrench
Funnel (medium size)
Safety goggles
Jackstands (2)
Drain pan

Repair and overhaul tool set

These tools are essential for anyone who plans to perform major repairs and are in addition to those in the maintenance and minor repair tool kit. Included is a comprehensive set of sockets which, though expensive, are invaluable because of their versatility, especially when various extensions and drives are available. We recommend the 1/2-inch drive over the 3/8-inch drive. Although the larger drive is bulky and more expensive, it has the capacity of accepting a very wide range

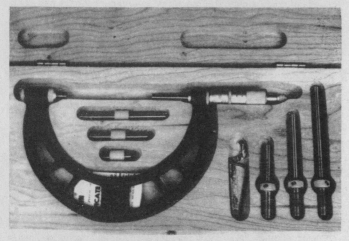

Micrometer set

Dial indicator set

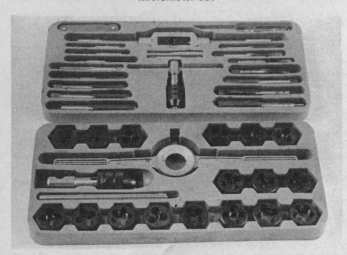

Tap and die set

of large sockets. Ideally, however, the mechanic should have a 3/8-inch drive set and a 1/2-inch drive set).

Socket set(s)
Reversible ratchet
Extension — 10 inch
Universal joint
Torque wrench (same size drive as sockets)
Ball peen hammer — 8 ounce
Soft-face hammer (plastic/rubber)
Standard screwdriver (1/4-inch x 6 inch)
Standard screwdriver (stubby — 5/16-inch)
Phillips screwdriver (No. 3 x 8 inch)
Phillips screwdriver (stubby — No. 2)
Pliers — vise grip
Pliers — lineman's
Pliers — needle nose
Pliers — snap-ring (internal and external)
Cold chisel — 1/2-inch
Scribe
Scraper (made from flattened copper tubing)
Centerpunch
Pin punches (1/16, 1/8, 3/16-inch)
Steel rule/straightedge — 12 inch
Allen wrench set (1/8 to 3/8-inch or 4 mm to 10 mm)
A selection of files
Wire brush (large)
Jackstands (second set)
Jack (scissor or hydraulic type)

Note: *Another tool which is often useful is an electric drill motor with a chuck capacity of 3/8-inch and a set of good quality drill bits.*

Special tools

The tools in this list include those which are not used regularly, are expensive to buy, or which need to be used in accordance with their manufacturer's instructions. Unless these tools will be used frequently, it is not very economical to purchase many of them. A consideration would be to split the cost and use between yourself and a friend or friends. In addition, most of these tools can be obtained from a tool rental shop on a temporary basis.

This list primarily contains only those tools and instruments widely available to the public, and not those special tools produced by the vehicle manufacturer for distribution to dealer service departments. Occasionally, references to the manufacturer's special tools are included in the text of this manual. Generally, an alternative method of doing the job without the special tool is offered. However, sometimes there is no alternative to their use. Where this is the case, and the tool cannot be purchased or borrowed, the work should be turned over to the dealer service department or an automotive repair shop.

Piston ring groove cleaning tool
Piston ring compressor
Piston ring installation tool
Cylinder ridge reamer
Cylinder surfacing hone
Cylinder bore gauge
Micrometers and/or dial calipers
Balljoint separator
Universal-type puller
Impact screwdriver
Dial indicator set
Hand operated vacuum/pressure pump
Universal electrical multimeter
Cable hoist
Brake spring removal and installation tools
Floor jack

Buying tools

For the do-it-yourselfer who is just starting to get involved in vehicle maintenance and repair, there are a number of options available when purchasing tools. If maintenance and minor repair is the extent of the work to be done, the purchase of individual tools is satisfactory. If, on the other hand, extensive work is planned, it would be a good idea to purchase a modest tool set from one of the large retail chain stores. A set can usually be bought at a substantial savings over the individual tool prices, and they often come with a tool box. As additional tools are needed, add-on sets, individual tools and a larger tool box can be purchased to expand the tool selection. Building a tool set gradually allows the cost of the tools to be spread over a longer period of time and gives the mechanic the freedom to choose only those tools that will actually be used.

Dial caliper

Hand-operated vacuum pump

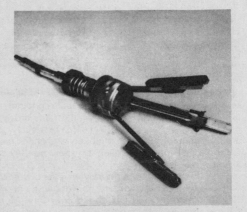
Cylinder hone

Ring compressor

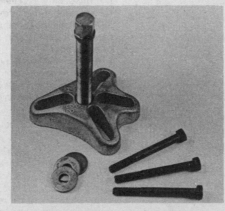
Damper/steering wheel puller

General purpose puller

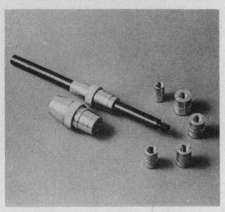
Clutch plate alignment tool

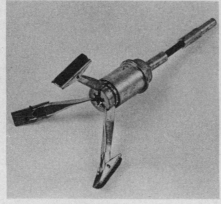
Brake cylinder hone

Brake hold-down spring tool

Ridge reamer

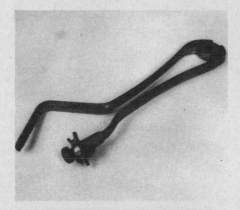
Piston ring groove cleaning tool

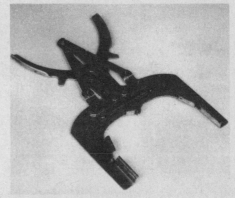
Ring removal/installation tool

Tool stores will often be the only source of some of the special tools that are needed, but regardless of where tools are bought, try to avoid cheap ones, especially when buying screwdrivers and sockets, because they won't last very long. The expense involved in replacing cheap tools will eventually be greater than the initial cost of quality tools.

Care and maintenance of tools

Good tools are expensive, so it makes sense to treat them with respect. Keep them clean and in usable condition and store them properly when not in use. Always wipe off any dirt, grease or metal chips before putting them away. Never leave tools lying around in the work area. Upon completion of a job, always check closely under the hood for tools that may have been left there so they won't get lost during a test drive.

Some tools, such as screwdrivers, pliers, wrenches and sockets, can be hung on a panel mounted on the garage or workshop wall, while others should be kept in a tool box or tray. Measuring instruments, gauges, meters, etc. must be carefully stored where they cannot be damaged by weather or impact from other tools.

When tools are used with care and stored properly, they will last a very long time. Even with the best of care, though, tools will wear out if used frequently. When a tool is damaged or worn out, replace it. Subsequent jobs will be safer and more enjoyable if you do.

Working facilities

Not to be overlooked when discussing tools is the workshop. If anything more than routine maintenance is to be carried out, some sort of suitable work area is essential.

It is understood, and appreciated, that many home mechanics do not have a good workshop or garage available, and end up removing an engine or doing major repairs outside. It is recommended, however, that the overhaul or repair be completed under the cover of a roof.

A clean, flat workbench or table of comfortable working height is an absolute necessity. The workbench should be equipped with a vise that has a jaw opening of at least four inches.

As mentioned previously, some clean, dry storage space is also required for tools, as well as the lubricants, fluids, cleaning solvents, etc. which soon become necessary.

Sometimes waste oil and fluids, drained from the engine or cooling system during normal maintenance or repairs, present a disposal problem. To avoid pouring them on the ground or into a sewage system, pour the used fluids into large containers, seal them with caps and take them to an authorized disposal site or recycling center (common in the U.S.). Plastic jugs, such as old antifreeze containers, are ideal for this purpose.

Always keep a supply of old newspapers and clean rags available. Old towels are excellent for mopping up spills. Many mechanics use rolls of paper towels for most work because they are readily available and disposable. To help keep the area under the vehicle clean, a large cardboard box can be cut open and flattened to protect the garage or shop floor.

Whenever working over a painted surface, such as when leaning over a fender to service something under the hood, always cover it with an old blanket or bedspread to protect the finish. Vinyl covered pads, made especially for this purpose, are available at auto parts stores.

Booster battery (jump) starting

Certain precautions must be observed when using a booster battery to jump start a vehicle.

    a) Before connecting the booster battery, make sure that the ignition switch is in the Off position.
    b) Turn off the lights, heater and other electrical loads.
    c) The eyes should be shielded. Safety goggles are a good idea.
    d) Make sure the booster battery is the same voltage as the dead one in the vehicle.
    e) The two vehicles must not touch each other.
    f) Make sure the transmission is in Neutral (manual transmission) or Park (automatic transmission).
    g) If the booster battery is not a maintenance-free type, remove the vent caps and lay a cloth over the vent holes.

Connect the red jumper cable to the *positive* (+) terminals of each battery.

Connect one end of the black jumper cable to the *negative* (–) terminal of the booster battery. The other end of this cable should be connected to a good ground on the vehicle to be started, such as a bolt or bracket on the engine block. Use caution to insure that the cable will not come into contact with the fan, drivebelts or other moving parts of the engine.

Start the engine using the booster battery, then, with the engine running at idle speed, disconnect the jumper cables in the reverse order of connection.

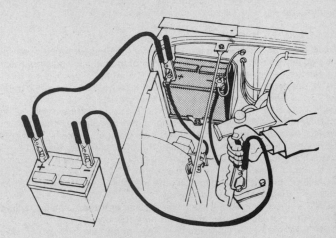

Booster cable connections (note that the negative cable is *not* attached to the negative terminal of the dead battery)

Jacking and towing

Jacking

The jack supplied with the vehicle should only be used for raising the vehicle when changing a tire or placing jackstands under the frame. **Caution:** *Never work under the vehicle or start the engine while this jack is being used as the only means of support.*

The vehicle should be on level ground with the wheels blocked, the parking brake applied and the transmission in Park (automatic) or Reverse (manual). If the wheels are to be removed from the vehicle, pry off the hub cap (if equipped) using the tapered end of the lug wrench and loosen the wheel bolts one-half turn. Do not loosen the bolts any more than this until the vehicle is off the ground. Refer to Chapter 10 for the complete tire changing procedure.

Insert the jack into the jacking point in the side of the vehicle. Operate the jack with a slow, smooth motion until the wheel is raised off the ground.

Lower the vehicle, remove the jack and tighten the bolts (if loosened or removed) in a criss-cross sequence by turning the wrench clockwise. Replace the hub cap (if equipped) by placing it in position and using the heel of your hand or a rubber mallet to seat it.

Towing

The vehicle can be towed with all four wheels on the ground, provided that speeds do not exceed 30 mph and the distance is not over 75 miles, otherwise transmission damage can result.

Towing equipment specifically designed for this purpose should be used and should be attached to the towing eyes under the bumpers which are connected to structural members of the vehicle and not the bumper or brackets.

The jack is inserted into the rocker panel jacking points

Safety is a major consideration when towing and all applicable laws must be obeyed. A safety chain system must be used for all towing.

While towing, the parking brake should be released and the transmission should be in Neutral. The steering must be unlocked (ignition switch in the Off position). Remember that power steering and power brakes will not work with the engine off.

Safety first!

Regardless of how enthusiastic you may be about getting on with the job at hand, take the time to ensure that your safety is not jeopardized. A moment's lack of attention can result in an accident, as can failure to observe certain simple safety precautions. The possibility of an accident will always exist, and the following points should not be considered a comprehensive list of all dangers. Rather, they are intended to make you aware of the risks and to encourage a safety conscious approach to all work you carry out on your vehicle.

Essential DOs and DON'Ts

DON'T rely on a jack when working under the vehicle. Always use approved jackstands to support the weight of the vehicle and place them under the recommended lift or support points.

DON'T attempt to loosen extremely tight fasteners (i.e. wheel lug nuts) while the vehicle is on a jack — it may fall.

DON'T start the engine without first making sure that the transmission is in Neutral (or Park where applicable) and the parking brake is set.

DON'T remove the radiator cap from a hot cooling system — let it cool or cover it with a cloth and release the pressure gradually.

DON'T attempt to drain the engine oil until you are sure it has cooled to the point that it will not burn you.

DON'T touch any part of the engine or exhaust system until it has cooled sufficiently to avoid burns.

DON'T siphon toxic liquids such as gasoline, antifreeze and brake fluid by mouth, or allow them to remain on your skin.

DON'T inhale brake lining dust — it is potentially hazardous (see *Asbestos* below)

DON'T allow spilled oil or grease to remain on the floor — wipe it up before someone slips on it.

DON'T use loose fitting wrenches or other tools which may slip and cause injury.

DON'T push on wrenches when loosening or tightening nuts or bolts. Always try to pull the wrench toward you. If the situation calls for pushing the wrench away, push with an open hand to avoid scraped knuckles if the wrench should slip.

DON'T attempt to lift a heavy component alone — get someone to help you.

DON'T rush or take unsafe shortcuts to finish a job.

DON'T allow children or animals in or around the vehicle while you are working on it.

DO wear eye protection when using power tools such as a drill, sander, bench grinder, etc. and when working under a vehicle.

DO keep loose clothing and long hair well out of the way of moving parts.

DO make sure that any hoist used has a safe working load rating adequate for the job.

DO get someone to check on you periodically when working alone on a vehicle.

DO carry out work in a logical sequence and make sure that everything is correctly assembled and tightened.

DO keep chemicals and fluids tightly capped and out of the reach of children and pets.

DO remember that your vehicle's safety affects that of yourself and others. If in doubt on any point, get professional advice.

Asbestos

Certain friction, insulating, sealing, and other products — such as brake linings, brake bands, clutch linings, torque converters, gaskets, etc. — contain asbestos. *Extreme care must be taken to avoid inhalation of dust from such products since it is hazardous to health.* If in doubt, assume that they *do* contain asbestos.

Fire

Remember at all times that gasoline is highly flammable. Never smoke or have any kind of open flame around when working on a vehicle. But the risk does not end there. A spark caused by an electrical short circuit, by two metal surfaces contacting each other, or even by static electricity built up in your body under certain conditions, can ignite gasoline vapors, which in a confined space are highly explosive. Do not, under any circumstances, use gasoline for cleaning parts. Use an approved safety solvent.

Always disconnect the battery ground (–) cable *at the battery* before working on any part of the fuel system or electrical system. Never risk spilling fuel on a hot engine or exhaust component.

It is strongly recommended that a fire extinguisher suitable for use on fuel and electrical fires be kept handy in the garage or workshop at all times. Never try to extinguish a fuel or electrical fire with water.

Torch (flashlight in the US)

Any reference to a "torch" appearing in this manual should always be taken to mean a hand-held, battery-operated electric light or flashlight. It DOES NOT mean a welding or propane torch or blowtorch.

Fumes

Certain fumes are highly toxic and can quickly cause unconsciousness and even death if inhaled to any extent. Gasoline vapor falls into this category, as do the vapors from some cleaning solvents. Any draining or pouring of such volatile fluids should be done in a well ventilated area.

When using cleaning fluids and solvents, read the instructions on the container carefully. Never use materials from unmarked containers.

Never run the engine in an enclosed space, such as a garage. Exhaust fumes contain carbon monoxide, which is extremely poisonous. If you need to run the engine, always do so in the open air, or at least have the rear of the vehicle outside the work area.

If you are fortunate enough to have the use of an inspection pit, never drain or pour gasoline and never run the engine while the vehicle is over the pit. The fumes, being heavier than air, will concentrate in the pit with possibly lethal results.

The battery

Never create a spark or allow a bare light bulb near a battery. They normally give off a certain amount of hydrogen gas, which is highly explosive.

Always disconnect the battery ground (–) cable *at the battery* before working on the fuel or electrical systems.

If possible, loosen the filler caps or cover when charging the battery from an external source (this does not apply to sealed or maintenance-free batteries). Do not charge at an excessive rate or the battery may burst.

Take care when adding water to a non maintenance-free battery and when carrying a battery. The electrolyte, even when diluted, is very corrosive and should not be allowed to contact clothing or skin.

Always wear eye protection when cleaning the battery to prevent the caustic deposits from entering your eyes.

Mains electricity (household current in the US)

When using an electric power tool, inspection light, etc., which operates on household current, always make sure that the tool is correctly connected to its plug and that, where necessary, it is properly grounded. Do not use such items in damp conditions and, again, do not create a spark or apply excessive heat in the vicinity of fuel or fuel vapor.

Secondary ignition system voltage

A severe electric shock can result from touching certain parts of the ignition system (such as the spark plug wires) when the engine is running or being cranked, particularly if components are damp or the insulation is defective. In the case of an electronic ignition system, the secondary system voltage is much higher and could prove fatal.

Automotive chemicals and lubricants

A number of automotive chemicals and lubricants are available for use during vehicle maintenance and repair. They include a wide variety of products ranging from cleaning solvents and degreasers to lubricants and protective sprays for rubber, plastic and vinyl.

Cleaners

Brake system cleaner is used to remove grease and brake fluid from the brake system where clean surfaces are absolutely necessary. It leaves no residue and often eliminates brake squeal caused by contaminants.

Electrical cleaner removes oxidation, corrosion and carbon deposits from electrical contacts, restoring full current flow. It can also be used to clean voltage regulators and other parts where an oil-free surface is desired.

Demoisturants remove water and moisture from electrical components such as alternators, voltage regulators, electrical connectors and fuse blocks. It is non-conductive, non-corrosive and non-flammable.

Degreasers are heavy-duty solvents used to remove grease from the outside of the engine and from chassis components. They can be sprayed or brushed on, and, depending on the type, are rinsed off either with water or solvent.

Lubricants

Motor oil is the lubricant formulated for use in engines. It normally contains a wide variety of additives to prevent corrosion and reduce foaming and wear. Motor oil comes in various weights (viscosity ratings) from 5 to 80. The recommended weight of the oil depends on the season, temperature and the demands on the engine. Light oil is used in cold climates and under light load conditions. Heavy oil is used in hot climates and where high loads are encountered. Multi-viscosity oils are designed to have characteristics of both light and heavy oils and are available in a number of weights from 5W-20 to 20W-50.

Gear oil is designed to be used in differentials, manual transmissions and other areas where high-temperature lubrication is required.

Chassis and wheel bearing grease is a heavy grease used where increased loads and friction are encountered, such as for wheel bearings, balljoints, tie rod ends and universal joints.

High temperature wheel bearing grease is designed to withstand the extreme temperatures encountered by wheel bearings in disc brake equipped vehicles. It usually contains molybdenun disulfide (moly), which is a dry-type lubricant.

White grease is a heavy grease for metal to metal applications where water is a problem. White grease stays soft under both low and high temperatures (usually from −100°F to +190°F), and will not wash off or dilute in the presence of water.

Assembly lube is a special extreme pressure lubricant, usually containing moly, used to lubricate high-load parts such as main and rod bearings and cam lobes for initial start-up of a new engine. The assembly lube lubricates the parts without being squeezed out or washed away until the engine oiling system begins to function.

Silicone lubricants are used to protect rubber, plastic, vinyl and nylon parts.

Graphite lubricants are used where oils cannot be used due to contamination problems, such as in locks. The dry graphite will lubricate metal parts while remaining uncontaminated by dirt, water, oil or acids. It is electrically conductive and will not foul electrical contacts in locks such as the ignition switch.

Moly penetrants loosen and lubricate frozen, rusted and corroded fasteners and prevent future rusting or freezing.

Heat-sink grease is a special electrically non-conductive grease that is used for mounting HEI ignition modules where it is essential that heat be transferred away from the module.

Sealants

RTV sealant is one of the most widely used gasket compounds. Made from silicone, RTV is air curing, it seals, bonds, waterproofs, fills surface irregularities, remains flexible, doesn't shrink, is relatively easy to remove, and is used as a supplementary sealer with almost all low and medium temperature gaskets.

Anaerobic sealant is much like RTV in that it can be used either to seal gaskets or to form gaskets by itself. It remains flexible, is solvent resistant and fills surface imperfections. The difference between an anaerobic sealant and an RTV-type sealant is in the curing. RTV cures when exposed to air, while an anaerobic sealant cures only in the absence of air. This means that an anaerobic sealant cures only after the assembly of parts, sealing them together.

Thread and pipe sealant is used for sealing hydraulic and pneumatic fittings and vacuum lines. It is usually made from a teflon compound, and comes in a spray, a paint-on liquid and as a wrap-around tape.

Chemicals

Anti-seize compound prevents seizing, galling, cold welding, rust and corrosion in fasteners. High temperature anti-seize, usually made with copper and graphite lubricants, is used for exhaust system and manifold bolts.

Anaerobic locking compounds are used to keep fasteners from vibrating or working loose, and cure only after installation, in the absence of air. Medium strength locking compound is used for small nuts, bolts and screws that you expect to be removing later. High strength locking compound is for large nuts, bolts and studs which you don't intend to be removing on a regular basis.

Oil additives range from viscosity index improvers to chemical treatments that claim to reduce internal engine friction. It should be noted that most oil manufacturers caution against using additives with their oils.

Fuel additives perform several functions, depending on their chemical makeup. They usually contain solvents that help dissolve carbon deposits that form on the inside surfaces of the combustion chambers. Some additives contain upper cylinder lubricants for valves and piston rings, and others chemicals to remove condensation from the fuel tank.

Other

Brake fluid is specially formulated hydraulic fluid that can withstand the heat and pressure encountered in brake systems. Care must be taken that this fluid does not come in contact with painted surfaces or plastics. An opened container should always be resealed to prevent contamination by water or dirt.

Weatherstrip adhesive is used to bond weatherstripping around doors, windows and trunk lids. It is sometimes used to attach trim pieces.

Undercoating is a petroleum-based tar-like substance that is designed to protect metal surfaces on the underside of the vehicle from corrosion. It also acts as a sound-deadening agent by insulating the bottom of the vehicle.

Waxes and polishes are used to help protect painted and plated surfaces from the weather. Different types of paint may require the use of different types of wax and polish. Some polishes utilize a chemical or abrasive cleaner to help remove the top layer of oxidized (dull) paint on older vehicles. In recent years many non-wax polishes that contain a wide variety of chemicals such as polymers and silicones have been introduced. These non-wax polishes are usually easier to apply and last longer than conventional waxes and polishes.

Conversion factors

Length (distance)

Inches (in)	X	25.4	=	Millimetres (mm)	X	0.0394	=	Inches (in)
Feet (ft)	X	0.305	=	Metres (m)	X	3.281	=	Feet (ft)
Miles	X	1.609	=	Kilometres (km)	X	0.621	=	Miles

Volume (capacity)

Cubic inches (cu in; in³)	X	16.387	=	Cubic centimetres (cc; cm³)	X	0.061	=	Cubic inches (cu in; in³)
Imperial pints (Imp pt)	X	0.568	=	Litres (l)	X	1.76	=	Imperial pints (Imp pt)
Imperial quarts (Imp qt)	X	1.137	=	Litres (l)	X	0.88	=	Imperial quarts (Imp qt)
Imperial quarts (Imp qt)	X	1.201	=	US quarts (US qt)	X	0.833	=	Imperial quarts (Imp qt)
US quarts (US qt)	X	0.946	=	Litres (l)	X	1.057	=	US quarts (US qt)
Imperial gallons (Imp gal)	X	4.546	=	Litres (l)	X	0.22	=	Imperial gallons (Imp gal)
Imperial gallons (Imp gal)	X	1.201	=	US gallons (US gal)	X	0.833	=	Imperial gallons (Imp gal)
US gallons (US gal)	X	3.785	=	Litres (l)	X	0.264	=	US gallons (US gal)

Mass (weight)

Ounces (oz)	X	28.35	=	Grams (g)	X	0.035	=	Ounces (oz)
Pounds (lb)	X	0.454	=	Kilograms (kg)	X	2.205	=	Pounds (lb)

Force

Ounces-force (ozf; oz)	X	0.278	=	Newtons (N)	X	3.6	=	Ounces-force (ozf; oz)
Pounds-force (lbf; lb)	X	4.448	=	Newtons (N)	X	0.225	=	Pounds-force (lbf; lb)
Newtons (N)	X	0.1	=	Kilograms-force (kgf; kg)	X	9.81	=	Newtons (N)

Pressure

Pounds-force per square inch (psi; lbf/in²; lb/in²)	X	0.070	=	Kilograms-force per square centimetre (kgf/cm²; kg/cm²)	X	14.223	=	Pounds-force per square inch (psi; lbf/in²; lb/in²)
Pounds-force per square inch (psi; lbf/in²; lb/in²)	X	0.068	=	Atmospheres (atm)	X	14.696	=	Pounds-force per square inch (psi; lbf/in²; lb/in²)
Pounds-force per square inch (psi; lbf/in²; lb/in²)	X	0.069	=	Bars	X	14.5	=	Pounds-force per square inch (psi; lbf/in²; lb/in²)
Pounds-force per square inch (psi; lbf/in²; lb/in²)	X	6.895	=	Kilopascals (kPa)	X	0.145	=	Pounds-force per square inch (psi; lbf/in²; lb/in²)
Kilopascals (kPa)	X	0.01	=	Kilograms-force per square centimetre (kgf/cm²; kg/cm²)	X	98.1	=	Kilopascals (kPa)
Millibar (mbar)	X	100	=	Pascals (Pa)	X	0.01	=	Millibar (mbar)
Millibar (mbar)	X	0.0145	=	Pounds-force per square inch (psi; lbf/in²; lb/in²)	X	68.947	=	Millibar (mbar)
Millibar (mbar)	X	0.75	=	Millimetres of mercury (mmHg)	X	1.333	=	Millibar (mbar)
Millibar (mbar)	X	0.401	=	Inches of water (inH₂O)	X	2.491	=	Millibar (mbar)
Millimetres of mercury (mmHg)	X	0.535	=	Inches of water (inH₂O)	X	1.868	=	Millimetres of mercury (mmHg)
Inches of water (inH₂O)	X	0.036	=	Pounds-force per square inch (psi; lbf/in²; lb/in²)	X	27.68	=	Inches of water (inH₂O)

Torque (moment of force)

Pounds-force inches (lbf in; lb in)	X	1.152	=	Kilograms-force centimetre (kgf cm; kg cm)	X	0.868	=	Pounds-force inches (lbf in; lb in)
Pounds-force inches (lbf in; lb in)	X	0.113	=	Newton metres (Nm)	X	8.85	=	Pounds-force inches (lbf in; lb in)
Pounds-force inches (lbf in; lb in)	X	0.083	=	Pounds-force feet (lbf ft; lb ft)	X	12	=	Pounds-force inches (lbf in; lb in)
Pounds-force feet (lbf ft; lb ft)	X	0.138	=	Kilograms-force metres (kgf m; kg m)	X	7.233	=	Pounds-force feet (lbf ft; lb ft)
Pounds-force feet (lbf ft; lb ft)	X	1.356	=	Newton metres (Nm)	X	0.738	=	Pounds-force feet (lbf ft; lb ft)
Newton metres (Nm)	X	0.102	=	Kilograms-force metres (kgf m; kg m)	X	9.804	=	Newton metres (Nm)

Power

Horsepower (hp)	X	745.7	=	Watts (W)	X	0.0013	=	Horsepower (hp)

Velocity (speed)

Miles per hour (miles/hr; mph)	X	1.609	=	Kilometres per hour (km/hr; kph)	X	0.621	=	Miles per hour (miles/hr; mph)

Fuel consumption*

Miles per gallon, Imperial (mpg)	X	0.354	=	Kilometres per litre (km/l)	X	2.825	=	Miles per gallon, Imperial (mpg)
Miles per gallon, US (mpg)	X	0.425	=	Kilometres per litre (km/l)	X	2.352	=	Miles per gallon, US (mpg)

Temperature

Degrees Fahrenheit = (°C x 1.8) + 32

Degrees Celsius (Degrees Centigrade; °C) = (°F - 32) x 0.56

*It is common practice to convert from miles per gallon (mpg) to litres/100 kilometres (l/100km), where mpg (Imperial) x l/100 km = 282 and mpg (US) x l/100 km = 235

Troubleshooting

Contents

Symptom	Section
Engine	
Engine continues to run after switching off	18
Engine hard to start when cold	4
Engine hard to start when hot	5
Engine lacks power	15
Engine lopes while idling or idles erratically	9
Engine misses at idle speed	10
Engine misses throughout driving speed range	11
Engine rotates but will not start	2
Engine runs with oil pressure light on	17
Engine stalls	14
Engine starts but stops immediately	7
Engine stumbles on acceleration	12
Engine surges while holding accelerator steady	13
Engine will not rotate when attempting to start	1
Oil puddle under engine	8
Pinging or knocking engine sounds during acceleration or uphill	16
Starter motor noisy or excessively rough in engagement	6
Starter motor operates without rotating engine	3

Symptom	Section
Engine electrical system	
Alternator light fails to go out	20
Battery will not hold a charge	19
Ignition and/or preglow light fails to come on when key is turned on	21

Symptom	Section
Fuel system	
Excessive fuel consumption	22
Fuel leakage and/or fuel odor	23

Symptom	Section
Cooling system	
Coolant loss	28
External coolant leakage	26
Internal coolant leakage	27
Overcooling	25
Overheating	24
Poor coolant circulation	29

Symptom	Section
Clutch	
Clutch slips (engine speed increases with no increase in vehicle speed)	31
Clutch pedal stays on floor when disengaged	35
Fails to release (pedal pressed to the floor — shift lever does not move freely in and out of Reverse)	30
Grabbing (chattering) as clutch is engaged	32
Squeal or rumble with clutch fully disengaged (pedal depressed)	34
Squeal or rumble with clutch fully engaged (pedal released)	33

Symptom	Section
Manual transmission	
Difficulty in engaging gears	40
Noisy in all gears	37
Noisy in Neutral with engine running	36
Noisy in one particular gear	38
Oil leakage	41
Slips out of gear	39

Symptom	Section
Automatic transmission	
Engine will start in gears other than Park or Neutral	46
Fluid leakage	42
General shift mechanism problems	44
Transmission slips, shifts rough, is noisy or has no drive in forward or reverse gears	47

Symptom	Section
Transmission will not downshift with accelerator pedal pressed to the floor	45
Transmission fluid brown or has burned smell	43

Symptom	Section
Driveshaft	
Knock or clunk when transmission is put under initial load (just after transmission is put into gear)	49
Leakage of fluid at front of driveshaft	48
Metallic grating sound consistent with road speed	50
Vibration	51

Symptom	Section
Differential/final drive unit	
Noise — same when in drive as when vehicle is coasting	52
Oil leakage	54
Vibration	53

Symptom	Section
Brakes	
Brake pedal feels spongy when depressed	58
Brake pedal pulsates during brake application	61
Excessive brake pedal travel	57
Excessive effort required to stop vehicle	59
Noise (high-pitched squeal without the brakes applied)	56
Pedal travels to the floor with little resistance	60
Parking brake does not hold	62
Vehicle pulls to one side during braking	55

Symptom	Section
Suspension and steering systems	
Excessive pitching and/or rolling around corners or during braking	65
Excessive play in steering	67
Excessive tire wear (not specific to one area)	69
Excessive tire wear on inside edge	71
Excessive tire wear on outside edge	70
Excessively stiff steering	66
Lack of power assistance	68
Shimmy, shake or vibration	64
Tire tread worn in one place	72
Vehicle pulls to one side	63

This section provides an easy reference guide to the more common problems which may occur during the operation of your vehicle. These problems and possible causes are grouped under various components or systems; i.e. Engine, Cooling system, etc., and also refer to the Chapter and/or Section which deals with the problem.

Remember that successful troubleshooting is not a mysterious *black art* practiced only by professional mechanics. It's simply the result of a bit of knowledge combined with an intelligent, systematic approach to the problem. Always work by a process of elimination, starting with the simplest solution and working through to the most complex — and never overlook the obvious. Anyone can forget to fill the fuel tank or leave the lights on overnight, so don't assume that you are above such oversights.

Finally, always get clear in your mind why a problem has occurred and take steps to ensure that it doesn't happen again. If the electrical system fails because of a poor connection, check all other connections in the system to make sure that they don't fail as well. If a particular fuse continues to blow, find out why — don't just go on replacing fuses. Remember, failure of a small component can often be indicative of potential failure or incorrect functioning of a more important component or system.

Engine

1   Engine will not rotate when attempting to start

1   Battery terminal connections loose or corroded. Check the cable terminals at the battery. Tighten the cable or remove corrosion as necessary.
2   Battery discharged or faulty. If the cable connections are clean and tight on the battery posts, turn the key to the On position and switch on the headlights and/or windshield wipers. If they fail to function, the battery is discharged.
3   Automatic transmission not completely engaged in Park or clutch not completely depressed.
4   Broken, loose or disconnected wiring in the starting circuit. Inspect all wiring and connectors at the battery, starter solenoid and ignition switch.
5   Starter motor pinion jammed in flywheel ring gear. If manual transmission, place transmission in gear and rock the vehicle to manually turn the engine. Remove starter and inspect pinion and flywheel at earliest convenience.
6   Starter solenoid faulty (Chapter 5).
7   Starter motor faulty (Chapter 5).
8   Steering lock and/or ignition switch faulty (Chapter 10).

2   Engine rotates but will not start

1   Fuel tank empty.
2   Battery discharged (engine rotates slowly). Check the operation of electrical components as described in previous Section.
3   Battery terminal connections loose or corroded. See previous Section.
4   Fuel injection timing or start of delivery incorrect (Chapter 4).
5   Fuel injection pump faulty (Chapter 4).
6   Broken, loose or disconnected wiring in the starting circuit (see previous Section).
7   Broken or damaged glow plug(s) (Chapter 5).
8   Broken, loose or disconnected glow plug wires.
9   Loose or leaking fuel injection lines.
10   Contaminated fuel.

3   Starter motor operates without rotating engine

1   Starter pinion sticking. Remove the starter (Chapter 5) and inspect.
2   Starter pinion or flywheel teeth worn or broken. Remove the cover at the rear of the engine and inspect.

4   Engine hard to start when cold

1   Battery discharged or low. Check as described in Section 1.
2   Glow plug wires loose or damaged (Chapter 5).
3   Fuel injection timing or start of delivery out of adjustment (Chapter 4).
4   Leaking fuel injection line.
5   Leaking fuel injector.

5   Engine hard to start when hot

1   Air filter clogged (Chapter 1).
2   Fuel not reaching the injectors (see Section 2).
3   Fuel injector nozzle clogged (Chapter 5).
4   Leaking fuel injection line.

6   Starter motor noisy or excessively rough in engagement

1   Pinion or flywheel gear teeth worn or broken. Remove the cover at the rear of the engine (if so equipped) and inspect.
2   Starter motor mounting bolts loose or missing.

7   Engine starts but stops immediately

1   Insufficient fuel reaching the fuel injector(s) (Chapter 5).
2   Idle speed set too low (Chapter 1).
3   Air in fuel injection lines.
4   Contaminated fuel.

8   Oil puddle under engine

1   Oil pan gasket and/or oil plug seal leaking. Check and replace if necessary.
2   Camshaft cover gasket leaking at front or rear of engine.
3   Engine oil seals leaking at front or rear of engine.
4   Leaking oil filter housing.
5   Leaking oil cooler or associated lines.
6   Oil pressure gauge sender line.
7   Leaking turbocharger oil feed or return line.

9   Engine lopes while idling or idles erratically

1   Air filter clogged (Chapter 1).
2   Fault in the fuel injection pump or timer.
3   Clogged fuel injector.
4   Leaking head gasket. If this is suspected, take the vehicle to a repair shop or dealer where the engine can be pressure checked.
5   Timing chain worn (Chapter 2).
6   Camshaft lobes worn (Chapter 2).
7   Contaminated fuel.

10   Engine misses at idle speed

Clogged fuel injector

11   Engine misses throughout driving speed range

1   Fuel filter clogged and/or impurities in the fuel system (Chapter 1).
2   Clogged fuel injector.
3   Low or uneven cylinder compression pressures. Have the compression checked.
4   Fault in the fuel injection pump or timer.

12   Engine stumbles on acceleration

1   Fuel injection timing device out of adjustment.
2   Fuel filter clogged. Replace filter.
4   Fault in the fuel injection system.

13   Engine surges while holding accelerator steady

Fuel injection pump fault.

14   Engine stalls

1   Idle speed incorrect (Chapter 1).
2   Fuel filter clogged and/or water and impurities in the fuel system (Chapter 1).
3   Valve clearances incorrectly set (Chapter 2).
4   Fuel injection pump fault.
5   Leaking fuel injection line.

15 Engine lacks power

1 Fuel injection system fault.
2 Fuel injection start of delivery out of adjustment (Chapter 4).
3 Brakes binding (Chapter 1).
4 Automatic transmission fluid level incorrect (Chapter 1).
5 Clutch slipping (Chapter 8).
6 Fuel filter clogged and/or impurities in the fuel system (Chapter 1).
7 Use of substandard fuel. Fill tank with proper fuel.
8 Low or uneven cylinder compression pressures. Have the compression tested, which will detect leaking valves and/or blown head gasket.
9 Turbocharger fault.

16 Pinging or knocking engine sounds during acceleration or uphill

1 Incorrect grade of fuel. Fill tank with fuel of the proper grade.
2 Fuel injection unit in need of adjustment (Chapter 4).

17 Engine runs with oil pressure light on

1 Low oil level. Check oil level and add oil if necessary (Chapter 1).
2 Idle rpm below specification (Chapter 1).
3 Short in wiring circuit. Repair or replace damaged wire.
4 Faulty oil pressure sender. Replace sender.
5 Worn engine bearings and/or oil pump.
6 Oil pressure gauge line leak.

18 Engine continues to run after switching off

Fault in fuel system cut off solenoid: turn off the engine by pressing the Stop lever located on the rear of the fuel injection pump.

Engine electrical system

19 Battery will not hold a charge

1 Alternator drivebelt defective or not adjusted properly (Chapter 1).
2 Electrolyte level low or battery discharged (Chapter 1).
3 Battery terminals loose or corroded (Chapter 1).
4 Alternator not charging properly (Chapter 5).
5 Loose, broken or faulty wiring in the charging circuit (Chapter 5).
6 Short in vehicle wiring causing a continual drain on battery.
7 Battery defective internally.

20 Alternator light fails to go out

1 Fault in alternator or charging circuit (Chapter 5).
2 Alternator drivebelt defective or not properly adjusted (Chapter 1).
3 Alternator voltage regulator inoperative (Chapter 5).

21 Ignition and/or preglow light fails to come on when key is turned on

1 Warning and/or preglow light bulb(s) defective (Chapter 12).
2 Alternator faulty (Chapter 5).
3 Fault in the instrument cluster wiring or bulb holder (Chapter 12).
4 Preglow system fault.

Fuel system

22 Excessive fuel consumption

1 Dirty or clogged air filter element (Chapter 1).
2 Fuel injection system excessively worn or damaged (Chapter 4).
3 Low tire pressure or incorrect tire size (Chapter 1).

23 Fuel leakage and/or fuel odor

1 Leak in a fuel feed or vent line (Chapters 1 and 4).
2 Tank overfilled. Fill only to automatic shut off.
3 Vapor leaks from system lines (Chapter 4).
4 Fuel injection system internal parts excessively worn or out of adjustment (Chapter 4).
5 Fuel injection lines loose or leaking.
6 Loose or leaking fuel injection lines.
7 Fuel injection pump leak.

Cooling system

24 Overheating

1 Insufficient coolant in system (Chapter 1).
2 Water pump drivebelt defective or not adjusted properly (Chapter 1).
3 Radiator core blocked or radiator grille dirty and restricted (Chapter 3).
4 Thermostat faulty (Chapter 3).
5 Fan blades broken or cracked (Chapter 3).
6 Radiator cap not maintaining proper pressure. Have cap pressure tested by gas station or repair shop.
7 Idle speed incorrect (Chapter 1).
8 Defective water pump (Chapter 3).
9 Blown head gasket.

25 Overcooling

1 Thermostat faulty (Chapter 3).
2 Inaccurate temperature gauge (Chapter 12)

26 External coolant leakage

1 Deteriorated or damaged hoses or loose clamps. Replace hoses and/or tighten clamps at hose connections (Chapter 1).
2 Water pump seals defective. If this is the case, water will drip from the weep hole in the water pump body (Chapter 1).
3 Leakage from radiator core or header tank. This will require the radiator to be professionally repaired (see Chapter 3 for removal procedures).
4 Engine drain plugs or water jacket core plugs leaking (see Chapter 2).

27 Internal coolant leakage

Note: Internal coolant leaks can usually be detected by examining the oil. Check the dipstick and inside of the camshaft cover for water deposits and an oil consistency like that of a milkshake.

1 Leaking cylinder head gasket. Have the cooling system pressure tested.
2 Cracked cylinder bore or cylinder head. Dismantle engine and inspect (Chapter 2).
3 Loose cylinder head bolts (Chapter 2).

28   Coolant loss

1   Too much coolant in system (Chapter 1).
2   Coolant boiling away due to overheating (see Section 16).
3   Internal or external leakage (see Sections 25 and 26).
4   Faulty radiator cap. Have the cap pressure tested.

29   Poor coolant circulation

1   Inoperative water pump. A quick test is to pinch the top radiator hose closed with your hand while the engine is idling, then let it loose. You should feel the surge of coolant if the pump is working properly (Chapter 1).
2   Restriction in cooling system. Drain, flush and refill the system (Chapter 1). If necessary, remove the radiator (Chapter 3) and have it reverse flushed.
3   Water pump drivebelt defective or not adjusted properly (Chapter 1).
4   Thermostat sticking (Chapter 3).

Clutch

30   Fails to release (pedal pressed to the floor — shift lever does not move freely in and out of Reverse)

1   Air in clutch hydraulic system (Chapter 8).
2   Clutch disc sticking on the input shaft splines.
3   Clutch plate warped or damaged (Chapter 8).

31   Clutch slips (engine speed increases with no increase in vehicle speed)

1   Clutch plate oil soaked or lining worn. Remove clutch (Chapter 8) and inspect.
2   Clutch plate not seated. It may take 30 or 40 normal starts for a new one to seat.
3   Weak or damaged diaphragm spring.

32   Grabbing (chattering) as clutch is engaged

1   Oil on clutch plate lining. Remove (Chapter 8) and inspect. Correct any leakage source.
2   Worn or loose engine or transmission mounts. These units move slightly when clutch is released. Inspect mounts and bolts.
3   Worn splines on clutch plate hub. Remove clutch components (Chapter 8) and inspect.
4   Warped pressure plate or flywheel. Remove clutch components and inspect.
5   Hardened or warped clutch disc facing.

33   Squeal or rumble with clutch fully engaged (pedal released)

1   Release bearing binding on transmission bearing retainer. Remove clutch components (Chapter 8) and check bearing. Remove any burrs or nicks, clean and relubricate before reinstallation.
2   Cracked clutch disc.

34   Squeal or rumble with clutch fully disengaged (pedal depressed)

1   Worn, defective or broken release bearing (Chapter 8).
2   Worn or broken pressure plate springs or diaphragm fingers (Chapter 8).

35   Clutch pedal stays on floor when disengaged

1   Bind in linkage or release bearing. Inspect linkage or remove clutch components as necessary.
2   Fault in the clutch hydraulic system or slave cylinder (Chapter 8)

Manual transmission

36   Noisy in Neutral with engine running

1   Input shaft bearing worn.
2   Damaged main drive gear bearing.
3   Worn countershaft bearings.

37   Noisy in all gears

1   Any of the above causes, and/or:
2   Insufficient lubricant (see checking procedures in Chapter 1).
3   Worn or damaged output shaft or bearings.

38   Noisy in one particular gear

1   Worn, damaged or chipped gear teeth for that particular gear.
2   Worn or damaged synchronizer for that particular gear.

39   Slips out of gear

1   Transmission loose on clutch housing (Chapter 7).
2   Shift rods not working freely (Chapter 7).
3   Dirt between transmission case and engine or misalignment of transmission (Chapter 7).
4   Worn or improperly adjusted linkage (Chapter 7).
5   Worn synchro units.

40   Difficulty in engaging gears

1   Clutch not releasing completely (see hydraulic system bleeding in Chapter 8).
2   Loose, damaged or out-of-adjustment shift linkage. Make a thorough inspection, replacing parts as necessary (Chapter 7).
3   Input shaft bearing seized.

41   Oil leakage

1   Excessive amount of lubricant in transmission (see Chapter 1 for correct checking procedures). Drain lubricant as required.
2   Side cover loose or gasket damaged.
3   Rear oil seal or speedometer oil seal in need of replacement (Chapter 7).

Automatic transmission

Note: *Due to the complexity of the automatic transmission, it is difficult for the home mechanic to properly diagnose and service this component. For problems other than the following, the vehicle should be taken to a dealer or reputable mechanic.*

42   Fluid leakage

1   Automatic transmission fluid is a deep red color. Fluid leaks should not be confused with engine oil, which can easily be blown by air flow to the transmission.
2   To pinpoint a leak, first remove all built-up dirt and grime from

around the transmission. Degreasing agents and/or steam cleaning will achieve this. With the underside clean, drive the vehicle at low speeds so air flow will not blow the leak far from its source. Raise the vehicle and determine where the leak is coming from. Common areas of leakage are:

    a) Pan: Tighten mounting bolts and/or replace pan gasket as necessary (see Chapters 1 and 7).

    b) Filler pipe: Replace the rubber seal where pipe enters transmission case.

    c) Transmission oil lines: Tighten connectors where lines enter transmission case and/or replace lines.

    d) Speedometer connector: Replace the O-ring where speedometer cable enters transmission case (Chapter 7).

43 Transmission fluid brown or has a burned smell

1 Transmission low on fluid. Replace fluid. Do not overfill.
2 Transmission fault.

44 General shift mechanism problems

1 Chapter 7B deals with checking and adjusting the shift linkage on automatic transmissions. Common problems which may be attributed to poorly adjusted linkage are:

    a) Engine starting in gears other than Park or Neutral.

    b) Indicator on shifter pointing to a gear other than the one actually being used.

    c) Vehicle moves when in Park.

2 Refer to Chapter 7B to adjust the linkage.

45 Transmission will not downshift with accelerator pedal pressed to the floor

Chapter 7B deals with adjusting the throttle linkage to enable the transmission to downshift properly.

46 Engine will start in gears other than Park or Neutral

Chapter 7B deals with adjusting the starter inhibitor/backup light switches used on automatic transmissions.

47 Transmission slips, shifts rough, is noisy or has no drive in forward or reverse gears

1 There are many probable causes for the above problems, but the home mechanic should be concerned with only one possibility — fluid level.
2 Before taking the vehicle to a repair shop, check the level and condition of the fluid as described in Chapter 1. Correct fluid level as necessary or change the fluid and filter if needed. If the problem persists, have a professional diagnose the probable cause.

Driveshaft

48 Leakage of fluid at front of driveshaft

Defective transmission rear oil seal. See Chapter 7 for replacement procedures.

49 Knock or clunk when transmission is put under initial load (just after transmission is put into gear)

1 Loose or disconnected rear suspension components. Check all mounting bolts and bushings (Chapter 10).

2 Loose driveshaft bolts. Inspect all bolts and nuts and tighten to specification (Chapter 8).
3 Worn or damaged universal joint bearings. Test for wear (Chapter 8).
4 Worn or damaged flex plates and centering sleeves.
5 Worn sliding sleeve splines.

50 Metallic grating sound consistent with road speed

1 Pronounced wear in the universal joint bearings. Test for wear (Chapter 8).
2 Worn or damaged centering sleeves, flex plates or center bearing.

51 Vibration

Note: *Before it can be assumed that the driveshaft is at fault, make sure the tires are perfectly balanced and perform the following test.*

1 Install a tachometer if necessary inside the car to monitor engine speed as the car is driven. Drive the car and note the engine speed at which the vibration is most pronounced. Now shift the transmission to a different gear and bring the engine speed to the same point.
2 If the vibration occurs at the same engine speed (rpm) regardless of which gear the transmission is in, the driveshaft is *Not* at fault since the driveshaft speed varies.
3 If the vibration decreases or is eliminated when the transmission is in a different gear at the same engine speed, refer to the following probable causes:
4 Bent or dented driveshaft. Inspect and replace as necessary (Chapter 8).
5 Undercoating or built-up dirt, etc. on the driveshaft. Clean the shaft thoroughly and test.
6 Worn universal joint bearings. Remove and inspect (Chapter 8).
7 Driveshaft and/or companion flange out of balance. Check for missing weights on the shaft. Have driveshaft professionally balanced if problem persists.
8 Driveshaft improperly installed (Chapter 8).
9 Worn flex plates and centering sleeves (Chapter 8).
10 Worn center bearing and rubber mount.
11 Worn sliding spleeve splines.
12 Worn center universal joint.

Differential/final drive unit

52 Noise — same when in drive as when vehicle is coasting

1 Road noise. No corrective procedures available.
2 Tire noise. Inspect tires and check tire pressures (Chapter 1).
3 Front wheel bearings loose, worn or damaged (Chapter 1).
4 Insufficient differential oil (whining noise consistent with vehicle speed changes).
5 Worn axleshaft joints.
6 Loose or damaged differential/final drive unit mounts.

53 Vibration

See probable causes under *Driveshaft*. Proceed under the guidelines listed for the driveshaft. If the problem persists, check the rear wheel bearings by raising the rear of the car and spinning the wheels by hand. Listen for evidence of rough bearings.

54 Oil leakage

1 Differential/final drive oil seals damaged (Chapter 8).
2 Axleshaft oil seals or boots damaged (Chapter 8).
3 Differential cover leaking. Tighten mounting bolts or replace the gasket as required (Chapter 8).

Brakes

Note: *Before assuming that a brake problem exists, make sure that the tires are in good condition and inflated properly (see Chapter 1), that the front end alignment is correct and that the vehicle is not loaded with weight in an unequal manner.*

55   Vehicle pulls to one side during braking

1   Defective, damaged or oil contaminated disc brake pads on one side. Inspect as described in Chapter 1.
2   Excessive wear of brake pad material or disc on one side. Inspect and correct as necessary.
3   Loose or disconnected front suspension components. Inspect and tighten all bolts to the specified torque (Chapter 10).
4   Defective caliper assembly. Remove caliper and inspect for stuck piston or other damage (Chapter 9).

56   Noise (high-pitched squeal without the brakes applied)

Disc brake pads worn out. Replace pads with new ones immediately (Chapter 9).

57   Excessive brake pedal travel

1   Partial brake system failure. Inspect entire system (Chapter 1) and correct as required.
2   Insufficient fluid in master cylinder. Check (Chapter 1), add fluid and bleed system if necessary (Chapter 9).
3   Brake system fluid leak.

58   Brake pedal feels spongy when depressed

1   Air in hydraulic lines. Bleed the brake system (Chapter 9).
2   Faulty flexible hoses. Inspect all system hoses and lines. Replace parts as necessary.
3   Master cylinder mounting bolts/nuts loose.
4   Master cylinder defective (Chapter 9).

59   Excessive effort required to stop vehicle

1   Power brake booster not operating properly (Chapter 9).
2   Excessively worn linings or pads. Inspect and replace if necessary (Chapter 1).
3   One or more caliper pistons seized or sticking.
4   Brake linings or pads contaminated with oil or grease. Inspect and replace as required (Chapter 1).
5   New pads or shoes installed and not yet seated. It will take a while for the new material to seat against the drum or rotor.
6   Fault in the vacuum pump or check valve (Chapter 9).

60   Pedal travels to the floor with little resistance

1   Little or no fluid in the master cylinder reservoir caused by leaking caliper piston(s), loose, damaged or disconnected brake lines. Inspect entire system and correct as necessary.
2   Fault in master cylinder.

61   Brake pedal pulsates during brake application

1   Wheel bearings not adjusted properly or in need of replacement (Chapter 1).
2   Caliper not sliding properly due to improper installation or obstructions. Remove and inspect (Chapter 9).

3   Rotor defective. Remove the rotor (Chapter 9) and check for excessive lateral runout and parallelism. Have the rotor resurfaced or replace it with a new one.

62   Parking brake does not hold

1   Mechanical parking brake linkage or shoes improperly adjusted. Adjust according to procedure in Chapter 9.
2   Parking brake shoes worn. (Chapter 9).
3   Parking brake shoes soaked with oil or brake fluid.

Suspension and steering systems

63   Vehicle pulls to one side

1   Tire pressures uneven (Chapter 1).
2   Defective tire (Chapter 1).
3   Excessive wear in suspension or steering components (Chapter 10).
4   Front end in need of alignment.
5   Front brakes dragging. Inspect brakes as described in Chapter 9.
6   Wheel bearings improperly adjusted.

64   Shimmy, shake or vibration

1   Tire or wheel out-of-balance or out-of-round. Have professionally balanced.
2   Loose, worn or out-of-adjustment wheel bearings (Chapter 1).
3   Shock absorbers and/or suspension components worn or damaged (Chapter 10).

65   Excessive pitching and/or rolling around corners or during braking

1   Defective shock absorbers. Replace as a set (Chapter 10).
2   Broken or weak springs and/or suspension components. Inspect as described in Chapter 10.

66   Excessively stiff steering

1   Lack of fluid in power steering fluid reservoir (Chapter 1).
2   Incorrect tire pressures (Chapter 1).
3   Lack of lubrication at steering joints (Chapter 1).
4   Front end out of alignment.
5   Air in power steering system. Bleed the system (Chapter 10).
6   Low tire pressure.
7   Power steering pump faulty.
8   Power steering pump drivebelt loose or worn.
9   Fault in the steering gearbox.

67   Excessive play in steering

1   Loose front wheel bearings (Chapter 1).
2   Excessive wear in suspension or steering components (Chapter 10).
3   Steering gearbox damaged or out of adjustment (Chapter 10).

68   Lack of power assistance

1   Steering pump drivebelt faulty or not adjusted properly (Chapter 1).
2   Fluid level low (Chapter 1).
3   Hoses or lines restricted. Inspect and replace parts as necessary.
4   Air in power steering system. Bleed system (Chapter 10).
5   Fault in power steering pump or steering gear.

69 Excessive tire wear (not specific to one area)

1 Incorrect tire pressures (Chapter 1).
2 Tires out of balance. Have professionally balanced.
3 Wheels damaged. Inspect and replace as necessary.
4 Suspension or steering components excessively worn (Chapter 10).

70 Excessive tire wear on outside edge

1 Inflation pressures incorrect (Chapter 1).
2 Excessive speed in turns.
3 Front end alignment incorrect (excessive toe-in). Have professionally aligned.
4 Suspension arm bent or twisted (Chapter 10).

71 Excessive tire wear on inside edge

1 Inflation pressures incorrect (Chapter 1).
2 Front end alignment incorrect (toe-out). Have professionally aligned.
3 Loose or damaged steering components (Chapter 10).
4 Rear suspension front mount bushing(s) worn, replace as a set (Chapter 10).
5 Excessive cornering speeds.

72 Tire tread worn in one place

1 Tires out of balance.
2 Damaged or buckled wheel. Inspect and replace if necessary.
3 Defective tire (Chapter 1).

Chapter 1 Routine maintenance

Contents

Air filter cleaning and replacement 25
Automatic transmission fluid and filter change............ 24
Battery check and maintenance 5
Brake check 13
Brake fluid replacement .... See Chapter 9
Chassis lubrication 10
Clutch disc wear check 21
Cooling system check............................. 7
Cooling system servicing (draining, flushing and refilling) 22
Driveline check................................. 19
Drivebelt check and adjustment 6
Differential oil change 29
Engine idle speed check and adjustment 14
Engine oil and filter change........................ 15
Engine routine maintenance 2
Exhaust Gas Recirculation (EGR) valve check
    (US models only)............................. 26

Exhaust system check 11
Fluid level checks 4
Front wheel bearing check, repack and adjustment 23
Fuel injection start of fuel delivery — check and adjustment . 32
Fuel filter replacement 17
Fuel system bleeding 30
Fuel system check 16
Idle speed adjusting knob — check and adjustment 28
Introduction and routine maintenance schedule 1
Manual transmission oil change...................... 31
Suspension and steering check 12
Throttle linkage check and lubrication 18
Tire and tire pressure checks 3
Tire rotation 20
Underhood hose check and replacement 8
Valve adjustment 27
Wiper blade inspection and replacement 9

Specifications

Recommended lubricants, fluids and capacities

Engine oil type* .... Grade CC or CD (US only)
Engine oil viscosity .... Consult your owner's manual or local dealer for oil viscosity recommendations for your area, special driving conditions and climate

Engine oil capacity (including filter)*
    Non-turbocharged engine .... 6.5 liters (6.0 US qts)
    Turbocharged engine .... 7.5 liters (7.9 US qts)
Coolant type* .... 45/55 mix of ethylene glycol antifreeze and water
Cooling system capacity** .... 11 liters (11.6 US qts)
Manual transmission oil type* .... Type A automatic transmission fluid
Manual transmission oil capacity** .... 1.6 liters (1.7 US qts)
Automatic transmission fluid type* .... Dexron II ATF
Automatic transmission fluid capacity (fluid change)*
    Non-turbo .... 4.81 liters (5.1 US qts)
    Turbo .... 6.11 liters (6.5 US qts)
Differential oil type** .... SAE 90W hypoid gear oil
Differential oil capacity* .... 1.01 liters (1.1 US qts)
Brake fluid type* .... DOT 3 or 4
Power steering fluid type* .... ATF
Manual steering gear box oil .... SAE 90W hypoid gear oil
Front wheel bearing lubricant .... No. 2 lithium or moly base wheel bearing grease
Level control system oil type* .... Hydraulic oil

*Consult dealer for specific approved types and brands

**Note: Capacity is approximate; actual fluid level should be measured as described in the appropriate Section.

Manual steering gear box oil .... SAE 90W hypoid oil
Front wheel bearing lubricant .... No. 2 lithium or moly base wheel bearing grease
Level control system oil type* .... Hydraulic oil

*Consult dealer for specific approved types and brands

Note: *Capacity is approximate; actual fluid level should be measured as described in the appropriate Section.*

General

Radiator cap opening pressure	103 kPa (15 psi)
Thermostat	
Starts to open	175 degrees F (80 degrees C)
Fully open	200 degrees F (94 degrees C)
Valve clearance (engine cold)	
Intake	0.10 mm (0.0039 in)
Exhaust	
Non-turbo	0.30 mm (0.0118 in)
Turbo	0.35 mm (0.0138 in)
Injection order	
Four-cylinder	1-3-4-2
Five-cylinder	1-2-4-5-3

Brakes

Pad lining minimum thickness	2 mm (0.0788 in)
Engine idle speed	
1975	700 to 800 rpm
1976	
616 engine	700 to 780 rpm
617 engine	680 to 760 rpm
1978 on	750 rpm

Engine drivebelt tension

Gates gauge	New belt	Used belt
616, 617.91 engine	50	45 to 50
617.95 engine		
Alternator/water pump (double V-belt)	30	20 to 25
Air conditioner/power steering pump	50	40 to 45
Borroughs gauge (part number 902 589 00 23 00)		
V-belt measuring 0.374 in (9.5 mm) (green zone)	10 to 10.5	9 to 10
V-belt measuring 0.492 in (12.5 mm) (red zone)	11 to 12	10.5 to 11
Dual belt (each belt) (green zone)	10	9.5

Torque specifications	Nm	Ft-lbs
Automatic transmission filter screws...................	7	5.2
Automatic transmission pan bolts	7	5.2
Automatic transmission drain plug	14	10
Automatic transmission torque converter drain plug	15	11
Brake caliper mounting bolts........................	35	26
Camshaft cover bolt	14	10
Engine oil drain plug	35 to 45	26 to 33
Engine oil filter cover bolts	20 to 25	15 to 18
Exhaust system bolts and nuts	20	15
Manual transmission drain and fill plugs	60	44
Steering gear box bolts.............................	72 to 81	53 to 60
Wheel lug bolts	110	81

1 Introduction and routine maintenance schedule

This Chapter was designed to help the home mechanic maintain his (or her) vehicle for peak performance, economy, safety and long life.

On the following pages you will find a maintenance schedule along with Sections which deal specifically with each item on the schedule. Included are visual checks, adjustments and item replacements.

Servicing your vehicle using the time/mileage maintenance schedule and the sequenced Sections will give you a planned program of maintenance. Keep in mind that it is a full plan, and maintaining only a few items at the specified intervals will not give you the same results.

You will find as you service your vehicle that many of the procedures can, and should, be grouped together, due to the nature of the job at hand. Examples of this are as follows:

If the vehicle is fully raised for a chassis lubrication for example, this is the ideal time for the following checks; exhaust system, suspension, steering and fuel system.

If the tires and wheels are removed, as during a routine tire rotation, go ahead and check the brakes and wheel bearings at the same time.

If you must borrow or rent a torque wrench, it is a good idea to check the fuel injection system, wheel nut and other torques all in the same day to save time and money.

The first step of this or any maintenance plan is to prepare yourself before the actual work begins. Read through the appropriate Sections for all work that is to be performed before you begin. Gather together all the necessary parts and tools. If it appears that you could have a problem during a particular job, don't hesitate to seek advice from your local parts man or dealer service department.

Fig. 1.1 Typical engine compartment component layout

1 Battery (Sec 5)
2 Air cleaner nut (Sec 5)
3 Ventilation hose (Chapter 6)
4 Camshaft cover (Chapter 2)
5 Throttle linkage (Sec 18)
6 Oil filter (Sec 15)

7 Windshield wiper (Sec 9)
8 Brake master cylinder (Sec 4)
9 Fuse box (Chapter 12)
10 Fuel filter housing (Sec 17)
11 Windshield washer reservoir
   (Sec 4)

12 Headlight (Chapter 12)
13 Oil cooler (Chapter 2)
14 Power steering pump (Sec 4)
15 Radiator hose (Sec 7)
16 Radiator (Sec 22)
17 Oil filler cap (Sec 4)

18 Hood latch (Sec 10)
19 EGR valve (Sec 26)
20 Level control system dipstick
   location (Sec 4)
21 Coolant reservoir (Sec 4)
22 Coolant cap (Sec 4)

1

Fig. 1.2 Typical view of the underside of the front of the vehicle

1 Lower radiator hose (Sec 8)
2 Radiator (Sec 7)
3 Drivebelt (Sec 6)
4 Engine oil drain plug (Sec 15)
5 Steering box (Sec 12)
6 Automatic transmission (Sec 25)
7 Steering damper (Sec 12)
8 Exhaust pipe (Sec 11)
9 Starter motor (Chapter 5)
10 Grease boot (Sec 10)
11 Brake hose (Sec 13)
12 Brake caliper and pad (Sec 13)
13 Balljoint (Sec 12)
14 Tire (Sec 3)

Fig. 1.3 Typical view of the underside of the rear of the vehicle

1 Level control system actuator
  (Sec 12)
2 Parking brake cable (Sec 13)
3 Driveshaft flex plate (Sec 19)
4 Differential seal (Sec 19)

5 Rear axle carrier bumper
  (Sec 12)
6 Lower shock absorber mount
  (Chapter 10)
7 Muffler hanger (Sec 11).

8 Muffler (Sec 11)
9 Differential drain plug
  (Sec 29)
10 Differential axleshaft boot
  (Sec 19)

11 Fuel hose (Sec 16)
12 Inner axleshaft boot (Sec 19)
13 Outer axleshaft boot (Sec 19)
14 Brake hose (Sec 13)
15 Brake caliper (Sec 13)

Routine maintenance intervals

The following recommendations are given with the assumption that the vehicle owner will be doing the maintenance or service work (as opposed to having a dealer service department do the work). The following are factory maintenance recommendations; however, due to the large number of models covered by this manual refer to your vehicle owner's manual for maintenance interval information specific to your own vehicle.

When the vehicle is new, it should be serviced initially by a factory authorized dealer service department to protect the factory warranty. In many cases the initial maintenance check is done at no cost to the owner.

Note: *The following maintenance intervals are recommended by the manufacturer. In the interest of vehicle longevity, we recommend shorter intervals on certain operations, such as fluid and filter replacement.*

Every 250 miles or weekly, whichever comes first

Check the engine oil level (Sec 4)
Check the engine coolant level (Sec 4)
Check the windshield washer fluid level (Sec 4)
Check the tires and tire pressures (Sec 3)
Check the automatic transmission fluid level (Sec 4)
Check the power steering fluid level (Sec 4)
Check the operation of all lights (Chapter 12)
Check the horn operation (Chapter 12)

Every 5000 miles (7500 km) or 5 months whichever comes first (UK models after August 1982 — 6000 miles (10,000 km)

Change the engine oil and oil filter (Sec 15)
Check the exhaust system and mounting nut tightness (Sec 11)
Check the brake master cylinder fluid level (Sec 4)
Check the wheel bolt tightness (Sec 12)
Check the differential oil level (Sec 4)
Check the disc brake pads (Sec 13)
Check the brake system (Sec 13)
Check and service the battery (Sec 5)
Check and lubricate the throttle linkage (Sec 18)

UK: Every 10,000 miles (15,000 km) up to August 1982; every 12,000 miles (20,000 km) after August, 1982
US: Every 15,000 miles or 15 months, whichever comes first

Check the cooling system (Sec 7)
Check the manual transmission fluid level (Sec 4)
Check and adjust (if necessary) the engine valve clearances (Sec 27)
Check and replace (if necessary) the windshield wiper blades (Sec 9)
Check and lubricate the chassis components (Sec 10)
Check the steering and suspension components (Sec 12)
Check and adjust (if necessary) the engine drivebelts (Sec 6)
Check the parking brake (Sec 13)
Check and adjust if necessary the engine idle speed (through 1979 models) (Sec 14)
Check the driveline components (Sec 19)
Rotate the tires (Sec 20)
Check the fuel system components (Sec 16)
Check the clutch disc wear (Sec 21)
Check, clean (or, if necessary) replace the air filter element (Sec 25)
Replace the brake fluid (once a year) (Chapter 9)
Check (and adjust if necessary) the idle speed adjusting knob (non-turbo models) (Sec 28)

US: Every 30,000 miles or 30 months, whichever comes first
UK: Every 28,000 miles (45,000 km) up to August 1982; every 36,000 miles (60,000 km) after August 1982

Drain, flush and refill the cooling system (Sec 22)
Drain and refill the manual transmission oil (Sec 31)
Replace the automatic transmission fluid and filter (Sec 24)
Replace the fuel filter and prefilter (Sec 17)
Lubricate and adjust the front wheel bearings (Sec 23)
Have the idle speed checked and (if necessary) adjusted (1980 and later models) (Sec 14)
Check the operation of the EGR valve (US models only) (Sec 27)
Check and adjust (if necessary) the fuel injection start of delivery (Sec 32)
Replace the air filter element (Sec 25)
Drain and refill the differential oil (Sec 29)

Severe operating conditions

Severe operating conditions are defined as:
  Frequent short trips or long periods of idling
  Driving at sustained high speeds during hot weather (over 90° F [+ 32°C])
  Driving in severe dust conditions
  Driving in temperatures below 10° F (−12°C) for 60 or more miles
  Towing a trailer
  Driving 2000 miles or more per month
  Driving in extremely humid conditions
  Continuous mountain driving or where the brakes are used extensively
If the vehicle has been operated under severe conditions, follow these maintenance intervals:
  Change the air filter every 15,000 miles (22,500 km)
  Change the engine oil and oil filter every 2500 miles (3750 km) or two months
  Drain and refill the automatic transmission every 15,000 miles (22,500 km)

---

2 Engine routine maintenance

A combination of individual routine maintenance operations, such as checking the glow plugs, having the fuel injection timing set and adjusting the idle speed, etc., is necessary to keep the engine running properly.

If, from the time the vehicle is new, the routine maintenance schedule (Section 1) is followed closely and frequent checks are made of fluid levels and high wear items, as suggested throughout this manual, the engine will be kept in relatively good running condition and the need for additional routine maintenance will be minimized.

More likely than not, however, there will be times when the engine is running poorly due to lack of regular maintenance. This is even more likely if a used vehicle (which has not received regular and frequent maintenance checks) is purchased. In such cases, engine maintenance will be needed outside of the regular routine maintenance intervals.

The following series of operations constitute engine routine maintenance procedures.

Clean, inspect and test battery (Sec 5)
Check all engine-related fluids (Sec 4)
Check and adjust drivebelts (Sec 6)
Check the glow plugs (Chapter 5)
Check and adjust the idle speed (Sec 14)
Check the idle speed adjusting knob (Sec 28)
Replace fuel filters (Sec 17)
Check air cleaner (Sec 25)
Check cooling system (Sec 7)
Check EGR system (Sec 26)
Check the engine electrical system (Chapter 5)
Check fuel system (Sec 16)

4.4a   The engine oil dipstick has a white plastic handle on most models

4.4b   The engine oil level should be kept between the indentation on the dipstick (arrows); do not overfill the crankcase

3   Tire and tire pressure checks

1   Periodically inspecting the tires may not only prevent you from being stranded with a flat tire, but can also give you clues as to possible problems with the steering and suspension systems before major damage occurs.

2   Proper tire inflation adds miles to the lifespan of the tires, allows the vehicle to achieve maximum miles per gallon figures and contributes to the overall quality of the ride.

3   When inspecting the tires, first check the wear of the tread. Irregularities in the tread pattern (cupping, flat spots, more wear on one side than the other) are indications of front end alignment and/or balance problems. If any of these conditions are noted, take the vehicle to a reputable repair shop to correct the problem. Chapter 10 contains information on front end alignment.

4   Also check the tread area for cuts and punctures. Many times a nail or tack will embed itself into the tire tread and yet the tire will hold its air pressure for a short time. In most cases, a repair shop or gas station can repair the punctured tire.

5   It is also important to check the sidewalls of the tires, both inside and outside. Check for deteriorated rubber, cuts, and punctures. Also inspect the inboard side of the tire for signs of brake fluid leakage, indicating that a thorough brake inspection is needed immediately.

6   Incorrect tire pressure cannot be determined merely by looking at the tire. This is especially true for radial tires. A tire pressure gauge must be used. If you do not already have a reliable gauge, it is a good idea to purchase one and keep it in the glovebox. Built-in pressure gauges at gas stations are often unreliable.

7   Always check tire inflation when the tires are cold. Cold, in this case, means the vehicle has not been driven more than one mile after sitting for three hours or more. It is normal for the pressure to increase four to eight pounds or more when the tires are hot.

8   Unscrew the valve cap protruding from the wheel or hubcap and press the gauge firmly onto the valve stem. Observe the reading on the gauge and compare the figure to the recommended tire pressure listed on the tire placard. The tire placard is usually attached to the driver's door jamb.

9   Check all tires and add air as necessary to bring them up to the recommended pressure levels. Do not forget the spare tire. Be sure to reinstall the valve caps (which will keep dirt and moisture out of the valve stem mechanism).

4   Fluid level checks

1   There are a number of components on a vehicle which rely on the use of fluids to perform their job. During normal operation of the vehicle, these fluids are used up and must be replenished before damage occurs. See *Recommended lubricants and fluids* at the front of this Chapter for the specific fluid to be used when addition is required. When checking fluid levels, it is important to have the vehicle on a level surface.

Engine oil

2   The engine oil level is checked with a dipstick which is located at the side of the engine block. The dipstick travels through a tube and into the oil pan to the bottom of the engine.

3   The oil level should be checked preferably before the vehicle has been driven, or about 15 minutes after the engine has been shut off. If the oil is checked immediately after driving the vehicle, some of the oil will remain in the upper engine components, producing an inaccurate reading on the dipstick.

4   Pull the dipstick from the tube and wipe all the oil from the end with a clean rag or paper towel. Insert the clean dipstick all the way back into the oil pan and pull it out again. Observe the oil at the end of the dipstick. At its highest point, the level should be between the two indentations on the dipstick (photos).

5   It takes approximately one quart of oil to raise the level from the lower indentation to the upper one. Do not allow the level to drop below the lower indentation as engine damage due to oil starvation may occur. On the other hand, do not overfill the engine by adding oil above the upper indentation since it may result in oil leaks or oil seal failures.

6   Oil is added to the engine after removing a twist-off cap located on the camshaft cover. An oil can spout or funnel will reduce spills as the oil is poured in.

7   Checking the oil level can also be an important preventative maintenance step. If you find the oil level dropping abnormally, it is an indication of oil leakage or internal engine wear which should be corrected. If there are water droplets in the oil, or if it is milky looking, component failure is indicated and the engine should be checked immediately. The condition of the oil can also be checked along with the level. With the dipstick removed from the engine, take your thumb and index finger and wipe the oil up the dipstick, looking for small dirt or metal particles which will cling to the dipstick. This is an indication that the oil should be drained and fresh oil added (Section 15).

Engine coolant

8   Many vehicles covered by this manual are equipped with a pressurized coolant recovery system which makes coolant level checks very easy. A white coolant reservoir attached to the inner fender panel is connected by a hose to the radiator cap. As the engine heats up during operation, coolant is forced from the radiator, through the connecting tube and into the reservoir. As the engine cools, the coolant is automatically drawn back into the radiator to keep the level correct.

4.9   The coolant level should be kept at the line marked by the arrow

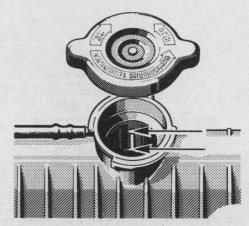

Fig. 1.4   On radiators without a remote reservoir, the coolant level should be at the tab in the filler neck (arrows) (Sec 4)

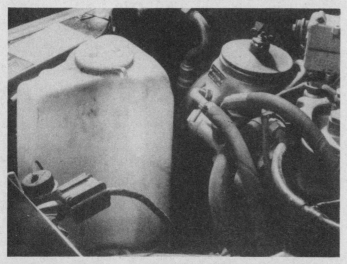

4.15   The windshield washer reservoir is located next to the radiator on most models. Do not confuse it with the coolant recovery tank which is similar in appearance but has a tube leading to the radiator

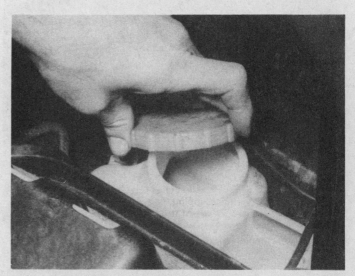

4.17   Checking the rear window washer level after removing the cap

9   The coolant level should be checked when the engine is hot. Merely observe the level of fluid in the reservoir, which should be at or near the line marked by the arrow on the side of the reservoir (photo). Periodically the coolant level in the radiator should also be checked by removing the cap.

10   **Warning**: *Under no circumstances should the radiator cap or the coolant recovery reservoir cap be removed when the system is hot, because escaping steam and scalding liquid could cause serious personal injury.* In the case of the radiator, wait until the system has cooled completely, then wrap a thick cloth around the cap and turn it to the first stop. If any steam escapes, wait until the system has cooled further, then remove the cap. The coolant recovery cap may be removed carefully after it is apparent that the system is sufficiently cool.

11   If only a small amount of coolant is required to bring the system up to the proper level, regular water can be used. However, to maintain the proper antifreeze/water mixture in the system, both should be mixed together to replenish a low level. High-quality antifreeze offering protection to −20°F should be mixed with water in the proportion specified on the container. Do not allow antifreeze to come in contact with your skin or painted surfaces of the vehicle. Flush contacted areas immediately with plenty of water.

12   Coolant should be added to the reservoir until it reaches the Full mark.

13   As the coolant level is checked, note the condition of the coolant. It should be relatively clear. If it is brown or a rust color, the system should be drained, flushed and refilled (Section 23).

14   If the cooling system requires repeated additions to maintain the proper level, have the radiator cap checked for proper sealing ability. Also check for leaks in the system (cracked hoses, loose hose connections, leaking gaskets, etc.).

Windshield washer fluid

15   Fluid for the windshield washer system is located in a plastic reservoir located in the engine compartment (photo). The reservoir should be kept no more than 2/3 full to allow for expansion should the fluid freeze. The use of an additive such as windshield washer fluid available at auto parts stores will help lower the freezing point of the fluid and will result in better cleaning of the windshield surface. Do not use antifreeze because it will cause damage to the vehicle's paint.

16   Also, to help prevent icing in cold weather, warm the windshield with the defroster before using the washer.

Rear window washer

17   On models equipped with rear window washers, the reservoir is accessible behind a panel in the rear compartment and should also be kept at the 2/3 full level using the same fluid as in the windshield washer (photo).

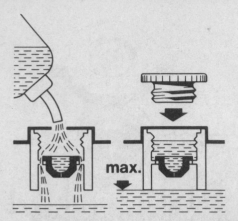

Fig. 1.5   On maintenance-type batteries, water is added until the overflow no longer drains off the excess (Sec 4)

4.22   The brake master cylinder fluid level can be viewed through the transluscent plastic reservoir. The fluid cap breather hole (arrow) should be checked for obstructions.

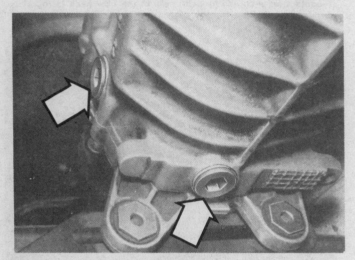

Fig. 1.6   Manual transmission drain and fill plugs (arrows) (Sec 4)

Headlight washer

18   Some models are equipped with headlight washers, the reservoir for which is located in the engine compartment. Because of the variety of reservoir configurations used, trace the tubes leading from the washers to the reservoir to determine its location. The reservoir should be kept at the 2/3 full level with the same fluid used in the windshield and rear window washer reservoirs.

Battery electrolyte

19   Vehicles equipped with maintenance-free batteries require no maintenance because the battery case is permanently sealed (except for vent holes) and has no filler caps. Water does not have to be added to these batteries at any time.
20   On maintenance-type batteries, the electrolyte level can be checked after removing the caps on the top of the battery. On some batteries the case is translucent and the level can be checked without removing the caps. Add distilled water until water no longer runs off through the overflow. If it is necessary to test the electrolyte, the tip of the tester can be inserted through the overflow.

Brake and clutch fluid

21   The brake master cylinder is mounted on the front of the power booster unit in the engine compartment. The clutch cylinder used on manual transmissions is mounted adjacent to the master cylinder.
22   The master cylinder and clutch cylinder reservoirs are translucent plastic, which allow checking the fluid level without removal of the reservoir cover. The level should be maintained at the Max marking on the reservoir and the breather hole in the cap should be kept clean (photo).

23   If a low level is indicated, be sure to wipe the top of the reservoir cover with a clean rag, to prevent contamination of the brake and/or clutch system, before lifting the cover.
24   When adding fluid, pour it carefully into the reservoir, taking care not to spill any onto surrounding painted surfaces. Be sure the specified fluid is used, since mixing different types of brake fluid can cause damage to the system. See *Recommended lubricants and fluids* or your owner's manual.
25   At this time the fluid and cylinder can be inspected for contamination. The manufacturer recommends that the brake system should be drained and refilled at the specified intervals (Chapter 9). The system should also be drained and refilled if deposits, dirt particles or water droplets are seen in the fluid.
26   After filling the reservoir to the proper level, make sure the lid is properly seated to prevent fluid leakage and/or system pressure loss.
27   The brake fluid in the master cylinder will drop slightly as the brake shoes or pads at each wheel wear down during normal operation. If the master cylinder requires repeated replenishing to keep it at the proper level, this is an indication of leakage in the brake system, which should be corrected immediately. Check all brake lines and connections, along with the wheel cylinders and booster (see Section 13 for more information).
28   If upon checking the master cylinder fluid level you discover one or both reservoirs empty or nearly empty, the brake system should be bled of all air before driving the vehicle (Chapter 9).

Manual transmission oil

29   Manual transmissions do not have a dipstick. The fluid level is checked with the engine cold by removing a plug in the side of the transmission case. Locate the plug and use a rag to clean the plug and the area around it, then remove it with a wrench.
30   If oil immediately starts leaking out, thread the plug back into the transmission because the level is all right. If there is no leakage, completely remove the plug and place you little finger inside the hole. The oil level should be just at the bottom of the plug hole.
31   If the transmission needs more oil, use a syringe if necessary to squeeze the appropriate lubricant into the plug hole until the level is correct.
32   Drive the vehicle a short distance, then check to make sure the plug is not leaking.

Automatic transmission fluid

33   The level of the automatic transmission fluid should be carefully maintained. Low fluid level can lead to slipping or loss of drive, while overfilling can cause foaming and loss of fluid.

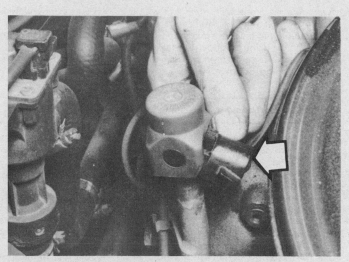

4.35   Flip the retaining lever (arrow) up before removing the automatic transmission dipstick

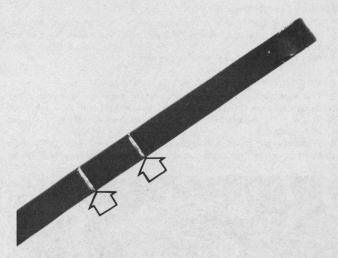

4.38   The automatic transmission fluid level should be kept between the marks (arrows) on the dipstick; do not overfill

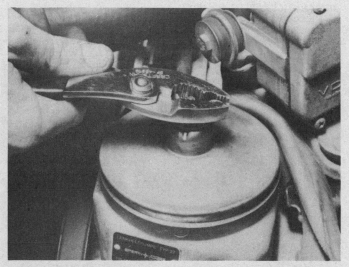

4.46a   A pair of pliers can be used to remove the power steering reservoir cover wingnut

4.46b   The power steering reservoir fluid level must be maintained at a level even with the washer on the shaft (arrow)

34   With the parking brake set, start the engine, then move the shift lever through all the gear ranges, ending in Park. The fluid level must be checked with the vehicle level and the engine running at idle. **Note:** *Incorrect fluid level readings will result if the vehicle has just been driven at high speeds for an extended period, in city traffic during hot weather, or if it's been pulling a trailer. If any of these conditions apply, wait until the fluid has cooled (about 30 minutes).*
35   With the transmission at normal operating temperature, release the locking lever and remove the dipstick from the filler tube (photo).
36   Wipe the fluid from the dipstick with a clean rag and push it back into the filler tube until the cap seats.
37   Pull the dipstick out again and note the fluid level.
38   The level should be in the area between the Maximum and Minimum marks on the dipstick (photo).
39   Add just enough of the recommended fluid to fill the transmission to the proper level. It takes about one pint to raise the level from the Minimum mark to the Maximum mark with a hot transmission, so add the fluid a little at a time and keep checking the level until it is correct.
40   The condition of the fluid should also be checked along with the level. If the fluid at the end of the dipstick is a dark reddish-brown color, or if the fluid has a burnt smell, the transmission fluid should be changed. If you are in doubt about the condition of the fluid, purchase some new fluid and compare the two for color and smell. Be sure to engage the locking lever after reinserting the dipstick.

Power steering fluid

41   Unlike manual steering, the power steering system relies on fluid which may, over a period of time, require replenishing.
42   The fluid reservoir for the power steering pump is located behind the radiator near the front of the engine.
43   For the check, the front wheels should be pointed straight ahead and the engine should be off.
44   Use a clean rag to wipe off the reservoir cap and the area around the cap. This will help prevent any foreign matter from entering the reservoir during the check.
45   Make sure the engine is at normal operating temperature.
46   Remove the nut, lift the cover from the reservoir and set it aside. The level should be near the mark below the reservoir rim (photos).
47   If additional fluid is required, pour the specified type directly into the reservoir.
48   Place the cap in position, making sure the gasket is seated and install the retaining nut securely.
49   If the reservoir requires frequent fluid additions, all power steering hoses, hose connections, the power steering pump and steering gear assembly should be carefully checked for leaks.

Manual steering gear box oil level

50 With the steering centered, remove the threaded plug in the steering box and check that the oil level is even with the lower edge of the threaded hole.
51 Add differential gear oil, if necessary.

Level control system reservoir

52 The rear suspension hydraulic system reservoir (located in the engine compartment) fluid level should be checked with the engine off.
53 Remove the dipstick from the reservoir, wipe it off with a clean rag and reinsert it.
54 Withdraw the dipstick and check the fluid level. With the vehicle unloaded (level control system not activated), the level should be be

Fig. 1.7   Remove the threaded plug (40) to check the manual steering gear box lubricant level (Sec 4)

4.54a   Removing the level control system reservoir dipstick

5.5a   Cleaning the battery cable with a wire brush

tween the Max. and Min. mark and with it loaded (system activated) it should be at the Min. mark (photos).
55 If additional fluid is required, pour the specified type directly into the reservoir using a funnel to prevent spills.
56 Further information on the level control system can be found in Section 12 and Chapter 10.

5   Battery check and maintenance

1 Tools and materials required for battery maintenance include eye and hand protection, baking soda, petroleum jelly, a battery cable puller and cable/terminal post cleaning tools.
2 Check the water level on non-maintenance free batteries as described in Section 4. Although they never require the addition of water, sealed maintenance free batteries should also nevertheless be routinely maintained according to the procedures which follow. **Warning:** *Hydrogen gas in small quantities is present in the area of the side vents on sealed batteries, so keep lighted tobacco and open flames or sparks away from them.*
3 The external condition of the battery should be monitored periodically for damage such as a cracked case or cover.
4 Check the tightness of the battery cable clamps to ensure good electrical connections and check the entire length of each cable for cracks and frayed conductors.
5 If corrosion (visible as white, fluffy deposits) is evident, remove the cables from the terminals, clean them with a battery brush and reinstall the cables (photos). Corrosion can be kept to a minimum by

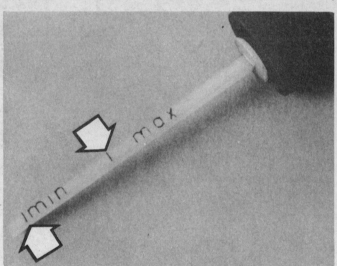

4.54b   The level control system reservoir fluid level must be kept between the marks on the dipstick (arrows)

5.5b   Cleaning corrosion from the battery post with a battery cleaning tool applying a layer of petroleum jelly on the terminals or by using a special treated washer.

6 If so equipped, make sure that the rubber protector over the positive terminal is not torn or missing. It should completely cover the terminal.

7 Make sure that the battery carrier is in good condition and that the hold-down clamp bolts are tight. If the battery is removed from the carrier, make sure that no parts remain in the bottom of the carrier when the battery is reinstalled. When reinstalling the hold-down clamp bolts, do not overtighten them.

8 Corrosion on the hold-down components, battery case and surrounding areas may be removed with a solution of water and baking soda, but take care to prevent any solution from coming in contact with your eyes, skin or clothes, as it contains acid. Protective gloves should be worn. Thoroughly wash all cleaned areas with plain water.

9 Any metal parts of the vehicle damaged by corrosion should be covered with a zinc-based primer, then painted after the affected areas have been cleaned and dried.

10 Further information on the battery, charging and jump-starting can be found in Chapter 5 and at the front of this manual.

6 Drivebelt check and adjustment

1 The drivebelts, or V-belts as they are sometimes called, are located at the front of the engine and play an important role in the overall operation of the vehicle and its components. Due to their function and material make-up, the belts are prone to failure after a period of time and should be inspected and adjusted periodically to prevent major engine damage.

2 These vehicles use ribbed belts of a special design which must always be replaced with belts of the same or equivalent design.

3 The number of belts used on a particular vehicle depends on the accessories installed. Drivebelts are used to turn the generator/alternator, power steering pump, water pump, vacuum pump and air-conditioning compressor. Depending on the pulley arrangement, a single belt may be used to drive more than one of these components.

4 With the engine off, open the hood and locate the various belts at the front of the engine. Using your fingers (and a flashlight, if necessary), move along the belts checking for cracks and separation of the belt plies. Also check for fraying and glazing, which gives the belt a shiny appearance. Both sides of the belt should be inspected, which means you will have to twist the belt to check the underside.

5 The tension of each belt can be checked either of two ways. The manufacturer recommends using a Gates or Borroughs tension gauge available at your dealer or auto parts stores. Refer to Specifications for tension readings. If a gauge is not available or a simple check of

the belts is required, check by pushing on the belt at a distance halfway between the pulleys. Push firmly with your thumb and see how much the belt moves (deflects). A rule of thumb is that if the distance from pulley center-to-pulley center is between 7 and 11 inches, the belt should deflect 1/4-inch. If the belt is longer and travels between pulleys spaced 12 to 16 inches apart, the belt should deflect 1/2 inch.

6 If it is necessary to adjust the belt tension, either to make the belt tighter or looser, it is done by moving the belt-driven accessory on the bracket.

7 For each component there will be an adjusting bolt and a pivot bolt. Both bolts must be loosened slightly to enable you to move the component. Hold the accessory in position and check the belt tension. If it is correct, tighten the two bolts until just snug, then recheck the tension. If the tension is all right, tighten the bolts.

8 It will often be necessary to use some sort of pry bar to move the accessory while the belt is adjusted. If this must be done to gain the proper leverage, be very careful not to damage the component being moved or the part being pried against.

7 Cooling system check

1 Many major engine failures can be attributed to a faulty cooling system. If the vehicle is equipped with an automatic transmission, the cooling system also plays an important role in prolonging its life.

2 The cooling system should be checked with the engine cold. Do this before the vehicle is driven for the day or after it has been shut off for at least three hours.

3 Remove the radiator cap and thoroughly clean the cap (inside and out) with clean water. Also clean the filler neck on the radiator. All traces of corrosion should be removed.

4 Carefully check the upper and lower radiator hoses along with the smaller diameter heater hoses. Inspect each hose along its entire length, replacing any hose which is cracked, swollen or shows signs of deterioration. Cracks may become more apparent if the hose is squeezed (photo).

5 Also make sure that all hose connections are tight. A leak in the cooling system will usually show up as white or rust colored deposits on the areas adjoining the leak.

6 Use compressed air or a soft brush to remove bugs, leaves, etc. from the front of the radiator or air-conditioning condenser. Be careful not to damage the delicate cooling fins or cut yourself on them.

7 Finally, have the cap and system pressure tested. If you do not have a pressure tester, most gas stations and repair shops will do this for a minimal charge.

8 Underhood hose check and replacement

Caution: *Replacement of air-conditioner hoses must be left to a dealer or air-conditioning specialist who has the proper equipment to depressurize the system safely. Never remove air conditioning components or hoses until the system has been depressurized.*

Vacuum hoses

1 High temperatures under the hood can cause the deterioration of the rubber and plastic hoses used for engine, accessory and emission systems operation.

2 Periodic inspection should be made for cracks, loose clamps, material hardening and leaks.

3 Some, but not all, vacuum hoses use clamps to secure the hoses to fittings. Where clamps are used, check to be sure they haven't lost their tension, allowing the hose to leak. Where clamps are not used, make sure the hose has not expanded and/or hardened where it slips over the fitting, allowing it to leak.

4 It is quite common for vacuum hoses, especially those in the emissions system, to be color coded or identified by colored stripes molded into the hose. Various systems require hoses with different wall thicknesses, collapse resistance and temperature resistance. When replacing hoses be sure to use the same hose material on the new hose.

5 Often the only effective way to check a hose is to remove it completely from the vehicle. Where more than one hose is removed, be sure to label the hoses and their attaching points to ensure proper reattachment.

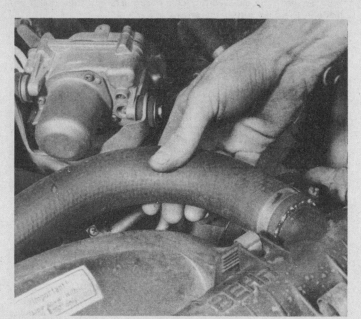

7.4 Squeezing the radiator hose is a good way to check for cracks and leaks

9.3   Swing the wiper arm out and then rotate the arm and trim cover toward the glass for access to the retaining nut

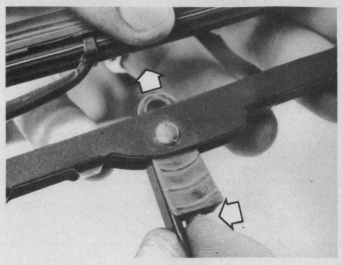

9.5   Press the lever and then slide the wiper blade assembly down the wiper arm (arrows)

6   When checking vacuum hoses, be sure to include any plastic T-fittings in the check. Check the fittings for cracks, and the hose where it fits over the fitting for enlargement, which could cause leakage.

7   A small piece of vacuum hose (1/4-inch inside diameter) can be used as a stethoscope to detect vacuum leaks. Hold one end of the hose to your ear and probe around vacuum hoses and fittings, listening for the ''hissing'' sound characteristic of a vacuum leak. **Caution:** *When probing with the vacuum hose stethoscope, be careful not to allow your body or the hose to come into contact with moving engine components such as drivebelts, the cooling fan, etc.*

Fuel hose

8   **Warning:** *There are certain precautions which must be taken when inspecting or servicing fuel system components. Work in a well ventilated area and do not allow open flames (cigarettes, appliance pilot lights, etc.) or bare light bulbs near the work area. Mop up any spills immediately and do not store fuel-soaked rags where they could ignite.*

9   Check all rubber fuel lines for deterioration and chafing. Check especially for cracking in areas where the hose bends and just before clamping points, such as where a hose attaches to the fuel pump, fuel filter and fuel injection unit.

10   Only factory replacement fuel line, should be used for new lines because of the high pressures involved. Under no circumstances should unreinforced vacuum line, clear plastic tubing or water hose be used for fuel line replacement.

11   Spring-type clamps are used on some fuel lines. These clamps often lose their tension over a period of time, and can be ''sprung'' during the removal process. Therefore it is recommended that all spring-type clamps be replaced with screw clamps whenever a hose is replaced.

Metal lines

12   Sections of metal line are often used for fuel line between the fuel pump and fuel injection unit. Check carefully to be sure the line has not been bent and crimped and that cracks have not started in the line in the area of bends.

13   If a section of metal fuel line must be replaced, only factory replacement lines, complete with fittings, should be used, since the lengths of the tubing are critical and aluminum or copper tubing do not have the strength necessary to withstand normal engine operating vibration.

14   Check the metal brake lines where they enter the master cylinder and brake proportioning unit (if used) for cracks in the lines or loose fittings. Any sign of brake fluid leakage calls for an immediate thorough inspection of the brake system.

---

9   Wiper blade inspection and replacement

---

1   The windshield and rear window (if equipped) wiper and blade assembly should be inspected periodically for damage, loose com-

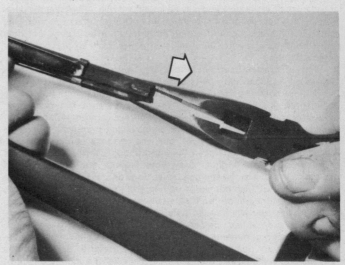

9.6   Squeeze the clips with needle nose pliers and then pull the blade in the direction of the arrow

ponents and cracked or worn blade elements.

2   Road film can build up on the wiper blades and affect their efficiency so they should be washed regularly with a mild detergent solution.

3   The action of the wiping mechanism can loosen the bolts, nuts and fasteners so they should be checked and tightened, as necessary, at the same time the wiper blades are checked (photo).

4   If the wiper blade elements are cracked, worn or warped, they should be replaced with new ones.

5   Lift the arm assembly away from the glass for clearance and remove the blade assembly by depressing the release lever and pushing it down the arm (photo)

6   Squeeze the retaining clip with needle nose pliers and slide the blade element out (photo).

7   Insert the new blade element and snap the retaining clip in place.

8   Install the blade assembly on the wiper arm.

---

10   Chassis lubrication

---

1   There is no provision for lubricaton of chassis or steering components on these models as they are lubed for life. The suspension grease boots, however, should be periodically inspected for leaks (Sec 12). Only the front wheel bearings (Section 23) require periodic lubrication.

10.3   Use a small brush to lubricate the hood latch

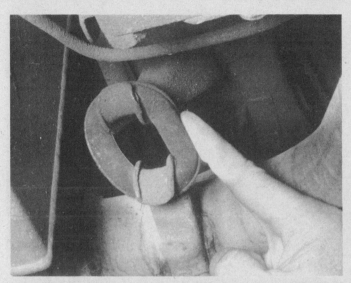

11.4   Push on the exhaust pipe hanger to check for cracks

11.5   Use a wrench or socket to check the exhaust system nuts and bolts for tightness

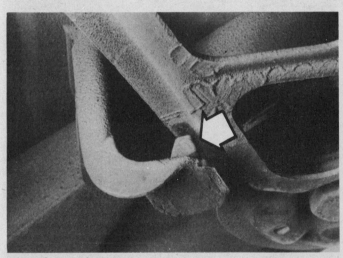

12.4   Check the rear axle carrier clearance at the point shown (arrow)

2   Lubricate all the hinges (door, hood, hatch) with a few drops of light engine oil to keep them in proper working order.
3   Open the hood and lubricate the latch mechanism with lithium base white grease (photo).
4   Lubricate the door and trunk or liftgate weatherstripping with silicone spray. This will reduce chafing and retard wear.
5   Finally, the key lock cylinders can be lubricated with spray-on graphite which is available at auto parts stores.

11   Exhaust system check

1   With the engine cold (at least three hours after the vehicle has been driven), check the complete exhaust system from its starting point at the engine to the end of the tailpipe. This should be done on a hoist where unrestricted access is available.
2   Check the pipes and connections for signs of leakage and/or corrosion indicating a potential failure. Make sure that all brackets and hangers are in good condition and tight.
3   At the same time, inspect the underside of the body for holes, corrosion, open seams, etc. which may allow exhaust gases to enter the passenger compartment. Seal all body openings with silicone or body putty.
4   Rattles and other noises can often be traced to the exhaust system, especially the mounts and hangers. Try to move the pipes and muffler.

If the components can come in contact with the body or suspension parts, secure the exhaust system with new mounts (photo).
5   This is also an ideal time to check the tightness of the intake and exhaust manifolds, exhaust pipe-to-manifold and turbocharger (if equipped) bolts and nuts (photo).

12   Suspension and steering check

1   It is a good idea to raise the vehicle periodically and visually check the suspension and steering components for wear.
2   Indications of a fault in these systems are excessive play in the steering wheel before the front wheels react, excessive sway around corners, body movement over rough roads or binding at some point as the steering wheel is turned.
3   Before the vehicle is raised for inspection, test the shock absorbers by pushing down to rock the vehicle at each corner. If you push down and the vehicle does not come back to a level position within one or two bounces, the shocks/struts are worn and must be replaced. As this is done, check for squeaks and strange noises coming from the suspension components. Information on suspension components can be found in Chapter 11.
4   With the vehicle weight resting on the suspension, check the clearance of the rear axle carrier. The clearance between the buffer and support plate should be approximately 20 mm (photo). The

12.7a   Check the balljoint grease boots (arrow) and...

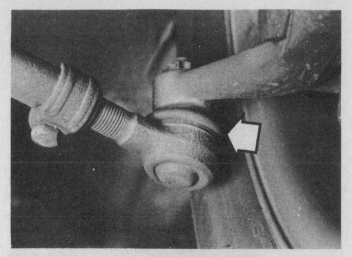

12.7b   ... steering arm boots for tears and leaks

12.8   This shock absorber is leaking and should be replaced

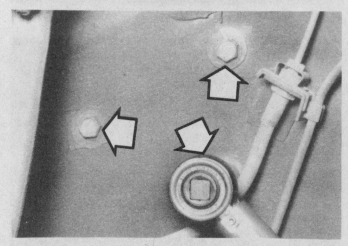

12.9   The steering box bolts (arrows) are accessible through the left front wheel well. The lower bolt is obscured by the ratchet and socket

12.10   Check the steering damper for leaks and looseness, indicating damage

clearance can be adjusted by loosening the nut at the top of the detent.
5   Now raise the vehicle and support it securely on jackstands placed under the frame rails. Because of the work to be done, make sure the vehicle cannot fall from the stands.
6   Check the wheel bearings (see Section 23).
7   Crawl under the vehicle and check for loose bolts, broken or disconnected parts and deteriorated rubber boots located on the suspension and steering components. These boots contain the chassis lubricant

and torn or leaking boots will soon lead to damaged suspension and steering because of the lost lubricant (photos). Further information on these boots can be found in Chapter 10.
8   Look for grease or fluid leaking from the steering assembly and check the shock absorbers, power steering hoses and connections for leaks (photo). Check the balljoints for wear.
9   Have an assistant turn the steering wheel from side-to-side and check the steering components for free movement, chafing and binding. If the steering does not react with the movement of the steering wheel, try to determine where the slack is located. Check the tightness of the steering gear bolts (photo).
10   On models so equipped, check the steering damper for damage and fluid leaks (photo).
11   Inspect the level control system (if equipped) for damage and fluid leaks (photo).
12   The manufacturer recommends periodically checking the wheel bolt tightness using a torque wrench with the wheels cold, i.e. before the vehicle is driven for the day. Tighten the bolts in a criss-cross pattern (photo). A further check of the wheels recommended by the manufacturer is to dismount each of the tires and visually inspect the entire wheel for cracks, dents and any imperfections. Obviously, this is a task which must be left to a dealer.

13   Brake check

Note: *For detailed photographs of the brake system, refer to Chapter 9.*
1   The brakes should be inspected every time the wheels are removed

12.11 Inspect the level control mechanism for damage and leaks

12.12 Tighten the wheel bolts using a torque wrench

1

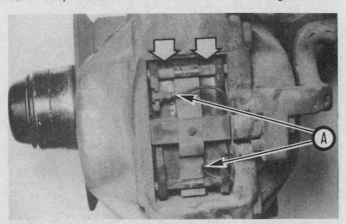

13.5a The thickness of the remaining brake pad material (arrows) can be viewed through the cutout in the caliper. Check the wear sensor wires (A)

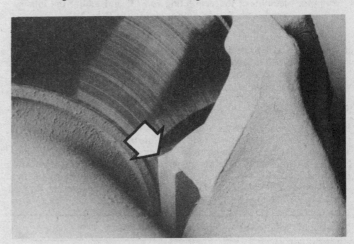

13.5b Check the rear brake pad material thickness (arrow) by viewing the caliper from in front and above

13.7 Check the brake hose and sensor wire (A) for damage

or whenever a defect is suspected. These models are equipped with sensors in the front brake pads. The sensors cause a light in the instrument panel to come on when driving and braking when the pads are worn beyond limits but it is a good idea to also periodically check the brakes visually. Indications of a potential brake system defect are: the vehicle pulls to one side when the brake pedal is depressed; noises coming from the brakes when they are applied; excessive brake pedal travel; pulsating pedal; and leakage of fluid, usually seen on the inside of the tire or wheel.

Disc brakes

2   These models are equipped with disc brakes on all four wheels and the pads can be visually checked without removing any parts except the wheels.

3   Raise the vehicle and place it securely on jackstands. Remove the wheels (see *Jacking and towing* at the front of the manual, if necessary).

4   The disc brake calipers, which contain the pads, are now visible. There is an outer pad and an inner pad in each caliper. All pads should be inspected.

5   Check the pad thickness by looking at each end of the caliper and through the inspection hole in the caliper body (front) or from above and in front of the caliper (rear) (photos). If the lining material is 5/64-inch or less in thickness, the pads should be replaced. Keep in mind that the lining material is riveted or bonded to a metal backing shoe and the metal portion is not included in this measurement.

6   Since it will be difficult, if not impossible, to measure the exact thickness of the remaining lining material, remove the pads (Chap-

ter 9) for further inspection or replacement if you are in doubt as to the condition of the pad.

7   Before installing the wheels, check for leakage around the brake hose connections leading to the caliper and damage (cracking, splitting, etc.) to the brake hose (photo). Replace the hose or fittings as necessary, referring to Chapter 9.

8   Also check the condition of the rotor. Look for scoring, gouging and burnt spots. If these conditions exist, the hub/rotor assembly should be removed for servicing (Chapter 9).

and lower the vehicle to the ground.

Fig. 1.8 On pneumatic governor equipped fuel injection pumps, disconnect the regulating rod (3) and adjust the idle speed with the adjusting screw (4) (Sec 14)

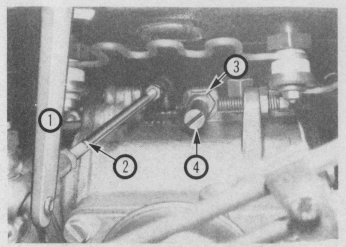

Fig. 1.9 On fuel injection pumps with mechanical governors, disconnect the regulating rod (2) from the lever (1), loosen the locknut (3) and adjust the idle speed by turning the screw (4) (Sec 14)

8   Also check the condition of the rotor. Look for scoring, gouging and burnt spots. If these conditions exist, the hub/rotor assembly should be removed for servicing (Chapter 9). Install the wheels and lower the vehicle to the ground.

Parking brake

9   Apply the parking brake and make sure the brake engages between two and four clicks. If it does not, adjust the parking brake (Chapter 9).
10 The easiest way to check the actual operation of the parking brake is to park the vehicle on a steep hill with the parking brake set and the transmission in Neutral. If the parking brake cannot prevent the vehicle from rolling, it is in need of adjustment (see Chapter 9).

14 Engine idle speed — check and adjustment

1   The engine idle speed should be checked and adjusted at the specified intervals. On 1979 and earlier models this is a fairly straight-forward procedure which is detailed below. On 1980 and later models idle speed adjustment requires the use of special tools and techniques and the job should be left to a dealer.
2   Warm the engine up to normal operating temperature.
3   Turn the idle speed adjusting knob fully to the right.
4   On models equipped with a fuel injection pump with a pneumatic governor, disconnect the regulating rod and adjust the idle speed on the throttle unit as shown in the accompanying illustration.
5   On mechanical governor equipped fuel injection pumps, disconnect the regulating rod and adjust the idle by turning the screw after loosening the locknut as shown in the illustration.
6   After adjustment of the idle speed, check the cruise control (if equipped) Bowden wire adjustment. Push the Stop lever against the regulating lever. The wire should now be free of tension and rest against the regulating lever. Adjust the wire with the adjusting nut as shown in the accompanying illustration if necessary.

15 Engine oil and filter change

1   Frequent oil changes may be the best form of preventive mainte-nance available to the home mechanic. When engine oil ages, it gets diluted and contaminated, which ultimately leads to premature engine wear.
2   Although some sources recommend oil filter changes every other oil change, we feel that the minimal cost of an oil filter and the relative ease with which it is installed dictate that a new filter be used whenever the oil is changed.
3   The tools necessary for a normal oil and filter change are a wrench to fit the drain plug at the bottom of the oil pan, a suitable size wrench

Fig. 1.10 Adjust the cruise control Bowden wire tension (arrow) after loosening the adjusting locknut (arrow) (Sec 14)

to remove the filter cover, a container with at least an eight-quart capacity to drain the old oil into and a funnel or oil can spout to help pour fresh oil into the engine.
4   In addition, you should have plenty of clean rags and newspapers handy to mop up any spills. Access to the underside of the vehicle is greatly improved if the vehicle can be lifted on a hoist, driven onto ramps or supported by jackstands. **Warning:** *Do not work under a ve-hicle which is supported only by a bumper, hydraulic or scissors-type jack.*
5   If this is your first oil change on the vehicle, it is a good idea to crawl underneath and familiarize yourself with the location of the oil drain plug. The engine and exhaust components will be warm during the actual work, so it is a good idea to figure out any potential problems before the engine and its accessories are hot.
6   Allow the engine to warm up to normal operating temperature. If the new oil or any tools are needed, use this warm-up time to gather everything necessary for the job. The correct type of oil to buy for your application can be found in *Recommended lubricants and fluids* at the beginning of this Chapter.
7   With the engine oil warm (warm engine oil will drain better and more built-up sludge will be removed with the oil), raise and support the vehicle. Make sure it is firmly supported. If jackstands are used, they should be placed toward the front of the frame rails which run the length of the vehicle.

15.8   Engine oil filter cover nuts (arrows)

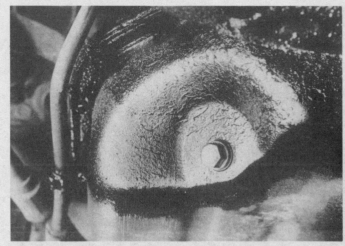

15.10   Oil pan drain plug location

1

15.15   The filter has a wire loop at the top to aid in removal

15.18   Inserting the oil filter cover and shaft into the housing

8   Remove the nuts and lift off the filter housing cover (photo).
9   Move all necessary tools, rags and newspapers under the vehicle. Position the drain pan under the drain plug. Keep in mind that the oil will initially flow from the pan with some force, so place the pan accordingly.
10   Being careful not to touch any of the hot exhaust pipe components, use the wrench to remove the drain plug near the bottom of the oil pan (photo). Depending on how hot the oil has become, you may want to wear rubber gloves while unscrewing the plug the final few turns.
11   Allow the old oil to drain into the pan. It may be necessary to move the pan farther under the engine as the oil flow slows to a trickle.
12   After all the oil has drained, wipe off the drain plug with a clean rag. Small metal particles may cling to the plug and would immediately contaminate the new oil.
13   Clean the area around the drain plug opening and reinstall the plug. Tighten the plug securely with the wrench. If a torque wrench is available, use it to tighten the plug.
14   Remove all tools, rags, etc. from under the vehicle, being careful not to spill the oil in the drain pan. Lower the vehicle.
15   Lift the old filter element out of the housing (photo).
16   Compare the old filter with the new one to make sure they are the same type.
17   Lower the new filter into the housing, making sure to seat it securely.
18   Install the filter housing cover, making sure the gasket seats securely and install the nuts (photo).
19   If an oil can spout is used, push the spout into the top of the oil can. A funnel may also be used.

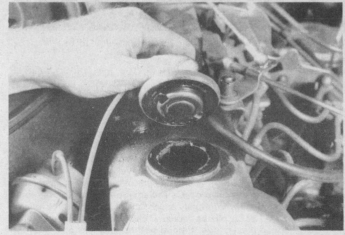

15.20   Engine oil is added through the filler cap in the camshaft cover

20   Remove the oil filler cap (photo). Pour about one quart (one liter) less than the specified amount of fresh oil into the engine (see *Recommended lubricants* for proper type of oil). Wait a few minutes to allow the oil to drain into the pan, then check the level on the oil dipstick (see Section 4 if necessary). If the oil level is at or near the upper mark on the dipstick, start the engine and allow the new oil to circulate.

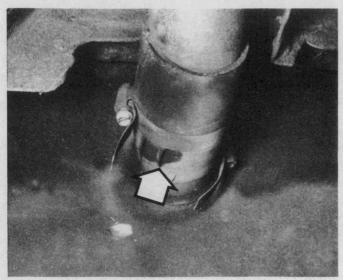

16.5 This fuel filler hose has cracked and is leaking (arrow) so it should be replaced

17.3 Loosening the fuel filter center bolt with a wrench

to get near the work area. Mop up spills immediately and do not store fuel-soaked rags where they could ignite.

1   The fuel system is under some pressure, so if any fuel lines are disconnected for servicing, be prepared to catch the fuel as it spurts out. Plug all disconnected fuel lines immediately after disconnection.

2   The fuel system is most easily checked with the vehicle raised on a hoist so the components underneath the vehicle are readily visible and accessible.

3   If the smell of diesel fuel is noticed while driving or after the vehicle has been in the sun, the system should be thoroughly inspected immediately.

4   Remove the fuel tank filler cap and check for damage, corrosion and an unbroken sealing imprint on the gasket. Replace the cap with a new one, if necessary.

5   With the vehicle raised, inspect the fuel tank and filler neck for punctures, cracks and other damage. The connection between the filler neck and the tank is especially critical. Sometimes a rubber filler neck will leak due to loose clamps or deteriorated rubber, problems a home mechanic can usually rectify (photo). **Warning:** *Do not, under any circumstances, try to repair a fuel tank yourself (except rubber components) unless you have had considerable experience. A welding torch or any open flame can easily cause the fuel vapors to explode if the proper precautions are not taken.*

6   Carefully check all rubber hoses and metal lines leading away from the fuel tank. Check for loose connections, deteriorated hoses, crimped lines and other damage. Follow the lines up to the front of the vehicle, carefully inspecting them all the way. Repair or replace damaged sections as necessary.

17.4   Holding the center bolt allows the fuel filter to be unscrewed

21   Run the engine for only about a minute and then shut it off. Immediately look under the vehicle and check for leaks at the oil pan drain plug. If it is leaking, tighten with a bit more force.

22   With the new oil circulated and the filter now completely full, recheck the level on the dipstick and if necessary, add enough oil to bring the level to the upper mark on the dipstick.

23   During the first few trips after an oil change, make it a point to check frequently for leaks and proper oil level.

24   The old oil drained from the engine cannot be reused in its present state and should be disposed of. Oil reclamation centers, auto repair shops and gas stations will normally accept the oil, which can be refined and used again. After the oil has cooled, it can be drained into a suitable container (capped plastic jugs, topped bottles, milk cartons, etc.) for transport to one of these disposal sites.

16 Fuel system check

Caution: *There are certain precautions to take when inspecting or servicing the fuel system components. Although diesel fuel is not as volatile as gasoline it is a good idea to work in a well-ventilated area and do not allow open flames (cigarettes, appliance pilot lights, etc.)*

17 Fuel filter replacement

1   These models are equipped with two filters: a main spin-on type mounted on a housing adjacent to the front of the cylinder head and a prefilter in the fuel line located on the left side of the engine compartment. Both are of the disposable type and should be replaced at the specified intervals.

2   Place some rags or newspapers under the fuel filter and prefilter to catch spilled fuel.

Main filter

3   Loosen the large bolt at the top of the housing using a suitable wrench (photo).

4   Unscrew the filter while holding the bolt (photo).

5   Install the new filter and tighten the bolt securely. Refer to Step 9 below.

17.6 Loosening the fuel prefilter screws with a screwdriver

17.9 When no air bubbles can be seen in the fuel flowing from the filter bolt (arrow), tighten the bolt to complete the bleeding procedure

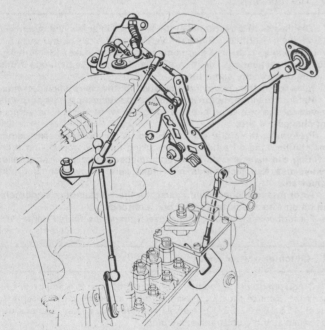

Fig. 1.11 Typical throttle linkage component layout (Sec 18)

18.4a Disconnect the throttle linkage joints by prying with a screwdriver

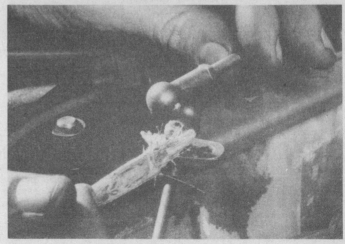

18.4b Use a small brush to lubricate the throttle linkage joints

Prefilter

6 Loosen the clamps with a screwdriver and slide the clamps back on the fuel line hoses (photo).
7 Note the direction in which the prefilter is installed and remove the hoses.
8 Install the hoses on the new prefilter and secure them with the clamps.
9 After replacing either filter, all air must be bled from the system. Loosen the large bolt at the top of the filter housing, loosen the hand pump (Section 31) and pump until no air bubbles can be seen escaping. Tighten the bolt (photo).

18 Throttle linkage check and lubrication

1 The throttle linkage should be checked and lubricated periodically to assure its proper function.

2 Check the operation of the linkage to make sure that it is not binding.
3 Inspect the linkage joints for looseness and the rods for corrosion and damage, replacing parts as necessary.
4 Use a screwdriver to carefully pry each joint off the ball, lubricate with white lithium grease and snap the joint back in place (photos).

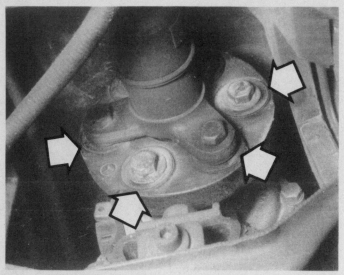

19.3   Check the driveshaft flex discs for loose bolts and damage to the rubber (arrows)

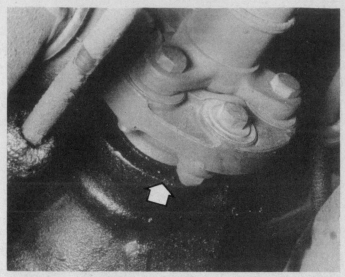

19.4   The leaking oil (arrow) is evidence the pinion seal is leaking and needs replacing

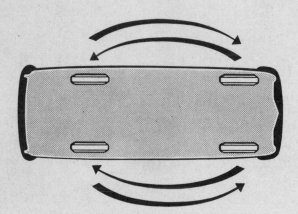

Fig. 1.12   Radial tires should be rotated front to rear (arrows) (Sec 20)

19   Driveline check

1   At the recommended intervals the transmission and differential output seals, driveshaft flex discs as well as the axleshaft boots should be inspected for leaks and damage. At the same time, it is a good idea to check the driveshaft universal joints and center bearings (Chapter 8).
2   Raise the vehicle and support it securely on jackstands.
3   Inspect the flex discs located at each end of the driveshaft for damage and distortion at the points where the bolts go through the discs (photo).
4   Check for lubricant leaks located at the point where the driveshaft exits the transmission (output seal) and enters the differential (pinion seal) or the axleshafts exit from it (output seals). It may be necessary to clean these areas before inspection. If there is any oil leaking from any of the junctions, the seal(s) must be replaced (Chapters 7 and 8) (photo).
5   The axleshaft boots are very important because they prevent dirt, water and other foreign material from entering and damaging the constant velocity (CV) joints. Inspect the condition of all four boots (two on each axleshaft). It is a good idea to clean the boots using soap and water as oil or grease will cause the boot material to deteriorate prematurely. If there is any damage or evidence of leaking lubricant, the boots must be replaced. Also, check the tightness of the boot clamps. If they are loose and can't be tightened, the clamp must be replaced.

20   Tire rotation

1   The tires should be rotated at the specified intervals and whenever uneven wear is noticed. Since the vehicle will be raised and the tires removed anyway, this is a good time to check the brakes (Section 13) and the wheel bearings (Section 23). Read over these Sections if this is to be done at the same time.
2   Refer to the accompanying illustration for the tire rotation patterns.
3   Refer to the information in *Jacking and towing* at the front of this manual for the proper procedures to follow when raising the vehicle and changing a tire.
4   Preferably, the entire vehicle should be raised at the same time. This can be done on a hoist or by jacking up each corner and then lowering the vehicle onto jackstands placed under the frame rails. Always use four jackstands and make sure the vehicle is firmly supported.
5   After rotation, check and adjust the tire pressures as necessary and be sure to check the wheel bolt tightness.
6   For further information on the wheels and tires, refer to Chapter 10.

21   Clutch disc wear check

1   If equipped with a manual shift transmission, it is important to check the wear of the clutch disc material at the specified intervals. A tool (115 589 07 23 00) is available from your dealer to check the disc wear at the clutch slave cylinder.
2   Insert the gauge between the clutch housing and the slave cylinder as shown in the accompanying illustration.
3   If the gauge notches are not visible when the gauge is fully inserted, the disc wear is within specifications. If they are visible the clutch should be replaced (Chapter 8).

22   Cooling system servicing (draining, flushing and refilling)

1   Periodically, the cooling system should be drained, flushed and refilled to replenish the antifreeze mixture and prevent formation of rust and corrosion which can impair the performance of the cooling system and ultimately cause engine damage.
2   At the same time the cooling system is serviced, all hoses and the radiator cap should be inspected and replaced if defective (see Section 7).
3   Since antifreeze is a corrosive and poisonous solution, be careful not to spill any of the coolant mixture on the vehicle's paint or your skin. If this happens, rinse immediately with plenty of clean water. Also,

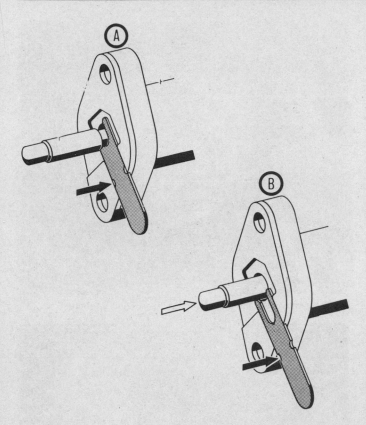

Fig. 1.13 Checking clutch disc friction material wear (Sec 21)

A   The disc is within specifications if the gauge can be inserted fully so the notches (arrow) cannot be seen
B   If the gauge notches (arrow) are visible, the disc is in need of replacement

22.6   Removing the radiator drain plug with a screwdriver

23.5   Hang the caliper out of the way using a piece of wire. Be careful that the rubber fluid hoses are not crimped or damaged

consult your local authorities about the dumping of antifreeze before draining the cooling system. In many areas of the U.S., reclamation centers have been set up to collect automobile oil and drained antifreeze/water mixtures rather than allowing them to be added to the sewage system.

4   With the engine cold, remove the radiator cap.

5   Move a large container under the radiator to catch the coolant as it is drained.

6   Drain the radiator by removing the drain plug at the bottom (photo). Be careful that none of the coolant is splashed on your skin or in your eyes.

7   Remove the engine drain plug located on the right side of the engine. This will allow the coolant to drain from the engine itself.

8   Disconnect the hose from the coolant reservoir and remove the reservoir. Flush it out with clean water.

9   Place a garden hose in the radiator filler neck at the top of the radiator and flush the system until the water runs clear at all drain points.

10   In severe cases of contamination or clogging of the radiator, remove it (see Chapter 3) and reverse flush it. This involves simply inserting the hose in the bottom radiator outlet to allow the clear water to run against the normal flow, draining through the top. A radiator repair shop should be consulted if further cleaning or repair is necessary.

11   When the coolant is regularly drained and the system refilled with the correct antifreeze/water mixture, there should be no need to use chemical cleaners or descalers.

12   To refill the system, install the radiator drain plug, reservoir and the overflow hose as well as the engine block drain plug.

13   Fill the radiator to the base of the filler neck and then add more coolant to the reservoir until it reaches the mark.

14   Run the engine until normal operating temperature is reached and, with the engine idling, add coolant up to the Full level. Install the radiator and reservoir caps.

15   Always refill the system with a mixture of high quality antifreeze and water in the proportion called for on the antifreeze container or in your owner's manual. Chapter 3 also contains information on antifreeze mixtures.

16   Keep a close watch on the coolant level and the various cooling system hoses during the first few miles of driving. Tighten the hose clamps and/or add more coolant as necessary.

23   Front wheel bearing check, repack and adjustment

Check

1   With the vehicle securely supported on jackstands, spin the front wheels and check for noise, rolling resistance and free play. Now grab the top of the tire with one hand and the bottom of the tire with the other. Move the tire in-and-out. If it moves more than 0.005-inch, the bearings should be removed for inspection and replaced if necessary.

2   The front wheel bearings on these models should be repacked with fresh grease and adjusted as part of the routine maintenance procedure.

Repack

3   Raise the front of the vehicle and support it securely on jackstands.

4   Remove the wheels.

5   Remove the brake caliper retaining bolts and hang the caliper out of the way using a coathanger or piece of wire (photo).

23.6   Large pliers can be used to remove the grease cap

23.7   Remove the locknut using an Allen head wrench

23.8   Remove the radio suppressor with needle nosed pliers

23.10   Hold the outer bearing in place while withdrawing the hub/disc

23.12a   Using a hammer and chisel to deform the grease seal

23.12b   Prying out the seal with a large screwdriver

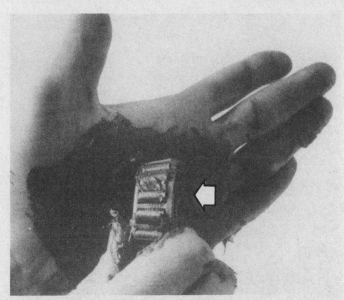

23.15 Work the grease into the bearing rollers from the back of the race in the direction shown (arrow)

23.19 Lubricating the inner circumference of the seal

23.20a Use a large socket, approximately the same diameter as the seal, to press the seal evenly into place. Note the direction the seal must face

23.20b Tapping the seal into the hub with the socket

6   Remove the grease cap (photo).
7   Loosen the locknut with an Allen wrench (photo).
8   Remove the radio static suppressor (photo).
9   Remove the locknut.
10 Remove the hub, holding the outer bearing in place with your thumbs (photo).
11 Remove the outer bearing.
12 Place the hub on a suitable working surface and remove the inner bearing seal using a hammer and chisel to deform it and then prying out with a screwdriver (photos).
13 Use solvent to remove all traces of the old grease from the bearings, hub and spindle. A small brush may prove useful; however, make sure no bristles from the brush embed themselves inside the bearing rollers. Allow the parts to air dry.
14 Carefully inspect the bearings for cracks, scoring and uneven surfaces. If the bearing races are defective, the hubs should be taken to a machine shop with the facilities to remove the old race and press new ones in.
15 Use an approved high temperature-wheel bearing grease to pack the bearings (see *Recommended lubricants* at the front of this Chapter). Work the grease completely into the bearings, forcing it between the rollers, cone and cage (photo).
16 Apply a thin coat of grease to the spindle at the outer bearing seat, inner bearing seat, shoulder and seal seat.
17 Put a small quantity of grease inboard of each bearing race inside the hub. Using your finger, form a dam at these points to provide extra grease availability and to keep thinned grease from flowing out of the bearing.
18 Install the grease-packed inner bearing into the rear of the hub and put a little more grease outboard of the bearing.
19 Lubricate the inner circumference of the new inner seal with a light coat of grease (photo).
20 Place the seal over the inner bearing and tap it evenly into place using a hammer and suitable size socket (photos).
21 Carefully place the hub assembly onto the spindle and push the grease-packed outer bearing into position.
22 Install the locknut and adjust the bearing preload using the following procedure.

23.23a Rotating the hub while tightening the locknut

23.23b Back off the locknut one third of a turn (arrow)

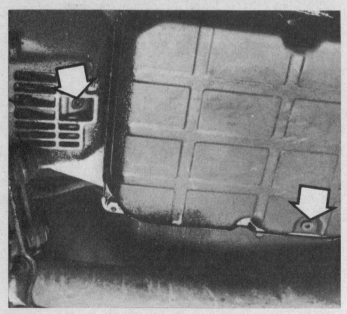

24.7 The torque converter and automatic transmission drain plugs (arrows)

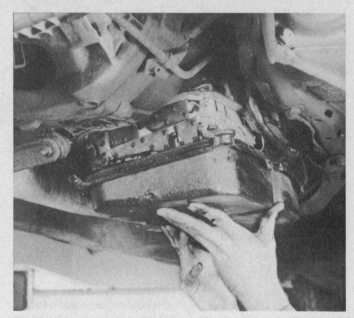

24.10 Hold the transmission oil pan level as it is lowered because there is still fluid in it

Adjustment

23 Rotate the hub while tightening the locknut until the bearings will no longer turn and then back off the locknut 1/3 turn (photos).
24 Give the kingpin a sharp blow with a hammer to loosen the bearing tension and then tighten the locknut Allen head screw securely and install the radio static suppressor.
25 Pack the cap with grease up to the bead and install it, tapping around the outer circumference with a hammer and punch to seat it.
26 Install the brake caliper(s).
27 Install the wheels and check the wheel bearing play as described in Step 1. Lower the vehicle.

24 Automatic transmission fluid and filter change

1 At the specified time intervals, the transmission fluid and filter should be drained and replaced.
2 Before beginning work, purchase the specified transmission fluid

(see *Recommended fluids* at the front of this Chapter) and a new filter. If a cork gasket oil pan is used, obtain a new one at this time. The rubber gasket used on later models can be reused if it is is in good condition.
3 Other tools necessary for this job include jackstands to support the vehicle in a raised position, a drain pan capable of holding at least 8 pints, newspapers and clean rags.
4 The fluid should be drained immediately after the vehicle has been driven. This will remove any built-up sediment better than if the fluid were cold. Because of this, beware of hot engine and exhaust components.
5 After the vehicle has been driven to warm up the fluid, raise it and place on jackstands for access underneath.
6 Move the necessary equipment under the vehicle, being careful not to touch any of the hot exhaust components.
7 Have an assistant rotate the engine with the starter or use a wrench to turn the engine over until the torque converter drain plug is accessible (photo). Place the drain pan under the transmission and torque converter and remove the drain plugs. Be sure the drain pan is in position, as

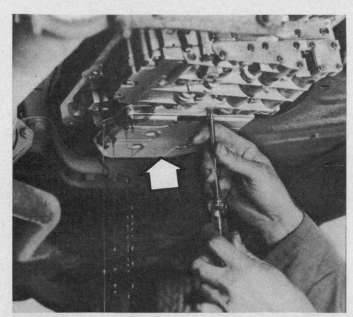

24.12 Be careful when removing the automatic transmission filter (arrow) because it contains residual fluid

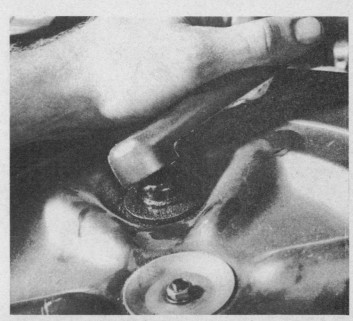

25.2 Removing the ventilation hose from the air cleaner

25.4 Lifting out the filter element

fluid will come out with some force.

8   After the fluid has drained completely, clean the torque converter and transmission drain plugs and reinstall them. Tighten the plugs securely.

9   On some models it will be necessary to use wire cutters to cut the strap retaining the wires to the transmission oil pan to allow removal of the pan.

10 Remove the retaining screws and lower the transmission oil pan carefully as there will still be fluid in it (photo).

11 Drain the residual fluid and inspect the drain pan for metal filings which would indicate that the transmission is in need of immediate repair. Wipe the pan clean with a lint-free rag.

12 Remove the filter screws (photo).

13 Lower the filter from the transmission, taking care as fluid will drain out as it is removed.

14 Place the new filter in position, seating it securely and install the screws. Tighten the screws to the specified torque.

15 Install the oil pan (using a new gasket if necessary) and tighten the screws to the specified torque.

16 Lower the vehicle.

17 Open the hood and remove the transmission fluid dipstick.

18 Add the specified amount and type of fluid to the transmission through the filler tube (use a funnel to prevent spills). It is best to add a little fluid at a time, continually checking the level with the dipstick (Section 4). Allow the fluid time to drain into the pan.

19 With the selector lever in Park, apply the parking brake and start the engine without depressing the accelerator pedal (if possible). Do not race the engine at high speed; run at slow idle only.

20 With the engine still idling, check the level on the dipstick. Look under the vehicle for leaks around the transmission oil drain plug.

21 Check the fluid level to make sure it is just below the Maximum mark on the dipstick. Do not allow the fluid level to go above this point as the transmission would then be overfilled, necessitating the draining of the excess fluid.

22 Push the dipstick firmly back into the tube and drive the vehicle to reach normal operating temperature (15 miles/24 kilometers of highway driving or its equivalent in the city). Park the vehicle on a level surface and check the fluid level on the dipstick with the engine idling and the transmission in Park. The level should now be at the Maximum mark on the dipstick. If not add more fluid to bring the level up to this point. Again, do not overfill.

25 Air filter cleaning and replacement

1   At the specified intervals, the air filter should be cleaned, or if specified, replaced with a new one. A thorough program of preventative maintenance would call for the filter to be inspected between changes.

2   The air filter is located inside the air cleaner housing on the top of the engine. The filter is replaced by removing the ventilation hose and the nut at the top of the air cleaner assembly, releasing the clips and lifting off the top plate (photo).

3   While the top plate is off, be careful not to drop anything down into the manifold opening.

4   Lift the air filter element out of the housing (photo).

5   Wipe out the inside of the air cleaner housing with a clean rag.

6   Strike the filter sharply on the floor, workbench or similar surface to dislodge the dust and dirt. If excessive, the filter should be replaced with a new one regardless of elapsed time.

7   If a new filter is being installed, compare it to the old one to make sure it is the same type and size.

8   Place the filter into the air cleaner housing. Make sure it seats properly in the bottom of the housing.

9   Install the top plate and the ventilation hose.

26.2   When vacuum is applied, the EGR shaft should be seen to move through the slot (arrow)

27.1   Unplug the emissions connector hoses

27.2a   Use a screwdriver to disconnect the throttle linkage

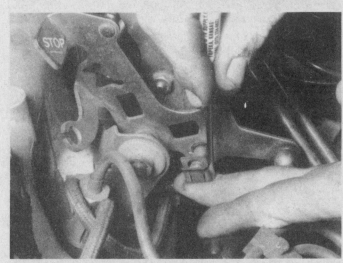

27.2b   Use a small screwdriver to remove the throttle linkage clip on the camshaft cover

2   With the engine cold to prevent burns, connect a vacuum pump to the valve and apply vacuum while watching the diaphragm rod through the slot in the valve (photo).
3   If the diaphragm does not move, replace the EGR valve with a new one. If in doubt about the condition of the valve, compare the free movement of your EGR valve with a new valve.
4   Refer to Chapter 6 for more information on the EGR system.

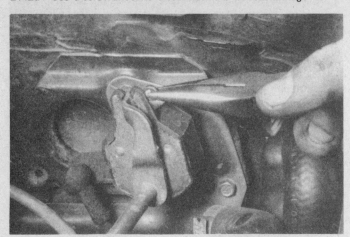

27.2c   Use needle-nose pliers to remove the throttle rod pin

26   Exhaust Gas Recirculation (EGR) valve check (US models only)

1   The EGR valve is located on the intake manifold, adjacent to the air cleaner. Most of the time when a problem develops in this emissions system, it is due to a stuck or corroded EGR valve.

27   Valve adjustment

1   Remove the ventilation hose and unplug the vacuum connectors (if equipped) on the camshaft cover (photo).
2   Disconnect throttle linkage (photos).
3   Unbolt the linkage and move it out of the way (photo).
4   Remove the bolts and lift the camshaft cover and gasket from the engine.
5   The valve clearance on these models is checked between the rocker arm and the camshaft base circle with the lobe positioned opposite the arm as shown in the accompanying illustration.
6   Slowly turn the engine over in a clockwise direction by slipping a socket over the large bolt at the front of the crankshaft until the first rocker arm and camshaft lobe (this will be the exhaust valve on all models) are correctly positioned so the clearance can be checked. Repeat the procedure on each valve in turn, working from the front of the engine to the rear. Refer to the accompanying illustrations to

27.3 Throttle linkage assembly-to-camshaft cover bolts (arrows)

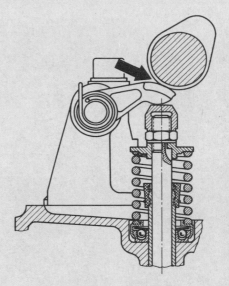

Fig. 1.14 The valve clearance must be measured between the rocker arm and the camshaft base circle (arrow) which is opposite the lobe (Sec 27)

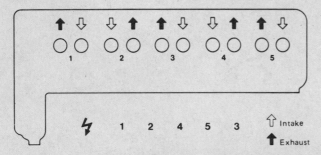

Fig. 1.15 Five-cylinder engine valve adjustment sequence (Sec 27)

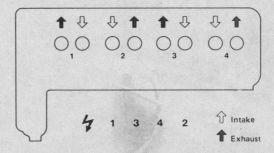

Fig. 1.16 Four-cylinder engine valve adjustment sequence (Sec 27)

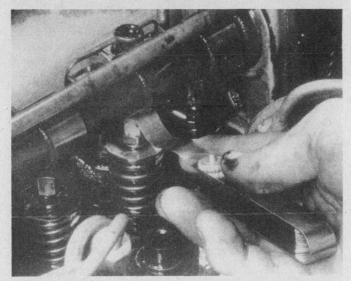

27.7 When inserted between the camshaft and rocker arm, the feeler gauge should be able to be withdrawn with a slight drag

27.8 The valve adjusting nut (A), locknut (B) and valve spring collar (C)

differentiate between the intake and exhaust valves as the clearance specifications between the two differ on some models.

7   Insert an appropriate size feeler gauge (refer to Specifications) between the rocker arm and the camshaft (photo). If the feeler gauge fits between the rocker arm and camshaft with a slight drag, then the clearance is correct and no adjustment is required.

8   If the feeler gauge will not fit between the rocker and the camshaft, or if it is loose, use two wrenches to loosen the adjusting nut locknut. It may also be necessary to hold the valve spring collar so it cannot move with a large wrench (photo).

27.9 Make sure the high-point of the camshaft lobe (arrow) is opposite the rocker arm when checking valve clearance

27.10 Use two wrenches to tighten the locknut

Fig. 1.17 To adjust the engine idle speed knob on mechanical governor equipped fuel injection pumps, measure the clearance between the adjusting ring or nipple and the spring (arrow) (models prior to 1979) (Sec 28)

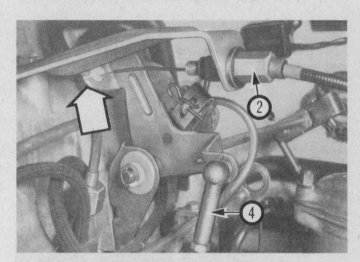

Fig. 1.18 1980 and later models idle speed adjust knob cable showing the locking grommet (arrow), adjusting nut (2) and throttle rod (4) (Sec 28)

9 Carefully tighten or loosen the adjusting nut until you can feel a slight drag on the feeler gauge as it is withdrawn from between the valve stem and adjusting nut (photo).
10 Hold the adjusting nut with one wrench, to keep it from turning, and tighten the locknut securely (photo). Recheck the clearance to make sure it hasn't changed.
11 After checking (and adjusting, if necessary) all the valves, Install the camshaft cover (use new a gasket if the old one is dried out or brittle) and tighten the mounting bolts evenly and securely to the specified torque.
12 Install the throttle linkage and vacuum line connector. The throttle linkage can be checked as described in Section 18.
13 Start the engine and check for oil leakage between the camshaft cover and the cylinder head.

28 Idle speed adjusting knob check and adjustment

1 Some models are equipped with an idle speed adjuster with a knob on the instrument panel so that engine idle speed can be adjusted manually for ease of starting and drivability. The idle speed adjuster clearance must be checked and adjusted at the specified intervals.

2 On models with pneumatic governor equipped fuel injection pumps, turn the preglow starter switch fully clockwise, then turn it counter-clockwise. Make sure there is a half turn of travel until the idle speed increases. Adjust the locknut on the cable at the bracket as necessary.
3 On injection pumps with mechanical governors, turn the idle speed adjusting knob fully to the right and make sure the clearance between the adjusting nipple or ring and spring is 1 mm as shown in the illustration.
4 With the engine off, depress the accelerator pedal while turning the knob fully clockwise. Start the engine and check that it runs at no more than 1000 rpm as otherwise the engine speed can climb to full throttle. Adjust by turning the adjusting screw on the end of the cable wire early models or the adjusting nut on the cable and bracket.

29 Differential oil change

Note: *Carefully read through this Section before undertaking this procedure. You will need to purchase the correct type and amount of differential oil before draining the old oil out of the vehicle (see Recommended lubricants at the front of this Chapter). It may also be necessary to obtain a metric Allen wrench to remove and install the drain/fill plugs.*

29.2   The differential drain and fill plugs (arrows)

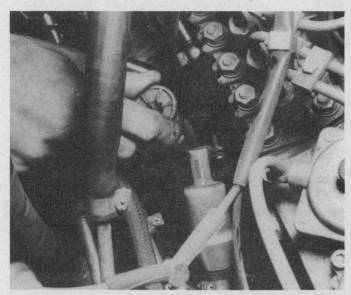

30.3   Unlock the hand pump by unscrewing the round handle

30   Fuel system bleeding

1   The fuel system must be kept free of air all times and a primer pump is incorporated for this purpose.
2   In the event that air enters the system such as when the fuel tank is run completely dry or the fuel filters are changed (Section 17) the system must be bled.
3   Make sure the fuel tank is full and unscrew the pump handle by rotating it in a counterclockwise direction (photo).
4   Operate the pump until air can be heard (a hissing noise) at the bypass valve located in the fuel filter housing (photo).
5   After bleeding, tighten the pump handle.
6   Refer to Sections 16 and 17 for more information on the fuel system.

30.4   A hissing noise can be heard in the area of the fuel filter nut (arrow) when the pump is operated

1   The vehicle should be driven for several minutes before draining the differential oil. This will warm up the oil and ensure complete drainage.
2   Move a drain pan, rags, newspapers and tools under the vehicle. With the drain pan under the differential, remove the drain plug from the bottom of the housing. Remove the inspection/fill plug to help vent the differential and aid the draining process (photo).
3   After the oil has completely drained, wipe the area around the drain hole with clean rag and install the drain plug, tightening it securely.
4   Fill the housing (through the inspection/fill plug hole) with the recommended lubricant until the level is even with the bottom of the inspection hole. Install the inspection plug after cleaning it and the threads in the housing.
5   Drive the vehicle and then check for leaks at the drain and inspection plugs.
6   After the job is complete, check for metal particles or chips in the drained oil, which indicate that the differential should be thoroughly inspected and repaired.

31   Manual transmission oil change

Note: *Carefully read through this Section before undertaking this procedure. You will need to purchase the correct type and amount of the specified oil before draining the old oil out of the vehicle (see Recommended lubricants at the front of this Chapter). It may also be necessary to obtain a suitable size Allen head wrench to remove and fill drain plugs.*

1   Raise the vehicle and support it securely on jackstands.
2   Move the drain pan, rags, newspapers and wrench under the transmission.
3   Move the transmission drain and fill plugs and allow the oil to drain into the pan.
4   After the oil has drained completely, reinstall the drain plug and tighten it securely.
5   Using a hand pump, syringe or funnel, fill the transmission with the specified lubricant.
6   Lower the vehicle. With the vehicle on a level surface, check the oil level, adding more oil if necessary and install the fill plug securely.

32   Fuel injection start of fuel delivery check and adjustment

The fuel injection start of fuel delivery must be checked and adjusted at the specified intervals. This procedure is described in Chapter 4A.

Chapter 2 Part A   Engine

Contents

Air filter replacement . . . . See Chapter 1	Front oil seal — replacement 4
Camshaft cover — removal and installation 2	General information 1
Camshaft — removal and installation 6	Intake and exhaust manifold and gasket — removal
Cylinder head — removal and installation 8	and installation 3
Drivebelt check and adjustment . . . . See Chapter 1	Lower oil pan — removal and installation 10
Engine mounts — replacement with engine in vehicle 12	Oil cooler — removal and installation 9
Engine oil and filter change . . . . See Chapter 1	Repair operations possible with the engine in
Engine oil level check . . . . See Chapter 1	the vehicle . . . . See Chapter 2B
Engine overhaul — general information . . . . See Chapter 2B	Rocker arm assemblies — removal and installation 7
Engine removal — methods and precautions . . . . See Chapter 2B	Timing chain — replacement in vehicle 5
Engine — removal and installation 11	Water pump — removal and installation . . . . See Chapter 3
Engine and transmission — separation and connection 13	

Specifications

Note: *Additional specifications can be found in Part B of Chapter 2.*

Torque specifications	Nm	Ft-lbs
Cylinder head bolts and camshaft bearing mount bolts		
Hexagon socket bolt*		
1st step	70	52
2nd step	90	66
10 minute settling time		
3rd step	100	74
Twelve-point socket bolt		
1st step	40	30
2nd step	70	52
10 minute settling time		
3rd step	rotate bolt head an additional 90°	
4th step	rotate bolt head an additional 90°	

* Hexagon socket-type head bolts must be retightened after 500 to 1000 Km (300 to 600 miles) (except US models from 1977 on)

	Nm	Ft-lbs
Camshaft cover		
Bolt	5	3.7
Nut	15	11
Camshaft sprocket bolt	80	59
Camshaft bearing mount nuts	25	18
Crankshaft pulley bolts	35	26
Crankshaft balancer bolt	270 to 330	199 to 244
Engine mount bolts		
Front engine mount adjustment screw	130	96
Rear engine mount adjustment screw	40	30
Engine mount bearer-to-engine block		
10 mm	40	30
12 mm	70	52
Bracket-to-oil pan	25 to 35	18 to 26
Rear engine mount-to-bearer	25	18
Transmission-to-engine mount nut	70	52
Rocker arm bracket-to-cylinder head bolts	38	28
Oil pan drain plug	40	30
Oil pan bolt		
10 mm	40	30
12 mm	70	52

2A

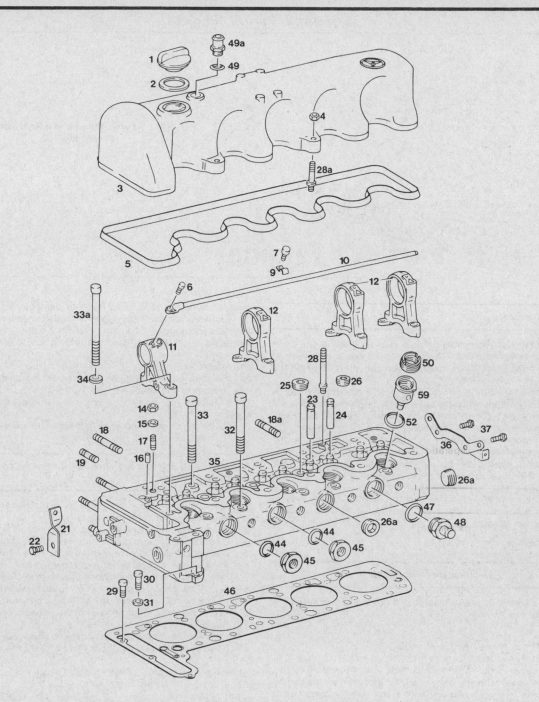

Fig. 2A.1 Cylinder head component layout details (Sec 2, 5, 7 and 8)

1 Filler cap	18a Stud	33 Cylinder head bolts
2 Seal	19 Stud	(12 mm by 119 or 120 mm)
3 Camshaft cover	21 Cylinder head lifting eye	33a Cylinder head bolts
4 Nut	22 Lifting eye retaining screw	(12 mm by 145 or 146 mm)
5 Cover gasket	23 Intake valve guides	34 Washers
6 Front oil pipe screw	24 Exhaust valve guides	35 Cylinder head
7 Oil pipe screws	25 Closing plugs	36 Rear cylinder head lifting eye
9 Oil pipe clips	26 Closing plugs	37 Screw
10 Oil pipe	26a Closing plugs	44 Sealing ring
11 Camshaft bearing mount	28 Studs	45 Screw connection
(front)	28a Studs	46 Cylinder head gasket
12 Camshaft bearing mounts	29 Screws	47 Sealing ring
14 Bearing mount nuts	30 Screws	48 Heater connection
15 Bearing mount washers	31 Washers	49 Sealing ring
16 Mounting pins	32 Cylinder head bolts	50 Threaded rings
17 Studs	(12 mm by 104 or 105 mm)	52 Sealing rings
18 Studs		59 Combustion prechambers

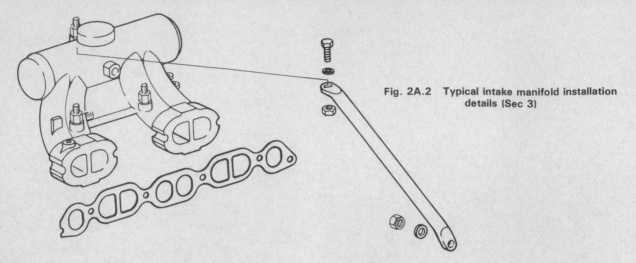

Fig. 2A.2   Typical intake manifold installation
details (Sec 3)

1   General information

This engine features replaceable cylinder sleeves and both the block and the removable head are made of cast iron. The camshaft is located in the cylinder head. The timing chain-driven camshaft actuates the valves via rocker arms.

The forward Sections in this Part of Chapter 2 are devoted to ''in vehicle'' repair procedures while the latter Sections involve the removal and installation procedures. Information concerning engine block and cylinder head servicing can be found in Part B of this Chapter.

The repair procedures included in this part are based on the assumption that the engine is still installed in the vehicle. Therefore, if this information is being used during a complete engine overhaul, with the engine already out of the vehicle and on a stand, many of the steps included here will not apply.

The specifications included in this part of Chapter 2 apply only to the engine and procedures found here. Part B of Chapter 2 contains the specifications necessary for engine block and cylinder head rebuilding.

2   Camshaft cover — removal and installation

Note: *Refer to Chapter 1 ''Valve clearance adjustment'' for additional illustrations and information.*

Removal

1   Disconnect the battery negative cable.
2   Disconnect the ventilation hose from the cover.
3   Carefully disconnect the throttle linkage and move it aside.
4   Remove the cover retaining bolts and lift the cover from the engine. It may be necessary to use a plastic hammer to break the gasket seal;

do not pry on the sealing surfaces or damage could result.
5   Clean the camshaft cover gasket mating surfaces and inspect them for nicks and gouges. Check the rubber gasket to make sure it has not hardened or cracked, replacing it with a new one if necessary.

Installation

6   Place the cover and gasket in position. Install the attaching bolts and tighten to the specified torque.
7   Install the throttle linkage and ventilation hose. Connect the battery cable.
8   Check the throttle operation before placing the vehicle into service.

3   Intake and exhaust manifold and gasket — removal and installation

1   Disconnect the negative cable from the battery.
2   Remove the air cleaner assembly.
3   On non-turbocharged engines, disconnect the throttle linkage.
4   Disconnect the choke vacuum lines (if equipped).
5   Disconnect the turbocharger pressure line at the manifold (photo).
6   Remove the turbocharger assembly (Chapter 4).
7   Disconnect the automatic transmission pipe and brace (if equipped).
8   On US models, disconnect the vacuum line from the EGR valve, loosen the bolt and remove the EGR pipe (photo).
9   Disconnect the vacuum line at the exhaust manifold.
10   Remove the manifold braces.
11   Remove the intake and exhaust manifold retaining nuts.
12   Remove the intake manifold, followed by the exhaust manifold.

3.5   Turbocharger pressure line bolt (arrow)

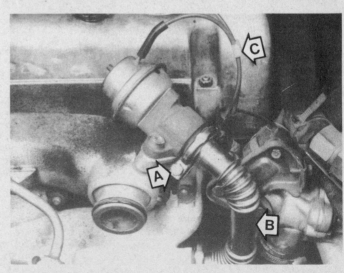

3.8   Removing the EGR valve pipe bolt (A), pipe (B) and vacuum hoses (C)

13 Use a scraper to remove the gasket. Carefully clean the contact surfaces of the manifolds and cylinder head, taking care to remove all traces of gasket material (photo).

14 Install a new gasket, place the manifolds in position and install the retaining nuts. Tighten the nuts securely.

15 The remainder of installation is the reverse of removal.

---

4 Front oil seal — replacement

1 Remove the radiator and cooling fan (Chapter 3).
2 Remove the drivebelts.
3 Mark the relationship of the crankshaft pulley to the damper, and remove the six Allen head screws. Remove the pulley.

3.13 Using a scraper to clean the manifold gasket surface

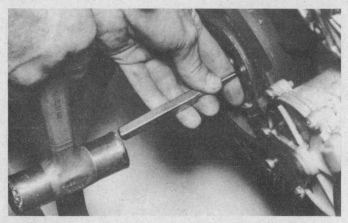

4.5 Marking the shaft-to-balancer relationship with a hammer and punch

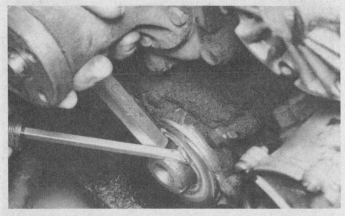

4.7 Use a screwdriver and a brass rod as a fulcrum to pry out the old seal

4 Lock the front balancer so that it can't turn and remove the bolt (photo).
5 Use a hammer and punch to mark the relationship of the balancer and crankshaft so the balancer will be reinstalled in its original position (photo).
6 Draw the balancer off the crankshaft with a suitable puller tool (photo).
7 Pry the old seal out of the bore with a screwdriver (photo).
8 Inspect the sealing ring on the crankshaft, replacing with a new one (a puller tool will be required) if it is worn or damaged (photo).

4.4 A bar (arrow) can be used to lock the balancer so it won't turn while the crankshaft bolt is removed

4.6 Remove the balancer with a puller tool using the crankshaft bolt and locking the balancer with a punch

4.8 Inspect the sealing ring on the crankshaft (arrow) for damage

2A

9   Inspect the front and back contact surfaces for corrosion, damage and burrs. A badly damaged balancer should be replaced with a new one but since this will require rebalancing the engine, minor imperfections can be removed with fine sandpaper (photos).
10   Lubricate the inner circumference of the new seal (photo).
11   If there are signs of oil leakage at the seal bore, it is a good idea to coat the outer circumference of the new seal with sealant.
12   Place the seal in position and draw it fully into the bore with the pulley bolt using a suitable size socket or piece of pipe and washers (photos).
13   Align the punch marks made during removal, place the balancer on the crankshaft and draw it on using the pulley bolt and washers. Note that the two alignment dowels must fit properly into the cutouts in the crankshaft or the balancer will have to be withdrawn and fitted again.
14   Place the pulley on the balancer, align the marks and install the retaining bolts, tightening them securely.
15   Install the drivebelts, fan and radiator.

---

5   Timing chain — replacement in vehicle

Note: *The timing chain can only be replaced with the engine in the vehicle by using a timing chain with a split link available from your dealer. Installing this link will require the use of Mercedes-Benz tool 000 589.58.43.00. A grinding tool for cutting the link such as a grinding wheel on a drill motor will also be necessary; a chisel or hacksaw are not acceptable. This procedure, if not done properly and with the recommended tools, can lead to major engine damage. Thus, in most cases timing chain replacement should be performed by a Mercedes dealer only.*

1   Disconnect the negative cable from the battery.
2   Remove the glow plugs (Chapter 5).
3   Remove the camshaft cover (Section 2) and align the TDC marks on the camshaft sprocket and tower (refer to illustration 2A.5 and photo 6.5).
4   Remove the EGR tube (if equipped) and chain tensioner lock bolt.
5   On engines with the Type A hooked steel tensioning rail, remove the rail (Section 6).
6   Place clean rags in the timing chain cavity and cover the top of the cylinder head to keep foreign material from entering the engine.

4.9a   Inspect the balancer-to-seal contact surface (arrow)

4.9b   Check the back side of the balancer for damage and corrosion. Note the two alignment dowels (arrows) which must fit into the cutout areas on the end of the crankshaft

4.10   Lubricating the seal with grease

4.12a   Draw the seal into place with a suitable socket and the pulley bolt

4.12b   The seal fully installed in the bore

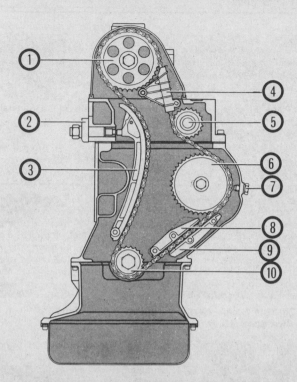

Fig. 2A.3   Timing chain component layout (Sec 5 and 6)

1 Camshaft sprocket	6 Injection timing device
2 Chain tensioner	7 Chain idler
3 Tension rail	8 Inner slide rail
4 Slide rail	9 Outer slide rail
5 Idler	10 Crankshaft sprocket

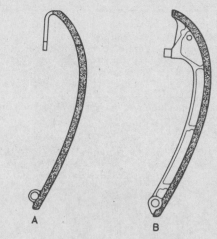

Fig. 2A.4   The Type A hooked chain tensioner must be removed prior to timing chain replacement while the Type B can remain in place (Sec 5 and 6)

2A

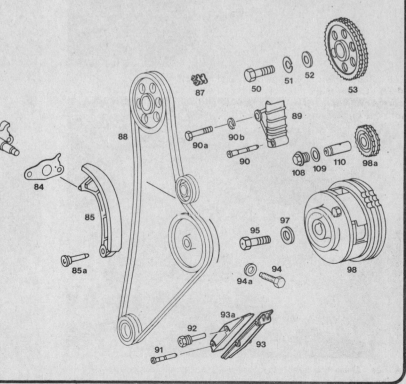

Fig. 2A.5   The camshaft sprocket and bearing tower marks aligned at TDC (arrow) (Sec 5)

Fig. 2A.6   The timing chain and tensioner component layout (Sec 5 and 6)

50 Camshaft sprocket bolt
51 Snap-ring
52 Washer
53 Camshaft sprocket
80 Chain tension bolts
84 Gasket
85 Tensioning rail
85a Bearing bolt
87 Replacement chain connecting link
88 Timing chain
89 Slide rail
90 Slide rail bearing bolt
90a Slide rail pivot bolt
91 Outer slide rail bearing bolt
92 Outer slide rail closing plug and bearing bolt
93 Outer slide rail
94 Chain locking screw
95 Injection timer bolt
97 Washer
98 Injection timer
98a Guide wheel
108 Closing plug
109 Sealing ring
110 Guide wheel shaft
a Chain tensioner assembly

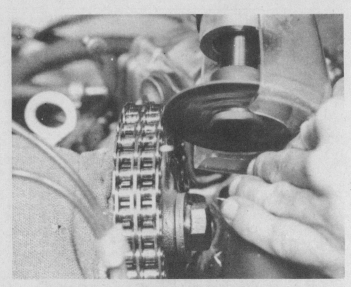

5.7a A suitable grinder must be used to remove the timing chain link heads

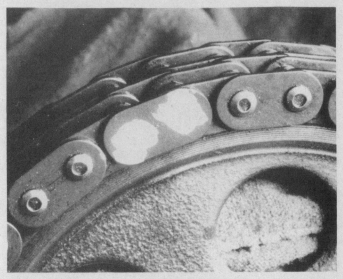

5.7b The timing chain link head should be ground off flush with the link plate face

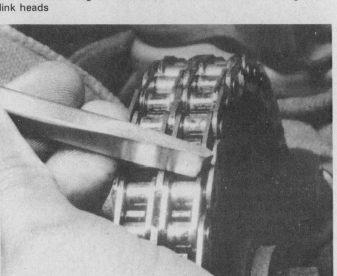

5.8 Remove the link plate with a chisel and hammer

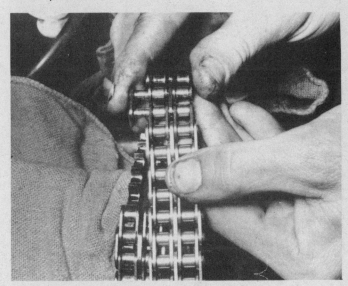

5.9 Fasten the new chain to the old with the link

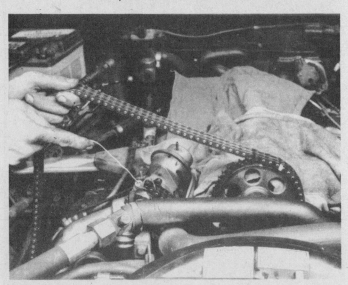

5.10 Maintain tension on the timing chain at all times as it is drawn through the engine

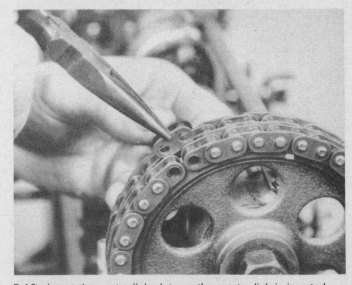

5.12 Insert the center link plate as the master link is inserted into the chain

5.13a Place the outer link in the tool

7 Use the grinder to cut off the heads of the uppermost link (photos).
8 Knock the outer link plate off the chain with a hammer and punch or chisel (photo).
9 Connect the new chain to the old using the new master link (photo).
Caution: *Maintain tension on both ends of the chain at all times; if it becomes slack the chain could jam on one of the tensioners, requiring disassembly of the engine to free it.*
10 Have an assistant turn the engine over in the direction of normal rotation (clockwise, facing the radiator) with a socket on the crankshaft pulley bolt while tension is maintained and the chain is drawn through (photo).
11 Once the new chain has been drawn through the engine, check to make sure the TDC mark on the camshaft sprocket and bearing tower and on the balancer are all aligned. If they are not, with the balancer at TDC, pull the chain off the camshaft sprocket (while maintaining tension) rotate the camshaft until the marks are in alignment and reinstall the chain.
12 Install the link and center link plate (photo).
13 Insert the outer link plate into the tool and install the plate on the chain link (photos).
14 Rotate the tool anvil for the final crimping operation (photo).
15 Use the tool to crimp the ends of the master link (photos).
16 Install the type-A chain tensioner.
17 The remainder of installation is the reverse of removal.

2A

5.13b Install the outer link on the chain with the tool

5.14 Turn the anvil in the tool around so the groove faces the chain for the final crimping operation

5.15a Crimp the master link with the tool (note the direction the anvil faces)

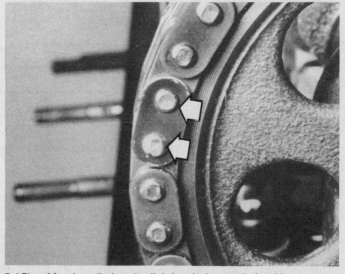

5.15b After installation the link heads (arrows) should appear very similar to the other link if properly crimped

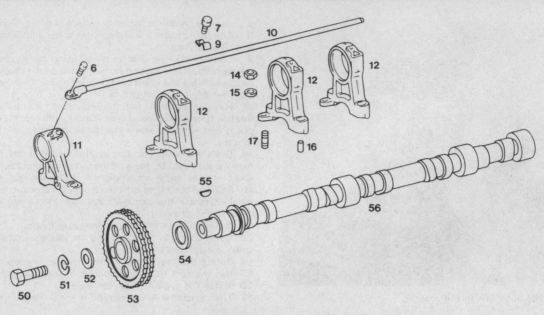

Fig. 2A.7 Camshaft and bearing mount component layout (Sec 6)

6	Oil pipe screws	11	Camshaft front bearing mount	16	Mounting pins	52	Flat washer
7	Oil pipe-to-bearing mount	12	Camshaft bearing mounts	17	Studs	53	Camshaft sprocket
	screws	14	Bearing mount nuts	50	Camshaft sprocket bolt	54	Shim
9	Oil pipe clip	15	Bearing nut washers	51	Lock washer	55	Woodruf key
10	Oil pipe					56	Camshaft

6.2   The air cleaner assembly retaining nut locations (arrows)

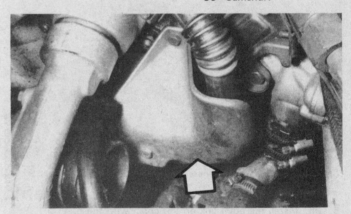

6.3   Turbocharger heat shield location (arrow)

6.5   The engine is at Top Dead Center (TDC) when the camshaft washer and bearing mount marks (arrows) are aligned

6   Camshaft — removal and installation

Removal

1   Disconnect the negative battery cable.
2   Remove the air cleaner assembly (photo).
3   Remove the turbocharger heat shield and EGR tube (if equipped) (photo).
4   Remove the camshaft cover (Section 2).
5   Rotate the engine with a wrench or socket on the balancer bolt until the marks on the camshaft and bearing tower are aligned, indicating the engine is at Top Dead Center (TDC) (photo). Remove the rocker arm assemblies (Sec 7).
6   Remove the level control hydraulic pump (if equipped) and fuel injection timer wheel (photos).
7   Remove the tensioning rail on models with type-A hooked steel tension rail or on models with the plastic tensioning rail, remove the timing chain tensioner closing plug and spring (photo).
8   Remove the slide rail retaining bolt (photo).

9   Remove the slide rail bearing bolt from the cylinder head with a slide hammer. Alternatively, use a suitable size bolt threaded into the bearing bolt with nuts and washers as spacers to draw the bearing bolt out, adding more spacers as necessary (photos).

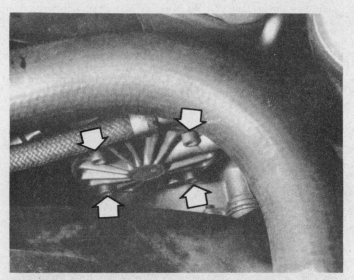

6.6a   Remove only the pump retaining bolts (arrows) and not the very similar bolts holding the housing together

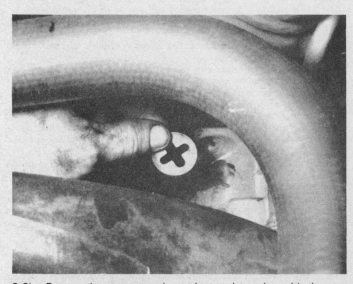

6.6b   Be sure the pump gear is not lost and remains with the pump itself

2A

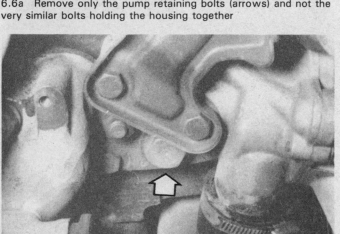

6.7   The timing chain tensioner closing plug (arrow) has a spring behind it so be careful during removal

6.8   The slide rail retaining bolt (arrow)

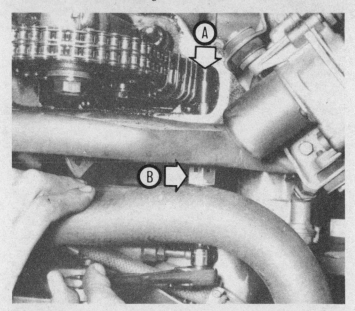

6.9a   Drawing the bearing bolt (arrow A) out of the cylinder block, using nuts (arrow B) and washers as spacers

6.9b   A suitable bolt and spacers can be used to remove the bearing bolt

10 Lift the slide rail out of the cylinder head cavity (photo).

11 Mark the relationship of the timing chain and sprocket with white paint (photo).

12 Lock the camshaft sprocket with a bar so it can't turn and remove the sprocket bolt (photo).

13 Remove the sprocket and washer and use a piece of wire to hold tension on the timing chain (photo).

14 Remove the camshaft bearing tower nuts and keep them in order for installation in their original positions (photo).

15 Remove the camshaft bearing tower bolts, loosening first the inside bolts then the outside before removing them. Keep them in order in a marked box or piece of cardboard for installation in their original locations (photos).

16 Rock the camshaft, bearing tower and oil pipe assembly gently back and forth to disengage it from the cylinder head and then lift it from the engine (photo).

17 Place the camshaft, bearing tower and oil pipe assembly on a clean working surface. The camshaft can be removed by sliding it rearward out of the bearing towers, tapping lightly with a plastic hammer to loosen the bearings, if necessary.

Installation

18 If the camshaft was removed from the bearing towers, lubricate the journals, lobes, bearings and bearing surfaces with clean engine oil prior to insertion into the towers.

19 Lower the camshaft and bearing tower assembly into position on the cylinder head, locate it on the dowels and install the bolts finger-tight. Since these bolts also retain the cylinder head, tightening them is a critical operation. Tighten the camshaft bearing tower bolts to the specified torque working from the inside out. **Note:** *On engines with hexagonal socket cylinder head bolts only, loosen each of the 14 remaining cylinder head bolts slightly and then tighten to the specified torque working from the inside out, one at a time.*

20 Install the camshaft bearing tower nuts and tighten to the specified torque, working from the inside out.

6.10 Lifting the slide rail from the engine

6.11 Use white paint to mark the relationship of the chain and camshaft sprocket with the engine at TDC

6.12 Insert a bar through the camshaft sprocket to keep it from turning as the bolt is removed

6.13 Fasten the timing chain securely with a piece of wire to maintain tension on it

6.14 Removing the camshaft bearing tower nuts

21 Install the camshaft washer, aligning the mark with the TDC mark on the camshaft tower and making sure the TDC mark on the balancer is lined up with the pointer (photos).
22 Install the timing chain on the sprocket, aligning the painted marks.
23 Install the timing chain, sprocket and bolt onto the camshaft. Lock the sprocket from turning and tighten the bolt to the specified torque.
24 Install the timing chain guide rail.
25 Lubricate the camshaft lobes and valve gear with assembly lube or clean engine oil (photo).
26 Install the tensioning spring.
27 Install the rocker arm assemblies (Section 7).
28 Adjust the valve clearance (Chapter 1).
29 Install the camshaft cover, air cleaner assembly and any other components which were removed.
30 Connect the battery cable.

2A

6.15a Removing the camshaft bearing tower bolts

6.15b Keep the camshaft bolts in order in a marked box for reinstallation to their original positions

6.16 Lifting the camshaft assembly from the engine

6.21a The TDC marks on the camshaft tower and washer must be aligned and...

6.21b ...at the same time the TDC mark and pointer on the balancer must also line up

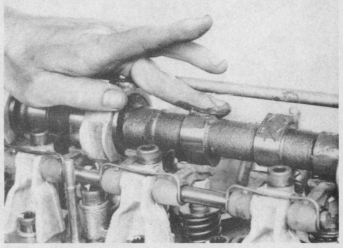

6.25 Lubricate the camshaft and valve gear before starting the engine

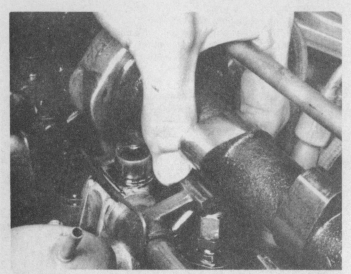

7.3   Move the rocker arm with your fingers to make sure it is free of camshaft load

7.4a   Work the rocker back and forth to release it from the protrusions on the cylinder head and then lift straight up

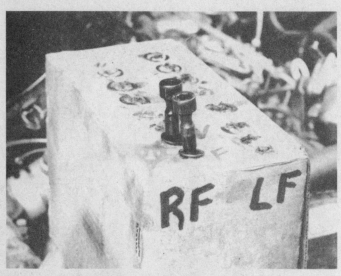

7.4b   Keep the rocker bolts in a marked box

7.4c   Dislodge the rocker, if necessary, by gently tapping with a rubber mallet

7.5a   With the camshaft assembly removed for clarity, the procedure for loosening the valve locknut (2) while holding the adjustment nut (1) can be seen

7.5b   The adjustment nut can now be turned and if the spring is to be considerably compressed, the spring collar should be held from turning with a wrench

7 Rocker arm assemblies — removal and installation

Removal

1   Disconnect the battery negative cable.
2   Remove the camshaft cover.
3   The rocker arms must be free of pressure from the camshaft lobes prior to removal. To accomplish this, turn the engine over slowly with a wrench or socket on the crankshaft pulley until each rocker arm group (starting at the front) is free of pressure. There are two rocker arms in each group except on the rear set on five cylinder engine which have three. Check for free movement by grasping the rockers and moving them back and forth with your fingers (photo).
4   Remove the bolts and lift the front rocker arm group from the engine, keeping the rocker arms and bolts in order for reinstallation to the original locations (photos). It may be necessary to dislodge the rocker towers from the mounting protrusions on the cylinder head by tapping with a rubber mallet (photo).
5   On the rear rocker arm groups it may be necessary to back off the valve adjuster to release camshaft pressure. Hold a wrench on the valve spring collar to keep it from turning (photos).

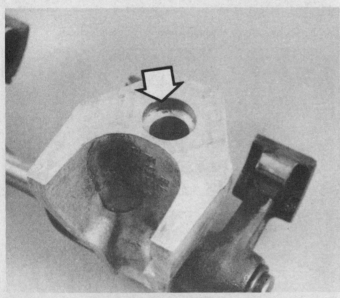

7.6   The rocker arm indentation (arrow) must be securely installed over the protrusion on the cylinder head

8.8   Disconnect all of the hoses at the right front corner of the engine except the air conditioning hose (arrow)

Installation

6   Place the rocker assemblies in position and seat them securely on the cylinder head protrusions (photo).
7   Install the rocker arm bolts and tighten them to the specified torque.
8   Adjust the valve clearances (Chapter 1), install the camshaft cover and connect the battery.

8 Cylinder head — removal and installation

Removal

1   Prior to removal, obtain a new head gasket and trace its outline and the location of all cylinder head bolts on a piece of cardboard (such as the back of the gasket package). Punch holes for all of the bolts. This will provide an easily referenced place to store the bolts so they can be installed in their original locations (photo).
2   Remove the hood (Chapter 11) and disconnect the negative cable from the battery.
3   Drain the cooling system (Chapter 1).
4   Remove the air cleaner assembly.
5   Remove the intake and exhaust manifold (Section 3) and (if equipped) turbocharger (Chapter 4).
6   Remove the camshaft cover.
7   Remove the camshaft, bearing tower and oil pipe assembly (Section 6) placing the bolts in a marked piece of cardboard.
8   Disconnect all hoses at the right front corner of the cylinder head which would affect removal, except for the air conditioning hose (if equipped) (photo).
9   Remove the thermostat housing (Chapter 3).
10   Remove the coolant bleed line between the cylinder head and engine block (photo).

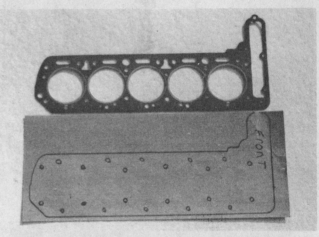

8.1   Trace the head gasket and bolt locations on a piece of cardboard so the head bolts can be kept in order

8.10   The bleed line connection between the cylinder block and head (arrows)

2A

11 Remove (if equipped) the cruise control and bracket assembly (photo).

12 Remove the power steering drivebelt.

13 Unbolt the cruise control-to-engine bracket (photo).

14 Remove the fuel filter (photo).

15 Disengage the power steering bracket and move it away from the cylinder head.

16 Disconnect the fuel injection lines at the pump and injector and the return hose from the fuel filter (photo).

17 Disconnect the vacuum line at the vacuum pump.

18 Disconnect the heater hose from the rear of the cylinder head.

19 Using the proper socket tool, remove the cylinder head bolts in the reverse order of the tightening sequence shown in the accompanying illustration (photos).

20 Connect a lifting device to the cylinder head (photo).

21 If the cylinder head will not lift off easily when the lifting device is raised, use a hammer and piece of wood to break it loose (photo).

22 As the cylinder head is raised, guide the timing chain through the opening and then fasten the chain securely out of the way with wire to maintain tension on it (photo).

23 Place the cylinder head on a clean working surface.

24 Remove the gasket. If the gasket is stuck a scraper can be inserted under the corner and a hammer can be used to break it loose (photo).

25 Clean the contact surfaces of the cylinder head and engine block, removing all traces of gasket material (photo).

8.11 Cruise control assembly-to-bracket bolts (arrows)

8.13 Cruise control bracket bolts (arrows)

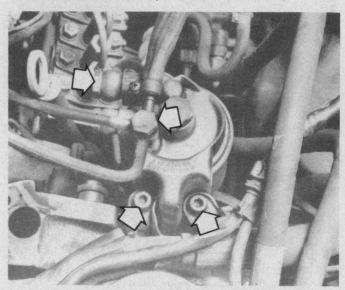

8.14 Fuel filter assembly bolts and hose connections (arrows)

8.16 After disconnecting and removing the fuel injection pipes, cover the pump with clean rags

8.19a A long breaker bar may be necessary to remove the cylinder head bolts

8.19b Don't forget to remove the cylinder head bolts in the timing chain cavity

8.20 The cylinder head is quite heavy and a hoist should be used for removal

8.21 Break the cylinder head gasket seal using a block of wood and rubber mallet

8.22 Lower the timing chain through the cavity as the cylinder head is raised. Keep tension on the chain at all times

8.24 Removing the old gasket with a hammer and scraper

8.25 Use the scraper to clean the block surface

Installation

26   Place the new gasket in position.

27   Lower the cylinder head into place, making sure it seats on the locating sleeves.

28   Clean the cylinder head bolt threads and then lubricate with clean engine oil.

29   Install the cylinder head bolts finger-tight and then tighten them to the specified torque. The hexagon head and 12-point socket head bolts require two different torquing procedures. The hexagon bolts are tighened in three steps with a ten minute waiting period between the second and third step. The 12-point socket bolts are tightened in four steps with a ten minute waiting period after the first two steps. Because the bolt heads are turned 90° on the last two steps, mark the bolt heads with paint so this movement can be easily checked. Also, use a bar and not the torque wrench for turning the bolts on these steps (photos). Refer to the Specifications section for the respective tightening torques.

30   The remainder of installation is the reverse of removal.

---

9   Oil cooler — removal and installation

1   Drain the engine oil (Chapter 1).

2   Disconnect and plug the oil cooler hoses.

3   Remove the retaining screws, disengage the oil cooler from the mount and lift it from the engine compartment.

4   Installation is the reverse of removal.

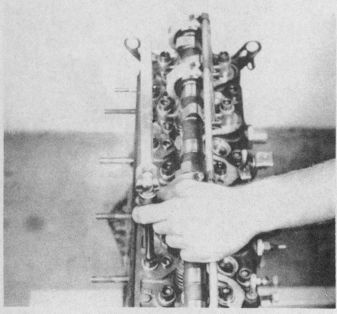

8.29b   After the bolts have been tightened to the specified torque . . .

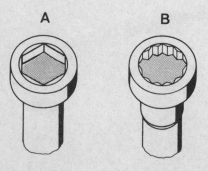

Fig. 2A.8   The two types of cylinder head bolts (Sec 8)

A   Hexagonal socket   *B   12-point socket*

---

10   Lower oil pan — removal and installation

Removal

1   Raise the front of the vehicle and support it securely on jackstands.

2   Drain the engine oil (Chapter 1).

8.29a   Install the cylinder head bolts finger-tight

8.29c   . . . turn each bolt an additional 90°

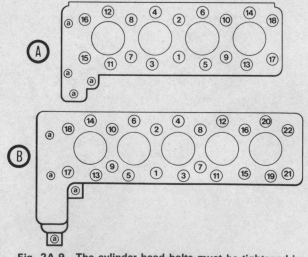

Fig. 2A.9   The cylinder head bolts must be tightened in the numbered sequence shown (Sec 8)

A   4-cylinder engines   *B   5-cylinder engines*

3 Remove all but one of the lower oil pan bolts and carefully lower the pan, taking care because it may contain residual oil.
4 Remove the gasket and carefully clean the contact surfaces of the pan and engine block.

Installation

5 Place the oil pan and gasket in position and install the bolts finger-tight. Tighten the bolts to the specified torque.
6 Lower the vehicle and refill with oil (Chapter 1).

---

11 Engine — removal and installation

Note: *On some air conditioned models the air conditioning hoses and lines may interfere with engine removal. Take the vehicle to a qualified shop and have the system discharged so the lines can be safely disconnected. Never remove air conditioning components or hoses until the system has been depressurized.*

Removal

1 Remove the hood and disconnect the battery negative cable.
2 Drain the cooling system, engine oil and transmission.
3 Remove the radiator, hoses and fan assembly (Chapter 3).
4 Remove the air cleaner assembly.
5 Disconnect the throttle linkage (photos).

6 Unbolt the throttle linkage from the camshaft cover and move it out of the way (photo). On automatic transmission models, disconnect the throttle cable.
7 Loosen the oil filter housing nuts and lift up on the housing and cover to break the suction and release the oil in the filter (photo).

11.5a Use pliers to pull off the longitudinal throttle linkage clip

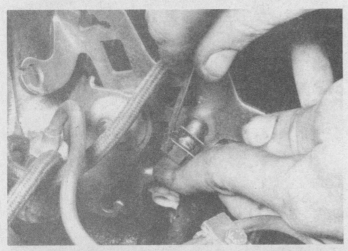

11.5b Pry the throttle rod clip off with a screwdriver

11.5c A long screwdriver is useful in disconnecting the linkage joints

11.6 Remove the bolts and lift the linkage junction box from the camshaft cover

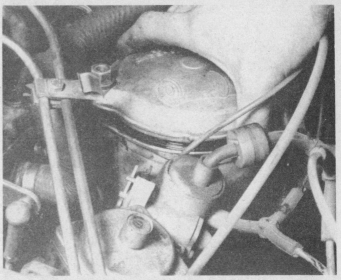

11.7 Lift the oil filter cover and element up to break the suction so the oil will drain

2A

8   Remove the oil cooler (if equipped).
9   Remove the fluid from the power steering pump reservoir using a suction pump, disconnect the hoses and fasten them out of the way.
10 Disconnect any air conditioning hoses which would interfere with engine removal after the system has been discharged.
11 Disconnect the engine electrical harness (photo).
12 Disconnect the heating system coolant hoses, marking their locations with tape.
13 Disconnect all fuel and vacuum lines which would interfere with engine removal, marking them with pieces of tape for ease of installation to their original locations.
14 Unplug the wire from the air conditioner compressor and remove the clamp.
15 Disconnect the wire at the alternator (photo).
16 Disconnect the starter cables at the battery and the junction box (photo).
17 Disconnect the oil pressure guage hose at the oil filter (photo).
18 Unbolt the level control system pump (if equipped) and fasten it out of the way with the hoses attached (photo).
19 Disconnect the vacuum pump line (photo).
20 Disconnect the exhaust pipe (photo).
21 Raise the vehicle and support it securely on jackstands.
22 Disconnect the exhaust pipe mount (photo).
23 Disconnect the body grounding strap at the bellhousing (photo).
24 Unscrew the front engine mounts (photo).
25 Remove the engine shock absorber nut while holding the shaft from turning with a wrench on the flat section of the shaft (photo).

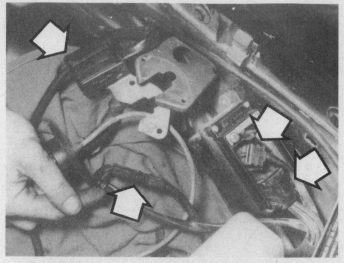

11.11   Engine electrical harness connections (arrows)

11.15   Alternator wire connection (arrow)

11.16   Disconnecting the starter cables at the junction box (arrow)

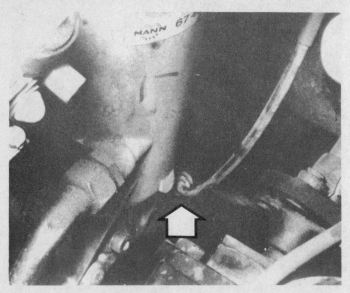

11.17   Oil pressure gauge connection at the oil filter housing

11.18   Level control pump retaining bolts (arrows)

11.19   Use two wrenches to disconnect the vacuum pump lines

11.20   Exhaust pipe nuts (arrows) (turbocharged model shown)

2A

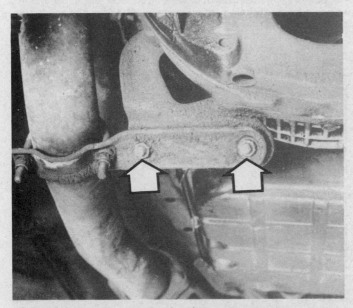

11.22   Exhaust pipe mounting bracket nuts

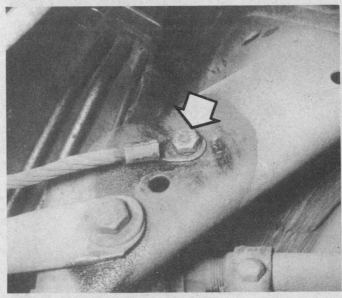

11.23   Body grounding strap (arrow)

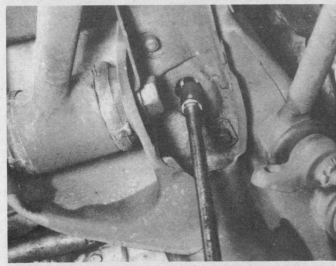

11.24   Removing the front engine mount bolts

11.25   Hold the engine shock absorber shaft with a wrench while unscrewing the nut

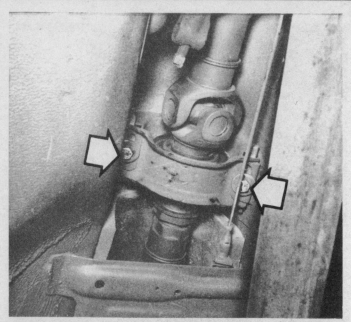

11.26   Driveshaft intermediate bearing mount bolts (arrows)

26 Remove the driveshaft intermediate bearing mount (photo).
27 Mark the driveshaft-to-flexible disc relationship with paint, remove the bolts and pry the driveshaft away from the disc with a pry bar or large screwdriver (photos).
28 On manual transmission models, disconnect the shift linkage (Chapter 7).
29 On automatic transmission models, use a screwdriver to put the white plastic locking plate up and then disconnect the electrical connector (photos).
30 Remove the automatic transmission shift rod thru-bolt.
31 Pry the cover off the automatic transmission speedometer sensor electrical connector and remove the screw (photo).
32 Remove the sensor wire and reinstall the screw so it won't be lost.
33 Remove the speedometer sensor cable bolt.
34 Remove the transmission mount bolts (photo).
35 Lower the vehicle and attach a lifting device to the engine. On five-cylinder engines, a lifting device with a swivel should be used to allow angling the engine and transmission unit to clear the radiator brace.
36 Lift the engine slowly and carefully from the engine compartment. It will be necessary to angle the engine/transmission unit as it is raised to clear the radiator brace and firewall (photo).
37 Lower the engine and transmission unit onto a clean working area, supporting the engine with the lifting device while disconnecting the transmission. The engine can now be mounted on an engine stand or placed on a sturdy workbench or working surface. Remember that the engine is extremely heavy, so take care to use blocks of wood to support it so it won't fall over.

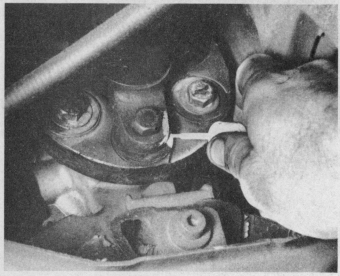

11.27a   Marking the driveshaft and disc relative positions

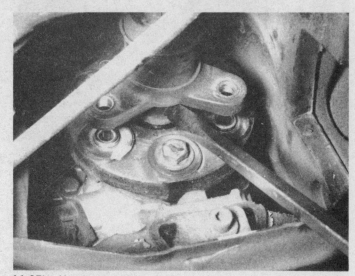

11.27b   Use a screwdriver to disconnect the driveshaft from the disc

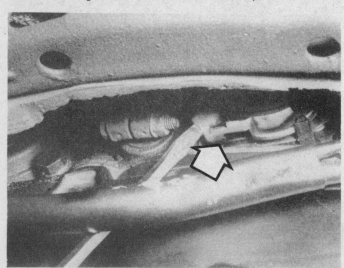

11.29a   Push up on the locking plate (arrow)

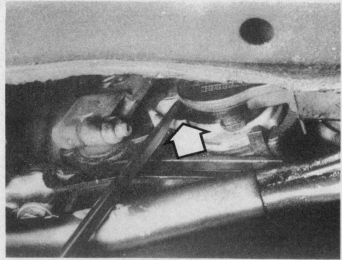

11.29b   Pry the connector off in the direction of the arrow

Installation

38 After reconnecting the transmission to the engine, the engine and transmission unit can be lowered into the vehicle and the remainder of installation is the reverse of removal.

39 Although the manufacturer recommends installing the engine and transmission as a unit, the length of the five-cylinder engine can make installation difficult. On these engines it may be easier to install the transmission first and then the engine using the following procedure.

40 Raise the transmission into position with a jack and install the rear mount bolts finger-tight.

41 Lower the engine into place on the engine mounts.

42 From under the vehicle, install the transmission-to-engine bolts, adjusting the position of the transmission with the jack if necessary.

43 On automatic transmissions, install the torque converter-to-flex plate bolt, rotating the engine using a wrench on the front crankshaft bolt for access to each bolt in turn.

44 Tighten the transmission mount bolts securely.

45 Once the engine and transmission have been connected in the vehicle, the remainder of installation is the reverse of removal. Work slowly and carefully installing all components, wires, etc. to their original positions.

12 Engine mounts — replacement with engine in vehicle

1 These models have a variety of engine and transmission mounts as well as shock absorbers to isolate the chassis from the considerable vibration of the diesel engine. The engine mounts and shock absorbers can be replaced with the engine/transmission still in the vehicle. Pry

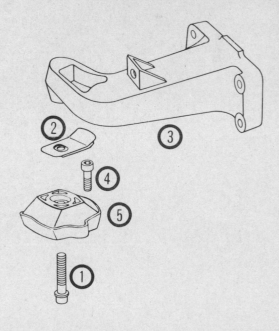

11.34 Transmission mount bolts (arrows)

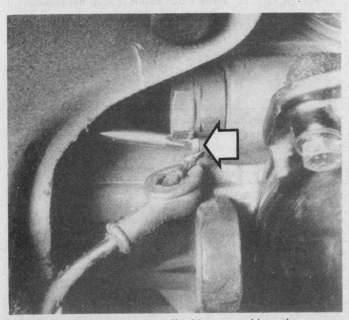

11.31 After prying the cover off with a screwdriver, the speedometer sensor screw (arrow) can be removed

11.36 The engine and transmission unit must be lifted out at an extreme angle to avoid contacting the firewall

Fig. 2A.10 Typical front engine mount installation details (Sec 12)

1 Bolt
2 Shield
3 Engine bearer
4 Bolt
5 Engine mount

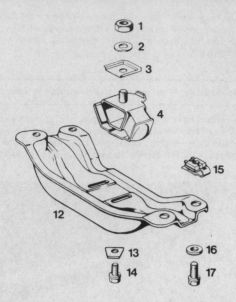

Fig. 2A.11   Typical rear engine mount installation details
(Sec 12)

1 Nut	13 Washer
2 Spring washer	14 Bolt
3 Supporting plate	15 Cage nut
4 Engine mount	16 Washer
12 Engine bearer	17 Bolt

on the rubber mounts with a bar to determine if they have become hard, split or separated from the metal backing. Fluid leakage indicates the seals are damaged and the shock absorbers require replacement.
2   Disconnect the negative cable from the battery.
3   Raise the vehicle and support it securely on jackstands.
4   Support the engine or transmission with a jack.
5   Remove the retaining bolts and replace the mount.

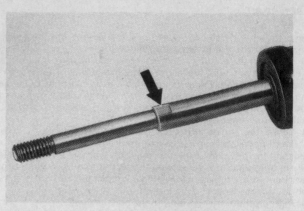

Fig. 2A.12   The engine shock absorber shaft flat section
(arrow) (Sec 12)

6   With the engine still supported with the jack, the shock absorber can be replaced. Hold the shock absorber shaft from turning using a wrench on the flat section. Remove the nuts from the ends of the shafts and replace the shock absorber.

13   Engine and transmission — separation and connection

1   Remove the starter motor.
2   On automatic transmission models, lock the starter ring gear teeth with a large screwdriver and remove the torque converter retaining bolts, rotating the crankshaft pulley with a wrench on the pulley bolt to bring each bolt into position.
3   Remove the transmission-to-engine bolts.
4   Insert a large screwdriver between the engine and transmission to separate them, working around the bellhousing until the transmission can be removed. On automatic transmission models, make sure the torque converter stays in place as the transmission is moved away from the engine.
5   The connection procedure is the reverse of separation.

Chapter 2 Part B
General engine overhaul procedures

Contents

Camshaft — inspection................................ 16
Crankshaft — inspection............................. 18
Crankshaft — installation and main bearing oil
  clearance check 22
Crankshaft — removal 13
Cylinder head — cleaning and inspection............. 8
Cylinder head — disassembly 7
Cylinder head — reassembly 10
Engine auxiliary components — installation 24
Engine auxiliary components — removal 11
Engine block — cleaning 14
Engine block — inspection 15
Engine overhaul — disassembly sequence 6
Engine overhaul — general information 3

Engine rebuilding alternatives 4
Engine removal — methods and precautions 5
General information 1
Initial start-up and break-in after overhaul 25
Main and connecting rod bearings — inspection 18
Piston/connecting rod assembly — inspection 17
Piston/connecting rod assembly — installation and bearing
  oil clearance check 23
Piston/connecting rod assembly — removal 12
Piston rings — installation 20
Rear oil seal — replacement 21
Repair operations possible with the engine in the vehicle 2
Valves — servicing.................................. 9

2B

Specifications

Note: *Additional specifications can be found in Part A of Chapter 2.*

General

Engine type	4-cycle diesel
Cylinder arrangement	Inline
Number of cylinders	4 or 5
Injection order	
Four-cylinder.......................................	1-3-4-2
Five-cylinder	1-2-4-5-3
Bore and stroke	
200D (UK) (123.120) engine 615.940...............	87 mm (3.428 in) X 83.6 mm (3.294 in)
220D (UK) (123.126) engine 615.912...............	87 mm (3.428 in) X 83.6 mm (3.294 in)
240D (UK) (123.123) engine 616.916...............	90.9 mm ((3.581 in) X 92.4 mm (3.641 in)
300D (UK) (123.130) engine 617.912...............	90.0 mm (3.581 in) X 92.4 mm (3.641 in)
240D (US) (123.123) engine 616.913...............	90.0 mm (3.581 in) X 92.4 mm (3.641 in)
240D (US) (123.123) engine 616.912	
Through 1977	90.0 mm (3.581 in) X 92.4 mm (3.641 in)
1978 on	87 mm (3.428 in) X 92.4 mm (3.641)
300D turbo (US) (123.133), 300CD turbo (US) (123.153),	
300TD turbo (US) (123.193) engine 617.952........	92.4 mm (3.641 in) X 92.4 mm (3.641 in)
300D (US) (123.130) engine 617.912...............	91 mm (3.585 in) X 92.4 mm (3.641 in)
300CD (US) (123.150) engine 617.912	91 mm (3.585 in) X 92.4 mm (3.641 in)
300TD (US) (123.190) engine 617.912..............	90.9 mm (3.581 in) X 92.4 mm (3.641 in)
Displacement	
200D (UK) (123.120) engine 615.940...............	1988 cc (121.3 cu in)
220D (UK) (123.126) engine 615.912...............	2197 cc (134 cu in)
240D (UK) (123.123) engine 616.912146.7	2404 cc (146.6 cu in)
240TD (UK) (123.183) engine 616.916..............	2399 cc (146.3 cu in)
240D (US) (123.123) engine 616.913...............	2404 cc (146.6 cu in)
240D (US) (123.123) engine 616.912	
Through 1977	2404 cc (146.6 cu in)
1978 on	2399 cc (146.3 cu in)
300D (UK) (123.130) engine 617.912..............	2998 cc (182.9 cu in)
300D (US) (123.130), 300CD (US) (123.150)	
engine 617.912	3005 cc (183.3 cu in)
300TD (123.190) engine 617.912	2998 cc (182.9 cu in)
300D turbo (US) (123.133), 300CD turbo (US) (123.153),	
300TD turbo (US) (123.193) engine 617.952........	2998 cc (182.9 cu in)
Compression ratio	
Turbo	21.5:1
Non-turbo	21:1

Valves and related components

Valve clearance

Cold	
Intake	0.10 mm (0.0039 in)*
Exhaust	
Non-turbo	0.30 mm (0.0118 in)
Turbo	0.35 mm (0.0138 in)

Valve clearance (continued)
Warm
  Intake .... 0.15 mm (0.0059 in)*
  Exhaust
    Non-turbo .... 0.35 mm (0.0138 in)
    Turbo .... 0.40 mm (0.0158 in)
*At ambient temperatures below -4 degrees F (-20 degrees C), add 0.05 mm (0.0019 in)

Valve face angle.. 30°
Valve seat angle.. 30°
Valve seat runout .... 0.03 mm (0.0012 in)
Valve head-to-cylinder head gasket — surface clearance (minimum)
  Turbo with new valves and seats
    Intake .... +0.17 to −0.23 mm (+0.0067 to −0.009 in)
    Exhaust .... +0.12 to −0.28 mm (+0.0047 to −0.011 in)
  Turbo with new valves and refaced seats (all) .... −1.0 mm (−0.0394 in)
  Non-turbo with new valves and seats
    Intake .... +0.03 to −0.43 mm (+0.0012 to −0.0169 in)
    Exhaust .... −0.38 to −0.78 mm (−0.0149 to −0.0307 in)
  Non-turbo with new valves and refaced seats (all) .... −1.5 mm (−0.0591 in)

Valve head seat thickness (margin)
Intake
  Non-turbo .... 2.34 mm (0.0922 in)
  Service limit .... 1.5 mm (0.0591 in)
  Turbo .... 2.54 mm (0.10 in)
  Service limit .... 2.0 mm (0.0788 in)
Exhaust
  Non-turbo .... 2.01 mm (0.0792 in)
  Service limit .... 1.5 mm (0.0591 in)
  Turbo .... 2.49 mm (0.0981 in)
  Service limit .... 2.0 mm (0.0788 in)

Valve stem diameter
All .... 9.92 to 9.94 mm (0.3908 to 0.3916 in)
Valve stem-to-guide clearance limit .... 0.105 mm (0.0041 in)

Valve length
Intake
  Non-turbo .... 131.3 to 131.7 mm (5.173 to 5.189 in)
  Turbo .... 131.5 mm (5.181 in)
Exhaust
  Non-turbo .... 130.8 to 131.2 mm (5.154 to 5.169 in)
  Turbo .... 131.5 mm (5.181 in)

Valve head diameter
Intake
  Four-cylinder .... 38.7 to 38.9 mm (1.525 to 1.533 in)
  Five-cylinder .... 39.7 to 39.9 mm (1.564 to 1.572 in)
Exhaust
  Four-cylinder .... 33.1 to 33.3 mm (1.304 to 1.312 in)
  Five-cylinder .... 34.1 to 34.3 mm (1.344 to 1.351 in)

Valve springs
Wire gauge
  Color-coded green-green or violet-green .... 3.8 mm (0.1497 in)
  Color-coded yellow-yellow or violet-yellow .... 3.9 mm (0.1537 in)
Free length
  Color-coded green-green or violet-green .... 50.5 mm (1.9897 in)
  Color-coded yellow-yellow or violet-yellow .... 51.2 mm (2.0173 in)
Preloaded length
  Color-coded green-green or violet-green .... 29.9 mm (1.1781 in)
  Color-coded yellow-yellow or violet-yellow .... 28.0 mm (1.1032 in)
Outside diameter
  Color-coded green-green or violet-green .... 30.2 mm (1.1899 in)
  Color-coded yellow-yellow or violet-yellow .... 30.4 mm (1.1978 in)

Rocker arm and shaft
Rocker arm bore.................................. 14.00 to 14.02 mm (0.5516 to 0.5524 in)
Bushing outside diameter .... 14.03 to 14.05 mm (0.5528 to 0.5536 in)
Inside diameter of bushing and rocker arm bore .... 12.0 to 12.02 mm (0.4728 to 0.4736 in)
Shaft diameter .... 11.96 to 11.98 mm (0.4712 to 0.4720 in)
Rocker arm radial play on shaft..................... 0.02 to 0.06 mm (0.0008 to 0.0024 in)
Rocker arm bracket bore........................... 11.98 to 12.0 mm (0.4720 to 0.4728 in)
Width of rocker arm bracket .... 24.07 to 24.20 mm (0.9484 to 0.9535 in)

Crankshaft and connecting rods
Crankshaft end play .... 0.1 to 0.25 mm (0.0039 to 0.0099 in)
Service limit................................... 0.03 mm (0.0012 in)

Connecting rod end play (side clearance)	0.12 to 0.26 mm (0.0047 to 0.0102 in)
Service limit	0.50 mm (0.019 in)

Main bearing journal diameter

Standard	69.96 to 69.95 mm (2.7564 to 2.7560 in)
First repair stage	69.70 to 69.71 (2.7462 to 2.7466 in))
Second repair stage	69.45 to 69.46 mm (2.7363 to 2.7367 in)
Third repair stage	69.20 to 69.21 mm (2.7265 to 2.7269 in)
Fourth repair stage	68.95 to 68.96 mm (2.7166 to 2.7170 in)

Thrust bearing journal width

Standard

0.0847 in (2.15 mm) thrust washer	34.00 to 34.03 mm (1.379 to 1.3408 in)
0.0867 in (2.20 mm) thrust washer	34.10 to 34.13 mm (1.3435 to 1.3447 in)

Repair stages 1 thru 4

0.0886 in (2.25 mm) thrust washer	34.20 to 34.23 mm (1.3475 to 1.3487 in)
0.0926 in (2.35 mm) thrust washer	34.40 to 34.43 mm (1.3554 to 1.3565 in)
0.0946 in (2.40 mm) thrust washer	34.50 to 34.53 mm (1.3593 to 1.3605 in)
Main bearing oil clearance	0.031 to 0.073 mm (0.0012 to 0.0029 in)

Connecting rod bearing journal diameter

Standard	51.95 to 51.96 mm (2.0468 to 2.0472 in)
First repair stage	51.70 to 51.71 mm (2.0369 to 2.0374 in)
Second repair stage	51.45 to 51.46 mm (2.0271 to 2.0275 in)
Third repair stage	51.20 to 51.21 mm (2.0173 to 2.0177 in)
Fourth repair stage	50.95 to 50.96 mm (2.0074 to 2.0078 in)
Connecting rod bearing bore diameter	55.60 to 55.62 mm (2.1906 to 2.1914 in)
Connecting rod bearing oil clearance	0.031 to 0.073 mm (0.0012 to to 0.0029 in)
Service limit	0.08 mm (0.0032 in)
Crankshaft journal taper/out-of-round limit	0.01 mm (0.0004 in)
Crankshaft runout limit	0.005 mm (0.0002 in)

Engine block

Engine bore diameter

Non-turbocharged

Engine number prefix 615

Number 1 cylinder

Group 0	87.009 to 87.018 mm (3.4282 to 3.4285 in)
Group 1	87.019 to 87.028 mm (3.4285 to 3.4289 in)
Group 2	87.029 to 87.038 mm (3.4289 to 3.4293 in)

Number 2 through 4 cylinders

Group 0	86.998 to 87.008 mm (3.4276 to 3.4281 in)
Group 1	87.009 to 87.018 mm (3.4282 to 3.4285 in)
Number 5 cylinder	87.019 to 87.028 mm (3.4285 to 3.4289 in)

Engine number prefix 616 and 617 (except turbo)

Number 1 cylinder

Group 0

1st version	91.009 to 91.018 mm (3.5858 to 3.5861 in)
2nd version	90.909 to 90.918 mm (3.5818 to 3.5822 in)

Group 1

1st version	91.019 to 91.028 mm (3.5861 to 3.5865 in)
2nd version	90.919 to 90.928 mm (3.5822 to 3.5826 in)

Group 2

1st version	91.029 to 91.038 mm (3.5865 to 3.5869 in)
2nd version	90.929 to 90.938 mm (3.5826 to 3.5829 in)

Number 2 through 4 cylinder

Group 0

1st version	90.998 to 91.008 mm (3.5853 to 3.5857 in)
2nd version	90.898 to 90.908 mm (3.5814 to 3.5818 in)

Group 1

1st version	91.00 to 91.018 mm (3.5854 to 3.5861 in)
2nd version	90.909 to 90.918 mm (3.5818 to 3.5822 in)

Number 5 cylinder

1st version	91.019 to 91.028 mm (3.5861 to 3.5865 in)
2nd version	90.919 to 90.928 mm (3.5819 ro 3.5826 in)

Turbocharged engines

Number 1 through 5 cylinders

Group 0	90.898 to 90.908 mm (3.5814 to 3.5818 in)
Group 1	90.908 to 90.918 mm (3.5818 to 3.5822 in)
Group 2	90.918 to 90.928 mm (3.5822 to 3.5826 in)
Out-of-round and taper	0.014 mm (0.0006 in)
Service limit	0.05 mm (0.0019 in)
Honing angle	25°

Pistons and rings

Piston diameter
Non-turbocharged engine
  Engine number prefix 615
    Number 1 cylinder
      Group 0 ....   86.98 mm (3.427 in)
      Group 1 ....   86.99 mm (3.4274 in)
      Group 2 ....   87.00 mm (3.4278 in)
    Number 2 through number 4 or 5 cylinders
      Group 0 ....   86.98 mm (3.427 in)
      Group 1 ....   86.99 mm 3.4274 in)
      Group 2 ....   87.00 mm (3.4278 in)
  Engine number prefix 616 and 617
    Number 1 cylinder
      Group 0
        1st version ....   90.98 mm (3.5846 in)
        2nd version ....   90.88 mm (3.5807 in)
      Group 1
        1st version ....   90.99 mm (3.585 in)
        2nd version ....   90.89 mm (3.5811 in)
      Group 2
        1st version ....   91.00 mm (3.5854 in)
        2nd version ....   90.90 mm (3.5815 in)
    Number 2 through number 4 cylinder
      Group 1
        1st version ....   90.00 mm (3.546 in)
        2nd version ....   90.89 mm (3.5811 in)
      Number 5 cylinder
        1st version ....   91.00 mm (3.5854 in)
        2nd version ....   90.90 mm (3.5815 in)
Turbocharged engines
  Number 1 through number 5 cylinder
    Group 0 ....   90.845 to 90.855 mm (3.5793 to 3.5797 in)
    Group 1 ....   90.855 to 90.865 mm (3.5787 to 3.5801 in)
    Group 2 ....   90.865 to 90.875 mm (3.5801 to 3.5805 in)

Piston-to-bore clearance
Non-turbocharged engines
  Number 1 cylinder ....   0.029 to 0.048 mm (0.0011 to 0.0019 in)
  All others ....   0.018 to 0.038 mm (0.0007 to 0.0015 in)
Turbocharged engine
  All ....   0.043 to 0.063 mm (0.0017 to 0.0025 in)
Service limit (all) ....   0.12 mm (0.005 in)

Piston ring-to-groove clearance
Non-turbocharged engine
  Top ....   0.1 to 0.132 mm (0.0039 to 0.0052 in)
  Service limit ....   0.2 mm (0.0079 in)
  Second ....   0.07 to 0.102 mm (0.0028 to 0.004 in)
  Service limit ....   0.15 mm (0.0059 in)
  Third ....   0.03 to 0.062 mm (0.0012 to 0.0024 in)
  Service limit ....   0.1 mm (0.0039 in)
Turbocharged engine
  Top ....   0.11 to 0.142 mm (0.0043 to 0.0056 in)
  Service limit ....   0.2 mm (0.0079 in)
  Second ....   0.07 to 0.112 mm (0.0028 to 0.0044 in)
  Service limit ....   0.15 mm (0.0059 in)
  Oil ....   0.03 to 0.062 mm (0.0012 to 0.0024 in)
  Service limit ....   0.1 mm (0.0039 in)

Piston ring end gap (all)
  Top ....   0.20 to 0.40 mm
  Service limit. ....   1.5 mm (0.0591 in)
  Second ....   0.20 to 0.40 mm
  Service limit ....   1.0 mm (0.0394 in)
  Oil ....   0.25 to 0.40 mm
  Service limit ....   1.0 mm (0.0394 in)

Piston pin diameter
  Non-turbocharged engine ....   25.995 to 26.000 mm (1.0242 to 1.0244 in)
  Turbocharged engine ....   27.995 to 28.000 mm (1.103 to 1.1032 in)
Pin-to-piston clearance
  In piston (all) ....   0.00 to 0.1 mm (0.00 to 0.0039 in)
Pin-to-rod clearance
  Non-turbocharged engine ....   0.012 to 0.023 mm (0.0005 to 0.0009 in)
  Turbocharged engine ....   0.018 to 0.029 mm (0.0007 to 0.0011 in)

Camshaft

Runout
  Non-turbocharged engine
    Camshaft code 00

Sprocket seat	0.02 mm (0.0008 in)
2nd bearing	0.03 mm (0.0012 in)
3rd bearing	0.025 mm (0.0009 in)

    Camshaft code 02

Sprocket seat	0.12 mm (0.0047 in)
2nd bearing	0.12 mm (0.0047 in)

    Camshaft code 06.10

Sprocket seat	0.025 mm (0.0009 in)
2nd bearing	0.025 mm (0.0009 in)

    Camshaft 08

Sprocket seat	0.02 mm (0.0008 in)
2nd bearing	0.03 mm (0.0012 in)
3rd bearing	0.025 mm (0.0009 in)

  Turbocharged engine
    Camshaft code 00

Sprocket seat	0.02 mm (0.0008 in)
2nd bearing	0.03 mm (0.0012 in)
3rd bearing	0.025 mm (0.0009 in)

    Camshaft code 05, 08

Sprocket seat	0.025 mm (0.0009 in)
2nd bearing	0.03 mm (0.0012 in)
3rd bearing	0.03 mm (0.0012 in)

Endplay	0.07 to 0.015 mm (0.0028 to 0.0006 in)

Bearing journal diameter
All except code 10
  Standard

Front journal	34.93 to 34.95 mm (1.3762 to 1.377 in)
Others	46.43 to 46.45 mm (1.8293 to 1.8301 in)

Code 10
  Standard

Front journal	34.93 to 34.95 mm (1.3762 to 1.377 in)
Others	48.93 to 48.95 mm (1.9278 to 1.9286 in)

Bearing oil clearance	0.05 to 0.084 mm (0.0019 to 0.0033 in)

Torque specifications	**Nm**	**Ft-lbs**
Camshaft sprocket bolt	80	59
Camshaft cover		
Nut	15	11
Bolt	5	3.7
Camshaft bearing mount nuts	25	18
Crankshaft main bearing bolts	90	66
Rocker arm bracket-to-cylinder head bolts	38	28
Timing chain tensioner closing plug	90	66
Fuel injection timing wheel bolt	40	30
Connecting rod nuts		
Initial torque	40 to 50	30 to 37
Final step	Rotate bolt head an additional 90 to 100°	
Cylinder head bolts and camshaft bearing mount bolts		
Hexagon socket bolt*		
1st step	70	52
2nd step	90	66
10 minute settling time		
3rd step	100	74
Twelve-point socket bolt		
1st step	40	30
2nd step	70	52
10 minute settling time		
3rd step	Rotate bolt head an additional 90°	
4th step	Rotate bolt head an additional 90°	

* Hexagon socket-type head bolts must be retightened after 300 to 600 miles (500 to 1000 km) (except US models from 1977 on)

	Nm	**Ft-lbs**
Crankshaft balancer bolt	270 to 330	199 to 244
Upper oil pan-to-crankcase		
6 mm bolts	9 to 11	7 to 8
8 mm bolts	20 to 25	15 to 18
Lower oil pan-to-upper pan bolt	10	7
Engine carrier-to-engine mount	70	52
Flywheel-to-crankshaft bolt		
Initial torque	30 to 40	22 to 30
Final step	Rotate bolt head an additional 90 to 100°	
Oil pump-to-crankcase bolt	20 to 25	15 to 18
Oil pump-to-flange bolt	9 to 11	7 to 8
Oil pump sprocket bolt	30 to 35	22 to 26

2B

1　General information

Included in this portion of Chapter 2 are the general overhaul procedures for the cylinder head and internal engine components. The information ranges from advice concerning preparation for an overhaul and the purchase of replacement parts to detailed, step-by-step procedures covering removal and installation of internal engine components and the inspection of parts.

The following Sections have been written based on the assumption that the engine has been removed from the vehicle. For information concerning in-vehicle engine repair, as well as removal and installation of the external components necessary for the overhaul, see Part A of this Chapter and Section 2 of this Part.

The specifications included here in Part B are only those necessary for the inspection and overhaul procedures which follow. Refer to Part A for additional specifications.

2　Repair operations possible with the engine in the vehicle

Many major repair operations can be accomplished without removing the engine from the vehicle.

It is a very good idea to clean the engine compartment and the exterior of the engine with some type of pressure washer before any work is begun. A clean engine will make the job easier and will prevent the possibility of getting dirt into internal areas of the engine.

Cover the fenders to prevent damage to the painted surfaces. In some cases, removal of the hood (Chapter 11) will provide additional working clearance and make the job easier.

If oil or coolant leaks develop, indicating a need for gasket or seal replacement, the repairs can generally be made with the engine in the vehicle. These models have a two-piece oil pan and the lower oil pan can be removed with the engine in place. The lower oil pan gasket, the cylinder head gasket, intake and exhaust manifold gaskets, vacuum pump gaskets and the front crankshaft oil seal are accessible with the engine in place.

Exterior engine components, such as the water pump, the starter motor, the alternator, the vacuum pump, the fuel pump and injectors, as well as the intake and exhaust manifolds, are quite easily removed for repair with the engine in place.

Since the cylinder head can be removed without pulling the engine, valve component servicing can also be accomplished with the engine in the vehicle.

Replacement of the timing chain and rails and fuel injection timing device are possible with the engine in place.

Detailed removal, inspection, repair and installation procedures for the above-mentioned components can be found in the appropriate Part of Chapter 2 or the other Chapters in this manual.

3　Engine overhaul — general information

It is not always easy to determine when, or if, an engine should be completely overhauled, as a number of factors must be considered.

High mileage is not necessarily an indication that an overhaul is needed, while low mileage, on the other hand, does not preclude the need for an overhaul. Frequency of servicing is probably the single most important consideration. An engine that has had regular (and frequent) oil and filter changes, as well as other required maintenance, will most likely give many thousands of miles of reliable service. Conversely, a neglected engine may require an overhaul very early in its life.

Excessive oil consumption is an indication that piston rings and/or valve guides are in need of attention (make sure that oil leaks are not responsible before deciding that the rings and guides are bad). Have a cylinder compression or leak-down test performed by an experienced mechanic to determine for certain the extent of the work required.

If the engine is making obvious knocking or rumbling noises (aside from the normal sounds of a diesel engine), the connecting rod and/or main bearings are probably at fault. If the oil pressure is extremely low, the bearings and/or oil pump are probably worn out.

Loss of power, rough running, excessive valve train noise and high fuel consumption rates may also point to the need for an overhaul (especially if they are all present at the same time). If checking and adjustment of the fuel injection system and timing do not remedy the situation, major mechanical work may be the only solution.

An engine overhaul generally involves restoring the internal parts to the specifications of a new engine. During an overhaul, the piston rings are replaced and the cylinder walls are reconditioned (rebored and/or honed). If a rebore is done, then new pistons are also required. The main and connecting rod bearings are replaced with new ones and, if necessary, the crankshaft may be reground to restore the journals. Generally, the valves are serviced as well, since they are usually in less-than-perfect condition at this point. While the engine is being overhauled, other components, such as the fuel injection system, starter and alternator can be rebuilt as well. The end result should be a like-new engine that will give as many trouble-free miles as the original.

Before beginning the engine overhaul, read through the entire procedure to familiarize yourself with the scope and requirements of the job. Overhauling an engine is not that difficult, but it is time consuming. Plan on the vehicle being tied up for a minimum of two weeks, especially if parts must be taken to an automotive machine shop for repair or reconditioning.

Check on availability of parts and make sure that any necessary special tools and equipment are obtained in advance. Most work can be done with typical shop hand tools, although a number of precision measuring tools are required for inspecting parts to determine if they must be replaced. Some of the checking and overhaul procedures, particularly those involving the cylinder head, should be left to your dealer or a properly equipped shop because of their specialized nature.

Often a reputable automotive machine shop will handle the inspection of parts and offer advice concerning reconditioning and replacement. **Note:** *Always wait until the engine has been completely disassembled and all components, especially the engine block, have been inspected before deciding what service and repair operations must be performed by an automotive machine shop. Since the block's condition will be the major factor to consider when determining whether to overhaul the original engine or buy a rebuilt one, never purchase parts or have machine work done on other components until the block has been thoroughly inspected and all possible options have been explored. As a general rule, time is the primary cost of an overhaul, so it does not pay to install worn or sub-standard parts.*

As a final note, to ensure maximum life and minimum trouble from a rebuilt engine, everything must be assembled with care in a spotlessly clean environment.

4　Engine rebuilding alternatives

The do-it-yourselfer is faced with a number of options when performing an engine overhaul. The decision to replace the engine block, piston/connecting rod assemblies and crankshaft depends on a number of factors, with the number one consideration being the condition of the block. Other considerations are cost, access to machine shop facilities, parts availability, time required to complete the project and experience.

Generally speaking the alternatives include:

Individual parts — If the inspection procedures reveal that the engine block and most engine components are in reusable condition, purchasing individual parts may be the most economical alternative. The block, crankshaft and piston/connecting rod assemblies should all be inspected carefully. Even if the block shows little wear, the cylinder bores should receive a finish hone; a job for an automotive machine shop.

New engine — A new engine purchased from the manufacturer and carrying a warranty is one option available when the engine is too badly worn or damaged.

Rebuilt engine — Ready to install rebuilt engines are available for most models. These are complete with oil pump, oil pan, cylinder head, camshaft cover, camshaft and valve train components, timing sprockets. All components are installed with new bearings, seals and gaskets incorporated throughout. The installation of manifolds and external parts may be all that is necessary. Some form of guarantee is usually included with the purchase.

Give careful thought to which alternative is best for you and discuss the situation with local automotive machine shops, auto parts dealers or dealership partsmen before ordering or purchasing replacement parts.

5 Engine removal — methods and precautions

If it has been decided that an engine must be removed for overhaul or major repair work, certain preliminary steps should be taken.

Locating a suitable work area is extremely important. A shop is, of course, the most desirable place to work. Adequate work space, along with storage space for the vehicle, is very important. If a shop or garage is not available, at the very least a flat, level, clean work surface made of concrete or asphalt is required.

Cleaning the engine compartment and engine prior to removal will help keep tools clean and organized.

An engine hoist or A-frame will also be necessary. Make sure that the equipment is rated in excess of the combined weight of the engine and its accessories. Safety is of primary importance, considering the potential hazards involved in lifting the engine out of the vehicle.

If the engine is being removed by a novice, a helper should be available. Advice and aid from someone more experienced would also be helpful. There are many instances when one person cannot simultaneously perform all of the operations required when lifting the engine out of the vehicle.

Plan the operation ahead of time. Arrange for or obtain all of the tools and equipment you will need prior to beginning the job. Some of the equipment necessary to perform engine removal and installation safely and with relative ease are (in addition to an engine hoist) a heavy duty floor jack, complete sets of wrenches and sockets as described in the front of this manual, wooden blocks and plenty of rags and cleaning solvent for mopping up the inevitable spills. If the hoist is to be rented, make sure that you arrange for it in advance and perform beforehand all of the operations possible without it. This will save you money and time.

Plan for the vehicle to be out of use for a considerable amount of time. A machine shop will be required to perform some of the work which the do-it-yourselfer cannot accomplish due to a lack of special

2B

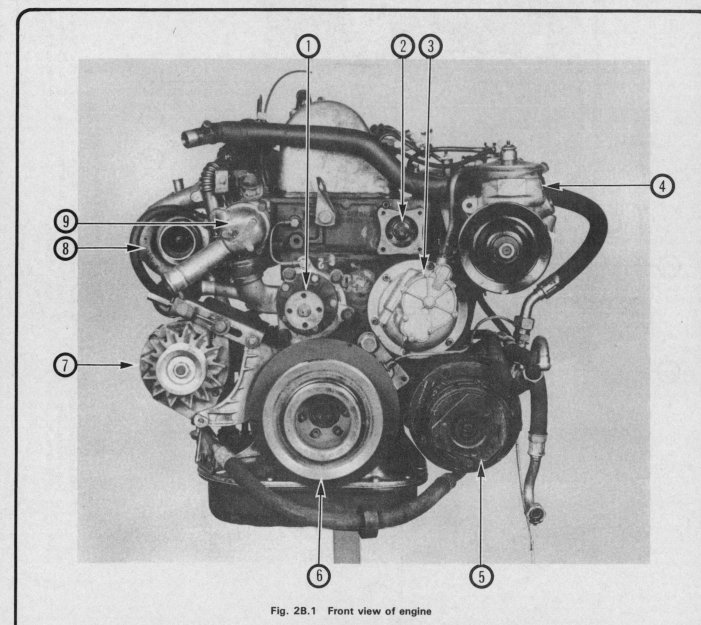

Fig. 2B.1 Front view of engine

1 Water pump	4 Power steering pump	7 Alternator
2 Level control pump drive	5 Air conditioning compressor	8 Turbocharger
3 Vacuum pump	6 Front balancer assembly	9 Thermostat housing

Fig. 2B.2 View of left side of engine

1 Power steering pump
2 Fuel filter housing
3 Oil filter housing
4 Fuel injection pump
5 Engine mount shock absorber
6 Upper oil pan
7 Lower oil pan
8 Air conditioning compressor
9 Vacuum pump

2B

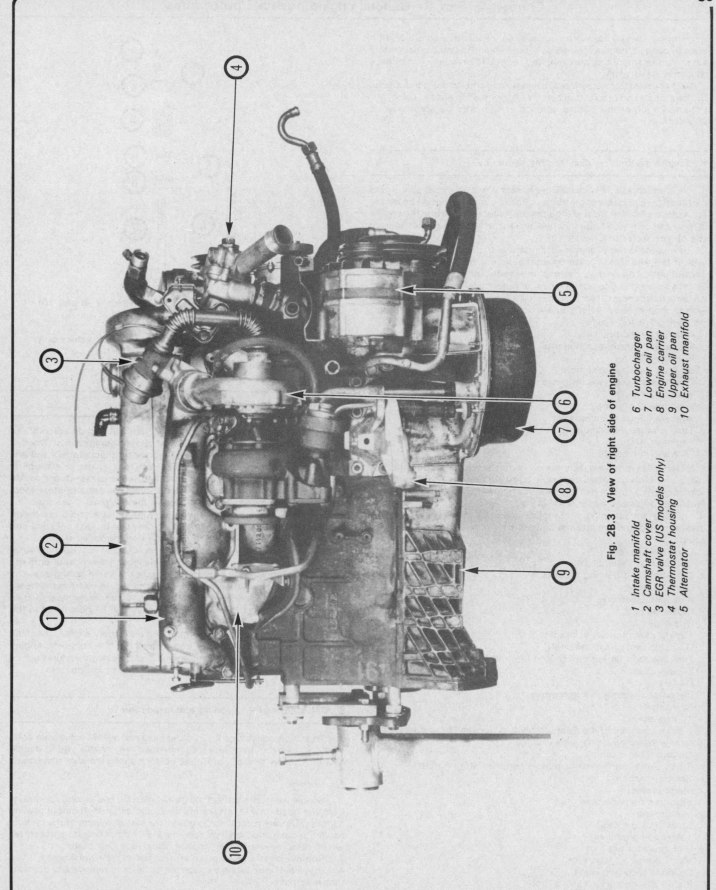

Fig. 2B.3 View of right side of engine

1 Intake manifold
2 Camshaft cover
3 EGR valve (US models only)
4 Thermostat housing
5 Alternator

6 Turbocharger
7 Lower oil pan
8 Engine carrier
9 Upper oil pan
10 Exhaust manifold

equipment. These shops often have a busy schedule, so it would be wise to consult them before removing the engine in order to accurately estimate the amount of time required to rebuild or repair components that may need work.

Always use extreme caution when removing and installing the engine. Serious injury can result from careless actions. Plan ahead. Take your time and a job of this nature, although major, can be accomplished successfully.

6　Engine overhaul — disassembly sequence

1　It is much easier to disassemble and work on the engine if it is mounted on a portable engine stand. These stands can often be rented for a reasonable fee from an equipment rental yard. Before the engine is mounted on a stand, the flywheel/driveplate should be removed from the engine (refer to Chapter 8).

2　If a stand is not available, it is possible to disassemble the engine with it blocked up on a sturdy workbench or on the floor. Be extra careful not to tip or drop the engine when working without a stand.

3　If you are going to obtain a new or rebuilt engine, all external components must come off first in order to be transferred to the replacement engine (just as they will if you are doing a complete engine overhaul yourself). These include:

Alternator and brackets
Emissions control components
Vacuum pump
Oil filter canister assembly
Thermostat and housing cover
Water pump
Fuel injection pump
Intake/exhaust manifolds
Turbocharger (if equipped)
Engine mounts
Flywheel/driveplate

Note: *When removing the external components from the engine, pay close attention to details that may be helpful or important during installation. Note the installed position of gaskets, seals, spacers, pins, washers, bolts and other small items.*

4　If you are planning a complete overhaul, the engine must be disassembled and the internal components removed in the following order:

Camshaft cover
Rocker arm assemblies
Camshaft and bearing mounts
Cylinder head
Balancer assembly
Lower oil pan
Upper oil pan
Timing chain tensioner assembly
Oil pump and chain assembly
Fuel injection timing device and intermediate shaft assembly
Timing chain rails
Oil jets
Piston/connecting rod assemblies
Crankshaft
Timing chain

6　Before beginning the disassembly and overhaul procedures, make sure the following items are available:

Common hand tools
Small cardboard boxes or plastic bags for storing parts
Gasket scraper
Ridge reamer
Vibration damper puller
Micrometers
Small hole gauges
Telescoping gauges
Dial indicator set
Valve spring compressor
Cylinder surfacing hone
Piston ring groove cleaning tool
Electric drill motor
Tap and die set
Wire brushes
Cleaning solvent

Fig. 2B.4　Valve component layout (Secs 7, 8 and 10)

1	Adjusting nut	5	Valve seals
2	Locknut	6	Rotocap (exhaust valves only)
3	Valve spring cap	7	Exhaust valve
4	Valve spring	8	Intake valve

7　Cylinder head — disassembly

1　Cylinder head disassembly involves removal and disassembly of the intake and exhaust valves and their related components. The cylinder heads used on these engines incorporate prechambers and any procedures involving these should be left to a dealer or a properly equipped shop. If they are still in place, remove the camshaft and rocker arm assemblies from the cylinder head. Label the parts or store them separately so they can be reinstalled in their original locations.

2　Before the valves are removed, arrange to label and store them, along with their related components, so they can be kept separate and reinstalled in the same valve guides they are removed from.

3　Hold the valve locknut and remove the adjusting nut. Hold the valve spring cap with a wrench and then slowly loosen the locknut until the valve spring pressure is released. Remove the valve spring cap, the spring, stem seal, rotocap (if equipped) and the valve from the head.

4　Repeat the procedure for the remaining valves. Remember to keep together all the parts for each valve so they can be reinstalled in the same locations.

5　Once the valves have been removed and safely stored, the head should be thoroughly cleaned and inspected. If a complete engine overhaul is being done, finish the engine disassembly procedures before beginning the cylinder head cleaning and inspection process.

8　Cylinder head — cleaning and inspection

1　Thorough cleaning of the cylinder head and related valve train components, followed by a detailed inspection, will enable you to decide how much valve service work must be done during the engine overhaul.

Cleaning

2　Scrape away all traces of old gasket material and sealing compound from the head gasket, intake manifold and exhaust manifold sealing surfaces. Be very careful not to gouge the soft aluminum of the cylinder head. Special gasket removal solvents are available at auto parts stores which dissolve the gasket, making removal much easier.

3　Remove any built-up scale around the coolant passages.

4　Run a stiff wire brush through the oil holes to remove any deposits that may have formed in them.

5　It is a good idea to run an appropriate size tap into each of the threaded holes to remove any corrosion and thread sealant that may be present. If compressed air is available, use it to clear the holes of debris produced by this operation.

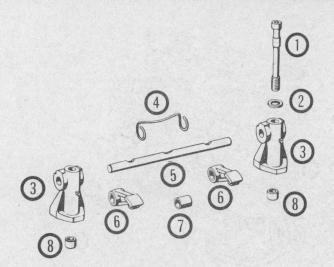

Fig. 2B.5   Rocker arm assembly component layout
(Secs 8 and 10)

1 *Bolt*
2 *Washer*
3 *Bearing brackets*
4 *Tensioning spring*
5 *Rocker arm shaft*
6 *Rocker arms*
7 *Bearing bushing*
8 *Bearing mount sleeves*

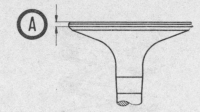

Fig. 2B.6   Valve seat thickness measurement dimension
(A) (Sec 9)

2B

6   Clean the exhaust and intake manifold stud threads in a similar manner with an appropriate size die. Clean the rocker arm bolt threads with a wire brush.

7   Clean the cylinder head with solvent and dry it thoroughly. Compressed air will speed the drying process and ensure that all holes and recessed areas are clean. **Note:** *Decarbonizing chemicals are available and may prove very useful when cleaning cylinder heads and valve train components. They are very caustic and should be used with caution. Be sure to follow the instructions on the container.*

8   Clean the rocker arm assemblies thoroughly. Compressed air will speed the drying process and can be used to clean out the oil passages.

9   Clean all the valve springs, nuts, spring caps and rotocaps with solvent and dry them thoroughly. Do the components from one valve at a time to avoid mixing up the parts.

10   Scrape off any heavy deposits that may have formed on the valves, then use a motorized wire brush to remove deposits from the valve heads and stems. Again, make sure the valves do not get mixed up.

Inspection

Cylinder head

11   Inspect the head very carefully for cracks, evidence of coolant leakage or other damage. If cracks are found, a new cylinder head should be obtained.

12   Using a straightedge and feeler gauge, check the head gasket mating surface for warpage. If the warpage exceeds 0.003-inch over the length of the head, it must be resurfaced at an automotive machine shop.

13   Examine the valve seats and the prechambers in each of the combustion chambers. If they are pitted, cracked or burned, the head will require service that is beyond the scope of the home mechanic.

14   Measure the inside diameters of the valve guides (at both ends and the center of each guide) with a small hole gauge and a 0-to-1-inch micrometer. Record the measurements for future reference. These clearances, when compared to the Specifications, will be one factor that will determine the extent of valve service work required. The guides are measured at the ends and at the center to determine if they are worn in a bell-mouth pattern (more wear at the ends). If they are, guide reconditioning or replacement is necessary. As an alternative, use a dial indicator to measure the lateral movement of each valve stem with the valve in the guide and approximately 1/16-inch off the seat.

Rocker arm components

15   Check the rocker arm faces (that contact the camshaft and valve adjustment nuts) for pits, wear and rough spots. Check the rocker shaft contact areas as well.

16   Inspect the rocker shaft sliding surfaces for scuffing and excessive wear.

17   Any damaged or excessively worn parts must be replaced with new ones.

Valves

Caution: *The exhaust valves are filled with sodium. The sodium could escape from a cracked valve and if mixed with water could explode as well as cause flammable hydrogen gas. Handle exhaust valves carefully.*

18   Carefully inspect each valve face for cracks, pits and burned spots. Check the valve stem and neck for cracks. Rotate the valve and check for any obvious indication that it is bent. Check the end of the stem for pits and excessive wear. The presence of any of these conditions indicates the need for valve service by a properly equipped professional.

19   Measure the thickness of the valve seat (on each valve) and compare it to Specifications. Any valve with a seat narrower than specified will have to be replaced with a new one.

20   Measure the valve stem diameter and compare this to Specifications.

Valve components

21   Check each valve spring for wear (on the ends) and pits. Measure the free length and compare it to the Specifications. Any springs that are shorter than specified have sagged and should not be reused.

22   Check the spring caps and nuts for obvious wear and cracks. Any questionable parts should be replaced with new ones, as extensive damage will occur in the event of failure during engine operation.

23   If the inspection process indicates that the valve components are in generally poor condition and worn beyond the limits specified, which is usually the case in an engine that is being overhauled, reassemble the valves in the cylinder head and refer to Section 9 for valve servicing recommendations.

24   If the inspection turns up no excessively worn parts, and if the valve faces and seats are in good condition, the valve train components can be reinstalled in the cylinder head without major servicing. Refer to the appropriate Section for cylinder head reassembly procedures.

9   Valves — servicing

1   Because of the complex nature of the job and the special tools and equipment needed, servicing of the valves, the valve seats, the valve guides, and valve seals (commonly known as a 'valve job') is best left to a professional.

2   The home mechanic can remove and disassemble the head, do the initial cleaning and inspection, then reassemble and deliver the head to a dealer service department or a reputable automotive machine shop for the actual valve servicing.

3   The dealer service department, or automotive machine shop, will remove the valves and springs, recondition or replace the valves and valve seats, recondition the valve guides, check and replace the valve springs, spring caps and nuts (as necessary), replace the valve seals with new ones, reassemble the valve components and make sure the installed valve-to-gasket surface distance is correct. The cylinder head gasket surface will also be resurfaced if it is warped.

4   After the valve job has been performed by a professional, the head will be in like-new condition. When the head is returned, be sure to clean it again, very thoroughly (before installation on the engine), to remove any metal particles and abrasive grit that may still be present from the valve service or head resurfacing operations. Use compressed air, if available, to blow out all the oil holes and passages.

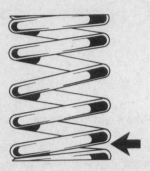

Fig. 2B.7   The valve spring must be installed with the dot
at the top and the tighter coils (arrow) against the
cylinder head (Sec 10)

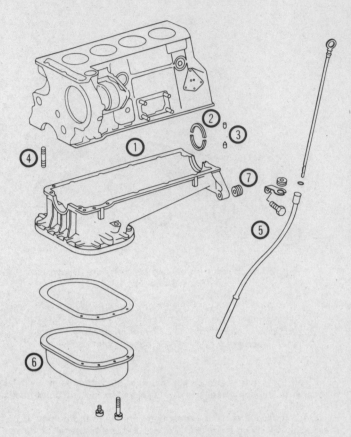

Fig. 2B.8   Oil pan assembly (Secs 11, 21 and 24)

1   Upper oil pan   5   Dipstick assembly
2   Rear oil seal   6   Lower oil pan
3   Pan-to-block aligning pins   7   Threaded insert
4   Studs

11.3   An Allen head wrench can be used on the hard to reach
pan bolts

10   Cylinder head — reassembly

1   Regardless of whether or not the head was sent to an automotive
repair shop for valve servicing, make sure it is clean before beginning
reassembly.
2   If the head was sent out for valve servicing, the valves and related
components will already be in place.
3   Lubricate the stems with clean engine oil and install the valves,
taking care not to damage the new valve stem oil seals. Make sure the
springs are installed with the tighter coils against the cylinder head.
Install the caps, rotocaps (exhaust valves) locknuts and adjusting nuts
loosely in place.
4   Compress the spring by holding the spring cap with a wrench and
tightening the locknut.
5   Lubricate the rocker arm and shaft assemblies with clean engine
oil. Install the assemblies and tighten the bolts to the specified torque
(Chapter 2, Part A).

11   Engine auxiliary components — removal

1   Several auxiliary components unique to these engines must removed before removal of the crankshaft, piston/connecting rods and

11.5   Use needle nose pliers to lift the oil pump chain tensioner
spring off

bearings can be carried out. These include:
   Upper oil pan
   Oil pump and chain assembly
   Vacuum pump
   Fuel injection timing device and intermediate shaft assembly
   Timing chain rails

11.6   The oil pump sprocket bolt (arrow)

11.7   Prying off the oil pump sprocket using two screwdrivers

2B

11.8   Oil pump retaining bolts (arrows)

11.9   Inspect the oil pump O-ring (arrow) for damage and cuts

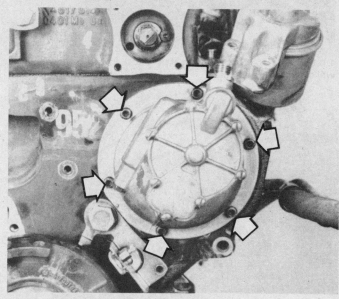

11.10   The vacuum pump retaining bolts (arrows)

Upper oil pan

2   After marking its position, remove the front balancer, using a puller tool.

3   Remove the nuts and Allen head screws retaining the upper oil pan to the cylinder block (photo).

4   Lift the upper oil pan from the engine.

Oil pump and chain assembly

5   Lift the spring off and swing the oil pump spring tensioner out of the way (photo).

6   Remove the oil pump sprocket bolt (photo).

7   Use two screwdrivers to pry the sprocket off the shaft. Unbolt and remove the front oil seal retainer to gain enough clearance around the oil pump chain. Use a soft faced hammer to dislodge the retainer, if necessary (photo).

8   Remove the retaining bolts and lift off the oil pump (photo).

9   Inspect the oil pump O-ring for cuts or damage and make sure it is soft and pliable, replacing it with a new one if necessary (photo).

Vacuum pump

10   Remove the retaining bolts and lift off the vacuum pump for access to the fuel injection timing device (photo).

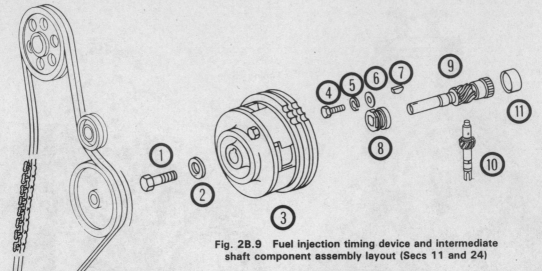

Fig. 2B.9 Fuel injection timing device and intermediate shaft component assembly layout (Secs 11 and 24)

1 Bolt
2 Washer
3 Fuel injection timing device
4 Bolt
5 Lock washer
6 Retaining washer
7 Woodruff key
8 Front bearing bushing
9 Intermediate shaft
10 Helical gear
11 Rear bearing bushing

11.11 Lock the fuel injection timing wheel with a screwdriver while removing the bolt

11.12 Use small screwdrivers to hold the timing chain out of the way so the timing device can be removed

11.13 Slide the spacer and washer out of the housing

11.14 Push the shaft out through the rear of the housing

Fuel injection timing device and intermediate shaft

11 Lock the timing device wheel so that it can't turn and remove the intermediate shaft nut (photo).

12 Removal of the injection timing device is complicated by the lack of clearance in the housing between the timing device teeth and the timing chain. Consequently several small screwdrivers can be used to hold the chain out of the way so the timing device wheel can be removed (photo). Grasp the timing wheel securely when lifting it off the shaft as it is rather heavy and dropping it can cause severe damage.

13 Slide the spacer (noting the direction in which it is installed) and washer off the shaft (photo).

14 Remove the intermediate shaft through the back of the housing (photo).

15 Remove the retaining bolt and slide the intermediate shaft bearing bushing out of the housing (photo).

Timing chain rails

16 Remove the timing chain tensioner and the chain retainer from the housing.

11.15 Remove the bolt (arrow) and intermediate shaft bushing

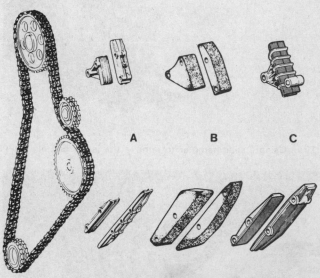

Fig. 2B.10 The three types of timing chain slide rails (Secs 11 and 24)

A Rubber backed   C Plastic
B Solid rubber

2B

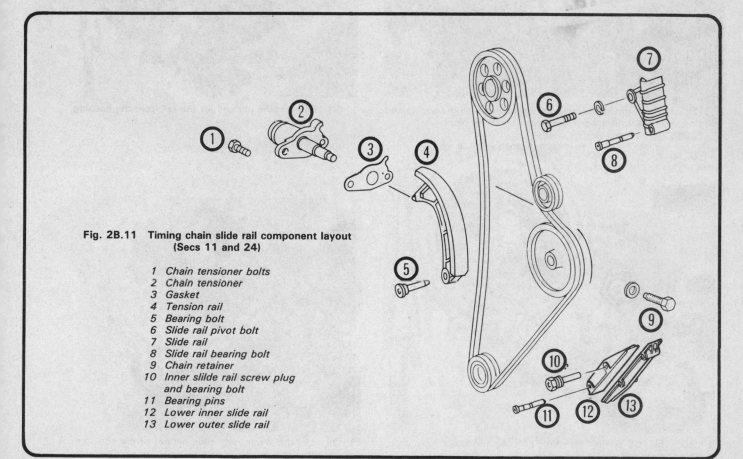

Fig. 2B.11 Timing chain slide rail component layout (Secs 11 and 24)

1 Chain tensioner bolts
2 Chain tensioner
3 Gasket
4 Tension rail
5 Bearing bolt
6 Slide rail pivot bolt
7 Slide rail
8 Slide rail bearing bolt
9 Chain retainer
10 Inner slilde rail screw plug and bearing bolt
11 Bearing pins
12 Lower inner slide rail
13 Lower outer slide rail

11.17a   Using a slide hammer to remove the lower bolt pin

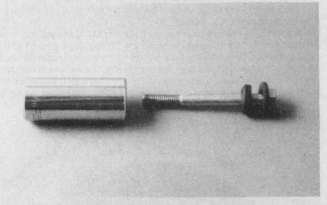

11.7b   A tool for drawing the slide rail bolt pins out of the block can be made from a socket or tubing, washers and a suitable bolt

11.7c   The bolt pin is removed by tightening with the socket and adding washers until the pin is drawn out of the block

11.18   Remove the pin and lift the rail from the housing

11.20   The TDC pointer assembly bolt (A) and lower inner slide rail closing plug (B)

11.21   Lift the lower inner slide rail out of the housing

Fig. 2B.12 Checking the connecting rod endplay with a dial indicator (Secs 12 and 23)

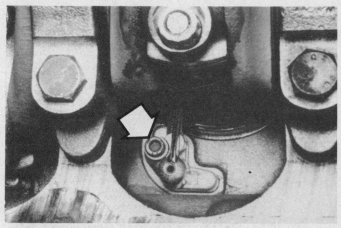

12.7a The oil jet bolt location (arrow)

12.7b Lift the oil jet out of the block and mark each oil jet – they are not interchangeable

12.8 The connecting rod bearing cap markings (arrows)

17 The timing chain rails can be removed after first removing the retaining bolts and bearing bolt pins. Bearing bolt pin removal can be accomplished with a slide hammer tool or by fabricating a tool using a bolt which threads into the pin and using washers and a socket or tube for a spacer to draw the pin out (photos).

Tension rail
18 Remove the upper rail pin and lift the rail from the housing (photo).

Upper slide rail
19 Remove the pivot bolt, draw out the rail pin and remove the rail.

Lower slide rails
20 Remove the TDC sensor and the closing plug (photo).
21 Remove the bolt pins and lift the inner and outer slide rails out (photo).

12 Piston/connecting rod assembly — removal

1 Prior to removal of the piston/connecting rod assemblies, the engine should be positioned upright. Inspect the top edges of the cylinder bores for a pronounced ridge. This can be easily seen or felt with the fingers. If only a slight ridge exists, fine emery cloth can be used to remove it.
2 If necessary, use a ridge reamer to completely remove the ridge at the top of each cylinder (follow the manufacturer's instructions provided with the ridge reaming tool). Failure to remove the ridge before attempting to remove the piston/connecting rod assemblies will result in piston breakage.
3 After all of the cylinder wear ridges have been removed, turn the engine upside-down.
4 Before the connecting rods are removed, check the end play as follows. Mount a dial indicator with its stem in line with the crankshaft and touching the side of the number one connecting rod cap.
5 Push the connecting rod backward, as far as possible, and zero the dial indicator. Next, push the connecting rod all the way to the

front and check the reading on the dial indicator. The distance that it moves is the end play. If the end play exceeds the service limit, a new connecting rod will be required. Repeat the procedure for the remaining connecting rods.
6 An alternative method is to slip feeler gauges between the connecting rod and the crankshaft throw until the play is removed.
7 Remove the oil jets from the cylinder block. It will be necessary to rotate the crankshaft to place each piston in turn at bottom dead center to allow removal of the jets. An Allen wrench socket will be necessary for removal because of lack of clearance (photos).
8 Check the connecting rods and connecting rod caps for identification marks. They should be plainly marked, with slashes across the cap and rod parting lines (photo). If they are not, identify each rod and cap, using a small punch to make the appropriate number of indentations to indicate the cylinders they are associated with.
9 Loosen each of the connecting rod cap nuts approximately 1/2 turn each. Remove the number one connecting rod cap and bearing insert. Do not drop the bearing insert out of the cap. Slip a short length of plastic or rubber hose over each connecting rod cap bolt to protect the crankshaft journal and cylinder wall when the piston is removed and push the connecting rod/piston assembly out through the top of the engine. Use a wooden tool to push on the upper bearing insert in the connecting rod. If resistance is felt, double-check to make sure that all of the ridge was removed from the cylinder.
10 Repeat the procedure for the remaining cylinders. After removal, reassemble the connecting rod caps and bearing inserts in their respective connecting rods and install the cap nuts finger tight. Leaving the old bearing inserts in place until reassembly will help prevent the connecting rod bearing surfaces from being accidentally nicked or gouged.

13 Crankshaft — removal

1 Before the crankshaft is removed, check the endplay as follows. Mount a dial indicator with the stem in line with the crankshaft and

Fig. 2B.13 Checking the crankshaft endplay with a dial indicator (Secs 13 and 22)

13.4   Main bearing cap number (arrow)

just touching one of the crank throws (see accompanying illustration).

2   Use a screwdriver to pry the crankshaft all the way to the rear and zero the dial indicator. Next, pry the crankshaft to the front as far as possible and check the reading on the dial indicator. The distance that it moves is the end play. If it is greater than specified, check the crankshaft thrust surfaces for wear. If no wear is apparent, new main bearings should correct the end play.

3   If a dial indicator is not available, feeler gauges can be used. Gently pry or push the crankshaft all the way to the front of the engine. Slip feeler gauges between the crankshaft and the front face of the thrust (center) main bearing to determine the clearance (which is equivalent to crankshaft end play).

4   Loosen each of the main bearing cap bolts 1/4-turn at a time, until they can be removed by hand. Check the main bearing caps to see if they are marked as to their locations. They are usually numbered consecutively (beginning with 1) from the front of the engine to the rear (photo). If they are not, mark them with number stamping dies or a centerpunch.

5   Gently tap the caps with a soft-faced hammer, then separate them from the engine block. If necessary, use the main bearing cap bolts as levers to remove the caps. Try not to drop the bearing insert if it comes out with the cap. The number 3 bearing is the thrust bearing which will either be flanged or have thrust washers installed on either side. Keep the thrust washer with the bearing cap.

6   Carefully lift the crankshaft, complete with the timing and oil pump chains, out of the engine. It is a good idea to have an assistant available, since the crankshaft is quite heavy. With the bearing inserts in place in the engine block and in the main bearing caps, return the caps to their respective locations on the engine block and tighten the bolts finger-tight. On models so equipped, remove the locking ring and pilot ball bearing assembly from the end of the crankshaft, using a slide hammer (available at tool rental stores).

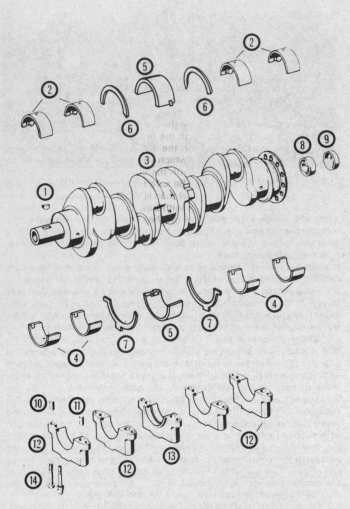

Fig. 2B.14 Crankshaft installation details (4-cylinder engine shown) (Secs 3, 17 and 21)

1   Woodruff key
2   Upper bearing shells
3   Crankshaft
4   Lower bearing shells
5   Thrust bearing shells
6   Upper thrust bearing halves
7   Lower thrust washer halves
8   Ball bearing
9   Locking ring
10 10 mm alignment pins
11 8 mm alignment pins
12 Bearing cap
13 Crankshaft thrust bearing cap
14 Bolts

14   Engine block — cleaning

1   Remove the soft plugs from the engine block. To do this, knock the plugs into the block (using a hammer and punch), then grasp them with large pliers and pull them back through the holes. There is one threaded plug on the side of the block which can be removed with a suitable Allen head socket and a long bar.

2   Using a gasket scraper, remove all traces of gasket material from the engine block. Be very careful not to nick or gouge the gasket sealing surfaces.

3   Remove the main bearing caps and separate the bearing inserts from the caps and the engine block. Tag the bearings according to which cylinder they removed from (and whether they were in the cap or the block) and set them aside.

4   The oil gallery plugs on these models consist of special steel balls which have been driven into place. Removal and installation of these balls should be left to your dealer or a shop with the special tools required.

5   If the engine is extremely dirty it should be taken to an automotive machine shop to be steam cleaned or hot tanked.

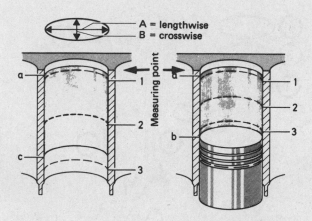

Fig. 2B.15 Cylinder bore measurement points (Sec 15)

A Top return point of the top piston ring
B Bottom dead center of the piston
C Bottom return point of the oil ring

6 After the block is returned, clean all oil holes and oil galleries one more time (brushes for cleaning oil holes and galleries are available at most auto parts stores). Flush the passages with warm water until the water runs clear, dry the block thoroughly and wipe all machined surfaces with a light, rust-preventative oil. If you have access to compressed air, use it to speed the drying process and to blow out all the oil holes and galleries.

7 If the block is not extremely dirty or sludged up, you can do an adequate cleaning job with warm soapy water and a stiff brush. Take plenty of time and do a thorough job. Regardless of the cleaning method used, be very sure to thoroughly clean all oil holes and galleries, dry the block completely and coat all machined surfaces with light oil.

8 The threaded holes in the block must be clean to ensure accurate torque readings during reassembly. Run the proper size tap into each of the holes to remove any rust, corrosion, thread sealant or sludge and to restore any damaged threads. If possible, use compressed air to clear the holes of debris produced by this operation. Now is a good time to thoroughly clean the threads on the head bolts and the main bearing cap bolts as well.

9 Reinstall the main bearing caps and tighten the bolts finger tight.

10 After coating the sealing surfaces of the new soft plugs with a good quality gasket sealer, install them in the engine block. Make sure they are driven in straight and seated properly or leakage could result. Special tools are available for this purpose, but equally good results can be obtained using a large socket (with an outside diameter that will just slip into the soft plug) and a hammer.

11 If the engine is not going to be reassembled right away, cover it with a large plastic bag to keep it clean.

---

15 Engine block — inspection

1 Thoroughly clean the engine block as described in Section 14 and double-check to make sure that the ridge at the top of each cylinder has been completely removed.

2 Visually check the block for cracks, rust and corrosion. Look for stripped threads in the threaded holes. It is also a good idea to have the block checked for hidden cracks by an automotive machine shop that has the special equipment to do this type of work. If defects are found, have the block repaired, if possible, or replaced.

3 Check the cylinder bores for scuffing and scoring.

4 Using the appropriate precision measuring tools, measure each cylinder's diameter at the top (just under the ridge), center and bottom of the cylinder bore, parallel to the crankshaft axis. Next, measure each cylinder's diameter at the same three locations across the crankshaft axis. Compare the results to the Specifications. If the cylinder walls are badly scuffed or scored, or if they are out-of-round or tapered beyond the limits given in the Specifications, have the engine block rebored and honed at an automotive machine shop. If a rebore is done,

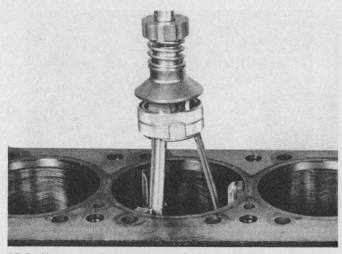

15.7 Honing a cylinder with a surfacing hone

oversize pistons and rings will be required.

5 If the cylinders are in reasonably good condition and not worn to the outside of the limits, and if the piston-to-cylinder clearances can be maintained properly, then they do not have to be rebored; honing is all that is necessary.

6 Before honing the cylinders, install the main bearing caps (without the bearings) and tighten the bolts to the specified torque.

7 To perform the honing operation you will need the proper size flexible hone (with fine stones), plenty of light oil or honing oil, some rags and an electric drill motor. Mount the hone in the drill motor, compress the stones and slip the hone into the first cylinder (photo). Lubricate the cylinder thoroughly, turn on the drill and move the hone up and down in the cylinder at a pace which will produce a fine cross-hatch pattern on the cylinder walls (with the cross-hatch lines intersecting at approximately a 60° angle). Be sure to use plenty of lubricant and do not take off any more material than is absolutely necessary to produce the desired finish. Do not withdraw the hone from the cylinder while it is running. Instead, shut off the drill and continue moving the hone up and down in the cylinder until it comes to a complete stop, then compress the stones and withdraw the hone. Wipe the oil out of the cylinder and repeat the procedure on the remaining cylinders. Remember, do not remove too much material from the cylinder wall. If you do not have the tools or do not desire to perform the honing operation, most automotive machine shops will do it for a reasonable fee.

8 After the honing job is complete, chamfer the top edges of the cylinder bores with a small file so the rings will not catch when the pistons are installed.

9 The entire engine block must be thoroughly washed again with warm, soapy water to remove all traces of the abrasive grit produced during the honing operation. Be sure to run a brush through all oil holes and galleries and flush them with running water. After rinsing, dry the block and apply a coat of light rust preventative oil to all machined surfaces. Wrap the block in a plastic bag to keep it clean and set it aside until reassembly.

---

16 Camshaft — Inspection

1 After the camshaft has been removed from the engine, cleaned with solvent and dried, inspect the bearing journals for uneven wear, pitting or evidence of seizure. If the journals are damaged, the bearing camshaft bearing towers are probably damaged as well. If the damage is severe, the camshaft, caps and the cylinder head will have to be replaced.

2 Inspect the camshaft lobes for obvious damage, heat discoloration, etc.

3 Measure the bearing journals with a micrometer to determine if they are excessively worn or out-of-round. If they are worn or out-of-round, the camshaft should be replaced with a new one. Measure the journals and the front oil seal surface and compare these measurements to Specifications to determine if wear is excessive.

Fig. 2B.16   Checking camshaft endplay with a dial indicator (Sec 16)

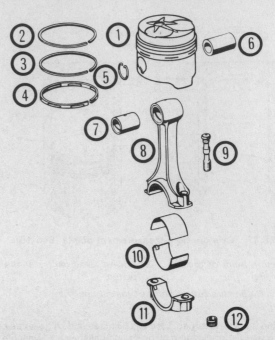

Fig. 2B.17   Piston and connecting rod component layout (Secs 17, 20 and 23)

1 Piston	7 Connecting rod bushing
2 Top piston ring (3 mm)	8 Connecting rod
3 Second piston ring (2 mm)	9 Connecting rod bolts
4 Chamfered oil with with	10 Connecting rod bearing
expanding spring	11 Connecting rod bearing cap
5 Piston pin locks	12 Connecting rod nuts
6 Piston pin	

17.4   Cleaning the piston ring grooves with a piston ring cleaning tool

4   With the camshaft mounted in V-blocks, check runout.
5   If the camshaft is installed in an assembled engine, the endplay can be checked with a dial indicator by pushing the camshaft fully rearward and then forward as shown in the accompanying illustration.
6   If the camshaft is worn, check with your dealer concerning reconditioning or replacement.

17   Piston/connecting rod assembly — inspection

1   Before the inspection process can be carried out, the piston/connecting rod assemblies must be cleaned and the original piston rings removed from the pistons. **Note:** *Always use new piston rings when the engine is reassembled.*
2   Using a piston ring installation tool, carefully remove the rings from the pistons. Do not nick or gouge the pistons in the process.
3   Scrape all traces of carbon from the top (or crown) of the piston. A hand-held wire brush or a piece of fine emery cloth can be used once the majority of the deposits have been scraped away. Do not, under any circumstances, use a wire brush mounted in a drill motor to remove deposits from the pistons. The piston material is soft and will be eroded away by the wire brush.
4   Use a piston ring groove cleaning tool to remove any carbon deposits from the ring grooves. If a tool is not available, a piece broken off the old ring will do the job. Be very careful to remove only the carbon deposits. Do not remove any metal and do not nick or scratch the sides of the ring grooves (photo).
5   Once the deposits have been removed, clean the piston/rod assemblies with solvent and dry them thoroughly. Make sure that all oil holes in the connecting rod and the piston are clear.
6   If the pistons are not damaged or worn excessively, and if the

engine block is not rebored, new pistons will not be necessary. Normal piston wear appears as even vertical wear on the piston thrust surfaces and slight looseness of the top ring in its groove. New piston rings, on the other hand, should always be used when an engine is rebuilt.
7   Carefully inspect each piston for cracks around the skirt, at the pin bosses and at the ring lands.
8   Look for scoring and scuffing on the thrust faces of the skirt, holes in the piston crown and burned areas at the edge of the crown. If the skirt is scored or scuffed, the engine may have been suffering from overheating and/or abnormal combustion, which caused excessively high operating temperatures. The cooling and lubrication systems should be checked thoroughly. A hole in the piston crown is an indication that abnormal combustion (preignition) was occurring. If any of the above problems exist, the causes must be corrected or the damage will occur again.
9   Corrosion of the piston (evidenced by pitting) indicates that coolant is leaking into the combustion chamber and/or the crankcase. Again, the cause must be corrected or the problem may persist in the rebuilt engine.
10   Measure the piston ring side clearance by laying a new piston ring in each ring groove and slipping a feeler gauge in between the ring and the edge of the ring groove (photo). Check the clearance at three or four locations around each groove. Be sure to use the correct ring for each groove; they are different. If the side clearance is greater than specified, new pistons and/or rings will have to be used.
11   Check the piston-to-bore clearance by measuring the bore (see Section 15) and the piston diameter. Make sure that the pistons and bores are correctly matched. Measure the piston across the skirt. Subtract the piston diameter from the bore diameter to obtain the clearance. If it is greater than specified, the block will have to be rebored and new pistons and rings installed. Check the piston-to-rod clearance by twisting the piston and rod in opposite directions. Any noticeable play indicates that there is excessive wear, which must be corrected. The piston/connecting rod assemblies should be taken to an automotive machine shop to have new piston pins installed and the pistons and connecting rods rebored.

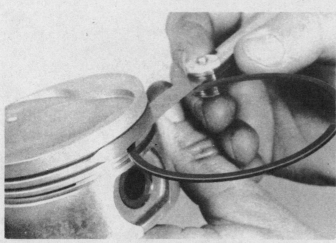

17.10 Checking the piston ring side clearance with a feeler gauge

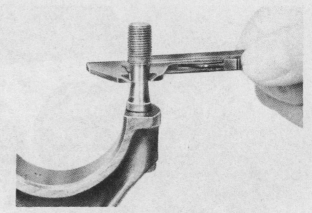

Fig. 2B.18 Measuring the connecting rod bolts for stretching (Sec 17)

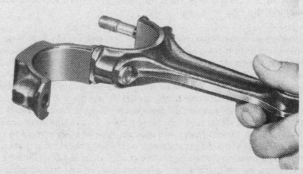

Fig. 2B.19 When slipped onto the connecting rod bolt as shown, the rod cap must not move downward under its own weight (Sec 17)

12 If the pistons must be removed from the connecting rods, such as when new pistons must be installed, or if the piston pins have too much play in them, they should be taken to an automotive machine shop. While they are there, have the connecting rods checked for bend and twist, as automotive machine shops have special equipment for this purpose. Unless new pistons or connecting rods must be installed, do not disassemble the pistons from the connecting rods.

13 Check the connecting rods for cracks and other damage. Temporarily remove the rod caps, lift out the old bearing inserts, wipe the rod and cap bearing surfaces clean and inspect them for nicks, gouges or scratches.

14 Measure the connecting rod clamp bolts at their thinnest point as shown in the accompanying illustration. If the measurement is less than 7.2 mm (0.2837 in), indicating the bolts have stretched, have them replaced.

15 Slip the bearing cap onto the clamp bolt as shown in the accompanying illustration and make sure the cap does not rotate downward. If it does, the connecting rod assembly must be replaced with a new one.

16 After checking the rods, replace the old bearings, slip the caps into place and tighten the nuts finger-tight.

18 Crankshaft — inspection

1   Clean the crankshaft with solvent and dry it thoroughly. Be sure to clean the oil holes with a stiff brush and flush them with solvent. Check the main and connecting rod bearing journals for uneven wear, scoring, pitting or cracks. Check the remainder of the crankshaft for cracks and damage.

2   Using an appropriate size micrometer, measure the diameter of the main and connecting rod journals and compare the results to the Specifications. By measuring the diameter at a number of points around the journal's circumference, you will be able to determine whether or not the journal is out of round. Take the measurement at each end of the journal, near the crank counterweights, to determine whether the journal is tapered.

3   If the crankshaft journals are damaged, tapered, out-of-round or worn beyond the limits given in the Specifications, have the crankshaft reground by a reputable automotive machine shop. Be sure to use the correct undersize bearing inserts if the crankshaft is reconditioned.

4   Refer to Section 19 and examine the main and rod bearing inserts. If the bearing inserts and journals are all in good condition, do not decide to reuse the bearings until the oil clearances have been checked.

19 Main and connecting rod bearings — inspection

1   Even though the main and connecting rod bearings should be replaced with new ones during the engine overhaul, the old bearings should be retained for close examination, as they may reveal valuable information about the condition of the engine.

2   Bearing failure occurs mainly because of lack of lubrication, the presence of dirt or other foreign particles, overloading the engine and corrosion. Regardless of the cause of bearing failure, it must be corrected before the engine is reassembled to prevent it from happening again.

3   When examining the bearings, remove them from the engine block, the main bearing caps, the connecting rods and the rod caps and lay them out on a clean surface in the same general position as their location in the engine. This will enable you to match any noted bearing problems with the corresponding crankshaft journal.

4   Dirt and other foreign particles get into the engine in a variety of ways. If may be left in the engine during assembly, or it may pass through filters or breathers. It may get into the oil, and from there into the bearings. Metal chips from machining operations and normal engine wear are often present. Abrasives are sometimes left in engine components after reconditioning, especially when parts are not thoroughly cleaned using the proper cleaning methods. Whatever the source, these foreign objects often end up embedded in the soft bearing material and are easily recognized. Large particles will not embed in the bearing and will score or gouge the bearing and shaft. The best prevention for this cause of bearing failure is to clean all parts thoroughly and keep everything spotlessly clean during engine assembly. Frequent and regular engine oil and filter changes are also recommended.

5   Lack of lubrication (or lubrication breakdown) has a number of interrelated causes. Excessive heat (which thins the oil), overloading (which squeezes the oil from the bearing face) and oil leakage or throwoff (from excessive bearing clearances, worn oil pump or high engine speeds) all contribute to lubrication breakdown. Blocked oil passages, which usually are the result of misaligned oil holes in a bearing shell, will also oil-starve a bearing and destroy it. When lack of lubrication is the cause of bearing failure, the bearing material is wiped or extruded from the steel backing of the bearing. Temperatures may increase to the point where the steel backing turns blue from overheating.

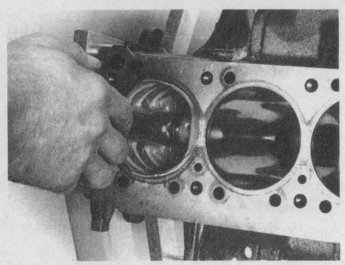

20.3a   Use the piston to square up the ring in the cylinder prior to checking the ring end gap

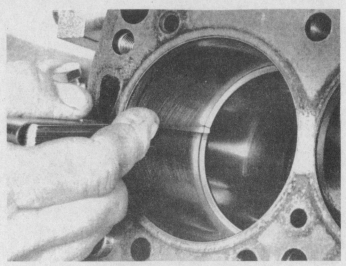

20.3b   Measure the ring end gap with a feeler gauge

6   Driving habits can have a definite effect on bearing life. Full-throttle, low-speed operation (or "lugging" the engine) puts very high loads on bearings, which tends to squeeze out the oil film. These loads cause the bearings to flex, which produces fine cracks in the bearing face (fatigue failure). Eventually the bearing material will loosen in pieces and tear away from the steel backing. Short-trip driving leads to corrosion of bearings because insufficient engine heat is produced to drive off the condensed water and corrosive gases. These products collect in the engine oil, forming acid and sludge. As the oil is carried to the engine bearings, the acid attacks and corrodes the bearing material.

7   Incorrect bearing installation during engine assembly will lead to bearing failure as well. Tight-fitting bearings leave insufficient bearing oil clearance and will result in oil starvation. Dirt or foreign particles trapped behind a bearing insert result in high spots on the bearing which lead to failure.

20   Piston rings — installation

1   Before installing the new piston rings, the ring end gaps must be checked. It is assumed that the piston ring side clearance has been checked and verified correct (Section 17).

2   Lay out the piston/connecting rod assemblies and the new ring sets so the ring sets will be matched with the same piston and cylinder during the end gap measurement and engine assembly.

3   Insert the top (number one) ring into the first cylinder and square it up with the cylinder walls by pushing it in with the top of the piston (photo). The ring should be near the bottom of the cylinder at the lower limit of ring travel. To measure the end gap, slip a feeler gauge between the ends of the ring (photo). Compare the measurement to the Specifications.

4   If the gap is larger or smaller than specified, double-check to make sure that you have the correct rings before proceeding.

5   If the gap is too small, it must be enlarged or the ring ends may come in contact with each other during engine operation, which can cause serious damage to the engine. The end gap can be increased by filing the ring ends very carefully with a fine file. Mount the file in a vise equipped with soft jaws, slip the ring over the file with the ends contacting the file face and slowly move the ring to remove material from the ends. When performing this operation, file only from the outside in.

6   Excess end gap is not critical unless it is greater than 0.040-inch (1 mm). Again, double-check to make sure you have the correct rings for your engine.

7   Repeat the procedure for each ring that will be installed in the first cylinder and for each ring in the remaining cylinders. Remember to keep rings, pistons and cylinders matched up.

8   Once the ring end gaps have been checked/corrected, the rings can be installed on the pistons.

9   The oil control ring (lowest one on the piston) is installed first. Use a piston ring installation tool to expand the ring and slip it into the groove.

10   After the oil ring has been installed, check to make sure that it can be turned smoothly in the ring groove.

11   The number two (middle) ring is installed next. **Note:** *Always follow the instructions printed on the ring package or box — different manufacturers may require different approaches. Do not mix up the top and middle rings, as they are of two different thicknesses.*

12   Use a piston ring installation tool and slip the ring into the middle groove on the piston. Do not expand the ring any more than is necessary to slide it over the piston.

13   Finally, install the number one (top) ring in the same manner. Be careful not to confuse the number one and number two rings because of their different thicknesses.

21   Rear oil seal — replacement

1   Pry the old seal out of the upper oil pan and (if not already removed) the cylinder block groove (photo).

2   Clean the seal grooves thoroughly, removing all foreign material.

3   Lay the seal in the seal groove in the upper oil pan and push it into place with your thumbs.

4   Seat it in the groove by rolling a large socket or piece of pipe along the entire length of the seal groove (photo).

5   Once you are satisfied that the seal is completely seated in the groove, cut off the excess on the ends with a single-edge razor blade or razor knife so the seal ends extend one millimeter (1 mm) above the pan surface (photo).

6   Repeat the entire procedure to install the other half of the seal in the cylinder block.

7   Apply a coat of engine oil to the contact surfaces of both seal halves.

22   Crankshaft — installation and main bearing oil clearance check

1   Crankshaft installation is generally one of the first steps in engine reassembly; it is assumed at this point that the engine block and crankshaft have been cleaned, inspected and repaired or reconditioned.

2   Position the engine with the bottom facing up.

3   Remove the main bearing cap bolts and lift out the caps. Lay them out in the proper order to help ensure that they are installed correctly.

4   If they are still in place, remove the old bearing inserts from the block and the main bearing caps. Wipe the main bearing surfaces of the block and caps with a clean, lint-free cloth (they must be kept spotlessly clean).

5   Clean the back sides of the new main bearing inserts and lay one

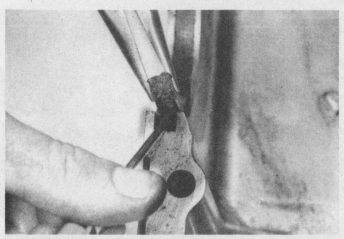

21.1 Use needle nose pliers and a screwdriver to remove the old oil seal

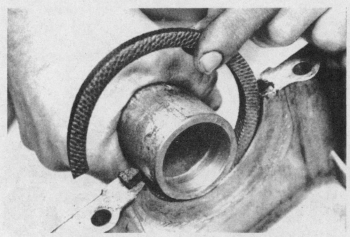

21.4 A large diameter piece of pipe can be used to press the new oil seal into the groove

21.5 Cut off the excess seal material with a razor blade

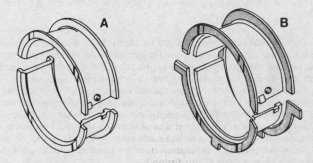

Fig. 2B.20 The two types of thrust bearings (Sec 22)

A *Flanged bearing*
B *Bearing with thrust washers*

bearing half in each main bearing saddle in the block. Lay the other bearing half from each bearing set in the corresponding main bearing cap. Make sure the tab on the bearing insert fits into the recess in the block or cap. Also, the oil holes in the block and cap must line up with the oil holes in the bearing insert. Do not hammer the bearing into place and do not nick or gouge the bearing faces. No lubrication should be used at this time.

6   The flanged thrust bearing or bearing with thrust washers must be installed in the number three (3) cap and saddle. There are also two thrust washers installed at both ends of the cylinder block (see illustrations).

7   Clean the faces of the bearings in the block and the crankshaft main bearing journals with a clean, lint-free cloth. Check or clean the oil holes in the crankshaft, as any dirt here can go only one way — straight through the new bearings.

8   Once you are certain that the crankshaft is clean, carefully lay it in position (an assistant would be very helpful here) in the main bearings.

9   Before the crankshaft can be permanently installed, the main bearing oil clearance must be checked (the oil and timing chains need not be installed for this procedure).

10   Trim several pieces of the appropriate size of Plastigage (so they are slightly shorter than the width of the main bearings) and place one piece on each crankshaft main bearing journal, parallel with the journal axis. Do not lay them across the oil holes.

11   Clean the faces of the bearings in the caps and install the caps in their respective positions (do not mix them up). Do not disturb the Plastigage.

12   Starting with the center main and working out toward the ends, tighten the main bearing cap bolts to the specified torque. Do not rotate the crankshaft at any time during this operation.

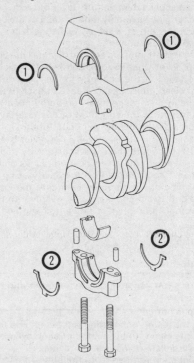

Fig. 2B.21 Crankshaft thrust washer locations (Sec 22)

1 *In crankcase*
2 *Adjacent to thrust bearing cap*

2B

22.18b   . . . rotate it a further 90°

22.18a   After tightening the connecting rod nut to the specified torque . . .

13 Remove the bolts and carefully lift off the main bearing caps. Keep them in order. Do not disturb the Plastigage or rotate the crankshaft. If any of the main bearing caps are difficult to remove, tap them gently from side-to-side with a soft-faced hammer to loosen them.

14 Compare the width of the crushed Plastigage on each journal to the scale printed on the Plastigage container to obtain the main bearing oil clearance. Check the Specifications to make sure it is correct.

15 If the clearance is not correct, double-check to make sure you have the right size bearing inserts. Also, make sure that no dirt or oil was between the bearing inserts and the main bearing caps or the block when the clearance was measured.

16 Carefully scrape all traces of the Plastigage material off the main bearing journals and/or the bearing faces. Do not nick or scratch the bearing faces — use a wood tool.

17 Carefully lift the crankshaft out of the engine. Clean the bearing faces in the block, then apply a thin, uniform layer of clean, high-quality moly-based grease or engine assembly lube to each of the bearing surfaces. Be sure to coat the thrust washers or flange faces as well as the journal face of the thrust bearing.

18 Make sure the crankshaft journals are clean, install the timing chain on the crankshaft sprocket, then lay the crankshaft back in place in the block. Clean the faces of the bearings in the caps, then apply a thin, uniform layer of clean, moly-based grease to each of the bearing faces. Install the caps in their respective numbered positions. Install the bolts and tighten them to the specified torque, starting with the center main and working out toward the ends (photos).

19 On manual transmission models, install a new pilot bearing in the end of the crankshaft. Lubricate the crankshaft cavity and the outer circumference of the bearing with clean bearing grease and place the ball bearing in position. Tap it evenly into the cavity using a suitable size drift or piece of pipe and a hammer. Lubricate the inside of the bearing with grease and tap the locking ring evenly into place.

20 Rotate the crankshaft a number of times by hand and check for any obvious binding.

21 The final step is to check the crankshaft endplay with a feeler gauge or a dial indicator as described in Section 13.

23 Piston/connecting rod assembly — installation and bearing oil clearance check

1   Before installing the piston/connecting rod assemblies the cylinder walls must be perfectly clean, the top edge of each cylinder must be chamfered, and the crankshaft must be in place.

2   Remove the connecting rod cap from the end of the number one connecting rod. Remove the old bearing inserts and wipe the bearing surfaces of the connecting rod and cap with a clean, lint-free cloth (they must be kept spotlessly clean).

3   Clean the back side of the new upper bearing half, then lay it in

Fig. 2B.22   Using a ring compressor tool and hammer handle to install the piston into the bore (Sec 22)

place in the connecting rod. Make sure that the tab on the bearing fits into the recess in the rod. Do not hammer the bearing insert into place and be very careful not to nick or gouge the bearing face. Do not lubricate the bearing at this time.

4   Clean the back side of the other bearing insert and install it in the rod cap. Again, make sure the tab on the bearing fits into the recess in the cap, and do not apply any lubricant. It is critically important that the mating surfaces of the bearing and connecting rod are perfectly clean and oil-free when they are assembled.

5   Position the piston ring gaps evenly an equal distance from one another, then slip a section of plastic or rubber hose over the connecting rod cap bolts.

6   Lubricate the piston and rings with clean engine oil and attach a piston ring compressor to the piston. Leave the skirt protruding about 1/4-inch to guide the piston into the cylinder. The rings must be compressed as far as possible.

7   Rotate the crankshaft until the number one connecting rod journal is as far from the number one cylinder as possible (bottom dead center), and apply a uniform coat of engine oil to the cylinder walls.

8   With the arrow on top of the piston facing to the front of the engine, gently place the piston/connecting rod assembly into the number one cylinder bore and rest the bottom edge of the ring compressor on the engine block. Tap the top edge of the ring compressor to make sure it is contacting the block around its entire circumference.

9   Clean the number one connecting rod journal on the crankshaft and the bearing faces in the rod.

10 Carefully tap on the top of the piston with the end of a wooden hammer handle while guiding the end of the connecting rod into place on the crankshaft journal. The piston rings may try to pop out of the ring compressor just before entering the cylinder bore, so keep some downward pressure on the ring compressor. Work slowly, and if any resistance is felt as the piston enters the cylinder, stop immediately. Find out what is hanging up and fix it before proceeding. Do not, for

23.12 Position the Plastigage strip on the bearing journal, parallel to the journal axis

23.13 The crushed Plastigage is compared to the scale printed on the container to obtain the bearing oil clearance

24.2a Pack heavy grease into the timing chain housing to hold the chain out of the way

24.2b With the grease adhering it to the side of the housing, hold the top of the chain to keep it from slipping down

any reason, force the piston into the cylinder, as you will break a ring and/or the piston.

11 Once the piston/connecting rod assembly is installed, the connecting rod bearing oil clearance must be checked before the rod cap is permanently bolted in place.

12 Cut a piece of the appropriate size Plastigage slightly shorter than the width of the connecting rod bearing and lay it in place on the number one connecting rod journal, parallel with the journal axis (it must not cross the oil hole in the journal) (photo).

13 Clean the connecting rod cap bearing face, remove the protective hoses from the connecting rod bolts and gently install the rod cap in place. Make sure the slash marks on the cap mate with those on the connecting rod. Install the nuts and tighten them to the specified torque, working up to it in three steps. Do not rotate the crankshaft at any time during this operation.

14 Remove the rod cap, being very careful not to disturb the Plastigage. Compare the width of the crushed Plastigage to the scale printed on the Plastigage container to obtain the oil clearance (photo). Compare it to the Specifications to make sure the clearance is correct. If the clearance is not correct, double-check to make sure that you have the correct size bearing inserts. Also, recheck the crankshaft connecting rod journal diameter and make sure that no dirt or oil was between the bearing inserts and the connecting rod or cap when the clearance was measured.

15 Carefully scrape all traces of the Plastigage material off the rod journal and/or bearing face (be very careful not to scratch the bearing — use your fingernail or a piece of hardwood). Make sure the bearing faces are perfectly clean, then apply a uniform layer of clean, high quality moly-based grease or engine assembly lube to both of them. You will have to push the piston into the cylinder to expose the face of the bearing insert in the connecting rod; be sure to slip the protective hoses

over the rod bolts first.

16 Slide the connecting rod back into place on the journal, remove the protective hoses from the rod cap bolts, install the rod cap and tighten the nuts to the specified torque. Again, work up to the torque in three steps.

17 Repeat the entire procedure for the remaining piston/connecting rod assemblies. Keep the back sides of the bearing inserts and the inside of the connecting rod and cap perfectly clean when assembling them. Make sure you have the correct piston for the cylinder and that the notch on the piston faces to the front of the engine when the piston is installed. Remember, use plenty of oil to lubricate the piston before installing the ring compressor. Also, when installing the rod caps for the final time, be sure to lubricate the bearing faces adequately.

18 After all the piston/connecting rod assemblies have been properly installed, rotate the crankshaft a number of times by hand and check for any obvious binding.

19 As a final step, the connecting rod end play must be checked. Refer to Section 12 for this procedure. Compare the measured end play to the Specifications to make sure it is correct.

20 Install the oil jets.

---

24 Engine auxiliary components — installation

Fuel injection timing device and intermediate shaft assembly

1 Install the intermediate shaft bushing and bolt. Lubricate the bushing with engine oil and insert the shaft from the rear of the housing.

2 Use heavy grease to hold the timing chain in place against the housing wall and hold it with your finger as well so the timing device wheel can be inserted (photos).

24.3 Carefully insert the timer wheel and then release the chain so it will engage the wheel teeth

24.7 The fuel injection timer wheel must be positioned with the recesses in the vertical position (arrows) prior to installing the vacuum pump

3   Slide the timing wheel carefully onto the shaft and then release the timing chain so that it meshes with the wheel gear teeth (photo).
4   Install the intermediate shaft bolt.

Timing chain rails
5   Pull the timing chain up through the cavity and fasten it with a piece of wire.
6   Install the rails, using new retaining pins (Section 11) and make sure that tension is maintained on the timing chain with the piece of wire.

Vacuum pump
7   Before installation, rotate the timing wheel so that the recesses on the cam face are situated vertically (photo).
8   Coat both sides of the new gasket with sealant, place the vacuum pump and gasket in position and install the bolts.

Oil pump
9   Place the oil pump in position and install the bolts. Tighten the bolts to the specified torque.
10 Install the chain, sprocket and bolt.
11 Swing the oil pump chain tensioner into position against the chain and secure it with the spring.

Upper oil pan
12 Form a 1/8 inch bead of RTV-type sealant on the cylinder block-to-pan contact surfaces.
13 Place the pan in position and install the bolts. Tighten the bolts to the specified torque.
14 Install the spacer on the crankshaft and install the front oil seal, tapping it evenly into place.

25 Initial start-up and break-in after overhaul

1   Once the engine has been properly installed in the vehicle, double check the engine oil and coolant levels. Using the hand pump on the side of the injection unit, prime the system until fuel begins flowing in the return line.
2   Crank the engine over until it starts running. It may take a few minutes to start, which is normal for a diesel engine. Make sure oil pressure registers on the gauge (if so equipped) or the oil light goes off.
3   As soon as the engine starts it should be set to idle at a fast idle (to ensure proper oil circulation) and allowed to warm up to normal operating temperature. While the engine is warming up, make a thorough check for oil and coolant leaks.
4   Shut the engine off and recheck the engine oil and coolant levels.
5   Drive the vehicle to an area with minimum traffic, accelerate at full throttle from 30 to 50 mph, then allow the vehicle to slow to 30 mph with the throttle closed. Repeat the procedure 10 or 12 times. This will load the piston rings and cause them to seat properly against the cylinder walls. Check again for oil and coolant leaks.
6   Drive the vehicle gently for the first 500 miles (no sustained high speeds) and keep a constant check on the oil level. It is not unusual for an engine to use oil during the break-in period.
7   At approximately 500 to 600 miles, change the oil and filter.
8   For the next few hundred miles, drive the vehicle normally. Do not either pamper it or abuse it.
9   After 2000 miles, change the oil and filter again and consider the engine fully broken in.

Chapter 3
Cooling, heating and air conditioning systems

Contents

Air conditioning compressor — removal and installation 14
Air conditioning system — servicing 13
Antifreeze — general information 2
Coolant level check . . . . See Chapter 1
Cooling system check . . . . See Chapter 1
Cooling system servicing . . . . See Chapter 1
Fan — removal and installation 6
Fan thermocouple — removal and installation 7
General information 1

Heater circulation pump — removal and installation 12
Heater control valve — removal and installation 11
Heater fan motor — removal and installation 10
Radiator — removal, servicing and installation 5
Thermostat — check 4
Thermostat — replacement 3
Water pump — check 8
Water pump — removal and installation 9

3

Specifications

Cooling system capacity (approximate)	12 US qts (11 liters)

Coolant type	55/45 mix of ethylene glycol antifreeze and water

Radiator cap opening pressure	103 kPa (15 psi)

Thermostat

Starts to open	175° to 193°F (80° to 90°C)
Fully open	193° to 200°F (90 to 94°C)

Torque specifications

	Nm	Ft-lbs
Fan-to-water pump hub	25	18
Fan thermocouple-to-fan bolt	25	18
Thermostat housing bolt	10	7
Water pump-to-block bolt	33	24

1 General information

The cooling system consists of a radiator, an engine-driven water pump and fan with thermostat controlled coolant flow. A fluid-type thermocouple allows the fan to free-wheel until air passing through the radiator is hot enough to activate it.

Later models are equipped with a coolant recovery system which consists of a plastic reservoir connected to the radiator by a tube. The reservoir retains coolant forced out of the radiator and through the tube by expansion. When the engine cools and the coolant contracts, it is drawn back into the radiator.

The heater utilizes the heat produced by the engine, which is absorbed by the coolant to warm the vehicle interior. The coolant, under pressure from the water pump and the auxiliary electrical heater circulation pump, passes through a heater core similar to a small radiator in the passenger compartment. Air directed through the core by the blower motor and duct system heats the vehicle interior. Coolant flow through the heater is controlled by the driver or passenger by way of the heater control valve.

Air conditioning is available as an option on these vehicles. The air conditioning system is located in the engine compartment and the compressor is turned by the crankshaft pulley-driven drivebelt.

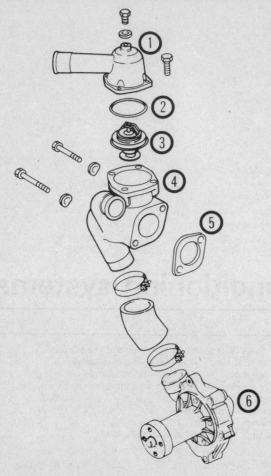

Fig. 3.1 Typical earlier model thermostat housing and water pump component layout (Sec 3, 4 and 9)

1 Thermostat housing cover   4 Thermostat housing
2 Rubber O-ring   5 Gasket
3 Thermostat   6 Water pump

2 Antifreeze — general information

Warning: *Do not allow antifreeze to come in contact with your skin or painted surfaces of the vehicle. Flush contacted areas immediately with plenty of water. Wipe up garage floor and drip pan coolant spills immediately. Keep antifreeze containers covered and repair leaks in your cooling system quickly.*

The cooling system should be filled with a water/ethylene glycol based antifreeze solution, which will prevent freezing down to at least −20°F at all times. It also provides protection against corrosion and increases the coolant boiling point.

The cooling system should be drained, flushed and refilled as per the scheduled intervals (see Chapter 1). The use of antifreeze solutions for periods longer than specified is likely to cause damage and encourage the formation of rust and scale in the system.

Before adding antifreeze to the system, check all hose connections. Antifreeze tends to search out and leak through very minute openings.

The exact mixture of antifreeze-to-water which you should use depends on the relative weather conditions. The mixture should contain at least 55 percent antifreeze, but should never contain more than 70 percent antifreeze.

3 Thermostat — replacement

Caution: *The engine must be completely cool before beginning this procedure.*

1 Refer to the Warning in Section 2.
2 Disconnect the negative cable at the battery. Place the cable out of the way so it cannot accidentally come in contact with the negative terminal of the battery, as this would once again allow power into the electrical system of the vehicle.
3 Drain the cooling system until the level is below the thermostat by loosening the radiator or coolant reservoir cap and removing the plug the bottom of the radiator. Install the plug when enough coolant has drained.
4 On later models, disconnect the lower radiator hose from the thermostat housing.
5 Remove the retaining bolts and separate the cover from the thermostat housing.
6 Grasp the housing cover securely, rock it back and forth to break the gasket seal and remove it from the engine.

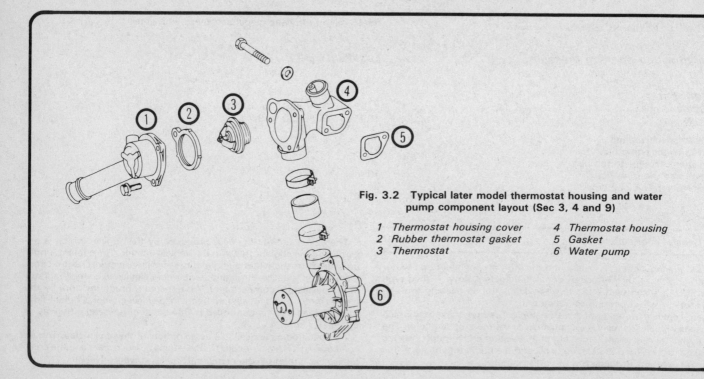

Fig. 3.2 Typical later model thermostat housing and water pump component layout (Sec 3, 4 and 9)

1 Thermostat housing cover   4 Thermostat housing
2 Rubber thermostat gasket   5 Gasket
3 Thermostat   6 Water pump

7   Remove the thermostat from the engine block cavity (photo).
8   Before installing the thermostat, clean the gasket sealing surfaces on the water outlet and thermostat housing. These surfaces must be perfectly smooth to prevent leakage.
9   On models so equipped, install the rubber gasket securely on the new thermostat (photo).
10   Place the thermostat in the housing.
11   On models so equipped, install the O-ring securely in the thermostat housing cover (photo).
12   Install the housing cover and bolts. Tighten the bolts to the specified torque.
13   Connect the lower radiator hose and tighten the hose clamp securely.
14   Fill the cooling system with the proper antifreeze/water mixture (refer to Chapter 1).

4   Thermostat — check

1   The best way to check the operation of the thermostat is with it removed from the engine. In most cases, if the thermostat is suspect, it is more economical to simply buy and install a replacement thermostat, as they are not very costly. However, the checking procedure is as follows.
2   Remove the thermostat as described in Section 3.
3   Inspect the thermostat for excessive corrosion and damage.

Replace it with a new one if either of these conditions is noted.
4   Place the thermostat in hot water (25 degrees above the temperature stamped on the thermostat). The water temperature should be approximately 200 degrees. When submerged in the water (which should be agitated thoroughly), the valve should open all the way.
5   Next, remove the thermostat using a piece of bent wire and place it in water which is 10 degrees below the temperature on the thermostat, or about 165 degrees. At this temperature, the thermostat valve should close completely.
6   Reinstall the thermostat if it operates properly. If it does not, purchase a new thermostat of the same temperature rating.

5   Radiator — removal, servicing and installation

Note: *The engine must be completely cool before beginning this procedure.*

1   Refer to the Warning in Section 2.
2   Disconnect the negative cable at the battery. Place the cable out of the way so it cannot accidentally come in contact with the negative terminal of the battery, as this would once again allow power into the electrical system of the vehicle.
3   Drain the radiator (refer to Chapter 1, if necessary).
4   Disconnect the coolant and recovery hoses from the radiator.
5   Remove the two radiator attaching clips and hang the fan shroud out of the way over the fan (photo).

3

3.7   Pull the thermostat from the cavity

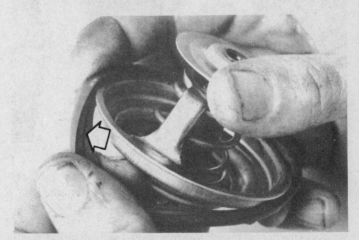

3.9   Work the gasket securely around the thermostat. Note that the thermostat edge fits into a slit (arrow) in the gasket

3.10   Insert the thermostat into the housing

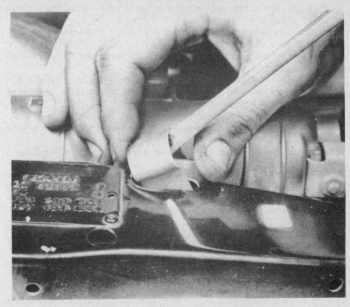

5.5   Release the radiator clips with a screwdriver

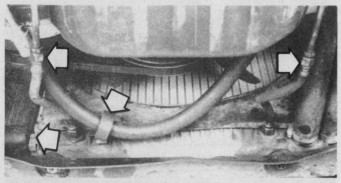

5.7   The locations of the oil cooler bracket (lower left arrow) and various automatic transmission cooler hose connections

5.8   Lift the radiator straight up and out of the engine compartment. Be careful, the fins are very fragile

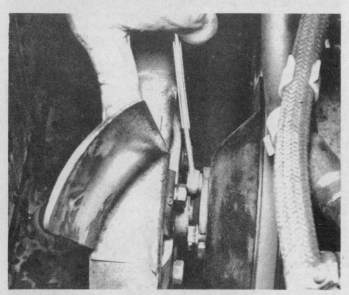

6.3a   The retaining bolts are accessible from the back side of the fan

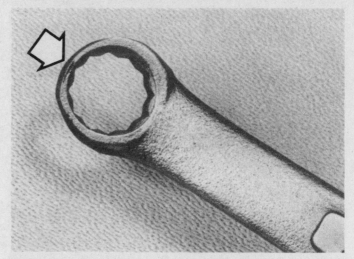

6.3b   Grind or file the end of a box wrench (arrow) to provide the clearance necessary to remove the fan bolts

6   Raise the front of the vehicle and support it securely on jackstands.

7   Disconnect the oil cooler bracket and automatic transmission cooler hose connections at the bottom of the radiator (photo). Plug the hose ends to prevent further draining and contamination while the radiator is out of place.

8   Lift the radiator carefully from the engine compartment (photo).

9   Carefully examine the radiator for evidence of leaks and damage. It is recommended that any necessary repairs be performed by a radiator repair shop.

10   With the radiator removed, brush accumulations of insects and leaves from the fins and examine and replace, if necessary, any hoses or clamps which have deteriorated.

11   The radiator can be flushed as described in Chapter 1.

12   If you are installing a new radiator, transfer the fittings from the old unit.

13   Installation is the reverse of removal, making sure the radiator seats securely in the mounts.

14   After installing the radiator, refill it with the proper coolant mixture (refer to Chapter 1). Also check the automatic transmission fluid level to replenish fluid which may have leaked from the hoses. Start the engine and check for leaks around the various hoses.

---

6   Fan — removal and installation

1   Disconnect the battery negative cable.

2   Remove the radiator (Section 5).

3   Remove the fan retaining bolts accessible on the back side of the hub. If only the fan is to be removed, the pulley and drivebelts can

be left in place. A suitable box wrench which has been ground down on one side for clearance will make removal easier because the area around the bolts is very restricted (photos).

4   Installation is the reverse of removal.

---

7   Fan thermocouple — removal and installation

1   Disconnect the negative battery cable.

2   Remove the radiator (Section 5) and the fan (Section 6).

3   Remove the retaining bolts and lift the thermocouple off of the fan (photo).

4   Installation is the reverse of removal.

---

8   Water pump — check

1   A failure of the water pump can cause overheating and serious engine damage (the pump will not circulate coolant through the engine).

2   There are three ways to check the operation of the water pump while it is still installed on the engine. If the pump is defective, it should

7.3   The thermocouple-to-fan retaining bolts (arrows)

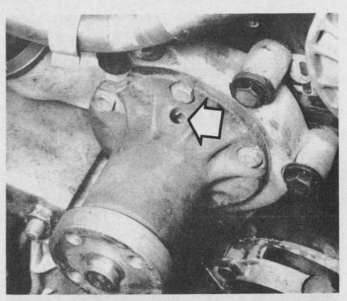

8.4   Check for leakage at the water pump 'weep' hole (arrow) (fan removed for clarity)

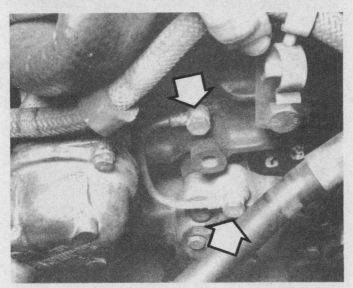

9.5   The water crossover pipe is held in place by two bolts (arrows)

9.6   The water pump retaining bolts (arrows); note that the balancer has be rotated so the notch provides access to the lower bolt

be replaced with a new or rebuilt unit.

3   With the engine at normal operating temperature, squeeze the upper radiator hose. If the water pump is working properly, a pressure surge will be felt as the hose is released.

4   Water pumps are equipped with "weep" or vent holes. If a pump seal failure occurs, small amounts of coolant will leak from the weep holes (photo).

5   If the water pump shaft bearings fail, there may be a squealing sound emitted from the front of the engine while it is running. Shaft wear can be felt if the water pump pulley is forced up and down.

9   Water pump — removal and installation

Note: *The engine must be completely cool before beginning this procedure.*

1   Refer to the Warning in Section 2.

2   Disconnect the negative battery cable.

3   Drain the cooling system (refer to Chapter 1, if necessary).

4   Remove the radiator, fan, upper and lower pulleys and the engine drivebelts.

5   Disconnect the radiator and heater hoses and remove the crossover pipe from the water pump housing (photo).

6   Remove the water pump bolts. If necessary, turn the balancer until the notch allows access to the lower bolt (photo).

7   Remove the water pump and housing assembly from the engine, using a rocking motion if necessary, to disengage it.

8   Carefully clean all gasket material from the mounting surfaces of the water pump and engine. These surfaces must be completely smooth in order to prevent leakage.

9   Coat both sides of the gasket with sealant and place it in position on the water pump housing.

10   Place the housing in position and install the retaining bolts finger-tight.

11   Tighten the bolts evenly in a criss-cross pattern to the specified torque.

12   The remainder of installation is the reverse of removal.

13   Refill the cooling system with a 50/50 mixture of water and antifreeze (Chapter 1).

14   Connect the battery negative cable, start the engine and run it until normal operating temperature is reached, then check for leaks.

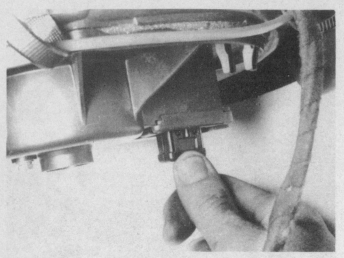

10.3 After the cover is removed, unplug the electrical connector which is now visible

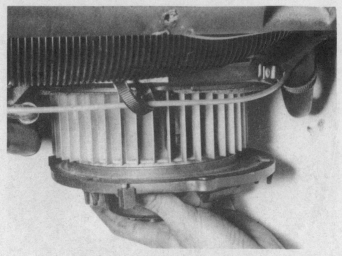

10.5 Lower the motor carefully from the housing

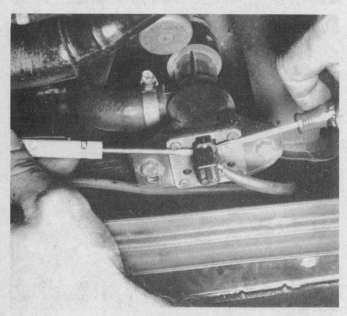

11.2 Pry upward using two screwdrivers to unplug the connector

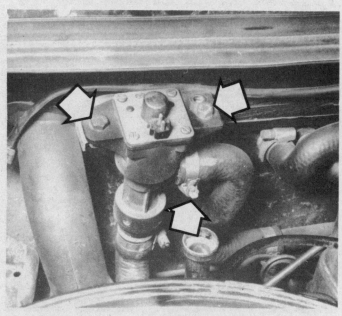

11.4 The heater control valve retaining bolts and heater hose connections (arrows)

10 Heater fan motor — removal and installation

1   Disconnect the battery negative cable.
2   Remove the cover panel under the right side of the dash.
3   Unplug the electrical connectors (photo).
4   Remove the retaining screws.
5   Lower the motor from the housing (photo).
6   Installation is the reverse of removal.

11 Heater control valve — removal and installation

1   Disconnect the negative battery cable.
2   Use two screwdrivers to unplug the electrical connector (photo).
3   Clamp the hose off with locking pliers or a similar tool or place a suitable size container under the valve to catch the coolant when the hose is disconnected.
4   Remove the two hose clamps and two retaining bolts and lift the valve from the engine compartment (photo).
5   Installation is the reverse of removal.

12 Heater circulation pump — removal and installation

1   The heater circulation pump is located in the engine compartment in-line with the heater hose. Begin removal by disconnecting the negative battery cable.
2   Place a container or newspapers under the pump to catch the coolant.
3   Unplug the electrical connector, disconnect the hoses and remove the pump (photo).
4   Installation is the reverse of removal.

13 Air conditioning system — servicing

Warning: *The air conditioning system is under high pressure. Do not disassemble any portion of the system (hoses, compressor, line fittings, etc.) without having the system depressurized by a dealer or competent repair facility.*

1   Raise the hood.
2   The condenser is located just forward of the radiator. Inspect the

12.3   Heater circulation pump electrical connector and hose connections (arrows)

13.2   The air conditioning condenser is located in front of the radiator and is easily checked with the hood open

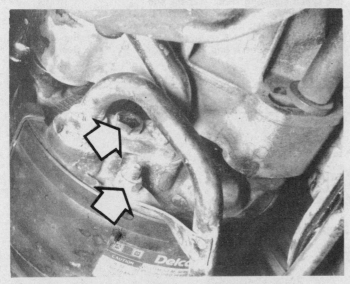

14.5   Air compressor pipe bracket nut and bolt (arrows)

14.6   Air conditioning compressor retaining bolts (arrows)

14   Air conditioning compressor — removal and installation

1   Take the vehicle to a properly equipped shop and have the air conditioning system depressurized.
2   Disconnect the battery negative cable.
3   Remove the compressor drivebelt.
4   Raise the front of the vehicle and support it securely on jackstands.
5   Working from under the engine compartment, disconnect the air conditioning hoses and the bracket at the compressor (photo). On vehicles with an automatic transmission, the fluid lines near the compressor may have to be disconnected to provide adequate working clearance.
6   Remove the retaining bolts and lower the compressor from the engine (photo).
7   Installation is the reverse of removal. Adjust the drivebelt tension as described in Chapter 1. Have the system recharged and check for proper operation.

condenser fins and brush away any leaves and bugs. Check the electric fan and wiring connectors which are also in this area. Replacement of these components is straightforward once the system has been depressurized (photo).
3   Check the condition of the system hoses. If there is any sign of deterioration or hardening, have them replaced by a dealer or air conditioning repair facility.
4   At the recommended intervals, check and adjust the compressor drivebelt as described in Chapter 1.
5   Because of the special tools, equipment and skills required to service air conditioning systems, and the differences between the various systems that may be installed on vehicles, air conditioning repair other than indicated here cannot be covered in this manual.

Chapter 4 Part A Fuel and exhaust systems

Contents

Air filter cleaning and replacement . . . . See Chapter 1
Air cleaner assembly — removal and installation 9
Engine idle speed check and adjustment . . . . See Chapter 1
Exhaust system check . . . . See Chapter 1
Exhaust system components — removal and installation 10
Fuel filter assembly — removal and installation 8
Fuel filter replacement . . . . See Chapter 1
Fuel injection pump — check 2
Fuel injection pump — removal and installation 4
Fuel injection pump start of delivery — check
  and adjustment 3
Fuel injection nozzles — removal and installation 7
Fuel injection timing device — removal and
  installation . . . . See Chapter 1
Fuel system bleeding . . . . See Chapter 1
Fuel system check . . . . See Chapter 1
Fuel tank — removal and installation 5
Fuel tank — repair 6
General information 1
Idle speed adjusting knob — check and
  adjustment . . . . See Chapter 1
Intake and exhaust manifold — removal and
  installation . . . . See Chapter 2
Throttle linkage check and lubrication . . . . See Chapter 1

Specifications

Fuel injection pump

Start of delivery (degrees Before Top Dead Center)
  Turbocharged models . . . .   23° to 25° BTDC
  Non-turbocharged models
    615.913/940 . . . .   26° BTDC
    615.912/941 . . . .   24° BTDC
    616 . . . .   24° BTDC

Torque specifications	Nm	Ft-lbs
Exhaust manifold-to-pipe self-locking nut	20 to 25	15 to 18
Exhaust pipe U-clamps	7	5
Exhaust pipe-to-transmission mount brace (turbocharged models)		
Exhaust pipe clamp nuts	7	5
Brace-to-transmission nuts	20	15
Turbocharger flange-to-exhaust pipe nut	20 to 25	15 to 18
Fuel injection lines	25	18
Fuel injection nozzles	70 to 80	52 to 59
Fuel tank		
Self-locking retaining nuts	26 to 34	19 to 25
Non-self-locking retaining nuts	35 to 43	26 to 32
Suction hose clamp screw	24 to 32	18 to 24
Fuel strainer nut	35 to 43	26 to 32
Fuel gauge immersion tube transmitter nut	35 to 43	26 to 32
Fuel delivery valve pipe connection	40 to 50	30 to 37

1 General information

The fuel system consists of a rear mounted fuel tank, a mechanically operated fuel injection pump with injector nozzles mounted in the cylinder head, the injection timer, the intake manifold and an air cleaner assembly. Some models are also equipped with an exhaust gas-driven turbocharger. The turbocharger is covered in Part B of this Chapter.

The exhaust system includes the muffler and associated pipes and hardware.

Fuel is drawn from the tank and through the filter by the injection pump. The fuel is injected directly into the precombustion and then the combustion chamber where it is ignited by the very high compression along with the air drawn in through the air cleaner and intake manifold. The fuel pressure and the point in the engine cycle at which it is injected into the cylinders is controlled by the timing chain-driven timing device and the internal governor in the fuel injection pump.

Because of the complexity of the diesel fuel injection system, checking (other than for leaks or obvious damage) and adjustment should be left to a dealer or a properly equipped shop. The home mechanic can adjust the fuel injection start of delivery (Section 3) using a simple factory tool. This is roughly similar to adjusting the distributor timing on a gasoline powered vehicle.

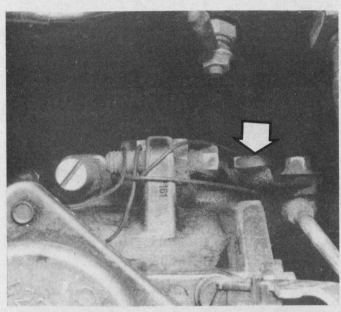

3.3 A piece of wire can be used to hold the pump lever (arrow) in the full load position

3.4a Unscrew the number one fuel element from the pump . . .

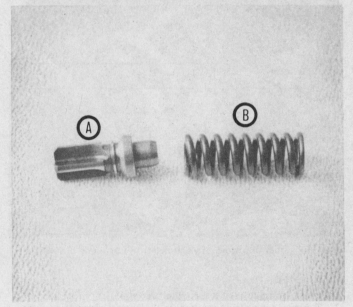

3.4b . . . and remove the valve (A) and spring (B)

3.6 The fuel injection start of delivery tool spout must be installed with the spout facing the engine in the direction of the arrow

2 Fuel injection pump — check

1   The fuel injection pump bolts to the cylinder block on the side of the engine.

2   The fuel injection pump is a complicated device which operates at very high pressure. Checking and adjustment (other than start of delivery, Section 3) requires special tools and techniques so this should be left to a dealer or properly equipped shop. Because of the high pressures involved, fuel leaks can seriously affect engine operation and the pump and lines should be checked periodically for leaks by the home mechanic.

3   Make sure that there is fuel in the fuel tank.

4   With the engine running, check for leaks at all fuel line connections between the fuel tank and the fuel pump. Tighten any loose connections. Inspect all lines for cracks as well as kinks which would restrict the fuel flow.

3 Fuel injection pump start of delivery — check and adjustment

Note: *This procedure determines the start of fuel delivery of the fuel injection pump number one element when the number one piston is at the start of the the compression stroke. Before beginning this procedure obtain a start of delivery overflow pipe spout tool number 636 589 02 23 00 from your dealer.*

1   Remove the fuel injection pump-to-injector pipe assembly.

2   Disconnect the vacuum hose from the fuel pump vacuum control unit.

3   Disconnect the throttle linkage from the pump and use a piece of wire to fasten the control lever in the full load position (photo).

4   Remove the number 1 pump element from the pump and then remove the delivery valve and spring from the element (photos).

5   Reinstall the element, minus the delivery valve and spring.

6   Install the overflow pipe tool in the number 1 pump element with

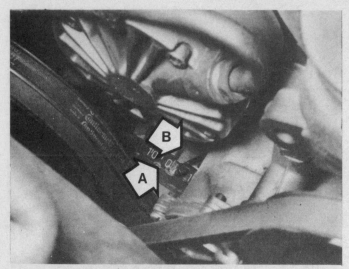

3.7 The engine timing marks (A) and pointer (B) (the engine is shown at Top Dead Center (TDC) here) are visible behind the drivebelt pulleys at the front of the engine; a flashlight is helpful in locating them

3.8a Loosen the fuel filter union bolt with a wrench while operating the hand pump until bubble-free fuel (arrow) can be seen escaping from the union and . . .

3.8b . . . the start of delivery tool spout (arrow)

3.9 Fuel must drip from the spout (arrow) at a one droplet per second rate

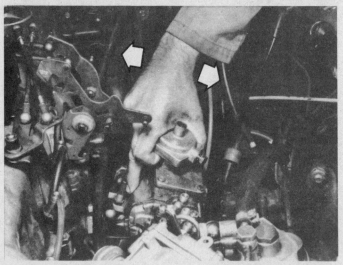

3.10 Rotate the fuel injection pump toward or away from the engine (arrows) to achieve the proper start of delivery

the spout facing toward the engine (photo).

7   Turn the engine over by hand in the normal direction of rotation (clockwise when facing the front of the vehicle) until the compression pressure can be felt beginning to build up. Rotate the engine until the timing pointer on the front of the engine is aligned with the specified start of delivery degrees on the balancer (refer to Specifications) (photo). Remove the oil filler cap. Check to see that both camshaft lobes for the front (number 1) cylinder are facing up. With this done, the number 1 piston is at the start of its compression stroke.

8   Loosen the fuel union bolt at the top of the fuel filter and bleed the air from the system by pumping the hand pump until fuel with no air bubbles issues from the top of the filter and the overflow tool spout (photos).

9   Stop pumping the hand pump and the flow from the spout of the overflow tool should slow until a rate of one droplet per second is reached (photo).

10 If the flow is not correct, loosen the fuel injection pump mounting bolts, repeat the procedure and rotate the pump until one droplet per second is achieved (photo).

11 Once the proper start of delivery is obtained, tighten the pump mounting bolts, remove the spout tool and reinstall the delivery valve and spring in the element. Install the fuel pipe assembly and connect the throttle linkage and vacuum hose.

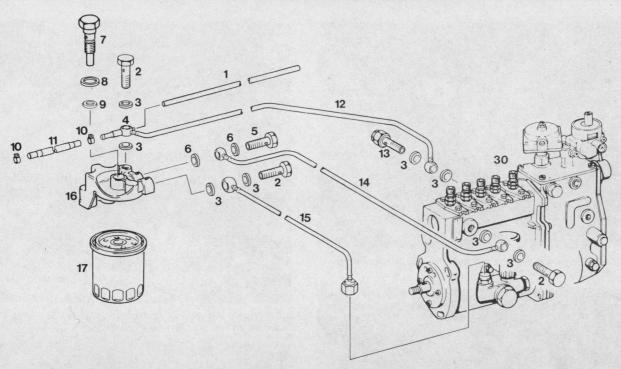

Fig. 4A.1 Fuel injection pump and filter assembly component layout (Sec 4 and 8)

1 Leak-off (overflow) hose from injection nozzle	5 Fuel union screw	10 Hose clamp	14 Fuel line
2 Fuel union screw	6 Sealing ring	11 Expansion hose	15 Fuel line
3 Sealing ring	7 Fuel union screw	12 Return line from bypass valve	16 Fuel filter housing
4 Banjo connector	8 Sealing ring		17 Fuel filter cartridge
	9 O-ring	13 Bypass valve	30 Fuel injection pump

4A

4.2 The oil cooler lines (A) and pressure gauge line (B) connections are accessible from the engine compartment

4.3 The turbocharger oil line is located at the bottom of the oil filter housing

4 Fuel injection pump — removal and installation

Removal

1 Disconnect the cable from the negative battery terminal.

2 On some models it will be necessary to remove the oil filter housing assembly. Drain the oil (Chapter 1) and in the engine compartment, disconnect the oil cooler line and the oil pressure gauge connection. Hold the cooler line nut fitting on the housing with a thin backup wrench while unscrewing the fitting to avoid twisting the line (photo).

3 If equipped, remove the turbocharger cooler line from under the

filter housing (photo). Remove the bolts using a suitable Allen head wrench and lift the housing from the engine. It may be necessary to cut off a short piece of an Allen wrench with a hacksaw and hold it with locking pliers to remove the bolts on some models because of the restricted working area around the oil filter housing.

4 Disconnect the throttle linkage at the fuel injection pump.

5 Mark the fuel injection pump vacuum hoses for ease of installation and disconnect them.

6 Remove the fuel injection pump-to-injector pipe assembly. Be sure to hold the fittings in the injection pump with a back-up wrench to prevent them from turning.

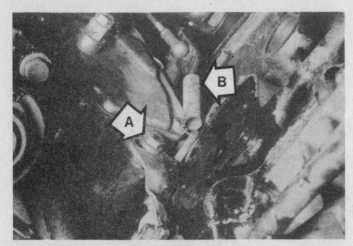

4.7   The fuel injection pump lower bolt (A) and throttle return spring (B) are accessible from below

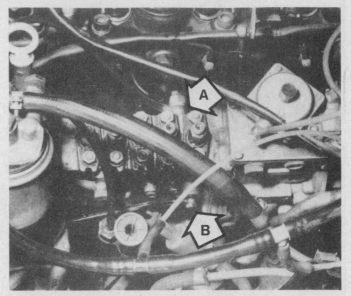

4.8   Prior to injection pump removal, the two fuel lines (A) and one oil feed line (B) must be disconnected

4.10   Slide the fuel injection pump rearward and then lift it from the engine compartment; be sure to get a good grip because the pump is heavy

7   From under the engine, disconnect the throttle return spring and remove the lower pump retaining bolts (photo).

8   Remove the fuel union bolts and disconnect the lines from the injection pump (photo).

9   Remove the remaining pump retaining bolts. Use a curved wrench to loosen the bottom one.

10   Grasp the pump securely (it is heavy), slide it rearward and then lift it from the engine compartment (photo).

4.11   The wide spline and the mark on the fuel injection pump (arrows) must be aligned before the pump is installed

Installation

11   Prior to installation, remove the front collar and align the mark on the splines with the mark on the housing (photo).

12   Install the collar on the pump. The engine must be at the specified start of delivery point (24 or 26° BTDC).

13   Install the pump into the engine as near as possible to it's original angle. A good way to check this is to place the fuel injection pipe assembly temporarily in place to make sure the connections line up.

14   Install the retaining bolts (but don't fully tighten them) and the fuel lines.

15   Bleed the air from the system with the hand pump and check and adjust the fuel start of delivery (Section 4). Fully tighten the pump mounting bolts.

16   The remainder of installation is the reverse of removal. **Note:** *Loosen the clamps between the fuel injection pipes to ease installation and prevent cross threading.*

5   Fuel tank — removal and installation

Warning: *While diesel fuel is not as flammable as gasoline, extra precau-*

tions should be taken when working on any part of the fuel system. Do not smoke or allow open flames or bare light bulbs near the work area. Also, do not work in a garage if a natural gas-type appliance with a pilot light is present. While performing any work on the fuel tank it is advisable to have a fire extinguisher on hand and to wear safety glasses.

1   Remove the cable from the negative battery terminal.

2   Remove the plug at the bottom of the tank and drain the fuel into a clean container.

Coupe and sedan

3   Loosen the hose clamps on the fuel suction and return hoses and disconnect, plugging the connections.

4   Remove the trunk floor mat and trim panel.

5   Loosen the retaining screws and remove the trunk rear wall panel for access to the fuel tank.

6   Loosen the retaining nuts, unplug the electrical connector and lift the fuel tank from the trunk, making sure the vent line is held in place.

7   Installation is the reverse of removal.

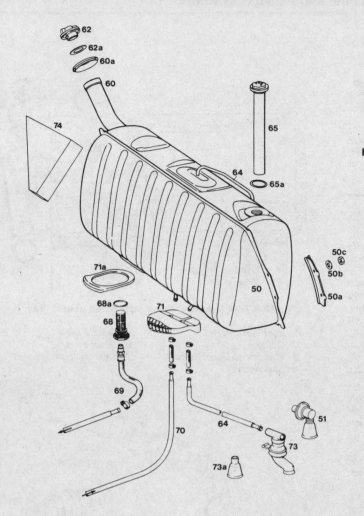

Fig. 4A.2 Sedan and coupe fuel tank installation details (Sec 5)

50   Fuel tank
50a   Reinforcing panel
50b   Washer
51   Vent valve (not all models)
60   Filler neck
60a   Sealing sleeve
62   Closing cover
62a   Sealing ring
64   Vent line
65   Immersion tube transmitter
65a   Sealing ring
68   Fuel strainer
68a   Sealing ring
69   Feed line
70   Return line
71   Gasket
71a   Gasket
73   Vent sleeve (later model)
73a   Protective sleeve (early model)
74   Damping shim

4A

Fig. 4A.3 Station wagon (touring sedan) fuel tank installation details (Sec 5)

50   Fuel tank
50a   Reinforcing panel
50b   Washer
50c   Self-locking nut
55   Later model expansion tank (not all models)
55a   Earlier model expansion tank (not all models)
60   Filler neck
60a   Sealing sleeve
62   Closing cover
62a   Sealing ring
64   Positive vent lines
64a   Negative vent lines
65   Immersion tube transmitter
65a   Sealing ring
68   Fuel strainer
68a   Sealing ring
69   Feed line
70   Return line
73   Later model venting sleeve
73a   Earlier model protective sleeve

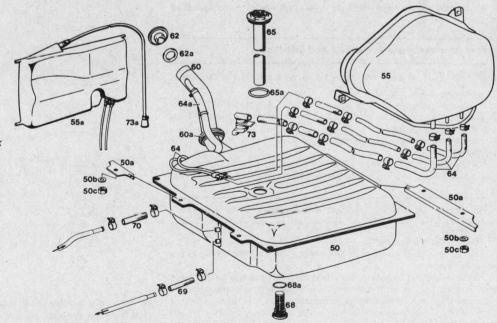

Station wagon (touring sedan)

8   Remove the trunk floor and intermediate shelf panels and remove the covers from the fuel guage sender and hose openings.

9   Unplug the sender connector.

10 Loosen the clamps with a screwdriver and disconnect the hoses.

11 From under the vehicle, loosen the clamps, disconnect and plug the fuel hose and return line placing a suitable container underneath to catch the residual fuel.

12 Remove the retaining bolts and lower the fuel tank from the vehicle.

13 Installation is the reverse of removal. Caution: Never perform any repair work involving heat or flame on the tank until it has been purged of fuel and vapors. All repair work should be performed by a professional (see the following Section).

6   Fuel tank — repair

1   Any repairs to the fuel tank or filler neck should be carried out by a professional who has experience in this critical and potentially dangerous work. Even after cleaning and flushing of the fuel system, explosive fumes can remain and ignite during repair of the tank.

2   If the fuel tank is removed from the vehicle, it should not be placed in an area where sparks or open flames could ignite the fumes coming from the tank. Be especially careful inside garages where a natural gas-type appliance is located, because the pilot light could cause an explosion.

7   Fuel injection nozzles — removal and installation

Warning: *Although diesel fuel is not as flammable as gasoline, extra precautions must be taken when working on any part of the fuel system. Do not smoke or allow open flames or bare light bulbs near the work area. Also, do not work in a garage if a natural gas type appliance with a pilot light is present.*

1   Remove the cable from the negative battery terminal.

2   Due to the rigid nature of the injection pipes, it is best to unscrew all the pipes from the nozzles even if only one nozzle is being serviced.

3   Pull off the overflow tube from the nozzle.

4   Unscrew the nozzle from the cylinder head with a socket wrench such as Mercedes tool number 000 589 68 03 00 available at your dealer. If such a tool is not available, remove the camshaft cover to provide the proper clearance and remove the nozzle with a suitable size wrench.

5   Installation is the reverse of removal, tightening to the specified torque.

8   Fuel filter assembly — removal and installation

Note: *If only the fuel filter cartridge is being replaced, refer to Chapter 1.*

1   Disconnect the negative battery cable.

2   Place newspapers or rags under the filter to catch the fuel.

3   Remove the four fuel union screws and disconnect the fuel lines from the filter housing.

4   Remove the retaining bolts and lift the assembly housing from the engine.

5   Installation is the reverse of removal, taking care to tighten the union screws securely. In order to prevent leaks, use new sealing rings.

9   Air cleaner assembly — removal and installation

Oil bath-type air filter

1   Loosen the hose clamp and disconnect the air filter top from the connector hose.

2   Remove the nut retaining the vibration mount to the fender inner panel and lift the housing assembly from the engine compartment.

3   Installation is the reverse of removal.

Dry-type air filter

4   Remove the top nut and remove the air filter cover and filter element.

5   Disconnect the intake hose (later models) and (if equipped) turbocharger hose.

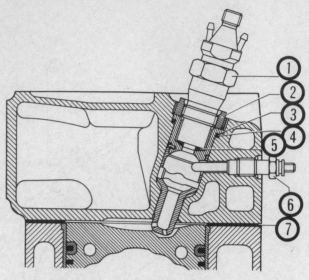

Fig. 4A.4 Fuel injection nozzle installation details (Sec 7)

1   Injection nozzle
2   Collar
3   Precombustion chamber
4   Sealing ring
5   Nozzle plate
6   Glow plug
7   Cylinder head gasket

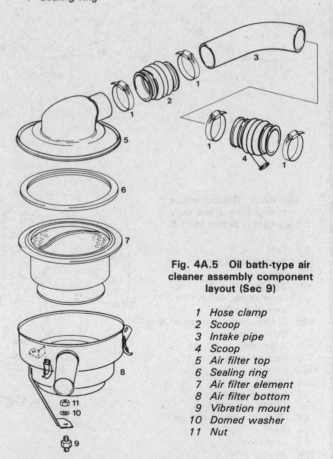

Fig. 4A.5 Oil bath-type air cleaner assembly component layout (Sec 9)

1   Hose clamp
2   Scoop
3   Intake pipe
4   Scoop
5   Air filter top
6   Sealing ring
7   Air filter element
8   Air filter bottom
9   Vibration mount
10 Domed washer
11 Nut

6   Remove the three nuts located inside the housing and lift the housing from the engine.

7   Remove the three bolts and lift the vibration mount from the manifold (photo). On turbocharged models it will be necessary to disconnect the oil pipe.

8   Installation is the reverse of removal, taking care to lubricate the intake manifold sealing ring with clean engine oil.

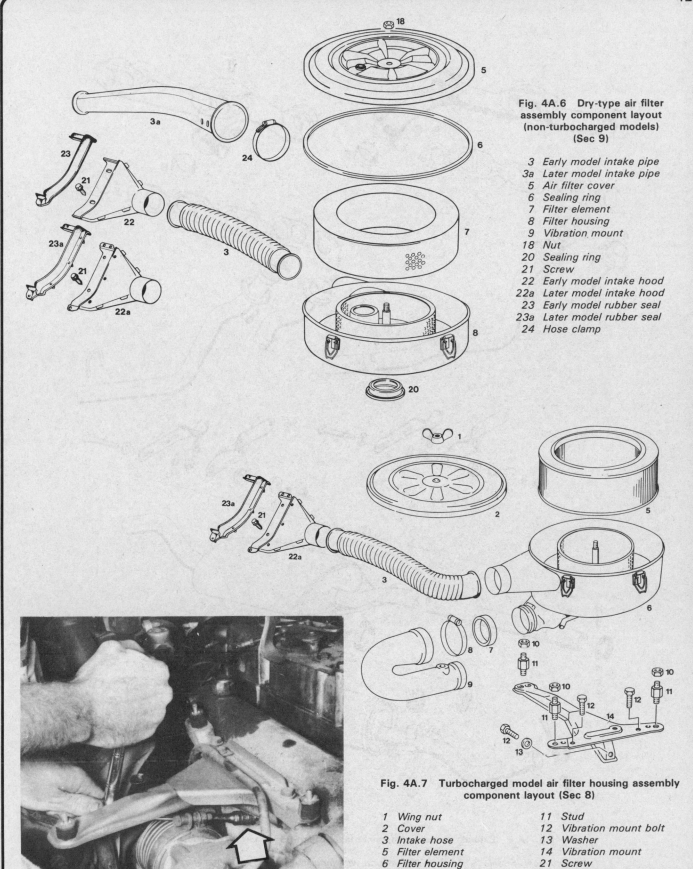

Fig. 4A.6 Dry-type air filter assembly component layout (non-turbocharged models) (Sec 9)

3   Early model intake pipe
3a Later model intake pipe
5   Air filter cover
6   Sealing ring
7   Filter element
8   Filter housing
9   Vibration mount
18 Nut
20 Sealing ring
21 Screw
22 Early model intake hood
22a Later model intake hood
23 Early model rubber seal
23a Later model rubber seal
24 Hose clamp

4A

Fig. 4A.7 Turbocharged model air filter housing assembly component layout (Sec 8)

1 Wing nut	11 Stud
2 Cover	12 Vibration mount bolt
3 Intake hose	13 Washer
5 Filter element	14 Vibration mount
6 Filter housing	21 Screw
7 Sealing ring	22 Early model intake hood
8 Clamp	22a Later model intake hood
9 Turbocharger intake pipe	23a Later model rubber seal
10 Nut	

9.7   The lower vibration mount bolt (arrow) is accessible with a socket on an extension

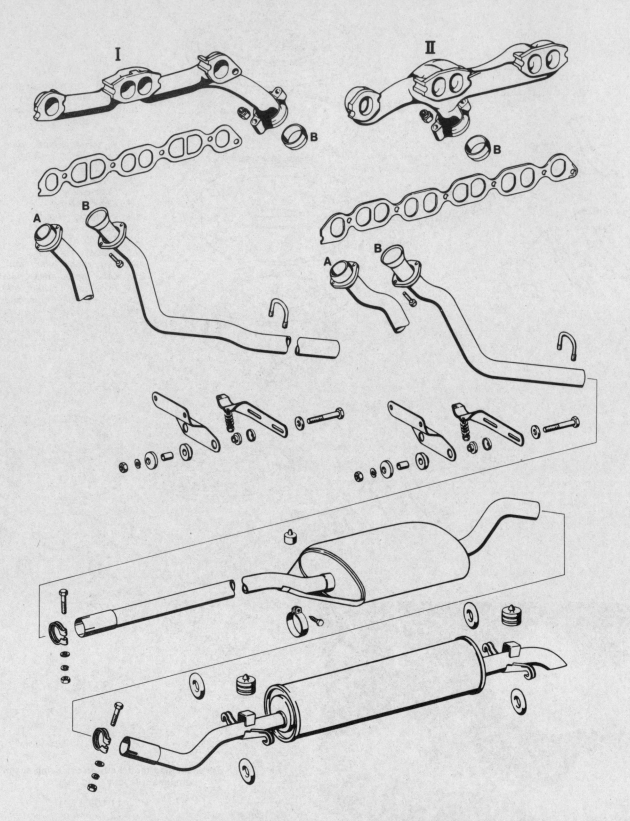

Fig. 4A.8 Exhaust system component layout (non-turbocharged models) (Sec 10)

I Four-cylinder models
II Five-cylinder models

A Earlier version with inner ball
   connection on exhaust manifold

B Later model with tulip
   connection on exhaust pipe

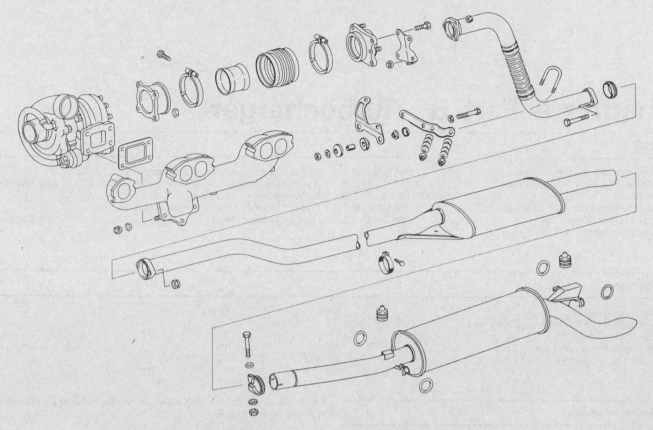

Fig. 4A.9 Turbocharged model exhaust system component layout (Sec 10)

10 Exhaust system components — removal and installation

Caution: *The vehicle's exhaust system generates very high temperatures and should be allowed to cool completely before any of the components are touched.*

1 Raise the vehicle and support it securely on jackstands.

2 Replacement of exhaust system components is basically a matter of removing any heat shields, disconnecting the component and installing a new one. Do not tighten any bolts or nuts fully until the exhaust system is in place and suspended from the rubber suspension rings.

3 The heat shields and exhaust system hangers must be reinstalled in the original locations or damage could result. Due to the high temperatures and exposed locations of the exhaust system components, rust and corrosion can "freeze" parts together. Penetrating oils are available to help loosen frozen fasteners. However, in some cases it may be necessary to cut the pieces apart with a hacksaw or cutting torch. The latter method should be employed only by persons experienced in this work.

4A

Chapter 4 Part B   Turbocharger

Contents

Air filter cleaning and replacement . . . .   See Chapter 1
Air cleaner assembly — removal and
  installation . . . .   See Chapter 4, Part A
Engine idle speed check and adjustment . . . .   See Chapter 1
Exhaust system check . . . .   See Chapter 1
General information   1
Intake and exhaust manifold — removal
  and installation . . . .   See Chapter 2
Turbocharger — checking   3
Turbocharger — removal and installation   2
Throttle linkage check . . . .   See Chapter 1

Specifications

Torque specifications	Nm	Ft-lbs
Exhaust pipe-to-transmission mount brace		
Exhaust pipe clamp nuts	7	5
Brace-to-transmission nuts	20	15
Turbocharger flange-to-exhaust pipe nut	20 to 25	15 to 18

1   General information

The turbocharger system increases power by using an exhaust gas turbine located between the exhaust manifold and the exhaust pipe to pressurize the fuel/air mixture as it enters the combustion chamber. Oil from the engine is used for turbocharger lubrication and cooling. The system incorporates a boost pressure control valve which vents all or part of the exhaust gases directly into the exhaust pipe depending on driving conditions.

2   Turbocharger — removal and installation

1   Disconnect the negative battery cable.
2   Remove the air cleaner and bracket assembly (Chapter 4, Part A,

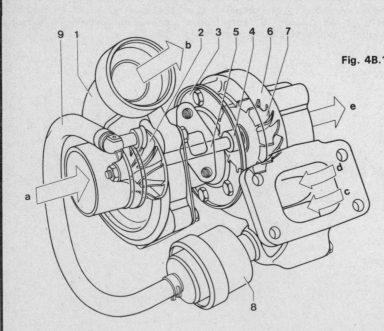

Fig. 4B.1   Turbocharger component layout (Sec 1)

1   Compressor housing
2   Compressor wheel
3   Center housing
4   Bearings
5   Shaft
6   Turbine housing
7   Turbine wheel
8   Boost pressure control valve
9   Connecting hose
a   Compressor intake (fresh air)
*b   Compressor discharge
  (compressed air)*
*c   Exhaust gases to the bypass
  duct*
*d   Exhaust gases to the turbine
  wheel*
e   Exhaust gas discharge

Fig. 4B.2   Turbocharger system operation (Sec 1)

2   Compressor wheel
7   Turbine wheel
8   Boost pressure control valve
9   Connecting hose
10 Exhaust manifold
11 Boost air pipe
14 Overload protection capsule
15 Pressure line
20 Boost pressure switch air pipe
21 Valve overload protection
c   Exhaust gas to bypass duct

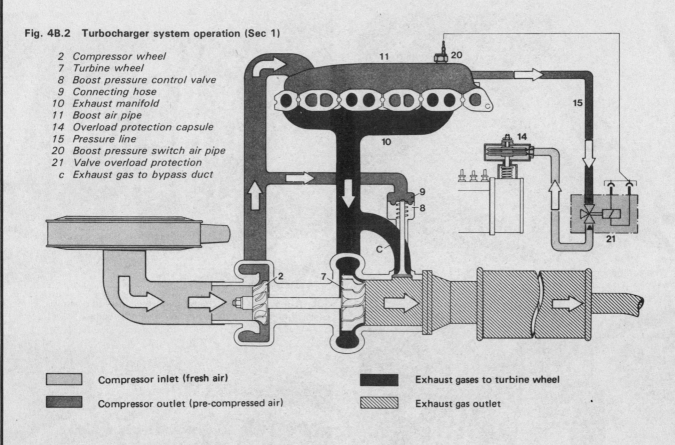

Compressor inlet (fresh air)

Compressor outlet (pre-compressed air)

Exhaust gases to turbine wheel

Exhaust gas outlet

4B

Fig. 4B.3   Turbocharger system component layout (Sec 2)

1   Intake hose
2   Hose clip
3   Air intake rubber sealing ring
4   Turbocharger
5   Outer rubber sealing ring
6   Adapter fitting
7   Inner rubber sealing
8   Flange gasket
9   Heat-resistant nut
10 Washer
11 Intake manifold
12 Pressure switch
13 Sealing ring
14 Delivery line from intake manifold
15 Union screw
16 Hose clip
17 Connecting hose
18 Switchover valve
19 Aneroid compensator delivery line
21 Nut
22 Washer
23 Gasket
70 Aneroid compensator

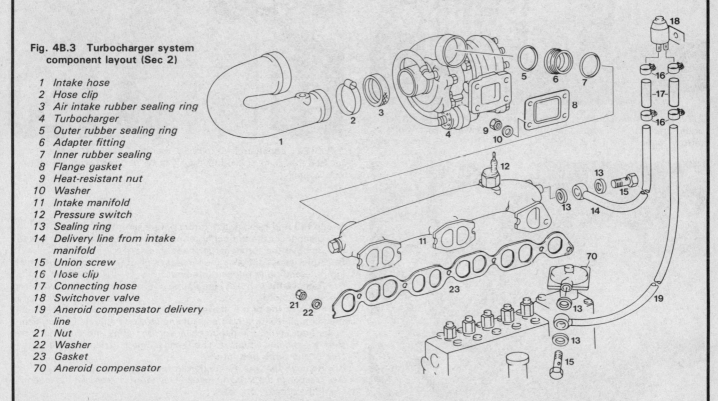

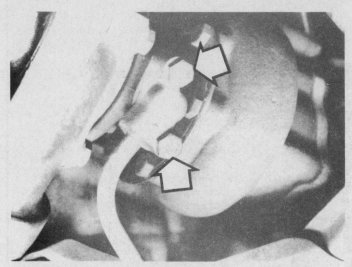

2.3   The turbocharger oil line is held in place by two bolts (arrows)

2.6   Removal of the exhaust pipe retaining nuts (arrows) is made easier if penetrating oil is applied to the threads

2.7   The flexible coupling is held in place by two straps with bolts (arrows). Also shown is one of the two flange collar bolts (arrow, upper left of photo)

2.8   The turbocharger-to-exhaust manifold nuts (arrows) are located in a tight space but they can be removed with an open end wrench

Section 8) and remove the turbocharger air intake hose.

3   Disconnect the turbocharger oil pipe at the turbocharger (photo).

4   Remove the turbocharger heat shield.

5   Apply penetrant oil to the threads of all of the turbocharger attaching nuts and bolts prior to removal.

6   Remove the exhaust pipe flange nuts and pry the pipe away from the studs (photo).

7   Remove the two bolts retaining the flexible coupling straps and then completely remove the retaining straps. Remove the two flange collar bolts, twist the flange collar for clearance and then pull it free from the flexible coupling. The flexible coupling can then be worked free of the turbo unit (photo).

8   Remove the four turbocharger retaining nuts (photo).

9   Disengage the turbocharger and oil return pipe and lift the assembly from lthe engine (photo).

10   Remove the trubocharger-to-intake manifold fitting, noting the direction in which it is installed.

11   Remove the flange gasket from the exhaust manifold and clean the contact surfaces of the manifold and turbocharger.

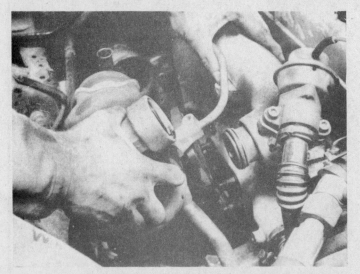

2.9   Grasp the turbocharger firmly and lift it away from the manifold while holding the oil line out of the way

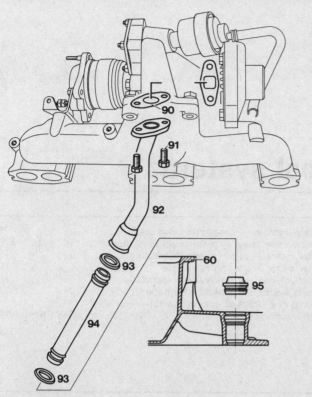

Fig. 4B.4 Turbocharger oil return pipe component layout (Sec 2)

60 Upper oil pan	93 O-ring
90 Gasket	94 Lower oil return pipe
91 Bolts	95 Seal
92 Upper oil return pipe	

12 Install a new flange gasket on the exhaust manifold, with the raised bead side against the manifold.

13 Install manifold fitting, place the turbocharger in postion and install the retaining nuts. New O-rings should be used on the turbocharger-to-intake manifold fitting. Tighten the nuts securely.

14 Install the flexible coupling and connect the exhaust pipe. Tighten all nuts and bolts securely.

15 Install the heat shield.

16 If a new turbocharger has been installed, pour approximately 1/4 pint (1/8 liter) of clean engine oil in the oil pipe opening.

17 Place the oil pipe and new gasket in position and install the bolts. Tighten the bolts securely.

18 Install the air cleaner assembly.

19 Connect the battery cable, start the engine and check for leaks.

3 Turbocharger — checking

1 While a comparatively simple design, the turbocharger is a precision device which can be severely damaged by an interrupted oil supply or loose or damaged ducting.

2 Due to the special techniques and equipment required, any hecking or diagnosis of suspected problems should be left to your dealer. The home mechanic can, however, check the connections and linkages for security, damage or obvious faults.

3 Because each turbocharger has its own distinctive sound, a change in the noise level can be a sign of potential problems.

4 A high-pitched or whistling sound is a symptom of an inlet air or exhaust gas leak. Another sign of a loose duct or an exhaust leak is low engine power. Check the air ducting between the air cleaner and the turbocharger connection to the exhaust manifold for loose connections or leaks.

5 White exhaust smoke and/or oil in the intake or exhaust is an indication of a faulty internal seal within the turbocharger.

6 If an unusual sound issues from the vicinity of the turbine, the ducting can be removed and the turbine wheel inspected. **Warning:** *All checks must be made with the engine off and cool to the touch and the turbocharger stopped or personal injury could result. Operating the turbocharger without all the ducts and filters installed is also dangerous and can result in damage to the turbine wheel blades.*

7 Check the operation of the turbine wheel to make sure it turns freely. If it does not, this could be a sign that the cooling oil has sludged or coked from overheating. Push inward on the shaft wheels and check for binding. The wheel should rotate freely with no binding or rubbing on the housing.

8 Inspect the exhaust manifold for cracks and loose connections.

9 Because the turbine wheel rotates at speeds up to 140,000 rpm, severe damage can result from the interruption or contamination of the oil supply to the turbine bearings. Check for leaks in the oil return pipe for obstructions, as this can cause severe oil loss through the turbocharger seals. Burned oil on the turbine housing is a sign of this. **Note:** *Any time a major engine bearing such as a main, connecting rod or camshaft bearing is replaced, the turbocharger should be flushed with clean oil.*

4B

Chapter 5 Engine electrical systems

Contents

Alternator — removal and installation   10
Battery cables — check and replacement   4
Battery — emergency jump starting   3
Battery — removal and installation   2
Charging system — check   9
Charging system — general information and precautions   8
General information   1
Engine idle speed check and adjustment . . . . See Chapter 1
Glow plugs — checking and replacement   6
Idle speed adjusting knob — check and
 adjustment . . . . See Chapter 1

Preglow system — description and testing   5
Preglow timer relay — removal and installation   7
Starter motor — removal and installation   13
Starter motor — testing in vehicle   12
Starter solenoid — removal and installation   14
Starting system — general information   11
Steering key lock and ignition switch — removal
 and installation . . . . See Chapter 10

Specifications

Torque specifications	Nm	Ft-lbs
Glow plug	50	37
Starter motor bolt	25	18
Steering track rod bolt	40	30

1 General information

The engine electrical system is composed of the battery, starter, alternator, preglow system and ignition switch.

Ignition timing changes on diesel engines are accomplished by the interaction of the fuel injection pump and timing device (Chapter 4). The ignition of the fuel/air mixture of a diesel engine is accomplished by the very high compression in the combustion chamber. Consequently, there is no ignition system as such on these vehicles. Therefore, the engine electrical system is involved with charging (alternator) and storage (battery) of electrical power as well as starting (starter and preglow systems).

The preglow system (Section 5) is used when the engine is first started, when there is insufficient temperature in the combustion chamber to support self-combustion.

2 Battery — removal and installation

1   The battery is located at the rear corner of the engine compartment. It is held in place by two clamps retained with nuts at the bottom of the case.
2   Hydrogen gas is produced by the battery, so keep open flames and lighted cigarettes away from it at all times.
3   Always keep the battery in an upright position. Spilled electrolyte should be rinsed off immediately with large quantities of water. Always wear eye protection when working around the battery.
4   Always disconnect the negative (–) battery cable first, followed by the positive (+) cable.
5   After the cables are disconnected from the battery, remove the nuts and the clamps (photo).
6   Carefully lift the battery out of the engine compartment.
7   Installation is the reverse of removal. The battery clamp nuts should

be tight, but do not overtighten them as damage to the battery case can occur. The battery posts and cable ends should be cleaned prior to connection (Chapter 1).

3 Battery — emergency jump starting

Refer to the booster battery (jump) starting procedure at the front of this manual.

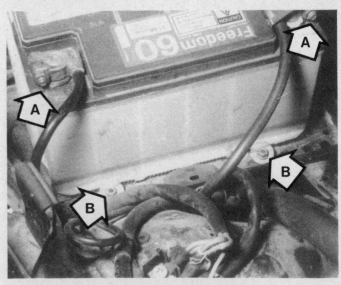

2.5 Battery cable (A) and retaining clamp (B) nuts

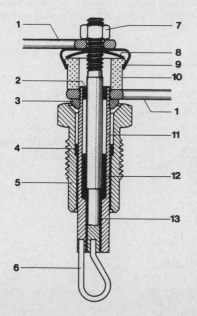

Fig. 5.1 Filament-type glow plug component layout (Sec 6)

1 Conductor
2 Plastic insulator
3 Outer electrode ring element
4 Insulating compound
5 Plug body
6 Glow filament
7 Nut
8 Domed washer
9 Sheet metal cap on connection insulator
10 Connection insulator
11 Outer electrode
12 Insulating compound
13 Center electrode

Fig. 5.2 Pencil-type glow plug component layout (Sec 6)

1 Control coil
2 Heater coil

5

4 Battery cables — check and replacement

1   Periodically inspect the entire length of each battery cable for damage, cracked or burned insulation and corrosion. Poor battery cable connections can cause starting problems and decreased engine performance.
2   Check the cable-to-terminal connections at the ends of the cables for cracks, loose wire strands and corrosion. The presence of white, fluffy deposits under the insulation at the cable terminal connection is a sign the cable is corroded and should be replaced. Check the terminals for distortion, missing mounting bolts or nuts and corrosion.
3   If only the positive cable is to be replaced, be sure to disconnect the negative cable from the battery first.
4   Disconnect and remove the cable from the vehicle. Make sure the replacement cable is the same length and diameter.
5   Clean the threads of the starter or ground connection with a wire brush to remove rust and corrosion. Apply a light coat of petroleum jelly to the threads to ease installation and prevent future corrosion. Inspect the connections frequently to make sure they are clean and tight.
6   Attach the cable to the starter or ground connection and tighten the mounting nut securely.
7   Before connecting the new cables to the battery, make sure they reach the terminals without having to be stretched.
8   Connect the positive cable first, followed by the negative cable. Tighten the nuts and apply a thin coat of petroleum jelly to the terminal and cable connection.

5 Preglow system — description and testing

1   The fuel/air mixture in a diesel engine self-ignites as it is sprayed into the highly compressed and therefore very hot combustion chamber. Since this high compression and heat are not present when the engine is first started when cold, these models are equipped with a preglow system using glow plugs in the combustion chambers to start ignition.
2   When the engine is switched on with the engine cold, battery voltage is sent through the glow plugs which ignite the fuel/air mixture until normal operating temperature is achieved.
3   Due to the variety of preglow systems used and the special equipment and techniques required, checking by the home mechanic is confined to checking for loose or damaged connections and wires and checking the glow plugs (Section 6).

6 Glow plugs — checking and replacement

1   Two types of glow plugs are used on these models. Early models (prior to 1980) use a filament type glow plug while later models are equipped with pencil-type glow plugs.
2   The filament type glow plugs are wired in series to maintain the proper resistance throughout the preglow system. The current flows from cylinder number four (number five on five cylinder engines) through to cylinder number one and then to ground. Consequently a failure or short circuit in one plug will cause problems in those wired in series after it.
3   Pencil-type glow plugs are wired in parallel so that if one plug fails the others will still function.
4   On later models a relay timer located in the engine compartment on the firewall or left inner fender panel controls current flow to the glow plugs.

Checking

Filament-type (serial) glow plug
5   With the preglow system on, connect the negative probe of a voltmeter (set at the 0 to 30 volt range) to a good ground and the positive probe to first the input and then the output of the number four (or five, if applicable) glow plug as shown in the accompanying illustration.

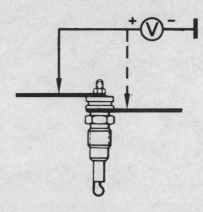

Fig. 5.3 Filament-type glow plug check (Sec 6)

6   If voltage is measured at the glow plug input and 0 volts at the output, the glow plug is faulty and must be replaced with a new one. If voltage passes through the plug, repeat the check on the remaining plugs, in order. **Caution:** *Do not short out the glow plugs to ground such as would happen if a screwdriver were placed between them and the engine block. This could seriously damage the timer relay.*

Pencil-type (parallel) glow plug
7   Unplug the glow plug connector at the relay (photo).

8   With the ignition Off, connect an ohmmeter (set on the 200 scale) to ground and each of the numbered glow plug terminals in turn (photo). An infinity reading on any plug terminal indicates that the plug or its related wiring is faulty and a new glow plug should be installed or the wiring repaired.

Replacement
9   Disconnect the negative battery cable.

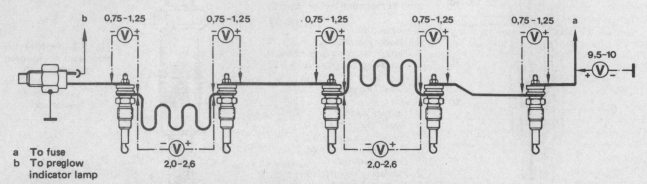

a   To fuse
b   To preglow
     indicator lamp

Fig. 5.4   Filament-type (series) glow plug electrical circuit

6.7   Grasp the glow plug connector securely and pull it off the timer relay in the direction shown

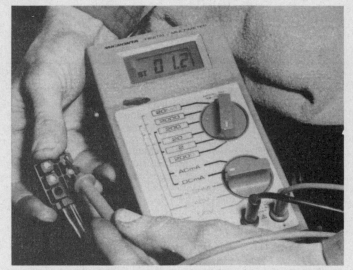

6.8   Checking the glow plug for continuity at the timer relay connector, using a voltmeter with the negative terminal probe grounded

6.10   The glow plug electrical connector is usually retained by a nut (arrow)

6.11   Unscrew the glow plug from the cylinder head using a wrench

10 Remove the nut and disconnect the glow plug wire (photo).
11 Unscrew the glow plug with a suitable wrench and remove it from the cylinder head (photo).
12 Screw the new glow plug into the cylinder head, tighten it securely and connect the wire.

7 Preglow timer relay — removal and installation

1 Disconnect the negative battery cable.
2 Remove the cover from the top of the relay and disconnect the electrical power lead retaining bolt and unplug the connectors from the relay (photo).
3 Remove the retaining bolts and lift the relay from the engine compartment.
4 Installation is the reverse of removal.

8 Charging system — general information and precautions

The charging system is made up of the alternator, voltage regulator and battery. These components work together to supply electrical power for the preglow system, lights, radio, etc.

The alternator is turned by a drivebelt at the front of the engine. When the engine is operating, voltage is generated by the internal components of the alternator to be sent to the battery for storage.

The purpose of the voltage regulator is to limit the alternator voltage to a preset value. This prevents power surges, circuit overloads, etc., during peak voltage output. On all models with which this manual is concerned, the voltage regulator is contained within the alternator housing.

The charging system does not ordinarily require periodic maintenance. The drivebelts, electrical wiring and connections should, however, be inspected at the intervals suggested in Chapter 1.

Take extreme care when making circuit connections to a vehicle equipped with an alternator and note the following. When making connections to the alternator from a battery, always match correct polarity. Before using arc welding equipment to repair any part of the vehicle, disconnect the wires from the alternator and the battery terminal. Never start the engine with a battery charger connected. Always disconnect both battery leads before using a battery charger.

9 Charging system — check

1 If a malfunction occurs in the charging circuit, do not immediately assume that the alternator is causing the problem.
First check the following items:
   a) The battery cables where they connect to the battery (make sure the connections are clean and tight).
   b) The battery electrolyte specific gravity (if it is low, charge the battery).
   c) Check the external alternator wiring and connections (they must be in good condition).
   d) Check the drivebelt condition and tension (see Chapter 1).
   e) Check the alternator mount and adjustment bolts for tightness.
   f) Run the engine and check the alternator for abnormal noise.
2 To check the overall operation of the charging system, connect a voltmeter to the battery terminals; positive (+) probe on the positive terminal and negative (−) probe on the negative terminal.
3 With the engine off, the voltage reading should be at least 12 volts. If it is not, have the battery charged. If it will not hold a charge so the reading is at least 12 volts, the battery should be replaced.
4 Turn the ignition On and check the voltage to make sure it drops slightly. Start the engine and run it at a fast idle. The voltage should now rise approximately 2 to 3 volts over the battery voltage of approximately 12 volts. Turn the headlights on and verify that the voltage does not rise or fall markedly.
5 If the voltage did not go up at all and remained below battery voltage, the indication is that the alternator or its related components are not operating properly. If the voltage continues to increase in relation to engine rpm or remains steady at a high reading (over 18 volts), the voltage regulator in the alternator is faulty. In either instance the system should be further checked by a properly equipped shop.

7.2 The glow plug timer relay (arrow) is located on the inner fender well on later models

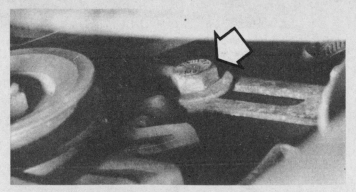

10.4a Alternator through-bolt location (arrow) as seen from under the vehicle

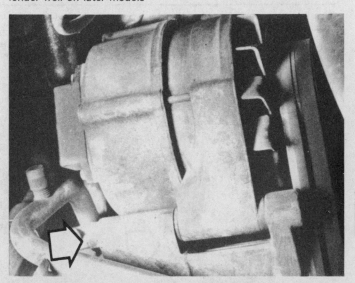

10.4b Alternator adjustment bolt (arrow) as seen from inside the engine compartment

10 Alternator — removal and installation

1 Disconnect the battery negative cable.
2 Loosen the adjustment and through-bolt, push the alternator toward the engine and remove the drivebelt.
3 Disconnect the wires from the alternator.
4 Remove the adjustment and through-bolts and lower the alternator from the engine (photos).
5 Installation is the reverse of removal.

11 Starting system — general information

The function of the starting system is to crank the engine. This system is composed of a starting motor, solenoid and battery. The battery supplies the electrical energy to the solenoid, which then completes the circuit to the starting motor, which does the actual work of cranking the engine.

The solenoid and starting motor are mounted together on the lower right side of the engine. No periodic lubrication or maintenance is required.

The electrical circuitry of the vehicle is arranged so that the starter motor can only be operated when the transmission selector lever is in Park or Neutral (automatic transmission) or when the clutch is depressed (manual transmission).

Never operate the starter motor for more than 30 seconds at a time without pausing to allow it to cool for at least two minutes. Excessive cranking can cause overheating, which can seriously damage the starter.

12 Starter motor — testing in vehicle

1   If the starter motor does not turn at all when the switch is operated, make sure that the shift lever is in Neutral or Park (automatic transmis-

sion) or Neutral with the clutch pedal all the way to the floor (manual transmission).

2   Make sure that the battery is charged and that all cables, both at the battery and starter solenoid terminals, are secure.

3   If, when the switch is actuated, the starter motor does not operate at all but the solenoid clicks, and the battery is fully charged, then the problem is in the main solenoid contacts or the starter motor itself.

4   If the solenoid plunger cannot be heard when the switch is actuated, the solenoid itself is defective or the solenoid circuit is open.

13 Starter motor — removal and installation

1   Disconnect the negative battery cable.

2   Raise the front of the vehicle and support it securely on jackstands.

3   Disconnect the wires from the starter solenoid (photo).

4   Remove the starter brace bolts from both the starter and the engine block (photo).

5   Remove the through-bolt and lower the steering track rod to provide clearance for the removal of the starter motor.

6   Remove the starter retaining bolts, using a suitable metric Allen head wrench (photo). On automatic transmission models, remove the filler tube bolt and have an assistant push the tube rearward to allow access to the upper bolt from in the engine compartment.

7   Lower the starter motor from the engine (photo).

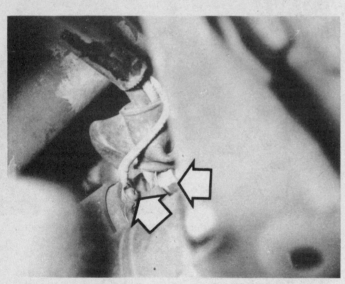

13.3   The starter electrical connections (arrows) can be reached from under the vehicle

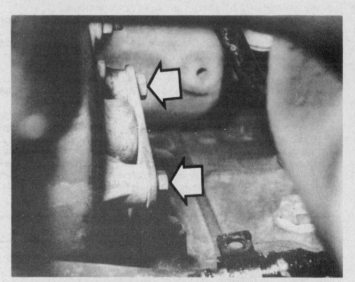

13.4   The starter brace bolts (arrows) are located at the front of the starter housing

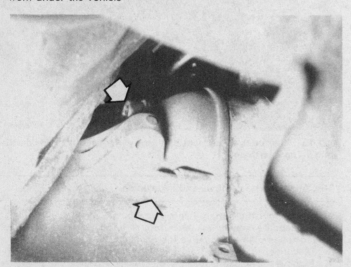

13.6   The starter bolts (arrows) are removed from the back of the bellhousing and are accessible from under the vehicle

13.7   Be sure to get a good grip on the starter motor because there is not a lot of room to maneuver it through the steering linkage and it is very heavy

14.2   The electrical cable is held on the starter solenoid by a nut (arrow)

8   Installation is the reverse of removal, taking care to tighten the steering track rod bolt to the specified torque.

14   Starter solenoid — removal and installation

1   Remove the starter motor (Section 13).
2   Disconnect the electrical lead from the rear of the solenoid (photo).
3   Remove the three screws retaining the solenoid to the starter housing (photo).
4   Slide the solenoid out of the starter housing (photo).
5   Installation is the reverse of removal.

14.3   The starter solenoid retaining screws (arrows)

14.4   Carefully withdraw the solenoid from the starter motor housing

5

Chapter 6 Emissions control systems

Contents

Exhaust Gas Recirculation (EGR) system (USA models) 2
General information 1

Positive Crankcase Ventilation (PCV) system 3

1 General information

To prevent pollution of the atmosphere from burned and evaporating gases, two emissions control systems are incorporated on the vehicles covered by this manual. These are:

Exhaust Gas Recirculation (EGR) (USA models only)
Positive Crankcase Ventilation (PCV)

The most frequent cause of emissions system problems is simply a loose or broken vacuum hose. Therefore, always check the hose connections first.

Pay close attention to any special precautions outlined in this Chapter. It should be noted that the illustrations of the various systems may not exactly match the system installed on your particular vehicle due to changes made by the manufacturer during production or from year to year.

A Vehicle Emissions Control Information label is located in the engine compartment of all vehicles sold in the USA and (on some models) the driver's door post. This label contains important emissions specifications as well as a vacuum hose schematic with emissions components identified. When servicing the engine or emissions systems, the VECI label in your particular vehicle should always be checked for up-to-date information.

Fig. 6.1 Typical vehicle emission control label locations on USA models (arrows) (Sec 1)

VEHICLE EMISSION CONTROL INFORMATION DAIMLER-BENZ AG. STUTTGART-UNTERTUERKHEIM

DISPLACEMENT: 2998 cm³ ENGINE FAMILY: BMB 3.0 D6JB5. APPROVED M.B. EMISSION CONTROL SYSTEM: DFI/EGR. INITIAL INJECTION: 24 DEG. BTDC. IDLE-RPM: 750 ± 50 MFR. ADJUSTED. TRANSMISSION IN NEUTRAL. ACCESSORIES NOT IN OPERATION. ADVERTISED HORSEPOWER: 83 HP. FUEL RATE AT ADV. HORSEPOWER: 41.5 mm³/STROKE. VALVE LASH AT WATER TEMP. BELOW 30°C: INTAKE 0.10 mm. EXHAUST 0.30 mm. VALVE LASH AT WATER TEMP. ABOVE 45°C: INTAKE 0.15 mm. EXHAUST 0.35 mm. MEASURED BETWEEN ROCKER ARM PAD AND CAM. THIS VEHICLE CONFORMS TO U. S. EPA AND STATE OF CALIFORNIA REGULATIONS APPLICABLE TO 1981 MODEL YEAR NEW MOTOR VEHICLES.

123 584 97 21

Fig. 6.2 Vehicle emission control labels contain important information (Sec 1)

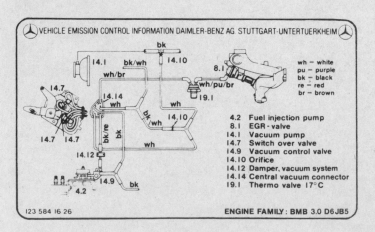

VEHICLE EMISSION CONTROL INFORMATION DAIMLER-BENZ AG. STUTTGART-UNTERTUERKHEIM

wh – white
pu – purple
bk – black
re – red
br – brown

4.2   Fuel injection pump
8.1   EGR - valve
14.1 Vacuum pump
14.7 Switch over valve
14.9 Vacuum control valve
14.10 Orifice
14.12 Damper, vacuum system
14.14 Central vacuum connector
19.1 Thermo valve 17°C

123 584 16 26

ENGINE FAMILY : BMB 3.0 D6JB5

Fig. 6.3 Some vehicles also have a label showing the vacuum hose routing (Sec 1)

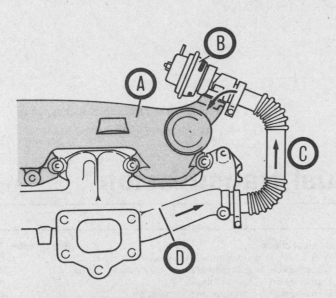

Fig. 6.4 Typical EGR system component layout (turbocharged model shown) (Sec 2)

A *Intake manifold*   C *Corrugated tubing*
B *EGR valve*   D *Exhaust manifold*

2.6   The EGR valve (at top of photo) can be removed after removing the bolts (arrows) and separating the flexible pipe

2 Exhaust Gas Recirculation (EGR) system (USA models)

General description

1   The EGR system meters exhaust gases into the engine induction system through passages cast into the intake manifold. From there the exhaust gases pass into the fuel/air mixture for the purpose of lowering combustion temperatures, thereby reducing the amount of oxides of nitrogen (NOX) formed.
2   The amount of exhaust gas admitted is regulated by a vacuum controlled EGR valve in response to engine operating conditions. A combination of temperature sensors threaded into the water passages, switchover valves and the throttle linkage control the operation of the EGR valve.
3   Common engine problems associated with the EGR system are poor engine performance, black or blue smoke, poor starting and combustion knocking under partial load.

Checking

4   Refer to Chapter 1 for EGR valve checking procedures.
5   If the EGR valve appears to be in proper operating condition, carefully check all hoses connected to the valve for breaks, leaks or kinks. Replace or repair the valve/hoses as necessary. Further checking should be left to your dealer or a properly equipped shop because of the special tools and techniques required.

Component Replacement

6   The EGR valve can be replaced by disconnecting the vacuum hose and valve-to-exhaust manifold crossover pipe and removing the retaining bolts (photo).

3 Positive Crankcase Ventilation (PCV) system

General description

1   The positive crankcase ventilation system reduces hydrocarbon emissions by circulating fresh air through the crankcase to pick up blow-by gases, which are then rerouted through the intake manifold to be burned in the engine.
2   The main components of this system are the vent insert, connection fitting, oil separator and the differential pressure valve which regulate the flow of gases according to engine speed and manifold vacuum.

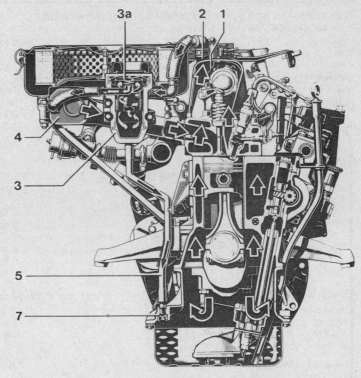

Fig. 6.5 Typical Positive Crankcase Ventilation (PCV) system component layout (Sec 3)

1 *Vent insert to make sure*   3a *Differential pressure valve*
   air is not drawn into it   4   *Intake manifold*
2 *Connection fitting*   5   *Return line*
3 *Oil separator*   7   *Check valve*

Checking

3   The PCV system is basically maintenance-free. Checking consists of inspecting the system hoses for damage or cracks, replacing as necessary.

Chapter 7 Part A Manual transmission

Contents

Countershaft and input shaft — disassembly and reassembly . 5
General information 1
Gearshift — adjustment 9
Housings and bearings — inspection 7
Manual transmission oil change .... See Chapter 1
Mainshaft — disassembly and reassembly 4
Oil level check.......................... See Chapter 1
Shift cover — disassembly and reassembly ....,... 6
Transmission — disassembly into major components 3
Transmission — reassembly 8
Transmission — removal and installation 2

Specifications

Transmission shift lever Neutral setting dimensions
4-speed (Fig. 7A.24)

A	142 mm (5.59 in)
B	58 mm (2.285 in)
C	111 mm (4.37 in)

5-speed (Fig. 7A.25)

A	168 mm (6.62 in)
B	86 mm (3.388 in)
C	95 mm (3.743 in)
Shift lever dimension a (Fig. 7A.26)	1.5 mm (0.059 in)

Overhaul dimensions

Speedometer input shaft-to-cover edge clearance A (Fig. 7A.20)	19 mm (0.749 in)
Endplay limits	
Input shaft	0 to 0.05 mm (0 to 0.00197 in)
Main shaft	0 to 0.05 mm (0 to 0.00197 in)
Countershaft......................................	0.07 to 0.15 mm (0.0027 to 0.0059 in)
Bearings	0 to 0.05 mm (0 to 0.00197 in)
Synchro ring-to-dog teeth wear limit	0.5 mm (0.0197) or less

Five-speed transmission selector rod coding (on end of fork)
Spacer thickness

Red dot	3.8 mm (0.149 in)
No dot	3.9 mm (0.154 in)
White dot	4.0 mm (0.158 in)

Torque specifications	Nm	Ft-lbs
Drive flange nut		
Four-speed	150	111
Five-speed	160	118
Mainshaft nut....................................	80	59
Countershaft nut	150	111
Filler and drain plugs	60	44
Cover bolts (four-speed)	15	11
Detent plug	24	18
Front and rear cover bolts		
7 mm bolts	20	15
10 mm bolts..................................	45	33
Shift cover bolts (5-speed)	15	11
Shift cover locking cage fastening bolt	25	18
Exhaust pipe brace bolts...........................	20	15

1 General information

The manual four-or five-speed transmission used on these models features synchromesh on all forward speeds. The four-speed and five-speed versions are very similar with the fifth gear of the five-speed located in a housing on the rear of the transmission. As a result, many of the repair procedures are similar.

When contemplating an overhaul of the transmission, due consideration should be given to the fact that it may be more economical to obain a rebuilt or good secondhand transmission rather than install new parts in the existing transmission.

2 Transmission — removal and installation

1 Raise the vehicle and support it securely on jackstands.
2 Disconnect the battery negative lead.
3 Remove the exhaust system, as described in Chapter 4.
4 Support the transmission with a jack and remove the rear transmission mount and the crossmember from the underbody.
5 Unscrew the nuts and clamp, and remove the exhaust bracket from the rear of the transmission, noting the direction in which it is installed.
6 Remove the driveshaft (Chapter 8).
7 Disconnect the shift linkage.
8 Disconnect the speedometer cable and fasten it out the way.
9 Remove the clutch slave cylinder and hydraulic line (Chapter 8) and fasten it out of the way with a piece of wire.
10 Remove the starter motor (Chapter 5).
11 Lower the jack a little and support the engine with another jack or blocks of wood.
12 Remove the bolts securing the transmission to the engine, then, with the help of an assistant, withdraw the transmission from the engine and remove it from under the car. Do not allow the weight of the transmission to hang on the input shaft and make sure that the car is adequately supported, since a little rocking may be necessary to free the transmission.
13 Installation is a reversal of removal, making sure to check that the clutch release arm and bearing are not binding and the clutch disc is aligned with the transmission input shaft. Lubricate the input shaft splines with a thin coat of moly-base grease. Check the transmission oil level, adding as necessary. When engaging the input shaft with the clutch disc it will be helpful to temporarily shift the transmission into top gear and then turn the rear drive flange.

3 Transmission — disassembly into major components

1 Clean the exterior of the transmission thoroughly with solvent and wipe dry.
2 Remove the clutch release arm and bearing, unscrew the nuts and remove the clutch housing from the front of the transmission using a plastic mallet, if necessary.
3 Unscrew the drain plug and drain the oil into a suitable container. Reinstall the drain plug.
4 From the left side of the transmission, loosen the clamp bolt on the center shift lever for revese gear (and, on five-speed versions, 5th gear), mark the lever in relation to the shaft then withdraw it from the spines.
5 Pry off the circlip and remove the washer from the shaft.
6 Unscrew the shift cover bolts and tap the cover from the locating dowels while at the same time tapping the reverse (and 5th if applicable) shaft inwards. Insert your fingers behind the cover and disconnect the shift forks from the rockers, then tilt the top of the cover outwards and lift it from the transmission.
7 Unbolt the front cover from the transmission housing, noting the location of the shims for adjustment of the bearing endplay.
Remove the gasket. Leave the clutch release bearing guide tube attached to the cover at this stage.
8 Hold the rear drive flange stationary with a metal bar bolted to it then use a slotted box wrench to unscrew the special nut.
9 Remove the drive flange from the splines with a suitable puller.
10 Remove the retaining bolts from the rear cover and tap it from the transmission casing. Remove the gasket.
11 Pull the speedometer worm drive gear from the rear end of the mainshaft.

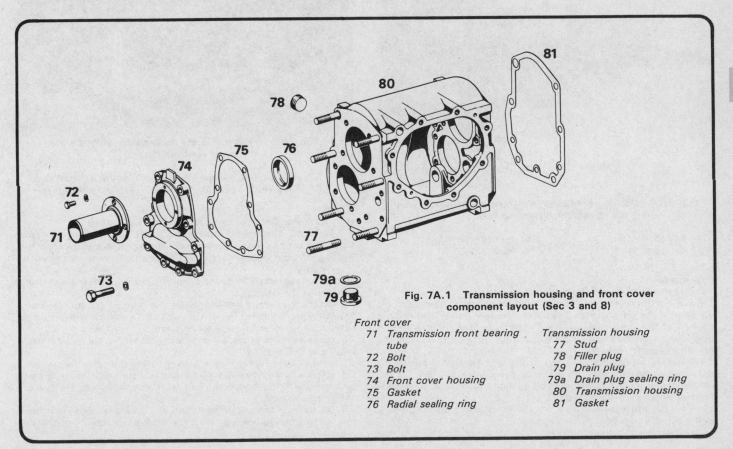

Fig. 7A.1 Transmission housing and front cover component layout (Sec 3 and 8)

Front cover
71 *Transmission front bearing tube*
72 *Bolt*
73 *Bolt*
74 *Front cover housing*
75 *Gasket*
76 *Radial sealing ring*

Transmission housing
77 *Stud*
78 *Filler plug*
79 *Drain plug*
79a *Drain plug sealing ring*
80 *Transmission housing*
81 *Gasket*

7A

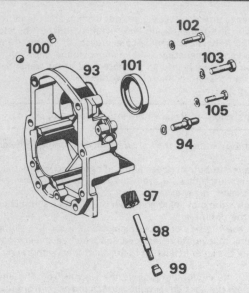

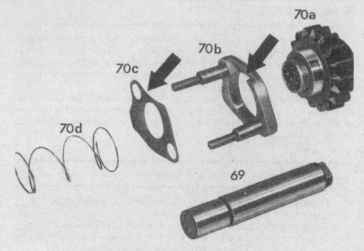

Fig. 7A.2 Transmission rear cover component layout
(Sec 3 and 8)

93	Rear cover housing	101	Mainshaft sealing ring
94	Collar bolt	102	Bolt
97	Speedometer drivegear	103	Bolt
98	Speedometer driveshaft	105	Bolt
100	Plug or steel ball		

Fig. 7A.3 Reverse idler gear synchronizer brake
component layout (Sec 3)

69	Idler shaft	70c	Thrust plate
70a	Reverse idler gear	70d	Spring
70b	Synchro ring		

Fig. 7A.4   Details of removing the input shaft bearing from
the transmission housing (Sec 3)

1a	Slotted nut	6	Oil thrower
3a	Bearing	7a	Input shaft

Fig. 7A.5   View inside the transmission with the shift
cover removed (Sec 3)

63	Reverse/5th selector dog	106	3rd/4th selector fork
65	Reverse/5th selector rod	107	1st/2nd selector fork

Four-speed

12 Pull the reverse gear from the mainshaft.

13 Pull out the reverse idler shaft then disconnect the idler gear from the fork on the selector rod. If necessary, screw a slide hammer into the end of the shaft to remove it. On some models the idler gear is fitted with a synchronizer brake which must be withdrawn from the housing together with the thrust plate and spring.

14 Remove the nut from the rear of the countershaft and lever off the reverse gear. In order to hold the countershaft stationary, temporarily install the drive flange and bolt a length of bar to it, then place the transmission in fourth gear.

15 With Neutral engaged, remove the selector forks from the grooves in the synchro sleeves.

16 Using a pin punch, drive the roll pin from the reverse selector dog

then withdraw the selector shaft and remove the dog.

17 Move the synchro unit sleeves to select two gears at the same time, then bend back the peened collar (if applicable) and unscrew the bearing nut from the front of the countershaft using a slotted wrench, if necessary.

18 Flatten the tab washers and unbolt the bearing retaining plate from the rear of the casing.

19 On models with a ball-bearing on the front of the countershaft, follow the procedure in Steps 20 through 25. On models with a tapered roller bearing, refer to Steps 26 through 33.

20 Using a bearing puller, extract the countershaft front and rear bearings from the housing.

21 Extract the mainshaft rear bearing, using the same procedure.

22 Install a suitable length of metal tube over the rear of the mainshaft and retain with the drive flange nut, in order to retain the 1st gear on the needle bearing.

23 Lift the rear of the mainshaft and withdraw the input shaft from the front of the housing. Remove the 4th gear synchro ring and the needle bearing.

Fig. 7A.6 Removing the mainshaft assembly (Sec 3)

11a Synchro sleeve in 3rd position

Fig. 7A.7 Driving the countershaft with tapered roller-type bearing from the housing (Sec 3)

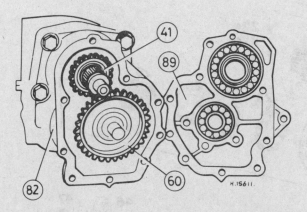

Fig. 7A.8 Removing the intermediate plate (5-speed transmission) (Sec 3)

41 5th gear (mainshaft)	*82 Intermediate housing*
60 5th gear (countershaft)	*89 Intermediate plate*

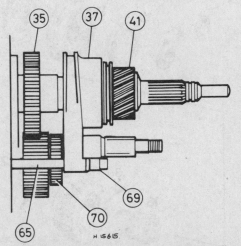

Fig. 7A.9 5-speed transmission gear layout (intermediate housing removed) (Sec 3)

35 Reverse gear (mainshaft)	*65 Reverse/5th selector rod*
37 5th synchro unit	*69 Reverse idler gear shaft*
41 5th gear (mainshaft)	*70 Reverse idler gear*

7A

24 Push the 3rd/4th synchro sleeve into 3rd speed position, then move the mainshaft assembly rearwards and withdraw it through the side aperture.

25 Move the countershaft rearwards, then withdraw it through the side aperture.

26 Use a bearing puller to extract the countershaft rear bearing from the housing.

27 Using a slotted box wrench, remove the slotted nut from the input shaft. Grip the input shaft in a soft jawed vice to hold it stationary.

28 Lever the input shaft bearing from the casing and shaft, using two screwdrivers.

29 Using a bearing puller, extract the mainshaft rear bearing from the housing.

30 With the help of an assistant, lift the input shaft and mainshaft together and use a plastic mallet to drive the countershaft and taper roller bearing rearwards from the housing, after first temporarily installing the nut on the front of the shaft.

31 With the countershaft in the bottom of the housing, withdraw the input shaft and bearing. Remove the 4th gear synchro ring and the needle bearing.

32 Push the 3rd/4th synchro sleeve into 3rd speed position, then move the mainshaft assembly rearwards and withdraw it through the opening in the side of the housing.

33 Move the countershaft rearwards, then withdraw it through the housing side opening.

Five-speed

34 Remove the selector forks from the grooves in the synchro sleeves.

35 Remove the nut from the rear of the countershaft using a slotted box wrench where applicable. In order to hold the countershaft stationary, temporarily move the synchro unit sleeves to select two gears at a time.

36 Unbolt the intermediate plate and withdraw it together with the bearings, using a soft-faced mallet to release it from the shafts. The countershaft bearing may in fact remain on the shaft if tight.

37 Using a two-legged puller, remove the 5th gear (and bearing if tight) from the countershaft.

38 Unbolt the intermediate housing from the casing, and remove the gasket.

39 Using a pin punch, drive the roll pin from the reverse/5th selector dog and move the dog forward as far as possible.

40 Extract the reverse/5th detent holder together with the detent spring and ball from the side of the casing.

41 Pull out the reverse idler shaft, then disconnect the idler gear from the fork on the selector rod.

42 Slide the 5th gear, together with the needle bearing and synchro ring from the mainshaft.

43 Using a two-legged puller on the reverse gear, pull the reverse gear and 5th synchro unit from the mainshaft. At the same time withdraw the reverse/5th selector rod from the housing and remove the dog. At this time also remove the 5th gear needle bearing race. Note that

there is a spacer between the synchro unit and reverse gear.

44 Pry the Wooduff key from the countershaft and slide off the spacer. Remove the reverse gear from the splines, using a puller if necessary.

45 Pry both Woodruff keys from the mainshaft.

46 Move the synchro unit sleeves to select two gears at the same time, then bend back the peening, if applicable, and unscrew the bearing nut from the front of the countershaft, using a slotted box wrench if applicable.

47 Unbolt the bearing retaining plate from the rear of the housing and recover the endplay shims.

48 Extract the inner circlip from the input shaft then use a bearing puller to remove the bearing from the housing and input shaft. Remove the oil thrower.

49 Remove the mainshaft rear bearing.

50 Place a suitable length of metal tube over the rear of the mainshaft and retain with the drive flange nut, in order to retain the 1st gear on the needle bearing.

51 On models with a ball-bearing on the front of the countershaft, use a bearing puller to extract the bearing from the housing and countershaft.

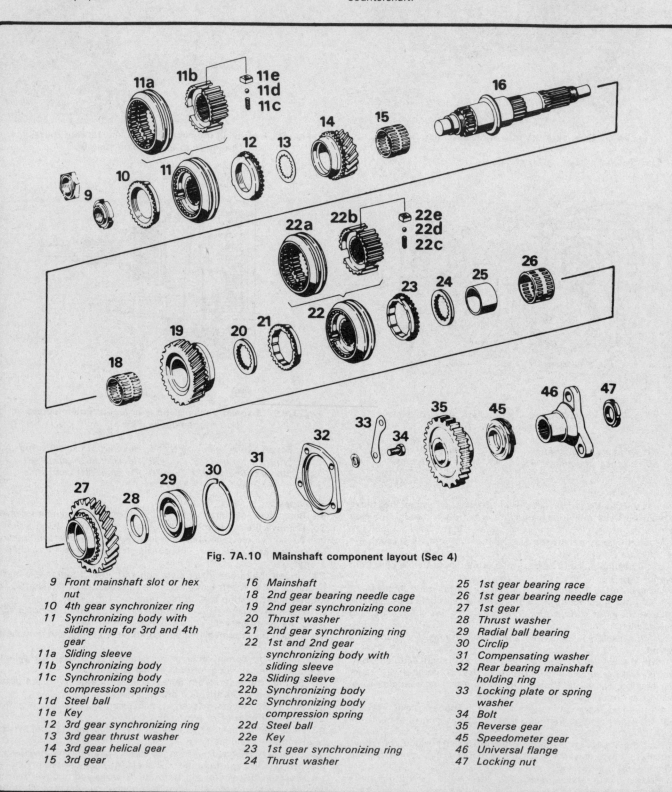

Fig. 7A.10 Mainshaft component layout (Sec 4)

9 Front mainshaft slot or hex nut	16 Mainshaft	25 1st gear bearing race
10 4th gear synchronizer ring	18 2nd gear bearing needle cage	26 1st gear bearing needle cage
11 Synchronizing body with sliding ring for 3rd and 4th gear	19 2nd gear synchronizing cone	27 1st gear
	20 Thrust washer	28 Thrust washer
11a Sliding sleeve	21 2nd gear synchronizing ring	29 Radial ball bearing
11b Synchronizing body	22 1st and 2nd gear synchronizing body with sliding sleeve	30 Circlip
11c Synchronizing body compression springs		31 Compensating washer
11d Steel ball	22a Sliding sleeve	32 Rear bearing mainshaft holding ring
11e Key	22b Synchronizing body	33 Locking plate or spring washer
12 3rd gear synchronizing ring	22c Synchronizing body compression spring	34 Bolt
13 3rd gear thrust washer	22d Steel ball	35 Reverse gear
14 3rd gear helical gear	22e Key	45 Speedometer gear
15 3rd gear	23 1st gear synchronizing ring	46 Universal flange
	24 Thrust washer	47 Locking nut

52 Using a soft-faced mallet, drive the countershaft (and front tapered roller bearing, if applicable) rearwards while an assistant lifts the mainshaft and input shaft.

53 With the countershaft in the bottom of the housing, withdraw the input shaft and bearing. Remove the 4th synchro ring and the needle bearing.

54 Push the 3rd/4th synchro sleeve into 3rd speed position then move the mainshaft assembly rearwards and withdraw it through the housing side opening.

55 Move the countershaft rearwards then withdraw it through the side opening.

4 Mainshaft — disassembly and reassembly

1 Temporarily install the drive flange to the rear of the mainshaft and place the flange securely in a vise with the mainshaft vertical.

2 Unscrew the nut from the front of the mainshaft using a slotted box wrench where necessary and remove the 3rd/4th synchro unit and synchro ring.

3 Remove the serrated thrust washer (if fitted) followed by 3rd gear and the needle bearing.

4 Remove the mainshaft from the vise, then from the rear, remove the thrust washer, 1st gear and the needle bearing rollers.

5 Place the mainshaft upright in the open vise with the 2nd gear at the bottom, then use a soft-faced mallet to drive the mainshaft down until the 1st gear needle bearing inner race is free.

6 Remove the mainshaft from the vise and withdraw the inner race followed by the thrust washer (if installed), 1st synchro ring, 1st/2nd synchro unit and 2nd synchro ring.

7 Remove the thrust washer (if installed), 2nd gear and needle bearing.

8 Clean all components in solvent, wipe dry and inspect them for wear and damage. Press each synchro ring onto its respective gear cone, then use a feeler blade to determine the clearance between the dog teeth. If the clearance is less than specified, replace the synchro ring. If the synchro unit is to be dismantled to replace worn components, first inspect the unit to see whether it incorporates coil or circular type springs.

9 To dismantle a coil spring type synchro unit, wrap a cloth around it, mark the hub in relation to the sleeve and then press the hub out of the sleeve. As the hub is ejected, the keys, balls and springs will be displaced (spring guides are provided on the 5th synchro). Replace the components as necessary and then reassemble them by inserting the springs and keys into the hub and, while holding the keys depressed partially insert the hub into the sleeve. Locate one ball at a time and when all three are installed, push the hub fully home. Install the hubs into the sleeves in accordance with the accompanying illustrations. Note that the 1st/2nd synchro keys have a chamfer on one corner.

Fig. 7A.11 Checking synchro-ring wear using a feeler gauge (Sec 4)

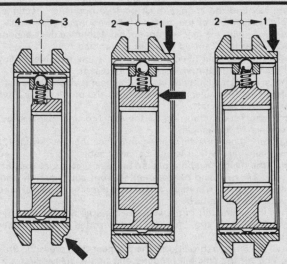

Fig. 7A.12 Cross-section view of the coil spring-type synchro units (Sec 4)

7A

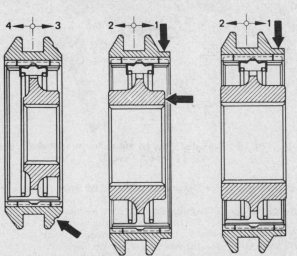

Fig. 7A.13 Cross-section view of the circular spring-type synchro units (Sec 4)

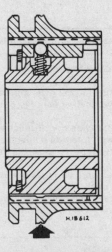

Fig. 7A.14 Cross-section view of the coil spring-type 5th synchro unit (Sec 4)

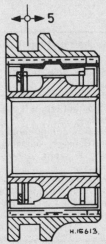

Fig. 7A.15 Cross-section view of the circular spring-type 5th synchro unit (Sec 4)

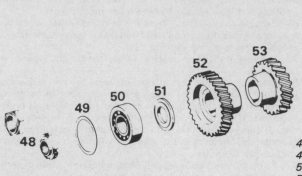

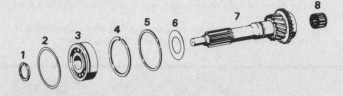

Fig. 7A.16 4-speed transmission countershaft component layout (Sec 5)

48　Slot or hex nut
49　Compensating washer
50　Radial ball bearing
51　Countershaft spacing washer
52　Countershaft helical gear
53　Countershaft helical gear (for 3rd gear)
54　Countershaft helical gear (for 1st and 2nd gear)
55　Woodruff key
57　Radial ball bearing
58　Reverse gear countershaft
62　Slot or hex nut

Make sure that the chamber faces toward the 2nd gear.

10　To dismantle a circular spring type synchro unit, mark the hub in relationship to the sleeve then remove the circlip (5th synchro only), push the hub from the sleeve and extract the keys and springs. replace components as necessary and then reassemble them so that the hub to sleeve relationship is in accordance with diagrams accompanying illustrations. Note that the angled ends of the springs must not be in the same key and the springs must point in opposite directions.

11　Begin reassembly of the mainshaft by mounting it vertically in a soft-jawed vise with the rear end uppermost. Lubricate the components with clean gear lubricant as they are assembled.

12　Install the 2nd gear needle bearing up to the shoulder, followed by 2nd gear and the thrust washer (if installed).

13　Install the 2nd synchro ring on the 2nd gear then press the 1st/2nd synchro unit on the splines with the flanged end of the sleeve towards the rear of the mainshaft.

14　Install the 1st synchro ring on the synchro unit followed by the thrust washer (if applicable).

15　Heat the 1st gear needle bearing inner race then quickly tap it fully onto the mainshaft with a length of metal tube.

16　Install the needle bearing rollers, 1st gear and thrust washer. To prevent the 1st gear and needle bearing from subsequently coming off, temporarily place a suitable metal tube over the mainshaft and retain it with the flange nut.

17　Invert the mainshaft in the vise, then install the 3rd gear needle bearing followed by the 3rd gear and serrated thrust washer (if applicable).

18　Install the 3rd synchro ring on the 3rd gear then press the 3rd/4th synchro unit on the splines, grooved end of the sleeve first.

19　Install the nut to the front of the mainshaft and tighten to the specified torque, then lock by peening the collar into the groove in the shaft.

5　Countershaft and input shaft — disassembly and reassembly

1　Where applicable, pull the tapered bearing from the front of the countershaft.

2　Rest the 3rd gear in the open vise with the largest gear uppermost and press the countershaft out in a downwards direction. Pry out the Woodruff key.

3　Clean all the components in solvent and wipe dry. Inspect them for wear and damage, replacing as necessary. Note that if the tapered-type bearing is worn, only a ball bearing-type is available for a replacement.

4　Install the Woodruff key and press the gears on in reverse order making sure that the gear shoulders face each other.

5　Pull the bearing from the input shaft and replace if necessary. Install in reverse order and tighten the nut securely where applicable.

6　Shift cover — disassembly and reassembly

1　Mark the shift levers in relation to the shafts then slide them from the splines.

Fig. 7A.17　Input shaft component layout (Sec 5)

1　Circlip
2　Compensating washer
3　Ball bearing
4　Circlip
5　Spacer
6　Oil thrower
7　Input shaft
8　Needle bearing

Fig. 7A.18　Exploded view of the earlier model shift cover (4-speed) (Sec 6)

108　Shift rocker for 3rd and 4th gear
108a　Shift lever for 3rd and 4th gear
109　Locking cage
110　Shift rocker for 1st and 2nd gear
111　O-ring
112　Shift finger for reverse gear
112a　Shift lever for reverse gear
114　Shift cover
116　Breather
118　Bushing
119　Needle bearing
120　Washer
121　Circlilp
122　Bolt
123　Lock or spring washer

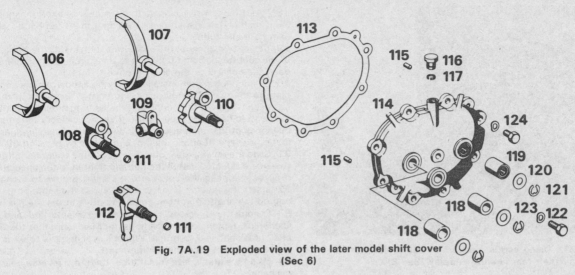

Fig. 7A.19   Exploded view of the later model shift cover
(Sec 6)

106	3rd and 4th speed shift fork	110	1st and 2nd speed
107	1st and 2nd speed shift fork		shift rocker
108	3rd and 4th speed shift	111	O-ring
	rocker	112	Reverse shift finger
109	Locking cage	113	Gasket
		114	Shift cover

115	Pin	120	Washer
116	Breather	121	Lock washer
117	Circlip	122	Bolt
118	Bushing	123	Lock or spring washer
119	Needle bearing	124	Bolt

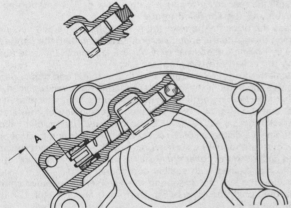

Fig. 7A.20   Cross-section view of the speedometer drive
gear (Sec 7)

A   Speedometer input shaft-to-
transmission cover clearance

2   Extract the C-clips from the shafts and remove the washers.
3   Pull out the shift rockers and finger.
4   Flatten the locktab (if installed) then unscrew the central bolt and pull out the locking cage. Note the locating pin in the cover.
5   Clean all the components in solvent and wipe dry. Inspect for wear and damage, replacing components as necessary. If the shaft bearings are worn, drive them out with a brass or aluminum drift and install new ones. Replace the O-ring seals.
6   Reassembly is a reversal of dismantling, taking care to lubricate the shafts with clean transmission oil.

7   Housings and bearings- inspection

1   Examine the housings for wear, cracks and damage and check the bearings for wear by spinning them by hand — replace the bearings if roughness or uneven movement is evident.
2   Replace all oil seals and gaskets. To replace the front cover oil seal, unbolt the clutch release bearing guide tube, then drive out the seal with a metal tube. The new seal should be driven in flush. Smear sealing compound on the guide tube bolts before inserting them, but do not fully tighten until after the transmission has been reassembled and the clutch housing installed.

3   To replace the rear cover oil seal, use a screwdriver or similar tool to pry it out. Use a hammer and a block of wood to drive the new seal in carefully and evenly so that it flush with the housing.
4   Check the speedometer drivegear in the rear cover for wear and replace it if necessary. To remove it use a soft metal drift to drive the shaft through the gear and out of the cover. Note that the sealing ball or plug will be pushed out, but the plug can be levered out first with a screwdriver. Extract the seal by screwing a bolt into it and pulling on the bolt. Installation is a reversal of removal, referring to the accompanying illustration. Before installing the sealing plug however, coat it with sealing compound.

8   Transmission — reassembly

1   Insert the countershaft through the housing side aperture and lower it to the bottom.
2   With the 3rd/4th synchro sleeve in the 3rd speed position, insert the mainshaft assembly into the housing.
3   Install the needle bearing in the input shaft and locate the 4th synchro ring onto the gear cone.

Five-speed
4   Insert the input shaft and engage it with the mainshaft.
5   While an assistant lifts the mainshaft and input shaft, raise the countershaft and, on tapered roller-type bearings, drive it forward until the bearing is in the housing. Install the rear (and front, where applicable) countershaft bearings, using suitable size metal tubes to drive them into the housing.
6   Install the oil thrower and bearing on the input shaft, then use a metal tube to drive the bearing fully into the housing. Support the mainshaft while installing the bearing, and make sure that the 4th synchro ring remains in place.
7   Install the inner circlip to the input shaft.
8   Remove the tube from the mainshaft and install the rear bearing into the housing using a suitable size metal tube while supporting the input shaft.
9   Move the synchro unit sleeves to select two gears at the same time then install the bearing nut to the front of the countershaft and tighten it to the specified torque. Where applicable peen the nut collar into the shaft groove.
10 Select neutral, then install the bearing endplay shims and retaining plate to the rear of the housing and tighten the bolts. If the bearing has been replaced, the endplay of the bearing outer track must be set

7A

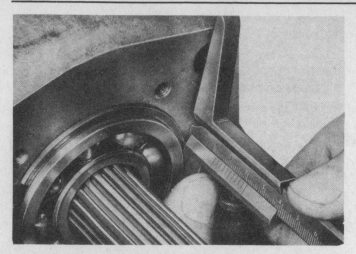

Fig. 7A.21 Using vernier calipers to determine the mainshaft rear bearing endplay (Sec 8)

to within the specified limits by using vernier calipers to determine the distances of the bearing circlip and retaining plate shoulder from the mating surface. If applicable, lock the bolts by bending the locktabs.

11 Install the spacer on the countershaft and press the reverse gear on the splines, then tap the Woodruff key in the groove.

12 Tap the two Woodruff keys into the mainshaft grooves.

13 Using a length of metal tubing, drive the reverse gear onto the mainshaft key, followed by the spacer. The correct thickness of the spacer is dependent on the length of the selector rod in accordance with the color code dot on the rod itself. Refer to the table in Specifications.

14 Engage the reverse/5th selector rod fork with the sleeve groove on the 5th synchro unit then slide them into the housing and onto the mainshaft. At the same time locate the dog on the selector rod in the housing aperture.

15 Warm the 5th gear needle bearing race (in the hand will suffice) and locate it on the mainshaft against the synchro unit, while pulling the mainshaft rearwards.

16 Locate the synchro ring on the 5th gear cone then install the needle bearing and slide the 5th gear on it.

17 Locate the reverse idler gear in the selector fork, then insert the idler shaft through the gear and into the housing.

18 Move the reverse/5th selector rod into its central position and insert the detent ball and spring, after applying a small amount of lithium base grease to the components. Drive the holder into the housing to retain it.

19 Align the dog with the hole in the selector rod, then drive in the roll pin.

20 Install the intermediate housing, together with a new gasket. Apply sealing compound to the threads of the bolts before inserting them and tightening them finger tight. Note that the locating pin on the reverse idler shaft must face outwards in order to engage the cut-out in the housing.

21 The intermediate housing must be centered in relation to the intermediate plate before finally tightening the bolts. To do this remove the bearings from the plate, install the plate to the housing and check that the bearings can be pushed freely into the plate. Re-position the housing as necessary then tighten the outer bolts. Remove the intermediate plate and bearings and tighten the inner bolts.

22 Using the metal tube, drive the 5th gear onto the end of the countershaft.

23 install a new gasket to the intermediate plate, having first installted the bearings, then locate the plate over the mainshaft and countershaft onto the locating pins, insert the bolts and tighten.

24 Temporarily locate the countershaft by selecting two gears at the same time, then install the nut to the countershaft and tighten to the specified torque. Where applicable peen the nut and lock it.

25 install the selector forks to the grooves in the synchro sleeves in the housing side aperture.

Four-speed

26 Insert the input shaft in the housing and engage it with the front of the mainshaft.

27 Remove the metal tube from the mainshaft then drive the rear bearing onto the mainshaft and into the housing while supporting the input shaft.

28 Invert the transmission so that the countershaft meshes with the input shaft and mainshaft gears then drive in the front and rear bearings using a metal tube.

29 Select two gears at the same time then install the nut to the front of the countershaft and tighten it to the specified torque. If applicable peen the collar into the shaft groove to lock it.

30 Select neutral then install the bearing endplay shims and retaining plate to the rear of the housing and tighten the bolts. If the bearing has been replaced, the endplay of the bearing outer track must be set to the specified clearance by using vernier calipers to determine the distances of the bearing circlip and retaining plate shoulder from the mating surface. If applicable, lock the bolts by bending the locktabs.

31 Slide the reverse gear onto the rear of the countershaft then, with two gears selected install the nut and tighten to the specified torque. If applicable peen the collar into the shaft groove to lock it.

32 Insert the reverse selector shaft and at the same time locate the dog on the shaft. Align the holes and drive in the roll pin to secure.

33 Engage the reverse idler gear with the selector fork and insert the idler shaft, tapping it into the housing. Make sure that the flat on the end of the shaft is uppermost. Where a synchronizer brake is installed, the recess must face the countershaft.

34 Using a suitable size metal tube, drive the reverse gear onto the mainshaft.

35 Install the selector forks to the grooves in the synchro sleeves in the housing side aperture and engage neutral.

All models

36 Using a metal tube, drive the speedometer worm drive gear onto the mainshaft with the chamfered end to the rear.

37 Install the rear cover together with a new gasket and tighten the bolts evenly to the specified torque.

38 Press the drive flange onto the mainshaft splines and secure by tightening the nut to the specified torque while holding the flange stationary by bolting a metal bar to it. Where applicable lock the nut by peening the collar into the groove.

39 Install the front cover together with the shims and a new gasket and tighten the bolts. If the input shaft bearing has been replaced, the endplay of the bearing outer track must be set to that specified. If the countershaft bearing has been replaced, the endplay of the bearing outer track must be set to within Specifications. Use vernier calipers to determine the distances of the cover shoulders, bearing track or bearing circlip from the mating surface, but add the thickness of the compressed gasket to the cover dimensions. Note that the threads of the bolts must be sealed with sealing compound.

40 Position the selector forks and the reverse/5th selector shaft in neutral, then push the reverse/5th shift shaft about 1 inch (24 mm) through the cover.

41 Install the shift cover, together with a new gasket, while at the same time engaging the reverse/5th finger with the dog and the selector

Fig. 7A.22 During 4-speed transmission rear cover installation, note the location of the fitted sleeve (A) and that the milled surface of the reverse shaft (arrow) is on top (Sec 8)

forks with the rockers. Apply sealing compound on the bolt threads prior to installation.

42 Place the washer on the reverse/5th shift shaft and install the circlip.

43 Press the shift lever on the splines in the previously noted position and tighten the clamp bolt.

44 Fill the transmission with the specified oil to the bottom of the filler plug hole, install the plug and tighten it securely.

45 Install the clutch housing to the front of the transmission and tighten the nuts. If the clutch release bearing guide tube has been removed, tighten the bolts now.

46 Install the clutch release arm and bearing (Chapter 8).

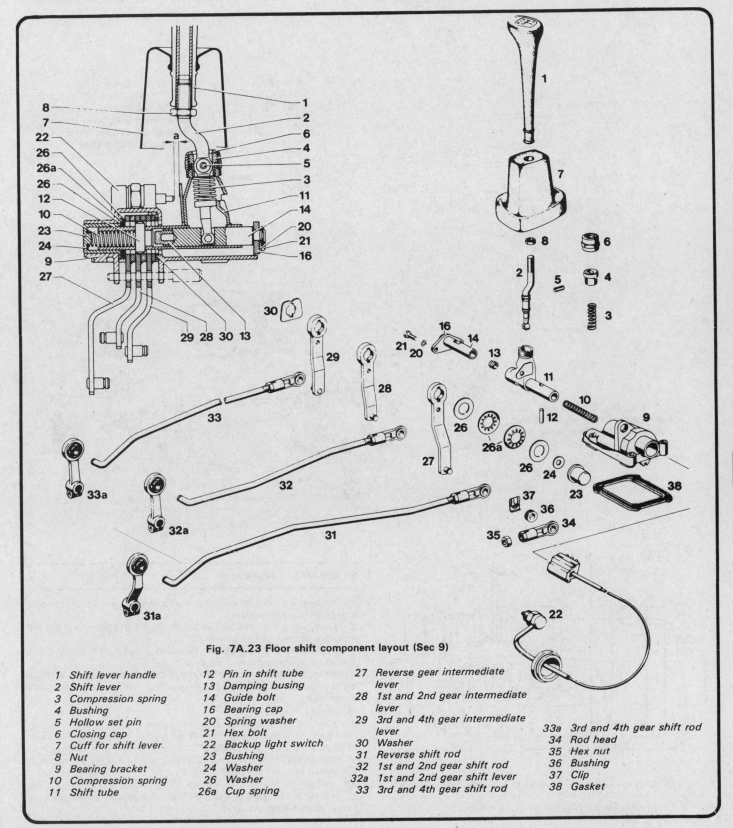

Fig. 7A.23 Floor shift component layout (Sec 9)

1 Shift lever handle	12 Pin in shift tube	27 Reverse gear intermediate lever
2 Shift lever	13 Damping busing	28 1st and 2nd gear intermediate lever
3 Compression spring	14 Guide bolt	29 3rd and 4th gear intermediate lever
4 Bushing	16 Bearing cap	30 Washer
5 Hollow set pin	20 Spring washer	31 Reverse shift rod
6 Closing cap	21 Hex bolt	32 1st and 2nd gear shift rod
7 Cuff for shift lever	22 Backup light switch	32a 1st and 2nd gear shift lever
8 Nut	23 Bushing	33 3rd and 4th gear shift rod
9 Bearing bracket	24 Washer	33a 3rd and 4th gear shift rod
10 Compression spring	26 Washer	34 Rod head
11 Shift tube	26a Cup spring	35 Hex nut
		36 Bushing
		37 Clip
		38 Gasket

7A

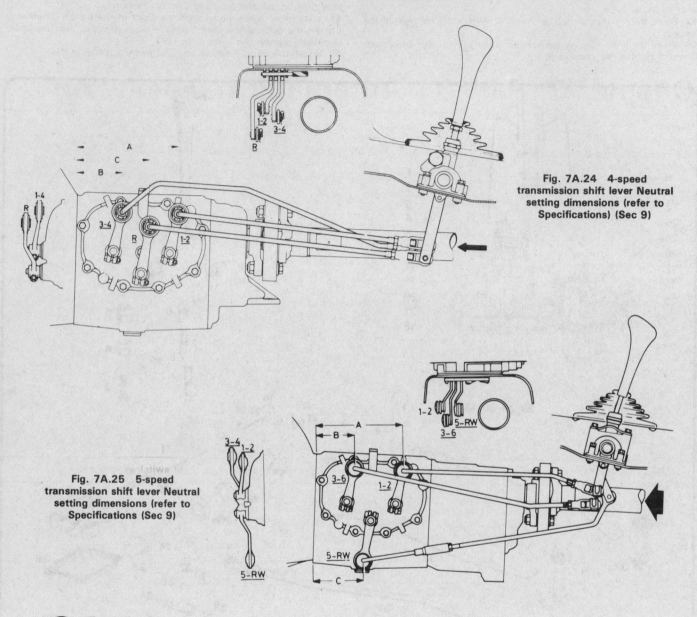

Fig. 7A.24 4-speed transmission shift lever Neutral setting dimensions (refer to Specifications) (Sec 9)

Fig. 7A.25 5-speed transmission shift lever Neutral setting dimensions (refer to Specifications (Sec 9)

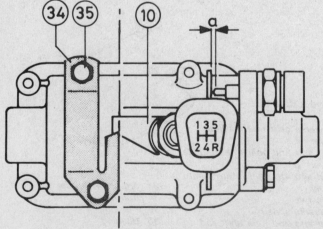

Fig. 7A.26 5-speed transmission gear lever alignment (Sec 9)

a	Refer to Specifications	34 Stop plate
10	Stop finger	35 Bolt

9 Gearshift — adjustment

1   Apply the parking brake, raise the front of the vehicle and support it securely on jackstands.
2   From under the vehicle, extract the clips and disconnect the rods from the bottom of the gearshift.
3   Lock the gearshift levers in Neutral by inserting a 0.24 in (6 mm) diameter pin through the hole provided.
4   Move the shift levers into Neutral and check the dimensions shown in the accompanying illustrations. Reposition the levers on the splines if necessary.

Five-speed models
5   Working inside the vehicle, remove the center console cover from the gear lever and push the gear lever fully to the right and forward. Make sure that the stop plate and finger are aligned as shown in the accompanying illustration, repositioning the stop plate if necessary.
6   Install the center console cover.

All models
7   Adjust the lengths of the shift rods so that they enter the levers freely, then install the clips.
8   Remove the locating pin and lower the vehicle

Chapter 7 Part B Automatic transmission

Contents

Automatic transmission fluid change . . . . See Chapter 1
Diagnosis — general 2
Fluid level check . . . . See Chapter 1
General information 1
Starter inhibitor/backup light switch — adjustment 3

Shift linkage — check and adjustment 4
Throttle linkage — adjustment 5
Throttle linkage check and lubrication . . . . See Chapter 1
Transmission — removal and installation 6

Specifications

Adjustment clearances

Dimension A in Fig. 7B.3	63 mm (2.48 in)
Dimension k in Fig. 7B.4	4 mm (0.158 in)

Torque specifications	Nm	Ft-lbs
Driveshaft clamping nut	30	22
Driveshaft intermediate bearing mount bolts	20	15
Exhaust pipe mount nuts	7	5
Torque converter bolt	42	31
Transmission-to-engine bolts		
10 mm	55	41
12 mm	65	48
Torque converter drain plug	14	10

1 General information

Due to the complexity of the clutches and the hydraulic control system, and because of the special tools and expertise required to perform an automatic transmission overhaul, this should not be undertaken by the home mechanic. Therefore, the procedures in this Chapter are limited to general diagnosis, routine maintenance and adjustment, transmission removal and installation and replacement of the input and output shaft seals.

If the transmission requires major repair work, it should be left to a dealer service department or a reputable automotive or transmission repair shop. You can, however, remove and install the transmission yourself and save the expense, even if the repair work is done by a transmission specialist.

Adjustments that the home mechanic may perform include those involving the starter inhibitor/backup light switch and the shift linkage. **Caution:** *Never tow a disabled vehicle at speeds greater than 30 mph or distances over 75 miles unless the rear wheels are off the ground. Failure to observe this precaution may result in severe transmission damage caused by lack of lubrication.*

2 Diagnosis — general

1 Automatic transmission malfunctions generally fall into four categories: poor engine performance, improper adjustments, hydraulic malfunctions and mechanical malfunctions. Diagnosis of these problems should always begin with a check of the easily repaired items: fluid level and condition, shift linkage adjustment and throttle linkage adjustment. Next, perform a road test to determine if the problem has been corrected or if more diagnosis is necessary. If the problem persists after the preliminary tests and corrections are completed, additional diagnosis should be done by a dealer service department or a reputable automotive or transmission repair shop.

3 Starter inhibitor/backup light switch — adjustment

1 Raise the vehicle and support it securely on jackstands.
2 Place the shifter in Neutral and disconnect the selector rod or cable from the transmission lever.
3 Loosen the switch adjusting screw and insert a suitable locating pin or piece of wire through the lever hole into the locating bore in the switch housing. Tighten the screw and remove the pin.
4 Reconnect the selector rod or cable and lower the vehicle.

7B

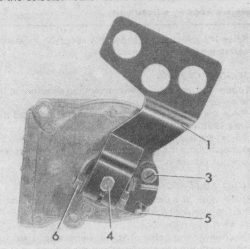

Fig. 7B.1 Automatic transmission starter/backup light switch (Sec 3)

1 *Transmission lever*	5 *Locating pin*
3 *Adjusting screw*	6 *Clamp nut*
4 *Shaft*	

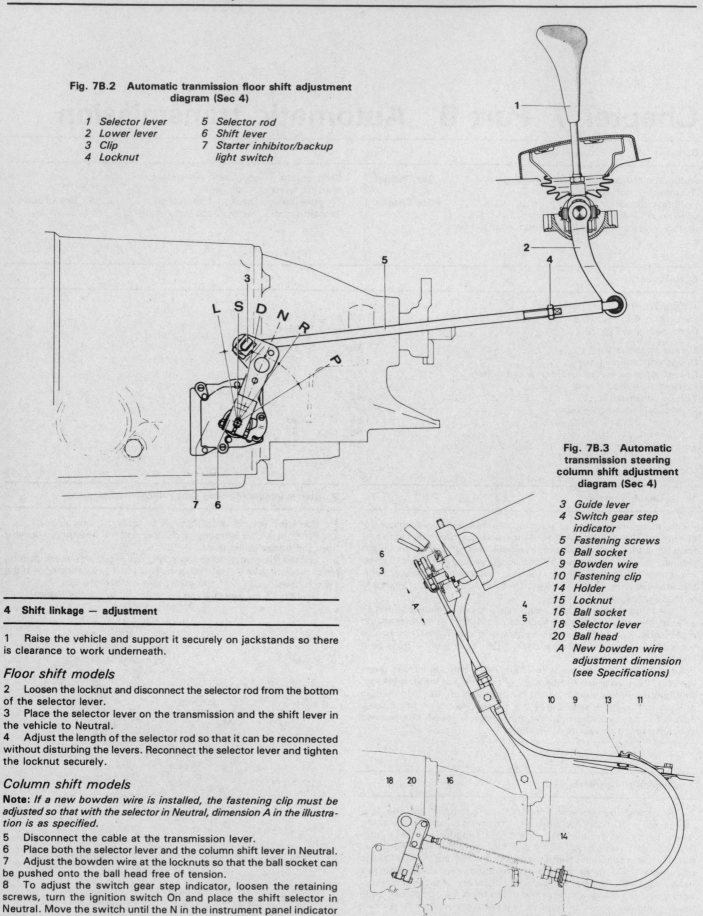

Fig. 7B.2 Automatic tranmission floor shift adjustment diagram (Sec 4)

1 Selector lever
2 Lower lever
3 Clip
4 Locknut
5 Selector rod
6 Shift lever
7 Starter inhibitor/backup light switch

Fig. 7B.3 Automatic transmission steering column shift adjustment diagram (Sec 4)

3 Guide lever
4 Switch gear step indicator
5 Fastening screws
6 Ball socket
9 Bowden wire
10 Fastening clip
14 Holder
15 Locknut
16 Ball socket
18 Selector lever
20 Ball head
A New bowden wire adjustment dimension (see Specifications)

4 Shift linkage — adjustment

1   Raise the vehicle and support it securely on jackstands so there is clearance to work underneath.

Floor shift models

2   Loosen the locknut and disconnect the selector rod from the bottom of the selector lever.
3   Place the selector lever on the transmission and the shift lever in the vehicle to Neutral.
4   Adjust the length of the selector rod so that it can be reconnected without disturbing the levers. Reconnect the selector lever and tighten the locknut securely.

Column shift models

Note: If a new bowden wire is installed, the fastening clip must be adjusted so that with the selector in Neutral, dimension A in the illustration is as specified.

5   Disconnect the cable at the transmission lever.
6   Place both the selector lever and the column shift lever in Neutral.
7   Adjust the bowden wire at the locknuts so that the ball socket can be pushed onto the ball head free of tension.
8   To adjust the switch gear step indicator, loosen the retaining screws, turn the ignition switch On and place the shift selector in Neutral. Move the switch until the N in the instrument panel indicator lights up and then tighten the screws.

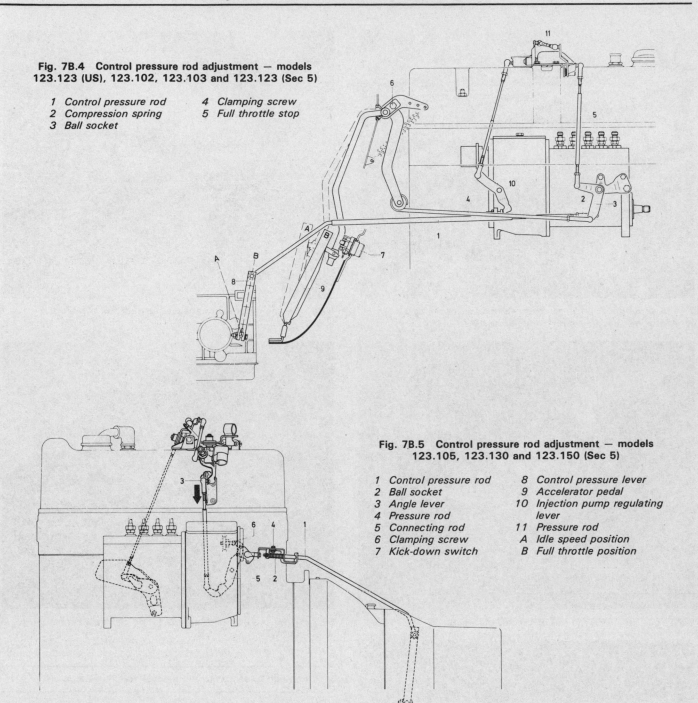

Fig. 7B.4 Control pressure rod adjustment — models
123.123 (US), 123.102, 123.103 and 123.123 (Sec 5)

1 Control pressure rod   4 Clamping screw
2 Compression spring   5 Full throttle stop
3 Ball socket

Fig. 7B.5 Control pressure rod adjustment — models
123.105, 123.130 and 123.150 (Sec 5)

1 Control pressure rod   8 Control pressure lever
2 Ball socket   9 Accelerator pedal
3 Angle lever   10 Injection pump regulating
4 Pressure rod   lever
5 Connecting rod   11 Pressure rod
6 Clamping screw   A Idle speed position
7 Kick-down switch   B Full throttle position

5 Throttle linkage — adjustment

1   The working pressure of the transmission is regulated by the throttle linkage control pressure rod. Since an incorrectly set pressure rod
can cause transmission damage, proper adjustment is critical. On the
models noted below, control pressure adjustment can be accomplished as described. On all other models, special tools are necessary
and this adjustment should be left to your dealer or a properly equipped
shop.

US model 123.123 as well as 123.102, 123.103 and 123.123 with key starting

2   Loosen the clamping screw (4 in the accompanying illustration).
3   Place the injection pump lever at full throttle by pushing the lever (3)

down so the regulating lever (5) is resting against the full throttle
stop (6).
4   The control pressure rod (1) should now be pulled to the full throttle
position by the compression spring (2). With the rod in this position,
tighten the clamping screw.

Models 123.105, 123.130, and 123.150

5   Disconnect the control pressure rod (1 in the illustration).
6   Push the throttle pedal (9) against the full throttle stop (not the
kick-down switch) with the injection pump regulating lever (10) resting
against the full throttle stop. If the regulating lever is not against the
stop, loosen the clamping screw (6) and readjust at the regulating shaft.
7   Pull the control pressure rod forward to the full throttle stop and
then adjust the rod length at the ball socket (2) so that the socket can
be pushed against the ball head with no binding.
8   Tighten the ball socket counternut (2).

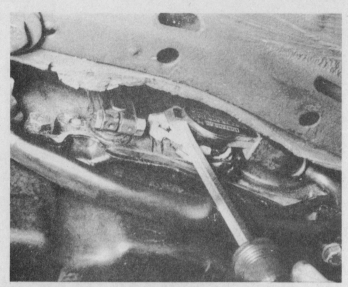

6.6   A screwdriver under the tab can be used to pry the connector off the later model inhibitor switch

6.7a   Pry the automatic transmission shift rod clip (arrow) and . . .

6.7b   . . . push the rod out of the selector lever

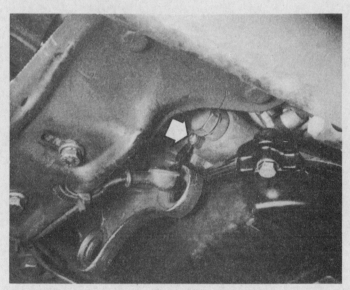

6.8   Pull off the cover for access to the electrical connector screw (arrow)

6.9   The exhaust pipe brace bolts and U-bolt nuts (arrows)

6   Automatic transmission — removal and installation

1   Disconnect the battery negative cable.
2   Raise the vehicle and support it securely on jackstands.
3   Drain the fluid from the transmission and torque converter (Chapter 1).
4   Mark the relative positions of the driveshaft bolts and remove the bolts. It may be necessary to loosen the driveshaft intermediate (center) bearing mount bolts and the clamping nuts on the driveshaft (Chapter 8).
5   Disconnect the speedometer connector at the transmission.
6   To disconnect the inhibitor switch, first rotate the locking ring clockwise to unlock it and then pry the cover off with a screwdriver (photo).
7   Disconnect the shift linkage (photos).
8   Disconnect any remaining electrical connections from the transmission (photo).
9   Disconnect the exhaust pipe mount from the transmission, loosen the U-bolt nuts and then move the pipe out of the way (photo).
10 Remove the transmission cooler oil pipe union bolts and disconnect the pipes. Plug the ends to prevent fluid loss and contamination.

6.11a Turn the engine over using a socket wrench on the crankshaft balancer bolt . . .

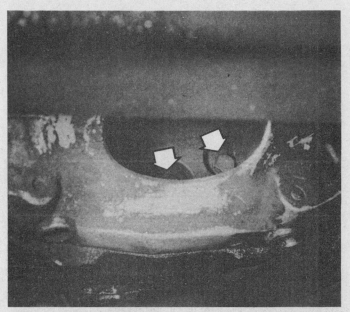

6.11b . . . to bring the torque converter bolts (arrows) around to where they can be reached through the access hole

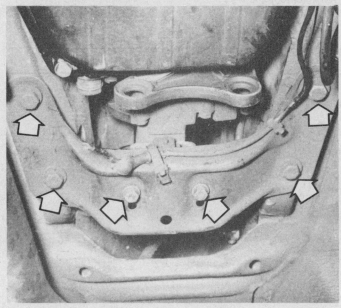

6.15 The transmission mount bolts (arrows)

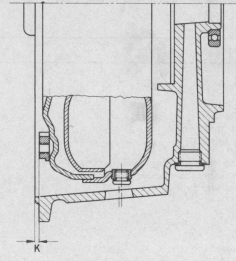

Fig. 7B.6 The torque converter must be installed on the transmission oil pump so the clearance (k) is as specified (Sec 6)

7B

11 Remove the torque converter bolts. Rotate the engine with a wrench on the crankshaft balancer bolt to bring each torque converter bolt in turn into position (photos).
12 Support the engine under the oil pan with a jack, using a block of wood to protect the pan surface.
13 Remove all but two of the transmission-to-engine retaining bolts.
14 Support the transmission with a jack. A transmission jack is the best device to use for this.
15 Unbolt and remove the transmission mount from the transmission and the vehicle (photo).
16 Remove the remaining two transmission-to-engine bolts.
17 Slide the transmission rearward and lower it carefully to the floor with the jack.
18 Installation is the reverse of removal, making sure the torque converter is fully engaged with the oil pump by checking the distance (k in the accompanying illustration). Tighten all fasteners to the specified torque.
19 After installation, push the torque converter forward through the vent slots to eliminate dimension A in the accompanying illustration.

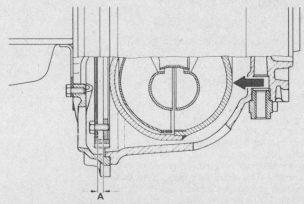

Fig. 7B.7 After transmission installation, the torque converter must be pushed forward (arrow) to cancel out any clearance at dimension A (Sec 6)

Chapter 8   Clutch and driveline

Contents

Axleshaft — removal and installation 15
Axleshaft boot — replacement 16
Clutch — general information 3
Clutch — removal, inspection and installation 8
Clutch master cylinder — removal, installation
  and adjustment 5
Clutch pedal assembly — removal, installation
  and adjustment 4
Clutch hydraulic system — bleeding 7
Clutch slave cylinder — removal and installation 6
Clutch release bearing and arm — removal and installation .. 9

Differential/final drive unit and
  axleshafts — general information 14
Differential/final drive unit — removal and installation 17
Differential/final drive unit oil seals — replacement 18
Driveline — checking 2
Driveshaft — general information 10
Driveshaft — removal and installation 11
Driveshaft center bearing — replacement 12
Driveshaft flex plates and centering sleeves — replacement .. 13
General information 1

Specifications

Clutch

Type	Hydraulically operated single dry plate, diaphragm spring
Clutch friction disc	
Lining thickness (new)............................	3.9 to 4.1 mm (0.154 to 0.162 in)
Wear limit (minimum)	1.9 to 2.1 mm (0.075 to 0.083 in)
Runout (maximum)	0.5 mm (0.02 in)
Clutch pedal	
Dead center spring spring measurement	
between retainers (dimension a in Fig. 8.1)	47.5 mm (1.87 in)
Pushrod-to-master cylinder clearance	0.2 mm (0.008 in)

Driveline

Driveshaft type	Two-piece tubular-type with universal joints and an intermediate (center) bearing
Axleshaft type	Ball and spider

Differential/final drive unit

Type	Unsprung, attached to the vehicle underbody and suspension crossmember
Pinion nut locking dimensions (Fig. 8.12)	
a	8.0 mm (0.315 in)
b	4.0 mm (0.158 in)

Torque specifications	**Nm**	**Ft-lbs**
Axleshaft bolt	30	22
Clutch cover bolts	24	18
Differential/final drive unit		
Rear mount-to-cover	119	89
Rear mount-to-underbody	30	22
Front mount	100	74
Differential/final drive pinion nut (minimum).............	179	132
Differential/final drive unit rear cover bolts	45	34
Driveshaft flange bolts and nuts		
10 mm	45	34
12 mm	65	48
Driveshaft intermediate (center) bearing bolts	24	18
Driveshaft sleeve nut	40	30

1   General information

Drive is transmitted from the clutch and through the manual transmission (or torque converter and automatic transmission — described in Chapter 7) to the differential/final drive unit by means of the two-section tubular driveshaft incorporating an intermediate (center) support ball bearing, center universal joint, and flexible universal joints at each end of the shaft. The drive then passes through the differential and to the rear wheels by way of axleshafts incorporating spider-type joints.

2   Driveline — checking

Clutch

1   The clutch should be periodically checked for wear as described in Chapter 1.
2   A simple check of clutch operation is to hold the clutch pedal approximately 1/2 inch (13 mm) from the floor with the engine running and then shift through the gears several times. If the shifts are smooth, the clutch is releasing properly. If they are not, the clutch is not releasing fully and the clutch master cylinder fluid level and linkage should be checked.

Driveshaft

3   The driveshaft bolts, flexible couplings and universal joints should be checked for looseness, wear and damage periodically.

Differential

4   Check the differential mounts and bolts for looseness and damage and inspect the input and output seals for lubricant leaks.

Axleshafts

5   The axleshaft joint boots should be inspected for damage, leaking lubricant or cuts. Leaking boots should be replaced immediately or the joints will be damaged.

3   Clutch — general information

The clutch is a single dry plate type with a diaphragm spring pressure plate. The pressure plate is actuated hydraulically by a release arm and sealed ball-bearing.
The clutch plate (or disc) is free to slide along the splined transmission input shaft, and is held in position between the flywheel and the pressure plate by the pressure of the diaphragm spring. Friction lining material is riveted to the clutch plate and it has a spring-cushioned hub to absorb transmission shocks and help ensure a smooth take-off.
The circular diaphragm spring is mounted on shoulder pins and held in the cover by two fulcrum rings. The spring is also held to the pressure plate by three steel spring clips which are riveted in position.
The clutch is actuated by a hydraulic master and slave cylinder. Wear of the friction linings is compensated for automatically by the hydraulic system.
Depressing the clutch pedal actuates the slave cylinder piston which moves the release arm. The release bearing on the arm is forced against the center fingers of the diaphragm spring and the pressure plate is released from the clutch plate.
When the clutch pedal is released, the diaphragm spring forces the pressure plate onto the clutch plate linings, and the clutch plate is also forced onto the flywheel. Drive from the engine is now transmitted directly through the clutch to the transmission.

4   Clutch pedal assembly — removal, installation and adjustment

1   Remove the panel covering the lower part of the steering column.
2   Remove the floor mat beneath the pedal assembly.
3   Remove the filler cap from the combination brake and clutch fluid reservoir and syphon out some of the fluid into a container.
4   Unscrew the union nut securing the outlet pipe to the clutch master cylinder and plug the outlet.
5   Disconnect the clutch master cylinder supply hose at the reservoir pivot bolt. Remove the bushing.

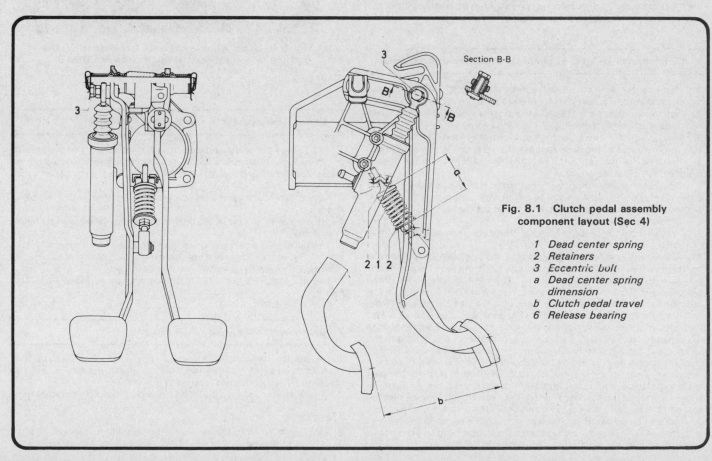

Section B-B

Fig. 8.1   Clutch pedal assembly component layout (Sec 4)

1   Dead center spring
2   Retainers
3   Eccentric bolt
a   Dead center spring dimension
b   Clutch pedal travel
6   Release bearing

8

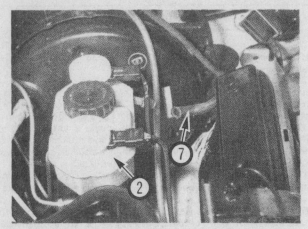

Fig. 8.2   The supply hose (7) which connects to the combination clutch master cylinder/brake and clutch fluid reservoir (2) (Sec 5)

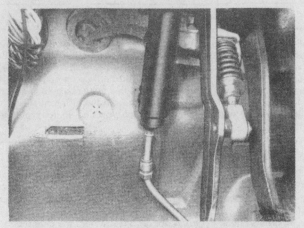

Fig. 8.3   Disconnecting the outlet pipe from the master cylinder (Sec 5)

6   Disconnect the pushrod from the brake pedal by unscrewing the pivot bolt. Remove the bush.
7   Disconnect the plug from the stop-light switch.
8   Unscrew the mounting nuts then withdraw the assembly rearwards and downwards through the bulkhead.
9   The clutch pedal may be removed after removing the clutch master cylinder and disconnecting the dead center spring.
10 Installation is a reversal of removal, installing the master cylinder as described in Section 5. Check that the distance across the dead center spring retainers is as specified with the pedal released. If it is not, loosen the locknut and turn the adjusting nut as necessary. Tighten the locknut when the dimension is correct. After installation, bleed the hydraulic system as described in Section 7.

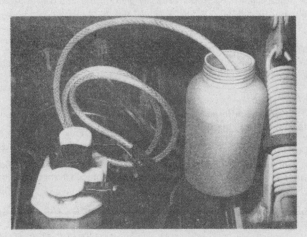

Fig. 8.4   Using a bottle of water and hose to set the clutch master cylinder pushrod clearance (Sec 5)

5   Clutch master cylinder — removal, installation and adjustment

1   Remove the floor covering beneath the pedals, and remove the panel covering the lower part of the steering column.
2   Syphon the fluid from the combination brake and clutch fluid reservoir until it is below the level of the clutch outlet.
3   Disconnect the clutch supply hose from the reservoir and immediately plug the end of the hose to prevent fluid loss and contamination.
4   Remove the fluid union nut securing the outlet pipe to the master cylinder and plug the outlet.
5   Remove the mounting bolt and withdraw the master cylinder downward (leaving the pushrod connected to the pedal) while withdrawing the supply hose through the bulkhead.
6   Disconnect the supply hose.
7   If the master cylinder is faulty it should be replaced with a new or rebuilt unit.
8   Installation is a reversal of removal, making sure the pushrod is adjusted so that there is a clearance between it and the master cylinder piston with the pedal fully released. The clearance is given in the Specification Section. Since the rod is not accessible, an approximate adjustment can be made by checking that the pad on the end of the pedal moves approximately 0.04 in (1.0 mm) before resistance is felt. If necessary loosen the locknut on the eccentric adjuster bolt connecting the pushrod to the pedal, turn the bolt as required, and retighten the locknut. An alternate method is to completely drain the system, disconnect the supply hose from the fluid reservoir and connect a hose from the supply hose to a container of water. A 0.06 in (1.5 mm) spacer is then placed between the pedal and the pedal stop, and air pressure supplied to the slave cylinder or master cylinder outlet. With air passing through the system, bubbles will be seen in the water, and the eccentric bolt can be adjusted so that just as the bubbles cease the locknut is tightened. With the spacer removed, the bubbles should start again. Bleed the hydraulic system, as described in Section 7.

6   Clutch slave cylinder — removal and installation

1   Raise the front of the vehicle and support it securely on jackstands.
2   Working beneath the vehicle, disconnect the hydraulic pipe from the slave cylinder and quickly cap the end of the pipe to prevent loss of fluid.
3   Unbolt and remove the slave cylinder, together with the slotted spacer.
4   If the slave cylinder is faulty it should be replaced with a new or rebuilt unit.
5   Installation is a reversal of removal, making sure that the slotted side of the spacer is against the transmission housing, and that the pushrod is correctly seated in the release lever.
6   After installation bleed the hydraulic system, as described in Section 7.

7   Clutch hydraulic system — bleeding

1   The clutch hydraulic system should be bled in reverse flow by forcing fluid through the slave cylinder via the master cylinder to the fluid reservoir by either of two methods.
2   Raise the front of the vehicle and support it securely on jackstands.

Method 1

3   Syphon fluid from the reservoir to the minimum level.
4   Using a pressurized brake bleeding kit (available at auto parts

Fig. 8.5 Using a centering tool to hold the clutch disc in place (Sec 8)

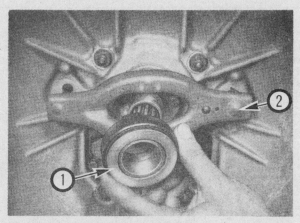

Fig. 8.6 The clutch release bearing (1) and lever (2) (Sec 8 and 9)

stores), connect the supply line to the bleed screw on the slave cylinder and open the screw half a turn.
5   Allow the fluid to fill the system until it reaches the maximum level in the reservoir then tighten the bleed screw.
6   Check the operation of the clutch. If necessary, bleed the system again to remove all the air.

Method 2

7   Fill the fluid reservoir to the maximum level mark.
8   Connect a hose which is long enough to connect the clutch slave cylinder bleed screw to the right front brake caliper bleed screw. Fill the hose with fluid by temporarily loosening the bleed screw and having an assistant depress the brake pedal slowly. Tighten the bleed screw.
9   Connect the hose to the clutch slave cylinder bleed screw and then loosen both bleed screws.
10 Have the assistant fully depress the brake pedal, then tighten the clutch bleed screw before releasing the pedal. Continue bleeding until the fluid reaching the reservoir is free of air bubbles, then tighten both bleed screws and remove the hose. Use the minimum number of strokes, otherwise there is a possibility of allowing aerated fluid to enter the brake hydraulic circuit. Also, do not allow the fluid level to drop below the maximum mark — this may occur if the clutch hydraulic circuit is initially empty.
11 Fill the fluid reservoir to the maximum level mark and lower the vehicle to the ground. Test the brake system and clutch operation before placing the vehicle into service.

8   Clutch — removal, inspection and installation

Removal

1   Remove the transmission (Chapter 7).
2   With a file or similar tool, mark the relative position of the clutch cover and flywheel to ensure identical positioning on installation. This is not necessary if a new clutch is to be installed.
3   Loosen the six bolts and spring washers securing the clutch cover to the flywheel, a little at a time and working in criss-cross pattern. This will prevent distortion of the cover and also preclude the cover from suddenly flying off if it was binding on the dowels.
4   With all the bolts removed, lift the assembly from the locating dowels. Note the direction in which the friction disc is installed and lift it from the clutch cover.

Inspection

5   Clean the dust out of the clutch housing, using a vacuum cleaner or clean cloth. Do not use compressed air as the dust can endanger your health if inhaled.
6   Inspect the friction surfaces of the clutch disc and flywheel for

signs of uneven contact, indicating improper mounting or damaged clutch springs. Also check the surfaces for burned areas, grooves, cracks or other signs of wear. It may be necessary to remove a badly grooved flywheel and have it machined to restore the surface. Light glazing of the flywheel surface can be removed with fine sandpaper. Inspect the clutch lining for contamination by oil, grease or any other substance and replace the disc with a new one if contamination is present. Slide the disc onto the input shaft temporarily to make sure the fit is snug and the splines are not burred or worn.
7   Remove the release bearing from the clutch housing as described in Section 9, and spin it to check for roughness. Also attempt to move the thrust surface laterally against the bearing housing. If any excessive movement or roughness is evident, replace the release bearing.

Installation

8   It is important that no oil or grease contacts the friction disc linings, or the pressure plate and flywheel faces. Install the clutch with clean hands and wipe down the pressure plate and flywheel faces with a clean rag before assembly begins. Lubricate the pilot bearing in the center of the crankshaft and the splines transmission input shaft with high moly-base grease.
9   Place the clutch friction disc in position on the flywheel, centering it with an alignment tool. The projecting torsion spring hub must face toward the rear.
10 With the friction disc held in place by the alignment tool, place the clutch cover assembly in position and align it with any marks made prior to removal.
11 Install the bolts and tighten them in a criss-cross pattern, one or two turns at a time, until they are tightened to the specified torque.
12 Install the clutch release bearing (Section 9).
13 Remove the alignment tool and install the transmission (Chapter 7).

9   Clutch release bearing and arm — removal and installation

1   With the transmission and engine separated to provide access to the clutch, inspect the release bearing located in the clutch housing over the input shaft.
2   Withdraw the release bearing from the guide sleeve.
3   Withdraw the release arm from the slave cylinder pushrod position, then pull it sideways from the ball-pin to disengage the spring clip.
4   Check the release bearing, as described in Section 8. Replace the bearing if there are any signs of grease leakage. Do not wash the bearing in solvent. Check the release arm for damage and wear.
5   Lubricate the guide sleeve, ball-pin, and the release bearing contact areas on the release arm with moly-base grease.
6   Installation is a reversal of removal, making sure that the release bearing seats securely in the arm.

8

10　Driveshaft — general information

Because the differential/final drive unit is solidly mounted to the chassis, angularity of the universal joints is small, so wear in the joints is likely to be minimal unless very high mileages have been completed. The driveshaft center bearing and flex plates can be replaced, but the center universal joint is of the sealed type and cannot be serviced.

11　Driveshaft — removal and installation

1　Raise the vehicle, support it securely on jackstands and remove the rear wheels.
2　It may be necessary to disconnect the handbrake/parking brake cables and compensating lever mechanism for access.
3　Use two large open-end wrenches to loosen the sleeve nut (ap-

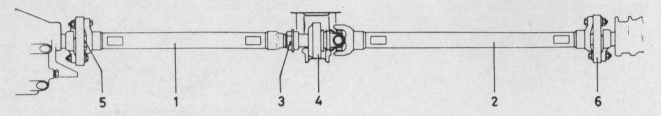

Fig. 8.7　Driveshaft component layout (Sec 10, 11, 12, 13 and 14)

1　Front section	3　Sleeve nut	5　Centering sleeve
2　Rear section	4　Intermediate (center) bearing	6　Rear flex plate

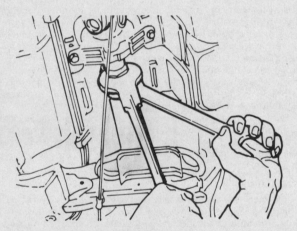

Fig. 8.8　Loosening the driveshaft sleeve nut using two wrenches (Sec 11)

11.4a　Mark the relative positions of the flex plate and driveshaft with white paint prior to removal

11.4b　Use a backup wrench (arrow) to hold the driveshaft nuts while removing the bolts

11.5　The driveshaft intermediate (center) bearing bolt locations (arrows)

proximately two turns) which is located on the front section of the shaft. This will permit the shaft to be slightly compressed to simplify removal. Do not push back on the rubber sleeve.

4   Mark their relative positions and remove the nuts and bolts securing the front and rear flex plates to the transmission and final drive unit (photos).

5   Remove the bolts securing the center bearing to the underbody, and lower the assembly onto a jack or suitable support (photo).

6   Mark the two sliding sections of the propeller shaft in relation to each other as a precaution in case the sections are inadvertently separated, otherwise the balance of the shaft may be upset.

7   Push the rear section of the shaft fowards so that it can be disconnected from the center pin on the final drive flange.

8   Pull the front section of the shaft from the transmission flange and lower the complete unit from the vehicle. Do not separate the two sections.

9   Upon installation, locate the front section of the shaft on the transmission flange pin, then push the rear section forwards (sleeve

nut still loose) and locate it on the final drive flange pin.

10   Lift the center bearing into position and install the bolts finger-tight.

11   Insert the coupling bolts (with their heads facing the center bearing) through the front and rear flanges, install new self-locking nuts and tighten them evenly to the specified torque.

12   Install the handbrake/parking brake cables and compensating lever mechanism, if removed.

13   Rotate the driveshaft several times to relieve any tension, making sure the front and rear sections to are not binding, then tighten the sleeve nut to the specified torque.

14   Fully tighten the center bearing bolts.

15   Lower the vehicle.

12   Driveshaft center bearing — replacement

1   Remove the driveshaft as described in Section 11.

2   Mark the relationships of the front and rear sections (photo).

3   With the sleeve nut already loosened for removal of the shaft, withdraw the front section.

4   Pull the rubber sleeve from the splines.

5   Extract the circlip using circlip pliers, then remove the cover plate (photo).

6   Using a suitable puller, pull the rubber mounting, together with the bearing, from the universal joint yoke (photo). Remove the inner cover plate.

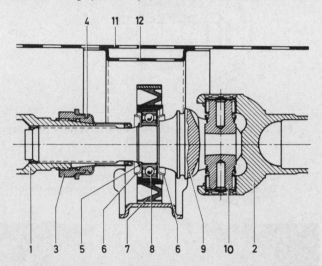

Fig. 8.9 Cross-section view of the driveshaft center bearing showing the component relationships (Sec 12)

1 *Front shaft*	8 *Ball bearing*
2 *Rear shaft*	9 *Yoke*
3 *Clamping nut*	10 *Spider with needle*
4 *Rubber sleeve*	*bearing and bushing*
5 *Locking ring*	11 *Chassis floor*
6 *Protective cap*	12 *Driveshaft tunnel*
7 *Driveshaft intermediate*	
(center) bearing	

12.2   Mark the relative positions of the front and rear driveshafts with paint before disassembling the bearing mount

12.5   Slide the snap-ring off the driveshaft, using snap-ring pliers

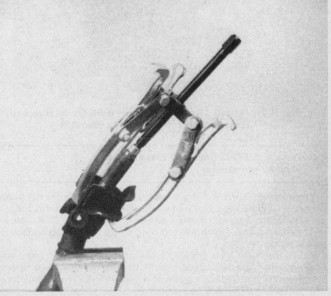

12.6   Draw the bearing mount off the driveshaft with a puller tool

8

7   Support the rubber mounting inner bore and, using a suitable diameter metal tube, drive out the bearing.

8   Clear the rubber mounting inner bore then support it on a block of wood and drive in the new bearing using a metal tube on the outer track only. The bearing should be driven in slowly up to the shoulder.

9   Install the inner cover plate.

10   Mount the universal joint in a soft-jawed vice and locate the bearing and rubber mounting on it with the inner V-fold of the mounting towards the joint. Using a metal tube on the inner track, drive the bearing fully onto the shaft.

11   Install the cover plate and retain it with the circlip with the inner crown against the plate.

12   Push the rubber sleeve over the splines.

13   Apply a little grease to the splines then connect the front section of the drive shaft, making sure that the previously made marks are correctly aligned.

14   Install the driveshaft.

13   Driveshaft flex plates and centering sleeves — replacement

1   Wear or deterioration of the driveshaft flex plates and centering sleeves may cause noise due to the driveshaft moving off center and becoming unbalanced. The centering sleeves also incorporate seals which, if worn, will allow grease from the inner cavities to leak out.

2   Remove the driveshaft (Section 8.)

3   If the flex plate is to be reinstalled, mark its relation to the driveshaft flange.

4   Remove the bolts and withdraw the flex plate.

5   Mount the driveshaft in a soft-jawed vice and drill a 0.4 in (10 mm) diameter hole through the centering sleeve approximately 0.6 in (15 mm) from its outer face.

6   Insert a suitable bar through the hole and use two screwdrivers or similar tools as levers to extract the sleeve from the driveshaft.

7   Clean the recess in the shaft and then locate the new sleeve squarely over the bore and drive it in fully, using a metal or wooden block.

8   Locate the flex plate on the driveshaft flange aligning any marks made during disassembly. Insert the bolts (with their heads facing the center bearing), then fit new self-locking nuts and tighten them evenly.

9   Install the driveshaft.

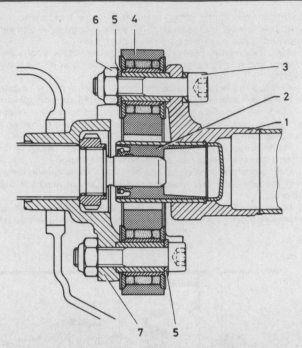

Fig. 8.10   Cross-section view of the driveshaft flex plate (Sec 13)

1 Driveshaft	5 Washer
2 Centering sleeve	6 Nut
3 Bolt	7 Transmission flange
4 Flex plate	

Fig. 8.11   Using a bar and two screwdrivers as levers to remove the centering sleeve (Sec 13)

14   Differential/final drive unit and axleshafts — general information

The differential unit is of the unsprung type with the entire differential/final drive unit housing attached to the rear underbody and suspension crossmember. Two axleshafts transmit drive from the final drive unit to the rear wheels which are attached to the fully independent rear suspension.

The differential/final drive unit pinion runs in two tapered roller bearings which are preloaded using a collapsible spacer. The differential incorporates two planetary gears on a single shaft. The axleshafts are of maintenance-free ball and spider type.

Overhaul of the differential/final drive unit is not covered in this manual because of the special tools and techniques required.

15.4   Lock the hub with a screwdriver and two lug bolts so it can't turn during axleshaft bolt removal

15   Axleshaft — removal and installation

1   Raise the vehicle, support it securely on jackstands and remove the rear wheels.

2   Drain the differential (Chapter 1). Install and tighten the drain plug.

3   Remove the brake caliper (Chapter 9) but do not disconnect the hydraulic hose. Hang the caliper to one side on a piece of wire.

4   Install two of the wheel bolts and insert a large screwdriver or similar too to keep the hub from turning while the axleshaft bolt is removed (photo).

15.5 Drive the axleshaft into the hub with a brass drift and a hammer

15.6 Carefully pry the axleshaft splined stub clear of the hub with a screwdriver

15.7 The differential/final drive unit upper mount bolts (arrows)

15.8a The tab of the axleshaft retaining clip (arrow) can be seen with the differential cover removed

5 Use a brass drift and a hammer to carefully drive the axleshaft in to disengage it from the rear hub (photo).

6 From under the vehicle, collapse the axleshaft sufficiently to allow the splines to be pried free of the hub (photo). It may be necessary to raise the differential/final drive unit with a jack to gain sufficient clearance to allow removal of the axleshaft from the hub.

7 Clean the final drive rear cover and surrounding components then unbolt and remove the rear cover. On some models it may be necessary to support the differential/final drive unit with a jack and remove the rear mount for access to the bolts (photo).

8 Use snap-ring pliers to extract the circlip from the differential side gear (photos). It will probably be necessary to rotate tne axleshaft until the clip tab comes into view.

9 The axleshaft can now be removed from the differential (noting the location of the spacer) and lowered from the vehicle. On early models the left- and right-hand axleshafts are identified by an L or R on the inner stub and this should be noted at the time of removal for reinstallation to the proper side.

10 Installation the reverse of removal, taking care not to compress or angle the axleshaft excessively, otherwise damage may occur.The circlip thickness must eliminate all endplay.

11 Clean the cover and housing mating surfaces thoroughly and apply a 1/4 in bead of RTV-type sealant around the gasket surface of the cover. Install the cover and tighten all bolts to the specified torque.

12 Fill the final drive unit with oil to the level of the filler hole with the vehicle on level ground (Chapter 1).

15.8b Use snap-ring pliers to pull the axleshaft retaining clip (painted white here for clarity) from the differential

8

16   Axleshaft boot — replacement

If the axleshaft boots are split or damaged they should be replaced immediately. However, because special tools and techniques are required this job should be left to your dealer or a properly equipped shop.

17   Differential/final drive unit — removal and installation

1   Block the front wheels, raise the vehicle, support it securely on jackstands and remove the rear wheels.
2   Drain the differential/final drive unit (Chapter 1) and reinstall the drain plug.
3   Remove the brake calipers with the fluid hoses still connected and hang them out of the way on pieces of wire.
4   Remove the axleshafts (Section 15).
5   Remove the driveshaft (Section 11).
6   If an rpm sensor is installed on the differential/final drive unit, unscrew the retaining bolt with an Allen wrench, remove the sensor and place it to one side.
7   Support the differential/final drive unit with a jack and remove the rear mount and the four main retaining bolts. These four bolts are on the top of the crossmember. It may be necessary to disconnect the handbrake/parking brake cable from the underbody to provide clearance.

Fig. 8.12   Locking the pinion nut (refer to Specifications for dimensions in inset (Sec 18)

8   With the help of an assistant, lower the differential/final drive unit to the floor and withdraw from under the vehicle.
9   Installation is a reversal of removal, making sure to tighten all nuts and bolts to the specified torque. On models equipped with an rpm sensor, make sure that the magnetic pick-up is free of any foreign particles.
10   Fill the differential/final drive unit with oil to the level of the filler hole with the vehicle on level ground.

18   Differential/final drive unit oil seals — replacement

Pinion oil seal

1   Remove the driveshaft (Section 11) and drain the oil from the differential/final drive unit.
2   In order that the correct bearing preload is maintained, the turning torque of the pinion must now be established. If a torque gauge is not

18.13   Use a screwdriver to pry the axleshaft seal from the bore

18.14   Lubricate the new axleshaft seal inner and outer circumferences (arrows) before installation

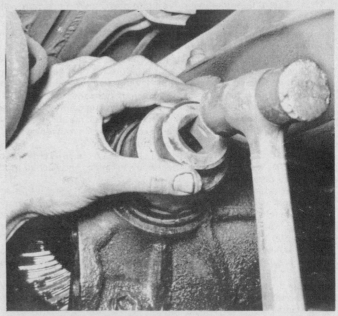

18.15   Tap the new seal carefully and evenly into the bore with suitable socket and a hammer

available, wind some string around the flange center pin and use a spring balance to record the force required to turn the flange slowly. Note that the axleshafts should be horizontal and the brake pads and shoes away from the discs.

3   Hold the flange stationary with a length of bar bolted to two of the bolt holes, then unscrew the pinion nut using a slotted box wrench.

4   Using a puller or slide hammer, draw the flange from the pinion splines.

5   Using a screwdriver, pry the oil seal from the differential/final drive housing.

6   Clean the oil seal and flange areas. Replace the flange if the oil seal shoulder is worn excessively.

7   Lubricate the outer edge and sealing lips of the new seal with oil. Place the seal in position and use a suitable size socket or tube and a hammer to drive it carefully and squarely into the housing.

8   Place the flange on the pinion splines and screw on a new pinion nut finger-tight.

9   Tighten the pinion nut gradually until the turning torque is the same as that recorded in paragraph 2. Do not overtighten the nut, otherwise

the collapsible spacer on the pinion will need to be replaced; and this work must be carried out by a dealer or properly equipped shop. The differential/final unit torque of the nut must be at least that given in Specifications. Remember, if this cannot be attained, the collapsible spacer must be replaced.

10   Using a blunt cold chisel lock the nut by peening the shoulder into the cut-out on the pinion.

11   Install the driveshaft, as described in Section 11, and fill the differential/final drive unit with oil to the level of the filler hole with the vehicle on level ground.

Axleshaft seal

12   Remove the axleshaft(s) (Section 15).

13   Pry the old seal out of the housing (photo).

14   Lubricate the outer seal circumference and the inner lip with clean lubricant (photo).

15   Place the seal in position and use a suitable size socket or similar tool and a hammer to drive it fully and evenly into the bore (photo).

16   Install the axleshaft(s).

8

Chapter 9 Brakes

Contents

Anti-lock Braking System (ABS) — description 19
Brake check .... See Chapter 1
Brake fluid — replacement 9
Brake pedal assembly — removal and installation 16
Brake system — bleeding 8
Disc brake caliper — removal, overhaul and installation 4
Disc brake pads — replacement 2
Disc brake rotor — inspection, removal and installation 5
Fluid level check .... See Chapter 1
General information 1
Hydraulic brake hoses and lines — inspection
  and replacement 7
Master cylinder — removal, overhaul and installation 6
Parking brake — checking and adjustment.............. 10
Parking brake cables — removal and installation 12
Parking brake hand lever (UK models) — removal and
  installation 14
Parking brake pedal (US models) — removal and installation . 13
Parking brake shoes — inspection and replacement 11
Power brake booster — description, removal and installation . 17
Stop light switch — removal and installation 15
Vacuum pump — testing and replacement.............. 18
Vacuum system — general information 3

Specifications

General

Type	Four-wheel disc with dual hydraulic circuits and vacuum booster assist with a cable operated parking brake actuating brake shoes against drums incorporated into the rear discs

Brake discs

Front

Thickness
New	12.6 mm (0.496 in)
Service limit	10.6 mm (0.418 in)
Runout (maximum)	0.12 mm (0.005 in)

Rear

Thickness
New	10 mm (0.394 in)
Service limit	8.3 mm (0.327 in)
Runout...	0.12 mm (0.005 in)
Parking brake drum diameter...................	160 mm (6.3 in)

Brake pad

Lining thickness (new)

Front
Pre-1979 models.................................	15.0 mm (0.59 in)
Post 1979 models................................	17.5 mm (0.69 in)

Rear
Pre-1979 models.................................	15.0 mm (0.59 in)
Post-1979 models................................	15.5 mm (0.61 in)
Service limit (all)	2 mm (0.079 in)

Parking brake lining service thickness
New	4.0 mm (0.157 in)
Service limit...................................	1.5 mm (0.059 in)

Stop light adjustment

Dimension a in Fig. 9.7	5 to 15 mm (0.197 to 0.591 in)
Pedal-to-switch clearance (fully released)	5 to 8 mm (0.197 to 0.315 in)

Torque specifications	Nm	Ft-lbs
Brake line union nut	15	11
Brake disc-to-front hub bolt	114	84
Brake caliper bolt		
Front	114	84
Rear	89	66
Brake vacuum booster unit nuts	15	11
Brake vacuum booster line	30	22
Master cylinder-to-brake booster nut	15	11
Parking brake carrier bolt	49	36

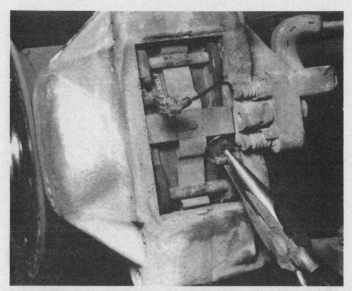

2.2 Use needle nose pliers to unplug the wear sensor connectors from the brake pads

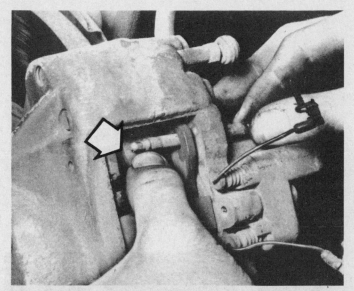

2.3a Push the brake pad anti-rattle spring down with your thumb (arrow) while withdrawing the pin

1 General information

All vehicles covered by this manual are equipped with hydraulically operated four-wheel disc brake systems. All brakes are self-adjusting because disc brakes automatically compensate for pad wear.

The hydraulic system consists of two separate front and rear circuits. The master cylinder has separate reservoirs for the two circuits and in the event of a leak or failure in one hydraulic circuit, the other circuit will remain operative. A visual warning of low fluid level or worn brake pads is given by a warning light activated by a switch in the master cylinder reservoir and sensors in the pads (some models).

Some later models are equipped with an ''Anti-lock Braking System'' (ABS) which is described within this Chapter.

The cable-operated handbrake/parking brake is of conventional brake shoe type on the rear wheels, with the drums being an integral part of the rear brake discs.

The cable-operated parking brake mechanically operates the rear brakes only. It is activated by a pull handle next to the front seats (right-hand drive models) or a foot pedal on the left side of the driver's compartment (left-hand drive models). The parking brake handle or pedal actuates brake shoes in the rear wheels only by way of a system of cables. The brake shoes are located in drums which are part of the rear brake disc rotor casting. The shoes are adjusted manually at specified intervals (Chapter 1).

The power brake booster, located in the engine compartment on the firewall, uses vacuum from the pump and atmospheric pressure to provide assistance to the hydraulically operated brakes.

After completing any operation involving the opening of the brake fluid lines or if the fluid level in the master cylinder runs extrmely low, always bleed the brakes of air as described in this Chapter. Also, after performing any brake system repairs test drive the vehicle to check for proper braking performance before resuming normal driving. Test the brakes while driving on a clean, dry, flat surface. Conditions other than these can lead to inaccurate test results. Test the brakes at various speeds with both light and heavy pedal pressure. The vehicle should stop evenly without pulling to one side or the other. Avoid locking the brakes because this slides the tires and diminishes braking efficiency and control.

Tires, vehicle load and front end alignment are factors which also affect braking performance. Check these items before assuming a brake system fault.

2 Disc brake pads — replacement

Warning: *The brake pad dust encountered during this procedure contains asbestos which is hazardous to your health. Carefully wipe the*

2.3b Use hammer and small punch to drive out the lower brake pad pin

fine dust from the components using a wet rag and avoid inhaling the dust at any time.

1   Raise the vehicle, support it securely on jackstands and remove the wheels.

2   Use needle nose pliers to unplug the wear sensor connectors (if equipped) (photo).

3   Remove the locking clips (if equipped) and drive the upper retaining pin out using a small punch. Remove the retaining spring and then drive out the lower pin (photos).

4   Grasp the ear of each pad with pliers and push the piston evenly into its bore, then withdraw the pad. It may be necessary to move the pad from side to side to dislodge any accumulated dust and dirt so it can be withdrawn.

5   Check each pad for wear and, if the lining thickness is below the minimun thickness (service limit) given in the Specifications, replace all the disc pads on the axle involved.

6   Wipe the dust and dirt from the caliper housing, pistons, disc and pads. Scrape any corrosion or foreign material from the brake rotor. Measure the thickness of the rotor and compare with the Specifications (refer to Section 5 for additional inspection procedures).

7   Draw out some of the fluid from the master cylinder reservoir so

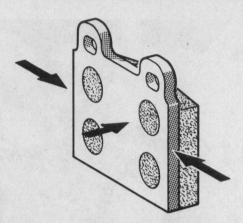

Fig. 9.1 Brake pad lubrication points (arrows) (Sec 2)

2.8 Insert the new pad into the caliper

2.9a Hold the brake pad anti-rattle spring down out of the way while tapping the pin into the caliper with a hammer

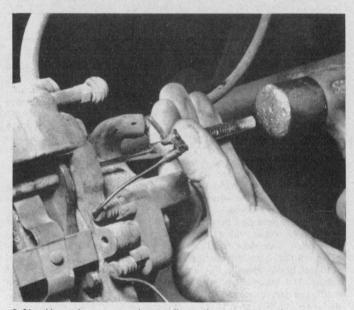

2.9b Use a hammer and a small punch to seat the pins

it won't overflow when the caliper pistons are pushed back to accommodate the new pads. Apply a little high melting-point brake grease to the contact surfaces of the back and edge of the new pad.

8   Push each piston fully into its bore and insert the new pads into the caliper (photo).

9   Place the retaining spring on the pads and insert the pins, tapping them fully into the caliper (photos).

10   Install any locking clips into the ends of the retaining pins and plug in the wear sensor wires.

11   Depress the brake pedal several times to seat the pads in their normal positions. On models with a pressure differential warning indicator on the master cylinder, the warning lamp may light up after removal and installation of the disc pads, in which case the reset pin on the master cylinder should be depressed.

3   Vacuum system — general information

Since diesel engines do not have any manifold vacuum, these models are equipped with a vacuum pump mounted on the front of the engine. The pump provides vacuum for the brake booster as well as various accessories such as the door lock system (Chapter 11).

The vacuum system consists of the vacuum pump, the rubber vacuum reservoirs located at various places in the vehicle and associated tubing.

4   Disc brake caliper — removal, overhaul and installation

Removal

1   Raise the vehicle, support it securely on jackstands and remove the relevant wheel(s).

2   Remove the disc pads, as described in Section 3.

3   Remove the brake fluid reservoir filler cap, place a piece of plastic sheeting over the opening and tighten the cap over it to reduce the loss of fluid in the subsequent operations. Alternatively, remove some of the fluid from the reservoir.

4   If not already removed, unplug the pad sensors and unbolt the bracket holding the wires to the caliper.

5   If the caliper is to be removed from the vehicle, disconnect and plug the brake hose at the caliper (photo).

6   Remove the mounting bolts and lift the caliper from the steering knuckle or hub (photo).

Overhaul

7   Prior to beginning work, obtain an overhaul kit.

8   Pry off the caliper dust caps, taking care on Bendix-type calipers

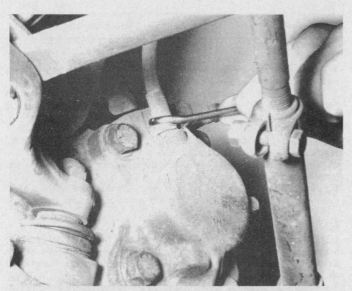

4.5   An open end wrench can be used to unscrew the brake hose from the caliper

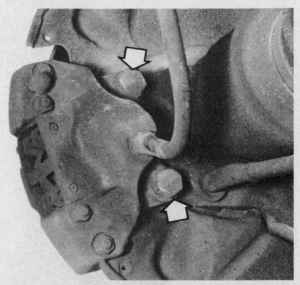

4.6   Rear brake caliper retaining bolts (arrows)

the caliper can be used to press the heat shield further into the piston. The heat shields are different for the inner and outer pistons and are not interchangeable.

Installation

16   Installation is a reversal of removal, making sure that the flexible brake fluid hose is not twisted when fully tightened and the mounting bolts are tightened to the specified torque. The manufacturer recommends using new bolts.
17   After installation, bleed the brake system, as described in Section 8.

---

5   Disc brake rotor — inspection, removal and installation

Inspection

1   Raise the vehicle and support it securely on jackstands.
2   Remove the appropriate wheel and tire.
3   Remove the brake caliper assembly (Section 4) and hang it out of the way on a piece of wire. Never hang the caliper by the brake hose because damage to the hose will occur.
4   Inspect the rotor surfaces. Light scoring or grooving is normal, but deep grooves or severe erosion is not. If pulsating has been noticed during application of the brakes, suspect disc runout.
5   Attach a dial indicator to the caliper mounting bracket, turn the rotor and note the amount of runout. Check both inboard and outboard surfaces. If the runout is more than the maximum allowable, the rotor must be removed from the car and taken to an automotive machine shop for resurfacing.
6   Using a micrometer, measure the thickness of the rotor. If it is less than the minimum specified, replace the rotor with a new one. Also measure the disc thickness at several points to determine variations in the surface. Any variation over 0.0005-inch may cause pedal pulsations during brake application. If this condition exists and the disc thickness is not below the minimum (usually found cast in the disc itself), the rotor can be removed and taken to an automotive machine shop for resurfacing.

Removal

7   To remove the front rotor, remove the hub (Chapter 1). The rotor can be unbolted from the hub using a suitable Allen head wrench (photo). It may be helpful to clamp the rotor in a vise and apply penetrent oil to the threads to ease the job of breaking the bolts loose.
8   The rear rotor is removed by simply withdrawing it from the hub after removing the caliper and hanging it out of the way on a wire. It may be necessary to adjust the parking brake shoes away from the integral drum cast in the rotor (Section 11) if the rotor does not come off easily.

5.7   An Allen head socket is needed to remove the front brake disc from the hub

not to remove the pressed-in ring. Remove the heat shields (if equipped).
9   Remove the pistons by applying low air pressure (a tire pump is perfect for this job) to the fluid inlet fitting using the following procedure. Hold one caliper depressed while ejecting the opposite piston. Hold a thick rubber pad or similar air-tight cover over the piston opening and eject the second piston. Mark the pistons and their respective bores with tape so they won't be interchanged.
10   Inspect the pistons and bores for scoring, corrosion and wear, replacing any damaged components with new ones.
11   Pry the old seals out of the bore grooves and discard them.
12   Clean the caliper and bore, using clean brake fluid, denatured alcohol or brake system cleaner.
13   Lubricate the bore and the new piston seal with clean brake fluid and install the seal into its groove, making sure the seal is not twisted.
14   Lubricate the pistons with clean brake fluid and insert them into their respective bores. Turn the pistons so that the recesses are at a 20° angle from the bottom of the caliper, push them in fully and install the dust caps.
15   Press the heat shields on, making sure that the raised part of the piston is at least 0.004 in (0.1 mm) above the heat shield surface. A short bolt and nut between the plate in the pad and the opening of

9

Installation

9   New rotors are covered with a protective coating which can be removed using spray carburetor cleaner and a rag (photo).

10   Installation is the reverse of removal, taking care to tighten the front rotor bolts to the specified torque. Lubricate the rear hub flange lightly with moly-base grease and place the rotor in position, making sure the locating pin on the hub fits securely in the hole in the rotor.

5.9   The protective coating can be removed from the new brake disc with carburetor cleaner and a rag

6   Master cylinder — removal, overhaul and installation

Removal

1   Completely cover the fender and affected engine compartment areas of the vehicle as brake fluid can ruin painted surfaces if it is spilled.

2   Place rags or newspapers under the master cylinder to soak up the fluid that will drain out, then disconnect and plug the brake line connections at the master cylinder.

3   Unplug the fluid level sensor connector(s) using a small screwdriver to release the clips. Disconnect the wiring from the pressure differential warning switch (if equipped).

4   On manual transmission models, disconnect the clutch hydraulic hose from the reservoir.

5   Remove the two master cylinder mounting nuts and lift the master cylinder from the front face of the vacuum booster unit (photo).

Overhaul

6   Obtain a rebuild kit which will contain all of the necessary replacement parts. The manufacturer recommends using a plastic sleeve assembly tool (available from a dealer) to make the job of installing the primary and secondary pistons easier.

7   Pry the sealing ring from the groove in the master cylinder flange.

8   Clean the exterior of the master cylinder with denatured alcohol or brake cleaner.

9   Remove the fluid reservoir and sealing plugs.

10   Depress the primary piston slightly and unscrew and remove the stop screw and seal.

11   Remove the circlip, withdraw the primary piston, stop washers, secondary and vacuum sleeve and intermediate ring.

12   Remove the secondary piston and spring assembly by tapping on the end of the master cylinder with a block of wood.

13   Unscrew the pressure differential warning switch (if equipped), unscrew the end plug and extract the control piston while tapping on the master cylinder with a block of wood.

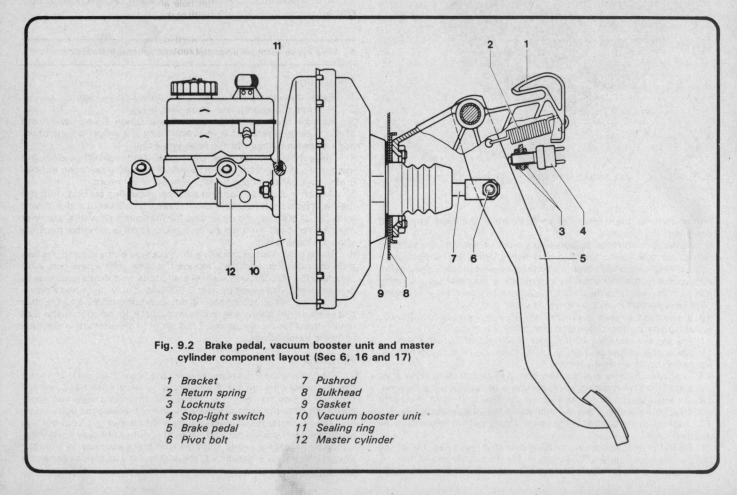

Fig. 9.2   Brake pedal, vacuum booster unit and master cylinder component layout (Sec 6, 16 and 17)

1 Bracket	7 Pushrod
2 Return spring	8 Bulkhead
3 Locknuts	9 Gasket
4 Stop-light switch	10 Vacuum booster unit
5 Brake pedal	11 Sealing ring
6 Pivot bolt	12 Master cylinder

6.5   The brake master cylinder electrical (A), hydraulic (B) and retaining nut (C) connections

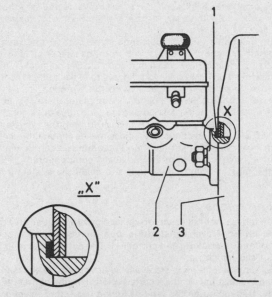

Fig. 9.3   Location of the sealing ring (1) between the master cylinder (2) and the vacuum booster unit (Sec 6)

14   Unscrew the reservoir filler cap and remove the strainer. The low fluid warning switch cannot be removed from the reservoir.

15   Clean the components thoroughly using clean brake fluid, denatured alcohol or brake cleaner. Inspect for worn or damaged components, replacing with new ones as necessary. Pay particular attention to the surfaces of the pistons and cylinder bore for scoring and corrosion.

16   Install the new seals from the overhaul kit on the pistons, using only your fingers to manipulate them into position.

17   Lubricate the master cylinder bore with clean brake fluid.

18   Dip the primary and secondary piston assemblies in clean brake fluid.

19   If an assembly sleeve tool is available, insert the secondary and primary pistons into the sleeve, place the sleeve in position on the bore and use a screwdriver to insert them in the master cylinder bore.

20   If an assembly tube is not available, carefully insert the primary and secondary pistons into the piston bore, taking care not to crimp the seals.

21   Install the secondary and vacuum sleeves, along with the intermediate ring and stop washers, retaining them with the circlip.

22   Depress the primary piston slightly and insert and tighten the stop screw using a new seal.

23   Clean the strainer with new brake fluid, insert it in the reservoir and install the cap.

24   Press the sealing plugs into the master cylinder and install the reservoir by pushing it into one plug, turning it 180° and then pushing it into the remaining plug.

25   Connect the pressure differential warning switch (if equipped) wiring.

26   Insert the fluid lines and tighten the union nuts.

27   Connect the low fluid warning wiring to the fluid reservoir.

Bench bleeding

28   If the fluid has been drained or a new master cylinder is being installed it is a good idea to bench bleed the master cylinder before installation using the following procedure.

29   Because it will be necessary to apply pressure to the master cylinder piston and, at the same time, control flow from the brake line outlets, it is recommended that the master cylinder be mounted in a vise. Use caution not to clamp the vise too tightly, or the master cylinder body might be cracked.

30   Insert threaded plugs into the brake line outlet holes and snug them down so that there will be no air leakage past them, but not so tight that they cannot be easily loosened.

31   Fill the reservoirs with brake fluid of the recommended type (see Recommended fluids and lubricants).

32   Remove one plug and push the piston assembly into the master

cylinder bore to expell the air from the master cylinder. A large Phillips screwdriver can be used to push on the piston assembly.

33   To prevent air from being drawn back into the master cylinder, the plug must be replaced and snugged down before releasing the pressure on the piston assembly.

34   Repeat the procedure until only brake fluid is expelled from the brake line outlet hole. When only brake fluid is expelled, repeat the procedure with the other outlet hole and plug. Be sure to keep the master cylinder reservoir filled with brake fluid to prevent the introduction of air into the system.

35   Since high pressure is not involved in the bench bleeding procedure, an alternative to the removal and replacement of the plugs with each stroke of the piston assembly is available. Before pushing in on the piston assembly, remove the plug as described in Step 33. Before releasing the piston, however, instead of replacing the plug, simply put your finger tightly over the hole to keep air from being drawn back into the master cylinder. Wait several seconds for brake fluid to be drawn from the reservoir into the piston bore, then depress the piston again, removing your finger as brake fluid is expelled. Be sure to put your finger back over the hole each time before releasing the piston, and when the bleeding procedure is complete for that outlet, replace the plug and snug it before going on to the other port.

Installation

36   Install a new O-ring on the vacuum booster unit, place the master cylinder in position and install the nuts. Tighten the nuts to the specified torque.

37   Connect the fluid lines and plug in the electrical connectors. Check the operation of fluid level sensor by pushing down on the black rubber bulb-like protrusions on the top of the reservoir to make sure the light on the instrument panel lights up.

38   On manual transmission models, bleed the clutch hydraulic system.

39   On pressure differential warning indicator equipped models, press on the reset pin projecting from the switch.

40   Bleed the brake system (Section 8).

---

7   Hydraulic brake hoses and lines — inspection and replacement

Flexible hoses

1   About every six months, with the vehicle raised and placed securely on jackstands, the flexible hoses which connect the steel brake lines with the front and rear brake assemblies should be inspected for cracks, chafing of the outer cover, leaks, blisters and other damage. These are important and vulnerable parts of the brake system and inspection

should be complete. A light and mirror will prove helpful for a thorough check. If a hose exhibits any of the above conditions, replace it as follows.

2   Using a suitable wrench, disconnect the hose at the connection with the rigid line and then unscrew it from the caliper or connectors.

3   When installing make sure all bolt and fluid line connection threads are clean. Thread on using only your fingers to make sure the connector is not cross-threaded, then tighten with the wrench.

4   When the brake hose installation is complete, there should be no kinks or twists in the hose. Also, make sure the hose does not contact any part of the suspension. Check this by turning the wheels to the extreme left and right positions. If the hose makes contact, the lockplate on the flexible hose bracket used on these models can be moved to position the hose away from any adjacent components.

5   Fill the master cylinder reservoir and bleed the system (refer to Section 8).

Steel brake lines

6   When it becomes necessary to replace steel lines, use only double wall steel tubing. Never substitute copper tubing because copper is subject to fatigue cracking and corrosion. The outside diameter of the tubing is used for sizing.

7   Direct replacement parts are available at your dealer and auto parts stores and brake supply houses carry various lengths of prefabricated brake line. Depending on the type of tubing used, these sections can either be bent by hand into the desired shape or bent in a tubing bender.

8   If prefabricated lengths are not available, obtain the recommended steel tubing and fittings to match the line to be replaced. Determine the correct length by measuring the old brake line, and cut the new tubing to length, leaving about 1/2-inch extra for flaring the ends.

9   Install the fittings onto the cut tubing and flare the ends using an ISO flaring tool.

10   Using a tubing bender, bend the tubing to match the shape of the old brake line.

11   Tube flaring and bending can usually be performed by a local auto parts store if the proper equipment is not available.

12   When installing the brake line, leave at least 3/4-inch clearance between the line and any moving parts.

8 Brake system — bleeding

1   Removal of all the air from the braking system is essential for the correct operation of the system. Before undertaking this task check the level of fluid in the reservoir and top up if necessary.

2   Check all brake line unions and connections for possible leakage, and at the same time check the condition of the rubber hoses, which may be cracked or worn.

3   If the condition of a caliper or wheel cylinder is in doubt, check for signs of fluid leakage.

4   If there is any possibility that incorrect fluid has been used in the system, drain all the fluid and flush with methylated spirits. Replace all piston seals and cups, as they will be affected and could possibly fail under pressure.

5   You will need a clean jar, a 12-inch length of rubber tubing which fits tightly over the bleed valve and the correct grade of brake fluid.

6   Bleed the master cylinder first by loosening the master cylinder-to-fluid line nut.

7   Wrap a rag around the tubing union to absorb the escaping fluid.

8   Have an assistant push the brake pedal slowly to the floor, which will force any air in the master cylinder to escape at the fitting.

9   With the pedal held to the floor, tighten the fitting. Release the brake pedal. Note: *Do not release the brake pedal until the fitting is tightened or air will enter the master cylinder.*

10   Repeat this procedure until air ceases to escape from the fitting.

11   The primary (front) and secondary (rear) hydraulic brake systems are bled separately. Always bleed the longest line (furthest away from the master cylinder) first.

12   To bleed the secondary system (rear), clean the area around the bleed valves. Remove the rubber cap (if equipped) over the bleed valve and fit the rubber tube over the bleed nipple.

13   Place the end of the rubber tube in the jar, which should contain sufficient brake fluid to keep the end of the tube submerged during the operation.

14   Open the bleed valve approximately 3/4-turn and have an assistant

8.21 Press down on the low fluid warning switch to check its operation

depress the brake pedal slowly through its full travel. Hold the brake pedal fully depressed.

15   Close the bleed valve and allow the pedal to return to the released position.

16   Continue this sequence until no more air bubbles issue from the bleed tube.

17   At regular intervals during the bleeding sequence make sure that the reservoir is kept topped up, otherwise air will enter again at this point. Do not reuse fluid bled from the system.

18   Repeat the procedure on the remaining rear brake line.

19   To bleed the primary system (front), the procedure is identical to that previously described.

20   Top up the master cylinder to within 1/4-inch of the top of the reservoir, check that the gasket is correctly located in the cover and install the cover.

21   The operation of the low fluid warning switch(es) can be checked by pressing down on the black rubber bulb on the top with the ignition switch on (photo). The brake light on the dash will light if the switch is operating properly.

9 Brake fluid — replacment

1   Brake fluid readily absorbs moisture and this lowers the boiling point while increasing the possibility of corrosion of the brake parts. Consequently the manufacturer recommends that the fluid in the brake system be replaced at the specified interval.

2   Replacing the brake fluid is basically the same as bleeding air from the brake system (Section 8) and the same procedures and sequence should be followed. The major difference is that fresh brake fluid from new, sealed containers should be used and, making sure the master cylinder reservoir is kept filled, an assistant should pump the brake pedal approximately ten strokes with the bleed screw of each caliper opened in turn. This will ensure that the lines and calipers are filled with fresh fluid.

10 Parking brake — checking and adjustment

Checking

1   Push on the parking brake pedal (left-hand drive models) and make sure it engages between 2 and 4. On hand brake equipped models (right-hand drive), pull up on the handle and make sure that it does not have to be pulled more than 2 clicks.

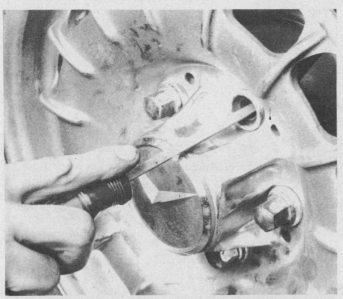

10.4 The parking brake adjustment starwheel is accessible through the wheel lug bolt opening with a screwdriver

10.5 With the brake rotor removed for clarity, the procedure for turning the starwheel to adjust the parking brake shoes can be seen

Adjustment

2 Block the wheels securely, remove one wheel bolt from each rear wheel and raise the rear of the vehicle.

3 Rotate the wheel until bolt hole is about 45° from vertical toward the front of the vehicle and the adjustment starwheel can be seen through the hole. A flashlight can be useful here.

4 Insert a flat bladed screwdriver into the hole until it engages the starwheel (photo).

5 Turn the starwheel with the screwdriver until the shoes are against the drum so the wheel won't turn and then back off 2 to 3 teeth so the wheel is just free to rotate without binding (photo).

6 After adjustment, lower the vehicle and install the wheel bolts. Recheck the adjustment and if it is still not within specification, adjust the cable by turning the bolt on the equalizer (photo).

---

11 Parking brake shoes — inspection and replacement

---

1 Remove the rear brake disc rotors (Section 5).

2 Carefully clean the dust from the brake assembly. **Caution:** *Do not inhale the brake dust as it is injurious to your health.*

3 Measure the thickness of the brake lining and if it is worn to less than that specified, replace the shoes as a set.

4 To remove the shoe retaining springs, align one of the wheel bolt holes with each spring in turn, compress the spring with a screwdriver and then rotate it 90° to disengage it.

5 Note the position of the return springs and then unhook and remove the lower spring.

6 Pull the bottom of the shoes apart and then withdraw the assembly, complete with the adjuster and upper return spring, over the axle flange.

7 Unhook the upper return spring and remove the shoes from the adjuster.

8 If necessary, remove the expander from the control cable by pushing the clevis pin out.

9 Wash the expander in solvent and wipe it dry. Lightly coat the contact surfaces with moly-base grease.

10 Connect the expander to the control cable and install the clevis pin. Hold the pin in place by pushing the expander against the brake backing plate.

11 Check the bolts retaining the backing plate and carrier housing with a suitable Allen wrench to make sure they are tightened securely.

12 Lubricate the adjuster threads lightly with moly-base grease and then set the adjuster at its shortest length.

13 Install the upper (large slot) ends in the adjuster so the adjuster wheel faces towards the front of the vehicle and hook the upper return springs to the shoes.

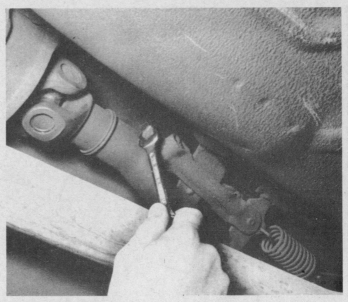

10.6 A small wrench can be used to adjust the parking brake cable adjustment bolt

14 Pull the bottom of the shoes apart, install the assembly over the axle flange and insert the expander into the smaller slots on the shoes.

15 Install the retaining springs.

16 Attach the small hook of the lower return spring to the front brake shoe and the large hook to the rear brake shoe.

17 Install the brake discs.

18 Adjust the parking brake (Section 10) and test for proper brake operation before placing the vehicle in service.

---

12 Parking brake cables — removal and installation

---

1 Raise the vehicle and support it securely on jackstands.

2 On some models, it may be necessary to lower the exhaust pipe for clearance, supporting it on a jackstand.

3 Unhook the return spring.

4 Unscrew the adjusting bolt completely, then release the intermediate lever from the underbody and adjusting bracket.

9

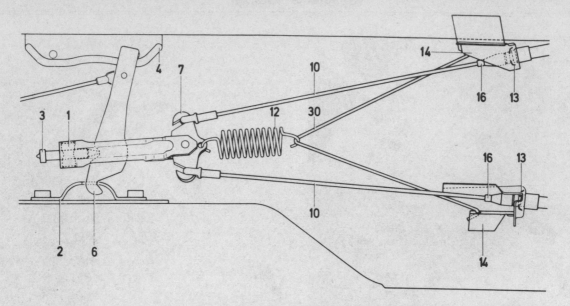

Fig. 9.4 Parking brake cable component layout (Sec 12)

1 Adjusting bracket	6 Intermediate lever	13 Spring clamp
2 Underbody mount	7 Compensating lever	14 Rear brake control cable
3 Adjusting screw	10 Rear brake control cable	16 Rubber sleeve
4 Intermediate lever guide		30 Spring holder

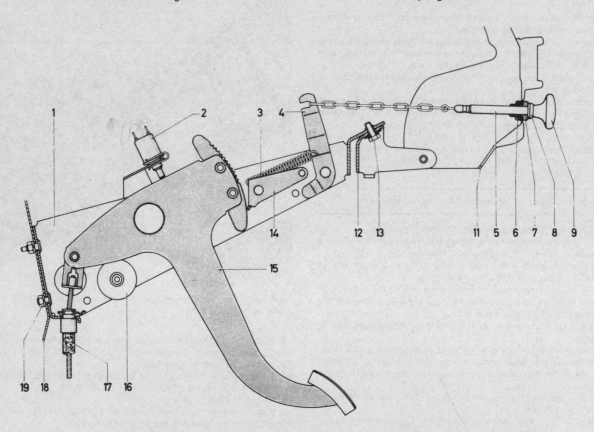

Fig. 9.5 Parking brake pedal component layout (left hand drive models) (Sec 13)

1 Bracket	7 Rosette	14 Detent
2 Warning light switch	8 Stop buffer	15 Pedal
3 Return spring	9 Actuating knob	16 Rubber stop
4 Releasing lever	11 Instrument panel	17 Brake control cable
5 Pull rod and chain	12 Panel holder	18 Bulkhead
6 Nut	13 Bolt	19 Bolt

Front cable

5   Remove the cotter pin and remove the clevis pin securing the front cable to the intermediate lever.
6   Pry off the spring clip securing the cable guide to the crossmember behind the transmission.
7   Inside the vehicle, remove the trim panel for access to the cable.
8   Disconnect the inner cable from the pedal or lever, pry out the spring clip and disconnect the outer cable.
9   Pull the cable through the rubber grommet from under the car.
10 Installation is the reverse of removal, adjusting the parking brake (Sec 10).

Rear cables

11 Disconnect the equalizer from both rear cables.
12 Pry off the spring clips and remove the cables from the underbody brackets.
13 Remove the parking brake shoe assemblies (Sec 11).
14 Remove the retaining bolts from the axleshaft housing and withdraw the cables.
15 Installation is the reverse of removal. After installing the shoes (Section 11), adjust the parking brake (Section 10).

13   Parking brake pedal (US models) — removal and installation

1   Raise the vehicle and support it securely on jackstands.
2   On some models it may be necessary to lower the exhaust system for clearance and support it on a jackstand.
3   Unhook the parking brake return spring.
4   Back the cable adjusting bolt completely out and release the in-termediate lever from the underbody and adjusting bracket.
5   Turn the steering all the way to the left stop and unscrew the pedal bracket nut from under the wheel well.
6   In the engine compartment, remove the bracket nut.
7   In the passenger compartment, remove the trim panel.
8   Disconnect the inner cable from the pedal and then pry the spring clip out and disconnect the outer cable.
9   Disconnect the wiring connector and warning switch wiring.
10 Disconnect the release knob chain from the lever.
11 Remove the upper retaining bolt and withdraw the pedal assembly from the vehicle.
12 Installation is the reverse of removal. After installation, adjust the parking brake (Section 10).

14   Parking brake hand lever (UK models) — removal and installation

1   Raise the vehicle and support it securely on jackstands.
2   If necessary for clearance, lower the exhaust system and support it on a jackstand.
3   Disconnect the parking brake return spring.
4   Back the cable adjusting bolt fully out and release the intermediate lever from the underbody and the adjusting bracket.
5   Inside the vehicle, remove the trim panel and disconnect the inner cable from the lever.
6   Unbolt the lever bracket from the side panel and disconnect the top of the lever from the pullrod by removing the clevis pin.
7   Installation is the reverse of removal. After installation, adjust the parking brake (Section 10).

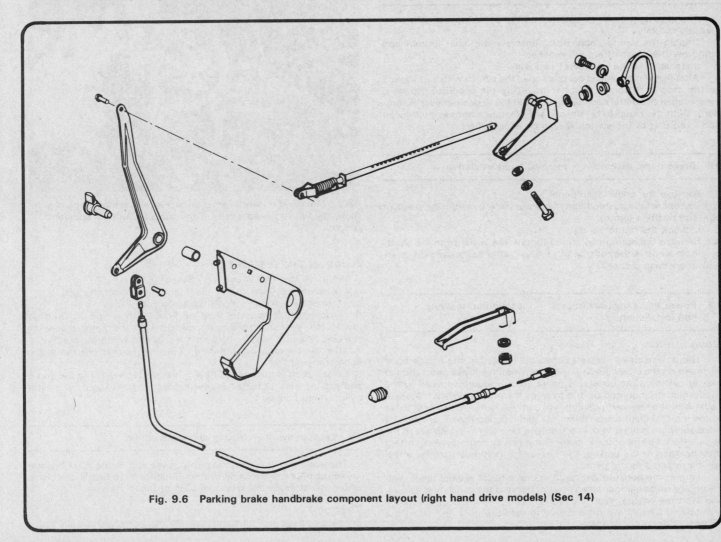

Fig. 9.6 Parking brake handbrake component layout (right hand drive models) (Sec 14)

9

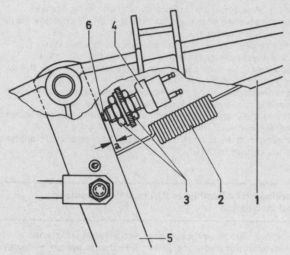

Fig. 9.7 Stop-light switch installation details (Sec 15)

1 Mounting bracket for brake   4 Brake lamp switch
   pedal   5 Brake pedal
2 Return spring   6 Contact button
3 Hex. nut   a = adjusting dimension

15 Stop light switch — removal and installation

1   The stop light switch is located on the pedal bracket below the steering column.
2   Unplug the wiring connectors, unscrew the inner locknut and withdraw the switch from the bracket.
3   Installation is the reverse of removal.
4   After installation, adjust the position of the switch with the locknuts so the stop light comes on after travelling the specified distance, measured at the pedal pad (dimension a in the accompanying illustration). With the pedal fully released the clearance between the pedal and fixed part of the switch should be as specified.

16 Brake pedal assembly — removal and installation

1   Remove the under dash panel.
2   Disconnect the pushrod from the brake pedal by removing the pivot bolt and bushing (photo).
3   Unhook the return spring.
4   Remove the spring clip and withdraw the pedal from the shaft.
5   Installation is the reverse of removal, after lubricating the shaft with moly-base grease.

17 Power brake vacuum booster — description, removal and installation

Description

1   The power brake vacuum booster is located in the engine compartment on the driver's side firewall between the brake pedal and the master cylinder. The booster is operated by vacuum supplied by the vacuum pump mounted on the front of the engine. When the brake pedal is in the released position, vacuum is channelled to both sides of the internal diaphragm. When the pedal is depressed, one side of the diaphragm is open to the atmosphere resulting in assistance to the pedal effort. Failure of the booster or the vacuum pump will not affect the operation of the braking system except that much greater effort will be required at the pedal.
2   To test the booster, depress the brake pedal several times with the engine off to dissipate the vacuum. Depress the pedal, hold it down and start the engine. With the engine idling, the vacuum assistance will draw the pedal a short distance toward the floor, indicating the booster is operating properly.

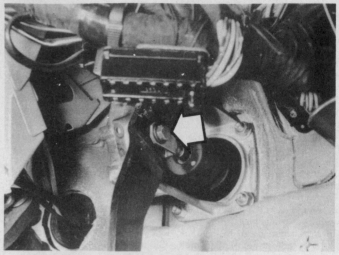

16.2   Brake pedal pivot bolt location (arrow)

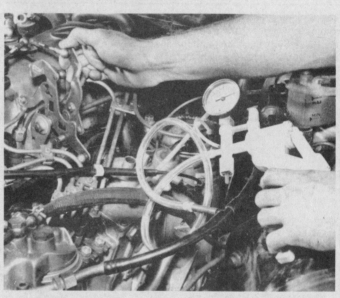

18.2   Moving the throttle lever to increase the engine speed will make the vacuum reading rise if the vacuum pump is operating properly

Removal and installation

3   Remove the master cylinder (Section 6).
4   Unscrew the vacuum line union and disconnect the line.
5   Inside the vehicle, remove the underdash panel.
6   Disconnect the booster pushrod from the brake pedal. On early models this is accomplished by removing the nut and then withdrawing the bolt. On later models, extract the clip and withdraw the pin.
7   Remove the mounting nuts and lift the booster unit from the engine compartment.
8   Installation is the reverse of removal with reference to Section 6 and making sure to install a new sealing ring between the master cylinder and booster.

18 Vacuum pump — testing and replacement

1   Because the vacuum pump provides vacuum for the brake booster as well as the central locking system (Chapter 11) a fault in the pump will manifest itself in a failure of both of these systems.

Testing

2   To check the vacuum pump, trace the line from the vacuum pump

and connect a hand operated vacuum pump which incorporates a gauge. Start the engine and make sure the vacuum reading increases along with engine speed when the throttle is opened, indicating the pump is operating (photo).

Replacement

3   Remove the radiator.
4   Disconnect the battery negative cable.
5   Remove any drivebelts which will interfere with removal.
6   Disconnect the vacuum connections at the pump by unscrewing the pipe union while holding the nut on the pipe.
7   Installation is the reverse of removal.

19 Anti-lock Braking System (ABS) — description

The components of this system include speed sensors mounted in the front steering knuckles, differential drive pinion and rear hubs, a hydraulic unit and the electronic control unit along with associated wiring. The hydraulic unit incorporates three fast switching valves which are controlled by the electrical signals from the wheel speed sensors by way of the electronic control unit to vary the fluid pressure elec-trically to keep the wheels from locking up.

In operation, once the vehicle has reached an initial speed of 6 mph (10 kmh), the ABS prevents the locking of the wheels at speeds over 3 mph (5 kmh). If one wheel starts to lock up, the ABS modulates the brake pressure and the brake pedal pulsates slightly to make the driver aware the system is operating.

An ABS indicator lamp in the instrument cluster comes on when the vehicle is first started. The light should go out as the vehicle starts off, at the very latest. The light will come on if the system isn't working or under certain conditions (such as if a wheel continues to spin on an icy road, for example) for more than 20 seconds. In this case the vehicle should be stopped and the engine shut off and restarted to reac-tivate the ABS. Also, if the vehicle voltage drops below 10 volts the light will also come on until the voltage rises above this point.

If the indicator lamp stays on, the ABS system has switched off because of a fault in which case the normal braking system will still be in operation, but without the anti-locking feature. In this instance the vehicle should be taken to a dealer to have the system checked as soon as possible.

The components and procedures described previously in this Chapter should apply to models equipped with ABS. If operational problems are encountered with this system, a Mercedes dealer should diagnose the system further.

Chapter 10 Suspension and steering systems

Contents

Bleeding the power steering system 21
Front shock absorber — removal and installation 5
Front stabilizer bar — removal and installation 6
Front wheel bearing check, repack and
  adjustment. . . . . See Chapter 1
General information 1
Level control system — description and checking 10
Power steering pump drive belt — adjustment . . See Chapter 1
Power steering pump drive belt — removal
  and installation. . . . . See Chapter 1
Power steering pump — removal and installation 20
Rear shock absorber — removal and installation 7
Rear stabilizer bar — removal and installation 8
Rear suspension front mount bushing — replacement 9
Steering column — removal and installation 12

Steering column coupling and corrugated tube — removal
  and installation 13
Steering damper — removal and installation 19
Steering gear — removal and installation 15
Steering idler arm — removal and installation 16
Steering linkage ends — check and replacement 18
Steering lock and ignition switch — removal
  and installation 14
Steering track rod and drag link — removal and installation . . 17
Steering wheel — removal and installation 11
Suspension and steering check . . . . See Chapter 1
Suspension system — inspection 4
Wheel bearing check, repack and adjustment . . . See Chapter 1
Wheels and tires — general information 2
Wheels and tires — removal and installation 3

Specifications

General
Front suspension
Type . . . .   Independent with coil springs, upper and lower control arms, telescopic shock absorbers and stabilizer bar

Rear suspension
Type . . . .   Independent with coil springs, semi-trailing arms, telescopic shock absorbers and stabilizer bar

Steering
Type . . . .   Recirculating ball with safety collapsible column and power assist
Dimension a (Fig. 10.4) . . . .   22.7 mm
Dimension b (Fig. 10.4) . . . .   165 mm

Tire pressures — cold

	Front	Rear
Standard sedans and coupes	196.2 kPa (28.4 psi)	215.8 kPa (31.3 psi)
Special sedans	245.2 kPa (35.6 psi)	294.3 kPa (42.7 psi)
Standard station wagon	196.2 kPa (28.4 psi)	215.8 kPa (31.3 psi)
Special station wagon	225.6 kPa (32.7 psi)	313.9 kPa (45.5 psi)

Torque specifications

	Nm	Ft-lbs
Front suspension		
Shock absorber lower mount bolt	19	14
Stabilizer bar end bolt.	65	48
Stabilizer bar mounting clamp bolt	19	14
Rear suspension		
Shock absorber lower mount bolt	45	33
Stabilizer bar mounting nut		
With lockwashers	19	14
Without lockwashers	30	22
Stabilizer bar link nut		
Metal	45	33
Plastic	30	22
Rear suspension front mount bushing bolt	119	89
Rear suspension front mount-to-underbody	40	30

Torque specifications (continued)

Steering

Track rod and drag link bolt	35	26
Track rod clamp bolt	20	15
Steering gear bolts	69 to 80	51 to 59
Pitman arm nut		
22 mm	140 to 179	103 to 132
24 mm	160 to 199	118 to 147
Steering arm nut	80	59
Steering damper bolt	45	33
Steering wheel nut or screw	80	59
Steering column bolt		
Upper mounting	9	6.6
Lower mounting	24	18
Steering shaft coupling bolt	25	18
Power steering pump bolt	34	25

Wheels

Wheel lug nuts	100 to 110	73 to 81

1 General information

The independent coil spring type front suspension features upper and lower control arms, support arms and telescopic shock absorbers. The front stabilizer bar is attached to the upper control arms and all suspension points are rubber mounted. The steering knuckle is attached to the upper control arms by sealed balljoints. The front wheel bearings are of the tapered roller type.

The independent rear suspension incorporates semi-trailing arms, coil springs and telescopic shock absorbers. A stabilizer bar is installed on all models. Some models are equipped with a hydraulic level control system on the rear suspension only. The recirculating ball-type steering features a collapsible steering column with power assist available.

Note: *Some later model vehicles are equipped with an ABS system (see Chapter 9). Some procedures in this Chapter may be affected by the presence of ABS components.*

2 Wheels and tires — general information

These models are equipped with metric size steel belted radial tires. Do not mix different types of tires such as radials and bias belted on the same car, as handling may be seriously affected.

It is recommended that tires be replaced in pairs on the same axle, but if only one tire is being replaced, be sure it is of the same size, structure and tread design as the other.

Because tire pressure has a substantial effect on handling and wear, the pressure on all tires should be checked at least once a month or before any extended trips and set to the correct pressure. Tire pressure should be checked and adjusted with the tires cold.

To achieve maximum life from your tires they should be rotated on the car as described in Chapter 1.

The tires should be replaced when the depth of the tread pattern is worn to the minimum specified depth. Some tires incorporate wear indicators which appear as bands across the tread when the tire is worn beyond limits. Tread wear can also be measured with a gauge inserted into the tread grooves. Correct tire pressures and driving techniques have an important influence on tire life. Hard cornering, excessively rapid acceleration or deceleration and heavy braking decrease tire wear. Extremely worn tires are very susceptible to punctures and are especially dangerous in wet weather conditions.

The tire tread pattern can give a good indication of problems in the maintenance or adjustment of tires and suspension components. If an abnormal tread wire pattern is seen, have the vehicle inspected by a Mercedes dealer for possible faults.

Wheels must be replaced if they are bent, rusted or corroded, buckled, leak air, have elongated bolt holes or if the lug nuts won't stay tight. Damaged wheels should be replaced with new ones rather than repaired as this can weaken the metal. Aluminum wheels are especially prone to corrosion and are easily scratched. When washing aluminum wheels use a soft cloth and a mild, non-abrasive detergent. If salty or alkaline water gets on aluminum wheels, they should be washed as soon as possible as salt and alkali can damage them.

Tire and wheel balance is important in the overall handling, braking and performance of the car. Unbalanced wheels can adversely affect handling and ride characteristics as well as tire life. Whenever a tire is installed on a wheel, the tire and wheel should be balanced by a qualified shop with the proper equipment.

3 Wheels and tires — removal and installation

1   With the car on a level surface, the parking brake on and the car in gear (manual transmissions should be in 'Reverse'; automatic transmissions should be in 'Park') remove the wheel cover (if equipped) and loosen, but do not remove, the wheel lug bolts or nuts.
2   Using a jack positioned in the proper location on the car, raise the car just enough so that the tire clears the ground surface.
3   Remove the wheel lug bolts.
4   Remove the wheel and tire.
5   If a flat tire is being replaced, ensure that there's adequate ground clearance for the new inflated tire, then mount the wheel and tire on the hub, holding it in place with one lug bolt.
6   Apply a light coat of spray lubricant or light oil to the wheel bolt threads and install them snugly with the cone shaped end facing the wheel.
7   Lower the car until the tire contacts the ground and the wheel stud or bolts are centered in their wheel holes.
8   Tighten the lug bolts evenly and in a cross pattern, and torque tighten to the specified torque.
9   Lower the car completely and remove the jack.
10 Replace the wheel cover.

4 Suspension system — inspection

1   The suspension components should normally last a long time, except in cases where damage has occurred due to an accident. The suspension parts, however, should be checked from time to time for signs of wear which will result in a loss of precision handling and riding comfort.
2   Because these models feature four wheel independent suspension, excessive wear on the inner edges of the rear as well as the front tires is an indication of both the front and rear suspension being out of adjustment or alignment. The vehicle should be taken to a dealer or properly equipped shop for further inspection and adjustment.
3   Check the condition of the steering. Grip the steering wheel at the top with both hands and rock it back and forth. Listen for any squeaks or metallic noises. Feel for free play. If any of these conditions is found, have an assistant do the rocking while the source of the trouble is located.
4   Check the shock absorbers, as these are the parts of the suspension system likely to wear out first. If there is any evidence of fluid leakage, they will definitely need replacing. Bounce the car up and down vigorously. It should feel stiff, and well damped by the shock absorbers. As soon as the bouncing is stopped the car should return to its normal

10

5.1a   Use a wrench to hold the lower shock absorber nut while loosening the locknut

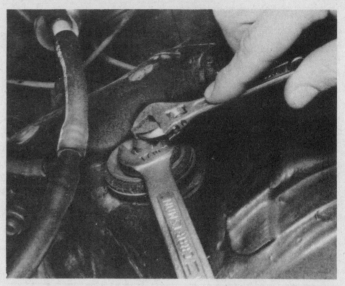

5.1b   Hold the top of the shock absorber shaft with a wrench while loosening the retaining nut; the shaft must not turn

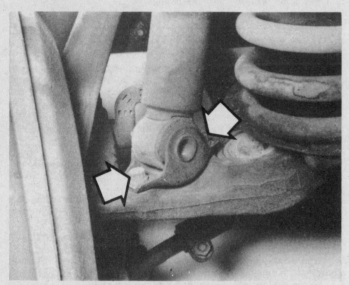

5.3   The front shock absorber lower retaining bolts (arrows)

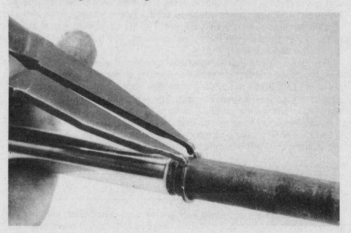

5.5   Remove the circlip from the shock absorber shaft

position without excessive up and down movement. Do not replace the shock absorbers as single units, but rather in pairs unless failure has occurred at low mileage.

5   Check all rubber bushings and grease seals for signs of deterioration, cracking and oil leakage. Have the damaged component replaced as soon as possible.

5   Front shock absorber — removal and installation

Warning: *On gas-charged shock absorbers, the strut shaft must not be allowed to rotate because this could loosen the internal seal resulting in a sudden extension of the shaft possibly causing personal injury. Consequently the shaft should always be held with a wrench on the flats at the end.*

1   In the engine compartment, remove the upper shock absorber locknut while holding the lower nut with a second wrench (photo). Now hold the top of the shock absorber shaft firmly with a wrench while the lower nut is removed (photo). Following this nut, remove the washers and rubber grommet.

2   Raise the front of the vehicle, support it securely on jackstands and remove the front wheel(s).

3   Remove the two lower shock absorber bolts, using a suitable socket. It may be necessary to use a box wrench on the inner bolt because of lack of clearance (photo).

4   Remove the shock absorber from the vehicle.

5   Depending on the style of the replacement shock absorber, some components may have to be transferred from the old shock absorber

5.7   Raising a gas charged shock absorber into place with a jack

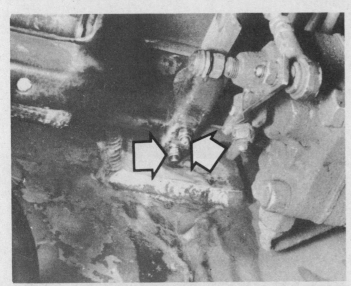

8.3 The level control unit link U-bolt-to-rear stabilizer bar nuts (arrows)

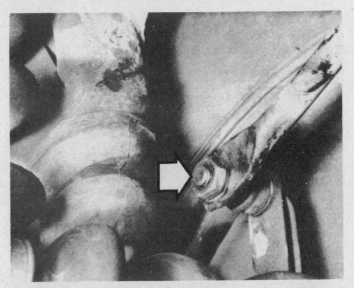

8.4 Stabilizer bar link nut location (arrow)

6 Slide the split rubber mounts from the stabilizer bar and remove the end covers from the body.
7 Withdraw the stabilizer bar from one side of the vehicle. Remove the rubber mounts from each end of the bar.
8 Check the rubber mounts for damage or wear, replacing them with new ones if necessary.
9 Installation is a reversal of removal, making sure that the bends on the bar where it exits the inner fender well faces downward and that the recesses in the clamps are located over the lugs on the rubber mounts.
10 Lower the vehicle weight onto the suspension and fully tighten the mounting nuts and bolts.

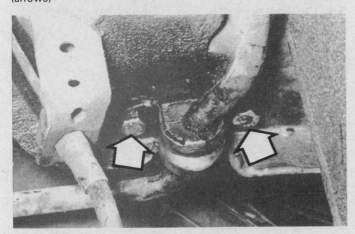

8.5 Stabilizer bar mounting clamp bolts

body to the new. If required, all components can be removed after removing the shaft circlip (photo).
6 Install the components on the new shock absorber.
7 Place the shock absorber in position with the shaft inserted in the upper mounting hole and install the lower mounting bolts. On gas charged shock absorbers it may be necessary to use a jack under the hub to further raise the shaft through the hole into the engine compartment (photo).
8 Install the mounting rubber, washer and nut. Hold the shaft with a wrench, tighten the nut securely and then install the locking nut. Tighten all fasteners to the proper torque after first lowering the vehicle to the ground.

7 Rear shock absorber — removal and installation

Note: *On level control equipped models, the rear shock absorber is part of the leveling system and removal and installation should be left to a dealer or properly equipped shop.*

1 Inside the vehicle, remove the rear seat and cushion (Chapter 11).
2 Block the front wheels, raise the rear of the vehicle and support it securely on jackstands.
3 Use a screwdriver or similar tool to pry out the access cover.
4 Remove the upper shock absorber nuts. **Warning:** *On gas-charged shock absorbers, the strut shaft must not be allowed to rotate because this could loosen the internal seal resulting in a sudden extension of the shaft possibly causing personal injury. Consequently the shaft should always be held with a wrench on the flats at the end.*
5 Under the vehicle, remove the lower mounting bolts and remove the shock absorber from the vehicle.
6 Installation is the reverse of removal. On gas-charged shock absorbers, it may be necessary to raise the strut up into the body, using a jack under the rear trailing arm.

6 Front stabilizer bar — removal and installation

1 Apply the parking brake, block the rear wheels, raise the front of the vehicle and support it securely on jackstands positioned beneath the lower control arms. Remove the front wheels.
2 Remove the mounting bolts from each end of the stabilizer bar, noting the position of the washers and mounting rubbers.
3 Remove the brake master cylinder and servo unit (Chapter 9) and battery and mount.
4 If necessary, remove the coolant hoses (drain cooling system first, as described in Chapter 1), linkage, vacuum lines and wiring which would interfere with access to the stabilizer bar.
5 Remove the mounting nuts on the bulkheads and remove the clamps.

8 Rear stabilizer bar — removal and installation

1 Block the front wheels, raise the rear of the vehicle and support it securely on jackstands.
2 Remove the rear wheels.
3 On level control equipped models, mark the location of the level control link on the stabilizer bar and disconnect the link (photo).
4 Remove the nuts securing the ends of the stabilizer bar to the links and pull out the links (photo).
5 Unbolt the mounting clamps from the underbody and remove the mounting plates and rubber mounts (photo).
6 Disconnect the rubber exhaust mount rings and lower the rear exhaust onto a jackstand or similar support.
7 Withdraw the stabilizer bar through the right side wheel well.

10

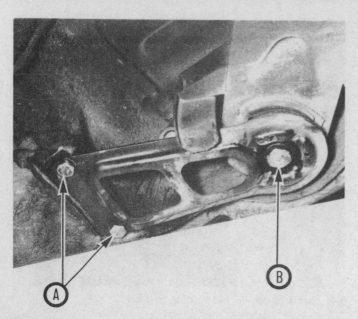

9.3   Rear suspension mount-to-underbody (A) and bushing (B) bolts

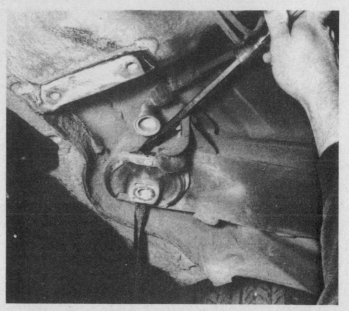

9.4   Use two screwdrivers to pry out the rear mount bushing

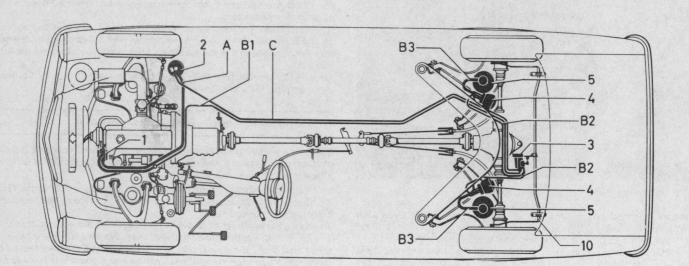

Fig. 10.1 Typical level control system component layout (Sec 10)

1 Hydraulic pressure pump	10 Stabilizer bar	B2 Pressure line from controller
2 Reservoir	A Suction line	to pressure reservoir
3 Level controller	B1 Pressure line to level	B3 Pressure return line from
4 Pressure reservoir	controller	pressure reservoir to strut
5 Suspension strut		C Return line

8   Inspect the rubber mounts for wear and damage, replacing as necessary.

9   Installation is the reverse of removal, making sure that the bends on the bar between the mount and the link face downward.

10 On level control equipped models have the rear body level checked by a dealer.

9   Rear suspension front mount bushing — replacement

1   Block the front wheels, raise the rear of the vehicle and support it on jackstands.

2   Support the suspension front mount with a jackstand or similar support.

3   Remove the suspension mount-to-underbody bolts, followed by the suspension mount-to-bushing bolt (photo).

4   Pry the old bushing out of the mount crossmember (photo).

5   Prior to installation, lubricate the new bushing with rubber lubricant or soapy water.

6   Press the bushing into place in the crossmember. It may be necessary to use the mounting bolt with a nut and several spacers as a tool to draw the bushing into place.

7   Install the front mount and tighten the bolts securely.

8   Lower the vehicle.

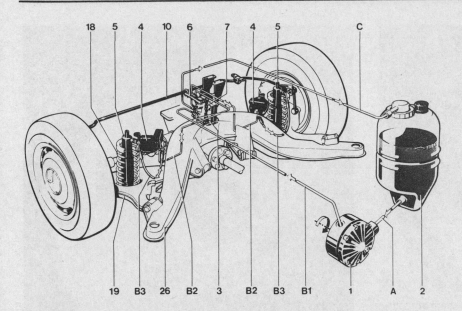

Fig. 10.2 Sedan and coupe model level control system details (Sec 10)

1 Hydraulic pressure pump
2 Oil supply tank
3 Level controller
4 Pressure reservoir
5 Suspension strut
6 Lever on stabilizer bar
7 Connecting rod
10 Stabilizer bar
18 Rear spring
19 Suspension arm
26 Rear axle carrier
A Oil supply tank to hydraulic pressure pump suction line
B1 Pressure oil pump to level controller pressure
B2 Level controller to pressure reservoir linel
B3 Pressure reservoir to suspension strut pressure line
C Level controller to oil supply tank return line

Fig.10.3 Station wagon level control system details (Sec 10)

1 Hydraulic pressure pump
2 Oil supply tank
3 Level controller
4 Pressure reservoir
5 Suspension strut
6 Lever on stabilizer bar
7 Connecting rod
10 Stabilizer bar
18 Rear spring
19 Suspension arm
26 Rear axle carrier
A Oil supply tank to hydraulic pressure pump line
B1 Hydraulic pressure pump to level controller line
B2 Level controller to pressure reservoir pressure line
B3 Pressure reservoir to suspension strut pressure line
C Level controller to oil supply tank return line

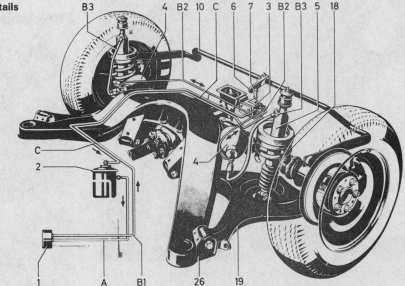

10 Level control system — description and checking

1   Some models are equipped with a level control system which hydraulically regulates the rear ride height of the vehicle. The system incorporates two struts fitted in place of the rear shock absorbers, and each strut is connected to its own pressure reservoir. A pump on the engine supplies the hydraulic fluid and the ride height is adjusted by a level controller attached to the rear stabilizer bar. The pressure reservoirs incorporate a gas-filled section which maintains the pressure during the deflection of the suspension.

2   The pump is driven by an auxiliary shaft which is driven by the timing chain.

3   Checking the level system consists of making sure the reservoir is filled to the proper level with the specified oil and inspecting all of the lines and connections for leaks and the level controller for damage and bent or loose linkage or levers (photo).

4   When filling the system, top up the reservoir to the maximum mark then run the engine at fast idling speed for approximately I minute with one or two persons, or an equivalent weight, in the rear luggage compartment. Stop the engine and top up the level. Note that, with the vehicle fully loaded and the engine running, the level will drop to the minimum mark.

10.3   The level control system unit (arrow) can be inspected from under the vehicle

10

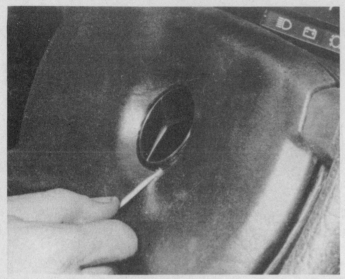

11.2   Use a small screwdriver to carefully pry out the motif logo from the steering wheel cover

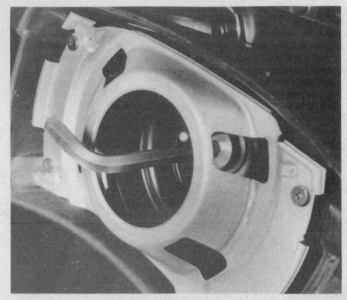

11.4   An Allen wrench can be used to remove the steering wheel screw on earlier models

12.7   Remove the steering column lower clamp bolt with an Allen wrench

5   Because of the special tools and techniques required, further checking or adjustment of the level control system should be left to a dealer or properly equipped shop.

11   Steering wheel — removal and installation

1   Disconnect the negative cable at the battery. Place the cable out of the way so it cannot accidentally come in contact with the negative terminal of the battery, as this would once again allow power into the electrical system of the vehicle.
2   Remove the horn pad (models produced prior to September, 1979) or pry the motif logo from the center of the steering wheel pad (later models) (photo).
3   With the front wheels point straight ahead, mark the relative positions of the steering wheel and inner column.
4   Remove the steering wheel retaining screw or nut using a suitable Allen head wrench or socket (photo).
5   Withdraw the steering wheel from the shaft splines.
6   Installation is the reverse of removal, taking care to align the marks made at the time of removal and tightening the screw or bolt to the specified torque.

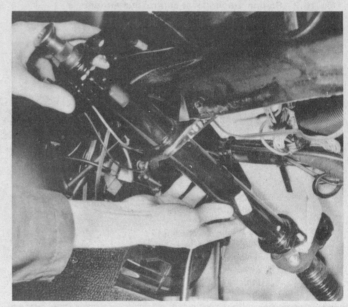

12.10   Support the steering column when removing it as it is easily damaged

12   Steering column — removal and installation

1   Disconnect the negative cable at the battery. Place the cable out of the way so it cannot accidentally come in contact with the negative terminal of the battery, as this would once again allow power into the electrical system of the vehicle.
2   Remove the lower under dash cover panels.
3   Remove the steering wheel (Section 11).
4   Remove the instrument panel (Chapter 11).
5   On automatic transmission equipped models with steering column shift, disconnect the shift linkage.
6   Remove the steering column lock (Section 14).
7   Remove the clamp bolt at the base of the steering column, using a suitable Allen head wrench (photo).
8   Remove the lower steering column retaining nuts and remove the heater hose bracket (if equipped).
9   Unplug the combination switch wiring connector.
10   Remove the upper mounting nuts, lower the column (taking care

14.4 With the tabs bent back, the key lock trim ring can be removed

not to damage the corrugated tube of the lower shaft) and withdraw it from the vehicle (photo).

11 Installation is the reverse of removal, taking care not to damage the lower shaft corrugated tube and making sure that the flat on the upper steering shaft faces the screw end of the steering coupling so the Allen head screw can be installed. Tighten all bolts to the proper torque.

13 Steering column coupling and corrugated tube — removal and installation

1 Disconnect the negative cable at the battery. Place the cable out of the way so it cannot accidentally come in contact with the negative terminal of the battery, as this would once again allow power into the electrical system of the vehicle.
2 Remove both under dash panels, for access.
3 Working in the engine compartment, use an Allen wrench to unscrew both clamp bolts from the coupling to the steering gear.
4 Push the coupling fully against the steering gear, removing the guard plate (if equipped).
5 Working inside the vehicle, use an Allen wrench to remove the clamp bolt at the bottom of the column on the coupling.
6 Push the coupling down into the opening in the firewall and then withdraw it from the vehicle, taking care not to damage the corrugated tube.
7 Installation is the reverse of removal, after lubricating the white plastic sealing ring at the bottom of the tube and the sealing lips of the rubber seal in the firewall with white lithium base grease. Make certain that the coupling clamp bolts are properly aligned and the coupling is securely mounted to both the upper steering shaft and the steering gear before tightening the bolts.

14 Steering lock and ignition switch — removal and installation

Note: *If the steering lock is defective and cannot be operated, the complete column must be removed (Section 12) and the locking pin drilled out.*

1 Disconnect the negative cable at the battery. Place the cable out of the way so it cannot accidentally come in contact with the negative terminal of the battery, as this would once again allow power into the electrical system of the vehicle.
2 Remove both under dash panels (Chapter 11).
3 Remove the instrument cluster (Chapter 12).
4 Bend back the tabs and remove the key lock trim ring from the dash (photo).
5 On early models use a hooked piece of wire to pull the plastic cap

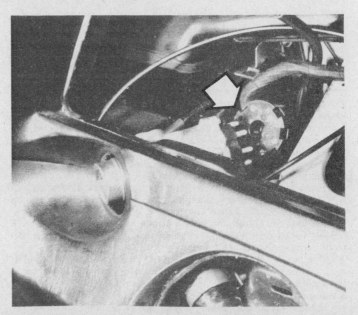

14.6 With the instrument cluster removed, the ignition switch (arrow) can be unplugged

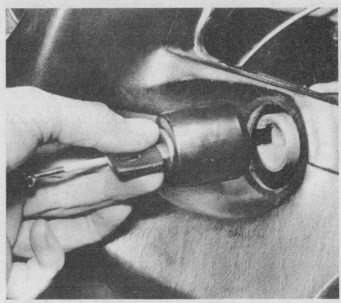

14.7 The ignition switch can be withdrawn with a small screwdriver or piece of wire inserted in the cutout

from the lock.
6 Unplug the connector from the ignition switch (photo).
7 On later models, insert the ignition key and turn it to the I position, then insert a piece of 0.05 in (1.25 mm) diameter wire in the locking cylinder cut-out, unscrew the cap and remove the locking cylinder (photo). Remove the wire, turn the key to the O position and remove it. Remove the cap, then insert the key in the I position and reinstall the locking cylinder in the housing while pushing down the detent. Disconnect the contact plug.
8 On all models with a steering lock starter switch, mark and disconnect the vacuum lines from the vacuum valve.
9 Loosen the steering lock clamp bolt. With the ignition key in the I position, depress the locking pin with a small screwdriver and turn the lock slightly, then turn the key to the O position and remove it.
10 Withdraw the steering lock from the column.
11 With the key in the I position, remove the contact switch or locking cylinder.
12 Installation is the reverse of removal, making sure to reconnect the vacuum lines securely to their original positions. On models which

10

don't have a steering lock starter switch, attach the preglow cable control to the steering lock making sure the dimensions are as specified, referring to the accompanying illustration.

15 Steering gear — removal and installation

1   Disconnect the negative cable at the battery. Place the cable out of the way so it cannot accidentally come in contact with the negative terminal of the battery, as this would once again allow power into the electrical system of the vehicle.

2   Set the front wheels in the straight-ahead position.

3   Syphon the fluid from the power steering pump reservoir and disconnect and plug the fluid hoses.

4   Raise the front of the vehicle and support it on jackstands.

5   Unscrew the coupling clamp bolts using a suitable Allen wrench and slide the coupling from the steering gear.

6   Remove the cotter pins and nuts securing the drag link and track rod end to the steering gear Pitman arm (photo). Use a separator tool to disconnect the link and arm.

7   Remove the self-locking nut and use a puller to remove the Pitman arm from the steering gear after marking the arm in relation to the sector shaft.

8   Support the steering gear (it's very heavy) and remove the mounting bolts which are accessible from the wheel well (photo). Lower the steering gear from the vehicle.

9   Installation is the reverse of removal, tighening all nuts and bolts to the specified torque. Make sure that the steering wheel and gear are in their central positions before sliding the coupling into place. Check that on full lock the Pitman arm or idler arm contacts the stops on the crossmember. If not, the track rod lengths may be unequal and should be checked by a dealer or properly equipped shop.

16 Steering idler arm — removal and installation

1   Raise the front of the vehicle and support it securely on jackstands.

2   Remove the cotter pins and nuts securing the drag link and track rod end to the steering idler, disconnect the link and arm using a suitable separator tool.

3   Remove the self-locking nut and the washer from the bottom of the idler.

4   Lift the idler arm out, noting the position of washers and dust caps.

5   When removing the bushings from the idler, it may be necessary to use a hammer and brass drift.

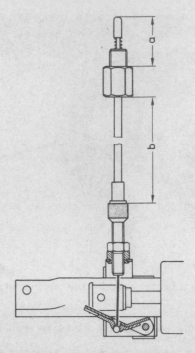

Fig. 10.4 Cable control installation details on models without a steering lock switch (refer to Specifications for dimensions a and b) (Sec 14)

6   Clean all the components and check them for wear, corrosion or damage.

7   Installation is a reversal of removal, after lubricating the bushings with oil. Tighten the nuts to the specified torque.

17 Steering track rod and drag link — removal and installation

1   Raise the front of the vehicle and support it securely on jackstands. If the track rod is being removed, remove the wheel from that side of the vehicle.

2   Remove the retaining cotter pins and nuts.

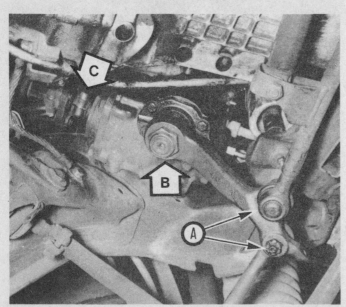

15.6   The steering gear connections accessible under the vehicle are the steering rod nuts (A), Pitman arm nut (B) and steering shaft bolt (C)

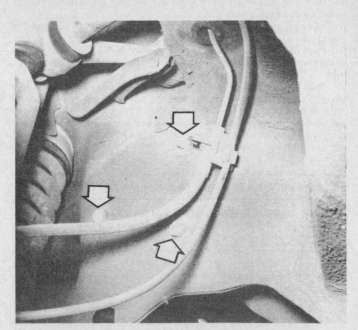

15.8   The retaining bolts for the steering gear (arrows) are accessible from the wheel well

3   Using a suitable separator tool disconnect the track rod ends from the arms (photo). When removing the drag link, disconnect the steering damper (Section 19), noting the position of washers and covers.
4   Installation is the reverse of removal.
5   Have the front wheel alignment checked.

18   Steering linkage ends — check and replacement

1   Block the rear wheels, raise the front of the vehicle and support securely on jackstands.
2   Attempt to turn the front wheel by hand alternately in opposite directions. If any play is evident check each rod end to determine which one is worn.
3   Remove the wheel.
4   Remove the cotter pin and nut.
5   Use a suitable separator tool to disconnect the track rod end from the steering arm.
6   Loosen the clamp bolt and remove the track rod end, either marking its position with white paint or noting the exact number of turns necessary to remove it.
7   Screw the new track rod end in to the marked or noted position and tighten the clamp bolt.
8   Install the track rod end on the steering arm, tighten the nut, and install a new cotter pin.
9   Have the front wheel alignment checked by a dealer or properly equipped shop.

19   Steering damper — removal and installation

1   Apply the parking brake, block the rear wheels and raise the front of the vehicle, supporting it securely on jackstands.
2   Remove the retaining nuts and bolts and lower the steering damper from the vehicle, noting the direction in which it is installed (photo).
3   Installation is the reverse of removal.

20   Power steering pump — removal and installation

1   Disconnect the negative cable at the battery. Place the cable out of the way so it cannot accidentally come in contact with the negative terminal of the battery, as this would once again allow power into the electrical system of the vehicle.
2   Remove the pump drivebelt.
3   Syphon the fluid out of the power steering pump fluid reservoir.
4   Disconnect the hoses from the pump (photo).
5   Remove the retaining bolts and lift the pump from the vehicle (photo).
6   Installation is the reverse of removal.
7   After installation refill the reservoir and bleed the air from the power steering system (Section 21).

19.2   Steering damper connections (arrows)

17.3   A separator tool is necessary when disconnecting the track rod

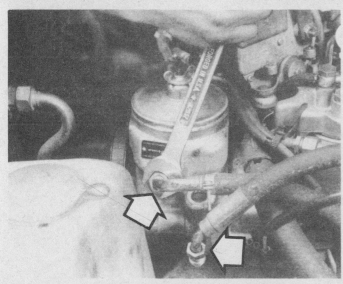

20.4   Power steering pump hose connections (arrows)

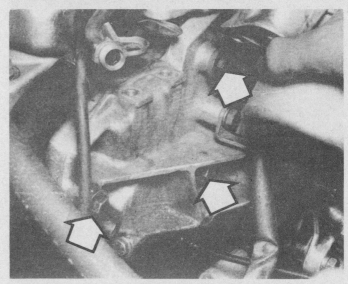

20.5   Power steering pump retaining bolts (arrows)

21   Bleeding the power steering system

1   Following any operation in which the power steering fluid lines have been disconnected, the power steering system must be bled of air to obtain proper steering performance.

2   Raise the front of the vehicle and support it on jackstands.

3   Turn the front wheels all the way to the left and right several times. Check the power steering fluid level (Chapter 1) and, if it has dropped, add fluid. Repeat this procedure until the fluid level does not drop.

4   Start the engine and allow it to run at fast idle. Recheck the fluid level and add more if necessary.

5   Bleed the system by turning the wheels from side to side without hitting the stops. This will work the air out of the ststem. Be careful that the reservoir does not run empty of fluid.

6   When the air is worked out of the system, return the wheels to the straight ahead position and leave the vehicle running for several more minutes before shutting it off.

7   Road test the vehicle to be sure the steering system is functioning normally and is free from noise.

8   Recheck the fluid level to be sure it is at or near the proper level while the engine is at normal operating temperature and add fluid if necessary.

Chapter 11 Body

Contents

Body — maintenance 2
Body repair — major damage 7
Body repair — minor damage 6
Bumpers — removal and installation 37
Center console and gearshift cover — removal
  and installation 36
Central locking system — general information 39
Door — removal and installation 20
Door retaining strap — removal and installation 21
Door trim panel — removal and installation 14
Exterior mirror — removal, repair and installation 27
Fixed glass replacement 40
Front door exterior handle — removal and installation 22
Front door lock — removal and installation 24
Front door window — removal and installation 17
Fuel filler door — removal and installation 28
General information 1
Glove compartment and lid — removal and installation 35
Hinges and locks — maintenance 5
Hood — removal, installation and adjustment 8
Hood lock cable — removal and installation 9
Instrument panel — removal and installation 34

Rear shelf (sedan models) — removal and installation 38
Rear door window — removal and installation 18
Rear door fixed glass — removal and installation 19
Rear door exterior handle — removal and installation 23
Rear door lock — removal and installation 25
Rear quarter window (coupe models) — removal
  and installation 31
Rear quarter window regulator — removal and installation ... 32
Seats — removal and installation 30
Sliding sunroof — adjustment 29
Station wagon tailgate lock — removal and installation 26
Tailgate (station wagon) — removal and installation 13
Tailgate strut (station wagon) — removal
  and installation 12
Trunk lid (sedan and coupe) — removal and installation 10
Trunk lid lock — removal and installation 11
Under dash panel — removal and installation 33
Upholstery and carpets — maintenance 3
Vinyl trim — maintenance 4
Window regulator (electric) — removal and installation 16
Window regulator (manual) — removal and installation 15

1 General information

All models are of unitized all steel welded construction incorporating a safety cell passenger compartment and impact absorbing front and rear sections. Due to this type of construction, it is very important that, in the event of collision damage, the underbody be thoroughly checked by a facility with the proper equipment to do so.

Body styles include sedan, coupe and station wagon models. A vacuum-operated central locking system using vacuum from the engine pump (Chapter 9) and a system of rubber reservoirs is featured.

Component replacement and repairs possible for the home mechanic are included in this Chapter.

2 Body — maintenance

1   The condition of your vehicle's body is very important, because this is very important in determining the second-hand or trade-in value. It is much more difficult to repair a neglected or damaged body than it is to repair mechanical components. The hidden areas of the body, such as the fender wells, the chassis, and the engine compartment, are equally important, although obviously do not require as frequent attention as the rest of the body.
2   Once a year, or every 12,000 miles, it is a good idea to have the underside of the body and the frame steam cleaned. All traces of dirt and oil will be removed and the underside can then be inspected carefully for rust, damaged brake lines, frayed electrical wiring, damaged cables, and other problems. The front suspension components should be greased after completion of this job.
3   At the same time, clean the engine and the engine compartment using either a steam cleaner or a water soluble degreaser.
4   The fender wells should be given particular attention, as undercoating can peel away and stones and dirt thrown up by the tires can cause the paint to chip and flake, allowing rust to set in. If rust is found, clean down to the bare metal and apply an anti-rust paint.

5   These models incorporate a drain system to ensure that water does not collect in the body or chassis. Check the drains whenever the vehicle is raised to make sure they are not clogged (photo).
6   The body should be washed once a week (or when dirty). Wet the vehicle thoroughly to soften the dirt, then wash it down with a soft sponge and plenty of clean soapy water. If the surplus dirt is not washed off very carefully, it will in time wear down the paint.
7   Spots of tar or asphalt coating thrown up from the road should be removed with a cloth soaked in solvent.
8   Once every six months, give the body and chrome trim a thorough wax job. If a chrome cleaner is used to remove rust from any of the vehicle's plated parts, remember that the cleaner also removes part of the chrome, so use it sparingly.

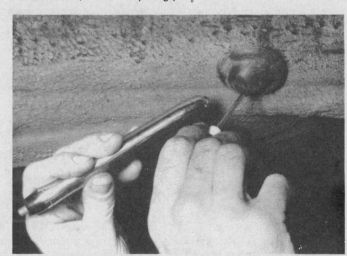

2.5   Use a screwdriver and a flashlight to make sure the body drains are clear

These photos illustrate a method of repairing simple dents. They are intended to supplement *Body repair - minor damage* in this Chapter and should not be used as the sole instructions for body repair on these vehicles.

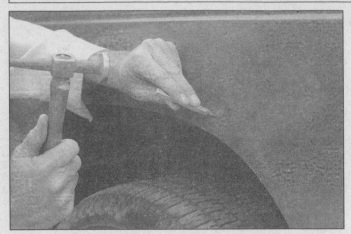

1   If you can't access the backside of the body panel to hammer out the dent, pull it out with a slide-hammer-type dent puller. In the deepest portion of the dent or along the crease line, drill or punch hole(s) at least one inch apart . . .

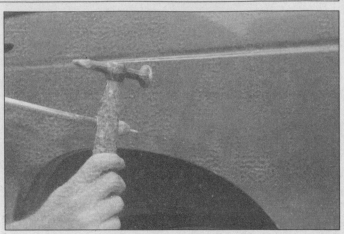

2   . . . then screw the slide-hammer into the hole and operate it. Tap with a hammer near the edge of the dent to help 'pop' the metal back to its original shape. When you're finished, the dent area should be close to its original contour and about 1/8-inch below the surface of the surrounding metal

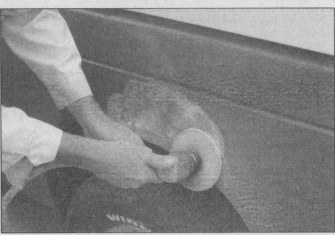

3   Using coarse-grit sandpaper, remove the paint down to the bare metal. Hand sanding works fine, but the disc sander shown here makes the job faster. Use finer (about 320-grit) sandpaper to feather-edge the paint at least one inch around the dent area

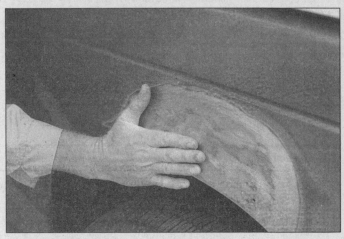

4   When the paint is removed, touch will probably be more helpful than sight for telling if the metal is straight. Hammer down the high spots or raise the low spots as necessary. Clean the repair area with wax/silicone remover

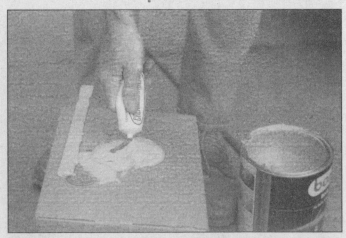

5   Following label instructions, mix up a batch of plastic filler and hardener. The ratio of filler to hardener is critical, and, if you mix it incorrectly, it will either not cure properly or cure too quickly (you won't have time to file and sand it into shape)

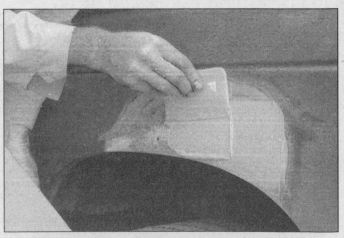

6   Working quickly so the filler doesn't harden, use a plastic applicator to press the body filler firmly into the metal, assuring it bonds completely. Work the filler until it matches the original contour and is slightly above the surrounding metal

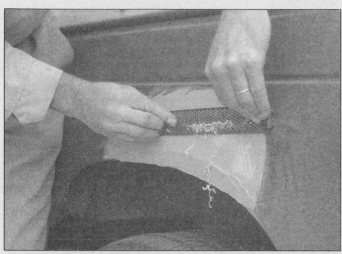

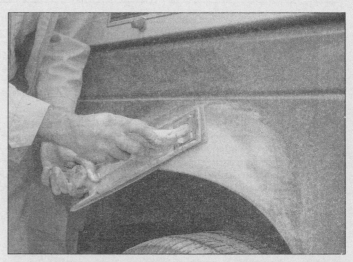

7 Let the filler harden until you can just dent it with your fingernail. Use a body file or Surform tool (shown here) to rough-shape the filler

8 Use coarse-grit sandpaper and a sanding board or block to work the filler down until it's smooth and even. Work down to finer grits of sandpaper - always using a board or block - ending up with 360 or 400 grit

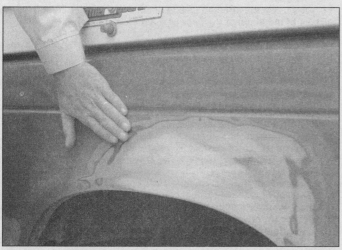

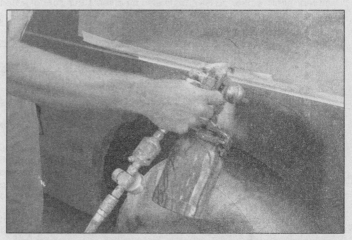

9 You shouldn't be able to feel any ridge at the transition from the filler to the bare metal or from the bare metal to the old paint. As soon as the repair is flat and uniform, remove the dust and mask off the adjacent panels or trim pieces

10 Apply several layers of primer to the area. Don't spray the primer on too heavy, so it sags or runs, and make sure each coat is dry before you spray on the next one. A professional-type spray gun is being used here, but aerosol spray primer is available inexpensively from auto parts stores

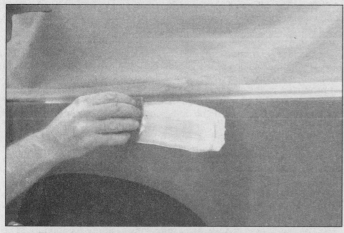

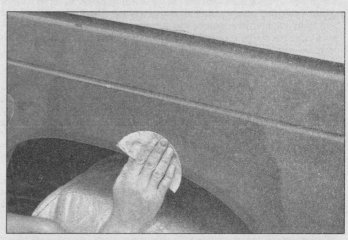

11 The primer will help reveal imperfections or scratches. Fill these with glazing compound. Follow the label instructions and sand it with 360 or 400-grit sandpaper until it's smooth. Repeat the glazing, sanding and respraying until the primer reveals a perfectly smooth surface

12 Finish sand the primer with very fine sandpaper (400 or 600-grit) to remove the primer overspray. Clean the area with water and allow it to dry. Use a tack rag to remove any dust, then apply the finish coat. Don't attempt to rub out or wax the repair area until the paint has dried completely (at least two weeks)

3 Upholstery and carpets — maintenance

1 Every three months, remove the carpets or mats and clean the interior of the vehicle (more frequently if necessary). Vacuum the upholstery and carpets to remove loose dirt and dust.

2 If the upholstery is soiled, apply upholstery cleaner with a damp sponge and wipe it off with a clean, dry cloth.

4 Vinyl trim — maintenance

Vinyl trim should not be cleaned with detergents, caustic soaps or petroleum-based cleaners. Plain soap and water or a mild vinyl cleaner is best for stains. Test a small area for color fastness. Bubbles under the vinyl can be corrected by piercing them with a pin and then working the air out.

5 Hinges and locks — maintenance

Every 3000 miles or three months, the door, hood and rear hatch hinges and locks should be lubricated with a few drops of oil. The door and rear hatch striker plates should also be given a thin coat of white lithium base grease to reduce wear and ensure free movement.

6 Body repair — minor damage

See color photo sequence "Repair of minor scratches"

1 If the scratch is superficial and does not penetrate to the metal of the body, repair is very simple. Lightly rub the scratched area with a fine rubbing compound to remove loose paint and built up wax. Rinse the area with clean water.

2 Apply touch-up paint to the scratch, using a small brush. Continue to apply thin layers of paint until the surface of the paint in the scratch is level with the surrounding paint. Allow the new paint at least two weeks to harden, then blend it into the surrounding paint by rubbing with a very fine rubbing compound. Finally, apply a coat of wax to the scratch area.

3 If the scratch has penetrated the paint and exposed the metal of the body, causing the metal to rust, a different repair technique is required. Remove all loose rust from the bottom of the scratch with a pocket knife, then apply rust inhibiting paint to prevent the formation of rust in the future. Using a rubber or nylon applicator, coat the scratched area with glaze-type filler. If required, the filler can be mixed with thinner to provide a very thin paste, which is ideal for filling narrow scratches. Before the glaze filler in the scratch hardens, wrap a piece of smooth cotton cloth around the tip of a finger. Dip the cloth in thinner and then quickly wipe it along the surface of the scratch. This will ensure that the surface of the filler is slightly hollow. The scratch can now be painted over as described earlier in this Section.

Repair of dents

4 When repairing dents, the first job is to pull the dent out until the affected area is as close as possible to its original shape. There is no point in trying to restore the original shape completely as the metal in the damaged area will have stretched on impact and cannot be restored to its original contours. It is better to bring the level of the dent up to a point which is about 1/8-inch below the level of the surrounding metal. In cases where the dent is very shallow, it is not worth trying to pull it out at all.

5 If the back side of the dent is accessible, it can be hammered out gently from behind using a soft-face hammer. While doing this, hold a block of wood firmly against the opposite side of the metal to absorb the hammer blows and prevent the metal from being stretched.

6 If the dent is in a section of the body which has double layers, or some other factor makes it inaccessible from behind, a different technique is required. Drill several small holes through the metal inside the damaged area, particularly in the deeper sections. Screw long, self tapping screws into the holes just enough for them to get a good grip in the metal. Now the dent can be pulled out by pulling on the protruding heads of the screws with locking pliers.

7 The next stage of repair is the removal of paint from the damaged area and from an inch or so of the surrounding metal. This is easily done with a wire brush or sanding disk in a drill motor, although it can be done just as effectively by hand with sandpaper. To complete the preparation for filling, score the surface of the bare metal with a screwdriver or the tang of a file or drill small holes in the affected area. This will provide a good grip for the filler material. To complete the repair, see the Section on filling and painting.

Repair of rust holes or gashes

8 Remove all paint from the affected area and from an inch or so of the surrounding metal using a sanding disk or wire brush mounted in a drill motor. If these are not available, a few sheets of sandpaper will do the job just as effectively.

9 With the paint removed, you will be able to determine the severity of the corrosion and decide whether to replace the whole panel, if possible, or repair the affected area. New body panels are not as expensive as most people think and it is often quicker to install a new panel than to repair large areas of rust.

10 Remove all trim pieces from the affected area except those which will act as a guide to the original shape of the damaged body, such as headlight shells, etc. Using metal snips or a hacksaw blade, remove all loose metal and any other metal that is badly affected by rust. Hammer the edges of the hole inward to create a slight depression for the filler material.

11 Wire brush the affected area to remove the powdery rust from the surface of the metal. If the back of the rusted area is accessible, treat it with rust-inhibiting paint.

12 Before filling is done, block the hole in some way. This can be done with sheet metal riveted or screwed into place, or by stuffing the hole with wire mesh.

13 Once the hole is blocked off, the affected area can be filled and painted. See the following sub-section on filling and painting.

Filling and painting

14 Many types of body fillers are available, but generally speaking, body repair kits which contain filler paste and a tube of resin hardener are best for this type of repair work. A wide, flexible plastic or nylon applicator will be necessary for imparting a smooth and contoured finish to the surface of the filler material. Mix up a small amount of filler on a clean piece of wood or cardboard (use the hardener sparingly). Follow the manufacturer's instructions on the package, otherwise the filler will set incorrectly.

15 Using the applicator, apply the filler paste to the prepared area. Draw the applicator across the surface of the filler to achieve the desired contour and to level the filler surface. As soon as a contour that approximates the original one is achieved, stop working the paste. If you continue, the paste will begin to stick to the applicator. Continue to add thin layers of paste at 20-minute intervals until the level of the filler is just above the surrounding metal.

16 Once the filler has hardened, the excess can be removed with a body file. From then on, progressively finer grades of sandpaper should be used, starting with a 180-grit paper and finishing with 600-grit wet-or-dry paper. Always wrap the sandpaper around a flat rubber or wooden block, otherwise the surface of the filler will not be completely flat. During the sanding of the filler surface, the wet-or-dry paper should be periodically rinsed in water. This will ensure that a very smooth finish is produced in the final stage.

17 At this point, the repair area should be surrounded by a ring of bare metal, which in turn should be encircled by the finely feathered edge of good paint. Rinse the repair area with clean water until all of the dust produced by the sanding operation is gone.

18 Spray the entire area with a light coat of primer. This will reveal any imperfections in the surface of the filler. Repair the imperfections with fresh filler paste or glaze filler and once more smooth the surface with sandpaper. Repeat this spray-and-repair procedure until you are satisfied that the surface of the filler and the feathered edge of the paint are perfect. Rinse the area with clean water and allow it to dry completely.

19 The repair area is now ready for painting. Spray painting must be carried out in a warm, dry, windless and dust free atmosphere. These conditions can be created if you have access to a large indoor work area, but if you are forced to work in the open, you will have to pick the day very carefully. If you are working indoors, dousing the floor in the work area with water will help settle the dust which would other-

wise be in the air. If the repair area is confined to one body panel, mask off the surrounding panels. This will help minimize the effects of a slight mismatch in paint color. Trim pieces such as chrome strips, door handles, etc., will also need to be masked off or removed. Use masking tape and several thicknesses of newspaper for the masking operations.
20 Before spraying, shake the paint can thoroughly, then spray a test area until the spray painting technique is mastered. Cover the repair area with a thick coat of primer. The thickness should be built up using several thin layers of primer rather than one thick one. Using 600-grit wet-or-dry sandpaper, rub down the surface of the primer until it is very smooth. While doing this, the work area should be thoroughly rinsed with water and the wet-or-dry sandpaper periodically rinsed as well. Allow the primer to dry before spraying additional coats.
21 Spray on the top coat, again building up the thickness by using several thin layers of paint. Begin spraying in the center of the repair area and then, using a circular motion, work out until the whole repair area and about two inches of the surrounding original paint is covered. Remove all masking material 10 to 15 minutes after spraying on the final coat of paint. Allow the new paint at least two weeks to harden, then use a very fine rubbing compound to blend the edges of the new paint into the existing paint. Finally, apply a coat of wax.

7 Body repair — major damage

1 Major damage must be repaired by an auto body shop specifically equipped to perform unibody repairs. These shops have available the specialized equipment required to do the job properly.
2 If the damage is extensive, the underbody must be checked for proper alignment or the vehicle's handling characteristics may be adversely affected and other components may wear at an accelerated rate.
3 Due to the fact that all of the major body components (hood, fenders, etc.) are separate and replaceable units, any seriously damaged components should be replaced rather than repaired. Sometimes these components can be found in a wrecking yard that specializes in used vehicle components (often at considerable savings over the cost of new parts).

8 Hood — removal, installation and adjustment

1 Fully open the hood and place some cloth pads beneath the two rear corners.
2 Disconnect the windscreen washer tube at the T-piece, release the clip and pull out the tube.
3 Mark the location of the hinge bolts on the hood with a pencil, then loosen them several turns (photo).

4 With the help of an assistant, support the hood then remove the bolts and lift the hood from the vehicle.
5 Installation is a reversal of removal, but set the hinges to their original positions before tightening the bolts. Check that the hood is central within its aperture and aligned correctly with the surrounding bodywork. Note that the lower edge at the front of the hood should align with the upper edge of the turn signal lamp cutouts.
6 To adjust the hood longitudinally, loosen the hinge bolts, reposition the hood, then tighten the bolts. To adjust the height, loosen the locknuts and turn the rubber stops under the front of the hood as required, then tighten the locknuts.

9 Hood lock cable — removal and installation

1 Remove the lower trim panel to gain access to the release cable (Section 33).
2 Unbolt the hood release lever from the side panel and disengage the cable (photo).
3 In the engine compartment, release the cable from the bracket and plastic straps retaining it to the body, then release it from the clip near the lock (photo).

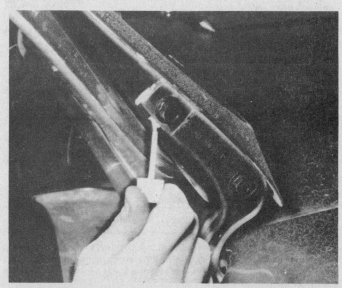

8.3 Marking the bolt position with white paint makes hood reinstallation easier

9.2 The upper hood release lever bolts (arrows) are accessible after removing the under dash panel

9.3 Use a small screwdriver to push off the clip (arrow) so the hood lock cable can be disengaged.

11

9.4 Loosen the hood release cable retaining nuts (arrows) so the cable can be removed

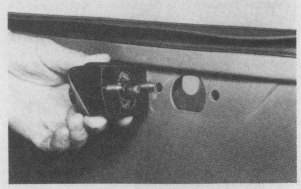

Fig. 11.1 Removing the trunk lid lock (Sec 11)

4   Disconnect the cable from the lock by loosening the locknuts and pushing the pin from the clip (photo).
5   Connect a string or thin wire to the end of the cable and remove it by pulling it through into the passenger compartment.
6   Installation is a reversal of removal after connecting the string or wire to the new cable and pulling it into position.
7   After installation, adjust the cable at the locknuts to eliminate any free-play.

10 Trunk lid (sedan and coupe) — removal and installation

1   Disconnect the negative cable at the battery. Place the cable out of the way so it cannot accidentally come in contact with the negative terminal of the battery, as this would once again allow power into the electrical system of the vehicle.
2   Remove both license plate lamps, as described in Chapter 12.
3   Remove the trunk light and switch (Chapter 12) and disconnect the wiring.
4   Place protective pads along the edges of the trunk opening to prevent damage to the painted surfaces.
5   Mark the location of the hinge bolts by scribing around them with a pencil, and loosen them several turns.
6   With an assistant supporting the weight, remove the bolts and lift the trunk lid from the vehicle.
7   Installation is a reversal of removal, taking care to align the bolts with the previously made marks before tightening them. Check the trunk lid to make sure it is centered in the opening and aligned with the surrounding bodywork. Make sure also that the lid seats correctly onto the weatherseal. Adjustment can be made if necessary by loosening the hinge bolts and removing or adding spacers under the trunk latch striker.

11 Trunk lid lock — removal and installation

1   Raise the trunk lid.
2   Remove the lid lock retaining nuts and washers.
3   Pry the plastic cover from the inside of the rear panel.
4   Remove the retaining bolt and withdraw the lower lock section through the cover opening and disconnect the central locking system links.
5   Installation is the reverse of removal, making sure the striker engages the lock securely.

12.3 Station wagon tailgate trim retaining screws

12 Tailgate strut (station wagon) — removal and installation

1   Disconnect the negative cable at the battery. Place the cable out of the way so it cannot accidentally come in contact with the negative terminal of the battery, as this would once again allow power into the electrical system of the vehicle.
2   Open the tailgate and remove (but do not disconnect) the rear compartment light.
3   Remove the retaining screws and withdraw the rear roof panel from the clips (photo).
4   Support the tailgate, pry out the strut retaining clip and extract the pin from the hinge.
5   Use an Allen wrench to remove the front mounting bolt, accessible through an access hole in the headliner. If there is no access hole in the headlining, carefully pull the headlining away.
6   Remove the strut by withdrawing it from the vehicle toward the rear, past the hinge.
7   To install, insert the strut into position and install the front retaining bolt. Tighten the bolt securely. Connect the strut to the tailgate and install the clip.
8   Install the roof panel and light.

13 Tailgate (station wagon) — removal and installation

1   Disconnect the negative cable at the battery. Place the cable out of the way so it cannot accidentally come in contact with the negative terminal of the battery, as this would once again allow power into the electrical system of the vehicle.
2   Remove the compartment light.
3   Remove the rear roof panel screws and remove the panel (photo).

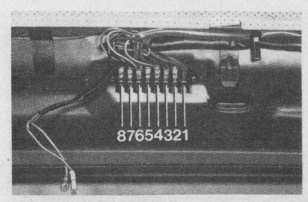

Fig. 11.2   **The station wagon tailgate wiring connections**
(Sec 13)

1	Light brown (ground)	5	Black/purple/white
2	Black/purple	6	Black
3	Black/blue/purple	7	Grey/purple
4	Purple/white	8	Brown/grey

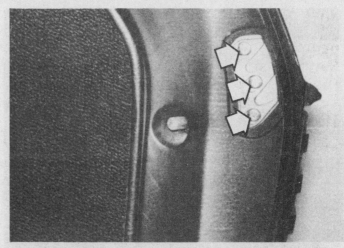

13.13   Station wagon tailgate side stop screws (arrows)

14.3   Slide the window crank trim cover out and toward the knob to disengage the handle

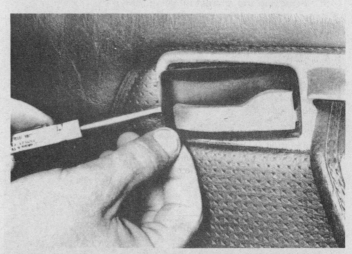

14.4a   Pry off the door handle trim cover with a screwdriver to . . .

4   Loosen the screws retaining the wiring connectors to the block on the roof frame and disconnect the wiring harness.

5   Remove and disconnect the rear speakers (if equipped).

6   Disconnect the rear window washer tube and the central locking system vacuum lines (if equipped). Support the tailgate and remove the struts (Section 12).

7   Mark the hinge bolt locations and loosen the bolts.

8   With an assistant supporting the weight, remove the bolts and carefully lower the tailgate complete with wiring harness, from the vehicle.

9   To install, place the tailgate in position and install the bolts to the marked positions. Tighten the bolts securely.

10   Install the tailgate struts.

11   Connect the wiring harness, referring to the wiring diagram in the accompanying illustration.

12   Connect any components which were removed and install the roof panel.

13   Check to make sure the tailgate is centered in the opening and is even with or no more than 0.04 in (1 mm) lower than the surrounding bodywork. The striker can be adjusted by slightly loosening the striker and side stop screws and then closing the tailgate until is is in the proper position (photo). Open the tailgate and tighten the screws. If necessary, spacers can be used to position the striker and side stops.

---

14   Door trim panel — removal and installation

Sedan and station wagon

1   Unscrew the locking knob from the top of the panel and raise the window fully up.

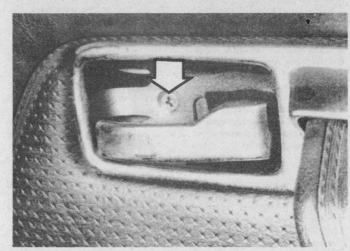

14.4b   . . . expose the door handle retaining screw

2   Disconnect the negative cable at the battery. Place the cable out of the way so it cannot accidentally come in contact with the negative terminal of the battery, as this would once again allow power into the electrical system of the vehicle.

3   Pry the plastic insert from the manual window regulator handle and slide the insert away from the knob to detach the handle (photo).

4   Pry out and remove the interior door handle trim cover for access to the retaining screw (photos).

11

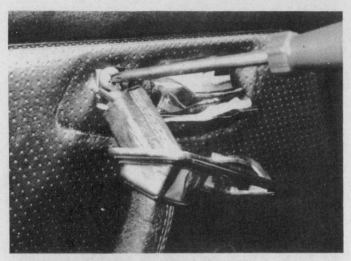

14.6   Removing the armrest retaining screw

14.8   Door latch trim retaining screws (arrows)

14.9   Use a small screwdriver to lift the clip so the ashtray housing can be removed from the door

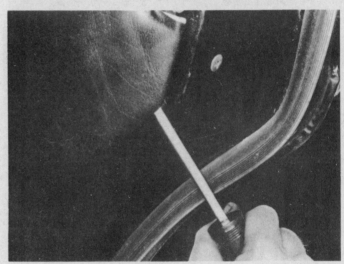

14.10   Disengage the door trim panel by prying the clips loose

5   On electric window models, disconnect the switch .
6   Remove the armrest upper mounting screw (photo).
7   Remove the lower screws and withdraw the armrest.
8   Remove the two screws and withdraw the door latch trim (photo).
9   On the rear door remove the ashtray, then pry the tab up and lift out the ashtray housing (photo).
10 Using a screwdriver or similar tool, carefully pry the trim panel from the door. Insert the screwdriver adjacent to the clips to prevent damage to the panel (photo).

Coupe

11 Remove the screws and withdraw the cover plate from the end of the door above the lock. Also remove the small bezel.
12 Where applicable, pry the plastic insert from the window regulator handle, move it towards the knob and remove it.
13 With the window glass fully up note the position of the handle then remove it together with the trim escutcheon (except on electric windows).
14 Remove the locking lever cover (one screw).
15 Pry the interior handle cover out, remove the screw and withdraw the trim piece. Remove the screws and lift the armrest off.
16 Using a wide-bladed screwdriver, pry the trim panel from the door. Insert the screwdriver adjacent to the clips to prevent damage to the panel. Note that there are additional clips at the front of the panel.
17 Lift the rear of the panel from the clips, at the same time prying it out from the locking lever.
18 Lift the front of the panel to disconnect the inner hook, then withdraw it from the door.

All

19 If necessary, peel the plastic sheet from the door, taking care not to tear it.
20 Installation is a reversal of removal, making sure that the retaining clips are correctly aligned before pressing them into the door.

---

15   Window regulator (manual) — removal and installation

---

1   Remove the door inner trim panel and plastic sheet (Section 14).

Front door

2   On sedan models, lower the window and pry the clips from the lift arms, then raise the window and support it with a block of wood. Remove the arms from the channel then unbolt the regulator and withdraw it through the opening.
3   On coupe models, lower the window and remove the screws from the lifting rail, then raise the window and support it with a block of wood. Unbolt the regulator and withdraw it through the opening.

Rear door

4   Lower the window and remove the screws from the lifting rail, then raise the window and support it with a block of wood.
5   Unbolt the regulator and withdraw it through the opening.
6   Installation the reverse of removal, making sure that all bolts and screws are tightened securely.

Fig. 11.3   The stop pad bolt on the electric window regulator (arrow) (Sec 16)

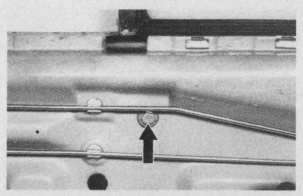

Fig. 11.4   The rear door fixed glass retaining channel lower retaining bolt (arrow) (Sec 19)

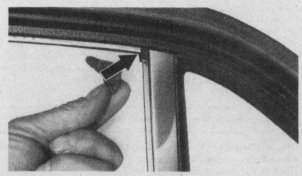

Fig. 11.5   Insert the rear door fixed glass seal, pressing it securely into place (Sec 19)

16   Window regulator (electric) — removal and installation

1   Remove the door inner trim panel and plastic sheet (Section 14).
2   Lower the window.
3   Disconnect the negative cable at the battery. Place the cable out of the way so it cannot accidentally come in contact with the negative terminal of the battery, as this would once again allow power into the electrical system of the vehicle.
4   Unscrew the bolts securing the lifting rail to the glass channel.
5   Raise the window and support it with a block of wood.
6   Mark the location of the wiring connectors so they can be reinstalled in the same positions and disconnect them from the terminals.
7   On the rear door, remove the rear window channel screws and push the channel forward.
8   Unscrew the retaining bolts and nuts and withdraw the regulator and motor assembly through the opening.
9   Installation is the reverse of removal. After installation the lower travel of the window can be adjusted as necessary by loosening the bolt and positioning the stop pad on the regulator arm as required.

17   Front door window — removal and installation

1   Remove the window regulator (Section 15 or 16).

Sedan and station wagon

2   Position the window so the lifting rail bolts are accessible in the openings and remove the bolts.
3   Remove the exterior mirror from the left-hand door and the inner cover from the right-hand door, pry off the moulding and then pry the inner and outer seals from the top of the door.
4   Lift the rear of the window, tilt it forward and withdraw it from the top of the door.
5   To install, place the window in position in the rails and move the window lift rail with the slides into the retaining rail from below. Install the bolts. The remainder of installation is the reverse of removal, but before tightening the rail bolts, fully lower the window, press it forward into the channel and at the same time press the lifting rail to the rear, then tighten the bolts. Fully raise the window and loosen the rear channel bolts. Press the window rearward into the channel, then tighten the bolts.

Coupe

6   Pry the inner seal from the top of the door.
7   Remove the top and bottom stops from the rear window channel.
8   Remove the bottom nut and top bolt and remove the rear window channel.
9   Remove the screws and withdraw the rear guide wedge.

10 Lift the window rearward from the door.
11 Installation is the reverse of removal, after which it should be adjusted as follows. Adjust the front guide retainer so that it lightly contacts the weatherstrip with the door closed. Check that, with the window closed, the front edge is aligned with the guide retainer. If necessary, adjust the upper stops, channels and lifting rail as required. Lateral adjustment is made at the guide pins. With the window fully open the upper edge must be flush with the seals — adjustment is made at the stop on the window lifting rail. Adjust the guide wedge so that it contacts the rear edge of the window. Apply a light coat of lithium base grease to the window guide rails before installing the door inner panel.

18   Rear door window — removal and installation

1   Remove the window regulator (Sections 15 or 16).
2   Remove the bolts and withdraw the rear window channel.
3   Pry off the moulding, followed by the inner and outer seals from the top of the door.
4   Lift the front of the window, tilt it toward the rear and withdraw it from the top of the door.
5   Installation is a reversal of removal, making sure the bolts are tightened securely and the rear channel is adjusted as required.

19   Rear door fixed glass — removal and installation

1   Remove the regulator and window.
2   Remove the bolt (in the door) and screw (in the window channel) securing the retaining channel and then rotate the channel forward and out of the door.
3   Slide the fixed glass and rubber frame forward and withdraw it from the door.
4   Installation is a reversal of removal, making sure the seal at the juncture of the fixed glass retaining channel and the upper window glass channel is securely installed.

11

20   Door — removal and installation

1   Open the door fully and support the lower edge on a jack or blocks of wood covered with pads to protect the surface.
2   Disconnect the retainer from the body pillar.
3   If the vehicle is equipped with electric windows, disconnect the electrical leads.
4   Mark the position of the hinge plates on the door frame with a pencil or white paint.
5   With an assistant supporting the weight, remove the bolts and lift the door from the vehicle.
6   Installation is a reversal of removal, making sure the hinges are bolted back into their original positions so the door alignment will be correct. If adjustment is required to lift or lower the door or to make the door panel flush with the body panels, loosen the hinge bolts and move the door as necessary. Check that the gap around the edge of the door is even on both sides and at the top.
7   Adjustment of the striker plate on the body pillar will affect the door closed position and also the flush appearance of the door edge with the body panel or pillar adjacent to it. The striker plate can be set by releasing the retaining screws (an Allen head wrench will be required for this) so that it moves stiffly and then closing the door. This will adjust the door closed position. Open the door carefully and fully tighten the screws. If necessary, shims can be removed or inserted behind the striker plate to ensure positive closing.

21   Door retaining strap — removal and installation

1   Remove the door trim panel and peel the plastic sheet from the area adjacent to the retaining strap.
2   Extract the clip and carefully drive out the pin securing the retaining strap to the pillar.
3   Remove the outer bolts and the inner nut and withdraw the retaining strap from the door.
4   Installation is a reversal of removal, after lubricating all contact surfaces with white lithium base grease.

22   Front door exterior handle — removal and installation

1   On sedan and station wagon models, pry the rubber grommet from the edge of the door for access to the two cross-head screws (photo). On coupe models, remove the cover plate at the top of the door and pry back the weatherseal for access to the screws.
2   Remove the three screws.
3   Push the handle forward, pull the grip, and withdraw the handle assembly.

22.1   After prying off the rubber grommet cover, two of the three front door handle retaining screws are accessible.

Fig. 11.6   The rear door exterior handle retaining screw (arrow), is accessible after pulling the weatherstripping back (Sec 23)

4   Before installing the handle, screw the front mounting screw in, leaving approximately the thickness of the door sheet metal.
5   Pull the handle grip bracket and insert the handle so that the operating rod enters the lock. If necessary tighten the front screw, and adjust the drive pin clearance to 1.0 mm (0.04 in) using a suitable Allen head wrench.
6   Tighten the rear screws and insert the grommet.

23   Rear door exterior handle — removal and installation

1   Pull back the weatherstripping for access and remove the handle retaining screw.
2   Push the handle forward, pull the grip and withdraw the handle assembly.
3   Before installing the handle, screw in the front mounting screw until there is approximately the thickness of the door sheet metal between the screw head and the handle surface.
4   Pull the grip and insert the handle, then push in the grip so that the drive screw engages. If necessary tighten the front screw, and adjust the drive screw clearance to 1.0 mm (0.04 in) by loosening the locknut.
5   Tighten the rear screw and install the weatherstripping.

24   Front door lock — removal and installation

1   Remove the door trim panel (Section 14).
2   Mark the position of the inside door remote control handle, remove retaining screws, disconnect the control rods and lift the handle from the door (photos).
3   Remove the exterior door handle (Section 23).
4   Remove the door lock retaining screws and withdraw the lock assembly downward through the opening in the door.
5   Place the door lock in position and install the retaining screws. Tighten the screws securely. The remainder of installation is the reverse of removal, adjusting the position of the remote handle after connecting the control rods to make sure there is no play before tightening the screws.

25   Rear door lock — removal and installation

1   Remove the door trim panel (Section 14).
2   Disconnect the linkage from the door lock and remove the remote control handle and linkage as an assembly.
3   On models equipped with electric windows or side impact reinforcements, remove the window regulator (Section 15 or 16).
4   Remove the cross-head screws and withdraw the lock downwards through the opening.

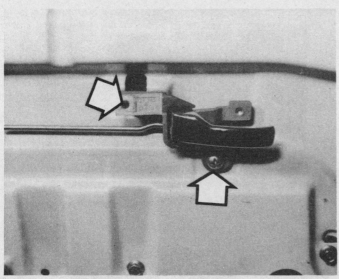

24.2a Inner door handle screw locations (arrows)

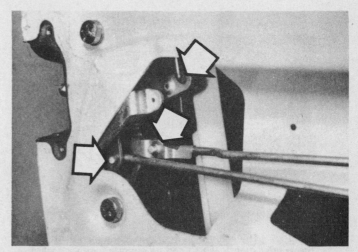

24.2b Inner door handle control rod connections (arrows)

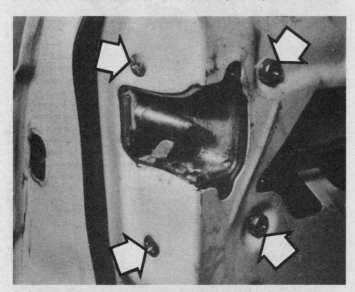

24.2c Door lock retaining screws (arrows)

5   Place the door lock in position and install the screws, tightening them securely. The remainder of installation is the reverse of removal.

---

26 Station wagon tailgate lock — removal and installation

1   With the tailgate open unscrew the locking knob and remove the tailgate trim panel (6 screws).
2   Remove the screw from the inner handle cover and remove the cover, then lift the trim panel from the clips.
3   Remove the screws and withdraw the bottom rail.
4   Remove the cross-head screw from the inner handle.
5   Pull the switch plug from the right-hand side of the lock and disconnect the locking rod from the left hand side of the lock.
6   On central locking system equipped models, disconnect the linkage from the vaccum unit.
7   Unscrew the lock mounting bolts and press the lock lever to the locked position. The lock can now be withdrawn through the opening.
8   Installation is a reversal of removal. After installation carry out the following adjustments. On models equipped with central locking, adjust the vacuum unit so that the linkage has no play when unlocked. The exterior handle free play should be 0.04 in (1 mm). If necessary, operate the safety plunger, then insert a screwdriver through the upper bolt hole to position the lock correctly and insert the bolt and tighten it.

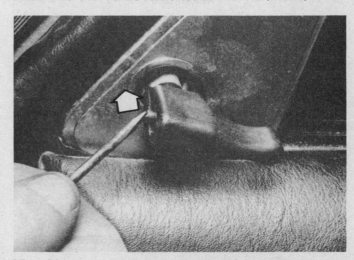

27.1 Push the mirror clip in the direction of the arrow to remove

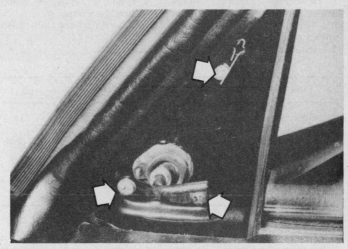

27.2 After prying off the trim panel the mirror retaining screws (arrows) can be removed

---

27 Exterior mirror — removal, repair and installation

1   Push the small plastic lock out of the mirror control handle using a small screwdriver and withdraw the handle (photo).
2   Pry off the cover plate to expose the three retaining screws, remove the screws and lift off the mirror (photo).

11

Fig. 11.7   The electric sunroof emergency key (left) and the winder (right), which can be operated with a socket wrench (Sec 29)

Fig. 11.9   Electric sunroof rear height adjustment (Sec 29)

3   If vibration causes the exterior mirror to alter its setting, the clamp screw can be tightened after the mirror has been removed.
4   The mirror glass can be replaced by prying it from the mirror head with a plastic or wooden lever.
5   Installation is a reversal of removal.

---

28   Fuel filler door — removal and installation

---

1   Open the door and pry out the cap retainer.
2   Unbolt the door and lift it from the body.
3   Installation is the reverse of removal, making sure that the seals are fitted correctly between the flap and the body.

---

29   Sliding sunroof — adjustment

Electrically-operated sunroof

1   Remove the headliner from the sliding roof. Loosen the slide bracket bolts, press the brackets inward while keeping the roof centered in its opening and then tighten the bolts.
2   To adjust the front height, loosen the slide rail screws and turn the slotted adjustment screws until the front edge is level with, or up to 0.04 in (1 mm) lower than the roof panel when closed. Tighten the slide rail bolts securely.
3   To adjust the rear height, close the sliding roof, then loosen the nut and turn the adjustment plate with a screwdriver until the rear edge is level with, or up to 0.04 in (1 mm) higher than the roof. Tighten the nut securely.
4   Install the headliner.

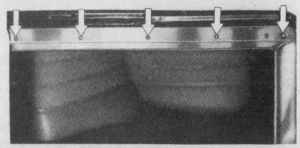

Fig. 11.8   The sunroof mounting height screws (arrows) (Sec 29)

29.5   The mechanical sliding roof slide bracket bolts (arrows)

29.6   The stop rod holder nut (arrow) is loosened to adjust front-to-rear clearance

Manually-operated sunroof

5   Remove the headliner from the sliding roof. Loosen the slide bracket bolts, press the brackets inward while keeping the roof centered in the opening and then tighten the bolts securely (photo).
6   To adjust the stop rods, loosen the stop rod holder nuts and position the sliding roof so that it is in full contact with the front seal and tighten the nuts securely (photo). Open the sunroof halfway, loosen the stop rod bolts and adjust so that the lever will operate with the roof in any position.
7   To adjust the front height, loosen the slide rail bolts and turn the slotted adjustment screws until the front edge is level with or no more

30.5   The left seat bracket bolt (arrow)

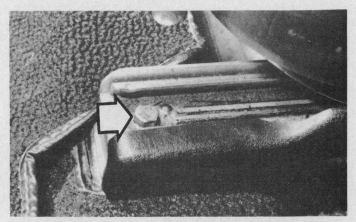

30.12   Passenger front seat side front guide rail bolt (arrow)

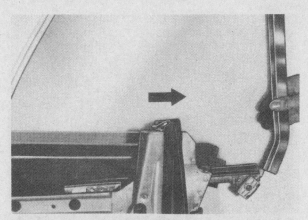

Fig. 11.10   Rear quarter window removal (Sec 31)

Fig. 11.11   Manual rear quarter window regulator bolts
(arrows) (Sec 32)

than 0.04 in (1 mm) lower than the roof panel when shut. Tighten the
slide rail screws.
8   To adjust the rear height, turn the bolts on the rear brackets until
the rear edge is even with or no less than 0.04 in (1 mm) higher than
the roof.
9   Install the headliner.

---

30   Seats — removal and installation

Front seat
Left
1   Set the seat in the highest position and push it fully forwards.
2   Disconnect the return spring.
3   Unscrew the bolt and pull out the slide rail.
4   Unscrew the rear guide rail bolts
5   Where applicable, on sedan models without height adjustment,
remove the bolt from the bracket at the side (photo).
6   Set the seat in the lowest position and push it fully rearwards.
7   Unscrew the front guide rail bolts and, on coupe models, disconnect
the vacuum line to the automatic locking system.
8   Lift the seat from the vehicle.
9   Installation is the reverse of removal.
Right
10   With the seat pushed fully forwards, remove the bolt and pull out
the slide rail.
11   Remove both bolts from the side bracket.
12   Push the seat fully rearwards, remove the front guide rail bolts and
lift the seat from the vehicle (photo).
13   Installation is a reversal of removal.

Rear seat
Rear seat and backrest (sedan models)
14   Push the safety catch and lift out the cushion, taking care not to
unfold the armrest.
15   Remove the backrest lower bolts, then unfold the armrest and
remove the center lower bolt.
16   Withdraw the backrest upwards to release the upper connections.
17   Installation is a reversal of the removal procedure.
Rear seat and backrest (station wagon models)
18   Push down the locking lever and fold the cushion forward.
19   Push on the rod safety catches to release them and lift out the
cushion.
20   Pry out the plastic covers, remove the bolts and withdraw the
backrest from the vehicle.
21   Installation is the reverse of removal.

**31   Rear quarter window (coupe models) — removal
and installation**

---

1   Remove the rear seat (Section 30).
2   Remove the cover plate (3 screws), regulator handle or electric
switch, trim and quarter panel.
3   Unbolt the shell cover and the access covers, then disconnect the
intermediate lever at the guide plate.
4   Unbolt the guide rail and lift the window forward from the vehicle.
5   Installation is a reversal of removal, making sure to adjust the window as necessary by loosening the relevant bolts.

---

32   Rear quarter window regulator — removal and installation

---

1   Remove the rear quarter trim panel.

Manual regulator
2   Remove the access cover (4 screws), then pry off the clip and
disconnect the intermediate lever at the guide plate.

11

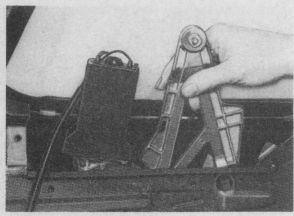

Fig. 11.12 Lifting out electric rear quarter window regulator (Sec 32)

Fig. 11.13 Use a backup wrench to hold the nut on the instrument panel center support bolt (arrow) (Sec 34)

3   Raise the window and support it with a wood block.
4   Remove the bolts and withdraw the regulator though the opening.
5   Installation the reverse of removal.

Electric regulator

6   Pry out the rocker switch and disconnect the wiring plug. Mark their locations for ease of installation to the original position and disconnect the wiring from the terminal block.
7   Remove the screws and both access covers.
8   Remove the trim cover.
9   Pry off the clip and disconnect the intermediate lever at the guide plate.
10 Unscrew the regulator mounting nuts, lower the window, then withdraw the regulator upward and remove it from the vehicle.
11 Installation is a reversal of the removal procedure.

33 Under dash panel — removal and installation

1   Remove the panel screw covers (photo).
2   Remove the lower panel screws by turning them a quarter turn.
3   Remove the three screws across the top, unsnap the clips and lower the panel from the instrument panel.
4   To install, place the panel securely in position, engage the clips and install the screws.

34 Instrument panel — removal and installation

1   Remove the glove compartment, as described in Section 35.
2   Remove both under dash panels from beneath the instrument panel.

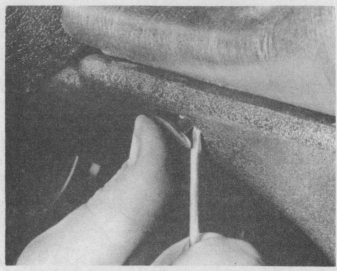

33.1 Use a small screwdriver to pry out the under dash panel screw covers

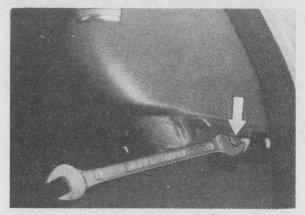

Fig. 11.14 Instrument panel retaining bolt (arrow) (Sec 34)

3   Pry out the windshield inner mouldings.
4   Remove the screws and disconnect the radio speaker covers, then remove the bolts from the instrument.
5   Remove the instrument cluster, as described in Chapter 12.
6   Use a screwdriver to carefully pry off the light switch control knob and unscrew the nut to release the switch.
7   Disconnect the parking brake chain (UK models).
8   Disconnect the left and right vent hoses.
9   Detach the fresh air flap lever and disconnect the fresh air hoses.
10 Disconnect the glove compartment light switch wires.
11 Remove the retaining bolt and nut at the center support and the two bolts at each end of the instrument panel.
12 Disconnect the radio speaker wires, if applicable.
13 Lift the instrument panel so that the defroster jets slide from the heater box, then withdraw the panel from the vehicle.
14 To install, slide the intrument panel from the right side into the left corner of the dash. Push the panel forward until the defroster jets are securely connected to the heater box. The remainder of installation is the reverse of removal, taking care to tighten the bolts securely.

35 Glove compartment and lid — removal and installation

1   Remove the striker (2 screws) and pry out the studs.
2   Press out the light and disconnect the plug.
3   Pull the glove compartment from the instrument panel.
4   Remove the cross-head screws from the lid.
5   Unscrew the slotted nuts retaining the lid hinge.

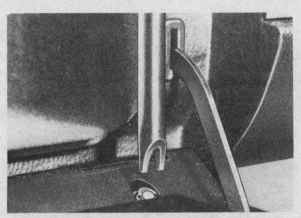

Fig. 11.15 Use a slotted wrench to remove the glove compartment door screws (Sec 35)

Fig. 11.16 Glove compartment lid lock pin (arrow) (Sec 35)

Fig. 11.17 Use pincer-type pliers to compress the glove compartment latch cams (Sec 35)

36.2a Use a small screwdriver to pry the console switches and lamps loose

36.2b Lift the tabs (arrows) and . . .

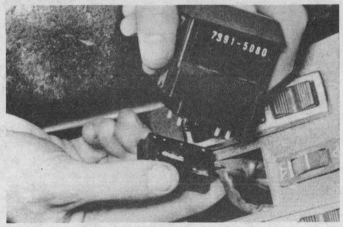

36.2c . . . then unplug the switches

6 Turn the lock pin on the outer edge of the lid to the vertical position, withdraw it and disconnect the stop bracket. The lock pin has a lock on one side only, so if it cannot be removed it should be turned through 180°.

7 Lift the inner lid and withdraw the outer lid, then withdraw the inner lid and stop bracket.

8 If necessary the lock may be removed by compressing the cams with pliers. Note that the top face of the lock is marked 'OBEN.'

9 Installation is a reversal of removal.

36 Center console and gearshift cover — removal and installation

1 Remove both front carpet mats.

2 Pry evenly at the top and bottom of the console switches and light covers and disconnect the switches (photos).

11

36.4a   Remove the ashtray bracket screws (top arrows) to expose the gearshift cover retaining screws (lower arrows)

36.4b   Lift out the gearshift cover

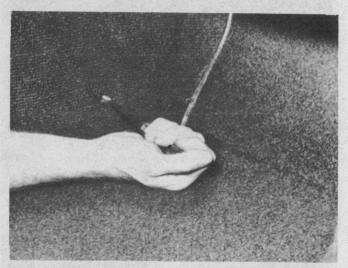

36.9a   Removing the front console retaining screws

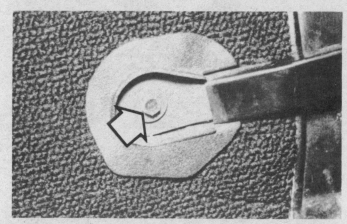

36.9b   The rear console retaining bolts (arrow)

3   Remove the ashtray and unplug the wiring connector.
4   Remove the ashtray frame and the front screws from the geashift lever cover, lift the cover slightly and push up the hazard warning light switch so that the plugs can be disconnected (photos).
5   Pull the gearshift lever cover from the center console.
6   Remove the radio (Chapter 12).
7   Pull off the heater control knobs, then unscrew the nuts.
8   Pull off the heater lever knob and withdraw the cover. Disconnect the light wire.
9   Remove the screws from the front tunnel and the rear bolts from the center console, peel back the carpet and remove the screw from the tray (photos).
10   Lift upward at the rear of the center console and withdraw it from the instrument panel, while holding the end of the console to prevent it spreading apart.
11   Installation is a reversal of removal, making sure to insert it securely into the instument panel.

---

37   Bumpers — removal and installation

Front

1   Loosen the bracket mounting nuts and withdraw the bumper forward (photo).
2   Installation is a reversal of removal, making sure to lubricate the rubber end covers with soapy water or rubber lubricant on models so equipped. On models which aren't equipped with rubber end covers, make sure that the bumper engages the side brackets.

36.9c   The rear console retaining screw is accessible after peeling back the carpet

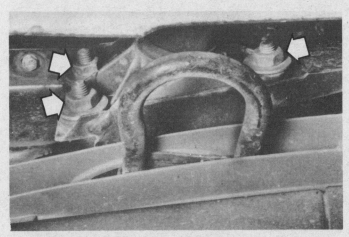

37.1 Front bumper retaining nuts (arrows)

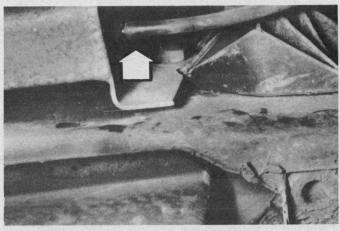

37.4 Disconnect the vacuum reservoir hose before removing the bumper

Rear

3 On station wagon models first remove the lens from the backup light and foglight, disconnect the wiring and remove the reflector.

4 On models equipped with central locking system, disconnect the vacuum reservoir tube (photo).

5 On all models remove the mounting nus and withdraw the bumper (and vacuum tank, if equipped) rearward.

6 Installation is a reversal of removal, making sure to lubricate the rubber end covers with soapy water or rubber lubricant (if equipped) or if not, make sure that the bumper engages the side brackets.

38 Rear shelf (sedan models) — removal and installation

1 Remove the rear seat backrest, as described in Section 30.

2 Remove the two screws from the first aid kit tray, lift the front of the tray, and withdraw it from the shelf.

3 Lift the center of the rear shelf and withdraw it forwards.

4 Installation is a reversal of removal.

39 Central locking system — general information

The central locking system uses vacuum from the vacuum pump mount on the front of the engine to automatically lock all doors, the trunk lid and the fuel tank flap when the driver's door is locked.

Vacuum from the vacuum pump (Chapter 9) is stored in the vacuum tank in the rear compartment and is channelled to the various elements by a switch on the driver's door. The vacuum tank permits the vehicle to be locked up to ten times with the engine stopped, after which the vehicle may be locked manually if required.

40 Fixed glass replacement

Due to the requirements for special handling techniques, the fixed glass such as the windshield, rear and side glass should be replaced by a dealer or auto glass shop.

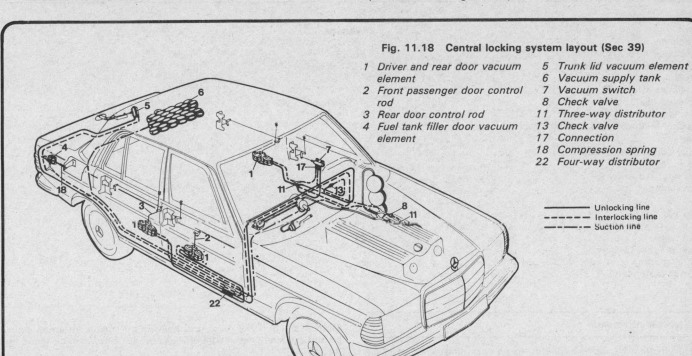

Fig. 11.18 Central locking system layout (Sec 39)

1 Driver and rear door vacuum element
2 Front passenger door control rod
3 Rear door control rod
4 Fuel tank filler door vacuum element

5 Trunk lid vacuum element
6 Vacuum supply tank
7 Vacuum switch
8 Check valve
11 Three-way distributor
13 Check valve
17 Connection
18 Compression spring
22 Four-way distributor

———— Unlocking line
– – – – Interlocking line
–·–·– Suction line

11

Chapter 12   Chassis electrical system

Contents

Bulb replacement 13
Combination switch — removal and installation 4
Courtesy light switch — removal and installation 5
Electrical troubleshooting — general information 2
Fuses — general information 3
General information 1
Headlamp and foglamp — adjustment 11
Headlamp and foglamp — removal and installation 12
Instrument cluster — removal and installation 8

Instrument cluster gauges — removal and installation 10
Instrument panel and center console switches — removal
   and installation 7
Lighting switch — removal and installation 6
Radio — removal and installation 17
Speedometer cable — removal and installation 9
Windshield wiper arm — removal and installation 14
Windshield wiper linkage — removal and installation 16
Windshield wiper motor — removal and installation 15

Specifications

Bulb

Front	Wattage
Headlamp	
Halogen bulb (UK)	60/55
Sealed beam unit (US)	(H3 halogen)
Fog lamp	
Halogen (UK)	55
Sealed beam (US)	(H3 halogen)
Sidelamp (UK)	4
Direction indicator and parking lamp	21

Interior	
Glove compartment lamp	5
Interior lamp	10
Sun visor mirror lamp	5
Trunk lamp	10

Rear	
Turn indicator	21
Tail/parking lamp	10
Stop lamp	21
Backup light	21
Rear fog lamp	21
License plate lamp	5

1   General information

The electrical system is a 12-volt, negative ground type. Power for the lights and all electrical accessories is supplied by a lead/acid-type battery which is charged by the alternator.

This Chapter covers repair and service procedures for the various electrical components not associated with the engine. Information on the battery, alternator, distributor and starter motor can be found in Chapter 5.

It should be noted that whenever portions of the electrical system are worked on, the negative battery cable should be disconnected to prevent electrical shorts and/or fires.

2 Electrical troubleshooting — general information

A typical electrical circuit consists of an electrical component, any switches, relays, motors, etc. related to that component and the wiring and connectors that connect the component to both the battery and the chassis. To aid in locating a problem in any electrical circuit, wiring diagrams are included at the end of this book.

Before tackling any troublesome electrical circuit, first study the appropriate diagrams to get a complete understanding of what makes up that individual circuit. Trouble spots, for instance, can often be narrowed down by noting if other components related to that circuit are operating properly or not. If several components or circuits fail at one time, chances are the problem lies in the fuse or ground connection, as several circuits often are routed through the same fuse and ground connections.

Electrical problems often stem from simple causes, such as loose or corroded connections or a blown fuse. Prior to any electrical troubleshooting, always visually check the condition of the fuse, wires and connections in the problem circuit.

If testing instruments are going to be utilized, use the diagrams to plan ahead of time where you will make the necessary connections in order to accurately pinpoint the trouble spot.

The basic tools needed for electrical troubleshooting include a circuit tester or voltmeter (a 12-volt bulb with a set of test leads can also be used), a continuity tester (which includes a bulb, battery and set of test leads) and a jumper wire, preferably with a circuit breaker incorporated, which can be used to bypass electrical components.

Voltage checks should be performed if a circuit is not functioning properly.

Connect one lead of a circuit tester to either the negative battery terminal or a known good ground. Connect the other lead to a connector in the circuit being tested, preferably nearest to the battery or fuse. If the bulb of the tester goes on, voltage is reaching that point (which means the part of the circuit between that connector and the battery is problem free). Continue checking along the entire circuit in the same fashion. When you reach a point where no voltage is present, the problem lies between there and the last good test point. Most of the time the problem is due to a loose connection. **Note:** *Keep in mind that some circuits receive voltage only when the ignition key is in the Accessory or Run position.*

A method of finding shorts in a circuit is to remove the fuse and connect a test light or voltmeter in its place to the fuse terminals. There should be no load in the circuit. Move the wiring harness from side-to-side while watching the test light. If the bulb goes on, there is a short to ground somewhere in that area, probably where insulation has rubbed off of a wire. The same test can be performed on other components of the circuit, including the switch.

A ground check should be done to see if a component is grounded properly. Disconnect the battery and connect one lead of a self powered test light such as a continuity tester to a known good ground. Connect the other lead to the wire or ground connection being tested. If the bulb goes on, the ground is good. If the bulb does not go on, the ground is not good.

A continuity check is performed to see if a circuit, section of circuit or individual component is passing electricity through it properly. Disconnect the battery and connect one lead of a self powered test light such as a continuity tester to one end of the circuit. If the bulb goes on, there is continuity, which means the circuit is passing electricity through it properly. Switches can be checked in the same way.

Remember that all electrical circuits are composed basically of electricity running from the battery, through the wires, switches, relays, etc. to the electrical component (light bulb, motor, etc.). From there it is run to the body (ground) where it is passed back to the battery. Any electrical problem is basically an interruption in the flow of electricity to and from the battery.

3 Fuses — general information

The electrical circuits of the vehicle are protected by relays and fuses. The individual relays are located in the wiring harness or in the fuse box. The fuse box is located on the engine firewall and access to the fuses is gained by unscrewing the two knurled knobs (photo).

Each of the fuses is designed to protect a specific circuit with the fuse application located on the inside of the cover. The in-line fuse for the radio is located next to the radio. The fuses in the fuse box are held in place by spring clips allowing easy replacement.

If an electrical component fails, your first check should be the fuse. A fuse which has "blown" is easily identified by inspecting the element on the ceramic fuse body or inside the clear plastic body. Also, the blade terminal tips are exposed in the fuse body, allowing for continuity checks.

It is important that the correct fuse be installed. The different electrical circuits need varying amounts of protection, indicated by the amperage rating molded in the fuse body and marked on the fuse box cover. **Caution:** *At no time should the fuse be bypassed with pieces of metal or foil. Serious damage to the electrical system could result. result.*

If the replacement fuse immediately fails, do not replace it again until the cause of the problem is isolated and corrected. In most cases, this will be a short circuit in the wiring caused by a broken or deteriorated wire.

3.1 Fuse box location

3.2 The fuses are accessible after removing the fuse box cover

12

4.3   Pull loose the rubber combination switch cover

4.4   Removing the combination switch screws

4.5   Remove the horn wires from the combination switch

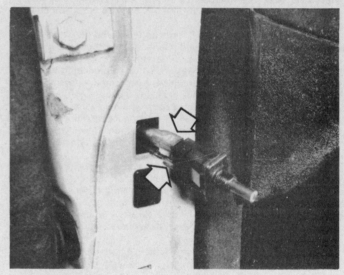

5.3   With the light switch pulled out of the door jamb, the wire connectors (arrows) can be unplugged

4   Combination switch — removal and installation

1   Disconnect the negative cable at the battery. Place the cable out of the way so it cannot accidentally come in contact with the negative terminal of the battery, as this would once again allow power into the electrical system of the vehicle.
2   Remove the under dash panel and disconnect the switch multiplug located under the steering column.
3   Remove the rubber sleeve covering the switch (photo).
4   Remove the switch mounting screws (photo).
5   Disconnect the horn wires by loosening the terminal screws (photo).
6   Withdraw the switch while feeding the wiring harness through the opening.
7   Installation is a reversal of removal.

5   Courtesy light switch — removal and installation

1   Disconnect the negative cable at the battery. Place the cable out of the way so it cannot accidentally come in contact with the negative terminal of the battery, as this would once again allow power into the electrical system of the vehicle.
2   Open the door and pry the switch from the door pillar.
3   Pull the switch out sufficiently for access to the wiring connector, unplug the wires and remove the switch (photo).
4   Installation is a reversal of removal.

6   Lighting switch — removal and installation

1   Disconnect the negative cable at the battery. Place the cable out of the way so it cannot accidentally come in contact with the negative terminal of the battery, as this would once again allow power into the

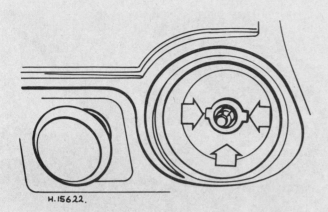

Fig. 12.1 The lighting switch must be engaged in the instrument panel lugs (arrows) before tightening the nut (Sec 6)

7.3 After prying the switch away from the dash the connector can be easily unplugged

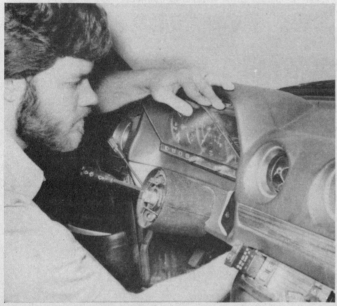

8.3 Push the instrument cluster out of the instrument panel from behind, while guiding it through the opening

electrical system of the vehicle.
2   Pull off the switch knob.
3   Remove the under dash panel (Chapter 11).
4   Unscrew the nut, withdraw the switch from the rear of the instrument panel and disconnect the wiring. Remove the cover.
5   Installation is a reversal of removal, making sure that the cover and switch engage securely in the recess lugs in the under dash panel.

7   Instrument panel and center console switches — removal and installation

1   Disconnect the negative cable at the battery. Place the cable out of the way so it cannot accidentally come in contact with the negative terminal of the battery, as this would once again allow power into the electrical system of the vehicle.
2   Carefully pry the switch out of the panel or instument panel.
3   Unplug the connector and remove the switch (photo).
4   Installation is a reversal of removal.

8   Instrument cluster — removal and installation

1   Disconnect the negative cable at the battery. Place the cable out of the way so it cannot accidentally come in contact with the negative

terminal of the battery, as this would once again allow power into the electrical system of the vehicle.
2   Remove the under dash panel (Chapter 11).
3   Reach up behind the cluster with one hand and push it out of the instrument panel from the rear while guiding the front with the other hand (photo). Alternatively, a hooked tool can be inserted into the gap between the cluster and instrument panel and the cluster can then be pulled away from the panel, working around its outer circumference.
4   Disconnect the speedometer, oil pressure and electrical connectors and withdraw the instrument cluster from the instrument panel.
5   Installation the reverse of removal, making sure the molded rubber strip around the cluster seats securely in the instrument panel.

9   Speedometer cable — removal and installation

Note: *This procedure applies only to mechanical-type speedometers.*
1   Disconnect the speedometer cable from the instrument panel.
2   Apply the handbrake/parking brake and block the rear wheels. Raise the front of the vehicle and support it on securely on jackstands.
3   Remove the retaining bolt from the transmission and pull out the speedometer cable.
4   Release the body clips and withdraw the cable.
5   Installation is a reversal of removal, but make sure that there are no sharp bends in the cable.

10   Instrument cluster gauges — removal and installation

1   Remove the instrument cluster (Section 8).

Clock
2   Remove the four screws and withdraw the clock from the back of the cluster.
3   Installation is the reverse of removal.

Speedometer
4   Remove the clock.
5   Remove the retaining screws, tilt the speedometer back and remove it from the cluster.
6   Installation is the reverse of removal, making sure the trip mileage reset lever engages the knob securely.

12

10.8   The gauge/dimmer potentiometer screw (arrow)

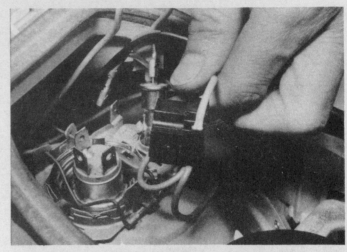

12.2A   Unplugging the headlamp connector (UK models)

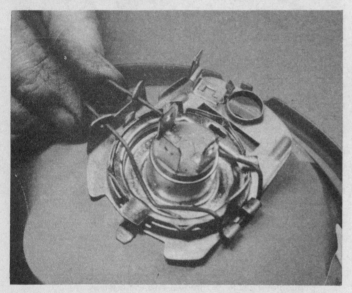

12.2B   Squeeze the headlamp bulb clip to release it (UK models)

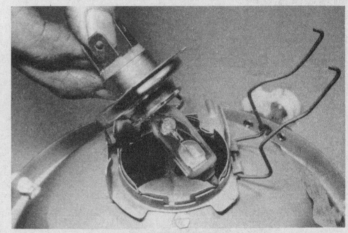

12.2C   Withdrawing the headlamp bulb (UK models)

Gauges

7   Remove the speedometer.
8   Remove the three retaining screws. The lower screw also retains the cluster adjustable lighting potentiometer (photo).
9   Pull the potentiometer out and withdraw the gauge from the cluster.
10   Installation is the reverse of removal.

11   Headlamp and foglamp — adjustment

1   While headlamp/foglamp adjustment should be left to a dealer or properly equipped shop, temporary adjustment is possible.
2   Position the vehicle as level as possible approximately 16 ft (5 m) from a wall.
3   Measure from the ground to the centers of the headlamps and mark the wall at this level.
4   With the headlamps on high beam, the light beams should not project above the points on the wall which are the same height as headlamp centers. The brightest points in the light pattern should be in direct alignment with the headlamps.
5   The foglamps can be adjusted using the same procedure.

12   Headlamp and foglamp — removal and installation

UK models

1   To remove a headlamp/foglamp bulb, open the hood and unclip and remove the headlamp unit rear cover.
2   Disconnect the wiring from the bulb, then either release the spring

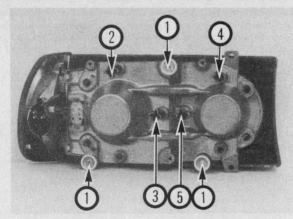

**Fig. 12.2   Bulb-type headlamp unit (UK models)
(Sec 12 and 13)**

1   White knurled
    retaining knobs
2   Headlamp height
    adjustment screw
3   Headlamp lateral
    adjustment screw

4   Foglamp height
    adjustment screw
5   Foglamp lateral
    adjustment screw

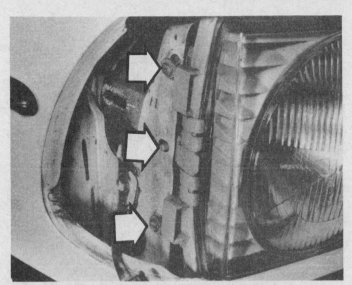

12.3 Headlamp mounting screws and locating lugs (arrows) (UK models)

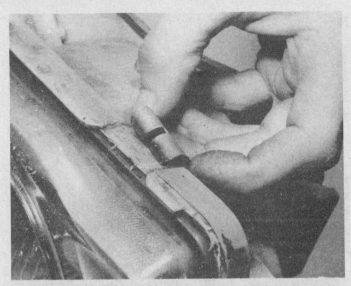

12.5A After prying it loose, the headlamp clip can be lifted off (UK models)

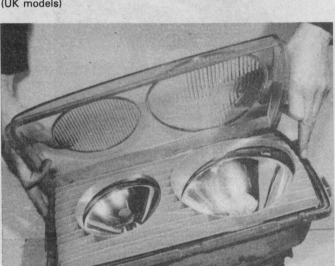

12.5B With the clips removed, the headlamp lens can be removed (UK models)

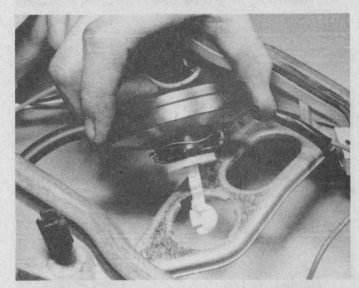

12.7 Removing the headlamp vacuum control unit (UK models)

clips or turn the bulbholder to extract the bulb (photos). Take care that the bulb glass is not be touched with the fingers as traces of oil from the skin will cause the bulb to burn out prematurely. If the bulb is touched, clean it with rubbing alcohol.

3 To remove the headlamp unit, first remove the direction indicator lamp, as described in Section 13, then remove the side mounting screws (photo).

4 Remove the inner mounting screws and withdraw the headlamp unit from the car.

5 To dismantle the headlamp, pry off the clips and remove the glass (photos).

6 Remove the headlamp assembly trim panel.

7 Release the clips and vacuum adjustment unit and remove the reflectors (photo).

8 Installation is a reversal of removal.

US models

9 These models are equipped with sealed beam unit headlamps and foglamps.

10 To remove a unit, first unscrew the knurled knobs from inside the engine compartment.

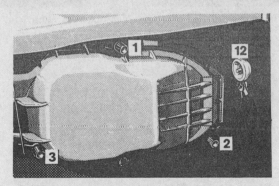

Fig. 12.3 Sealed beam headlamp (US models) installation details (Sec 12 and 13)

1 Headlamp vertical adjustment screw
2 Headlamp horizontal adjustment screw
3 Foglamp adjustment screw
12 White knurled parking lamp retaining knob

12

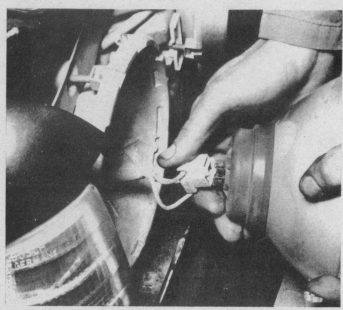

12.11   Support the sealed beam headlamp and unplug the connector (US models)

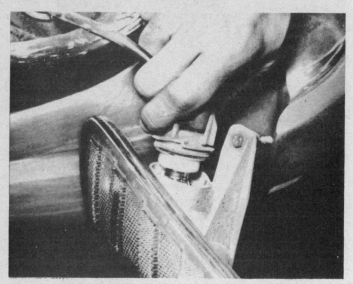

13.4   Twist the turn signal/parking bulb holder to remove it

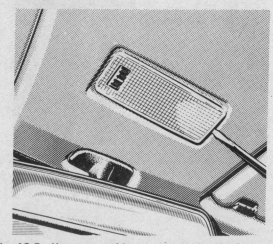

Fig. 12.5   Use a screwdriver to pry the interior lamp out (Sec 13)

13.3   The turn signal/parking lamp can be removed after unscrewing the white knob (arrow)

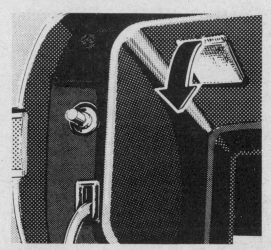

Fig. 12.4   Glove compartment lamp and bulb removal (Sec 13)

11   Remove the inner mounting screws and withdraw the unit to the side far enough to allow the wiring plugs to be disconnected (photo).
12   Unbolt the parking light/direction indicator unit from the headlamp unit (Section 13).
13   Installation is a reversal of removal.

13   Bulb replacement

Front

Front sidelamp (UK models)
1   Unclip the headlamp rear cover.
2   Pull the sidelamp holder out, depress the bulb and twist to remove.
Parking and turn signal light
3   Unscrew the white knurled knob in the engine compartment adjacent to the headlamp assembly and remove the lamp housing (photo).
4   Twist the bulb holder to remove it and then press the bulb and turn it for removal.

Interior

Glove compartment light
5   Pry the lamp from the top of the glove compartment and then remove the bulb from the spring terminals.

Interior light
6   Pry the lamp assembly carefully from the headlining (photo).
7   Disengage the bulb from the spring terminals.

13.6   Once the interior lamp is pried loose, the bulb is easily replaced

13.12   Use a screwdriver to push the automatic transmission bulb holder out for access to the bulb

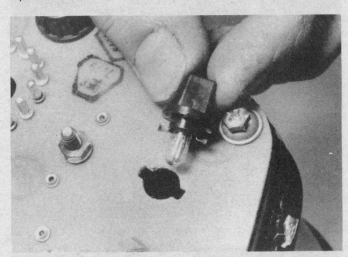

13.19   The instrument cluster bulb holder is removed after aligning the tabs with the slot in the housing

Fig. 12.6   Pry the sun visor mirror out at both sides for access to the lamp bulb (Sec 13)

Fig. 12.7   The trunk light (1) is accessible through an opening in the inner panel (Sec 13)

Hazard switch light
8   Pry the hazard switch from the center console.
9   Disconnect the plug.
10   Turn the bulb holder a quarter turn counterclockwise and withdraw it from the switch, depress the bulb and remove it.

Automatic transmission gearshift selector light
11   Remove the gearshift cover.
12   Pull the bulbholder out and remove the bulb (photo).

Heater control lights
13   Pull the heater control knobs off and then pull the knob illumination bulbs from the holders.
14   Pull the air flap control knob off, unscrew the nuts and withdraw the control cover.
15   Pull the bulb holders out and remove the bulbs.

Ashtray light
16   Remove the ashtray, unscrew the two screws and remove the cover.
17   Pull the bulb holder out and extract the bulb.

Instrument cluster light
18   Remove the instrument cluster (Section 8).
19   Turn the bulb holder a quarter turn to remove it and then pull the bulb from the holder (photo).

Sun visor mirror light
20   Pry alternately at both sides of the mirror with a small screwdriver to gain access to the bulb.

Trunk light
21   Open the trunk and remove the bulb from the spring terminals.

12

Fig. 12.8 The tail light bulb layout viewed from the rear (top) and facing the bulb holder (bottom)

1 *Turn signal*
2 *Tail/parking lamp*
3 *Stop lamp*
4 *Backup lamp (coupe and sedan)*
5 *Optional foglamp*

13.22   Removing the coupe and sedan tail light bulb holder assembly

13.23   Unsnap the station wagon bulb holder from the tail light housing

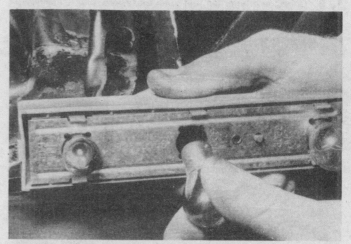

13.24   Push in, twist and remove the tail light bulb

13.25   License plate lamp screws (arrows)

13.26   Separate the license plate lamp bulb holder housing from the housing for access to the bulb

13.27 Station wagon back-up light screws (arrows)

13.28 Push in and rotate the back-up light bulb to remove it

Rear

Taillights

22 On sedan models, unscrew the white knurled knobs in the trunk and remove the bulb holder assembly (photo).
23 On station wagon models, remove the retaining nuts, push the taillight housing out of the body and remove the bulb holder (photo).
24 On all models, remove the bulb by depressing and twisting (photo).

License plate light

25 Remove the license plate lamp lens screws (photo).
26 Lower the lamp from the body, separate the lens and remove the bulb (photo).

Back-up light (station wagon models)

27 Remove the backup light lense retaining screws (photo).
28 Press the bulb in and rotate it to remove (photo).

---

14 Windshield wiper arm — removal and installation

1 Remove the wiper blades (Chapter 1).
2 Lift the wiper to the vertical position, grasp the wiper retaining nut cover and rotate the arm and cover together toward the windshield to lift the cover, exposing he nut.
3 Remove the nut and washer, mark the arm in relation to the spindle, and pull off the arm.
4 Installation is a reversal of removal, tightening the nut securely.

---

15 Windshield wiper motor — removal and installation

1 Disconnect the negative cable at the battery. Place the cable out of the way so it cannot accidentally come in contact with the negative terminal of the battery, as this would once again allow power into the electrical system of the vehicle.
2 Remove the wiper arms (Section 14).
3 Remove the plastic heater air intake grilles located in the cowl. Use a narrow screwdriver to push the clip center pins out, pry out the clips and then pull the grilles forward. Remove the wiper arm shaft cap and nut, where applicable.
4 Remove the screws, push out the center clip pins and withdraw the center panel.
5 Pry the operating rods from the wiper motor crank.
6 Remove the drain tube from the spindle, where applicable.
7 Disconnect the wiper motor multi-plug in the engine compartment.
8 Unclip the wiring plug, then unbolt the wiper motor from the center bracket.
9 Installation is a reversal of removal.

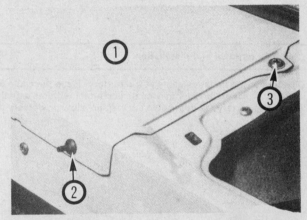

Fig. 12.9 Windshield wiper motor center cover panel (1), clips (2) and retaining screw (3) (Sec 15)

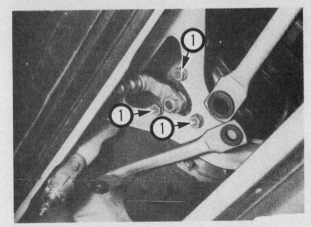

Fig. 12.10 Windshield wiper mounting bolts (1) (Sec 15)

---

16 Windshield wiper linkage — removal and installation

1 Remove the wiper motor (Section 13).
2 Remove the operating rods, then unbolt the spindle assemblies from the bulkhead in a downward direction.
3 Installation is the reverse of removal.

12

17.3 The radio retaining screws (arrows)

17.4 Pull the radio out sufficiently to allow the electrical connections to be unplugged

17 Radio — removal and installation

1   Disconnect the negative cable at the battery. Place the cable out of the way so it cannot accidentally come in contact with the negative terminal of the battery, as this would once again allow power into the electrical system of the vehicle.

2   Remove the knobs from the radio and pry off the cover panel.

3   Remove the two retaining screws and bars (photo).

4   Withdraw the radio from the opening, disconnect the electical plugs and remove the radio from the vehicle (photo).

5   Installation is the reverse of removal.

Key to early model (from chassis number 000 001) 240D (123.183) and 300TD (123.190) (UK) wiring diagram

1 Headlamp unit, left
  a High beam
  b Low beam
  c Parking lamp/standing lamp
  d Fog lamp
  e Turn signal lamp
2 Brake fluid indicator lamp switch
3 Contact sensor, brake pads, front, left
4 Contact sensor, brake pads, front, right
5 Instrument cluster
  a Turn signal indicator lamp, left
  b High beam indicator lamp
  c Coolant temperature gauge
  d Fuel gauge
  e Fuel reserve warning lamp
  f Charge indicator lamp
  g Brake pad wear indicator lamp
  h Brake fluid and parking brake indicator lamp
  i Instrument lamps
  j Rheostat, instrument lamps
  k Warning buzzer
  l Turn signal indicator lamp, right
  m Electronic clock
  n Preglow indicator lamp
6 Cigar lighter with ashtray illumina-illumination
7 Radio*
8 Headlamp unit, right
  a High beam
  b Low beam
  c Parking lamp/standing lamp
  d Fog lamp
  e Turn signal lamp
9 Automatic antenna*
10 Parking brake indicator lamp switch
11 Temperature sensor, coolant
12 Warning buzzer contact
13 Front dome lamp w/switch
14 Door contact switch, front, right
15 Door contact switch, front left
16 Dual-tone horn (fanfares)
17 Sensor, Tempomat*²)
18 Amplifier, Tempomat*²)
19 Actuator, Tempomat*²)
20 Warning flasher switch/timer
21 Horn contact
22 Switch, Tempomat*²)
  A Off
  V Decelerate/set
  SP Resume
  B Accelerate/set

23 Glove compartment lamp switch
24 Glove compartment lamp
25 Fuse box
26 Relay I, window lifts*
27 Relay II, window lifts*
28 Door contact switch, window lifts*
29 Combination switch
  a Turn signal lamp switch
  b Headlamp flasher switch
  c Dimmer switch
  d Washer switch
  e Switch wiping speed
    I Intermittent wiping
    II Slow wiping
    III Fast wiping
30 Wiper motor
31 Intermittent wiping timer
32 Steering locky starter switch
33 Lighting switch
34 Sliding roof motor*
35 Switch, electrically operated sliding roof*
36 Solenoid valve, automatic transmission*
37 Kick-down switch*
38 Starter lockout and back-up lamp switch*
39 Relay, air conditioner I*
40 Relay, air conditioner II*
41 Blower switch with lamp
42 Stop lamp switch
43 Washer pump
44 Wiper motor, headlamp, right*
45 Wiper motor, headlamp, left*
46 Relay, headlamp cleaning system*
47 Washer pump, headlamps*
48 Temperature sensor, preglowing indicator
49 Preglow time relay
50 Illumination
  a Air deflector control*
  b Heater control
  c Switch
51 Temperature switch 62 °C (144 °F) receiver drier, air conditioner*
52 Temperature switch 100 °C (212 °F)*
53 Auxiliary fan*
54 Relay, auxiliary fan*
55 Pressure switch, refrigerant compressor On 2.6 bar, Off 2.0 bar
56 Electromagnetic clutch, refrigerant compressor*
57 Temperature control w/lighting, air conditioner*

58 Pre-resistance, blower motor
59 Blower motor
60 Fuse box, glow plugs
61 Window lift motor, rear, left*
62 Switch, window, rear, left*
63 Switch cluster, window lifts*
  a Switch, window, rear, left
  b Safety switch
  c Switch, window, front, left
  d Switch, window, front, right
  e Switch, window, rear, right
64 Window lift motor, front, left*
65 Window lift motor, front, right*
66 Glow plugs and series resistor¹)
67 Detent switch, rear dome lamp
68 Plug connection, tail lamp cable harness
69 Time-lag relay, heated rear window
70 Switch, heated rear window
71 Wiper motor, rear door
72 Starter
73 Battery
74 Alternator w/electronic regulator
75 Door contact switch, rear, left
76 Door contact switch, rear, right
77 Fuel gauge sending unit
78 Rear dome lamp
79 Window lift motor, rear, right
80 Switch, window, rear, right
81 Tail lamp unit, left
  a Turn signal lamp
  b Tail/standing lamp
  c Stop lamp
82 Rear fog lamp
83 Washer pump, rear door
84 Detent switch, wiper motor rear door/push-button switch washer pump, rear door
85 License plate lamps
86 Rear door contact switch/rear door lock
87 Heated rear window
88 Illumination, shift plate
89 Ground connection, rear door
90 Back-up lamp
91 Tail lamp unit, right
  a Turn signal lamp
  b Tail/standing lamp
  c Stop lamp
* Special Equipment
¹) 240 TD, 4 glow plugs
²) On 300 TD only

Wire Color Code

bl	= blue	nf	= neutral	
br	= brown	rs	= pink	
el	= ivory	rt	= red	
ge	= yellow	sw	= black	
gn	= green	vi	= purple	
gr	= grey	ws	= white	

Example:
Wire designation 1.5 gr/rt
Basic color gr = grey
Identification color rt = red
Cross section of wire 1.5 = 1.5 mm²

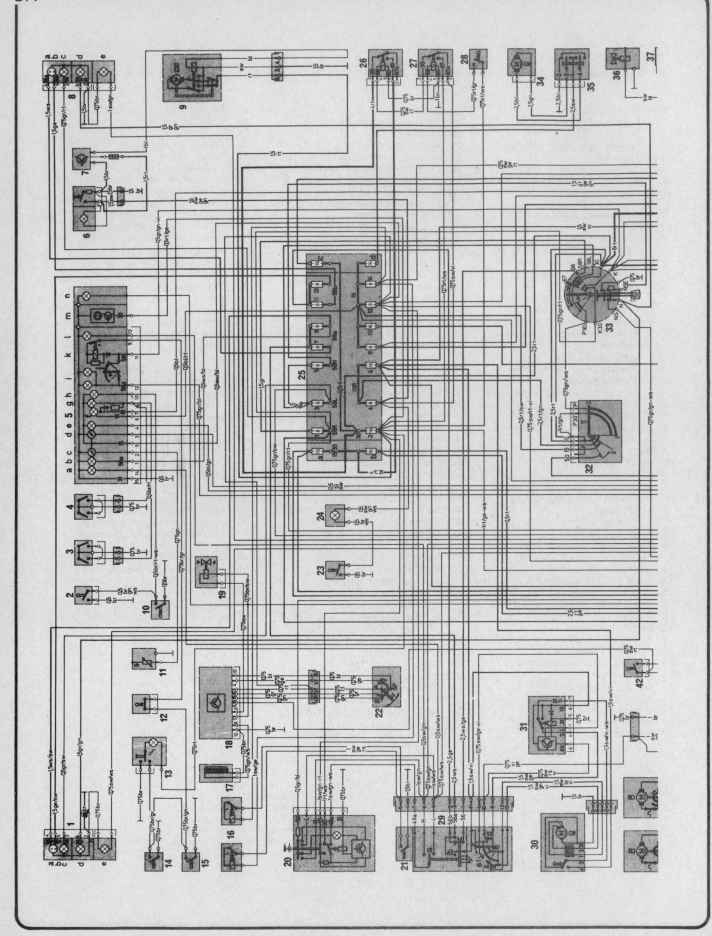

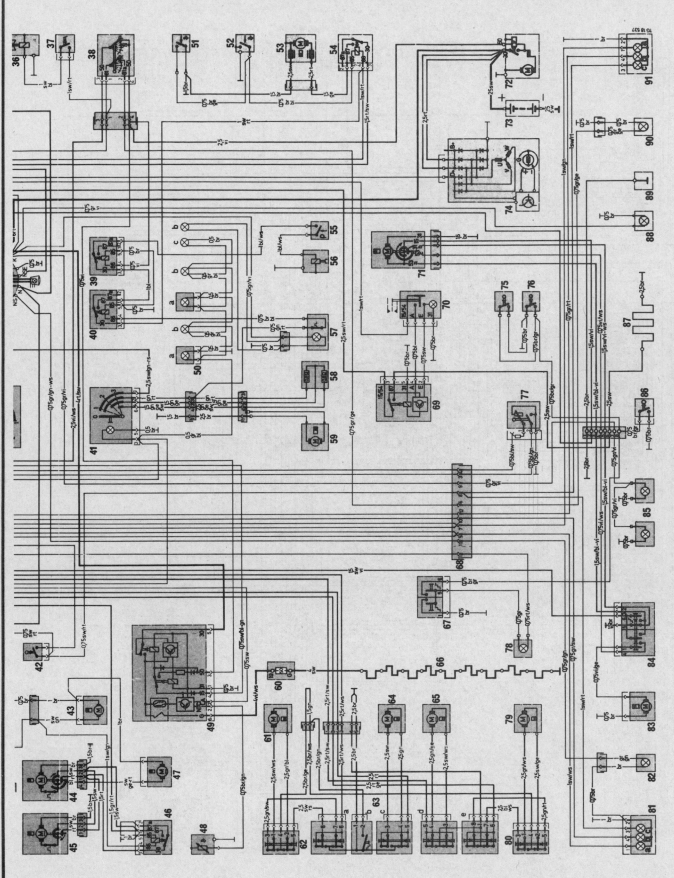

Early model (from chassis number 000 001) 240D (123.183) and 300TD (123.190) (UK) wiring diagram

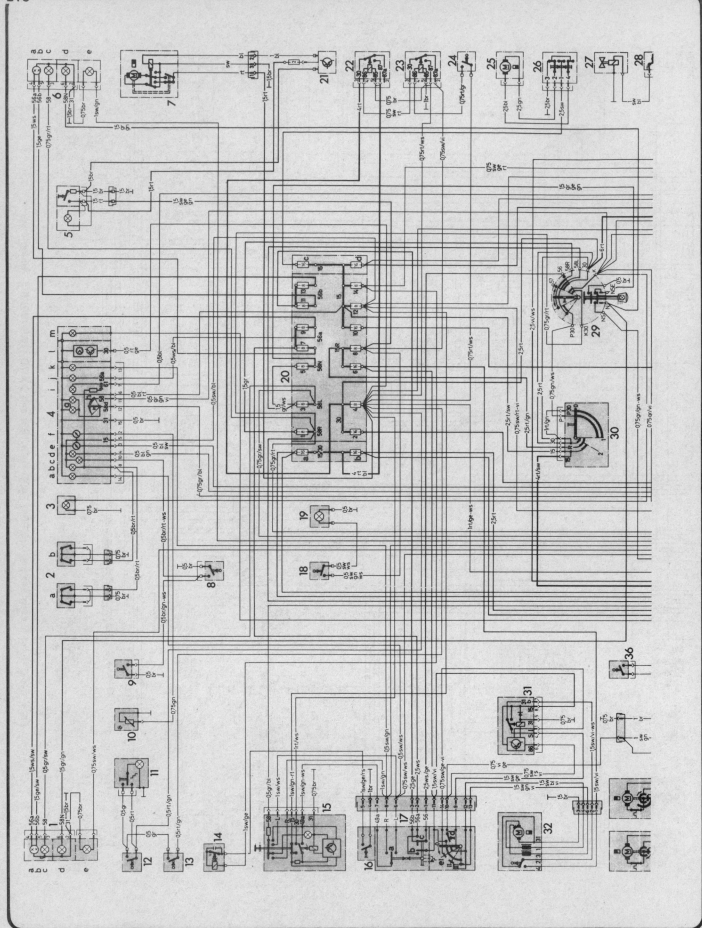

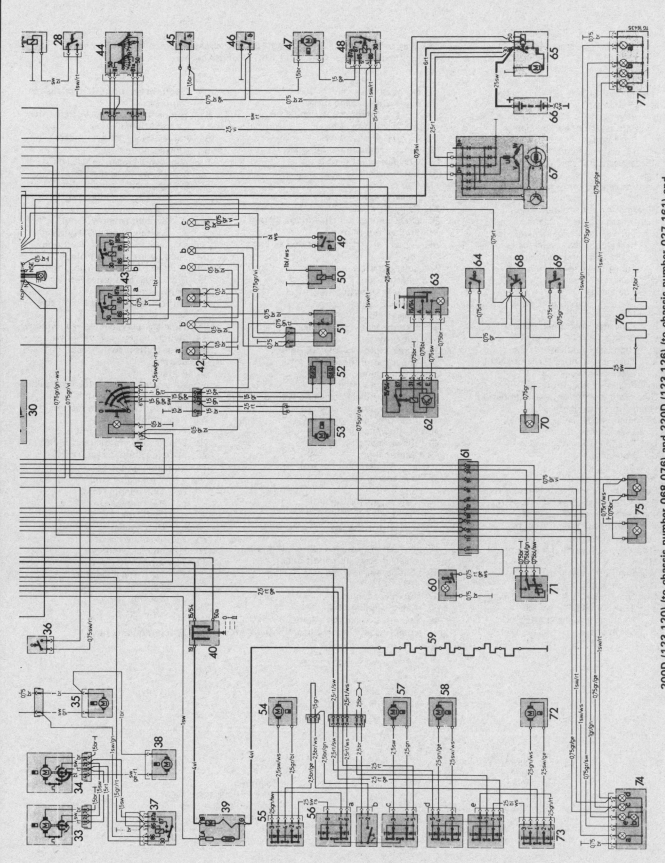

217

200D (123.120) (to chassis number 068 076) and 220D (123.126) (to chassis number 027 161) and 240D (123.123) (to chassis number 044 537) (UK) wiring diagram

Key to 200D (123.120) (to chassis number to 068 076), 220D (123.126) (to chassis number 027 161) and
240D (123.123) (to chassis number 044 537) (UK) wiring diagram

1   Headlamp unit, left
    a   High beam
    b   Low beam
    c   Parking lamp/standing lamp
    d   Fog lamp
    e   Turn signal lamp
2a Contact sensor, brake pads, front, right
2b Contact sensor, brake pads, front, left
3   Illumination, shift plate*
4   Instrument cluster
    a   Turn signal indicator lamp, left
    b   Brake pad wear indicator lamp
    c   Brake fluid and parking brake indicator lamp
    d   Fuel reserve warning lamp
    e   Fuel gauge
    f   Coolant temperature gauge
    g   Instrument lamps
    h   Rheostat, instrument lamps
    i   Charge indicator lamp
    j   High beam indicator lamp
    k   Turn signal indicator lamp, right
    l   Electronic clock
    m   Preglow indicator lamp
5   Cigar lighter with ashtray illumination
6   Headlamp unit, right
    a   High beam
    b   Low beam
    c   Parking lamp/standing lamp
    d   Fog lamp
    e   Turn signal lamp
7   Automatic antenna*
8   Parking brake indicator lamp switch
9   Brake fluid indicator lamp switch
10 Temperature sensor, coolant
11 Front dome lamp with switch
12 Door contact switch, front left
13 Door contact switch, front right
14 Horn
15 Warning flasher switch/timer
16 Horn contact
17 Combination switch
    a   Turn signal lamp switch
    b   Headlamp flasher switch
    c   Dimmer switch

    d   Washer switch
    e   Switch wiping speed
        I   Intermittent wiping
        II   Slow wiping
        III Fast wiping
18 Glove compartment lamp switch
19 Glove compartment lamp
20 Fuse box
21 Radio*
22 Relay I, window lifts*
23 Relay II, window lifts*
24 Door contact switch, window lifts*
25 Sliding roof motor*
26 Switch, electrically operated sliding roof*
27 Solenoid valve, automatic transmission*
28 Kick-down switch*
29 Lighting switch
30 Steering lock switch
31 Intermittent wiping timer
32 Wiper motor
33 Wiper motor, headlamp, right*
34 Wiper motor, headlamp, left*
35 Washer pump
36 Stop lamp switch
37 Relay, headlamp cleaning system*
38 Washer pump, headlamps*
39 Fuse box, glow plugs
40 Preglow/starter switch
41 Blower switch with lamp
42 Illumination
    a   Air deflector control
    b   Heater control
    c   Switch
43a Relay, air conditioner I*
43b Relay, air conditioner II*
44 Starter lockout and back-up lamp switch*
45 Temperature switch 62 °C (144 °F) receiver drier, air conditioner*
46 Temperature switch 100 °C (212 °F)*
47 Auxiliary fan*
48 Relay, auxiliary fan*
49 Pressure switch, refrigerant compressor* On 2.6 bar, Off 2.0 bar

50 Electromagnetic clutch, refrigerant compressor*
51 Temperature control with lighting, air conditioner*
52 Pre-resistance, blower motor
53 Blower motor
54 Window lift motor, rear, left*
55 Switch, window, rear, left*
56 Switch cluster, window lifts*
    a   Switch, window, rear, left
    b   Safety switch
    c   Switch, window, front, left
    d   Switch, window, front, right
    e   Switch, window, rear, right
57 Window lift motor, front, left*
58 Window lift motor, front, right*
59 Glow plugs and series resistor
60 Trunk lamp
61 Plug connection, tail lamp cable harness
62 Time-lag relay, heated rear window
63 Switch, heated rear window
64 Door contact switch, rear, left*
65 Starter
66 Battery
67 Alternator with electronic regulator
68 Rear dome lamp switch*
69 Door contact switch, rear, right*
70 Rear dome lamp*
71 Fuel gauge sending unit
72 Window lift motor, rear, right*
73 Switch, window, rear, right*
74 Tail lamp unit, left
    a   Turn signal lamp
    b   Tail/standing lamp
    c   Back-up lamp
    d   Stop lamp
    e   Rear fog lamp
75 License plate lamps
76 Heated rear window
77 Tail lamp unit, right
    a   Turn signal lamp
    b   Tail/standing lamp
    c   Back-up lamp
    d   Stop lamp

*   Special equipment

Wire Color Code

bl = blue
br = brown
el = ivory
ge = yellow
gn = green
gr = grey

nf = neutral
rs = pink
rt = red
sw = black
vi = purple
ws = white

Example:
Wire designation 1.5 gr/rt
Basic color gr = grey
Identification color rt = red
Cross section of wire 1.5 = 1.5 mm^2

Key to 240D (123.123) (from chassis number 044 538) and 300D (123.130) (from chassis number 057 327) (UK) wiring diagram

1 Headlamp unit, left
  a High beam
  b Low beam
  c Parking lamp/standing lamp
  d Fog lamp
  e Turn signal lamp
2 Brake fluid indicator lamp switch
3 Contact sensor, brake pads, front, left
4 Contact sensor, brake pads, front right
5 Instrument cluster
  a Turn signal indicator lamp
  b High beam indicator lamp
  c Coolant temperature gauge
  d Fuel gauge
  e Fuel reserve warning lamp
  f Charge indicator lamp
  g Brake pad wear indicator lamp
  h Brake fluid and parking indicator lamp
  i Instrument lamps
  j Rheostat, instrument lamps
  k Warning buzzer
  l Turn signal indicator lamp, right
  m Electronic clock
  n Preglow indicator lamp
6 Cigar lighter with ashtray illumination
7 Radio*
8 Headlamp unit, right
  a High beam
  b Low beam
  c Parking lamp/standing lamp
  d Fog lamp
  e Turn signal lamp
9 Automatic antenna*
10 Parking brake indicator lamp switch
11 Temperature sensor, coolant
12 Warning buzzer contact
13 Front dome lamp with switch
14 Door contact switch, front right
15 Door contact switch, front left
16 Dual-tone horn (fanfares)
17 Sensor, Tempomat*[2]
18 Amplifier, Tempomat*[2]
19 Actuator, Tempomat*[2]
20 Warning flasher switch/timer
21 Horn contact
22 Switch, Tempomat*[2]
  A Off
  V Decelerate/set

SP Resume
B Accelerate/set
23 Glove compartment lamp switch
24 Glove compartment lamp
25 Fuse box
26 Relay I, window lifts*
27 Relay II, window lifts*
28 Door contact switch, window lifts*
29 Combination switch
  a Turn signal lamp switch
  b Headlamp flasher switch
  c Dimmer switch
  d Washer switch
  e Switch wiping speed
    I Intermittent wiping
    II Slow wiping
    III Fast wiping
30 Wiper motor
31 Intermittent wiping timer
32 Steering lock switch
33 Lighting switch
34 Sliding roof motor*
35 Switch, electrically operated sliding roof*
36 Solenoid valve, automatic transmission*
37 Kick-down switch*
38 Starter lockout and back-up lamp switch*
39 Relay, air conditioner I*
40 Relay, air conditioner II*
41 Blower switch with lamp
42 Stop lamp switch
43 Washer pump
44 Wiper motor, headlamp, right*
45 Wiper motor, headlamp, left*
46 Relay, headlamp cleaning system*
47 Washer pump, headlamps*
48 Temperature sensor, preglowing indicator
49 Preglow time relay
50 Illumination
  a Air deflector control*
  b Heater control
  c Switch
51 Temperature switch 62 °C (144 °F) receiver drier, air conditioner*
52 Temperature switch 100 °C (212 °F)*
53 Auxiliary fan*
54 Relay, auxiliary fan*

55 Pressure switch, refrigerant compressor*
  On 2.6 bar, Off 2.0 bar
56 Electromagnetic clutch, refrigerant compressor*
57 Temperature control with lighting, air conditioner*
58 Pre-resistance, blower motor
59 Blower motor
60 Fuse box, glow plugs
61 Window lift motor, rear, left*
62 Switch, window, rear, left*
63 Switch cluster, window lifts*
  a Switch, window, rear, left
  b Safety switch
  c Switch, window, front, left
  d Switch, window, front, right
  e Switch, window, rear, right
64 Window lift motor, front, left*
65 Window lift motor, front, right*
66 Glow plugs and series resistor[1]
67 Trunk lamp
68 Plug connection, tail lamp cable harness
69 Time-lag relay, heated rear window
70 Switch, heated rear window
71 Starter
72 Battery
73 Alternator with electronic regulator
74 Door contact switch, rear, left*
75 Rear dome lamp switch*
76 Door contact switch, rear, right*
77 Rear dome lamp*
78 Fuel gauge sending unit
79 Window lift motor, rear, right*
80 Switch, window, rear, right*
81 Tail lamp unit, left
  a Turn signal lamp
  b Tail/standing lamp
  c Back-up lamp
  d Stop lamp
  e Rear fog lamp
82 License plate lamps
83 Heated rear window
84 Illumination, shift plate*
85 Tail lamp unit, right
  a Turn signal lamp
  b Tail/standing lamp
  c Back-up lamp
  d Stop lamp

* Special equipment
[1] 240 D, 4 glow plugs
[2] Only 300 D

Wire Color Code

bl	= blue	nf	= neutral
br	= brown	rs	= pink
el	= ivory	rt	= red
ge	= yellow	sw	= black
gn	= green	vi	= purple
gr	= grey	ws	= white

Example:
Wire designation 1.5 gr/rt
Basic color gr = grey
Identification color rt = red
Cross section of wire 1.5 = 1.5 mm²

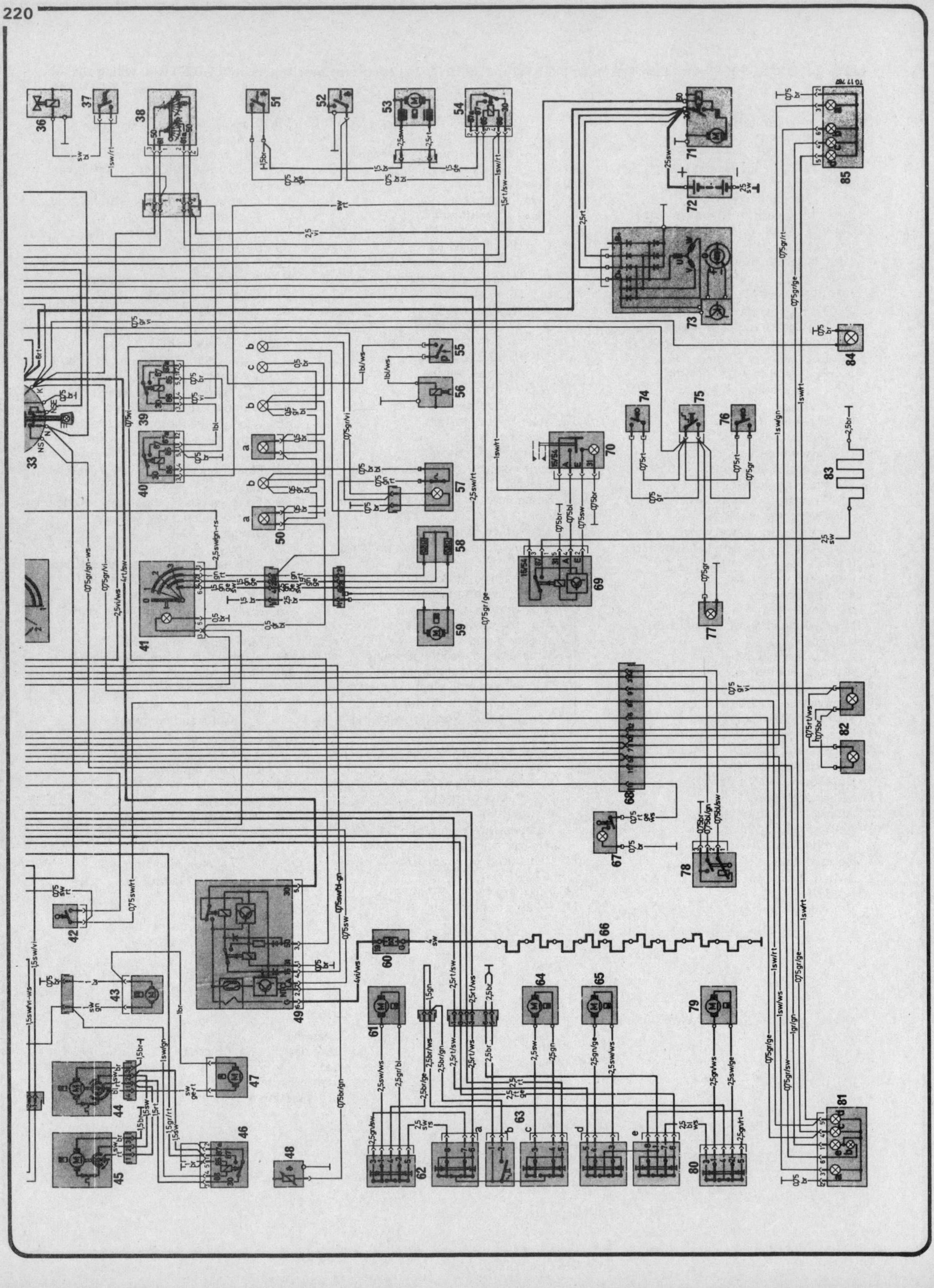

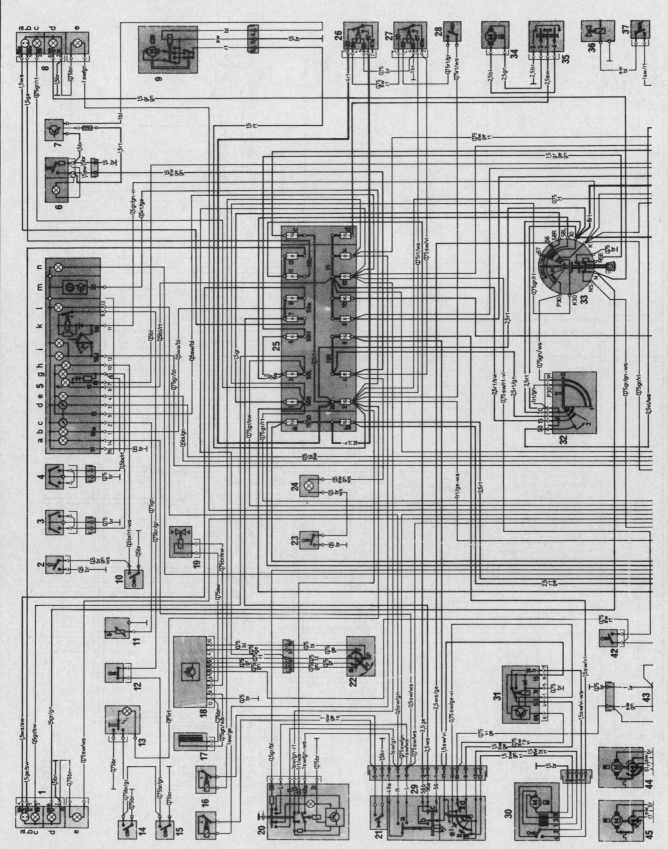

240D (123.123) (from chassis number 044 538) and 300D (123.130) (from chassis number 057 327 on) (UK) wiring diagram

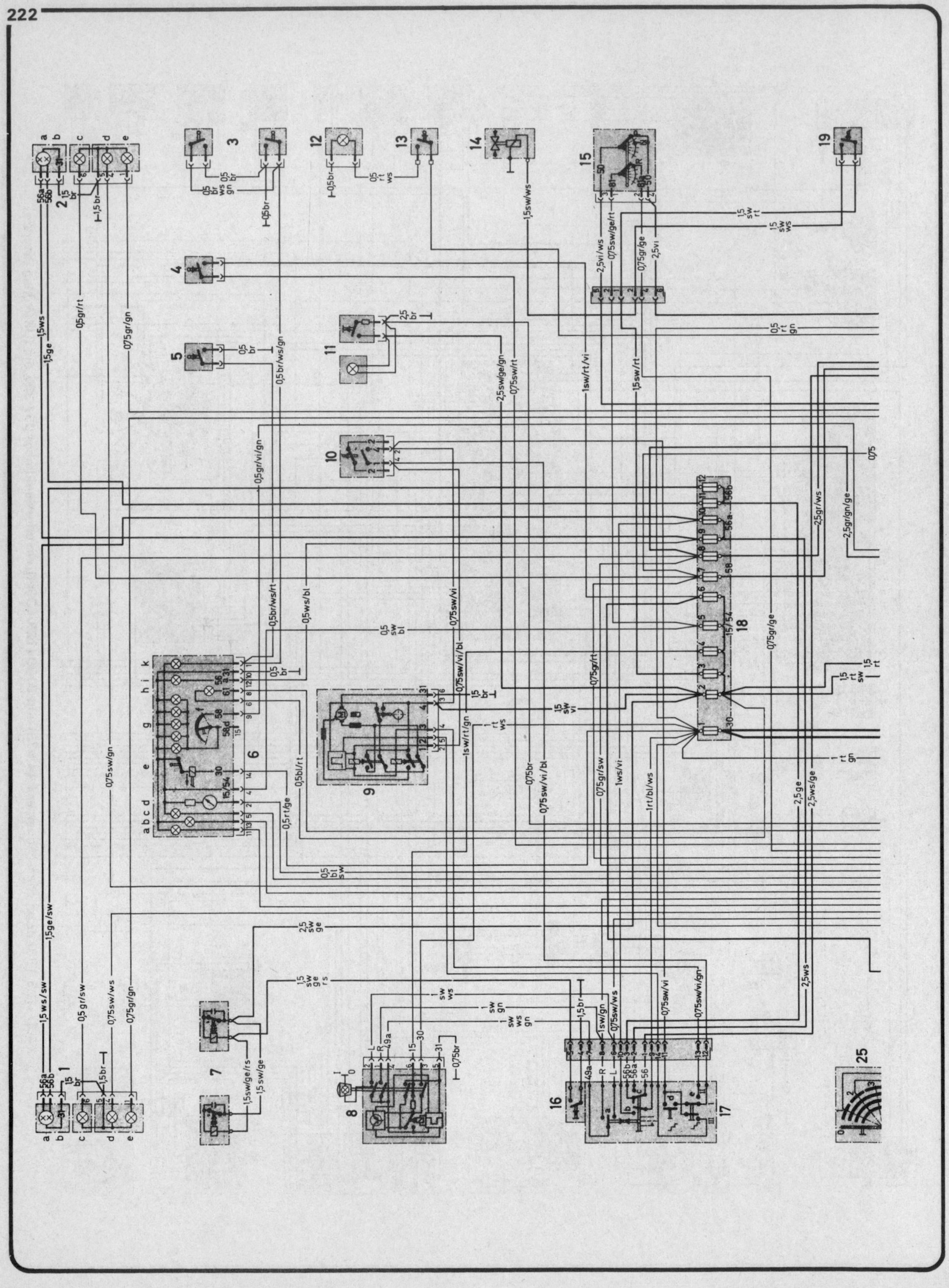
1
2
3
4
5
6
7
8
9
10
11
12
13
14
15
16
17
18
19
25

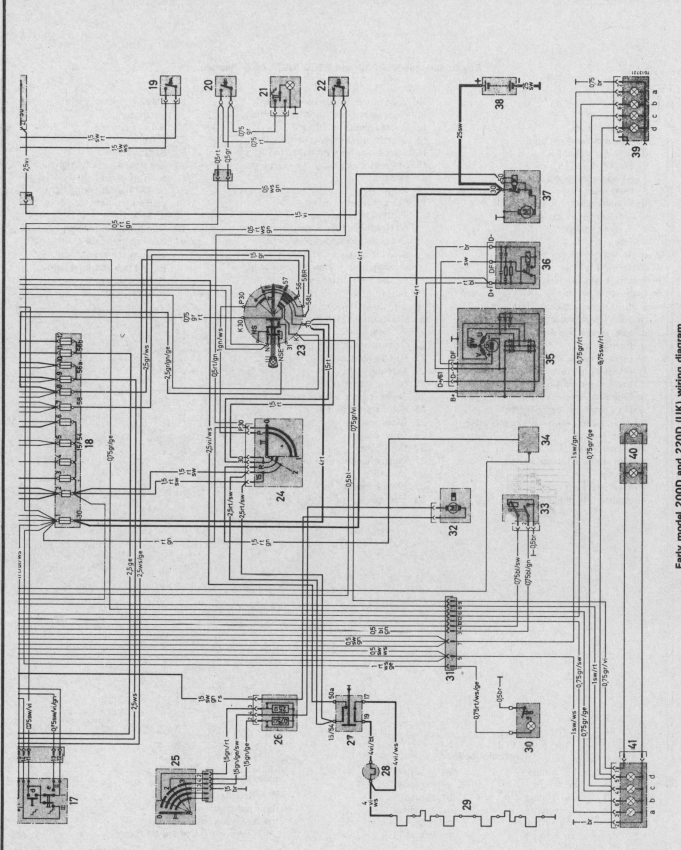

Early model 200D and 220D (UK) wiring diagram

Key to early model 200D and 220D (UK) wiring diagram

1 Light assembly, left
  a High beam
  b Dipped beam
  c Side light/parking light
  d Turn signal light
  e Fog light
2 Light assembly, right
  a High beam
  b Dipped beam
  c Side light/parking light
  d Turn signal light
  e Fog light
3 Brake fluid level warning light switch
4 Brake light switch
5 Parking brake warning light switch
6 Instrument cluster
  a Turn signal indicator, left
  b Turn signal indicator, right
  c Fuel reserve warning light
  d Fuel gauge
  e Electric clock
  f Rheostat for instrument lighting
  g Instrument lighting
  h Charging indicator light
  i High beam indicator light
  k Service and parking brake indicator
    light
7 Two-tone horn
8 Hazard warning flasher switch,
  electronic
9 Windscreen wiper motor with
  intermittent wiping electronics

10 Foot pump, windscreen washer
11 Cigar lighter with ashtray illumination
12 Glove compartment light
13 Switch, glove compartment light
14 Solenoid valve automatic transmission
15 Starter lock-out and reversing light
  switch
16 Horn ring
17 Combination switch
  a Blinker switch
  b Headlight flasher switch
  c Hand-operated dipper switch
  d Windscreen wiper switch
  e Switch for windscreen wiper speed
    and intermittent wiping
18 Fuses
19 Kickdown switch
20 Door contact, left front
21 Reading light
22 Door contact, right front
23 Rotary light switch
24 Steering lock
25 Blower switch
26 Series resistor blower switch
27 Glow starter switch
28 Glow control
29 Glow plugs
30 Boot light
31 Plug connection for tail light wiring
  harness
32 Blower motor
33 Fuel gauge sending unit

34 Radio (optional extra)
35 Generator
36 Voltage control
37 Starter
38 Battery
39 Tail light assembly, right
  a Turn signal light
  b Tail light/parking light
  c Back-up light
  d Stop light
40 Number plate lighting
41 Tail light assembly, left
  a Turn signal light
  b Tail light/parking light
  c Back-up light
  d Stop light

Wire color code

bl	= blue	ws	= white
rt	= red	gn	= green
sw	= black	br	= brown
el	= ivory	ge	= yellow
nf	= neutral	gr	= grey
vi	= violet	rs	= pink

Example:

Wire designation 1.5 gr/rt
Basic color gr = grey
Identification color rt = red
Cross section of wire 1.5 = 1.5 mm^2

Key to 200D (123.120) (from chassis number 068 077) and 220D (123.126) (from chassis number 027 162 to chassis number 056 736) (UK) wiring diagram

1 Headlamp unit, left
  a   High beam
  b   Low beam
  c   Parking lamp/standing lamp
  d   Fog lamp
  e   Turn signal lamp
2 Brake fluid indicator lamp switch
3 Contact sensor, brake pads, front, left
4 Contact sensor, brake pads, front, right
5 Instrument cluster
  a   Turn signal indicator lamp, left
  b   High beam indicator lamp
  c   Coolant temperature gauge
  d   Fuel gauge
  e   Fuel reserve warning lamp
  f   Charge indicator lamp
  g   Brake pad wear indicator lamp
  h   Brake fluid and parking brake indicator lamp
  i   Instrument lamps
  j   Rheostat, instrument lamps
  k   Warning buzzer
  l   Turn signal indicator lamp, right
  m   Electronic clock
  n   Preglow indicator lamp
6 Cigar lighter with ashtray illumination
7 Radio*
8 Headlamp unit, right
  a   High beam
  b   Low beam
  c   Parking lamp/standing lamp
  d   Fog lamp
  e   Turn signal lamp
9 Automatic antenna*
10 Parking brake indicator lamp switch
11 Temperature sensor, coolant
12 Warning buzzer contact
13 Front dome lamp with switch
14 Door contact switch, front left
15 Door contact switch, front right
16 Dual-tone horn (fanfares)
17 Warning flasher switch/timer
18 Glove compartment lamp switch
19 Glove compartment lamp
20 Fuse box
21 Relay I, window lifts*

22 Relay II, window lifts*
23 Door contact switch, window lifts*
24 Combination switch
  a   Turn signal lamp switch
  b   Headlamp flasher switch
  c   Dimmer switch
  d   Washer switch
  e   Switch wiping speed
     I   Intermittent wiping
     II Slow wiping
     III Fast wiping
25 Horn contact
26 Wiper motor
27 Intermittent wiping timer
28 Steering lock switch
29 Lighting switch
30 Sliding roof motor*
31 Switch, electrically operated sliding roof*
32 Solenoid valve, automatic transmission*
33 Kick-down switch*
34 Starter lockout and back-up lamp switch*
35 Relay, air conditioner II*
36 Relay, air conditioner I*
37 Blower switch with lamp
38 Stop lamp switch
39 Washer pump
40 Wiper motor, headlamp, left*
41 Wiper motor, headlamp, right*
42 Relay, headlamp cleaning system*
43 Washer pump, headlamps*
44 Fuse box, glow plugs
45 Preglow/starter switch
46 Illumination
  a   Air deflector control
  b   Heater control
  c   Switch
47 Temperature switch 62 °C (144 °F) receiver drier, air conditioner*
48 Temperature switch 100 °C (212 °F)*
49 Auxiliary fan*
50 Relay, auxiliary fan*
51 Pressure switch, refrigerant compressor* On 2.6 bar, Off 2.0 bar
52 Electromagnetic clutch, refrigerant compressor*

53 Temperature control with lighting, air conditioner*
54 Pre-resistance, blower motor
55 Blower motor
56 Window lift motor, rear, left*
57 Switch, window, rear, left*
58 Switch cluster, window lifts*
  a   Switch, window, rear, left
  b   Safety switch
  c   Switch, window, front, left
  d   Switch, window, front, right
  e   Switch, window, rear, right
59 Window lift motor, front, left*
60 Glow plugs and series resistor
61 Thermo-time switch, preglowing system
62 Time-lag relay, heated rear window
63 Switch, heated rear window
64 Starter
65 Battery
66 Alternator with electronic regulator
67 Door contact switch, rear, left*
68 Rear dome lamp switch
69 Door contact switch, rear, right*
70 Rear dome lamp
71 Plug connection, tail lamp cable harness
72 Trunk lamp
73 Window lift motor, front, right*
74 Switch, window, rear, right*
75 Window lift motor, rear right*
76 Fuel gauge sending unit
77 Tail lamp unit, left
  a   Turn signal lamp
  b   Tail/standing lamp
  c   Back-up lamp
  d   Stop lamp
  e   Rear fog lamp
78 License plate lamps
79 Heated rear window
80 Illumination, shift plate
81 Tail lamp unit, right
  a   Turn signal lamp
  b   Tail/standing lamp
  c   Back-up lamp
  d   Stop lamp

*   Special equipment

Wire Color Code

bl	=	blue	nf	=	neutral
br	=	brown	rs	=	pink
el	=	ivory	rt	=	red
ge	=	yellow	sw	=	black
gn	–	green	vi	=	purple
gr	=	grey	ws	=	white

Example:
Wire designation 1.5 gr/rt
Basic color gr = grey
Identification color rt = red
Cross section of wire 1.5 = 1.5 mm^2

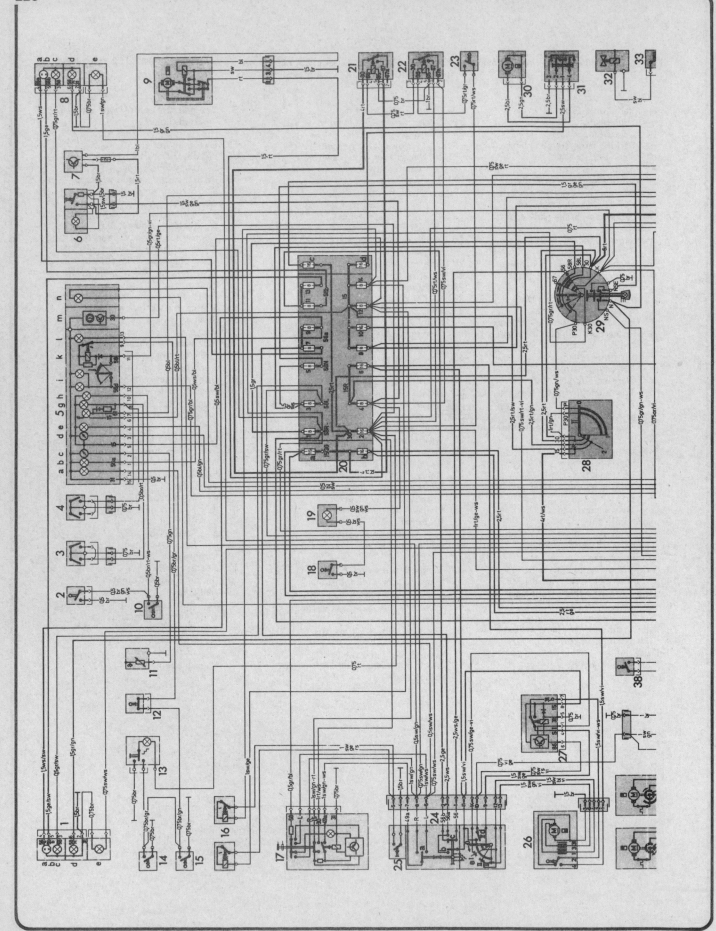

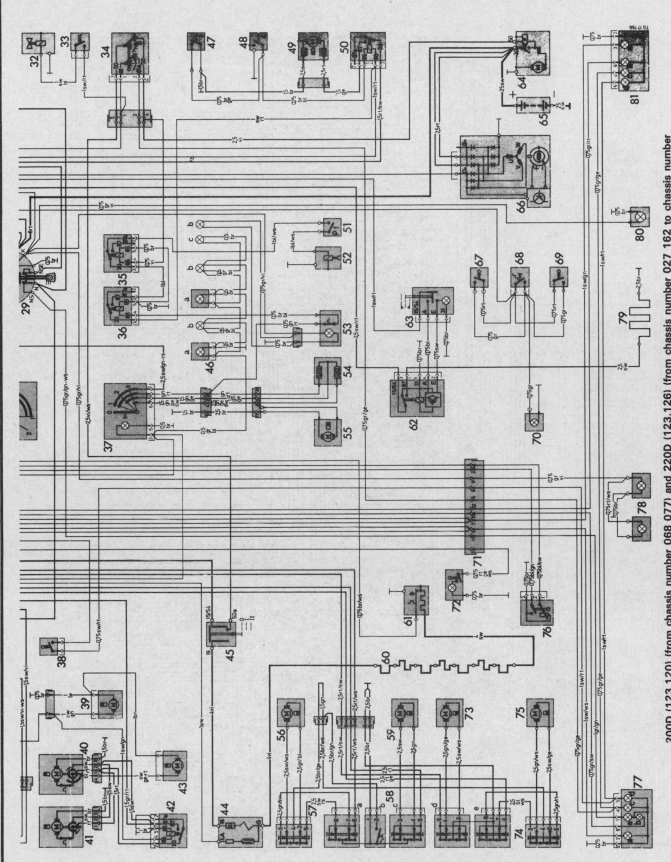

200D (123.120) (from chassis number 068 077) and 220D (123.126) (from chassis number 027 162 to chassis number 056 736) (UK) wiring diagram

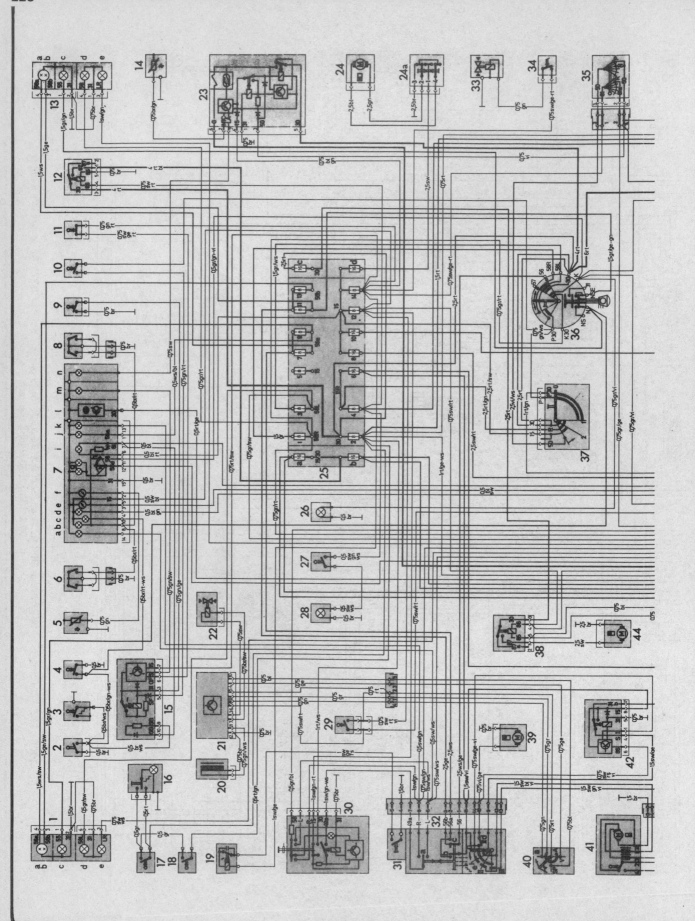

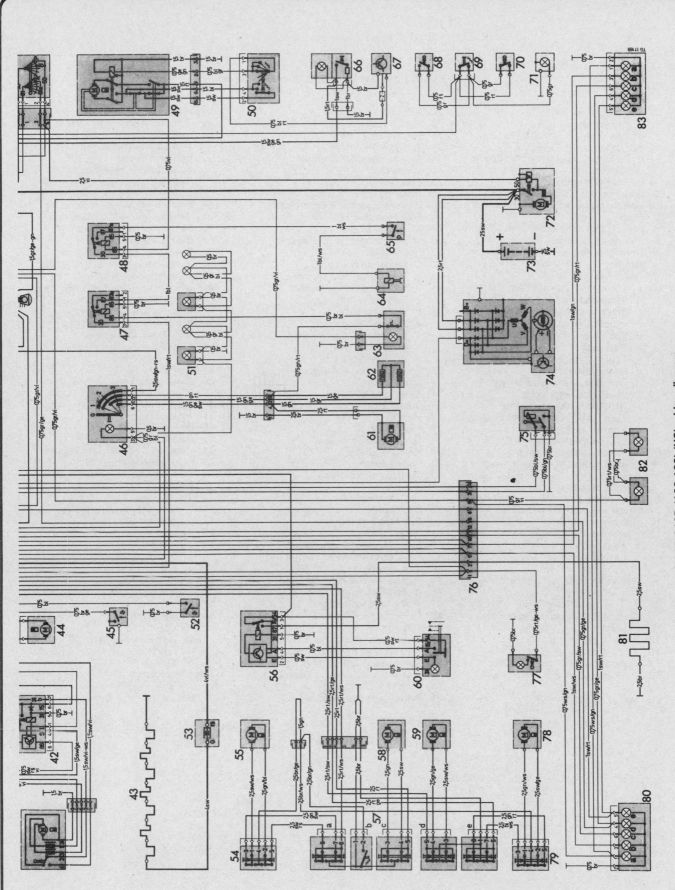

1977 240D (123.123) (US) wiring diagram

Key to 1977 240D (123.123) (US) wiring diagram

1 Headlamp unit, left
  a High beam
  b Low beam
  c Fog lamp
  d Parking lamp/standing lamp/side
    marker lamp
  e Turn signal lamp
2 Brake fluid indicator lamp switch
3 Switch, pressure differential indicator
  lamp
4 Parking brake indicator lamp switch
5 Temperature sensor, coolant
6 Contact sensor, brake pads, front,
  left
7 Instrument cluster
  a Turn signal indicator lamp, left
  b Brake pad wear indicator lamp
  c Brake fluid and parking brake
    indicator lamp
  d Fuel reserve warning lamp
  e Fuel gauge
  f Coolant temperature gauge
  g Instrument lamps
  h Rheostat, instrument lamps
  i Charge indicator lamp
  j High beam indicator lamp
  k Turn signal indicator lamp, right
  l Electronic clock
  m Seat belt warning lamp
  n Preglow indicator lamp
8 Contact sensor, brake pads, front,
  right
9 Warning buzzer contact
10 Door contact switch, warning buzzer
11 Driver's belt buckle switch
12 Relay, window lifts*
13 Headlamp unit, right
  a High beam
  b Low beam
  c Fog lamp
  d Parking lamp/standing lamp/side
    marker lamp
  e Turn signal lamp
14 Temperature sensor, preglowing
  indicator
15 Warning device
16 Front dome lamp w/switch
17 Door contact switch, front left
18 Door contact switch, front right
19 Horn
20 Sensor, cruise control*

21 Amplifier, cruise control*
22 Actuator, cruise control*
23 Preglow time relay
24 Sliding roof motor*
24a Switch, electrically operated
   sliding roof*
25 Fuse box
26 Illumination, shift plate*
27 Glove compartment lamp switch
28 Glove compartment lamp
29 Stop lamp switch
30 Warning flasher switch/timer
31 Horn contact
32 Combination switch
  a Turn signal lamp switch
  b Headlamp flasher switch
  c Dimmer switch
  d Washer switch
  e Switch wiping speed
    I Intermittent wiping
    II Slow wiping
    III Fast wiping
33 Solenoid valve, automatic
  transmission*
34 Kick-down switch*
35 Starter lockout and back-up lamp
  switch*
36 Lighting switch
37 Ignition starter switch
38 Relay, auxiliary fan*
39 Washer pump
40 Switch, cruise control*
  A Off
  V Decelerate/set
  SP Resume
  B Accelerate/set
41 Wiper motor
42 Intermittent wiping timer
43 Glow plugs and series resistors
44 Auxiliary fan*
45 Temperature switch 100 °C (212 °F)*
46 Blower switch with lamp
47 Relay, air conditioner I*
48 Relay, air conditioner II*
49 Automatic antenna*
50 Switch, automatic antenna*
51 Illumination, heater controls
52 Temperature switch 62 °C (144 °F)
  receiver drier, air conditioner*
53 Fuse box, glow plugs
54 Switch, window, rear, left*

55 Window lift motor, rear, left*
56 Time-lag relay, heated rear window
57 Switch cluster, window lifts*
  a Switch, window, rear, left
  b Safety switch
  c Switch, window, front, left
  d Switch, window, front, right
  e Switch, window, rear, right
58 Window lift motor, front, left*
59 Window lift motor, front, right*
60 Switch, heated rear window
61 Blower motor
62 Pre-resistance, blower motor
63 Temperature control w/lighting,
  air conditioner*
64 Electromagnetic clutch, refrigerant
  compressor*
65 Pressure switch, refrigerant
  compressor*
  On 2.6 bar, Off 2.0 bar
66 Cigar lighter with ashtray
  illumination
67 Radio*
68 Door contact switch, rear, left*
69 Rear dome lamp switch*
70 Door contact switch, rear, right*
71 Rear dome lamp*
72 Starter
73 Battery
74 Alternator w/electronic regulator
75 Fuel gauge sending unit
76 Plug connection, tail lamp cable
  harness
77 Trunk lamp
78 Window lift motor, rear, right*
79 Switch, window, rear, right*
80 Tail lamp unit, left
  a Side marker lamp
  b Turn signal lamp
  c Tail/standing lamp
  d Back-up lamp
81 Heated rear window
82 License plate lamps
83 Tail lamp unit, right
  a Side marker lamp
  b Turn signal lamp
  c Tail/standing lamp
  d Back-up lamp
  e Stop lamp

* Special equipment

Wire Color Code

bl = blue   nf = neutral
br = brown   rs = pink
el = ivory   rt = red
ge = yellow   sw = black
gn = green   vi = purple
gr = grey   ws = white

Example:
Wire designation 1.5 gr/rt
Basic color gr = grey
Identification color rt = red
Cross section of wire 1.5 = 1.5 mm²

Key to 1977 300D (123.130) (from chassis number 000 001 to chassis number 000 326) (UK) wiring diagram

1 Headlamp unit, left
  a High beam
  b Low beam
  c Parking lamp/standing lamp
  d Fog lamp
  e Turn signal lamp
2a Contact sensor, brake pads, front, right
2b Contact sensor, brake pads, front, left
3 Illumination, shift plate*
4 Instrument cluster
  a Turn signal indicator lamp, left
  b Brake pad wear indicator lamp
  c Brake fluid and parking brake indicator lamp
  d Fuel reserve warning lamp
  e Fuel gauge
  f Coolant temperature gauge
  g Instrument lamps
  h Rheostat, instrument lamps
  i Charge indicator lamp
  j High beam indicator lamp
  k Turn signal indicator lamp, right
  l Electronic clock
  m Preglow indicator lamp
5 Cigar lighter with ashtray illumination
6 Headlamp unit, right
  a High beam
  b Low beam
  c Parking lamp/standing lamp
  d Fog lamp
  e Turn signal lamp
7 Automatic antenna*
8 Parking brake indicator lamp switch
9 Actuator, Tempomat*
10 Amplifier, Tempomat*
11 Brake fluid indicator lamp switch
12 Temperature sensor, coolant
13 Front dome lamp with switch
14 Sensor, Tempomat*
15 Door contact switch, front left
16 Door contact switch, front right
17 Horn
18 Warning flasher switch/timer
19 Horn contact
20 Combination switch
  a Turn signal lamp switch
  b Headlamp flasher switch
  c Dimmer switch
  d Washer switch

  e Switch wiping speed
    I Intermittent wiping
    II Slow wiping
    III Fast wiping
21 Glove compartment lamp switch
22 Glove compartment lamp
23 Fuse box
24 Radio*
25 Relay I, window lifts*
26 Relay II, window lifts*
27 Door contact switch, window lifts*
28 Sliding roof motor*
29 Switch, electrically operated sliding roof*
30 Solenoid valve, automatic transmission*
31 Kick-down switch*
32 Lighting switch
33 Steering lock switch
34 Intermittent wiping timer
35 Switch, Tempomat*
  A Off
  V Decelerate/set
  SP Resume
  B Accelerate/set
36 Wiper motor
37 Wiper motor, headlamp, right*
38 Wiper motor, headlamp, left*
39 Washer pump
40 Stop lamp switch
41 Relay, headlamp cleaning system*
42 Washer pump, headlamps*
43 Temperature sensor, preglowing indicator
44 Preglow time relay
45 Blower switch with lamp
46 Illumination
  a Air deflector control
  b Heater control
  c Switch
47 Relay, air conditioner I*
48 Relay, air conditioner II*
49 Starter lockout and back-up lamp switch
50 Temperature switch 62 °C (144 °F) receiver drier, air conditioner*
51 Temperature switch 100 °C (212 °F)*
52 Auxiliary fan*
53 Relay, auxiliary fan*
54 Pressure switch, refrigerant compressor*
  On 2.6 bar, Off 2.0 bar

55 Electromagnetic clutch, refrigerant compressor*
56 Temperature control with lighting, air conditioner*
57 Pre-resistance, blower motor
58 Blower motor
59 Fuse box, glow plugs
60 Window lift motor, rear, left*
61 Switch, window, rear, left*
62 Switch cluster, window lifts*
  a Switch, window, rear, left
  b Safety switch
  c Switch, window, front, left
  d Switch, window, front, right
  e Switch, window, rear, right
63 Glow plugs and series resistor
64 Window lift motor, front, left*
65 Window lift motor, front, right*
66 Trunk lamp
67 Switch, window, rear, right*
68 Window lift motor, rear, right*
69 Fuel gauge sending unit
70 Plug connection, tail lamp cable harness
71 Rear dome lamp*
72 Time-lag relay, heated rear window
73 Switch, heated rear window
74 Door contact switch, rear, left*
75 Rear dome lamp switch*
76 Door contact switch, rear, right*
77 Alternator with electronic regulator
78 Battery
79 Starter
80 Tail lamp unit, right
  a Turn signal lamp
  b Tail/standing lamp
  c Back-up lamp
  d Stop lamp
81 Heated rear window
82 License plate lamps
83 Tail lamp unit, left
  a Turn signal lamp
  b Tail/standing lamp
  c Back-up lamp
  d Stop lamp
  e Rear fog lamp

* Special equipment

Wire Color Code

bl	=	blue	nf	= neutral
br	=	brown	rs	= pink
el	=	ivory	rt	= red
ge	=	yellow	sw	= black
gn	=	green	vi	= purple
gr	=	grey	ws	= white

Example:
Wire designation 1.5 gr/rt
Basic color gr = grey
Identification color rt = red
Cross section of wire 1.5 = 1.5 mm^2

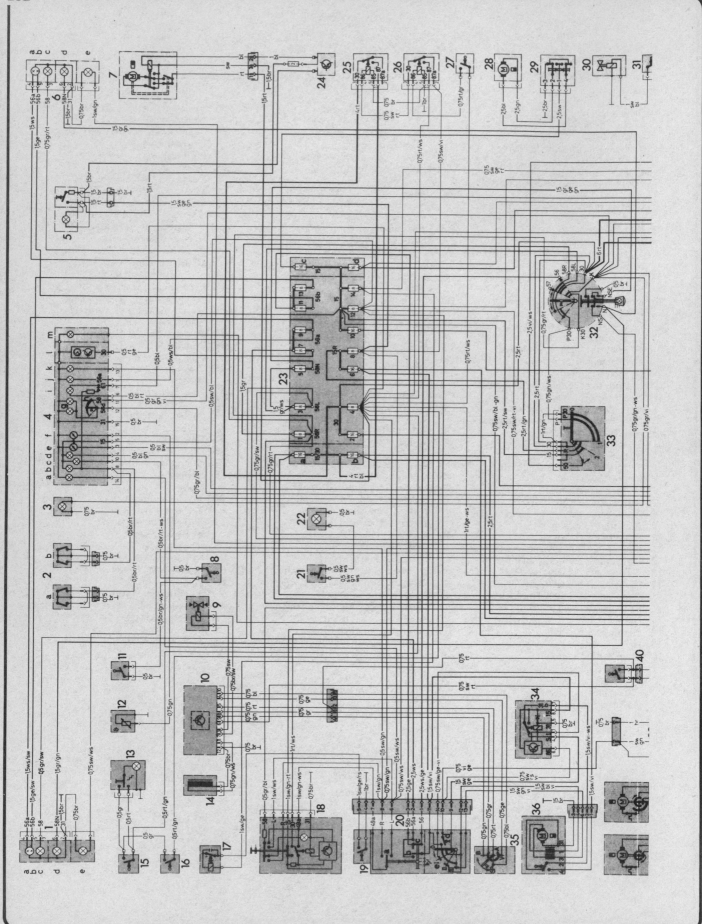

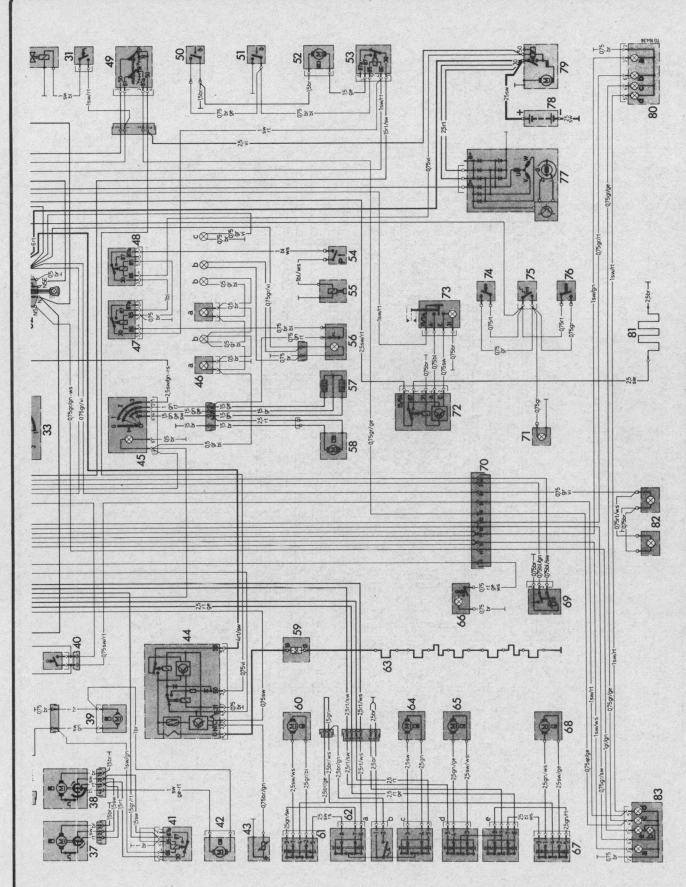

1977 300D (123.130) (from chassis number 000 001 to chassis number 057 326) (UK) wiring diagram

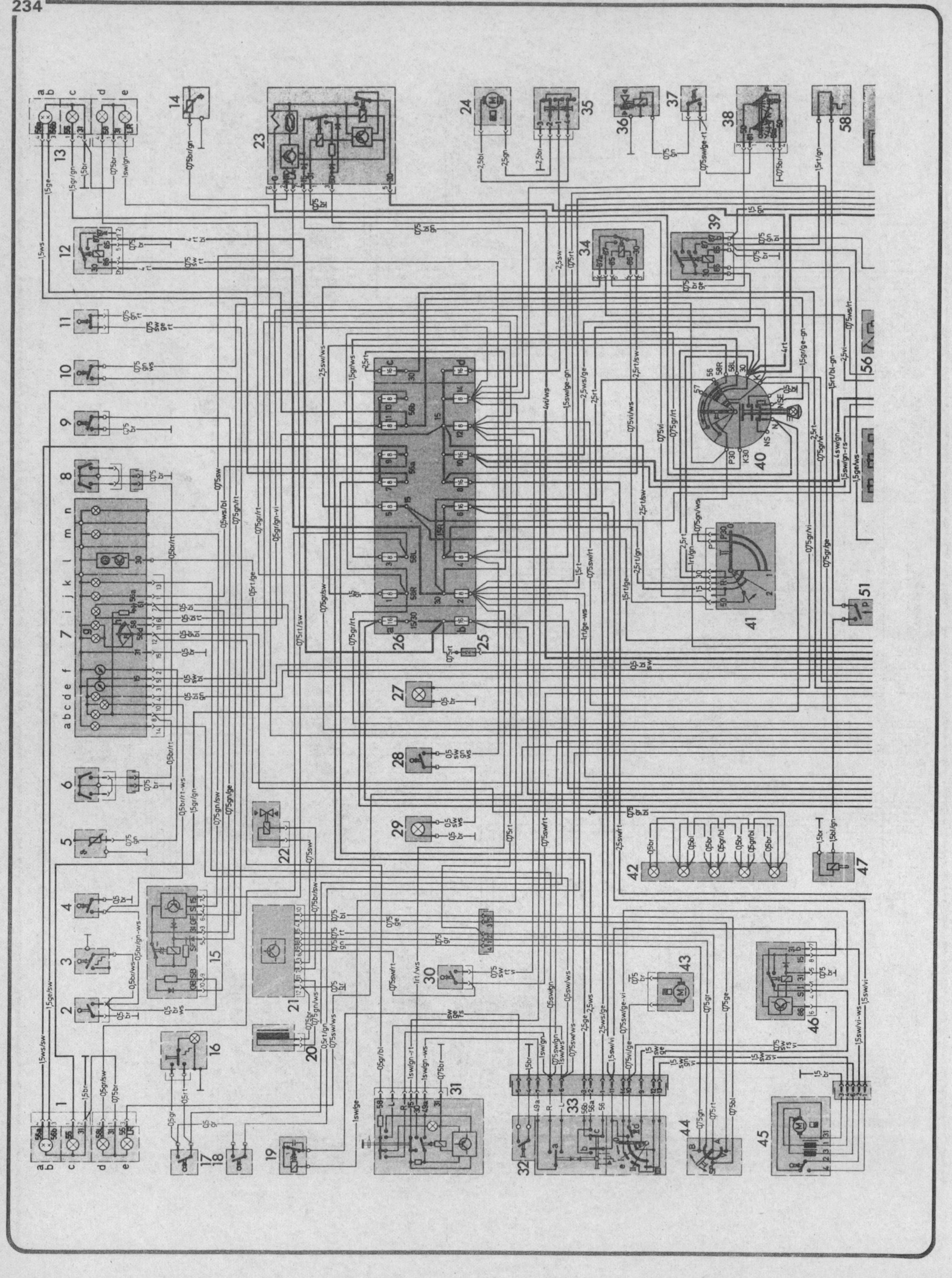

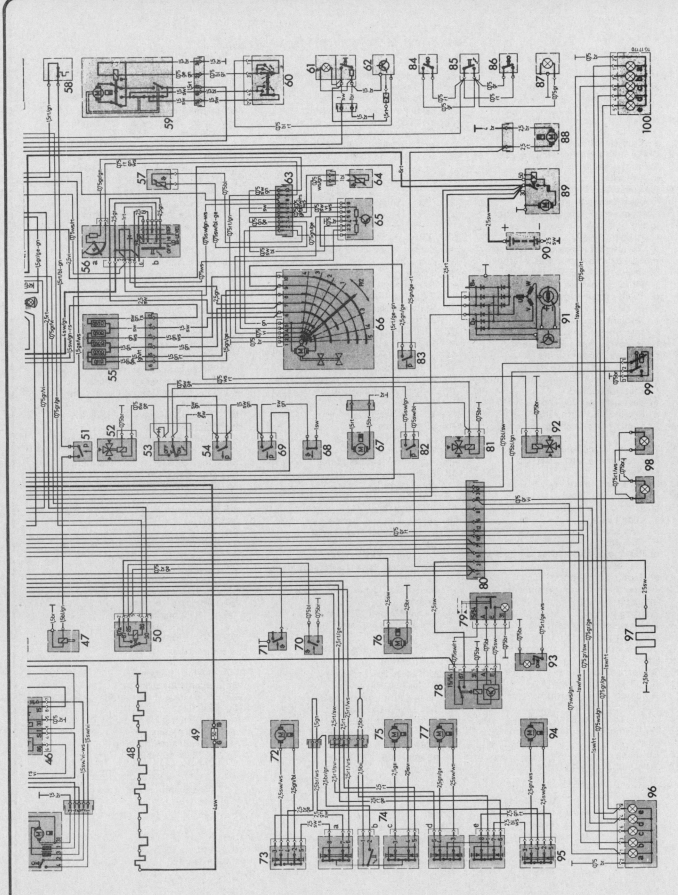

1977 300D (123.130) (US) wiring diagram

16 Key to 1977 300D (123.130) (US) wiring diagram

1 Headlamp unit, left
  a High beam
  b Low beam
  c Fog lamp
  d Parking lamp/standing lamp/side marker lamp
  e Turn signal lamp
2 Brake fluid indicator lamp switch
3 Switch, pressure differential indicator lamp
4 Parking brake indicator lamp switch
5 Coolant temperature gauge
6 Contact sensor, brake pads, front, left
7 Instrument cluster
  a Turn signal indicator lamp, left
  b Brake pad wear indicator lamp
  c Brake fluid and parking brake indicator lamp
  d Fuel reserve warning lamp
  e Fuel gauge
  f Coolant temperature gauge
  g Instrument lamps
  h Rheostat, instrument lamps
  i Charge indicator lamp
  j High beam indicator lamp
  k Turn signal indicator lamp, right
  l Electronic clock
  m Seat belt warning lamp
  n Preglow indicator lamp
8 Contact sensor, brake pads, front, right
9 Warning buzzer contact
10 Door contact switch, warning buzzer
11 Driver's belt buckle switch
12 Relay window lifts
13 Headlamp unit, right
  a High beam
  b Low beam
  c Fog lamp
  d Parking lamp/standing lamp/side marker lamp
  e Turn signal lamp
14 Temperature sensor, preglowing indicator
15 Warning device
16 Front dome lamp w/switch
17 Door contact switch, front left
18 Door contact switch, front right
19 Horn
20 Sensor, cruise control
21 Amplifier, cruise control
22 Actuator, cruise control
23 Preglow time relay
24 Sliding roof motor*
25 Fuse, amplifier, automatic climate control
26 Fuse box
27 Illumination, shift plate

28 Glove compartment lamp switch
29 Glove compartment lamp
30 Stop lamp switch
31 Warning flasher switch/timer
32 Horn contact
33 Combination switch
  a Turn signal lamp switch
  b Headlamp flasher switch
  c Dimmer switch
  d Washer switch
  e Switch wiping speed
    I   Intermittent wiping
    II   Slow wiping
    III Fast wiping
34 Relay, starter/air conditioning
35 Switch, electrically operated sliding roof*
36 Solenoid valve, automatic transmission
37 Kick-down switch
38 Starter lockout and back-up lamp switch
39 Dual contact relay
40 Lighting switch
41 Ignition starter switch
42 Illumination, heater controls
43 Washer pump
44 Switch, cruise control
  A   Off
  V   Decelerate/set
  SP Resume
  B   Accelerate/set
45 Wiper motor
46 Intermittent wiping timer
47 Electromagnetic clutch, refrigerant compressor
48 Glow plugs and series resistor
49 Fuse box, glow plugs
50 Relay, auxiliary fan
51 Pressure switch, refrigerant compressor
    On 2.6 bar, Off 2.0 bar
52 Switch-over valve, fresh/recirculating air flap
53 Switch, refrigerant compressor, on/off
54 Vacuum switch, 78.5 mbar, refrigerant compressor "DEF" and "BI-level"
55 Pre-resistance, blower motor
56 Control unit
  a Temperature selector
  b Push button switch
57 Temperature sensor, outside
58 Temperature switch 2 °C (36 °F)
59 Automatic antenna*
60 Switch, automatic antenna*
61 Cigar lighter with ashtray illumination
62 Radio*

63 Plug for tester, automatic climate control system
64 Temperature sensor, inside
65 Amplifier, automatic climate control
66 Servo assembly, automatic climate control
67 Auxiliary water pump for heater, automatic climate control
68 Temperature switch, On 16 °C, Off 26 °C (On 61 °F, Off 79 °F)
69 Vacuum switch, 78.5 mbar
70 Temperature switch 62 °C (144 °F) receiver drier, air conditioner
71 Temperature switch 100 °C (212 °F)
72 Window lift motor, rear, left
73 Switch, window, rear, left
74 Switch cluster, window lifts
  a Switch, window, rear, left
  b Safety switch
  c Switch, window, front, left
  d Switch, window, front, right
  e Switch, window, rear, right
75 Window lift motor, front, left
76 Auxiliary fan
77 Window lift motor, front, right
78 Time-lag relay, heated rear window
79 Switch, heated rear window
80 Plug connection, tail lamp cable harness
81 Switch-over valve, footwell flap
82 Vacuum switch, BI-level
83 Vacuum switch, 175 mbar, master switch
84 Door contact switch, rear, left
85 Rear dome lamp switch
86 Door contact switch, rear, right
87 Rear dome lamp
88 Blower motor
89 Starter
90 Battery
91 Alternator w/electronic regulator
92 Vacuum switch, BI-level
93 Trunk lamp
94 Window lift motor, rear, right
95 Switch, window, rear, right
96 Tail lamp unit, left
  a Side marker lamp
  b Turn signal lamp
  c Tail/standing lamp
  d Back-up lamp
  e Stop lamp
97 Heated rear window
98 License plate lamps
99 Fuel gauge sending unit
100 Tail lamp unit, right
  a Side marker lamp
  b Turn signal lamp
  c Tail/standing lamp
  d Back-up lamp
  e Stop lamp

* Special equipment

Wire Color Code

bl	=	blue	nf	=	neutral
br	=	brown	rs	=	pink
el	=	ivory	rt	=	red
ge	=	yellow	sw	=	black
gn	=	green	vi	=	purple
gr	=	grey	ws	=	white

Example:
Wire designation 1.5 gr/rt
Basic color gr = grey
Identification color rt = red
Cross section of wire 1.5 = 1.5 mm^2

Key to 1978/1979 240D (123.123) (UK) wiring diagram

1 Headlamp unit, left
  a High beam
  b Low beam
  c Fog lamp
  d Parking/side marker/standing
     lamp
  e Turn signal lamp
2 Brake fluid indicator switch
3 Switch, pressure differential
  indicator lamp
4 Parking brake indicator lamp switch
5 Temperature sensor, coolant
6 Contact sensor, brake pads, front, left
7 Instrument cluster
  a Turn signal indicator lamp, left
  b Brake pad wear indicator lamp
  c Brake fluid and parking brake
     indicator lamp
  d Fuel reserve warning lamp
  e Fuel gauge
  f Coolant temperature gauge
  g Instrument lamps
  h Rheostat, instrument lamps
  i Charge indicator lamp
  j High beam indicator lamp
  k Turn signal indicator lamp, right
  l Electronic clock
  m Seat-belt warning lamp
  n Preglow indicator lamp
8 Contact sensor, brake pads, front, right
9 Warning buzzer contact
10 Driver's belt buckle switch
11 Relay window lifts
12 Headlamp unit, right
  a High beam
  b Low beam
  c Fog lamp
  d Parking/side marker/standing
     lamp
  e Turn signal lamp
13 Temperature sensor, preglowing
  indicator
14 Warning device
15 Front dome lamp w/switch
16 Door contact switch, front, left
17 Door contact switch, front, right
18 Horn
19 Sensor, cruise control*
20 Amplifier, cruise control*

21 Actuator, cruise control*
22 Preglow time relay
23 Sliding roof motor*
24 Switch, electrically operated
  sliding roof*
25 Fuse box
26 Shift gate illumination lamp*
27 Glove compartment lamp switch
28 Glove compartment lamp
29 Stop lamp
30 Warning flasher switch/timer
31 Horn contact switch
32 Combination switch
  a Turn signal lamp switch
  b Headlamp flasher switch
  c Dimmer switch
  d Washer switch
  e Switch wiping speed
     I   Interval wiping
     II Slow wiping
     III Fast wiping
33 Solenoid valve, automatic transmission
34 Kick-down-switch*
35 Starter-lockout and back-up lamp
  switch*
36 Lighting switch
37 Steering lock, starter switch
38 Relay, auxiliary fan*
39 Washer pump
40 Switch, cruise control*
  A   Off
  V   Decelerate/set
  SP Resume
  B   Accelerate/set
41 Wiper motor
42 Interval wiping timer
43 Glow plugs and pre-resistance
44 Auxiliary fan*
45 Temperature switch 100° C (212° F)
46 Blower switch with lamp
47 Relay, air conditioner I*
48 Relay, air conditioner II*
49 Automatic antenna*
50 Switch automatic antenna*
51 Illumination, lamps heater controls
52 Temperature switch 62° C (144° F)
  receiver drier, air conditioner
53 Fuse box, glow plugs
54 Switch, window, rear, left*

55 Window lift motor, rear, left*
56 Time-lag relay, heated rear window
57 Switch cluster, window lifts*
  a Switch, window, rear, left
  b Safety switch
  c Switch, window, front, left
  d Switch, window, front, right
  e Switch, window, rear, right
58 Window lift motor, front, left*
59 Window lift motor, front, right*
60 Push button switch, heated rear window
61 Blower motor
62 Pre-resistance, blower motor
63 Temperature control w/illumination,
  air conditioner*
64 Solenoid clutch, refrigerant compressor*
65 Pressure switch, refrigerant compressor
  On 2.6 bar, Off 2.0 bar*
66 Cigar lighter with ashtray illumination*
67 Radio*
68 Door contact switch, rear, left*
69 Rear dome lamp switch*
70 Door contact switch, rear, right*
71 Rear dome lamp*
72 Starter
73 Battery
74 Alternator w/electronic regulator
75 Fuel gauge sending unit
76 Plug connection, cable to rear
  components
77 Trunk lamp
78 Window lift motor, rear, right*
79 Switch, window, rear, right*
80 Tail lamp unit, left
  a Side marker lamp
  b Turn signal lamp
  c Tail/parking lamp
  d Back-up lamp
  e Stop lamp
81 Heated rear window
82 License plate lamp
83 Tail lamp unit, right
  a Side marker lamp
  b Turn signal lamp
  c Tail/parking lamp
  d Stop lamp

* Special equipment

Wire Color Code

bl =	blue	nr =	neutral	
br =	brown	rs =	pink	
el =	ivory	rt =	red	
ge =	yellow	sw =	black	
gn =	green	vi =	purple	
gr =	grey	ws =	white	

Example:
Wire designation 1.5 gr/rt
Basic color gr = grey
Identification color rt = red
Cross section of wire 1.5 = 1.5 mm^2

238

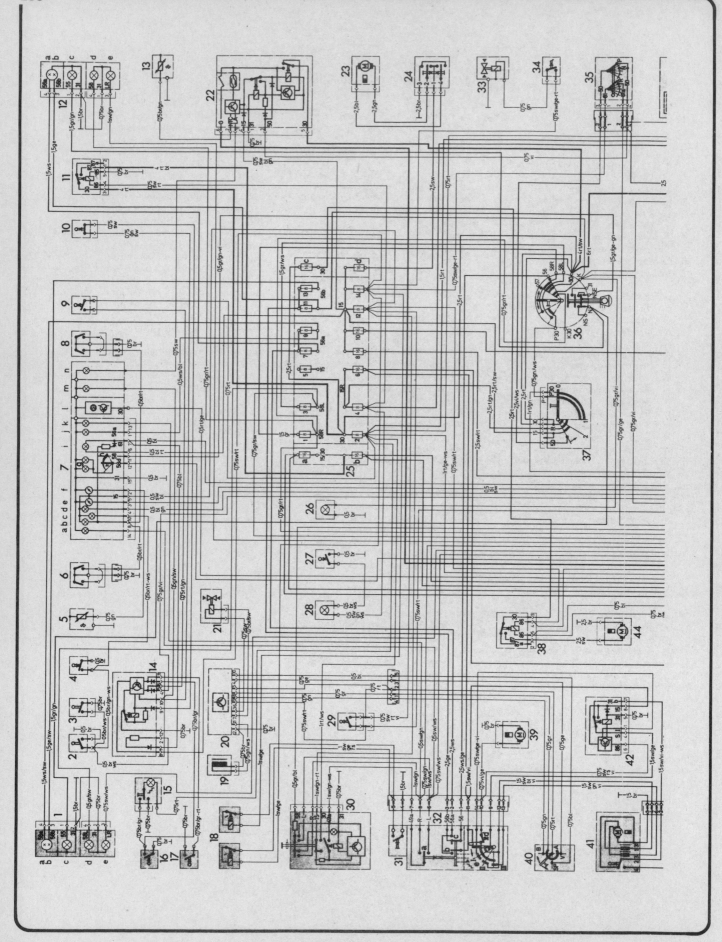

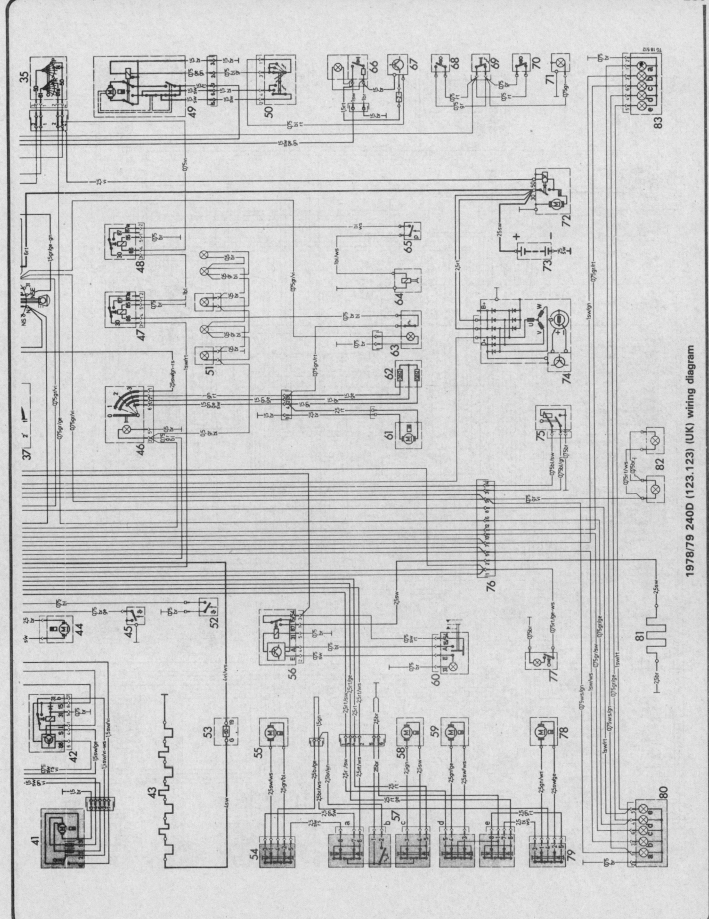

1978/79 240D (123.123) (UK) wiring diagram

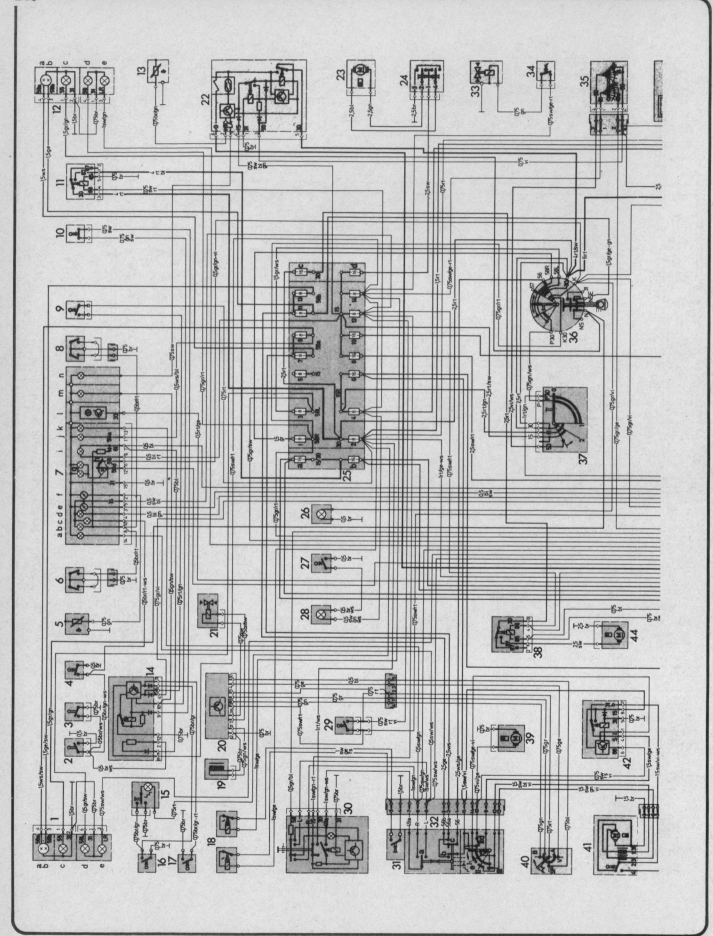

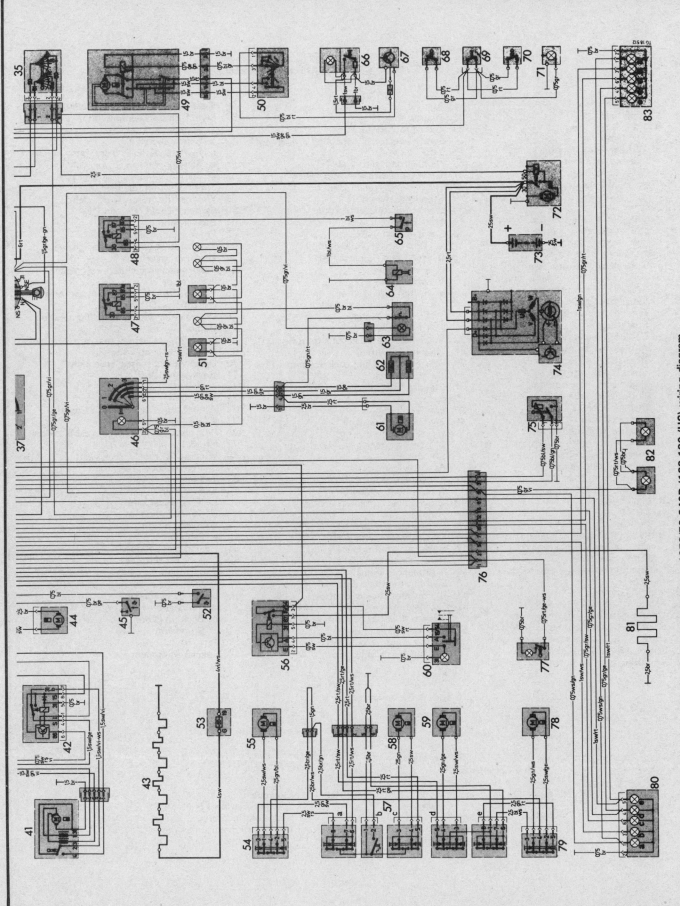

1978/79 240D (123.130 (US) wiring diagram

Key to 1978/79 240D (123.130) (US) wiring diagram

1 Headlamp unit, left
  a High beam
  b Low beam
  c Fog lamp
  d Parking lamp/standing lamp/
    side marker lamp
  e Turn signal lamp
2 Brake fluid indicator lamp switch
3 Switch, pressure differential indicator
  lamp
4 Parking brake indicator lamp switch
5 Temperature sensor, coolant
6 Contact sensor, brake pads, front, left
7 Instrument cluster
  a Turn signal indicator lamp, left
  b Brake pad weat indicator lamp
  c Brake fluid and parking brake
    indicator lamp
  d Fuel reserve warning lamp
  e Fuel gauge
  f Coolant temperature gauge
  g Instrument lamps
  h Rheostat, instrument lamps
  i Charge indicator lamp
  j High beam indicator lamp
  k Turn signal indicator lamp, right
  l Electronic clock
  m Seat belt warning lamp
  n Preglow indicator lamp
8 Contact sensor, brake pads, front, right
9 Warning buzzer contact
10 Driver's belt buckle switch
11 Relay window lifts*
12 Headlamp unit, right
  a High beam
  b Low beam
  c Fog lamp
  d Parking lamp/standing lamp/
    side marker lamp
  e Turn signal lamp
13 Temperature sensor, preglowing
  indicator
14 Warning device
15 Front dome lamp with switch
16 Door contact switch, front, left
17 Door contact switch, front, right
18 Horn
19 Sensor, cruise control*
20 Amplifier, cruise control*

21 Actuator, cruise control*
22 Preglow time relay
23 Sliding roof motor*
24 Switch, electrically operated sliding roof*
25 Fuse box
26 Illumination, shift plate*
27 Glove compartment lamp switch
28 Glove compartment lamp
29 Stop lamp switch
30 Warning flasher switch/timer
31 Horn contact
32 Combination switch
  a Turn signal lamp switch
  b Headlamp flasher switch
  c Dimmer switch
  d Washer switch
  e Switch wiping speed
    I   Intermittent wiping
    II   Slow wiping
    III Fast Wiping
33 Solenoid valve, automatic transmission*
34 Kick-down switch*
35 Starter lockout and back-up lamp switch*
36 Lighting switch
37 Steering lock, starter switch
38 Relay, auxiliary fan*
39 Washer pump
40 Switch, cruise control*
  A Off
  V Decelerate/set
  SP Resume
  B Accelerate/set
41 Wiper motor
42 Intermittent wiping timer
43 Glow plugs and series resistors
44 Auxiliary fan*
45 Temperature switch 100 °C (212 °F)*
46 Blower switch with lamp
47 Relay, air conditioner I*
48 Relay, air conditioner II*
49 Automatic antenna*
50 Switch, automatic antenna*
51 Illumination, heater controls
52 Temperature switch 62 °C (144 °F)
  receiver drier, air conditioner*
53 Fuse box, glow plugs
54 Switch, window, rear, left*
55 Window lift motor, rear, left*

56 Time-lag relay, heated rear window
57 Switch cluster, window lifts*
  a Switch, window, rear, left
  b Safety switch
  c Switch, window, front, left
  d Switch, window, front, right
  e Switch, window, rear, right
58 Window lift motor, front, left*
59 Window lift motor, front, right*
60 Switch, heated rear window
61 Blower motor
62 Pre-resistance blower motor
63 Temperature control with lighting,
  air conditioner*
64 Electromagnetic clutch, refrigerant
  compressor*
65 Pressure switch, refrigerant compressor
  On 2.6 bar, Off 2.0 bar*
66 Cigar lighter with ashtray illumination
67 Radio*
68 Door contact switch, rear, left*
69 Rear dome lamp switch*
70 Door contact switch, rear, right*
71 Rear dome lamp*
72 Starter
73 Battery
74 Alternator with electronic regulator
75 Fuel gauge sending unit
76 Plug connection, tail lamp cable harness
77 Trunk lamp
78 Window lift motor, rear, right*
79 Switch, window, rear, right*
80 Tail lamp unit, left
  a Side marker lamp
  b Turn signal lamp
  c Tail/standing lamp
  d Back-up lamp
  e Stop lamp
81 Heated rear window
82 License plate lamps
83 Tail lamp unit, right
  a Side marker lamp
  b Turn signal lamp
  c Tail/standing lamp
  d Back-up lamp
  e Stop lamp

* Special equipment

Wire Color Code

bl	= blue	nf	= neutral
br	= brown	rs	= pink
el	= ivory	rt	= red
ge	= yellow	sw	= black
gn	= green	vi	= purple
gr	= grey	ws	= white

Example:
Wire designation 1.5 gr/rt
Basic color gr = grey
Identification color rt = red
Cross section of wire 1.5 = 1.5 mm^2

22 Key to 1978/79 300D/CD (123.130/150) (UK) wiring diagram

1 Headlamp unit, left
  a High beam
  b Low beam
  c Fog lamp
  d Parking/side marker/standing lamp
  e Turn signal lamp
2 Brake fluid indicator lamp switch I
3 Brake fluid indicator lamp switch II
4 Parking brake indicator lamp switch
5 Temperature sensor, coolant
6 Contact sensor, brake pads, front, left
7 Instrument cluster
  a Turn signal indicator lamp, left
  b Brake pad wear indicator lamp
  c Brake fluid and parking brake indicator lamp
  d Fuel reserve warning lamp
  e Fuel gauge
  f Coolant temperature gauge
  g Instrument lamps
  h Rheostat, instrument lamps
  i Charge indicator lamp
  j High beam indicator lamp
  k Turn signal indicator lamp, right
  l Electronic clock
  m Seat-belt warning lamp
  n Preglow indicator lamp
8 Contact sensor, brake pads, front, right
9 Warning buzzer contact
10 Driver's belt buckle switch
11 Relay window lifts
12 Headlamp unit, right
  a High beam
  b Low beam
  c Fog lamp
  d Parking/side marker/standing lamp
  e Turn signal lamp
13 Temperature sensor, preglowing indicator
14 Warning device
15 Front dome lamp w/switch
16 Door contact switch, front, left
17 Door contact switch, front, right
18 Dual-tone horns (fanfares)
19 Sensor, cruise control
20 Amplifier, cruise control
21 Actuator, cruise control
22 Preglow time relay
23 Fuse box
24 Fuse, amplifier, automatic climate control
25 Shift gate illumination lamp
27 Glove compartment lamp
28 Stop lamp switch
29 Warning flasher switch/timer
30 Horn contact switch

31 Combination switch
  a Turn signal lamp switch
  b Headlamp flasher switch
  c Dimmer switch
  d Washer switch
  e Switch wiping speed
    I Interval wiping
    II Slow wiping
    III Fast wiping
32 Switch, cruise control
  A Off
  V Decelerate/set
  SP Resume
  B Accelerate/set
33 Washer pump
34 Illumination lamps, heater controls
35 Ignition starter switch
36 Lighting switch
37 Double-pole relay
38 Relay, air conditioner/starter
39 Sliding roof motor*
40 Switch, electrically operated sliding roof*
41 Solenoid valve, automatic transmission
42 Kick-down switch
43 Starter-lockout and back-up lamp switch
44 Temperature switch, 2° C (36° F)
45 Automatic antenna
46 Control unit
  a Temperature selector
  b Push button switch
47 Pre-resistance, blower motor
48 Switch-over valve (fresh/recirculating air flap)
49 Switch, refrigerant compressor, on/off
50 Vacuum switch 78.5 mbar, refrigerant compressor (,,DEF" and ,,BI-LEVEL.")
51 Pressure switch, refrigerant compressor On 2.6 bar, Off 2.0 bar
52 Relay, auxiliary fan
53 Solenoid clutch, refrigerant compressor
54 Interval wiping timer
55 Wiper motor
56 Glow plugs and series resistor
57 Fuse box, glow plugs
58 Temperature sensor, outside
59 Switch, window, rear, left
60 Window lift motor, rear, left
61 Temperature switch 100° C (212° F)
62 Temperature switch 62°, receiver drier, automatic climate control
63 Vacuum switch, 78.5 mbar
64 Temperature switch, On 16° C – Off 26° C
65 Plug for tester, automatic climate control system

66 Switch automatic antenna
67 Cigar lighter with ashtray illumination
68 Radio*
69 Temperature sensor, outside
70 Amplifier, automatic climate control
71 Servo assembly, automatic climate control system
72 Auxiliary water pump for heater, automatic climate control system
73 Auxiliary fan
74 Window lift motor, front, left
75 Switch cluster, window lifts
  a Switch, window, rear, left
  b Safety switch
  c Switch, window, front, left
  d Switch, window, front, right
  e Switch, window, rear, right
76 Window lift motor, front, left
77 Time-lag relay, heated rear window
78 Push button switch, heated rear window
79 Plug connection, cable to rear components
80 Vacuum switch (,,BI-LEVEL")
81 Switch-over valve (footwell flaps)
82 Vacuum switch, 175 mbar, master switch
83 Door contact switch, rear, left
84 Rear dome lamp switch
85 Door contact switch, rear, right
86 Rear dome lamp
87 Blower motor
88 Starter
89 Battery
90 Alternator w/electronic regulator
91 Switch-over valve (,,BI-LEVEL")
92 Trunk lamp
93 Window lift motor, rear, right
94 Switch, window, rear, right
95 Tail lamp unit, left
  a Side marker lamp
  b Turn signal lamp
  c Tail/parking lamp
  d Back-up lamp
  e Stop lamp
96 Heated rear window
97 License plate lamp
98 Fuel gauge sending unit
99 Tail lamp unit, right
  a Side marker lamp
  b Turn signal lamp
  c Tail/parking lamp
  d Back-up lamp
  e Stop lamp

* Special equipment

Wire color Code

bl = blue
br = brown
el = ivory
ge = yellow
gn = green
gr = grey
nf = neutral
rs = pink
rt = red
sw = black
vi = purple
ws = white

Example:
Wire designation 1.5 gr/rt
Basic color gr = grey
Identification color rt = red
Cross section of wire 1.5 = 1.5 mm^2

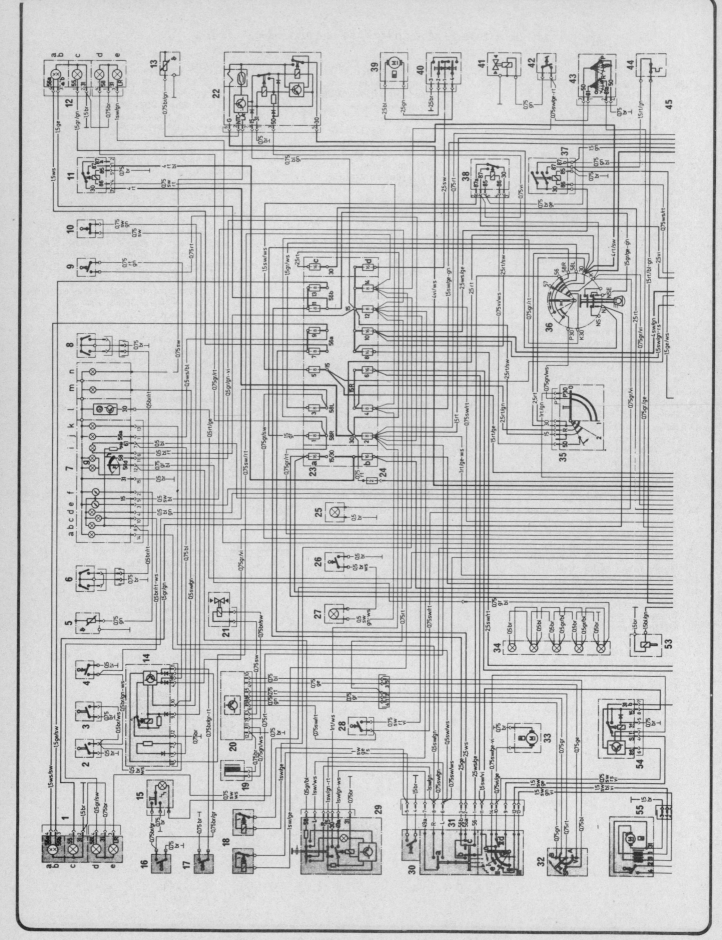

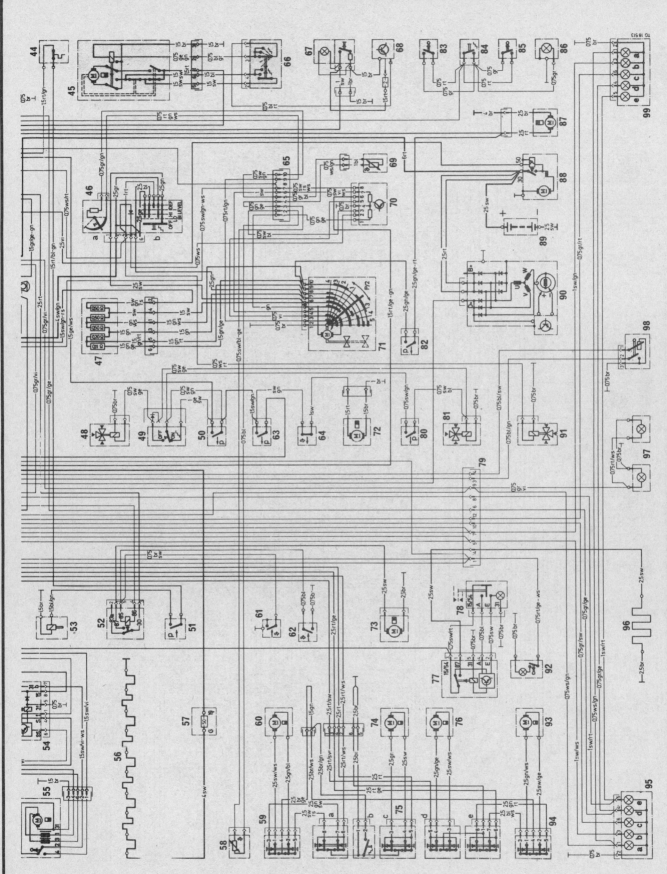

245

1978/79 300D/CD (123.130/150) (UK) wiring diagram

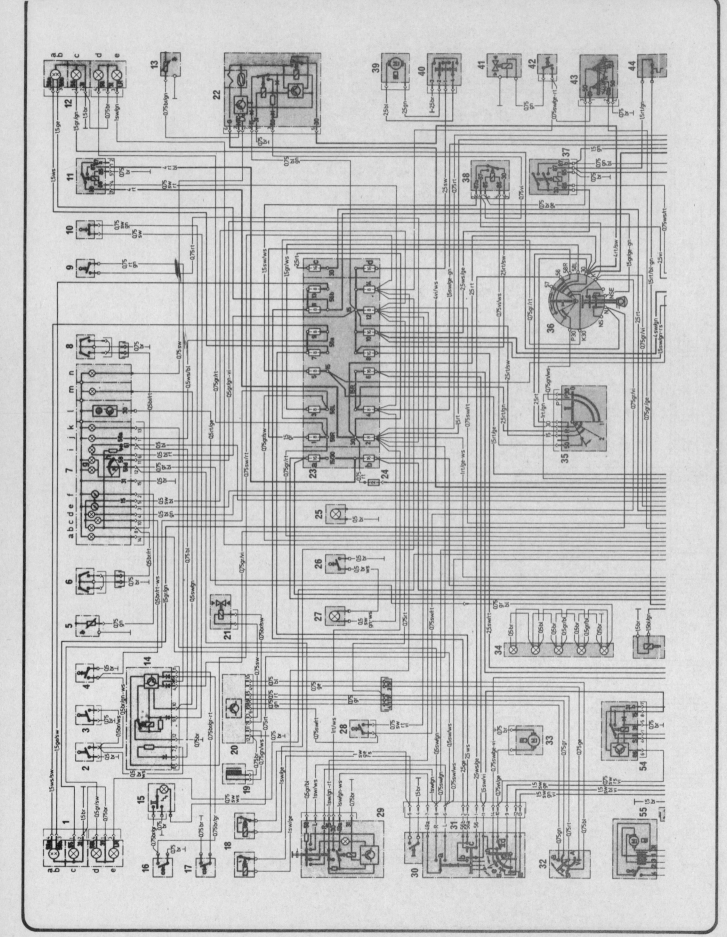

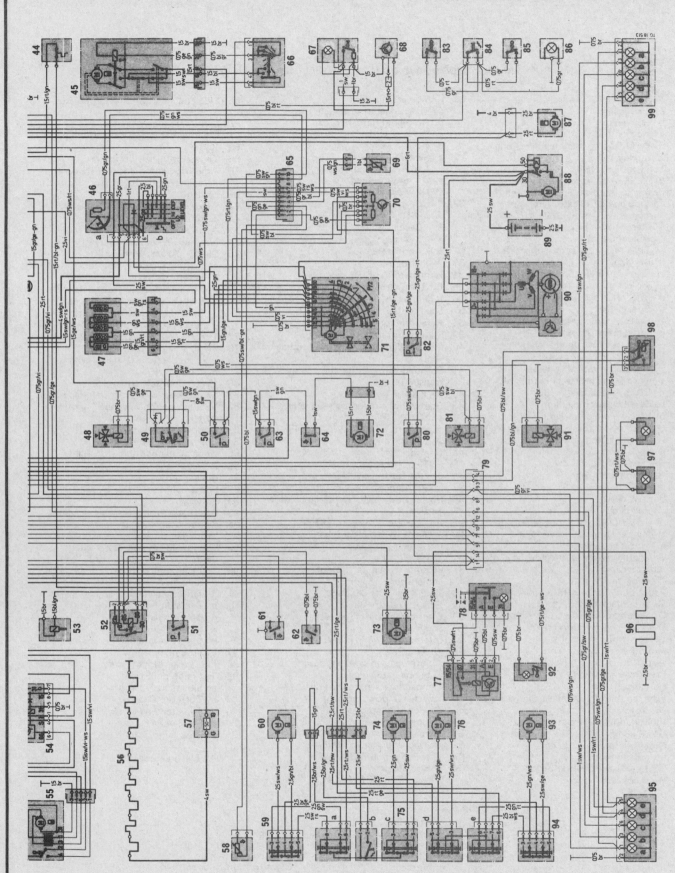

1978/79 300D/CD (123.130/150) (US) wiring diagram

Key to 1978/79 300D/CD (123.130/150) (US) wiring diagram

1 Headlamp unit, left
  a High beam
  b Low beam
  c Fog lamp
  d Parking lamp/standing lamp/side marker lamp
  e Turn signal lamp
2 Brake fluid indicator lamp switch I
3 Brake fluid indicator lamp switch II
4 Parking brake indicator lamp switch
5 Temperature sensor, coolant
6 Contact sensor, brake pads, front, left
7 Instrument cluster
  a Turn signal indicator lamp, left
  b Brake pad wear indicator lamp
  c Brake fluid and parking brake indicator lamp
  d Fuel reserve warning lamp
  e Fuel gauge
  f Coolant temperature gauge
  g Instrument lamps
  h Rheostat, instrument lamps
  i Charge indicator lamp
  j High beam indicator lamp
  k Turn signal indicator lamp, right
  l Electronic clock
  m Seat belt warning lamp
  n Preglow indicator lamp
8 Contact sensor, brake pads, front, right
9 Warning buzzer contact
10 Driver's belt buckle switch
11 Relay, window lifts
12 Headlamp unit, right
  a High beam
  b Low beam
  c Fog lamp
  d Parking lamp/standing lamp/side marker lamp
  e Turn signal lamp
13 Temperature sensor, preglowing indicator
14 Warning device
15 Front dome lamp with switch
16 Door contact switch, front, left
17 Door contact switch, front, right
18 Dual-tone horn (fanfares)
19 Sensor, cruise control
20 Amplifier, cruise control
21 Actuator, cruise control
22 Preglow time relay
23 Fuse box
24 Fuse, amplifier, automatic climate control
25 Illumination, shift plate
26 Glove compartment lamp switch
27 Glove compartment lamp
28 Stop lamp switch
29 Warning flasher switch/timer
30 Horn contact

31 Combination switch
  a Turn signal lamp switch
  b Headlamp flasher switch
  c Dimmer switch
  d Washer switch
  e Switch wiping speed
    I   Intermittent wiping
    II Slow wiping
    III Fast wiping
32 Switch, cruise control
  A Off
  V Decelerate/set
  SP Resume
  B Accelerate/set
33 Washer pump
34 Illumination, heater controls
35 Ignition starter switch
36 Lighting switch
37 Dual contact relay
38 Relay, air conditioner/starter
39 Sliding roof motor*
40 Switch, electrically operated sliding roof*
41 Solenoid valve, automatic transmission
42 Kick-down switch
43 Starter lockout and back-up lamp switch
44 Temperature switch 2 °C (36 °F)
45 Automatic antenna
46 Control unit
  a Temperature selector
  b Push button switch
47 Pre-resistance blower motor
48 Switch-over valve, fresh/recirculating air flap
49 Switch, compressor, on/off
50 Vacuum switch, 78.5 mbar, refrigerant compressor "DEF" and "BI-level"
51 Pressure switch, refrigerant compressor On 2.6 bar, Off 2.0 bar
52 Relay, auxiliary fan
53 Electromagnetic clutch, refrigerant compressor
54 Intermittent wiping timer
55 Wiper motor
56 Glow plugs and series resistor
57 Fuse box, glow plugs
58 Temperature sensor, outside
59 Switch, window, rear, left
60 Window lift motor, rear left
61 Temperature switch 100 °C (212 °F)
62 Temperature switch 62 °C (144 °F) receiver drier, air conditioner
63 Vacuum switch 78.5 mbar
64 Temperature switch, On 16 °C, Off 26 °C (On 61 °F, Off 79 °F)

65 Plug connection, tester, automatic climate control
66 Switch, automatic antenna
67 Cigar lighter with ashtray illumination
68 Radio
69 Temperature sensor, inside
70 Amplifier, automatic climate control
71 Servo assembly, automatic climate control
72 Auxiliary water pump for heater, automatic climate control
73 Auxiliary fan
74 Window lift motor, front, left
75 Switch cluster, window lifts
  a Switch, window, rear, left
  b Safety switch
  c Switch, window, front, left
  d Switch, window, front, right
  e Switch, window, rear, right
76 Window lift motor, front, left
77 Time-lag relay, heated rear window
78 Switch, heated rear window
79 Plug connection, tail lamp cable harness
80 Vacuum switch, BI-level
81 Switch-over valve, footwell flap
82 Vacuum switch 175 mbar, master switch
83 Door contact switch, rear, left
84 Rear dome lamp switch
85 Door contact switch, rear, right
86 Rear dome lamp
87 Blower motor
88 Starter
89 Battery
90 Alternator with electronic regulator
91 Switch-over valve, BI-level
92 Trunk lamp
93 Window lift motor, rear, right
94 Switch, window, rear, right
95 Tail lamp unit, left
  a Side marker lamp
  b Turn signal lamp
  c Tail/standing lamp
  d Back-up lamp
  e Stop lamp
96 Heated rear window
97 License plate lamps
98 Fuel gauge sending unit
99 Tail lamp unit, right
  a Side marker lamp
  b Turn signal lamp
  c Tail/standing lamp
  d Back-up lamp
  e Stop lamp

* Special equipment

Wire Color Code

bl	=	blue	nf	=	neutral
br	=	brown	rs	=	pink
el	=	ivory	rt	=	red
ge	=	yellow	sw	=	black
gn	=	green	vi	=	purple
gr	=	grey	ws	=	white

Example:
Wire designation 1.5 gr/rt
Basic color gr = grey
Identification color rt = red
Cross section of wire 1.5 = 1.5 mm^2

Key to 1979 300TD (123.190) (UK) wiring diagram

1 Headlamp unit, left
  a High beam
  b Low beam
  c Fog lamp
  d Parking lamp/standing lamp/
      side marker lamp
2 Brake fluid indicator lamp switch I
3 Brake fluid indicator lamp switch II
4 Parking brake indicator lamp switch
5 Temperature sensor, coolant
6 Contakt sensor, brake pads, front, left
7 Instrument cluster
  a Turn signal indicator lamp, left
  b Brake pad wear indicator lamp
  c Brake fluid and parking brake
      indicator lamp
  d Fuel reserve warning lamp
  e Fuel gauge
  f Coolant temperature gauge
  g Instrument lamps
  h Rheostat, instrument lamps
  i Charge indicator lamp
  j High beam indicator lamp
  k Turn signal indicator lamp, right
  l Electronic clock
  m Seat belt warning lamp
  n Preglow indicator lamp
8 Contact sensor, brake pads, front, right
9 Warning buzzer contact
11 Driver's belt buckle switch
12 Relay, window lifts
13 Headlamp unit, right
  a High beam
  b Low beam
  c Fog lamp
  d Parking lamp/standing lamp/
      side marker lamp
  e Turn signal lamp
14 Temperature sensor, preglowing indicator
15 Warning device
16 Front dome lamp w/switch
17 Door contact switch, front, left
18 Door contact switch, front, right
19 Horn
20 Sensor, cruise control system
21 Amplifier, cruise control
22 Actuator, cruise control
23 Preglow time relay
24 Sliding roof motor*
25 Fuse, amplifier, automatic climate control
26 Fuse box
27 Illumination, shift plate
28 Glove compartment lamp switch
29 Glove compartment lamp
30 Stop lamp switch
31 Warning flasher switch/timer
32 Horn contact

33 Combination switch
  a Turn signal lamp switch
  b Headlamp flasher switch
  c Dimmer switch
  d Washer switch
  e Switch, wiping speed
     I   Intermittent wiping
     II Slow wiping
     III Fast wiping
34 Relay, starter/air conditioning
35 Switch, electrically operated sliding roof*
36 Solenoid valve, automatic transmission
37 Kick-down switch
38 Starter lockout and back-up lamp switch
39 Dual contact relay
40 Lighting switch
41 Steering lock starter switch
42 Illumination, heater control
43 Washer pump
44 Switch, cruise control
  A Off
  V Decelerate/set
  SP Resume
  B Accelerate/set
45 Wiper motor
46 Intermittent wiping timer
47 Electromagnetic clutch, refrigerant
    compressor
48 Glow plugs and series resistor
49 Fuse box, glow plugs
50 Relay, auxiliary fan
51 Pressure switch, refrigerant compressor
    On 2.6 bar, Off 2.0 bar
52 Switch-over valve, fresh/recirculating
    air flap
53 Switch, refrigerant compressor, on/off
54 Vacuum switch, 78.5 mbar, refrigerant
    compressor ,,DEF'' and ,,BI-level''
55 Pre-resistance, blower-motor
56 Control unit
  a Temperature selector
  b Push button switch
57 Temperature sensor, outside
58 Temperature switch 2 °C (36 °F)
59 Automatic antenna
60 Switch, automatic antenna
61 Cigar lighter with ashtray illumination
62 Radio
63 Plug connection tester, automatic
    climate control system
64 Temperature sensor, inside
65 Amplifier, automatic climate control
66 Servo assembly, automati climate
    control
67 Auxiliary water pump for heater,
    automatic climate control
68 Temperature switch, On 16 °C –
    Off 26 °C (On 61 °F, Off 79 °F)

69 Vacuum switch, 78.5 mbar, refrigerant
    compressor
70 Temperature switch 62 °C (144 °F)
    receiver drier, air conditioner
71 Temperature switch 100 °C (212 °F)
72 Window lift motor, rear, left
73 Switch, window, rear, left
74 Switch cluster, window lifts
  a Switch, window, rear, left
  b Safety switch
  c Switch, window, front, left
  d Switch, window, front, right
  e Switch, window, rear, right
75 Window lift motor, front, left
76 Auxiliary fan
77 Window lift motor, front, right
78 Time-lag relay, heated rear window
79 Switch, heated rear window
80 Plug connection, tail lamp cable harness
81 Switch-over valve, footwell flaps
82 Vacuum switch, BI-level
83 Vacuum switch, 175 mbar, master
    switch
84 Switch-over valve, BI-level
85 Door contact switch, rear, left
86 Door contact switch, rear, right
87 Blower motor
88 Starter
89 Battery
90 Alternator w/electronic regulator
91 Wiper motor, rear door
92 Fuel gauge sending unit
93 Detent switch, rear dome lamp
94 Rear dome lamp
95 Window lift motor, rear, right
96 Switch, window, rear, right
97 Tail lamp unit, left
  a Turn signal lamp
  b Tail/standing lamp
  c Stop lamp
98 Back-up lamp
99 Washer pump, rear door
100 Detent switch, wiper motor rear door/
     push-button switch washer pump,
     rear door
101 License plate lamp
102 Rear door contact switch
103 Heated rear window
104 Ground connection,
     rear door
105 Back-up lamp
106 Tail lamp unit, right
  a Turn signal lamp
  b Tail/standing lamp
  c Stop lamp

* Special equipment

Wire Color Code

bl = blue
br = brown
el = ivory
ge = yellow
gn = green
gr = grey

nf = neutral
rs = pink
rt = red
sw = black
vi = purple
ws = white

Example:
Wire designation 1.5 gr/rt
Basic color gr = grey
Identification color rt = red
Cross section of wire 1.5 = 1.5 mm²

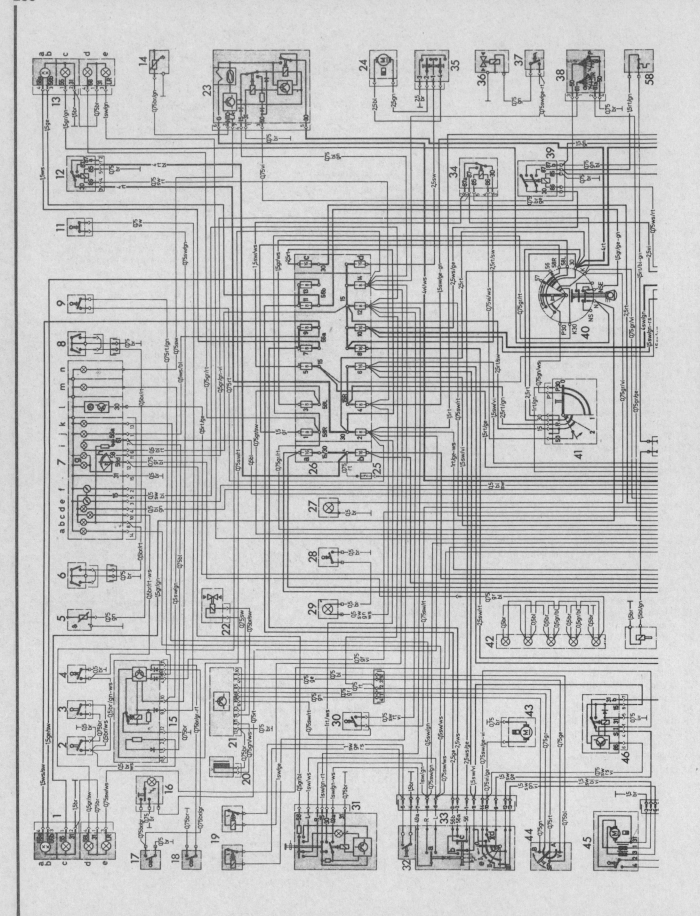

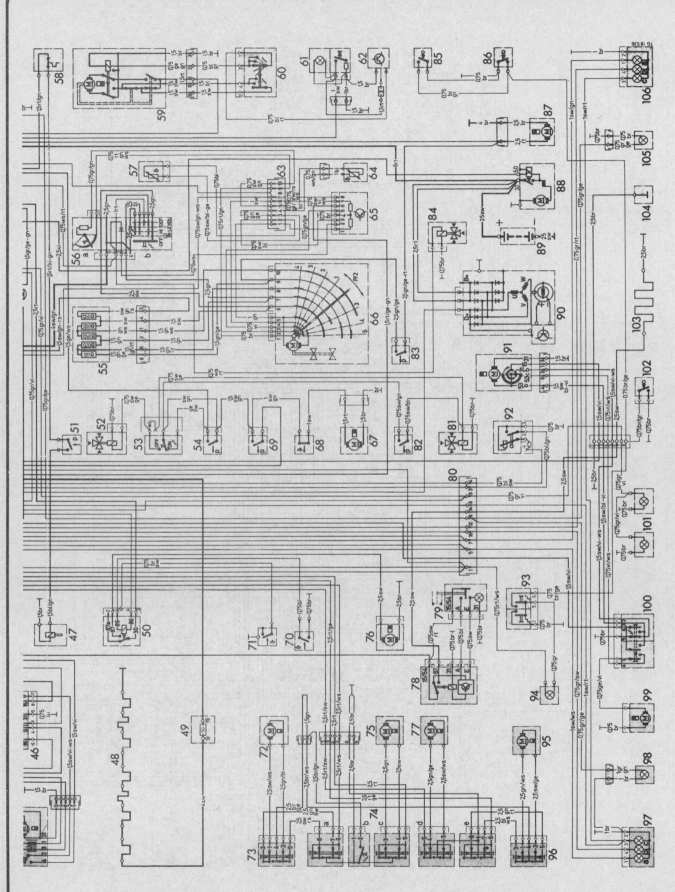

1979 300TD (123.190) (UK) wiring diagram

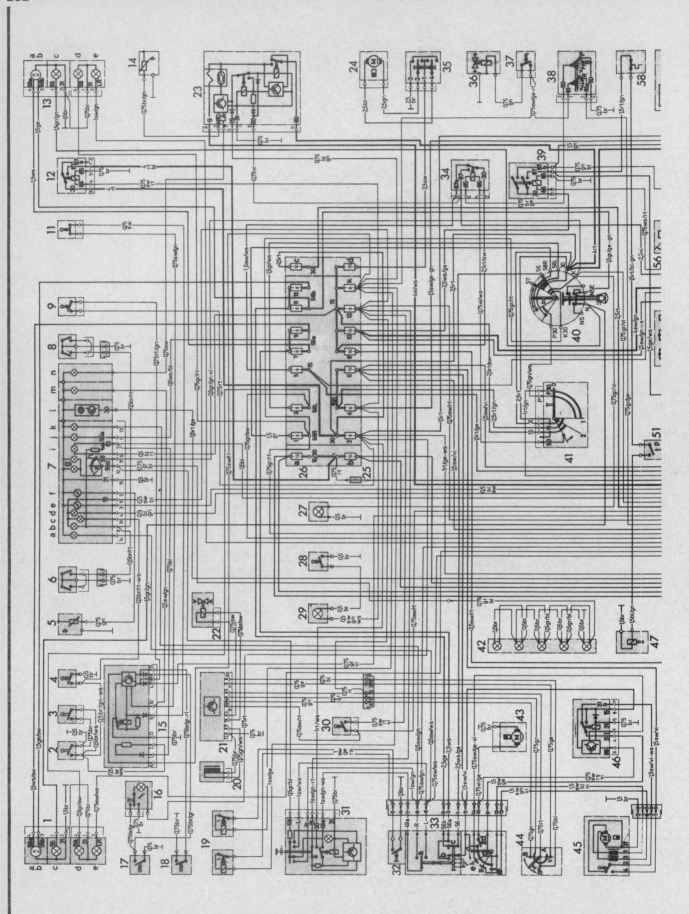

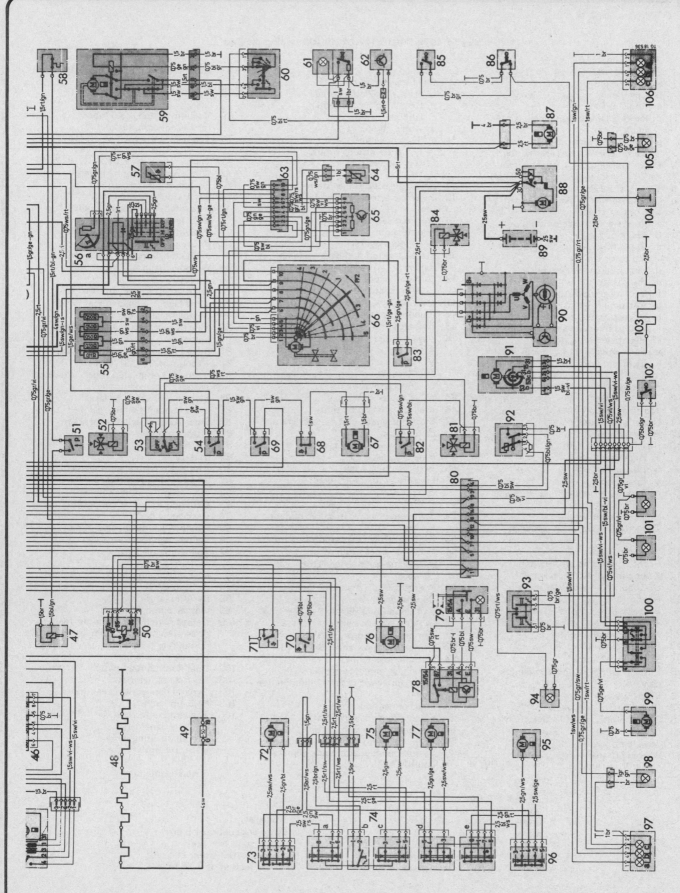

27 1979 300TD (123.190) (US) wiring diagram

Key to 1979 300TD (123.190) (US) wiring diagram

1 Headlamp unit, left
  a High beam
  b Low beam
  c Fog lamp
  d Parking lamp/standing lamp/side marker lamp
  e Turn signal lamp
2 Brake fluid indicator lamp switch I
3 Brake fluid indicator lamp switch II
4 Parking brake indicator lamp switch
5 Temperature sensor, coolant
6 Contact sensor, brake pads, front, left
7 Instrument cluster
  a Turn signal indicator lamp, left
  b Brake pad wear indicator lamp
  c Brake fluid and parking brake indicator lamp
  d Fuel reserve warning lamp
  e Fuel gauge
  f Coolant temperature gauge
  g Instrument lamps
  h Rheostat, instrument lamps
  i Charge indicator lamp
  j High beam indicator lamp
  k Turn signal indicator lamp, right
  l Electronic clock
  m Seat belt warning lamp
  n Preglow indicator lamp
8 Contact sensor, brake pads, front, right
9 Warning buzzer contact
11 Driver's belt buckle switch
12 Relay, window lifts
13 Headlamp unit, right
  a High beam
  b Low beam
  c Fog lamp
  d Parking lamp/standing lamp/side marker lamp
  e Turn signal lamp
14 Temperature sensor, preglowing indicator
15 Warning device
16 Front dome lamp with switch
17 Door contact switch, front, left
18 Door contact switch, front, right
19 Horn
20 Sensor, cruise control
21 Amplifier, cruise control
22 Actuator, cruise control
23 Preglow time relay
24 Sliding roof motor*
25 Fuse, amplifier, automatic climate control
26 Fuse box
27 Illumination, shift plate
28 Glove compartment lamp switch
29 Glove compartment lamp
30 Stop lamp switch
31 Warning flasher switch/timer

32 Horn contact
33 Combination switch
  a Turn signal lamp switch
  b Headlamp flasher switch
  c Dimmer switch
  d Washer switch
  e Switch, wiping speed
    I   Intermittent wiping
    II Slow wiping
    III Fast wiping
34 Relay, air conditioner/starter
35 Switch, electrically operated sliding roof*
36 Solenoid valve, automatic transmission
37 Kick-down switch
38 Starter lockout and back-up lamp switch
39 Dual contact relay
40 Lighting switch
41 Steering lock, starter switch
42 Illumination, heater controls
43 Washer pump
44 Switch cruise control
  A Off
  V Decelerate/set
  SP Resume
  B Accelerate/set
45 Wiper motor
46 Intermittent wiping timer
47 Electromagnetic clutch, refrigerant compressor
48 Glow plus and series resistor
49 Fuse box, glow plugs
50 Relay, auxiliary fan
51 Pressure switch, refrigerant compressor
  On 2.6 bar, Off 2.0 bar
52 Switch-over valve, fresh/recirculating air flap
53 Switch, refrigerant compressor, on/off
54 Vacuum switch, 78.5 mbar, refrigerant compressor "DEF" and "BI-level"
55 Pre-resistance, blower motor
56 Control unit
  a Temperature selector
  b Plush button switch
57 Temperature sensor, outside
58 Temperature switch 2 °C (36 °F)
59 Automatic antenna
60 Switch, automatic antenna
61 Cigar lighter with ashtray illumination
62 Radio
63 Plug connection, tester, automatic climate control
64 Temperature sensor, inside
65 Amplifier, automatic climate control
66 Servo assembly, automatic climate control

67 Auxiliary water pump for heater, automatic climate control
68 Temperature switch, On 16 °C Off 26 °C (On 61 °F, Off 79 °F)
69 Vacuum switch, 78.5 mbar, refrigerant compressor
70 Temperature switch 62 °C (144 °F) receiver drier, air conditioner
71 Temperature switch 100 °C (212 °F)
72 Window lift motor, rear, left
73 Switch, window, rear, left
74 Switch cluster, window lifts
  a Switch, window, rear, left
  b Safety switch
  c Switch, window, front, left
  d Switch, window, front, right
  e Switch, window, rear, right
75 Window lift motor, front, left
76 Auxiliary fan
77 Window lift motor, front, right
78 Time-lag relay, heated rear window
79 Switch, heated rear window
80 Plug connection, tail lamp cable harness
81 Switch-over valve, footwell flaps
82 Vacuum switch, BI-level
83 Vacuum switch, 175 mbar, master switch
84 Switch-over valve, BI-level
85 Door contact switch, rear, left
86 Door contact switch, rear, right
87 Blower motor
88 Starter
89 Battery
90 Alternator with electronic regulator
91 Wiper motor, rear door
92 Fuel gauge sending unit
93 Detent switch, rear dome lamp
94 Rear dome lamp
95 Window lift motor, rear, right
96 Switch, window, rear, right
97 Tail lamp unit, left
  a Turn signal lamp
  b Tail/standing lamp
  d Stop lamp
98 Back-up lamp
99 Washer pump, rear door
100 Detent switch, wiper motor, rear door/push button switch, washer pump, rear door
101 License plate lamps
102 Rear door contact switch
103 Heated rear window
104 Ground connection, rear door
105 Back-up lamps
106 Tail lamp unit, right
  a Turn signal lamp
  b Tail/standing lamp
  c Stop lamp

* Special equipment

Wire Color Code

bl	= blue	nf	= neutral
br	= brown	rs	= pink
el	= ivory	rt	= red
ge	= yellow	sw	= black
gn	= green	vi	= purple
gr	= grey	ws	= white

Example:
Wire designation 1.5 gr/rt
Basic color gr = grey
Identification color rt = red
Cross section of wire 1.5 = 1.5 mm^2

Key to 1980 240D (123.123) (UK) wiring diagam

1 Headlamp unit, left
  a High beam
  b Low beam
  c Fog lamp
  d Parking/standing/side marker lamp
  e Turn signal lamp
2 Brake fluid indicator lamp switch I
3 Brake fluid indicator lamp switch II
4 Parking brake indicator lamp switch
5 Temperature sensor, coolant
6 Contact sensor, brake pads, front, left
  a Turn signal indicator lamp, left
  b Brake pad wear indicator lamp
  c Brake fluid and parking brake indicator lamp
  d Fuel reserve warning lamp
  e Fuel gauge
  f Coolant temperature gauge
  g Instrument lamps
  h Rheostat, instrument lamps
  i Charge indicator lamp
  j High beam indicator lamp
  k Turn signal indicator lamp, right
  l Electronic clock
  m Seat belt warning lamp
  n Preglow indicator lamp
7 Instrument cluster
8 Contact sensor, brake pads, front, right
9 Warning buzzer contact
10 Driver's belt buckle switch
11 Relay window lifts
12 Headlamp unit, right
  a High beam
  b Low beam
  c Fog lamp
  d Parking/standing/side marker lamp
  e Turn signal lamp
13 Temperature sensor, preglow indicator
14 Warning device
15 Front dome lamp w/switch
16 Door contact switch, left
17 Door contact switch, right
18 Dual-tone horn (fanfare)
19 Sensor, cruise control system*
20 Amplifier, cruise control*
21 Actuator, cruise control*
22 Electromagnetic clutch, refrigerant compressor*

22a Pressure switch, refrigerant compressor On 2.6 bar, Off 2.0 bar*
23 Sliding roof motor*
24 Switch, electrically operated sliding roof*
25 Fuse box
26 Illumination, shift plate*
27 Glove compartment lamp switch
28 Glove compartment lamp
29 Stop lamp switch
30 Warning flasher switch/timer
31 Horn contact
32 Combination switch
  a Turn signal lamp switch
  b Headlamp flasher switch
  c Dimmer switch
  d Washer switch
  e Switch, wiping speed
    I Intermittent wiping
    II Slow wiping
    III Fast wiping
33 Solenoid valve, automatic transmission*
34 Kick-down switch*
35 Starter lockout and backup lamp switch*
36 Lighting switch
37 Ignition starter switch
38 Relay, auxiliary fan*
39 Washer pump
40 Switch, cruise control*
  A Off
  V Decelerate/set
  SP Resume
  B Accelerate/set
41 Wiper motor
42 Intermittent wiping timer
43 Pencil element glow plugs
44 Auxiliary fan*
46 Blower switch with lamp
48 Relay, air conditioner II*
49 Automatic antenna*
50 Switch, automatic antenna*
51 Illumination
  a Air defelctor control
  b Heater control
  c Switch
52 Temperature switch 62 °C (144 °F) receiver drier*
53 Preglow time relay
54 Switch, window, rear, left*

55 Window lift motor, rear, left*
56 Time-lag relay, heated rear window
57 Switch cluster, window lifts*
  a Switch, window, rear, left
  b Safety switch
  c Switch, window, front, left
  d Switch, window, front, right
  e Switch, window, rear, right
58 Window lift motor, front, left*
59 Window lift motor, front, right*
60 Switch, heated rear window
61 Blower motor
62 Pre-resistance, blower motor
63 Temperature control w/lighting, air conditioner*
66 Cigar lighter with ashtray illumination
67 Radio*
68 Door contact switch, rear, left*
69 Rear dome lamp switch*
70 Door contact switch, rear, right*
71 Rear dome lamp*
72 Starter
73 Battery
74 Alternator w/electronic regulator
75 Fuel gauge sending unit
76 Plug connection, tail lamp cable harness
77 Trunk lamp
78 Window lift motor, rear, right*
79 Switch, window, rear, right*
80 Tail lamp unit, left
  a Side marker lamp
  b Turn signal lamp
  c Tail/standing lamp
  d Backup lamp
  e Stop lamp
81 Heated rear window
82 License plate lamp
83 Tail lamp unit, right
  a Side marker lamp
  b Turn signal lamp
  c Tail/standing lamp
  d Backup lamp
  e Stop lamp

* Special equipment

Wire Color Code

bl = blue
br = brown
el = ivory
ge = yellow
gn = green
gr = grey

nf = neutral
rs = pink
rt = red
sw = black
vi = purple
ws = white

Example:
Wire designation 1.5 gr/rt
Basic color gr = grey
Identification color rt = red
Cross section of wire 1.5 = 1.5 mm^2

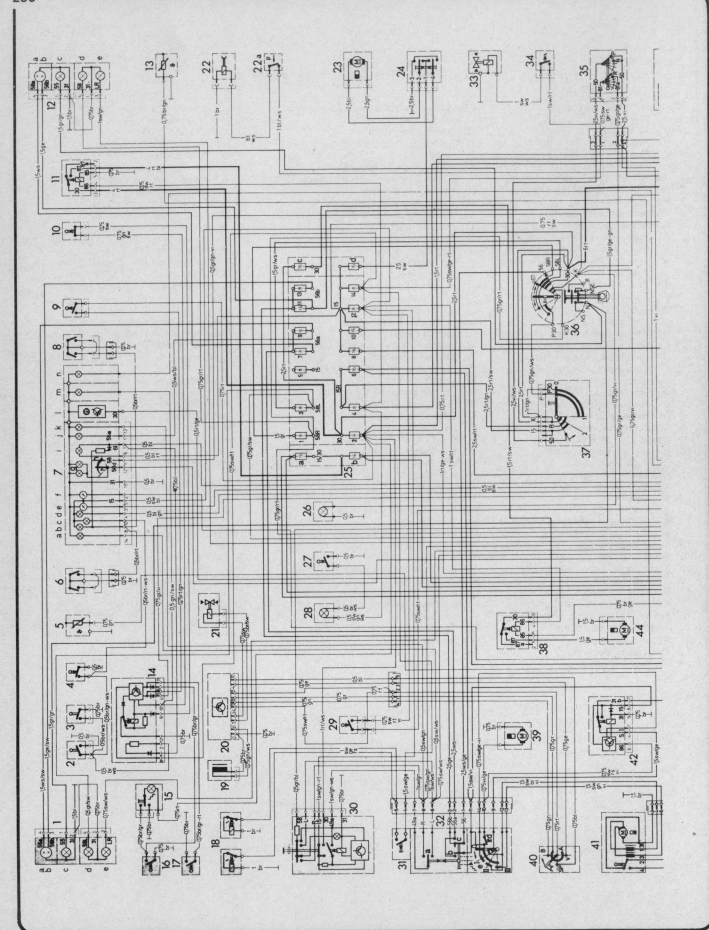

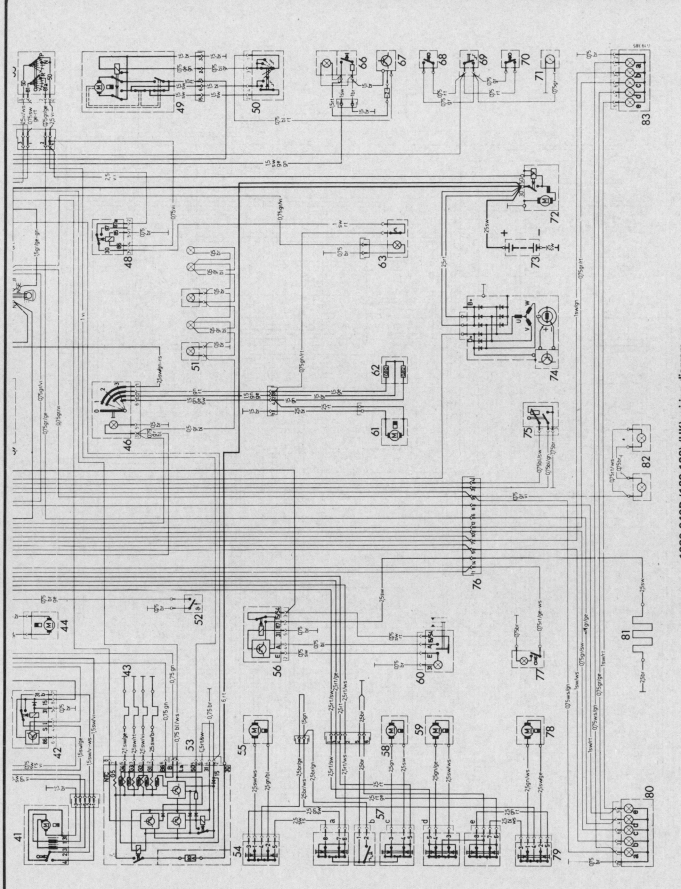

1980 240D (123.123) (UK) wiring diagram

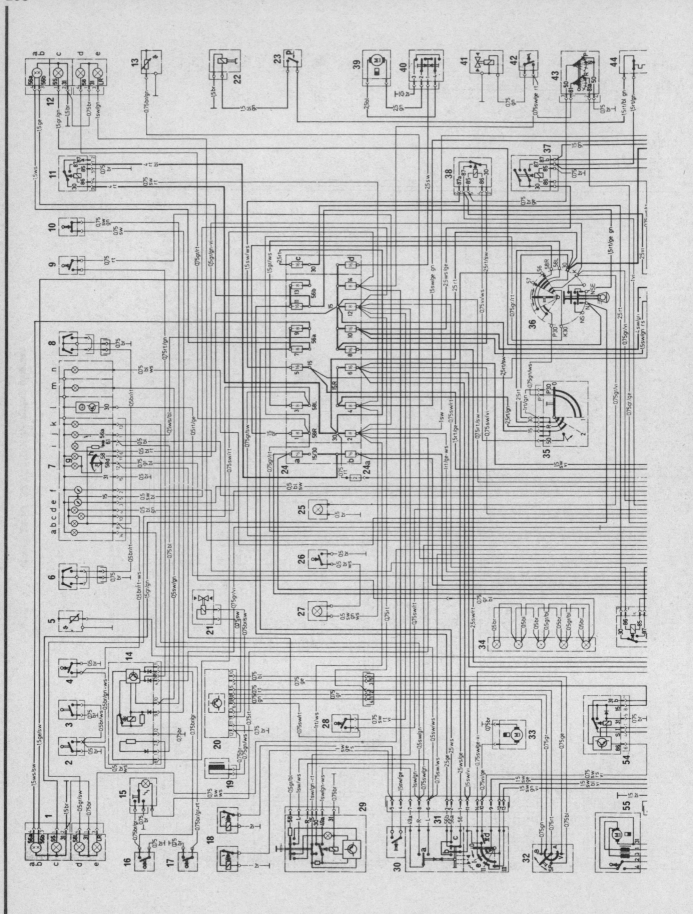

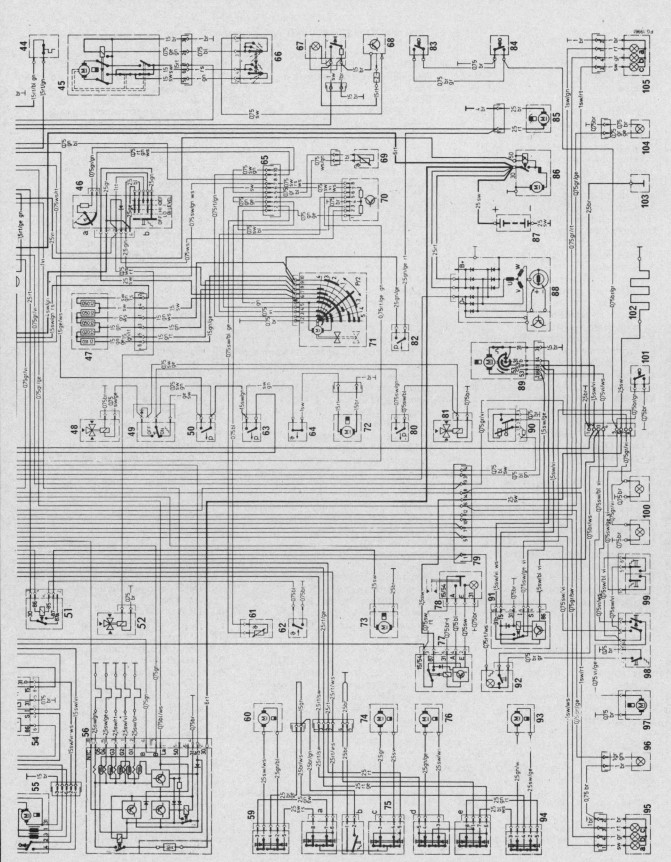

1980 300TD (123.190) (UK) wiring diagram

Key to 1980 300TD (123.190) (UK) wiring diagram

1 Headlamp unit, left
  a High beam
  b Low beam
  c Fog lamp
  d Parking/standing/side marker lamp
  e Turn signal lamp
2 Brake fluid indicator lamp switch I
3 Brake fluid indicator lamp switch II
4 Parking brake indicator lamp switch
5 Temperature sensor, coolant
6 Contact sensor, brake pads, front, left
7 Instrument cluster
  a Turn signal indicator lamp, left
  b Brake pad wear indicator lamp
  c Brake fluid and parking brake
    indicator lamp
  d Fuel reserve warning lamp
  e Fuel gauge
  f Coolant temperature gauge
  g Instrument lamps
  h Rheostat, instrument lamps
  i Charge indicator lamp
  j High beam indicator lamp
  k Turn signal indicator lamp, right
  l Electronic clock
  m Seat belt warning lamp
  n Preglow indicator lamp
8 Contact sensor, brake pads, front, right
9 Warning buzzer contact
10 Driver's belt buckle switch
11 Relay window lifts
12 Headlamp unit, right
  a High beam
  b Low beam
  c Fog lamp
  d Parking/standing/side marker lamp
  e Turn signal lamp
13 Temperature sensor, preglow indicator
14 Warning device
15 Front dome lamp w/switch
16 Door contact switch, front right
17 Door contact switch, front left
18 Dual-tone horn (fanfare)
19 Sensor, cruise control system
20 Amplifier, cruise control
21 Actuator, cruise control
22 Electromagnetic clutch, refrigerant
  compressor
23 Pressure switch, refrigerant compressor
  On 2.6 bar, Off 2.0 bar
24 Fuse box
24a Fuse, amplifier, automatic climate
  control
25 Illumination, shift plate
26 Glove compartment lamp switch
27 Glove compartment lamp

28 Stop lamp switch
29 Warning flasher switch/timer
30 Horn contact
31 Combination switch
  a Turn signal lamp switch
  b Headlamp flasher switch
  c Dimmer switch
  d Washer switch
  e Switch, wiping speed
    I   Intermittent wiping
    II Slow wiping
    III Fast wiping
32 Switch, cruise control
  A Off
  V Decelerate/set
  SP Resume
  B Accelerate/set
33 Washer pump
34 Illumination, heater controls
35 Starter switch
36 Lighting switch
37 Dual contact relay
38 Relay, air conditioner/starter
39 Sliding roof motor *
40 Switch, electrically operated sliding roof*
41 Solenoid valve, automatic transmission
42 Kick-down switch
43 Starter lockout and backup lamp switch
44 Temperature switch 2 °C (36 °F)
45 Automatic antenna
46 Control unit
  a Temperature selector
  b Push button switch
47 Pre-resistance, blower motor
48 Switch-over valve, fresh/recirculating
  air flap
49 Switch, refrigerant compressor, on/off
50 Vacuum switch, 78.5 mbar, refrigerant
  compressor "DEF" and "BI-level"
51 Switch-over valve, BI-level
52 Relay, auxiliary fan
54 Intermittent wiping timer
55 Wiper motor
56 Preglow time relay with glow plugs
59 Switch, window, rear, left
60 Window lift motor, rear, left
61 Temperature sensor, outside
62 Temperature switch 62 °C (144 °F)
  receiver drier air conditioner
63 Vacuum switch 78.5 mbar
64 Temperature switch, On 16 °C Off
  Off 26 °C (On 61 °F, Off 79 °F)
65 Plug tester, automatic climate control
66 Switch, automatic antenna
67 Cigar lighter with ashtray illumination
68 Radio

69 Temperature sensor, inside
70 Amplifier, automatic climate control
71 Servo assembly, automatic climate
  control
72 Auxiliary water pump for heater
  automatic climate control
73 Auxiliary fan
74 Window lift motor, front, left
75 Switch cluster, window lifts
  a Switch, window, rear, left
  b Safety switch
  c Switch, window, front, left
  d Switch, window, front, right
  e Switch, window, rear, right
76 Window lift motor, front, right
77 Time-lag relay, heated rear window
78 Switch, heated rear window
79 Plug connection, tail lamp cable harness
80 Vacuum switch, BI-level
81 Switch-over valve, footwell flaps
82 Vacuum switch, 175 mbar, master
  switch
83 Door contact switch, rear, left
84 Door contact switch, rear, right
85 Blower motor
86 Starter
87 Battery
88 Alternator w/electronic regulator
89 Wiper motor, rear door
90 Fuel gauge sending unit
91 Intermittent wiping timer, rear door
92 Rear dome lamp w/switch
93 Window lift motor, rear, right
94 Switch, window, rear right
95 Tail lamp unit, left
  a Turn signal lamp
  b Tail/standing lamp
  c Stop lamp
96 Backup lamp, left
97 Washer pump, rear door
98 Detent switch, rear dome lamp
  Push-button switch washer pump,
  rear door
99 Detent switch, wiper motor rear door
  Detent switch, intermittent wipe,
  rear door
100 License plate lamp
101 Rear door contact switch
102 Heated rear window
103 Ground connection, rear door
104 Backup lamp, right
105 Tail lamp unit, right
  a Turn signal lamp
  b Tail/standing lamp
  c Stop lamp

*   Special equipment

Wire Color Code

bl = blue	nf = neutral	
br = brown	rs = pink	**Example:**
el = ivory	rt = red	Wire designation 1.5 gr/rt
ge = yellow	sw = black	Basic color gr = grey
gn = green	vi = purple	Identification color rt = red
gr = grey	ws = white	Cross section of wire 1.5 = 1.5 mm^2

Key to 1980 300TD (123.190) (US) wiring diagram

1 Headlamp unit, left
  a High beam
  b Low beam
  c Fog lamp
  d Parking/standing/side marker lamp
  e Turn signal lamp
2 Brake fluid indicator lamp switch I
3 Brake fluid indicator lamp switch II
4 Parking brake indicator lamp switch
5 Temperature sensor, coolant
6 Contact sensor, brake pads, front, left
7 Instrument cluster
  a Turn signal indicator lamp, left
  b Brake pad wear indicator lamp
  c Brake fluid and parking brake
    indicator lamp
  d Fuel reserve warning lamp
  e Fuel gauge
  f Coolant temperature gauge
  g Instrument lamps
  h Rheostat, instrument lamps
  i Charge indicator lamp
  j High beam indicator lamp
  k Turn signal indicator lamp, right
  l Electronic clock
  m Seat belt warning lamp
  n Preglow indicator lamp
8 Contact sensor, brake pads, front, right
9 Warning buzzer contact
10 Driver's belt buckle switch
11 Relay window lifts
12 Headlamp unit, right
  a High beam
  b Low beam
  c Fog lamp
  d Parking/standing/side marker lamp
  e Turn signal lamp
13 Temperature sensor, preglow indicator
14 Warning device
15 Front dome lamp w/switch
16 Door contact switch, front right
17 Door contact switch, front left
18 Dual-tone horn (fanfare)
19 Sensor, cruise control system
20 Amplifier, cruise control
21 Actuator, cruise control
22 Electromagnetic clutch, refrigerant
  compressor
23 Pressure switch, refrigerant compressor
  On 2.6 bar, Off 2.0 bar
24 Fuse box
24a Fuse, amplifier, automatic climate
  control
25 Illumination, shift plate
26 Glove compartment lamp switch
27 Glove compartment lamp

28 Stop lamp switch
29 Warning flasher switch/timer
30 Horn contact
31 Combination switch
  a Turn signal lamp switch
  b Headlamp flasher switch
  c Dimmer switch
  d Washer switch
  e Switch, wiping speed
    I Intermittent wiping
    II Slow wiping
    III Fast wiping
32 Switch, cruise control
  A Off
  V Decelerate/set
  SP Resume
  B Accelerate/set
33 Washer pump
34 Illumination, heater controls
35 Starter switch
36 Lighting switch
37 Dual contact relay
38 Relay, air conditioner/starter
39 Sliding roof motor *
40 Switch, electrically operated sliding roof*
41 Solenoid valve, automatic transmission
42 Kick-down switch
43 Starter lockout and backup lamp switch
44 Temperature switch 2 °C (36 °F)
45 Automatic antenna
46 Control unit
  a Temperature selector
  b Push button switch
47 Pre-resistance, blower motor
48 Switch-over valve, fresh/recirculating
  air flap
49 Switch, refrigerant compressor, on/off
50 Vacuum switch, 78.5 mbar, refrigerant
  compressor "DEF" and "BI-level"
51 Switch-over valve, BI-level
52 Relay, auxiliary fan
54 Intermittent wiping timer
55 Wiper motor
56 Preglow time relay with glow plugs
59 Switch, window, rear, left
60 Window lift motor, rear, left
61 Temperature sensor, outside
62 Temperature switch 62 °C (144 °F)
  receiver drier air conditioner
63 Vacuum switch 78.5 mbar
64 Temperature switch, On 16 °C Off
  Off 26 °C (On 61 °F, Off 79 °F)
65 Plug tester, automatic climate control
66 Switch, automatic antenna
67 Cigar lighter with ashtray illumination
68 Radio

69 Temperature sensor, inside
70 Amplifier, automatic climate control
71 Servo assembly, automatic climate
  control
72 Auxiliary water pump for heater
  automatic climate control
73 Auxiliary fan
74 Window lift motor, front, left
75 Switch cluster, window lifts
  a Switch, window, rear, left
  b Safety switch
  c Switch, window, front, left
  d Switch, window, front, right
  e Switch, window, rear, right
76 Window lift motor, front, right
77 Time-lag relay, heated rear window
78 Switch, heated rear window
79 Plug connection, tail lamp cable harness
80 Vacuum switch, BI-level
81 Switch-over valve, footwell flaps
82 Vacuum switch, 175 mbar, master
  switch
83 Door contact switch, rear, left
84 Door contact switch, rear, right
85 Blower motor
86 Starter
87 Battery
88 Alternator w/electronic regulator
89 Wiper motor, rear door
90 Fuel gauge sending unit
91 Intermittent wiping timer, rear door
92 Rear dome lamp w/switch
93 Window lift motor, rear, right
94 Switch, window, rear right
95 Tail lamp unit, left
  a Turn signal lamp
  b Tail/standing lamp
  c Stop lamp
96 Backup lamp, left
97 Washer pump, rear door
98 Detent switch, rear dome lamp
  Push-button switch washer pump,
  rear door
99 Detent switch, wiper motor rear door
  Detent switch, intermittent wipe,
  rear door
100 License plate lamp
101 Rear door contact switch
102 Heated rear window
103 Ground connection, rear door
104 Backup lamp, right
105 Tail lamp unit, right
  a Turn signal lamp
  b Tail/standing lamp
  c Stop lamp

* Special equipment

Wire Color Code

bl = blue	nf = neutral
br = brown	rs = pink
el = ivory	rt = red
ge = yellow	sw = black
gn = green	vi = purple
gr = grey	ws = white

Example:
Wire designation 1.5 gr/rt
Basic color gr = grey
Identification color rt = red
Cross section of wire 1.5 = 1.5 mm^2

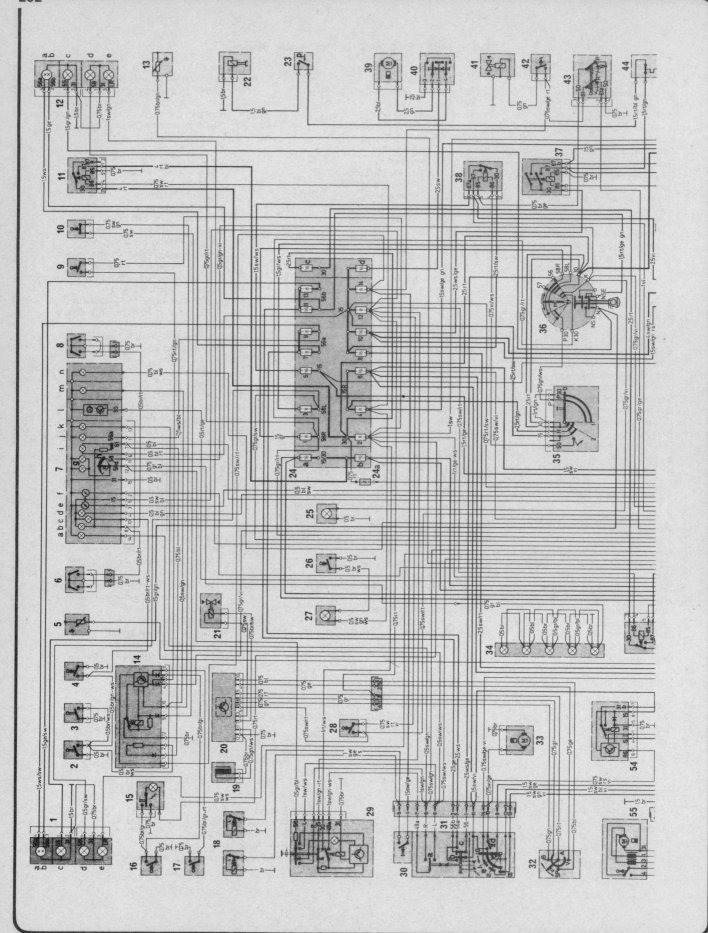

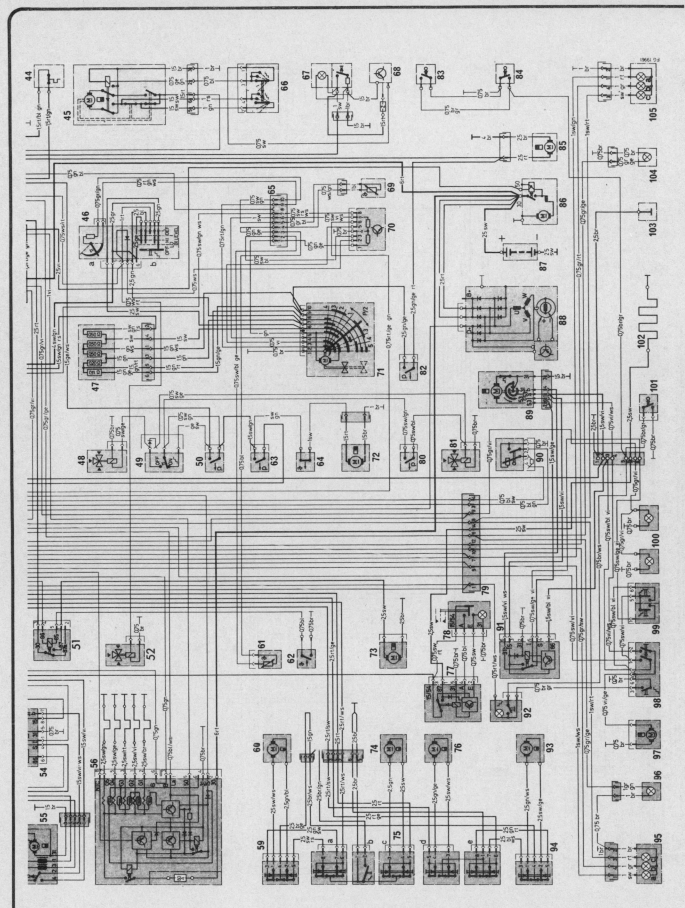

1980 300TD (123.190) (US) wiring diagram

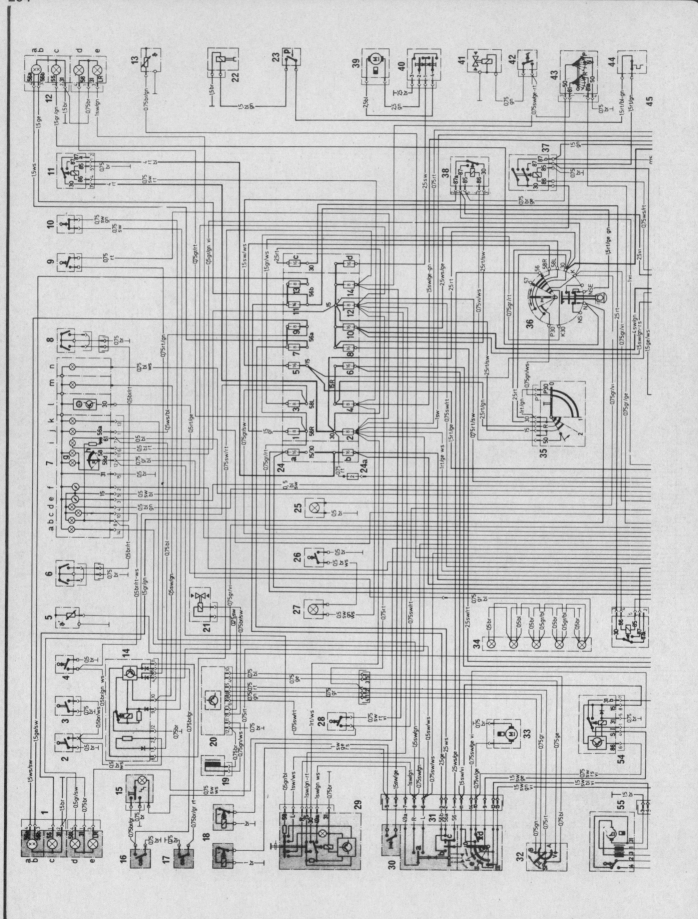

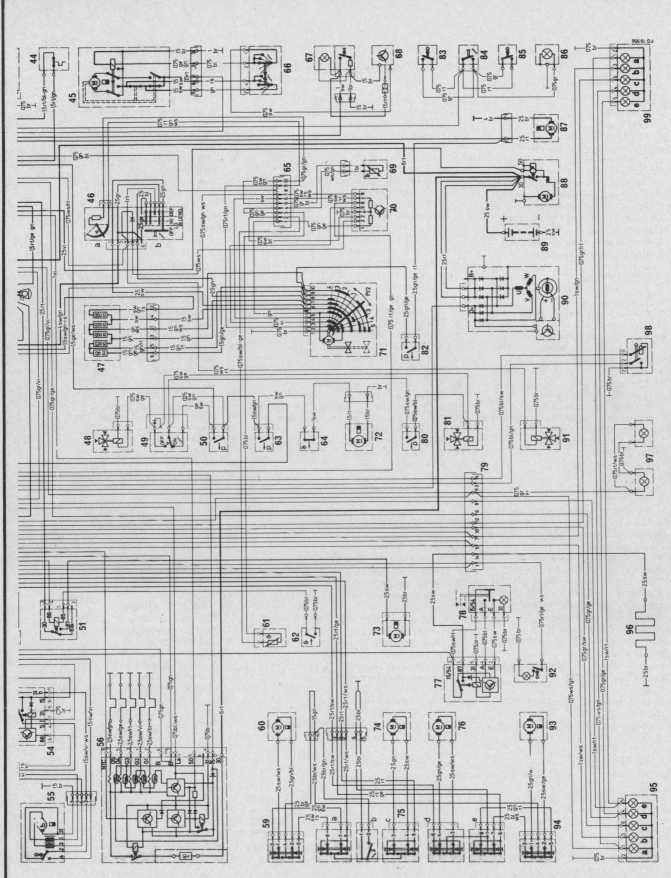

1980 300D/CD (123.130/150) (UK) wiring diagram

Key to 1980 300D/CD (123.130/150) (UK) wiring diagram

1 Headlamp unit, left
  a High beam
  b Low beam
  c Fog lamp
  d Parking/standing/side marker lamp
  e Turn signal lamp
2 Brake fluid indicator lamp switch I
3 Brake fluid indicator lamp switch II
4 Parking brake indicator lamp switch
5 Temperature sensor, coolant
6 Contact sensor, brake pads, front, left
7 Instrument cluster
  a Turn signal indicator lamp, left
  b Brake pad wear indicator lamp
  c Brake fluid and parking brake
    indicator lamp
  d Fuel reserve warning lamp
  e Fuel gauge
  f Coolant temperature gauge
  g Instrument lamps
  h Rheostat, instrument lamps
  i Charge indicator lamp
  j High beam indicator lamp
  k Turn signal indicator lamp, right
  l Electronic clock
  m Seat belt warning lamp
  n Preglow indicator lamp
8 Contact sensor, brake pads, front, right
9 Warning buzzer contact
10 Driver's belt buckle switch
11 Relay window lifts
12 Headlamp unit, right
  a High beam
  b Low beam
  c Fog lamp
  d Parking/standing/side marker lamp
  e Turn signal lamp
13 Temperature sensor, preglow indicator
14 Warning device
15 Front dome lamp w/switch
16 Door contact switch, front, right
17 Door contact switch, front, left
18 Dual-tone horn (fanfare)
19 Sensor, cruise control system
20 Amplifier, cruise control
21 Actuator, cruise control
22 Electromagnetic clutch, refrigerant
  compressor
23 Pressure switch, refrigerant compressor
  On 2.6 bar, Off 2.0 bar
24 Fuse box
24a Fuse, amplifier, automatic climate
  control
25 Illumination, shift plate

26 Glove compartment lamp switch
27 Glove compartment lamp
28 Stop lamp switch
29 Warning flasher switch/timer
30 Horn contact
31 Combination switch
  a Turn signal lamp switch
  b Headlamp flasher switch
  c Dimmer switch
  d Washer switch
  e Switch, wiping speed
    I   Intermittent wiping
    II Slow wiping
    III Fast wiping
32 Switch, cruise control
  A Off
  V Decelerate/set
  SP Resume
  B Accelerate/set
33 Washer pump
34 Illumination, heater controls
35 Starter switch
36 Lighting switch
37 Dual contact relay
38 Relay, air conditioner/starter
39 Sliding roof motor *
40 Switch, electrically operated sliding roof*
41 Solenoid valve, automatic transmission
42 Kick-down switch
43 Starter lockout and backup lamp switch
44 Temperature switch 2 °C (36 °F)
45 Automatic antenna
46 Control unit
  a Temperature selector
  b Push button switch
47 Pre-resistance, blower motor
48 Switch-over valve, fresh/recirculating
  air flap
49 Switch, refrigerant compressor, on/off
50 Vacuum switch, 78.5 mbar, refrigerant
  compressor "DEF" and "BI-level"
51 Relay, auxiliary fan
54 Intermittent wiping timer
55 Wiper motor
56 Preglow time relay with glow plugs
59 Switch, window, rear, left
60 Window lift motor, rear, left
61 Temperature sensor, outside
62 Temperature switch 62 °C (144 °F)
  receiver drier air conditioner
63 Vacuum switch 78.5 mbar
64 Temperature switch, On 16 °C —
  Off 26 °C (On 61 °F, Off 79 °F)
65 Plug tester, automatic climate control

66 Switch, automatic antenna
67 Cigar lighter with ashtray illumination
68 Radio
69 Temperature sensor, inside
70 Amplifier, automatic climate control
71 Servo assembly, automatic climate
  control
72 Auxiliary water pump for heater,
  automatic climate control
73 Auxiliary fan
74 Window lift motor, front, left
75 Switch cluster, window lifts
  a Switch, window, rear, left
  b Safety switch
  c Switch, window, front, left
  d Switch, window, front, right
  e Switch, window, rear, right
76 Window lift motor, front, right
77 Time-lag relay, heated rear window
78 Switch, heated rear window
79 Plug connection, tail lamp cable harness
80 Vacuum switch, BI-level
81 Switch-over valve, footwell flaps
82 Vacuum switch, 175 mbar, master
  switch
83 Door contact switch, rear, left
84 Rear dome lamp switch
85 Door contact switch, rear, right
86 Rear dome lamp
87 Blower motor
88 Starter
89 Battery
90 Alternator w/electronic regulator
91 Switch-over valve, Bi-level
92 Trunk lamp
93 Window lift motor, rear, right
94 Switch, window, rear right
95 Tail lamp unit, left
  a Side marker lamp
  b Turn signal lamp
  c Tail/standing lamp
  d Backup lamp
  e Stop lamp
96 Heated rear window
97 License plate lamp
98 Fuel gauge sending unit
99 Tail lamp unit, right
  a Side marker lamp
  b Turn signal lamp
  c Tail/standing lamp
  d Backup lamp
  e Stop lamp

* Special equipment

Wire Color Code

bl = blue
br = brown
el = ivory
ge = yellow
gn = green
gr = grey

nf = neutral
rs = pink
rt = red
sw = black
vi = purple
ws = white

Example:
Wire designation 1.5 gr/rt
Basic color gr = grey
Identification color rt = red
Cross section of wire 1.5 = 1.5 mm^2

Key to 1980 300D/CD (123.130/150) (US) wiring diagram

1 Headlamp unit, left
  a High beam
  b Low beam
  c Fog lamp
  d Parking/standing/side marker lamp
  e Turn signal lamp
2 Brake fluid indicator lamp switch I
3 Brake fluid indicator lamp switch II
4 Parking brake indicator lamp switch
5 Temperature sensor, coolant
6 Contact sensor, brake pads, front, left
7 Instrument cluster
  a Turn signal indicator lamp, left
  b Brake pad wear indicator lamp
  c Brake fluid and parking brake
    indicator lamp
  d Fuel reserve warning lamp
  e Fuel gauge
  f Coolant temperature gauge
  g Instrument lamps
  h Rheostat, instrument lamps
  i Charge indicator lamp
  j High beam indicator lamp
  k Turn signal indicator lamp, right
  l Electronic clock
  m Seat belt warning lamp
  n Preglow indicator lamp
8 Contact sensor, brake pads, front, right
9 Warning buzzer contact
10 Driver's belt buckle switch
11 Relay window lifts
12 Headlamp unit, right
  a High beam
  b Low beam
  c Fog lamp
  d Parking/standing/side marker lamp
  e Turn signal lamp
13 Temperature sensor, preglow indicator
14 Warning device
15 Front dome lamp w/switch
16 Door contact switch, front, right
17 Door contact switch, front, left
18 Dual-tone horn (fanfare)
19 Sensor, cruise control system
20 Amplifier, cruise control
21 Actuator, cruise control
22 Electromagnetic clutch, refrigerant
  compressor
23 Pressure switch, refrigerant compressor
  On 2.6 bar, Off 2.0 bar
24 Fuse box
24a Fuse, amplifier, automatic climate
  control
25 Illumination, shift plate

26 Glove compartment lamp switch
27 Glove compartment lamp
28 Stop lamp switch
29 Warning flasher switch/timer
30 Horn contact
31 Combination switch
  a Turn signal lamp switch
  b Headlamp flasher switch
  c Dimmer switch
  d Washer switch
  e Switch, wiping speed
    I   Intermittent wiping
    II Slow wiping
    III Fast wiping
32 Switch, cruise control
  A Off
  V Decelerate/set
  SP Resume
  B Accelerate/set
33 Washer pump
34 Illumination, heater controls
35 Starter switch
36 Lighting switch
37 Dual contact relay
38 Relay, air conditioner/starter
39 Sliding roof motor *
40 Switch, electrically operated sliding roof*
41 Solenoid valve, automatic transmission
42 Kick-down switch
43 Starter lockout and backup lamp switch
44 Temperature switch 2 °C (36 °F)
45 Automatic antenna
46 Control unit
  a Temperature selector
  b Push button switch
47 Pre-resistance, blower motor
48 Switch-over valve, fresh/recirculating
  air flap
49 Switch, refrigerant compressor, on/off
50 Vacuum switch, 78.5 mbar, refrigerant
  compressor "DEF" and "BI-level"
51 Relay, auxiliary fan
54 Intermittent wiping timer
55 Wiper motor
56 Preglow time relay with glow plugs
59 Switch, window, rear, left
60 Window lift motor, rear, left
61 Temperature sensor, outside
62 Temperature switch 62 °C (144 °F)
  receiver drier air conditioner
63 Vacuum switch 78.5 mbar
64 Temperature switch, On 16 °C —
  Off 26 °C (On 61 °F, Off 79 °F)
65 Plug tester, automatic climate control

66 Switch, automatic antenna
67 Cigar lighter with ashtray illumination
68 Radio
69 Temperature sensor, inside
70 Amplifier, automatic climate control
71 Servo assembly, automatic climate
  control
72 Auxiliary water pump for heater,
  automatic climate control
73 Auxiliary fan
74 Window lift motor, front, left
75 Switch cluster, window lifts
  a Switch, window, rear, left
  b Safety switch
  c Switch, window, front, left
  d Switch, window, front, right
  e Switch, window, rear, right
76 Window lift motor, front, right
77 Time-lag relay, heated rear window
78 Switch, heated rear window
79 Plug connection, tail lamp cable harness
80 Vacuum switch, BI-level
81 Switch-over valve, footwell flaps
82 Vacuum switch, 175 mbar, master
  switch
83 Door contact switch, rear, left
84 Rear dome lamp switch
85 Door contact switch, rear, right
86 Rear dome lamp
87 Blower motor
88 Starter
89 Battery
90 Alternator w/electronic regulator
91 Switch-over valve, Bi-level
92 Trunk lamp
93 Window lift motor, rear, right
94 Switch, window, rear right
95 Tail lamp unit, left
  a Side marker lamp
  b Turn signal lamp
  c Tail/standing lamp
  d Backup lamp
  e Stop lamp
96 Heated rear window
97 License plate lamp
98 Fuel gauge sending unit
99 Tail lamp unit, right
  a Side marker lamp
  b Turn signal lamp
  c Tail/standing lamp
  d Backup lamp
  e Stop lamp

*   Special equipment

Wire Color Code

bl = blue
br = brown
el = ivory
ge = yellow
gn = green
gr = grey

nf = neutral
rs = pink
rt = red
sw = black
vi = purple
ws = white

Example:
Wire designation 1.5 gr/rt
Basic color gr = grey
Identification color rt = red
Cross section of wire 1.5 = 1.5 mm^2

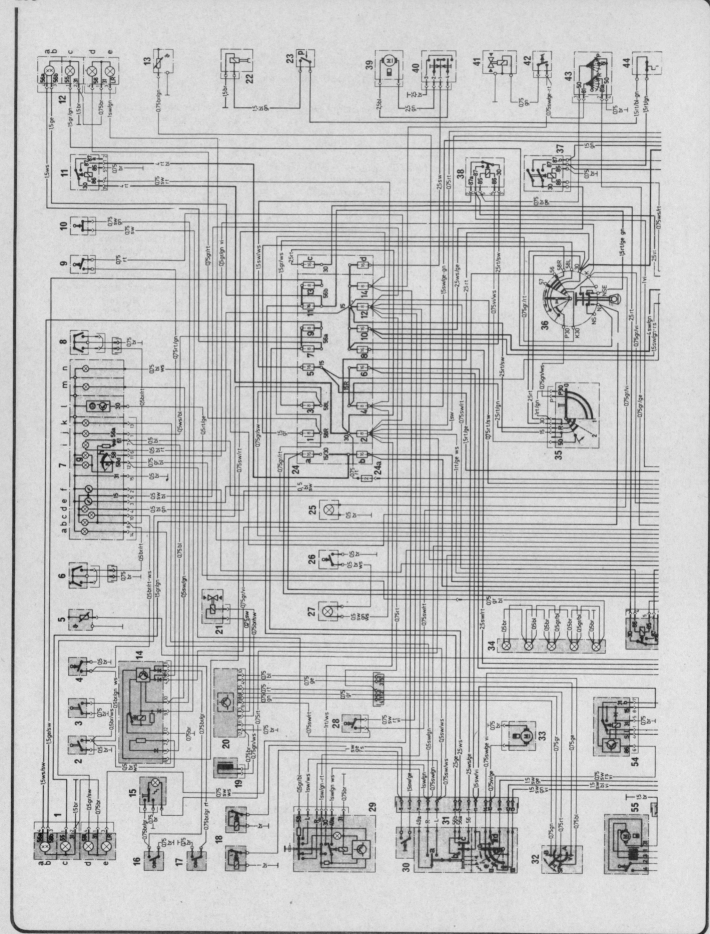

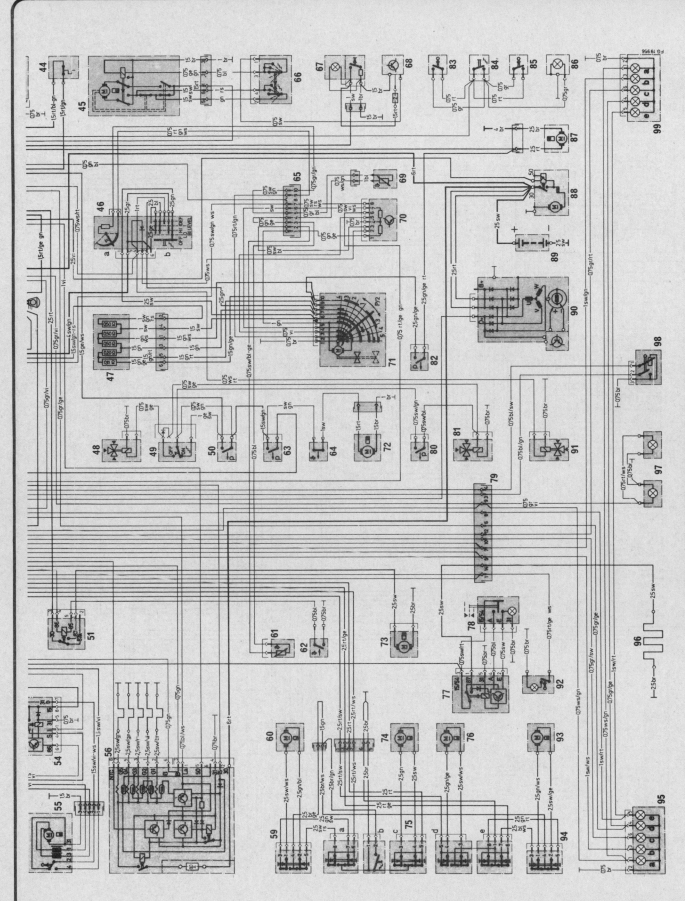

1980 300D/CD (123.130/150) (US) wiring diagram

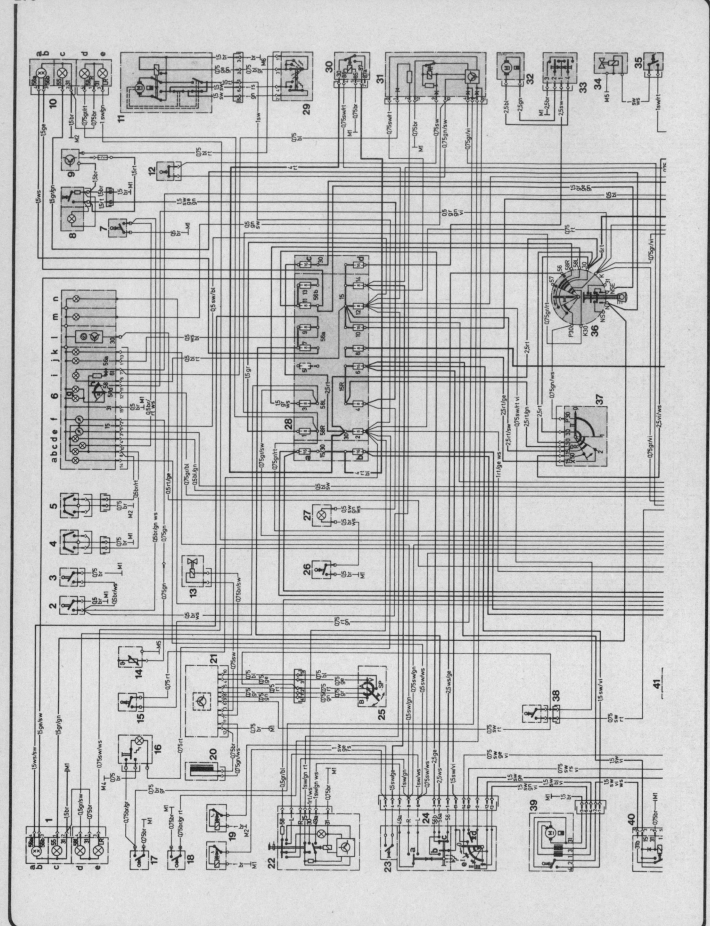

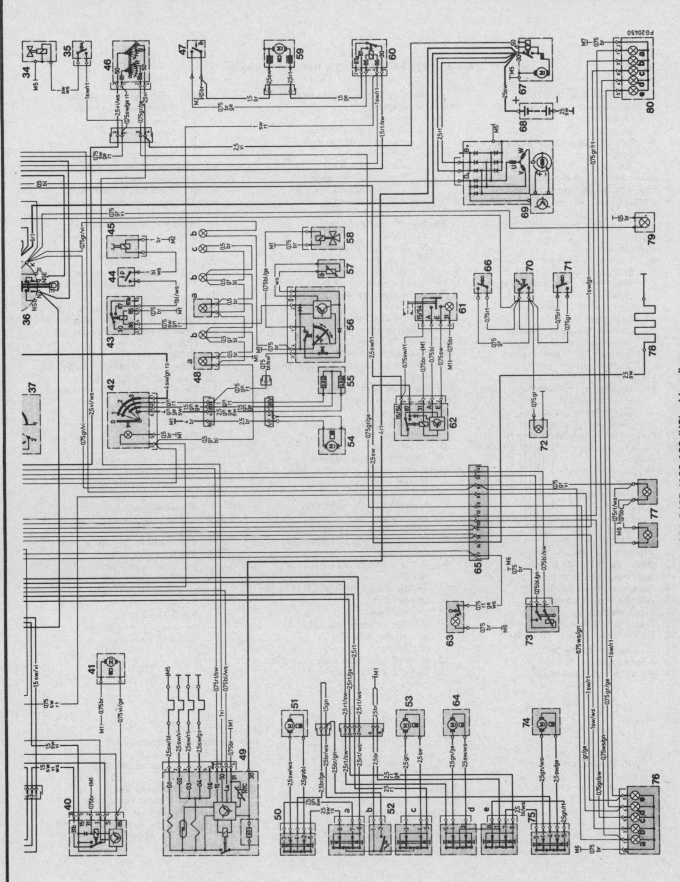

271

1981 240D (123.123) (US) wiring diagram

Key to 1981 240D (123.123) (US) wiring diagram

1 Headlamp unit, left
  a High beam
  b Low beam
  c Fog lamp
  d Parking/standing/side marker lamp
  e Turn signal lamp
2 Brake fluid indicator lamp switch I
3 Brake fluid indicator lamp switch II
4 Contact sensor, brake pads, front, left
5 Contact sensor, brake pads, front, right
6 Instrument cluster
  a Turn signal indicator lamp, left
  b Brake pad wear indicator lamp
  c Brake fluid and parking brake indicator lamp
  d Fuel reserve warning lamp
  e Fuel gauge
  f Coolant temperature gauge
  g Instrument lamps
  h Rheostat, instrument lamps
  i Charge indicator lamp
  j High beam indicator lamp
  k Turn signal indicator lamp, right
  l Electronic clock
  m Seat belt system warning lamp
  n Preglow indicator lamp
7 Parking brake indicator lamp switch
8 Cigar lighter with ashtray illumination
9 Radio*
10 Headlamp unit, right
  a High beam
  b Low beam
  c Fog lamp
  d Parking/standing/side marker lamp
  e Turn signal lamp
11 Automatic antenna
12 Driver's belt buckle switch
13 Actuator, cruise control*
14 Temperature sensor, coolant
15 Warning buzzer contact
16 Front dome lamp w/switch
17 Door contact switch, front, right
18 Door contact switch, front, left
19 Dual-tone horn (fanfare)
20 Sensor, cruise control*
21 Amplifier, cruise control*

22 Warning flasher switch/timer
23 Horn contact
24 Combination switch
  a Turn signal lamp switch
  b Headlamp flasher switch
  c Dimmer switch
  d Washer switch
  e Switch, wiping speed
    I Intermittent wiping
    II Slow wiping
    III Fast wiping
25 Switch, cruise control*
  A Off
  V Decelerate/set
  SP Resume
  B Accelerate/set
26 Glove compartment lamp switch
27 Glove compartment lamp
28 Fuse box
29 Switch, automatic antenna*
30 Relay, window lifts
31 Warning device
32 Sliding roof motor*
33 Switch, electrically operated sliding roof*
34 Solenoid valve, automatic transmission*
35 Kick-down switch*
36 Lighting switch
37 Starter switch
38 Stop lamp switch
39 Wiper motor
40 Intermittent wiping timer
41 Washer pump
42 Blower switch with lamp
43 Relay, air conditioner*
44 Pressure switch, refrigerant compressor*
  On 2.6 bar, Off 2.0 bar
45 Electromagnetic clutch, refrigerant compressor*
46 Starter lockout and backup lamp switch*
47 Temperature switch 52 °C (126 °F) receiver drier*
48 Illumination
  a Air deflector control
  b Heater control
  c Switch*
49 Preglow time relay with glow plugs
50 Switch, window, rear, left*

52 Switch cluster, window lifts*
  a Switch, window, rear, left
  b Safety switch
  c Switch, window, front, left
  d Switch, window, front, right
  e Switch, window, rear, right
53 Window lift motor, front, left*
54 Blower motor
55 Pre-resistance, blower motor
56 Temperature control, air conditioner*
57 Temperature control, air conditioner*
58 Switch-over valve, fresh/recirculating air flap*
59 Auxiliary fan*
60 Relay, auxiliary fan*
61 Switch, heated rear window
62 Time-lag relay, heated rear window
63 Trunk lamp
64 Window lift motor, front, right*
65 Connector, tail lamp cable harness
66 Door contact switch, rear, left*
67 Starter
68 Battery
69 Alternator w/electronic regulator
70 Rear dome lamp switch*
71 Door contact switch, rear, right*
72 Rear dome lamp*
73 Fuel gauge sending unit
74 Window lift motor, rear, right*
75 Switch, window, rear, right*
76 Tail lamp unit, left
  a Side marker lamp
  b Turn signal lamp
  c Tail/standing lamp
  d Backup lamp
  e Stop lamp
77 License plate lamp
78 Heated rear window
79 Illumination, shift plate*
80 Tail lamp unit, right
  a Side marker lamp
  b Turn signal lamp
  c Tail/standing lamp
  d Backup lamp
  e Stop lamp

* Special equipment

Wire Color Code

bl	= blue	nf	= neutral
br	= brown	rs	= pink
el	= ivory	rt	= red
ge	= yellow	sw	= black
gn	= green	vi	= purple
gr	= grey	ws	= white

Example:
Wire designation 1.5 gr/rt
Basic color gr = grey
Identifiaction color rt = red
Cross section of wire 1.5 = 1.5 mm^2

Ground connections

M1 Main ground (behind instrument cluster)
M2 Ground, front, right (near headlamp unit)
M4 Ground, dome lamp, front
M5 Ground, engine
M6 Ground, trunk, wheelhouse, left
M7 Ground, trunk, wheelhouse, right

Key to 1981 300D/CD (123.130/150) (UK) wiring diagram

1 Headlamp unit, left
  a High beam
  b Low beam
  c Fog lamp
  d Parking/standing/side marker lamp
  e Turn signal lamp
2 Brake fluid indicator lamp switch I
3 Brake fluid indicator lamp switch II
4 Parking brake indicator lamp switch
5 Temperature sensor, coolant
6 Contact sensor, brake pads, front, left
7 Instrument cluster
  a Turn signal indicator lamp, left
  b Brake pad wear indicator lamp
  c Brake fluid and parking brake indicator lamp
  d Fuel reserve warning lamp
  e Fuel gauge
  f Coolant temperature gauge
  g Instrument lamps
  h Rheostat, instrument lamps
  i Charge indicator lamp
  j High beam indicator lamp
  k Turn signal indicator lamp, right
  l Electronic clock
  m Seat belt warning lamp
  n Preglow indicator lamp
8 Contact sensor, brake pads, front, right
9 Warning buzzer contact
10 Driver's belt buckle switch
11 Relay, window lifts
12 Headlamp unit, right
  a High beam
  b Low beam
  c Fog lamp
  d Parking/standing/side marker lamp
  e Turn signal lamp
13 Illumination, heater controls
14 Warning device
15 Front dome lamp w/switch
16 Door contact switch, front, right
17 Door contact switch, front, left

18 Dual-tone horn (fanfare)
19 Sensor, cruise control
20 Amplifier, cruise control
21 Actuator, cruise control
22 Warning flasher switch/timer
21 Stop lamp switch
24 Glove compartment lamp
25 Glove compartment lamp switch
26 Illumination, shift plate
27 Fuse box
28 Sliding roof motor*
29 Switch, electrically operated sliding roof*
30 Horn contact
31 Combination switch
  a Turn signal lamp switch
  b Headlamp flasher switch
  c Dimmer switch
  d Washer switch
  e Switch, wiping speed
    I Intermittent wiping
    II Slow wiping
    III Fast wiping
32 Switch, cruise control
  A Off
  V Decelerate/set
  SP Resume
  B Accelerate/set
33 Washer pump
34 Solenoid valve, automatic transmission
35 Kick-down switch
36 Starter lockout and backup lamp switch
37 Connector, electronic radio
38 Lighting switch
39 Starter switch
40 Intermittent wiping timer
41 Wiper motor
42 Preglow time relay with glow plugs
43 Automatic antenna
44 Switch, automatic antenna
45 Door contact switch, rear, right
46 Door contact switch, rear, left

47 Rear door contact switch
48 Rear dome lamp
49 Window lift motor, rear, left
50 Switch, window, rear, left
51 Switch cluster, window lifts
  a Switch, window, rear, left
  b Safety switch
  c Switch, window, front, left
  d Switch, window, front, right
  e Switch, window, rear, right
52 Window lift motor, front, left
53 Window lift motor, front, right
54 Switch, window, rear, right
55 Window lift motor, rear, right
56 Time-lag relay, heated rear window
57 Trunk lamps
58 Switch, heated rear window
59 Plug connection, tail lamp cable harness
60 Alternator w/electronic regulator
61 Battery
62 Starter
63 Cigar lighter with ashtray illumination
64 Radio
65 Tail lamp unit, right
  a Side marker lamp
  b Turn signal lamp
  c Tail/standing lamp
  d Backup lamp
  e Stop lamp
66 Fuel gauge sendig unit
67 License plate lamp
68 Heated rear window
69 Tail lamp unit, left
  a Side marker lamp
  b Turn signal lamp
  c Tail/standing lamp
  d Backup lamp
  e Stop lamp

*   Special equipment
X   Automatic climate control connection

Wire Color Code

bl	= blue	nf	= neutral
br	= brown	rs	= pink
el	= ivory	rt	= red
ge	= yellow	sw	= black
gn	= green	vi	= purple
gr	= grey	ws	= white

Example:
Wire designation 1.5 gr/rt
Basic color gr = grey
Identification color rt = red
Cross section of wire 1.5 = 1.5 mm^2

Ground connections

M1 Main ground (behind instrument cluster)
M2 Ground, front, right (near headlamp unit)
M4 Ground, dome lamp, front
M5 Ground, engine
M6 Ground, trunk, wheelhouse, left
M7 Ground, trunk, wheelhouse, right

274

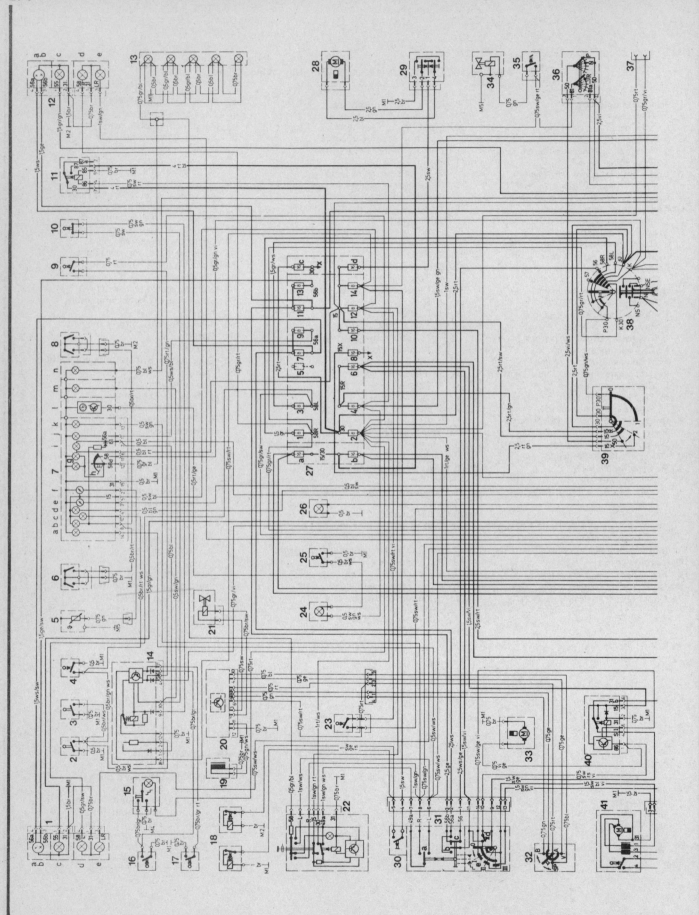

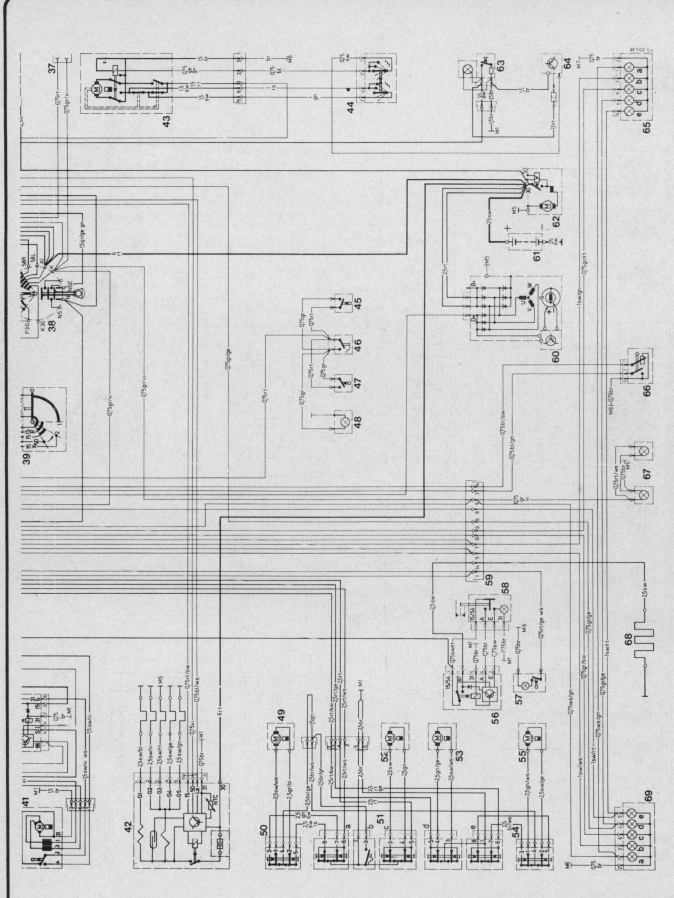

1981 300D/CD (123.130/150) (UK) wiring diagram

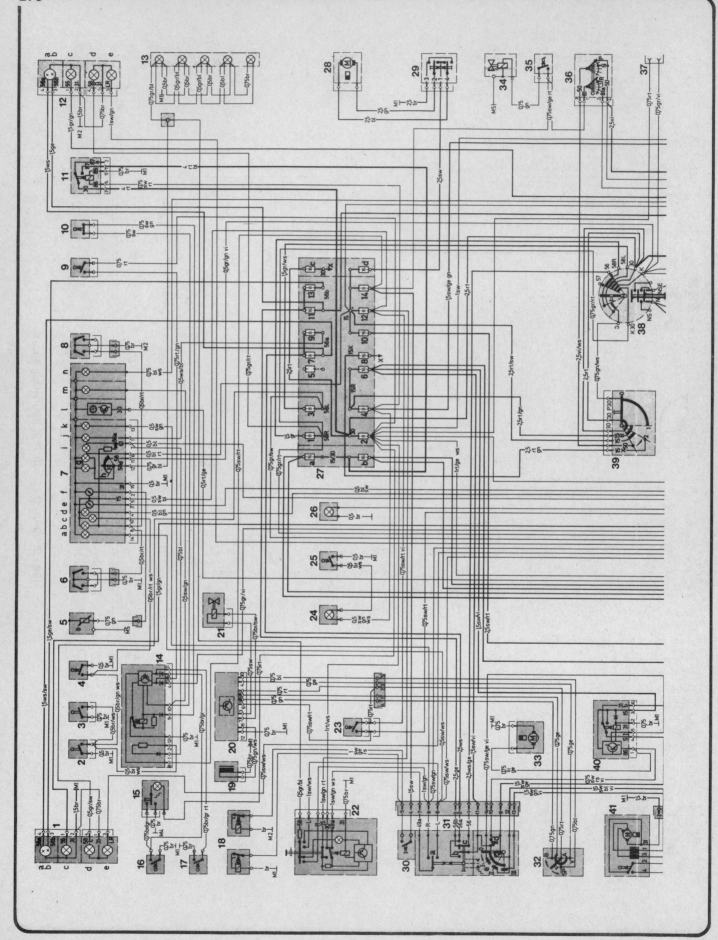

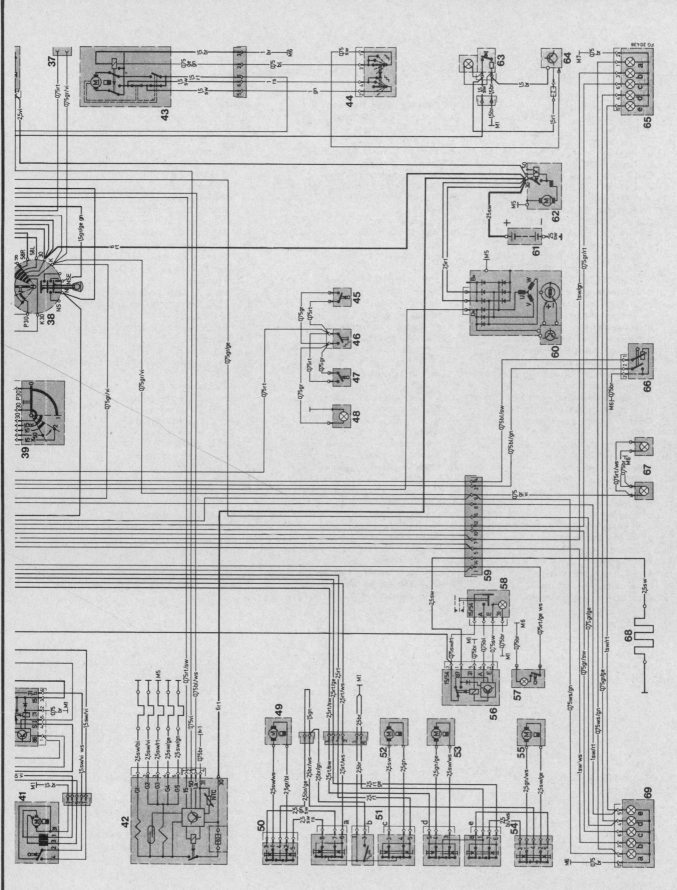

1981 300D/CD (123.130/150) (US) wiring diagram

Key to 1981 300D/CD (123.130/150) (US) wiring diagram

1 Headlamp unit, left
  a High beam
  b Low beam
  c Fog lamp
  d Parking/standing/side marker lamp
  e Turn signal lamp
2 Brake fluid indicator lamp switch I
3 Brake fluid indicator lamp switch II
4 Parking brake indicator lamp switch
5 Temperature sensor, coolant
6 Contact sensor, brake pads, front, left
7 Instrument cluster
  a Turn signal indicator lamp, left
  b Brake pad wear indicator lamp
  c Brake fluid and parking brake
    indicator lamp
  d Fuel reserve warning lamp
  e Fuel gauge
  f Coolant temperature gauge
  g Instrument lamps
  h Rheostat, instrument lamps
  i Charge indicator lamp
  j High beam indicator lamp
  k Turn signal indicator lamp, right
  l Electronic clock
  m Seat belt warning lamp
  n Preglow indicator lamp
8 Contact sensor, brake pads, front,
  right
9 Warning buzzer contact
10 Driver's belt buckle switch
11 Relay, window lifts
12 Headlamp unit, right
  a High beam
  b Low beam
  c Fog lamp
  d Parking/standing/side marker lamp
  e Turn signal lamp
13 Illumination, heater controls
14 Warning device
15 Front dome lamp w/switch
16 Door contact switch, front, right
17 Door contact switch, front, left

18 Dual-tone horn (fanfare)
19 Sensor, cruise control
20 Amplifier, cruise control
21 Actuator, cruise control
22 Warning flasher switch/timer
21 Stop lamp switch
24 Glove compartment lamp
25 Glove compartment lamp switch
26 Illumination, shift plate
27 Fuse box
28 Sliding roof motor*
29 Switch, electrically operated sliding
  roof*
30 Horn contact
31 Combination switch
  a Turn signal lamp switch
  b Headlamp flasher switch
  c Dimmer switch
  d Washer switch
  e Switch, wiping speed
    I Intermittent wiping
    II Slow wiping
    III Fast wiping
32 Switch, cruise control
  A Off
  V Decelerate/set
  SP Resume
  B Accelerate/set
33 Washer pump
34 Solenoid valve, automatic transmission
35 Kick-down switch
36 Starter lockout and backup lamp
  switch
37 Connector, electronic radio
38 Lighting switch
39 Starter switch
40 Intermittent wiping timer
41 Wiper motor
42 Preglow time relay with glow plugs
43 Automatic antenna
44 Switch, automatic antenna
45 Door contact switch, rear, right
46 Door contact switch, rear, left

47 Rear door contact switch
48 Rear dome lamp
49 Window lift motor, rear, left
50 Switch, window, rear, left
51 Switch cluster, window lifts
  a Switch, window, rear, left
  b Safety switch
  c Switch, window, front, left
  d Switch, window, front, right
  e Switch, window, rear, right
52 Window lift motor, front, left
53 Window lift motor, front, right
54 Switch, window, rear, right
55 Window lift motor, rear, right
56 Time-lag relay, heated rear window
57 Trunk lamps
58 Switch, heated rear window
59 Plug connection, tail lamp cable
  harness
60 Alternator w/electronic regulator
61 Battery
62 Starter
63 Cigar lighter with ashtray illumination
64 Radio
65 Tail lamp unit, right
  a Side marker lamp
  b Turn signal lamp
  c Tail/standing lamp
  d Backup lamp
  e Stop lamp
66 Fuel gauge sendig unit
67 License plate lamp
68 Heated rear window
69 Tail lamp unit, left
  a Side marker lamp
  b Turn signal lamp
  c Tail/standing lamp
  d Backup lamp
  e Stop lamp

* Special equipment
X Automatic climate control connection

Wire Color Code

bl	= blue	nf	= neutral
br	= brown	rs	= pink
el	= ivory	rt	= red
ge	= yellow	sw	= black
gn	= green	vi	= purple
gr	= grey	ws	= white

Example:
Wire designation 1.5 gr/rt
Basic color gr = grey
Identification color rt = red
Cross section of wire 1.5 = 1.5 mm^2

Ground connections

M1 Main ground
  (behind instrument cluster)
M2 Ground, front, right
  (near headlamp unit)
M4 Ground, dome lamp, front
M5 Ground, engine
M6 Ground, trunk, wheelhouse, left
M7 Ground, trunk, wheelhouse, right

Key to 1981 300TD (123.193) (US) wiring diagram

1 Headlamp unit, left
  a High beam
  b Low beam
  c Parking/standing lamp
  d Fog lamp
  e Turn signal lamp
2 Brake fluid indicator switch
3 Contact sensor, brake pads, left front
4 Contact sensor, brake pads, right front
5 Instrument cluster
  a Turn signal indicator, left
  b High beam indicator
  c Coolant temperature gauge
  d Fuel gauge
  e Fuel reserve warning lamp
  f Charge indicator
  g Brake pad wear indicator
  h Brake fluid and parking brake indicator
  i Instrument lamps
  j Rheostat, instrument lamps
  k Warning buzzer
  l Turn signal indicator, right
  m Electronic clock
  n Preglow indicator lamp
6 Headlamp unit, right
  a High beam
  b Low beam
  c Parking/standing lamp
  d Fog lamp
  e Turn signal lamp
7 Actuator, Tempomat*
8 Switch, Tempomat*
  A Off
  V Decelerate/set
  SP Resume
  B Accelerate/set
9 Sensor, Tempomat*
10 Parking brake indicator switch
11 Temperature sensor, coolant
12 Pressure switch, charge air pipe
13 Warning buzzer contact
14 Dome lamp, front, with switch
15 Door contact switch, left front
16 Door contact switch, right front
17 Dual-tone horn (fanfare)
18 Warning flasher switch/timer
19 Horn contact
20 Combination switch
  a Turn signal switch
  b Headlamp flasher switch
  c Dimmer switch
  d Washer switch
  e Switch, wiping speed
    I Intermittent wiping
    II Slow wiping
    III Fast wiping

21 Glove compartment lamp switch
22 Glove compartment lamp
23 Fuse box
24 Amplifier, Tempomat*
25 Relay I window lifts*
26 Relay II window lifts*
27 Door contact switch, window lifts*
28 Cable connector, stop light
29 TDC transmitter
30 Adapter, TDC transmitter
31 Switch-over valve, overload protection device
32 Lighting switch
33 Starter switch
34 Intermittent wiping timer
35 Wiper motor
36 Wiper motor, headlamp, right*
37 Wiper motor, headlamp, left*
38 Washer pump
39 Stop lamp switch
40 Relay, headlamp cleaning system*
41 Washer pump, headlamps*
42 Preglow time relay
43 Glow plugs
44 Blower switch with lamp
45 Illumination
  a Air deflector control
  b Heater control
  c Switch
  d Temperature control, air conditioning*
46 Relay, air conditioning (refrigerant compressor)*
47 Pressure switch, refrigerant compressor*
  On 2.6 bar, Off 2.0 bar
48 Electromagnetic clutch, refrigerant compressor*
49 Pressure switch, transmission
50 Switching unit, engine overload protection device
51 Solenoid valve, automatic transmission
52 Kickdown switch
53 Starter lockout and backup lamp switch*
54 Temperature switch 62 °C (144 °F) receiver drier*
55 Auxiliary fan*
56 Relay, auxiliary fan*
57 Switch-over valve, fresh/recirculating air flap
58 Temperature sensor, air conditioning
59 Temperature control, air conditioning
60 Pre-resistance, blower motor
61 Blower motor

62 Window lift motor, left rear*
63 Switch, window, left rear*
64 Switch cluster, window lifts*
  a Switch, window, left rear
  b Safety switch
  c Switch, window, left front
  d Switch, window, right front
  e Switch, window, right rear
65 Window lift motor, left front*
66 Window lift motor, right front*
67 Automatic antenna*
68 Plug connection, tail lamp cable harness
69 Time-lag relay, heated rear window
70 Fuel gauge sending unit
71 Detent switch, wiper motor, rear door/ Detent switch, intermittent wiping, rear door
72 Dome lamp, rear, with switch
73 Wiper motor, rear door
74 Switch, heated rear window
75 Illumination, shift plate*
76 Intermittent wiping timer, rear door
77 Alternator w/electronic regulator
79 Battery
80 Starter
81 Cigar lighter with ashtray illumination
82 Radio*
83 Window lift motor, right rear*
84 Switch, window, right rear*
85 Tail lamp unit, left
  a Turn signal lamp
  b Tail/standing lamp
  c Stop lamp
86 Rear fog lamp
87 Washer pump, rear door
88 Detent switch, rear dome lamp/ Push-button switch, washer pump, rear door
89 License plate lamp
90 Cable connector, rear door
91 Heated rear window
92 Door contact switch, left rear*
93 Door contact switch, right rear*
94 Rear door contact switch
95 Ground connection, rear door
96 Backup lamp
97 Tail lamp unit, right
  a Turn signal lamp
  b Tail/standing lamp
  c Stop lamp

*   Special equipment

Ground connections

M1 Main ground (behind instrument cluster)
M2 Ground, right front (near headlamp unit)
M3 Ground, wheelhouse, left front (ignition coil)
M4 Ground, dome lamp, front
M5 Ground engine
M6 Ground, trunk, wheelhouse, left
M7 Ground, trunk, wheelhouse, right
M8 Ground, rear door (8-pin connector)

M1 (60)
  └ Position number of the component over which the ground line is looped
  Ground connection

Wire Color Code

bl	=	blue	nf	=	neutral
br	=	brown	rs	=	pink
el	=	ivory	rt	=	red
ge	=	yellow	sw	=	black
gn	=	green	vi	=	purple
gr	=	grey	ws	=	white

Example:
Wire designation 1.5 gr/rt
Basic color gr = grey
Identification color rt = red
Cross section of wire 1.5 = 1.5 mm^2

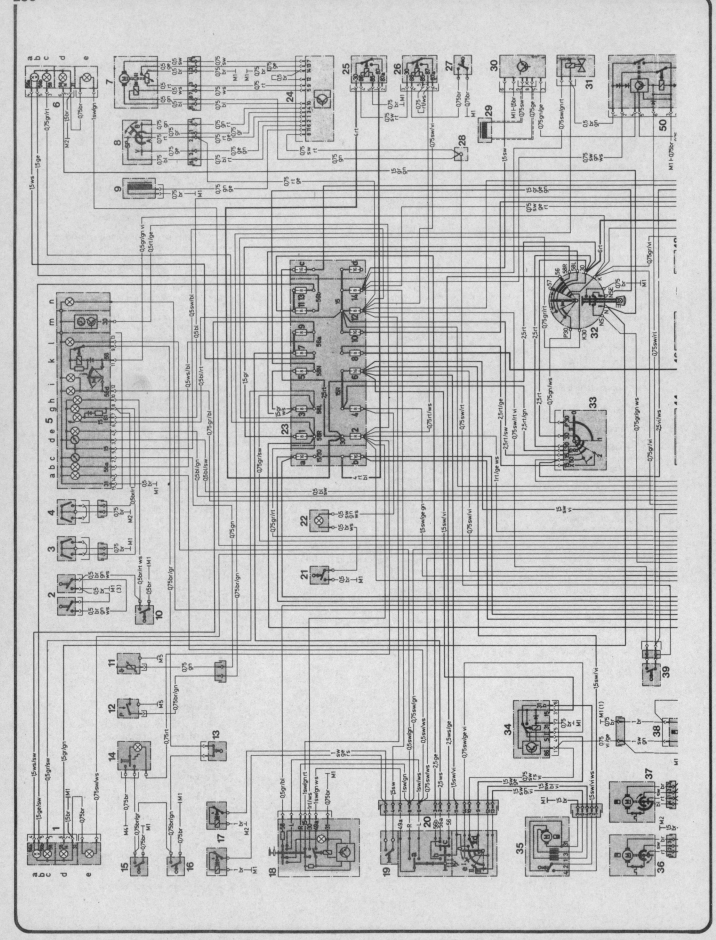

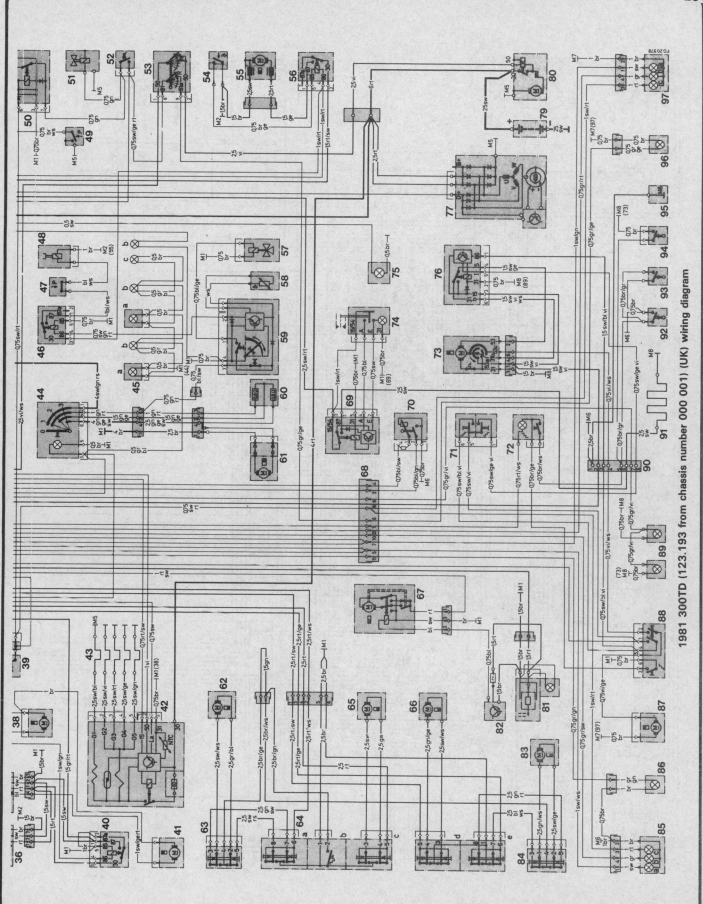

281

1981 300TD (123.193 from chassis number 000 001) (UK) wiring diagram

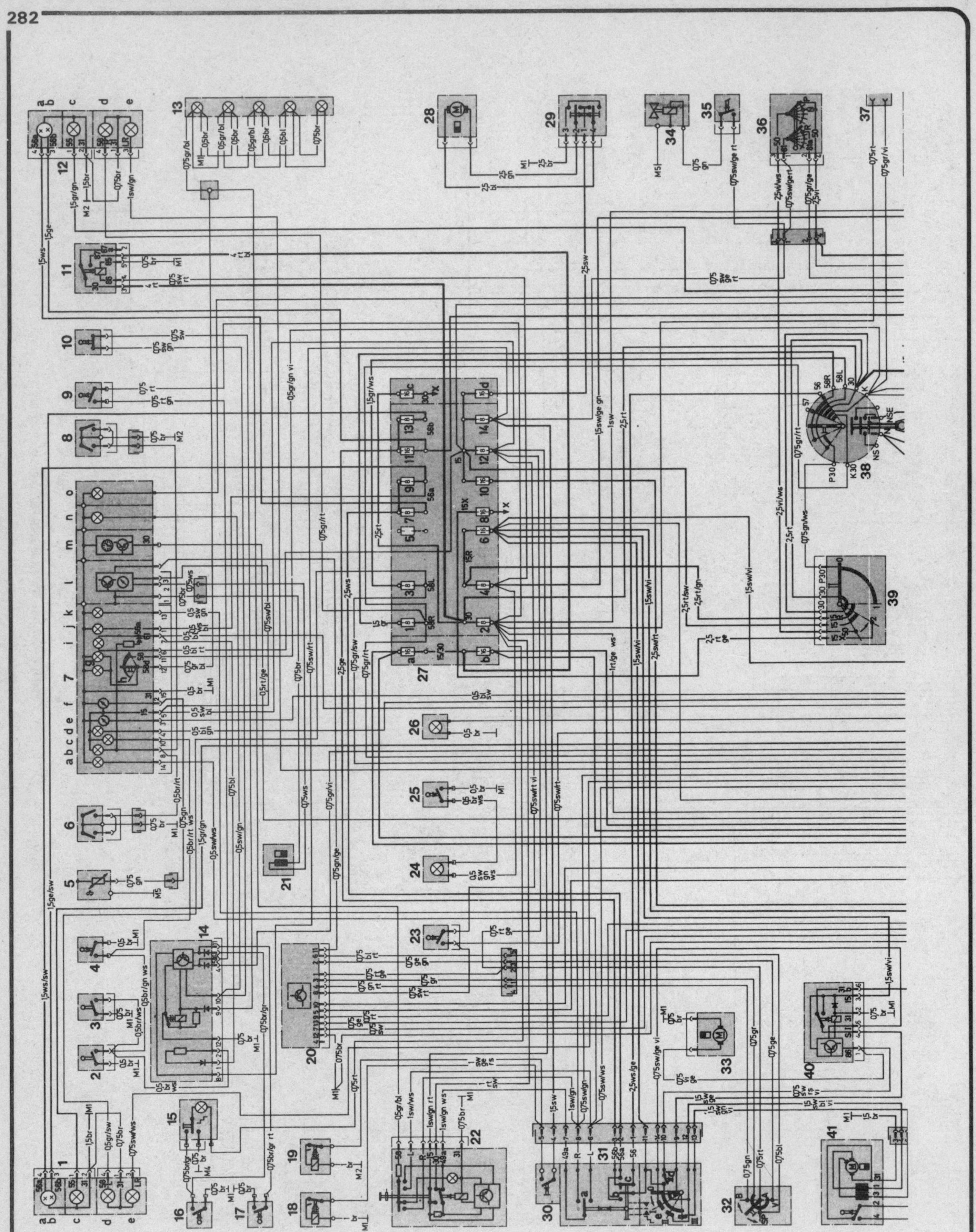
1
2
3
4
5
6
7
8
9
10
11
12
13
14
15
16
17
18
19
20
21
22
23
24
25
26
27
28
29
30
31
32
33
34
35
36
37
38
39
40
41

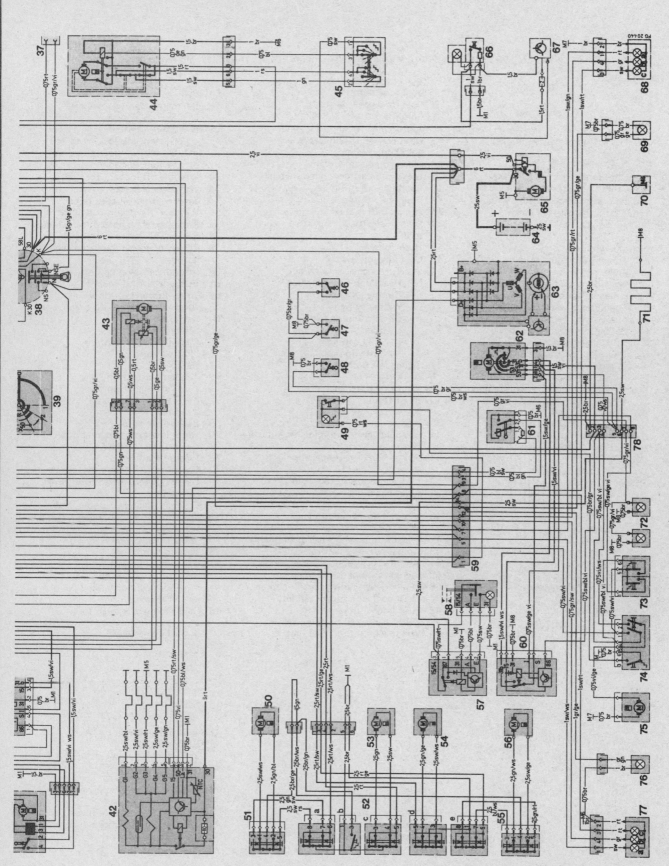

1981 300TD (123.193) (US) wiring diagram

Key to 1981 300TD (123.193 from chassis number 000 001) (UK) wiring diagram

1 Headlamp unit, left
  a High beam
  b Low beam
  c Fog lamp
  d Parking/standing/side marker lamp
  e Turn signal lamp
2 Brake fluid indicator lamp switch I
3 Brake fluid indicator lamp switch II
4 Parking brake indicator lamp switch
5 Temperature sensor, coolant
6 Contact sensor, brake pads, front, left
7 Instrument cluster
  a Turn signal indicator lamp, left
  b Brake pad wear indicator lamp
  c Brake fluid and parking brake indicator lamp
  d Fuel reserve warning lamp
  e Fuel gauge
  f Coolant temperature gauge
  g Instrument lamps
  h Rheostat, instrument lamps
  i Charge indicator lamp
  j High beam indicator lamp
  k Turn signal indicator lamp, right
  l Electronic speedometer
  m Electronic clock
  n Seat belt system warning lamp
  o Preglow indicator lamp
8 Contact sensor, brake pads, front, right
9 Warning buzzer contact
10 Driver's belt buckle switch
11 Relay, window lifts
12 Headlamp unit, right
  a High beam
  b Low beam
  c Fog lamp
  d Parking/standing/side marker lamp
  e Turn signal lamp
13 Illumination, heater controls
14 Warning device
15 Front dome lamp w/switch
16 Door contact switch, front, right
17 Door contact switch, front, left

18 Dual-tone horn (fanfare)
19 Dual-tone horn (fanfare)
20 Amplifier, cruise control
21 Sensor, electronic speedometer
22 Warning flasher switch/timer
23 Stop lamp switch
24 Glove compartment lamp
25 Glove compartment lamp switch
26 Illumination, shift plate
27 Fuse box
28 Sliding roof motor*
29 Switch, electrically operated sliding roof*
30 Horn contact
31 Combination switch
  a Turn signal lamp switch
  b Headlamp flasher switch
  c Dimmer switch
  d Washer switch
  e Switch, wiping speed
    I Intermittent wiping
    II Slow wiping
    III Fast wiping
32 Switch, cruise control
  A Off
  V Decelerate/set
  SP Resume
  B Accelerate/set
33 Washer pump
34 Solenoid valve, automatic transmission
35 Kick-down switch
36 Starter lockout and backup lamp switch
37 Connector, electronic radio
38 Lighting switch
39 Starter switch
40 Intermittent wiping timer
41 Wiper motor
42 Preglow time relay with glow plugs
43 Actuator, cruise control
44 Automatic antenna
45 Switch, automatic antenna
46 Door contact switch, rear, right
47 Door contact switch, rear, left
48 Rear door contact switch
49 Dome lamp, rear, with switch
50 Window lift motor, rear, left

51 Switch, window, rear, left
52 Switch cluster, window lifts
  a Switch, window, rear, left
  b Safety switch
  c Switch, window, front, left
  d Switch, window, front right
  e Switch, window, rear, right
53 Window lift motor, front, left
54 Window lift motor, front, right
55 Switch, window, rear, right
56 Window lift motor, rear, right
57 Time-lag relay, heated rear window
58 Switch, heated rear window
59 Plug connection, tail lamp cable harness
60 Intermittent wiping timer, rear door
61 Fuel guage sending unit
62 Wiper motor, rear door
63 Alternator w/electornic regulator
64 Battery
65 Starter
66 Cigar lighter with ashtray illumination
67 Radio
68 Tail lamp unit, right
  a Turn signal lamp
  b Tail/standing lamp
  c Stop lamp
69 Backup lamp, left
70 Ground connection, rear door
71 Heated rear window
72 License plate lamp
73 Detent switch, wiper motor rear door
   Detent switch, intermittent wipe, rear door
74 Detent switch, rear dome lamp
   Push-button switch, washer pump, rear door
75 Washer pump, rear door
76 Backup lamp, right
77 Tail lamp unit, left
  a Turn signal lamp
  b Tail/standing lamp
  c Stop lamp
78 Cable connector, rear door

*   Special equipment

Wire Color Code
bl = blue   nf = neutral
br = brown   rs = pink
el = ivory   rt = red
ge = yellow   sw = black
gn = green   vi = purple
gr = grey   ws = white

Example:
Wire designation 1.5 gr/rt
Basic color gr = grey
Identifiaction color rt = red
Cross section of wire 1.5 = 1.5 mm^2

Ground connections
M1 Main ground (behind instrument cluster)
M2 Ground, front, right (near headlamp unit)
M4 Ground, dome lamp, front
M5 Ground, engine
M6 Ground, trunk, wheelhouse, left
M7 Ground, trunk, wheelhouse, right
M8 Ground, rear door

Key to 1982 240D (123.123) (US) wiring diagram

1 Headlamp unit, left
  a High beam
  b Low beam
  c Fog lamp
  d Parking/standing/side marker lamp
  e Turn signal lamp
2 Brake fluid indicator lamp switch I
3 Brake fluid indicator lamp switch II
4 Parking brake indicator lamp switch
5 Temperature sensor, coolant
6 Contact sensor, brake pads, front, left
  a Turn signal indicator lamp, left
  b Brake pad wear indicator lamp
  c Brake fluid and parking brake
     indicator lamp
  d Fuel reserve warning lamp
  e Fuel gauge
  f Coolant temperature gauge
  g Instrument lamps
  h Rheostat, instrument lamps
  i Charge indicator lamp
  j High beam indicator lamp
  k Turn signal indicator lamp, right
  l Electronic clock
  m Seat belt warning lamp
  n Preglow indicator lamp
7 Instrument cluster
8 Contact sensor, brake pads, front, right
9 Warning buzzer contact
10 Driver's belt buckle switch
11 Relay window lifts
12 Headlamp unit, right
  a High beam
  b Low beam
  c Fog lamp
  d Parking/standing/side marker lamp
  e Turn signal lamp
13 Temperature sensor preglow indicator
14 Warning device
15 Front dome lamp w/switch
16 Door contact switch, left
17 Door contact switch, right
18 Dual-tone horn (fanfare)
19 Sensor, cruise control system*
20 Amplifier, cruise control*
21 Actuator, cruise control*
22 Electromagnetic clutch,
   refrigerant compressor*

22a Pressure switch, refrigerant compressor
    On 2.6 bar, Off 2.0 bar*
23 Sliding roof motor*
24 Switch, electrically operated sliding roof*
25 Fuse box
26 Illumination, shift plate*
27 Glove compartment lamp switch
28 Glove compartment lamp
29 Stop lamp switch
30 Warning flasher switch/timer
31 Horn contact
32 Combination switch
  a Turn signal lamp switch
  b Headlamp flasher switch
  c Dimmer switch
  d Washer switch
  e Switch, wiping speed
     I   Intermittent wiping
     II Slow wiping
     III Fast wiping
33 Solenoid valve, automatic transmission*
34 Kick-down switch*
35 Starter lockout and backup lamp switch*
36 Lighting switch
37 Ignition starter switch
38 Relay, auxiliary fan*
39 Washer pump
40 Switch, cruise control*
  A Off
  V Decelerate/set
  SP Resume
  B Accelerate/set
41 Wiper motor
42 Intermittent wiping timer
43 Pencil element glow plugs
44 Auxiliary fan*
46 Blower switch with lamp
48 Relay, air conditioner II*
49 Automatic antenna*
50 Switch, automatic antenna*
51 Illumination
  a Air defelctor control
  b Heater control
  c Switch
52 Temperature switch 62 °C (144 °F)
   receiver drier*
53 Preglow time relay
54 Switch, window, rear, left*

55 Window lift motor, rear, left*
56 Time-lag relay, heated rear window
57 Switch cluster, window lifts*
  a Switch, window, rear, left
  b Safety switch
  c Switch, window, front, left
  d Switch, window, front, right
  e Switch, window, rear, right
58 Window lift motor, front, left*
59 Window lift motor, front, right*
60 Switch, heated rear window
61 Blower motor
62 Pre-resistance, blower motor
63 Temperature control w/lighting,
   air conditioner*
66 Cigar lighter with ashtray illumination
67 Radio*
68 Door contact switch, rear, left*
69 Rear dome lamp switch*
70 Door contact switch, rear, right*
71 Rear dome lamp*
72 Starter
73 Battery
74 Alternator w/electronic regulator
75 Fuel gauge sending unit
76 Plug connection, tail lamp
   cable harness
77 Trunk lamp
78 Window lift motor, rear, right*
79 Switch, window, rear, right*
80 Tail lamp unit, left
  a Side marker lamp
  b Turn signal lamp
  c Tail/standing lamp
  d Backup lamp
  e Stop lamp
81 Heated rear window
82 License plate lamp
83 Tail lamp unit, right
  a Side marker lamp
  b Turn signal lamp
  c Tail/standing lamp
  d Backup lamp
  e Stop lamp

* Special equipment

Wire Color Code

bl = blue	nf = neutral	
br = brown	rs = pink	
el = ivory	rt = red	
ge = yellow	sw = black	
gn = green	vi = purple	
gr = grey	ws = white	

Example:
Wire designation 1.5 gr/rt
Basic color gr = grey
Identification color rt = red
Cross section of wire 1.5 = 1.5 mm²

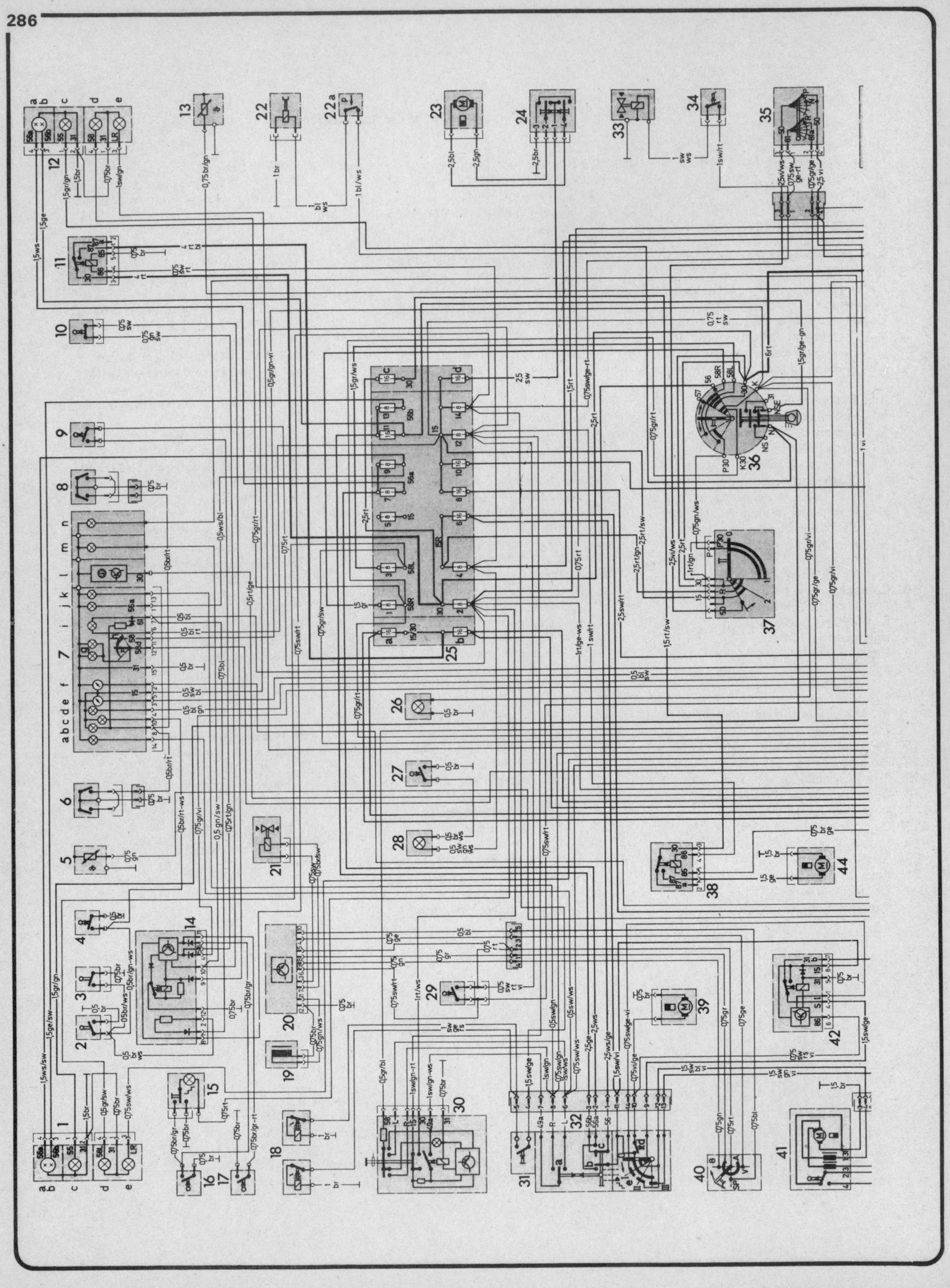

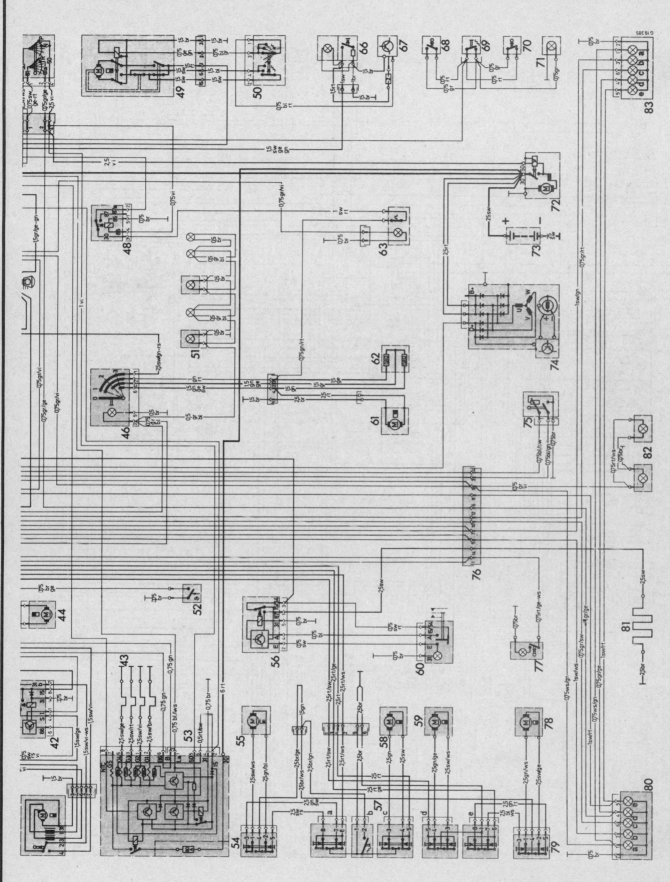

1982 240D (123.123) (US) wiring diagram

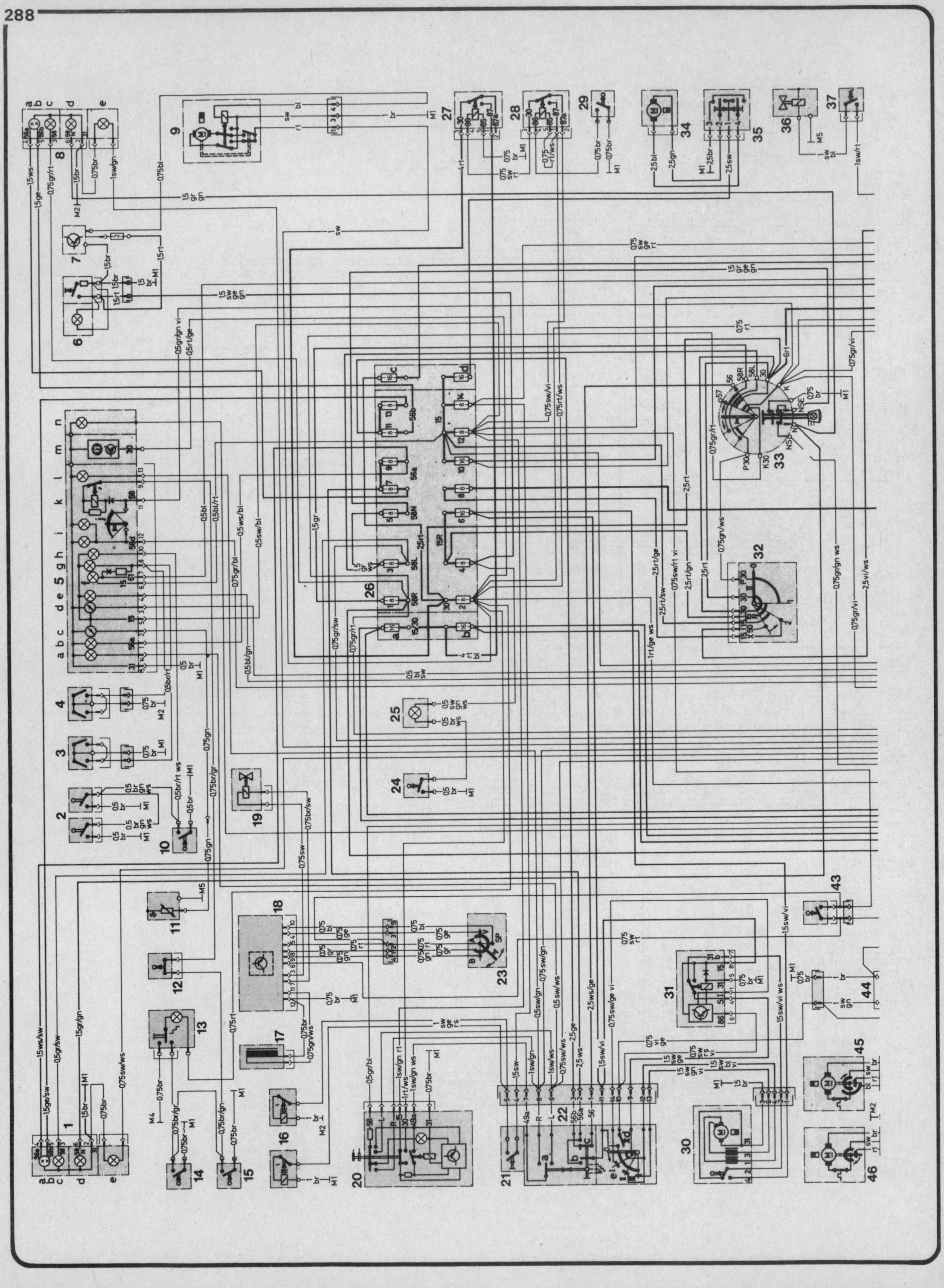

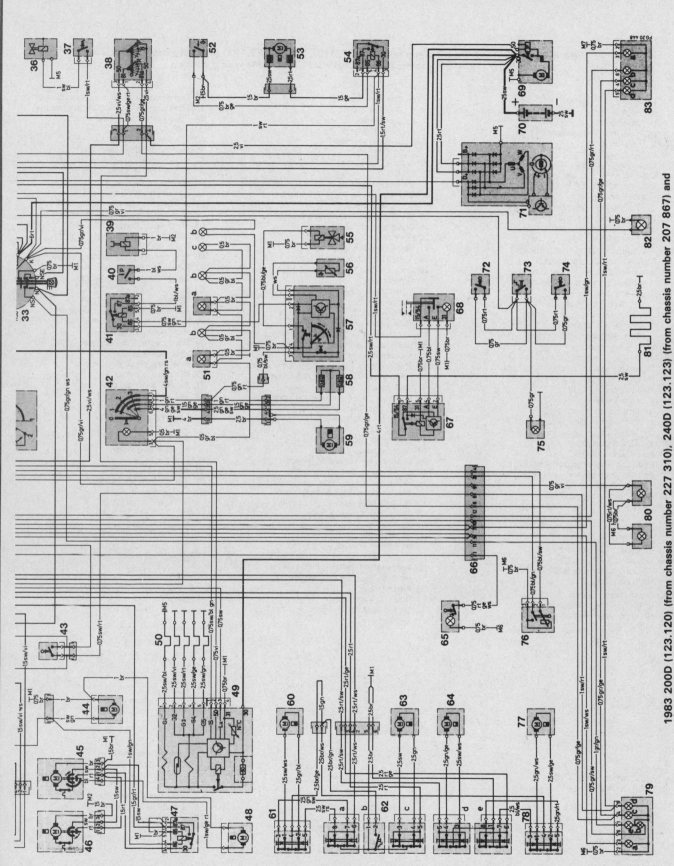

1983 200D (123.120) (from chassis number 227 310), 240D (123.123) (from chassis number 207 867) and 300D (123.130) (from chassis number 211 267) (UK) wiring diagram

Key to 1983 200D (123.120) (from chassis number 227 310), 240D (123.123) (from chassis number 207 867) and 300D (123.130) (from chassis number 211 267) (UK) wiring diagram

1 Headlamp unit, right
  a High beam
  b Low beam
  c Parking/standing lamp
  d Fog lamp
  e Turn signal lamp
2 Brake fluid indicator lamp switch
3 Contact sensor, brake pads, front, left
4 Contact sensor, brake pads, front, right
5 Instrument cluster
  a Turn signal indicator lamp, left
  b High beam indicator lamp
  c Coolant temperature gauge
  d Fuel gauge
  e Fuel reserve warning lamp
  f Charge indicator lamp
  g Brake pad wear indicator lamp
  h Brake fluid and parking brake indicator lamp
  i Instrument lamps
  j Rheostat, instrument lamps
  k Warning buzzer
  l Turn signal indicator lamp, right
  m Electronic clock
  n Preglow indicator lamp
6 Cigar lighter with ashtray illumination
7 Radio*
8 Headlamp unit, right
  a High beam
  b Low beam
  c Parking/standing lamp
  d Fog lamp
  e Turn signal lamp
9 Automatic antenna*
10 Parking brake indicator lamp switch
11 Temperature sensor, coolant
12 Warning buzzer contact
13 Front dome lamp w/switch
14 Door contact switch, front left
15 Door contact switch, front, right
16 Dual-tone horn (fanfare)
17 Sensor, Tempomat*[2]
18 Amplifier, Tempomat*[2]
19 Actuator, Tempomat*[2]
20 Warning flasher switch/timer
21 Horn contact
22 Combination switch
  a Turn signal lamp switch
  b Headlamp flasher switch

  c Dimmer switch
  d Washer switch
  e Switch, wiping speed
    I Intermittent wiping
    II Slow wiping
    III Fast wiping
23 Switch, Tempomat*[2]
  A Off
  V Decelerate/set
  SP Resume
  B Accelerate/set
24 Glove compartment lamp switch
25 Glove compartment lamp
26 Fuse box
27 Relay I window lifts*
28 Relay II window lifts*
29 Door contact switch, window lifts*
30 Wiper motor
31 Intermittent wiping timer
32 Starter switch
33 Lighting switch
34 Sliding roof motor*
35 Switch, electrically operated sliding roof*
36 Solenoid valve, automatic transmission*
37 Kick-down switch*
38 Starter lockout and backup lamp switch
39 Electromagnetic clutch, refrigerant compressor*
40 Pressure switch, refrigerant compressor On 2.6 bar, Off 2.0 bar
41 Relay, air conditioner*
42 Blower witch with lamp
43 Stop lamp switch
44 Washer pump
45 Wiper motor headlamp, right*
46 Wiper motor, headlamp, left*
47 Relay, headlamp cleaning system*
48 Washer pump, headlamps*
49 Preglow time relay
50 Pencil element glow plugs[1]
51 Illumination
  a Air deflector control
  b Heater control
  c Switch*
52 Temperature switch 52 °C (126 °F) receiver drier, air conditioner*
53 Auxiliary fan*
54 Relay, auxiliary fan*
55 Switch-over valve, fresh/recirculating air flap*

56 Temperature sensor, air conditioner*
57 Temperature control, air conditioner*
58 Pre-resistance, blower motor
59 Blower motor
60 Window lift motor, rear, left*
61 Switch, window, rear, left*
62 Switch cluster, window lifts*
  a Switch, window, rear, left
  b Safety switch
  c Switch, window, front, left
  d Switch, window, front, right
  e Switch, window, rear, right
63 Window lift motor, front, left*
64 Window lift motor, front, right*
65 Trunk lamp
66 Plug connection, tail lamp cable harness
67 Time-lag relay, heated rear window
68 Switch, heated rear window
69 Starter
70 Battery
71 Alternator w/electronic regulator
72 Door contact switch, rear, left*
73 Rear dome lamp switch*
74 Door contact switch, rear, right*
75 Rear dome lamp*
76 Fuel gauge sending unit
77 Window lift motor, rear, right*
78 Switch, window, rear, right*
79 Tail lamp unit, left
  a Turn signal lamp
  b Tail/standing lamp
  c Backup lamp
  d Stop lamp
  e Rear fog lamp
80 License plate lamps
81 Heated rear window
82 Illumination, shift plate
83 Tail lamp unit, right
  a Turn signal lamp
  b Tail/standing lamp
  c Backup lamp
  d Stop lamp

*Special equipment

[1] 200 D, 240 D
  4 Pencil element glow plugs
[2] only 300 D

Wire Color Code

bl	= blue	nf	= neutral
br	= brown	rs	= pink
el	= ivory	rt	= red
ge	= yellow	sw	= black
gn	= green	vi	= purple
gr	= grey	ws	= white

Example:
Wire designation 1.5 gr/rt
Basic color gr = grey
Identification color rt = red
Cross section of wire 1.5 = 1.5 mm^2

Ground connections
M1 Main ground (behind instrument cluster)
M2 Ground, front, right (near headlamp unit)
M4 Ground, dome lamp, front
M5 Ground, engine
M6 Ground, trunk, wheelhouse, left
M7 Ground, trunk, wheelhouse, right

Key to 1983 240TD (123.183) (from chassis number 013 252) and 300TD (123.190) (from chassis number 019 972) (UK) wiring diagram

1 Headlamp unit, left
  a High beam
  b Low beam
  c Parking/standing lamp
  d Fog lamp
  e Turn signal lamp
2 Brake fluid indicator lamp switch
3 Contact sensor, brake pads, front, left
4 Contact sensor, brake pads, front, right
5 Instrument cluster
  a Turn signal indicator lamp, left
  b High beam indicator lamp
  c Coolant temperature gauge
  d Fuel gauge
  e Fuel reserve warning lamp
  f Charge indicator lamp
  g Brake pad wear indicator lamp
  h Brake fluid and parking brake indicator lamp
  i Instrument lamps
  j Rheostat, instrument lamps
  k Warning buzzer
  l Turn signal indicator lamp, right
  m Electronic clock
  n Preglow indicator lamp
6 Cigar lighter with ashtray illumination
7 Radio*
8 Headlamp unit, right
  a High beam
  b Low beam
  c Parking/standing lamp
  d Fog lamp
  e Turn signal lamp
9 Automatic antenna*
10 Parking brake indicator lamp switch
11 Temperature sensor, coolant
12 Warning buzzer contact
13 Front dome lamp w/switch
14 Door contact switch, front left
15 Door contact switch, front, right
16 Dual-tone horn (fanfare)
17 Sensor, Tempomat*[2]
18 Amplifier, Tempomat*[2]
19 Actuator, Tempomat*[2]
20 Warning flasher switch/timer
21 Horn contact
22 Combination switch
  a Turn signal lamp switch
  b Headlamp flasher switch
  c Dimmer switch

  d Washer switch
  e Switch, wiping speed
    I Intermittent wiping
    II Slow wiping
    III Fast wiping
23 Switch, Tempomat*[2]
  A Off
  V Decelerate/set
  SP Resume
  B Accelerate/set
24 Glove compartment lamp switch
25 Glove compartment lamp
26 Fuse box
27 Relay I window lifts*
28 Relay II window lifts*
29 Door contact switch, window lifts*
30 Wiper motor
31 Intermittent wiping timer
32 Starter switch
33 Lighting switch
34 Sliding roof motor*
35 Switch, electrically operated sliding roof*
36 Solenoid valve, automatic transmission*
37 Kick-down switch*
38 Starter lockout and backup lamp switch
39 Electromagnetic clutch, refrigerant compressor*
40 Pressure switch, refrigerant compressor On 2.6 bar, Off 2.0 bar
41 Relay, air conditioner*
42 Blower switch with lamp
43 Stop lamp switch
44 Washer pump
45 Wiper motor, headlamp, right*
46 Wiper motor, headlamp, left*
47 Relay, headlamp cleaning system*
48 Washer pump, headlamps*
49 Preglow time relay
50 Pencil element glow plugs[1]
51 Illumination
  a Air deflector control
  b Heater control
  c Switch*
52 Temperature switch 52 °C (126 °F) receiver drier, air conditioner*
53 Auxiliary fan*
54 Relay, auxiliary fan*
55 Switch-over valve, fresh/recirculating air flap*

56 Temperature sensor, air conditioner*
57 Temperature control, air conditioner*
58 Pre-resistance, blower motor
59 Blower motor
60 Window lift motor, rear, left*
61 Switch, window, rear, left*
62 Switch cluster, window lifts*
  a Switch, window, rear, left
  b Safety switch
  c Switch, window, front, left
  d Switch, window, front, right
  e Switch, window, rear, right
63 Window lift motor, front, left*
64 Window lift motor, front, right*
65 Detent switch, wiper motor, rear door
    Detent switch, intermittent wiping, rear door
66 Time-lag relay, heated rear window
67 Switch, heated rear window
68 Illumination, shift plate
69 Starter
70 Battery
71 Alternator w/electronic regulator
72 Intermittent wiping timer, rear door
73 Wiper motor, rear door
74 Fuel gauge sending unit
75 Plug connection, tail lamp cable harness
76 Dome lamp, rear, with switch
77 Window lift motor, rear, right*
78 Switch, window, rear, right*
79 Tail lamp unit, left
  a Turn signal lamp
  b Tail/standing lamp
  c Stop lamp
80 Rear fog lamp
81 Washer pump, rear door
82 Detent switch, rear dome lamp
    Push-button switch washer pump, rear door
83 License plate lamp
84 Heated rear window
85 Door contact switch, rear, left*
86 Door contact switch, rear, right*
87 Rear door contact switch
88 Ground connection, rear door
89 Backup lamp
90 Tail lamp unit, right
  a Turn signal lamp
  b Tail/standing lamp
  c Stop lamp

*Special equipment
[1] 240 TD 4 Pencil element glow plugs
[2] only 300 TD

Ground connections
M1 Main ground (behind instrument cluster)
M2 Ground, front, right (near headlamp unit)
M4 Ground, dome lamp, front
M5 Ground, engine
M6 Ground, trunk, wheelhouse, left
M7 Ground, trunk, wheelhouse, right
M8 Ground, rear door

Wire Color Code

bl	= blue	nt	= neutral
br	= brown	rs	= pink
el	= ivory	rt	= red
ge	= yellow	sw	= black
gn	= green	vi	= purple
gr	= grey	ws	= white

Example:
Wire designation 1.5 gr/rt
Basic color gr = grey
Identification color rt = red
Cross section of wire 1.5 = 1.5 mm^2

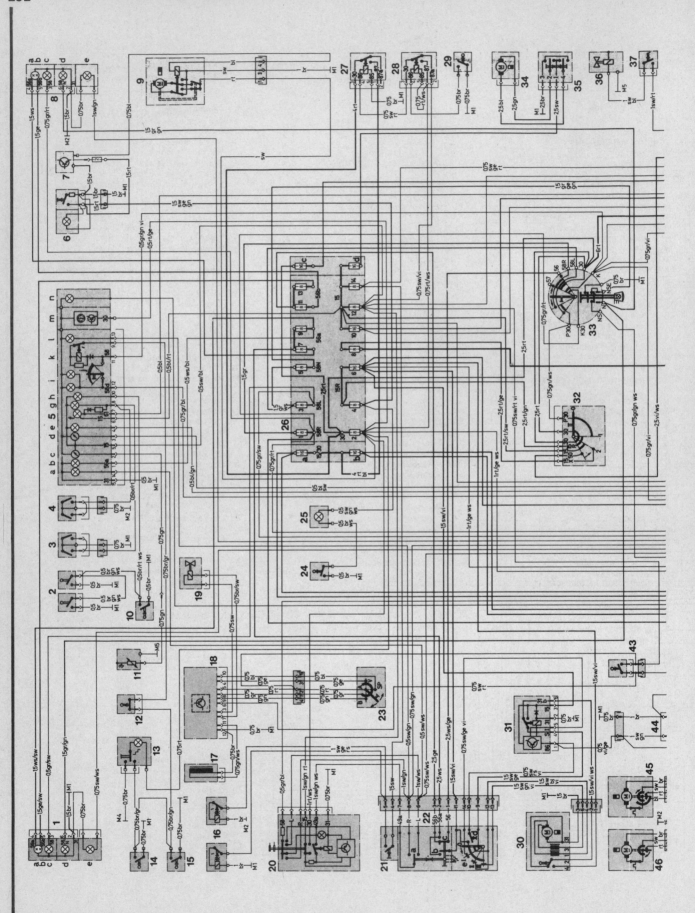

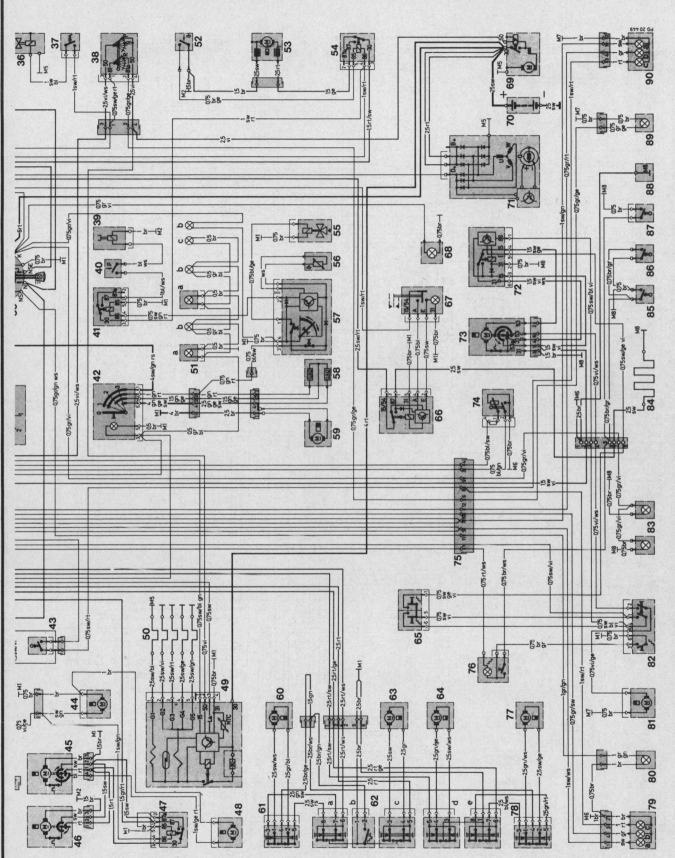

1983 240TD (123.183) (from chassis number 013 252) and 300TD (123.190) (from chassis number 019 972) (UK) wiring diagram

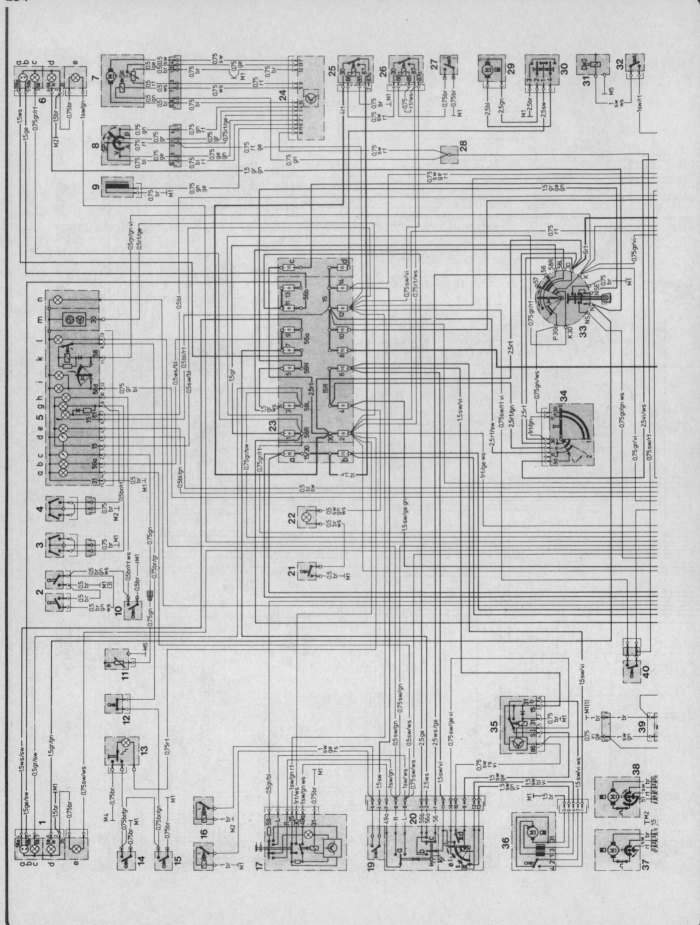

295

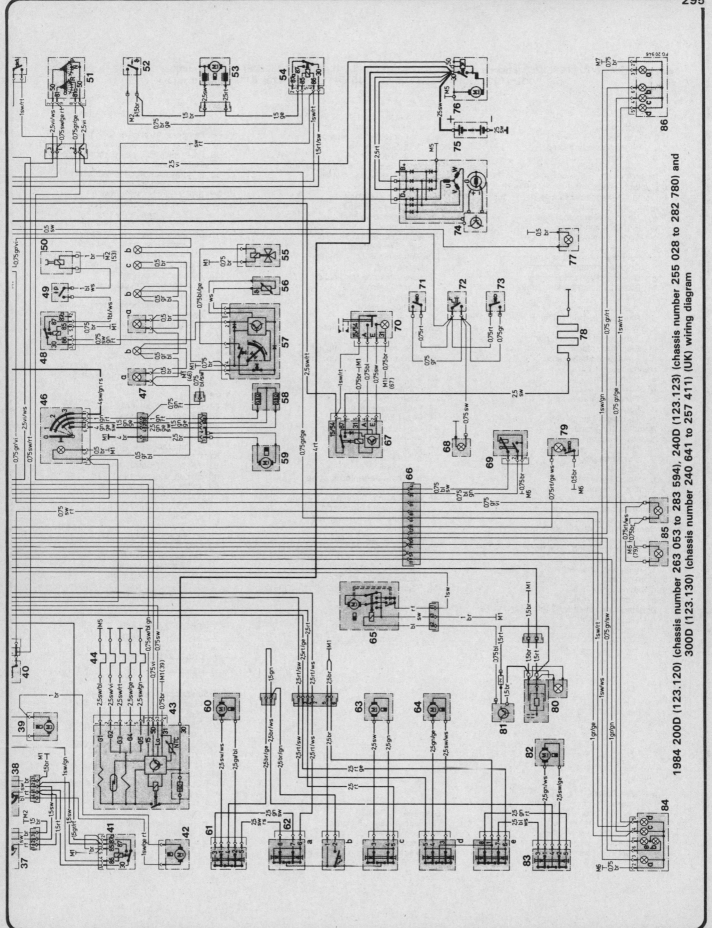

1984 200D (123.120) (chassis number 263 053 to 283 594), 240D (123.123) (chassis number 255 028 to 282 780) and 300D (123.130) (chassis number 240 641 to 257 411) (UK) wiring diagram

Key to 1984 200D (123.120) (chassis number 263 053 to 283 594), 240D (123.123) (chassis number 255 028 to 282 780) and 300D (123.130) (chassis number 240 641 to 257 411) (UK) wiring diagram

1 Headlamp unit, left
   a High beam
   b Low beam
   c Parking/standing lamp
   d Fog lamp
   e Turn signal lamp
2 Brake fluid indicator switch
3 Contact sensor, brake pads, left front
4 Contact sensor, brake pads, right front
5 Instrument cluster
   a Turn signal indicator, left
   b High beam indicator
   c Coolant temperature gauge
   d Fuel gauge
   e Fuel reserve warning lamp
   f Charge indicator
   g Brake pad wear indicator
   h Brake fluid and parking brake indicator
   i Instrument lamps
   j Rheostat, instrument lamps
   k Warning buzzer
   l Turn signal indicator, right
   m Electronic clock
   n Preglow indicator lamp
6 Headlamp unit, right
   a High beam
   b Low beam
   c Parking/standing lamp
   d Fog lamp
   e Turn signal lamp
7 Actuator, Tempomat[1]
8 Switch, Tempomat[1]
   A Off
   V Decelerate/set
   SP Resume
   B Accelerate/set
9 Sensor, Tempomat[1]
10 Parking brake indicator switch
11 Temperature sensor, coolant
12 Warning buzzer contact
13 Dome lamp, front, with switch
14 Door contact switch, left front
15 Door contact switch, right front
16 Dual-tone horn (fanfare)
17 Warning flasher switch/timer
19 Horn contact
20 Combination switch
   a Turn signal switch
   b Headlamp flasher switch
   c Dimmer switch

   d Washer switch
   e Switch, wiping speed
      I Intermittent wiping
      II Slow wiping
      III Fast wiping
21 Glove compartment lamp switch
22 Glove compartment lamp
23 Fuse box
24 Amplifier, Tempomat[1]
25 Relay I window lifts*
26 Relay II window lifts*
27 Door contact switch, window lifts*
28 Cable connector, stop light
29 Sliding roof motor*
30 Switch, electrically operated sliding roof*
31 Solenoid valve, automatic transmission*
32 Kickdown switch*
33 Lighting switch
34 Starter switch
35 Intermittent wiping timer
36 Wiper motor
37 Wiper motor, headlamp, left*
38 Wiper motor, headlamp, right*
39 Washer pump
40 Stop lamp switch
41 Relay, headlamp cleaning system*
42 Washer pump, headlamps*
43 Preglow time relay
44 Glow plugs[2]
46 Blower switch with lamp
47 Illumination
   a Air deflector control
   b Heater control
   c Switch
   d Temperature control, air conditioning*
48 Relay, air conditioning (refrigerant compressor)*
49 Pressure switch, refrigerant compressor*
   On 2.6 bar, Off 2.0 bar
50 Electromagnetic clutch, refrigerant compressor*
51 Starter lockout and backup lamp switch*
52 Temperature switch 62 °C (144 °F) receiver drier*
53 Auxiliary fan*
54 Relay, auxiliary fan*

55 Switch-over valve, fresh/recirculating air flap*
56 Temperature sensor, air conditioning*
57 Temperature control, air conditioning*
58 Pre-resistance, blower motor
59 Blower motor
60 Window lift motor, left rear*
61 Switch, window, left rear*
62 Switch cluster, window lifts*
   a Switch, window, left rear
   b Safety switch
   c Switch, window, left front
   d Switch, window, right front
   e Switch, window, right rear
63 Window lift motor, left front*
64 Window lift motor, right front*
65 Automatic antenna*
66 Plug connection, tail lamp cable harness
67 Time-lag relay, heated rear window
68 Dome lamp, rear*
69 Fuel gauge sending unit
70 Switch, heated rear window
71 Door contact switch, left rear*
72 Rear dome lamp switch*
73 Door contact switch, right rear*
74 Alternator w/electronic regulator
75 Battery
76 Starter
77 Illumination, shift plate*
78 Heated rear window
79 Trunk lamp
80 Cigar lighter with ashtray illumination
81 Radio*
82 Window lift motor, right rear*
83 Switch, window, right rear*
84 Tail lamp unit, left
   a Turn signal lamp
   b Tail/standing lamp
   c Backup lamp
   d Stop lamp
   e Rear fog lamp
85 License plate lamp
86 Tail lamp unit, right
   a Turn signal lamp
   b Tail/standing lamp
   c Backup lamp
   d Stop lamp

*   Special equipment
[1] Special equipment (only 300 D)
[2] 200 D, 240 D 4 Glow plugs

Ground connections
M1 Main ground (behind instrument cluster)
M2 Ground, right front (near headlamp unit)
M3 Ground, wheelhouse, left front (ignition coil)
M4 Ground, dome lamp, front
M5 Ground engine
M6 Ground, trunk, wheelhouse, left
M7 Ground, trunk, wheelhouse, right

M1 (60)
   └ Position number of the component over which the ground line is looped
   └─ Ground connection

Wire Color Code

bl	= blue	nf	= neutral
br	= brown	rs	= pink
el	= ivory	rt	= red
ge	= yellow	sw	= black
gn	= green	vi	= purple
gr	= grey	ws	= white

Example:
Wire designation 1.5 gr/rt
Basic color gr = grey
Identification color rt = red
Cross section of wire 1.5 = 1.5 mm^2

Key to 1984 200D (123.120) (from chassis number 283 595), 240D (123.123) (from chassis number 282 781) and 300D (123.130) (from chassis number 257 412) (UK) wiring diagram

1 Headlamp unit, left
   a   High beam
   b   Low beam
   c   Parking/standing lamp
   d   Fog lamp
   e   Turn signal lamp
2 Brake fluid indicator switch
3 Contact sensor, brake pads, left front
4 Contact sensor, brake pads, right front
5 Instrument cluster
   a   Turn signal indicator, left
   b   High beam indicator
   c   Coolant temperature gauge
   d   Fuel gauge
   e   Fuel reserve warning lamp
   f   Charge indicator
   g   Brake pad wear indicator
   h   Brake fluid and parking brake indicator
   i   Instrument lamps
   j   Rheostat, instrument lamps
   k   Warning buzzer
   l   Turn signal indicator, right
   m   Electronic clock
   n   Preglow indicator lamp
6 Headlamp unit, right
   a   High beam
   b   Low beam
   c   Parking/standing lamp
   d   Fog lamp
   e   Turn signal lamp
7 Actuator, Tempomat[1]
8 Switch, Tempomat[1]
   A   Off
   V   Decelerate/set
   SP   Resume
   B   Accelerate/set
9 Sensor, Tempomat[1]
10 Parking brake indicator switch
11 Temperature sensor, coolant
12 Warning buzzer contact
13 Dome lamp, front, with switch
14 Door contact switch, left front
15 Door contact switch, right front
16 Dual-tone horn (fanfare)
17 Warning flasher switch/timer
18 Turn signal and warning flasher relay
19 Horn contact
20 Combination switch
   a   Turn signal switch
   b   Headlamp flasher switch
   c   Dimmer switch

   d   Washer switch
   e   Switch, wiping speed
      I   Intermittent wiping
      II   Slow wiping
      III   Fast wiping
21 Glove compartment lamp switch
22 Glove compartment lamp
23 Fuse box
24 Amplifier, Tempomat[1]
25 Relay I window lifts*
26 Relay II window lifts*
27 Door contact switch, window lifts*
28 Cable connector, stop light
29 Sliding roof motor*
30 Switch, electrically operated sliding roof*
31 Solenoid valve, automatic transmission*
32 Kickdown switch*
33 Lighting switch
34 Starter switch
35 Intermittent wiping timer
36 Wiper motor
37 Wiper motor, headlamp, left*
38 Wiper motor, headlamp, right*
39 Washer pump
40 Stop lamp switch
41 Relay, headlamp cleaning system*
42 Washer pump, headlamps*
43 Preglow time relay
44 Glow plugs[2]
45 Cable connector, terminal 58 d
46 Blower switch with lamp
47 Illumination
   a   Air deflector control
   b   Heater control
   c   Switch
   d   Temperature control, air conditioning*
48 Relay, air conditioning (refrigerant compressor)*
49 Pressure switch, refrigerant compressor*
   On 2.6 bar, Off 2.0 bar
50 Electromagnetic clutch, refrigerant compressor*
51 Starter lockout and backup lamp switch*
52 Temperature switch 62 °C (144 °F) receiver drier*
53 Auxiliary fan*
54 Relay, auxiliary fan*

55 Switch-over valve, fresh/recirculating air flap*
56 Temperature sensor, air conditioning*
57 Temperature control, air conditioning*
58 Pre-resistance, blower motor
59 Blower motor
60 Window lift motor, left rear*
61 Switch, window, left rear*
62 Switch cluster, window lifts*
   a   Switch, window, left rear
   b   Safety switch
   c   Switch, window, left front
   d   Switch, window, right front
   e   Switch, window, right rear
63 Window lift motor, left front*
64 Window lift motor, right front*
65 Automatic antenna*
66 Plug connection, tail lamp cable harness
67 Time-lag relay, heated rear window
68 Dome lamp, rear*
69 Fuel gauge sending unit
70 Switch, heated rear window
71 Door contact switch, left rear*
72 Rear dome lamp switch*
73 Door contact switch, right rear*
74 Alternator w/electronic regulator
75 Battery
76 Starter
77 Illumination, shift plate*
78 Heated rear window
79 Trunk lamp
80 Cigar lighter with ashtray illumination
81 Radio*
82 Window lift motor, right rear*
83 Switch, window, right rear*
84 Tail lamp unit, left
   a   Turn signal lamp
   b   Tail/standing lamp
   c   Backup lamp
   d   Stop lamp
   e   Rear fog lamp
85 License plate lamp
86 Tail lamp unit, right
   a   Turn signal lamp
   b   Tail/standing lamp
   c   Backup lamp
   d   Stop lamp

*   Special equipment
[1]   Special equipment (only 300 D)
[2]   200 D, 240 D 4 Glow plugs

Ground connections
M1 Main ground (behind instrument cluster)
M2 Ground, right front (near headlamp unit)
M3 Ground, wheelhouse, left front (ignition coil)
M4 Ground, dome lamp, front
M5 Ground engine
M6 Ground, trunk, wheelhouse, left
M7 Ground, trunk, wheelhouse, right

M1 (60)
   └─ Position number of the component over which the ground line is looped
   └─── Ground connection

Wire Color Code

bl	=	blue	nf =	neutral
br	=	brown	rs =	pink
el	=	ivory	rt =	red
ge	=	yellow	sw =	black
gn	=	green	vi =	purple
gr	=	grey	ws =	white

Example:
Wire designation 1.5 gr/rt
Basic color gr = grey
Identification color rt = red
Cross section of wire 1.5 = 1.5 mm^2

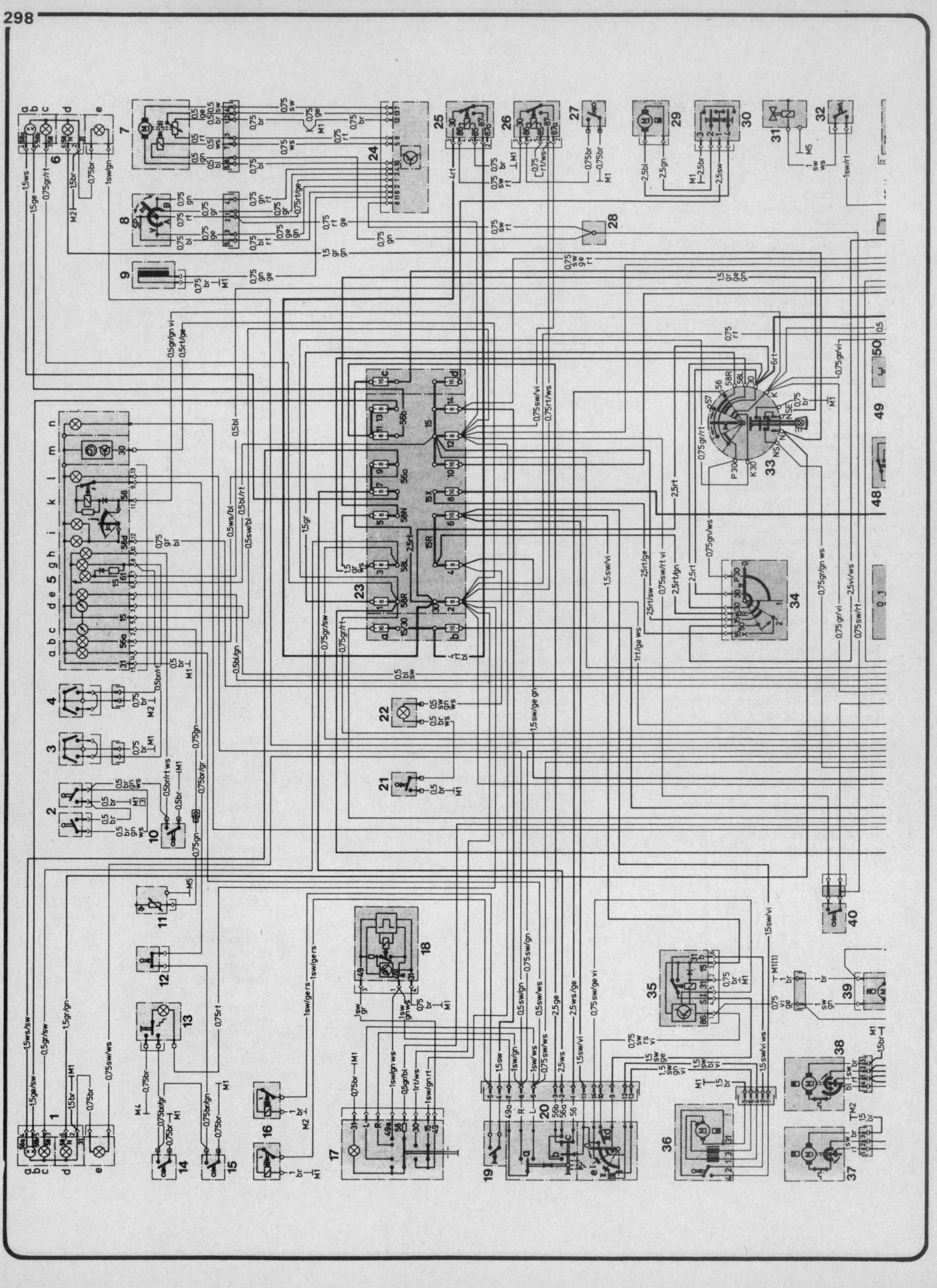

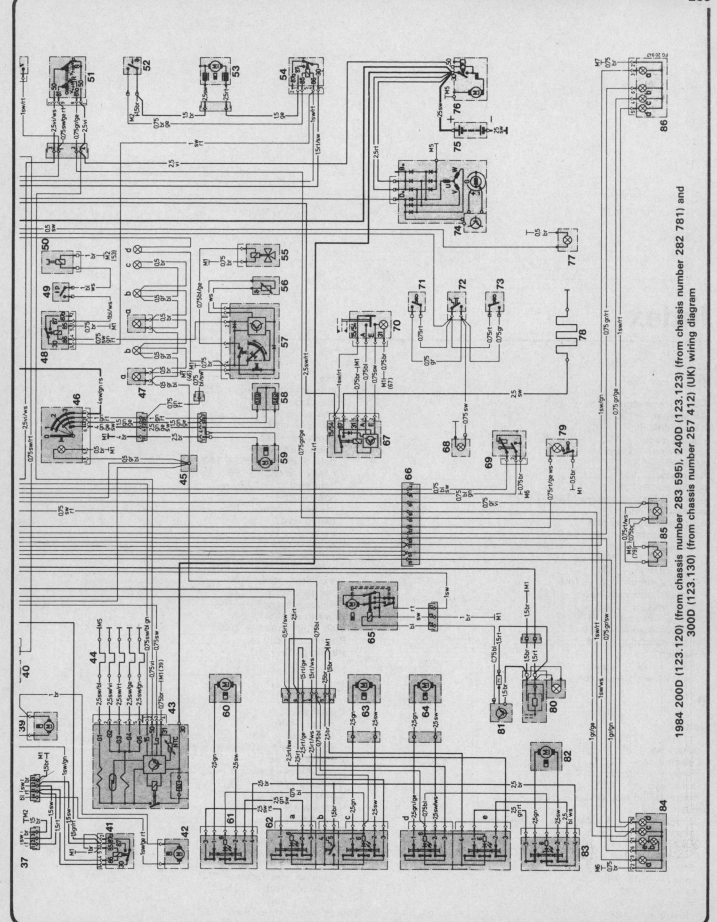

1984 200D (123.120) (from chassis number 283 595), 240D (123.123) (from chassis number 282 781) and 300D (123.130) (from chassis number 257 412) (UK) wiring diagram

Index

A

About this manual — 5
Air cleaner — 120
Air conditioning
    compressor — 113
    servicing — 112
Air filter — 53
Alternator — 131
Antifreeze — 108
Anti-lock braking system (ABS) — 173
Asbestos — 18
Automatic transmission
    backup light switch — 147
    diagnosis — 147
    filter change — 52
    fluid change — 52
    general information — 147
    removal and installation — 150
    shift linkage — 148
    starter inhibitor — 147
    throttle linkage — 149
    troubleshooting — 24
Axleshaft
    boot — 160
    removal and installation — 158

B

Battery
    cables — 129
    checking — 38
    electrolyte — 36
    general information — 18
    maintenance — 38
    removal and installation — 128
Body
    door removal and installation — 194
    general information — 185
    glass — 193, 197, 201
    hinges and locks — 188
    maintenance — 185
    repair — 188, 189
    tailgate — 190
    trunk lid — 190
    vinyl trim — 188
Booster battery starting — 17

Brake

    anti-locking system — 173
    bleeding — 168
    booster — 172
    caliper — 164
    checking — 42
    fluid — 36, 168
    general information — 163
    hoses and lines — 167
    light switch — 172
    lines — 167
    master cylinder — 166
    pads — 163
    parking — 168
    pedal — 172
    rotor — 165
    system bleeding — 168
    troubleshooting — 26
    vacuum pump — 172
    vacuum system — 164
Break-in — 106
Bulb replacement — 208
Bumpers — 200
Buying parts — 10

C

Camshaft
    cover — 60
    inspection — 99
    removal and installation — 66
Carpets — 198
Central locking system — 201
Charging system — 131
Chassis lubrication — 40
Chemicals — 19
Cleaners — 19
Clutch
    bleeding — 154
    checking — 48
    fluid — 36
    general information — 153
    master cylinder — 154
    pedal — 153
    release arm — 155
    release bearing — 155

removal and installation — 155
slave cylinder — 154
system bleeding — 154
throwout bearing — 155
troubleshooting — 24
Combination switch — 204
Component disassembly — 13
Connecting rod
bearing inspection — 101
inspection — 100
installation — 104
oil clearance check — 104
removal — 97
Console — 194
Console switches — 205
Conversion factors — 20
Coolant — 34, 108
Cooling system
checking — 39
coolant level — 34
fan — 110
fan switch — 110
general information — 107
hoses — 13, 37
radiator — 109
servicing — 48
thermostat — 108, 109
troubleshooting — 23
water pump — 110, 111
Courtesy light — 204
Crankshaft
inspection — 101
installation — 102
main bearing inspection — 101
oil clearance check — 102
oil seal — 61, 102
removal — 97
Cylinder head
assembly — 92
disassembly — 90
inspection — 90
removal and installation — 71

D

Dash panel — 198
Differential
general information — 158
oil change — 56
removal and installation — 160
seals — 160
troubleshooting — 25
Dimensions — 9
Dimmer switch — 204
Door
exterior handle — 194
fuel filler — 196
glass — 193
handle — 194
hinges and locks — 188
lock — 194
removal and installation — 194
retaining strap — 194
trim panel — 191
window glass — 193
Drivebelt
adjustment — 39
checking — 39
Driveshaft
center bearing — 157
centering sleeves — 158
flex plates — 158
general information — 156
removal and installation — 156

Drivetrain
checking — 48
general information — 153

E

EGR system — 135
EGR valve
checking — 54, 135
Electrical system
general information — 128, 202
troubleshooting — 23, 203
Emergency jump starting — 17
Emissions system
EGR valve — 54, 135
general information — 134
PCV valve — 135
Engine
auxiliary component installation — 105
auxiliary component removal — 92
block cleaning — 98
block inspection — 99
general information — 60, 86
maintenance — 33
mounts — 79
oil and filter change — 44
oil seals — 61, 102
overhaul — 86, 90
rebuilding alternatives — 86
removal and installation — 75, 87
transmission separation — 80
troubleshooting — 22
Exhaust gas recirculation valve — 54, 135
Exhaust system
checking — 41
component removal and installation — 123
manifold — 60
pipes — 123
Exterior door handle — 194
Exterior mirror — 195

F

Fan
removal and installation — 110
switch — 110
Fasteners — 10
Fire — 18
Fluid capacities — 28
Fluid level checks — 34
Foglamps — 206
Front oil seal — 61
Front wheel bearings — 49
Fuel injection nozzles — 120
Fuel injection pump
checking — 115
delivery adjustment — 115
removal and installation — 117
Fuel filler door — 196
Fuel filter — 46, 120
Fuel system
bleeding — 57
checking — 46
fuel delivery — 57
fuel filter — 46, 120
general information — 114
idle speed — 44, 56
injection nozzles — 120
injection pump — 115, 117
troubleshooting — 23
Fuel tank
removal and installation — 118
repair — 120
Fumes — 18
Fuses — 203

G

Gasket sealing surfaces — 13
Gearshift cover — 194
Gearshifter — 146, 148
General dimensions — 9
Glass
  fixed — 201
  front window — 193
  rear door — 193
  rear quarter — 197
Glove compartment — 198
Glow plugs — 129, 131

H

Head
  assembly — 92
  disassembly — 90
  inspection — 90
  removal and installation — 71
Headlamp washer fluid — 36
Headlamps — 206
Heater — 112
Hinges — 188
Hood — 189
Hose
  checking — 39
  removal — 13
  replacement — 39

I

Identification numbers — 7, 9
Idle speed — 44, 56
Ignition switch — 181
Initial start-up — 106
Instrument cluster — 205
Instrument panel
  removal and installation — 198
  switches — 205
Intake manifold — 60
Introduction — 5, 29

J

Jacking — 17
Jump starting — 17

L

Level control system
  description and checking — 179
  fluid level — 38
Light bulbs — 203, 206
Light switches — 204, 205
Locks — 188, 189, 190, 194, 195, 201
Lubricants — 19, 28
Lubrication — 40

M

Main bearing inspection — 101
Maintenance
  engine — 33
  routine — 29
  schedule — 29
  techniques — 10
Manual transmission
  assembly — 143
  bearings — 143
  countershaft — 142
  dismantling — 137
  general information — 137
  housing — 143
  input shaft — 142
  mainshaft — 141
  oil change — 57
  oil level — 36
  removal and installation — 137
  shift cover — 142
  troubleshooting — 24
Master cylinder — 166
Metric conversion table — 20
Mirrors — 195
Motor mounts — 79
Muffler — 123

O

Oil
  change — 44
  cooler — 74
  level — 34
  pan — 74
  seals — 61, 102

P

Parking brake
  adjustment — 168
  cables — 169
  checking — 168
  hand lever — 171
  pedal — 171
  shoes — 169
PCV system — 135
Piston
  inspection — 100
  installation — 104
  removal — 97
  rings — 102
Positive crankcase ventilation system — 135
Power brake booster — 172
Power steering
  bleeding — 184
  fluid level — 37
  pump — 183
Preglow
  system — 129
  timer relay — 131

Q

Quarter window
  regulator — 197
  removal and installation — 197

R

Radiator — 109
Radio — 212
Rear door lock — 194
Rear shelf — 201
Rear suspension bushing — 178
Rear quarter window — 197
Recommended fluids and lubricants — 28
Rings — 102
Rocker arms — 71

S

Safety — 18
Sealants — 19
Seats — 197
Shifter — 146, 148
Shifter cover — 194
Shock absorber
  front — 176
  rear — 177
Sliding roof — 196
Speedometer cable — 205
Stabilizer bar
  front — 177
  rear — 177
Starter
  general information — 132
  removal and installation — 132
  solenoid — 133
  testing — 132
Station wagon
  tailgate — 190
  tailgate lock — 195
  tailgate strut — 190
Steering
  checking — 41
  column — 180, 181
  damper — 183
  drag link — 182
  gear — 182
  gearbox oil level — 38
  idler arm — 182
  linkage end — 183
  lock — 181
  power — 183, 184
  track rod — 182
  troubleshooting — 26
  wheel — 180
Stop light switch — 172
Suspension
  checking — 41
  general information — 175
  inspection — 175
  level control system — 179
  rear mount bushing — 178
  troubleshooting — 26

T

Tailgate
  lock — 195
  removal and installation — 190
  strut — 190
Terminology — 8
Thermostat — 108, 109
Throttle linkage — 47
Tightening sequences — 12
Timing chain — 62
Tires
  general information — 34, 175
  pressure checking — 34
  removal and installation — 175
  rotation — 48
Tools — 13
Towing — 17
Transmission
  assembly — 143
  backup light switch — 147

  bearings — 143
  countershaft — 142
  diagnosis — 147
  dismantling — 137
  filter change — 52
  fluid change — 52
  fluid level — 36
  general information — 137, 147
  housing — 143
  input shaft — 142
  mainshaft — 141
  oil change — 57
  oil level — 36
  removal and installation — 137, 150
  separation — 80
  shift cover — 142
  shift linkage — 146, 148
  starter inhibitor switch — 147
  throttle linkage — 149
  troubleshooting — 24
Trim panels — 191
Troubleshooting — 21
Trunk lid — 190
Turbocharger
  checking — 127
  general information — 124
  removal and installation — 124
Turn signal — 204

U

Under dash panel — 198
Upholstery — 188
Use of English — 8

V

Vacuum pump — 172
Vacuum system — 164
Valve
  adjustment — 54
  servicing — 91
Vehicle identification numbers — 7, 9
Vinyl trim — 188

W

Water pump — 110, 111
Wheel bearings — 49
Wheelbase — 9
Wheels
  general information — 175
  removal and installation — 175
Window glass — 193, 197
Window regulators — 192, 193
Windshield washer fluid — 35
Windshield wiper
  arm — 211
  blades — 40
  linkage — 211
  motor — 211
Wiring diagrams — 213
Working facilities — 16

Haynes Automotive Manuals

NOTE: New manuals are added to this list on a periodic basis. If you do not see a listing for your vehicle, consult your local Haynes dealer for the latest product information.

ACURA
12020 Integra '86 thru '89 & Legend '86 thru '90
12021 Integra '90 thru '93 & Legend '91 thru '95

AMC
Jeep CJ - see JEEP (50020)
14020 Concord/Hornet/Gremlin/Spirit '70 thru '83
14025 (Renault) Alliance & Encore '83 thru '87

AUDI
15020 4000 all models '80 thru '87
15025 5000 all models '77 thru '83
15026 5000 all models '84 thru '88

AUSTIN
Healey Sprite - see MG Midget (66015)

BMW
*18020 3/5 Series '82 thru '92
18021 3 Series including Z3 models '92 thru '98
18025 320i all 4 cyl models '75 thru '83
18050 1500 thru 2002 except Turbo '59 thru '77

BUICK
*19010 Buick Century '97 thru '02
Century (FWD) - see GM (38005)
*19020 Buick, Oldsmobile & Pontiac Full-size (Front wheel drive) '85 thru '02
19025 Buick Oldsmobile & Pontiac Full-size (Rear wheel drive) '70 thru '90
19030 Mid-size Regal & Century '74 thru '87
Regal - see GENERAL MOTORS (38010)
Skyhawk - see GM (38030)
Skylark - see GM (38020, 38025)
Somerset - see GENERAL MOTORS (38025)

CADILLAC
21030 Cadillac Rear Wheel Drive '70 thru '93
Cimarron, Eldorado & Seville - see GM (38015, 38030, 38031)

CHEVROLET
10305 Chevrolet Engine Overhaul Manual
*24010 Astro & GMC Safari Mini-vans '85 thru '03
24015 Camaro V8 all models '70 thru '81
24016 Camaro all models '82 thru '92
Cavalier - see GM (38015)
Celebrity - see GM (38005)
24017 Camaro & Firebird '93 thru '02
24020 Chevelle, Malibu, El Camino '69 thru '87
24024 Chevette & Pontiac T1000 '76 thru '87
Citation - see GENERAL MOTORS (38020)
24032 Corsica/Beretta all models '87 thru '96
24040 Corvette all V8 models '68 thru '82
24041 Corvette all models '84 thru '96
24045 Full-size Sedans Caprice, Impala, Biscayne, Bel Air & Wagons '69 thru '90
24046 Impala SS & Caprice and Buick Roadmaster '91 thru '96
Lumina '90 thru '94 - see GM (38010)
*24048 Lumina & Monte Carlo '95 thru '03
Lumina APV - see GM (38035)
24050 Luv Pick-up all 2WD & 4WD '72 thru '82
Malibu - see GM (38026)
24055 Monte Carlo all models '70 thru '88
Monte Carlo '95 thru '01 - see LUMINA
24059 Nova all V8 models '69 thru '79
24060 Nova/Geo Prizm '85 thru '92
24064 Pick-ups '67 thru '87 - Chevrolet & GMC, all V8 & in-line 6 cyl, 2WD & 4WD '67 thru '87; Suburbans, Blazers & Jimmys '67 thru '91
24065 Pick-ups '88 thru '98 - Chevrolet & GMC, all full-size models '88 thru '98; C/K Classic '99 & '00; Blazer & Jimmy '92 thru '94; Suburban '92 thru '99; Tahoe & Yukon '95 thru '99
*24066 Pick-ups '99 thru '02 - Chevrolet Silverado & GMC Sierra '99 thru '02; Suburban/Tahoe/Yukon/Yukon XL '00 thru '02
24070 S-10 & GMC S-15 Pick-ups '82 thru '93
*24071 S-10, Gmc S-15 & Jimmy '94 thru '01
*24072 Chevrolet TrailBlazer & TrailBlazer EXT, GMC Envoy & Envoy XL, Oldsmobile Bravada '02 and '03
24075 Sprint '85 thru '88, Geo Metro '89 thru '01
24080 Vans - Chevrolet & GMC '68 thru '96

CHRYSLER
10310 Chrysler Engine Overhaul Manual
25015 Chrysler Cirrus, Dodge Stratus, Plymouth Breeze, '95 thru '98
25020 Full-size Front-Wheel Drive '88 thru '93
K-Cars - see DODGE Aries (30008)
Laser - see DODGE Daytona (30030)
25025 Chrysler LHS, Concorde & New Yorker, Dodge Intrepid, Eagle Vision, '93 thru '97
*25026 Chrysler LHS, Concorde, 300M, Dodge Intrepid '98 thru '03
25030 Chrysler/Plym. Mid-size '82 thru '95
Rear-wheel Drive - see DODGE (30050)
*25035 PT Cruiser all models '01 thru '03
*25040 Chrysler Sebring/Dodge Avenger '95 thru '02

DATSUN
28005 200SX all models '80 thru '83
28007 B-210 all models '73 thru '78
28009 210 all models '78 thru '82
28012 240Z, 260Z & 280Z Coupe '70 thru '78
28014 280ZX Coupe & 2+2 '79 thru '83
300ZX - see NISSAN (72010)
28016 310 all models '78 thru '82
28018 510 & PL521 Pick-up '68 thru '73
28020 510 all models '78 thru '81
28022 620 Series Pick-up all models '73 thru '79
720 Series Pick-up - NISSAN (72030)
28025 810/Maxima all gas models, '77 thru '84

DODGE
400 & 600 - see CHRYSLER (25030)
30008 Aries & Plymouth Reliant '81 thru '89
30010 Caravan & Ply. Voyager '84 thru '95
*30011 Caravan & Ply. Voyager '96 thru '02
30012 Challenger/Plymouth Saporro '78 thru '83
Challenger '67-'76 - see DART (30025)
30016 Colt/Plymouth Champ '78 thru '87
30020 Dakota Pick-ups all models '87 thru '96
30021 Durango '98 & '99, Dakota '97 thru '99
30025 Dart, Challenger/Plymouth Barracuda & Valiant 6 cyl models '67 thru '76
30030 Daytona & Chrysler Laser '84 thru '89
Intrepid - see Chrysler (25025, 25026)
*30034 Dodge & Plymouth Neon '95 thru '99
30035 Omni & Plymouth Horizon '78 thru '90
30040 Pick-ups all full-size models '74 thru '93
30041 Pick-ups all full-size models '94 thru '01
*30045 Ram 50/D50 Pick-ups & Raider and Plymouth Arrow Pick-ups '79 thru '93
30050 Dodge/Ply./Chrysler RWD '71 thru '89
30055 Shadow/Plymouth Sundance '87 thru '94
30060 Spirit & Plymouth Acclaim '89 thru '95
*30065 Vans - Dodge & Plymouth '71 thru '03

EAGLE
Talon - see MITSUBISHI (68030, 68031)
Vision - see CHRYSLER (25025)

FIAT
34010 124 Sport Coupe & Spider '68 thru '78
34025 X1/9 all models '74 thru '80

FORD
10355 Ford Automatic Transmission Overhaul
10320 Ford Engine Overhaul Manual
36004 Aerostar Mini-vans '86 thru '97
Aspire - see FORD Festiva (36030)
36006 Contour/Mercury Mystique '95 thru '00
36008 Courier Pick-up all models '72 thru '82
*36012 Crown Victoria & Mercury Grand Marquis '88 thru '00
36016 Escort/Mercury Lynx '81 thru '90
36020 Escort/Mercury Tracer '91 thru '00
Expedition - see FORD Pick-up (36059)
36022 Ford Escape & Mazda Tribute '01 thru '03
*36024 Explorer & Mazda Navajo '91 thru '01
36025 Ford Explorer & Mercury Mountaineer '02 and '03
36028 Fairmont & Mercury Zephyr '78 thru '83
36030 Festiva & Aspire '88 thru '97
36032 Fiesta all models '77 thru '80
*36034 Focus all models '00 and '01
36036 Ford & Mercury Full-size '75 thru '87
36044 Ford & Mercury Mid-size '75 thru '86
36048 Mustang V8 all models '64-1/2 thru '73
36049 Mustang II 4 cyl, V6 & V8 '74 thru '78
36050 Mustang & Mercury Capri '79 thru '86
*36051 Mustang all models '94 thru '03
36054 Pick-ups and Bronco '73 thru '79
36058 Pick-ups and Bronco '80 thru '96
*36059 Pick-ups, Expedition & Lincoln Navigator '97 thru '02
*36060 Super Duty Pick-up, Excursion '97 thru '02
36062 Pinto & Mercury Bobcat '75 thru '80
36066 Probe all models '89 thru '92
36070 Ranger/Bronco II gas models '83 thru '92
*36071 Ford Ranger '93 thru '00 & Mazda Pick-ups '94 thru '00
36074 Taurus & Mercury Sable '86 thru '95
*36075 Taurus & Mercury Sable '96 thru '01
36078 Tempo & Mercury Topaz '84 thru '94
36082 Thunderbird/Mercury Cougar '83 thru '88
36086 Thunderbird/Mercury Cougar '89 thru '97
36090 Vans all V8 Econoline models '69 thru '91
*36094 Vans full size '92 thru '01
*36097 Windstar Mini-van '95 thru '03

GENERAL MOTORS
10360 GM Automatic Transmission Overhaul
38005 Buick Century, Chevrolet Celebrity, Olds Cutlass Ciera & Pontiac 6000 '82 thru '96
*38010 Buick Regal, Chevrolet Lumina, Oldsmobile Cutlass Supreme & Pontiac Grand Prix front wheel drive '88 thru '02
38015 Buick Skyhawk, Cadillac Cimarron, Chevrolet Cavalier, Oldsmobile Firenza Pontiac J-2000 & Sunbird '82 thru '94
*38016 Chevrolet Cavalier/Pontiac Sunfire '95 thru '04
38020 Buick Skylark, Chevrolet Citation, Olds Omega, Pontiac Phoenix '80 thru '85
38025 Buick Skylark & Somerset, Olds Achieva, Calais & Pontiac Grand Am '85 thru '98
*38026 Chevrolet Malibu, Olds Alero & Cutlass, Pontiac Grand Am '97 thru '00
38030 Cadillac Eldorado & Oldsmobile Toronado '71 thru '85, Seville '80 thru '85, Buick Riviera '79 thru '85
*38031 Cadillac Eldorado & Seville '86 thru '91, DeVille & Buick Riviera '86 thru '93, Fleetwood & Olds Toronado '86 thru '92
38032 DeVille '94 thru '02, Seville '92 thru '02
38035 Chevrolet Lumina APV, Oldsmobile Silhouette & Pontiac Trans Sport '90 thru '96
*38036 Chevrolet Venture, Olds Silhouette, Pontiac Trans Sport & Montana '97 thru '01
General Motors Full-size Rear-wheel Drive - see BUICK (19025)

GEO
Metro - see CHEVROLET Sprint (24075)
Prizm - see CHEVROLET (24060) or TOYOTA (92036)
40030 Storm all models '90 thru '93
Tracker - see SUZUKI Samurai (90010)

GMC
Vans & Pick-ups - see CHEVROLET

HONDA
42010 Accord CVCC all models '76 thru '83
42011 Accord all models '84 thru '89
42012 Accord all models '90 thru '93
42013 Accord all models '94 thru '97
*42014 Accord all models '98 thru '02
42020 Civic 1200 all models '73 thru '79
42021 Civic 1300 & 1500 CVCC '80 thru '83
42022 Civic 1500 CVCC all models '75 thru '79
42023 Civic all models '84 thru '91
42024 Civic & del Sol '92 thru '95
*42025 Civic '96 thru '00, CR-V '97 thru '00, Acura Integra '94 thru '00
Passport - see ISUZU Rodeo (47017)
42026 Civic '01 thru '04, CR-V '02 thru '04
*42040 Prelude CVCC all models '79 thru '89

HYUNDAI
*43010 Elantra all models '96 thru '01
43015 Excel & Accent all models '86 thru '98

ISUZU
Hombre - see CHEVROLET S-10 (24071)
*47017 Rodeo '91 thru '02, Amigo '89 thru '02, Honda Passport '95 thru '02
47020 Trooper '84 thru '91, Pick-up '81 thru '93

JAGUAR
49010 XJ6 all 6 cyl models '68 thru '86
49011 XJ6 all models '88 thru '94
49015 XJ12 & XJS all 12 cyl models '72 thru '85

JEEP
50010 Cherokee, Comanche & Wagoneer Limited all models '84 thru '01
50020 CJ all models '49 thru '86
*50025 Grand Cherokee all models '93 thru '04
50029 Grand Wagoneer & Pick-up '72 thru '91
*50030 Wrangler all models '87 thru '00
50035 Liberty '02 thru '04

LEXUS
ES 300 - see TOYOTA Camry (92007)

LINCOLN
Navigator - see FORD Pick-up (36059)
*59010 Rear Wheel Drive all models '70 thru '01

MAZDA
61010 GLC (rear wheel drive) '77 thru '83
61011 GLC (front wheel drive) '81 thru '85
61015 323 & Protegé '90 thru '00
*61016 MX-5 Miata '90 thru '97
61020 MPV all models '89 thru '94
Navajo - see FORD Explorer (36024)
61030 Pick-ups '72 thru '93
Pick-ups '94 on - see Ford (36071)
61035 RX-7 all models '79 thru '85
61036 RX-7 all models '86 thru '91
61040 626 (rear wheel drive) '79 thru '82
61041 626 & MX-6 (front wheel drive) '83 thru '91
61042 626 '93 thru '01, & MX-6/Ford Probe '93 thru '97

MERCEDES-BENZ
63012 123 Series Diesel '76 thru '85
63015 190 Series 4-cyl gas models, '84 thru '88
63020 230, 250 & 280 6 cyl sohc '68 thru '72
63025 280 123 Series gas models '77 thru '81
63030 350 & 450 all models '71 thru '80

MERCURY
64200 Villager & Nissan Quest '93 thru '01
All other titles, see FORD listing.

MG
66010 MGB Roadster & GT Coupe '62 thru '80
66015 MG Midget & Austin Healey Sprite Roadster '58 thru '80

MITSUBISHI
68020 Cordia, Tredia, Galant, Precis & Mirage '83 thru '93
68030 Eclipse, Eagle Talon & Plymouth Laser '90 thru '94
*68031 Eclipse '95 thru '01, Eagle Talon '95 thru '98
68035 Mitsubishi Galant '94 thru '03
68040 Pick-up '83 thru '96, Montero '83 thru '93

NISSAN
72010 300ZX all models incl. Turbo '84 thru '89
72015 Altima all models '93 thru '04
72020 Maxima all models '85 thru '92
*72021 Maxima all models '93 thru '01
72030 Pick-ups '80 thru '97, Pathfinder '87 thru '95
*72031 Frontier Pick-up '98 thru '01, Xterra '00 & '01, Pathfinder '96 thru '01
72040 Pulsar all models '83 thru '86
72050 Sentra all models '82 thru '94
72051 Sentra & 200SX all models '95 thru '99
72060 Stanza all models '82 thru '90

OLDSMOBILE
*73015 Cutlass '74 thru '88
For other OLDSMOBILE titles, see BUICK, CHEVROLET or GM listings.

PLYMOUTH
For PLYMOUTH titles, see DODGE.

PONTIAC
79008 Fiero all models '84 thru '88
79018 Firebird V8 models except Turbo '70 thru '81
79019 Firebird all models '82 thru '92
79040 Mid-size Rear-wheel Drive '70 thru '87
For other PONTIAC titles, see BUICK, CHEVROLET or GM listings.

PORSCHE
80020 911 Coupe & Targa models '65 thru '89
80025 914 all 4 cyl models '69 thru '76
80030 924 all models incl. Turbo '76 thru '82
80035 944 all models incl. Turbo '83 thru '89

RENAULT
Alliance, Encore - see AMC (14020)

SAAB
*84010 900 including Turbo '79 thru '88

SATURN
*87010 Saturn all models '91 thru '02
87020 Saturn all L-series models '00 thru '04

SUBARU
89002 1100, 1300, 1400 & 1600 '71 thru '79
89003 1600 & 1800 2WD & 4WD '80 thru '94

SUZUKI
90010 Samurai/Sidekick/Geo Tracker '86 thru '01

TOYOTA
92005 Camry all models '83 thru '91
92006 Camry all models '92 thru '96
*92007 Camry/Avalon/Solara/Lexus ES 300 '97 thru '01
92015 Celica Rear Wheel Drive '71 thru '85
92020 Celica Front Wheel Drive '86 thru '99
92025 Celica Supra all models '79 thru '92
92030 Corolla all models '75 thru '79
92032 Corolla rear wheel drive models '80 thru '87
92035 Corolla front wheel drive models '84 thru '92
92036 Corolla & Geo Prizm '93 thru '02
92040 Corolla Tercel all models '80 thru '82
92045 Corona all models '74 thru '82
92050 Cressida all models '78 thru '82
92055 Land Cruiser FJ40/43/45/55 '68 thru '82
92056 Land Cruiser FJ60/62/80/FZJ80 '80 thru '96
92065 MR2 all models '85 thru '87
92070 Pick-up all models '69 thru '78
92075 Pick-up all models '79 thru '95
*92076 Tacoma '95 thru '00, 4Runner '96 thru '00, T100 '93 thru '98
*92078 Tundra '00 thru '02, Sequoia '01 thru '02
92080 Previa all models '91 thru '95
*92082 RAV4 all models '96 thru '02
92085 Tercel all models '87 thru '94

TRIUMPH
94007 Spitfire all models '62 thru '81
94010 TR7 all models '75 thru '81

VW
96008 Beetle & Karmann Ghia '54 thru '79
*96009 New Beetle '98 thru '00
96016 Rabbit, Jetta, Scirocco, & Pick-up gas models '74 thru '91 & Convertible '80 thru '92
96017 Golf, GTI & Jetta '93 thru '98, Cabrio '95 thru '98
*96018 Golf, GTI, Jetta & Cabrio '98 thru '02
96020 Rabbit, Jetta, Pick-up diesel '77 thru '84
96023 Passat '98 thru '01, Audi A4 '96 thru '01
96030 Transporter 1600 all models '68 thru '79
96035 Transporter 1700, 1800, 2000 '72 thru '79
96040 Type 3 1500 & 1600 '63 thru '73
96045 Vanagon air-cooled models '80 thru '83

VOLVO
97010 120, 130 Series & 1800 Sports '61 thru '73
97015 140 Series all models '66 thru '74
97020 240 Series all models '76 thru '93
97025 260 Series all models '75 thru '82
97040 740 & 760 Series all models '82 thru '88

TECHBOOK MANUALS
10205 Automotive Computer Codes
10210 Automotive Emissions Control Manual
10215 Fuel Injection Manual, 1978 thru 1985
10220 Fuel Injection Manual, 1986 thru 1999
10225 Holley Carburetor Manual
10230 Rochester Carburetor Manual
10240 Weber/Zenith/Stromberg/SU Carburetor
10305 Chevrolet Engine Overhaul Manual
10310 Chrysler Engine Overhaul Manual
10320 Ford Engine Overhaul Manual
10330 GM and Ford Diesel Engine Repair
10340 Small Engine Repair Manual
10345 Suspension, Steering & Driveline
10355 Ford Automatic Transmission Overhaul
10360 GM Automatic Transmission Overhaul
10405 Automotive Body Repair & Painting
10410 Automotive Brake Manual
10415 Automotive Detailing Manual
10420 Automotive Eelectrical Manual
10425 Automotive Heating & Air Conditioning
10430 Automotive Reference Dictionary
10435 Automotive Tools Manual
10440 Used Car Buying Guide
10445 Welding Manual
10450 ATV Basics

SPANISH MANUALS
98903 Reparación de Carrocería & Pintura
98905 Códigos Automotrices de la Computadora
98910 Frenos Automotriz
98915 Inyección de Combustible 1986 al 1999
99040 Chevrolet & GMC Camionetas '67 al '87
99041 Chevrolet & GMC Camionetas '88 al '98
99042 Chevrolet Camionetas Cerradas '68 al '95
99055 Dodge Caravan/Ply. Voyager '84 al '95
99075 Ford Camionetas y Bronco '80 al '94
99077 Ford Camionetas Cerradas '69 al '91
99088 Ford Modelos de Tamaño Mediano '75 al '86
99091 Ford Taurus & Mercury Sable '86 al '95
99095 GM Modelos de Tamaño Grande '70 al '90
99100 GM Modelos de Tamaño Mediano '70 al '88
99110 Nissan Camionetas '80 al '96, Pathfinder '87 al '95
99118 Nissan Sentra '82 al '94
99125 Toyota Camionetas y 4-Runner '79 al '95

Listings shown with an asterisk (*) indicate model coverage as of this printing. These titles will be periodically updated to include later model years - consult your Haynes dealer for more information.

Nearly 100 Haynes motorcycle manuals also available

2-05